Acclaim for

JOHN KERR'S

A Most Dangerous Method

"An invaluable corrective to received views about the Jung-Freud relationship. . . . We gain . . . insight into the sexual ethics of the earliest psychoanalysts and the sexual politics that affected the shaping of both Freudian and Jungian theory." —*The New York Review of Books*

"At some points, it reads like an epistolary novel; at others, it reads like one of Freud's or Jung's famous case histories. . . . [Kerr] superbly re-creates both the social and personal contexts for the emergence of the dominant mode of self-understanding of our time."
—*San Francisco Chronicle*

"*A Most Dangerous Method* amounts to a new history of the early years of psychoanalysis. . . . Kerr is clever and thorough, ingenious and reasonable. . . . His overall picture is convincing and in many ways surprising." —*The Independent on Sunday*

"John Kerr has written a detailed and enthralling book . . . fascinating. . . . Sabina Spielrein emerges as a still small voice of much endurance and integrity. . . . Now she takes her place as the original model for Jung's 'anima'—that archetypal feminine force by which men unconsciously are so often held in thrall." —*Daily Telegraph*

"Fiction could not better this. It would be difficult to imagine a more fascinating device to tell the story of Freud's acrimonious break-up with Jung . . . than the introduction of the character of Spielrein. . . . With tremendous skill Kerr has not only rescued her from obscurity, he has told an amazing story, and simultaneously given an authoritative history which deserves to be regarded as the unexpurgated rise of psychoanalysis." —*The Herald*

"Kerr eyeballs the human oddities that were preserved, like bugs in amber, in the text and texture of the new 'science.'" —*Village Voice*

JOHN KERR

A Most Dangerous Method

John Kerr was trained as a clinical psychologist at New York University and has worked as a staff psychologist in diverse inpatient and outpatient settings. In addition, for many years he was Senior Editor at The Analytic Press, a publisher of books for psychoanalysts and other mental health professions. He is the co-editor of *Freud and the History of Psychoanalysis* and *Attachment Theory: Social, Developmental, and Clinical Perspectives.* Currently, Mr. Kerr works as a private editor and is writing a play about the American psychiatrist, Harry Stack Sullivan, as well as a memoir about his years in Brooklyn.

A MOST DANGEROUS METHOD

A MOST DANGEROUS METHOD

The Story of Jung, Freud,
and Sabina Spielrein

JOHN KERR

VINTAGE BOOKS

A Division of Random House, Inc.

New York

FIRST VINTAGE BOOKS EDITION, AUGUST 1994

The Library of Congress has cataloged the Knopf edition as follows:
Kerr, John.
A most dangerous method: the story of Jung, Freud, and Sabina
Spielrein / John Kerr. — 1st ed.
p.   cm.
Includes bibliographical references and index.
ISBN 0-679-40412-0
1. Psychoanalysis—History.   2. Jung, C. G. (Carl Gustav),
1875–1961.   3. Freud, Sigmund, 1856–1939.   4. Spielrein, Sabina.
I. Title.
BF173.K42   1993
150.19'5'0922—dc20   92-54802
CIP

ISBN 978-0-679-73580-9

10 9 8 7 6 5 4 3 2 1

Some people are lucky enough to have three parents.
This book is dedicated to

my mother

my father

and Mabel Groom

I hope that Freud and his pupils will push their ideas to their utmost limits, so that we may learn what they are. They can't fail to throw light on human nature, but I confess that he made on me personally the impression of a man obsessed with fixed ideas. I can make nothing in my own case with his dream theories, and obviously "symbolism" is a most dangerous method.

—William James, letter of 28 September 1909 to Théodore Flournoy

Contents

PART FOUR   INTIMATE MATTERS

PART FIVE   THE AFTERMATH

Acknowledgments

THIS BOOK owes its existence to a small number of people whose interest, patience, and generosity outlasted my ability to exhaust the available supply of all three traits. First, I must thank Paul Schrader, who introduced me to the topic and facilitated the translation of Spielrein's early papers. An inadvertent mentor, Schrader not only intuited that an important story lay inside the tangle of available documents but pursued that story with a rare intellectual honesty.

Peter Swales, a friend as well as a colleague, deserves far more credit than space allows. Had I not early tumbled to Swales's researches, most of them then unpublished, which he made available with a generosity bordering on recklessness, I would have undoubtedly gotten off on the wrong track. Swales has done more independent archival research and has dug up more new information about Freud than almost any other living person. He has also gathered what is surely one of the finest private libraries in the world regarding Freud and the early history of psychoanalysis. He put all of it at my disposal. One has to be personally acquainted with Swales to grasp what a treasure-trove of information he is—and how willingly he will make time for discussion of elusive and difficult points, even at one in the morning if need be.

Schrader and Swales got me started, but the topic would still have lain there had not Robert Holt taken an interest and offered to sponsor an earlier version of this story as my doctoral dissertation. Holt's scholarly diligence is legendary within the field of psychology; I took advantage of it with multiple drafts. My indebtedness here to Professor Holt compounds multiple earlier debts for his patient instruction in the logic of scientific verification and the intricacies of Freudian theory.

What Swales and Holt have meant to me in terms of Freud, Sonu Shamdasani has meant in terms of Jung. Not only has Shamdasani made himself continuously available for discussion over the years, he has shared with me his own archival researches and his preparations for his forthcoming intellectual biography of Jung. In particular, I would like to thank him for discovering Jung's early association with Binet, for charting Jung's evolving intellectual debt to Myers and Flournoy, and, most especially, for identifying Spielrein's word association protocol. Eugene Taylor, Anthony Stadlen, and Ernst Falzeder have likewise been very generous with their time and erudition.

Over the course of the past decade, Anthony Econom, student of history and book-lover, has given me advice, instruction, offprints, and an occasional scolding. The original 1916 English version of Jung's "Transformations and Symbols" was once relatively hard to find; Econom found two copies, one for me and one so he could read along and keep an eye on where the argument was going. This book could not have been written without his support and guidance. Three other book-lovers, Jack Molloy, David Little, and Heather Waters, have also earned my gratitude for their constant support—and for listening to more about Freud, Jung, and Spielrein over the years than any person should have to endure.

Special thanks go to the members of New York Hospital/Cornell Medical Center's History of Psychiatry Section, founded by Eric Carlson. The Section gave my ideas a patient hearing and provided an education in return. Among the members I would particularly like to thank are Larry Friedman, Jacques Quen, Leonard Groopman, Dan Burston, Marianne Eckhardt, Nate Kravis, George Makari, Anna Antonovsky, Doris Nagel, Norman Dain, Ralph Baker, Barbara Fass Leavy, Leon Hankoff, Herb Spiegel, and Cornelius Clark. It is extremely rare to find people who are both historically sophisticated and well versed in psychiatric and psychoanalytic theory. Rarer still are people who combine these qualities with such graceful collegiality.

As I possess only rudimentary French and, beyond a few technical terms, no German at all, I have been dependent on the good offices of others for translations. Here I would like to thank Ursula Ofman, Peter Gachot, Julia Swales, Marie-Louise Schoelly, Tanaquil Taubes, Michael Münchow, and Michael Norton for their tireless assistance. Libraries and, even more, librarians were also indispensable. In particular I would like to thank Mr. Richard Wolf of the Rare Books Department of the Countway Library, Harvard Medical School; Ms. Taylor of the A. A. Brill Library, New York Psychoanalytic Society; and especially Doris Albrecht and Peggy Brooks of the Kristine Mann Library of the C. G. Jung Institute of New York.

Without Amy Bianco's intervention, this book might still be a manuscript. She found not only a publisher but also an editor: Peter Dimock, whose sensitivity to the narrative was matched by a seemingly endless supply of patient support. This book owes more to him than the reader can possibly guess. I would also like to acknowledge the diligent and inspired efforts of Melvin Rosenthal, Ellen Shapiro, and Carol Devine Carson in preparing this book for publication.

Research on this book was financed at times by borrowed money. Here I must thank those who lent it to me: Jack Molloy, David Little, Anthony Econom, Lester Berentsen, my parents, and my brothers Chris and Colin. I would also like to thank Jack Benson and Joseph and Michael Diliberto for extending credit—and their support—over the years. Similarly, I have to thank Sara Weber and Robert Langan, colleagues as well as friends, and Steven Cecere, for letting their upstairs tenant be late with the rent.

Ruth Ochroch, William Blackwell, Ted Coons, Paul Vitz, Richard Noll, Dennis Klein, and Carol Janeway all made valuable suggestions during the course of this project. Finally, I would also like to thank a number of people for their support and encouragement over the years: Gene Anderson and Judy Robinson (and Eleanor), Susan Coates, Vincent Russo, Paul Stepansky, Jackie Balzano, Frank Sulloway, Andrew Lubrano, Rosemarie Sand, John and Deanna Robins, Deborah and Daniel DeLosa, Mark Micale, Damien Dummigan, Richard Schimenti, Frank Kominsky, Eric Benson, James Van Meter, Phyllis Grosskurth, Peter Rudnytsky, Toby Gelfand, and Ralph Martin.

J.K.

A MOST
DANGEROUS
METHOD

Introduction

Sigmund Freud and Carl Jung met for the first time on 3 March 1907. They talked for thirteen hours straight. The last time the two men were together in the same room was at the Fourth International Psychoanalytic Congress, held in Munich on 7–8 September 1913. On that occasion, so far as is known, they said not a single word to each other. So it was in silence that one of the most vexed partnerships in the history of ideas ended. Yet, working together for little more than six years, these two men decisively altered the course of twentieth-century thought.

This is the story of that partnership. I tell it not primarily to round out the biographical understanding of either man; still less to take sides. I tell it in order to raise critical issues about the nature of their joint accomplishment.

During the years of their collaboration, Freud and Jung brought into prominence a new method of psychotherapy—psychoanalysis— and won widespread acceptance for the interpretive views, some of them quite radical, that helped make that method distinctive. Without them, more specifically without their collaboration, psychoanalysis as we know it today would not exist. But if Freud and Jung brought into being something radically new—something whose transformative value continues to be felt today—they also shaped their creation in ways that were scarcely inevitable, ways that reflected their own special needs of the moment, and ways that ultimately produced distortions which are important to recognize and understand.

Clearly, the relationship between Freud and Jung is an important story to tell. But it is not an easy story to tell critically. These are men we would prefer to admire. We would rather keep them as heroes, as the attractive, humane, skeptical, ultimately wise figures that emerge in so many later anecdotes. Having opened a new perspective on the human mind, and most especially on human limitations, Freud and

Jung were perforce the first thinkers to live with that peculiarly intense burden of self-reflection that distinguishes the psychology of modern man. They were, in that sense, the first citizens of the twentieth century. It both pleases and comforts us to think that they possessed the virtues that the new forms of self-awareness require to be humanly sustaining.

Neither man was ever so winning a personality as when he was in opposition. Later in their lives, if the logic of a situation called for them to be in opposition to their own theories, they could manage that gracefully, too. We are all familiar, I think, with Freud's unamused protest: "Sometimes a cigar is just a cigar." But more pertinent perhaps is his remark to Abram Kardiner, who during a training analysis questioned the logic of a particular psychoanalytic theorem: "Oh, don't take that too seriously. That's something I dreamed up on a rainy Sunday afternoon." The irreverence complemented the streak of indomitability in Freud's character. When the Nazi authorities required him to sign a propaganda statement attesting to their good treatment of him before he would be allowed to emigrate, Freud responded with a heroic flourish. After signing his name, he thoughtfully added a postscript: "I can heartily recommend the Gestapo to anybody."

Jung, too, could take a bemused distance from himself. During a panel discussion at the institute he founded, he confided quietly to a colleague: "Thank God I am not a Jungian." Jung's handling of patients could be equally straightforward. When one young woman tired of talking about her unrequited sexual transference and proposed that they lie down together on the couch, Jung replied on point: "Yes, we could—but then we would have to get up again." And Jung could wear the mantle of his reputation no less lightly than his former Viennese friend. During a trip to London later in life, Jung took an afternoon by himself to go to the reading room of the British Museum to look up a rare book. But at the entrance he was challenged politely by the guard: Where was his entrance pass? Jung replied that he had no pass, that he was Carl Jung from Zurich and did not know he needed one. The guard, obviously startled, queried: "Carl Jung? You mean Freud, Adler, Jung?" To which Jung answered wistfully, "No . . . just Jung." (He was allowed to enter.)

But these anecdotes come from late in the lives of the two men. The story of their partnership belongs to an earlier, much darker period. And though many of their more admirable qualities were also in evidence then, both men were more ambitious, more dogmatic, more intolerant—more possessed—than they would show themselves later on. Success improves most characters, but ambition usually does not. At the time of their collaboration, both Freud and Jung were being cruelly tantalized by the prospects of their own future greatness.

One has to keep in mind the context. At the beginning of this century, in both Europe and America, there was an explosion of interest in the psychology of what were then called "nervous" disorders. There was also a corresponding surge in experimentation with psychotherapy. This dual trend—the effort to understand better the nature of nervous complaints and to provide amelioration through purely "psychical" means—was the result of multiple factors which obtained generally throughout the Western world. To begin with, it was a period of general economic prosperity. Then, as now, when people have money to spend, one of the things they spend it on is themselves. Often enough, this entails seeking relief from troubles that in harder times one would pay less attention to. Then, too, it was a period when there was an extremely high incidence of "nervous" disorders generally. Few today remember an era when a proper Victorian household was equipped with decanters of smelling salts in all the downstairs rooms for the benefit of equally proper Victorian ladies who might be struck down by that common malady, the swoon. But not only women suffered. Men, too, commonly suffered from a variety of mental and physical symptoms to the point where it was generally conceded, even if the specific causes were disputed, that there was something about the pace of modern civilization that regularly resulted in a pathologically overtaxed nervous system.

Where it could, diagnosis followed gender. While hysteria was reserved largely, but not exclusively, for women, neurasthenia, compulsion neurosis, obsessional states, and other syndromes were generally the diagnostic prerogative of the male. Moreover, inside all these labels lay the more insidious secondary diagnosis of hereditary taint—that sneak thief of medical theory which satisfied the physician's need to say something while robbing the patient of all confidence in his or her future prospects for sanity. It was an age when many sensitive citizens, and not a few more robust ones, found themselves in the uneasy position of pleading a clear conscience as a way of staying one step ahead of unvoiced doubts; of exhausting their energies in overwork and in equally taxing trips to the spa to ward off an ominous, brooding lassitude; of endorsing all sorts of philosophical, political, and social causes as a way of deflecting their attention from an inward unhappiness that seemed to have no name. The resources of character—willpower and rectitude—seemed to have been mysteriously undermined from within.

Against all this, late-nineteenth-century neurology had proved itself singularly impotent. Though a few fundamental insights had been won concerning the basic functioning of the nervous system, their relevance to nervous complaints was confined to the introduction of a physicalist language of "energy" and "discharge," of "tension" and "fatigue," which only served to constrict what the patient could say. The available physicalist treatments—electricity, bromides, surgery—had generated no discernible pattern of success, and the suspicion was widespread that what success had been had was due rather to the power of suggestion. The use of hypnotism outright had proven more consistently effective, but it raised both eyebrows and questions. If the mind could be affected for the better in a trance, then why not in the waking state? And what did this say about the nature of the complaint, and about the functioning of the nervous system generally?

Nervous complaints thus entailed any number of intensely interesting and hitherto unsolved scientific questions. In an age when an important scientific discovery could guarantee lasting fame, this factor alone was sufficient to ensure that talented men would begin tackling the problem in earnest. Of all the factors conspiring to make the study of nervous complaints fashionable, however, perhaps the most important was philosophical. For this was the age that first accepted scientific materialism as its dominant worldview. It was now commonly assumed that science had decisively triumphed over religion and metaphysics and that a complete materialistic account of the external world was nearly at hand. But how then was man to conceptualize that other pole of experience—the self? There seemed no place in the material world, with its endlessly antecedent causes, for the thinking, feeling, willing agency of the self. The paradox was apparent to all. There was as yet no agreed upon way of resolving it.

The questions inherent in nervous complaints—the relation of the nervous system to the conscious and unconscious mind—occupied a crucial philosophical backwater. A satisfactory scheme which could relate the felt phenomena of human psychology with the findings of anatomy and physiology necessarily would have important philosophical ramifications. It ought not surprise us, therefore, to learn that medical men who occupied themselves with nervous patients also regularly tried their hand at philosophy. Nor that the phenomenology of nervous disorders was closely linked in the popular mind with all that seemed exceptional and marvelous, with séances, genius, telepathy, and the like—with all the places where there still seemed to be cracks in the materialist world order.

The net result of all these factors was that any number of discerning medical men elected to go in the only direction that was open, pursuing psychological investigations and experimenting with psychological treatments. The trend was quite general throughout the Western world. Its diversity notwithstanding, one can properly speak of a "psychotherapy movement." In only a few decades' time, however, this general movement virtually disappeared, consumed from within by just one of the many strands of which it was originally composed.

The rapid growth of psychoanalysis to a position of preeminence is astonishing in retrospect. As of 1900, the theories of Sigmund Freud about hysteria and other common nervous syndromes were known to most medical men, but they occupied no more prominence than the varied theories of numerous contemporaries. The specific method Freud used in arriving at these theories—his beloved "psychoanalysis"—was considered more a curiosity than a model. One could often hear the ostensibly reasonable view that in Freud's own hands psychoanalysis had indeed generated some interesting findings, but that it was neither teachable nor learnable and that in the hands of a less talented physician would generate nothing worthwhile.

By 1911, scarcely more than a decade later, this same marginally interesting method had become the focal point for a massive, extremely bitter controversy that was the chief preoccupation of the world of official neurology and psychiatry in Europe. By 1926, the year a secret governing "Committee" of its adherents disbanded, psychoanalysis had become the single most prominent school of psychology and psychotherapy in the world, one capable of attracting a steady stream of students and followers not only from the medical specialties but also from the arts and humanities. By 1939, the year of Freud's death, it had become, in the words of Auden's eulogy, "a whole climate of opinion." Freud's own stature had grown in proportion to the latent scientific and philosophical dimensions that had informed the topic of neurosis from the start. The niche had been there all along, and it was Freud whom the world called upon to fill it. Jung was left to find his own parallel niche, and he did so by leaving room in his system for some of the religious and mystical sentiments that Freud personally abhorred.

Such was the rapid rise of psychoanalysis to a position of predominance that it completely supplanted the discourse of an earlier age. Gone were the names and contributions of many other thinkers; gone, too, were the variety of original points of view that had made the earlier period so fertile a ground for theory. It was a situation ripe for the rewriting of history, and out of it there inexorably arose several sets of myths and half-truths, many of them initiated by Freud himself. One set of myths and half-truths involved a false portrayal of the era. It was said that originally Freud alone tackled the issues of human sexuality honestly, and likewise that Freud alone took the idea of the unconscious seriously. It was also maintained that for doing so he was roundly ignored or else unfairly attacked, forced by his contemporaries to live the life of a scientific nomad until the world caught up to him. All of this is demonstrably untrue, but it has only been in the last twenty-five years or so that historians have had the confidence to set the record straight.

A second set of myths and half-truths related to the origins of Freud's theories. It was said that his ideas first emerged in the course of his clinical work—indeed, that his conclusions were more or less forced on him by his patients—and that he then extended these findings by performing a heroic self-analysis upon himself. Here, too, there is more distortion than truth. It is now quite clear where Freud actually got his ideas—from his library principally—and it is equally clear that his novel application of these ideas to the testimony of his patients was often as likely to be tendentiously wide of the mark as on it. The ancillary myth of the self-analysis has only recently come under critical scrutiny, and while it is still too early to tell what the final judgment will be, it is already clear that some of the alleged theoretical "fruits" of this episode were available to Freud from other sources.

This book is principally concerned with a third set of myths and half-truths, those having to do with the early years of this century when psychoanalysis first came to controversial prominence. Because Freud's were the founding insights, it has seemed more or less natural to most commentators to tell the story of the psychoanalytic movement from the perspective of Vienna. Told in this way, it readily becomes the story of how Freud gradually refined his theories while simultaneously attracting a number of followers, some of whom were nonetheless ambivalent about all or part of psychoanalysis and later left to found their own schools. The view seems reasonable enough on the surface, and it makes the noisy schisms of the era less disturbing by robbing them of much of their significance. Paradoxically, the view is equally attractive to the adherents of the dissident figures, since it allows them to suppose that their champions held distinctive views of their own right from the start.

The essential problem with this view is that it reads Freud's later stature back into the earlier period, to the neglect of the prevailing realities within the European medical community. At the time, the people who mattered were Jung and his Zurich mentor, Eugen Bleuler, not Freud. Jung and Bleuler already possessed international reputations as pioneering psychiatrists. Moreover, they had the prestige of the Zurich medical school behind them and they commanded the Zurich Psychiatric Clinic with its attached psychological laboratory, where interested physicians could receive training. In short, it was Jung and Bleuler who possessed the institutional resources needed to turn psychoanalysis into a scientific movement. The rise of psychoanalysis directly reflected these institutional realities. It was when Jung and Bleuler first began reporting that they could confirm some of Freud's theories with their own patients that the controversies began in earnest. It was Zurich where almost all of Freud's most important early followers first received training in the new methods. And it was Zurich that ultimately provided psychoanalysis with its first official institutions: the first congress, the first journal, the International Association when it was founded—all these initially were run out of Zurich, not Vienna. It was Jung and Bleuler who put Freud on the scientific map, not the other way around.

The story of the psychoanalytic movement has to be understood in terms of the axis between Zurich and Vienna. This perspective forces us to recognize the fundamental change that psychoanalysis underwent shortly after Jung and Bleuler came upon the scene. Insofar as psychoanalysis was a science, its findings, in principle, had to be replicatable by others. Recognizing this, and seeking to capitalize on it, Freud in effect presented himself to Jung and Bleuler as a scientific asset to be acquired. They responded on their side by setting up the necessary practical institutions. Initially, the arrangement seemed straightforward. Freud's priority was unquestioned, and beyond priority science knows no property rights in its discoveries. There was no logical reason why Zurich should not be the international center for psychoanalysis, and at first Freud was very eager to see it become so.

But Freud's ambitions were not only scientific; his attentions were little diverted by such things as experimental validation, outcome studies, and the other accoutrements of collegial research. No sooner did psychoanalysis acquire the much-needed trappings of day-to-day science than it began branching off into other areas. By degrees, it ceased to be primarily a clinical method and became increasingly a literary, artistic, and cultural movement with general aspirations as a totalizing worldview. Jung, for his own reasons, was happy to hasten the transformation. Bleuler was not, and began to withdraw. As the essential character of the movement changed, so, too, did the reasonableness of the institutional arrangement. For in a literary, artistic, and cultural movement there are indeed such things as property rights. When Freud became distrustful of Jung, he decided he had to take back command of psychoanalysis.

The resulting confrontation was scientifically destructive and personally savage. It does not do Freud credit that in order to reassert his property rights, he turned all too readily to the means that lay closest at hand. Making out of his new therapeutic tool a weapon, Freud attempted to use what he knew about Jung's personal life to exert a measure of essentially ideological control that the younger man found intolerable. It does not do Jung credit that in trying to counteract this pressure while yet remaining the official president of the movement, he began to toy with the idea of introducing a Christianized version of psychoanalysis. This only accelerated the pace of Freud's insinuations, until finally Jung threatened to retaliate in kind by revealing what he knew about Freud's personal life. The actual outcome, in which each man found the liberty to go his own way, was predictable only in retrospect. For a time, it was all the two men could do to keep the more ruinous possibilities of their situation from running riot and wrecking everything they had worked so hard to build up. Their final act of collaboration was to accept the fact that they were stalemated.

The story is both complex and disturbing. Of all its manifold dimensions, perhaps the most important has also been the hardest to conceptualize: the relation between the personal factor and the theoretical struggle that arose out of it and ultimately supplanted it.

To be sure, Freud's imputations as to Jung's motives have been a matter of record since the publication of their correspondence in 1974. But heretofore there has been no way of appraising those charges objectively and thus of arriving at a final verdict about the whole episode. The ultimate break was so painful for Jung—he teetered close to insanity for several years—that afterward he put as much distance as he reasonably could between himself and this period of his life. Having arrived at last at his own distinctively "Jungian" views, he elected to obscure the essential continuity between his later endeavors and his earlier one. Even more to the point, he deliberately concealed the biographical keys that were needed to make that continuity meaningful. Yet the story of the psychoanalytic movement cannot be adequately told without Jung. Indeed, such was his pivotal role in it that were one to put it in the form of a drama, one would perforce make Jung the protagonist: dramatically speaking, he is the motor of the story, the engine that makes things happen.

Even with the red flag of Freud's imputations, it has not proved easy for commentators to keep the requisite attention focused on Jung's motives. The understandable wish of history to know those motives better has seemed to fare badly before the bar of a formidable but essentially right-headed contemporary philosophy of science which rules categorically that the animus of a discoverer ordinarily has no bearing whatsoever on the ultimate validity of the discovery. Not knowing what Jung's motives were, psychoanalytic historians have had no way of fashioning the rejoinder that needed to be made. In point of fact, Jung's incipient revisions of psychoanalytic theory, the very thing that first aroused Freud's distrust and instigated the runaway collapse of their partnership, stemmed directly from Jung's own reflections about his motives and about where they had led him psychologically. Accordingly, though it is only part of the story, an adequate historical account of the psychoanalytic movement must rescue Jung's various decisions during his career as a psychoanalyst from the deliberate mystification with which Jung subsequently surrounded them. I believe this will do Jung somewhat more justice than he was able to do to himself.

The possibility of reappraising both Jung's early career and his partnership with Freud depends to no small degree on a recent archival discovery that is as astonishing as it is improbable. In 1977 a carton of personal papers was discovered in the basement of the Palais Wilson in Geneva. Upon inspection these turned out to have been the property of one Sabina Spielrein, who had last been in Geneva in 1923. Spielrein had held a post as lecturer on psychoanalysis at the Rousseau Institute, an international pedagogical center, during the time when it was housed at the Palais Wilson. Then she had emigrated back to her native Russia. No one knows how or why this collection of personal papers was left behind, to molder or to be discovered as chance dictated.

One has to understand just how obscure a figure Spielrein was to appreciate the discovery. She was known to have been one of the first women psychoanalysts. Her bibliography comprised some thirty professional papers, a few of which had been cited in works by Jung and Freud. (One paper in particular had drawn an occasional mention in the secondary literature, for it was said to have anticipated Freud's later theory of a "death instinct.") At one time or another, she had been officially listed on the rosters of the Vienna, Berlin, Geneva, and Moscow psychoanalytic societies. But, beyond that, and beyond a few biographical facts that could be adduced from reading her professional papers, prior to 1974 virtually nothing more was known about this woman.

The first glimpse that Spielrein might be far more than a minor figure had come only with the publication of the Freud-Jung correspondence in 1974. There one could learn that before becoming an analyst, Spielrein had been Jung's patient. One could also learn that there had arisen a potentially disastrous scandal, barely covered up, implicating the two of them in an illicit romance. The Freud-Jung letters additionally made clear that when Spielrein later moved to Vienna she became personally acquainted with Freud. The documentary record expanded a bit further in 1975 with the publication of the third volume of the minutes of the Vienna Psychoanalytic Society. There one could read of Spielrein's participation in the weekly Wednesday Night Meetings of the Vienna group during the academic year 1911–1912. But the two documentary sources seemed out of joint. There was no easy way to combine them or use them together with her published papers to arrive at a coherent picture of who Spielrein was. Nonetheless, working largely on clinical intuition, a Jungian analyst based in Rome, Aldo Carotenuto, speculated in a book published in 1976 that Spielrein might have been far more important to Jung's development than had hitherto been appreciated.

Then came the discovery of the carton in the Palais Wilson. Included in the cache were portions of a diary Spielrein kept, letters and drafts of letters that she had written to Freud and Jung, and, no less important, hitherto unknown letters written back to her by both men. For being the first to speculate about her in print, Carotenuto found himself the beneficiary of this improbable find. After further research proved unavailing, Carotenuto published what he had in 1982 together with a somewhat anachronistic though thoroughly sympathetic commentary written from a Jungian perspective. In the wake of his book, a second carton was then discovered. This one was lodged at the family archive of the descendants of Edouard Claparède, a prominent Genevan psychologist who had known Spielrein personally. Still another cache has since been discovered in the personal archives of George de Morsier, once an important Swiss analyst.

Taken together, the different documentary sources allow one to sketch out large portions of what proves to have been an astonishing career. In a feminist age, I think, no one will object to the notion that the story of Spielrein's career within the psychoanalytic movement is worth telling for its own sake. Unfortunately, however, even with the new materials, it is not possible to tell that story with anything like the fullness of detail one would wish. About Spielrein's husband, for example, we know scarcely more than that he was a Jewish physician. Similarly, there are several long stretches in her life for which we have only the meagerest of ideas concerning with whom she associated or what she did. But perhaps we should be grateful that we know anything at all. As it turns out, she was a woman with a predilection for insisting on her point of view at exactly those moments when history began moving in opposing directions. In retrospect, it becomes clear why it was not accidental that her name has not come up before now.

Of all the important people who later wished Spielrein forgotten, none had so desperately pressing reasons as did Jung. Spielrein had been closest to him during that personal transformation that first made Jung into a Freudian. Likewise, she had been at the center of the sudden squall of distrust that led to the break with Freud. Ultimately, she alone was in a position to provide the missing biographical keys linking Jung's earlier endeavors with his later ones. But beyond shedding new light on Jung's early career and on his partnership with Freud, the Spielrein story, such as it can be known, has another significance. As the reader will discover, she had a crucial contribution of her own to make, one that was potentially central to the overall structure of psychoanalytic theory. Yet that contribution, like her earlier protests as a patient and as a lover, was ignored and then deliberately obscured. In this respect, Spielrein is an exemplar of the larger tale being told in this book. The silence that for so long attended her story is emblematic of a more insidious silence that gradually overtook psychoanalysis during this time. By listening in a new way, psychoanalysis gave nervous patients a voice they had not had before. But as psychoanalytic theory became increasingly restricted to suit the personal and political needs of the two men who ran it, the range of its listening narrowed. In the absence of anyone to hear, there began to be many things that patients were not permitted to say.

The philosopher Paul Ricoeur has defined history as a story about the past told to the present for present purposes. The present to which this story is addressed is the contemporary state of psychoanalysis. There are four salient features of the psychoanalytic scene today. First, it is in a period of institutional decline. Candidacies are down, patients are harder to come by, other therapeutic disciplines are clamoring for recognition. Having originally oversold itself to psychiatry, psychoanalysis now finds itself unwelcome in many of the major medical centers that used to be its bailiwick. Second, psychoanalysis is in the midst of a sustained period of remarkable theoretical fertility. A host of new theoreticians have lately taken center stage, and while some of them still claim fealty to Freud, others equally brilliant claim otherwise. Third, taken from a scientific perspective, psychoanalysis is badly in need of retrenchment. The distinguished psychologist Robert Holt has summed up the situation with regard to the current scientific status of the body of psychoanalytic doctrine: ". . . [t]he situation is not hopeless, but it *is* grave. Psychoanalysts have been living in a fool's paradise . . ." Fourth, psychoanalysis continues to exhibit an unconscionable disregard for its own history. No other contemporary intellectual endeavor, from conventional biomedical research to literary criticism, currently suffers from so profound a lack of a critical historical sense concerning its origins.

This book will argue that the seeds of the current situation were sown during the partnership between Freud and Jung. For it was during this period that historical accuracy first came to be less important than ideological correctness. Unchecked by a historical framework of accountability, the skew of ideology in turn created a context in which scientific claims could continue to be made without the needed critical tests being deemed necessary. The artificial restriction of the range of permissible interpretation, against which contemporary theorists are finally freeing themselves, also began at this time. Combined, these developments virtually guaranteed that psychoanalysis would eventually come to its present, problematic institutional status, once the remarkable momentum that Freud and Jung had won for it was finally spent.

In providing an account of the founding period of the psychoanalytic movement, this study joins a small number of similar studies which have sought to restore critical historical understanding to psychoanalysis. While such efforts cannot substitute for the efforts of practicing analysts to open fresh theoretical perspectives, nor for the much-needed efforts of scientific researchers to examine psychoanalytic hypotheses through empirical studies, they can serve as an important complement to both those endeavors. By surveying more carefully the ground upon which psychoanalysis was built, critical history can provide a map for those who wish to renovate it or build extensions. This book is written in the hope that it will significantly improve the prospects for psychoanalysis, now murkily hopeful at best.

Let me close this introduction with one final comment by way of a warning. The story that follows is not a nice one. It is not a love story. Nor is it one of those edifying stories about how a few intrepid men and women made a scientific breakthrough. If I could characterize it in a single phrase I would say that it is an unusually gruesome ghost story, where the ghost who finally devours all the people in the end is not a being but a theory—and a way of listening. When men first decided they had the power to understand one another in an entirely new way, it should not surprise us that the results could be tragic.

Part One

A Case of Hysteria

If . . . our much-plagued soul can lose its equilibrium for all time as a result of long-forgotten unpleasant sexual experiences, that would be the beginning of the end for the human race; nature would have played a gruesome trick on us!

—Emil Kraepelin, 1899

CHAPTER I

Her Father's Hand

It is in the milder cases of hysteria that such delirious states occur. . . .
Emotional disturbances seem to favor its outbreak. It is prone to
relapse. . . . Most frequently we find delusions of persecution, with
often very violent reactive fear . . . then religious and erotic delusions.
Hallucinations of all the senses are not uncommon. . . . The visual
hallucinations are mostly visions of animals, funerals, fantastic
processions swarming with corpses, devils, ghosts, and what not. . . .
The auditory delusions are simply noises in the ear (shrieks, crashes,
bangs), or actual hallucinations, often with sexual content.

—Krafft-Ebing, *Textbook of Insanity,* as cited by Jung, 1902

O N 17 AUGUST 1904, a young Russian girl named Sabina Spielrein, not yet nineteen years old, was brought over a thousand
miles from her home city of Rostov-on-Don to be admitted to the
Burghölzli Psychiatric Clinic in Zurich, Switzerland. Owing to that
hospital's formidable, if admirable, policy on the issue of patient privacy, Spielrein's hospital record is not available. Virtually everything
we know about her condition at the time of her admission, and about
the course of her illness up to that time, stems from a lecture delivered
three years later by Carl Jung, the physician in charge of her case.
That lecture has been the source of considerable misunderstanding,
because of the seeming gravity of the symptoms:

Puberty started when she was thirteen. From then on fantasies
developed of a thoroughly perverse nature which pursued her obses-
sively. These fantasies had a compulsive character: she could never
sit at a table without thinking of defecation while she was eating,
nor could she watch anyone else eating without thinking of the same
thing, and especially not her father. In particular, she could not see
her father's hands without feeling sexual excitement; for the same

reason she could no longer bear to touch his right hand. . . . If she was reproached or even corrected in any way, she answered by sticking out her tongue, or even with convulsive laughter, cries of disgust, and gestures of horror, because each time she had before her the vivid image of her father's chastising hand, coupled with sexual excitement, which immediately passed over into ill-concealed masturbation.

The seemingly grave course was matched by a vivid depiction of her state upon admission:

> . . . her condition had got so bad that she really did nothing else than alternate between deep depressions and fits of laughing, crying, and screaming. She could no longer look anyone in the face, kept her head bowed, and when anybody touched her stuck her tongue out with every sign of loathing.

This picture has led any number of contemporary commentators astray. Aldo Carotenuto, who published the first cache of Spielrein's rediscovered personal papers, has supposed that she suffered from a brief "psychotic episode" indicative of "schizophrenia." Bruno Bettelheim, whose trenchant comments on Carotenuto's book have since been added as a foreword to it, alternates between "either a schizophrenic disturbance or severe hysteria with schizoid features."

Thus does one age misjudge the illnesses of another. The fact is that there is absolutely no warrant in all the numerous personal documents left behind by Spielrein, nor in any other known document pertaining to her, for going beyond the diagnosis actually given by her physician in his lecture—"psychotic hysteria." Moreover, as will become clear in a later chapter, the whole point of that lecture, delivered under historic circumstances, was to illustrate a new approach to the specific syndrome of hysteria. The psychiatrist Anthony Storr, virtually alone among reviewers of Carotenuto's book, has seconded the diagnosis of "hysteria" while adding that because of

> . . . changed social circumstances, we rarely see the dramatic cases of conversion hysteria upon which the early theories of psychoanalysis were based. My guess is that Sabina Spielrein was one of those cases and that Jung's diagnosis underlines the fact that hysteria could indeed be so serious that it mimicked a psychotic break with reality.

Storr puts his finger on the problem: though such dramatic cases of hysteria are extremely rare nowadays, they were common enough at the turn of the century and had been well described, under a variety of labels, in the psychiatric literature. Krafft-Ebing, professor of psychiatry at the prestigious University of Vienna, had provided a comprehensive description of the phenomenology of such states in his *Textbook of Insanity,* for twenty years the premier psychiatric text in German-speaking Europe. Krafft-Ebing, anticipating his own subsequent researches into sexual pathology but confirming an ancient prejudice, rather stressed the role of erotic themes in the hallucinations of such patients. Jean-Martin Charcot, the legendary Parisian neurologist, had by contrast emphasized the theme of trauma. Charcot's view was that such delirious states regularly marked the third stage in a full-blown hysterical attack, itself understood as a manifestation of an underlying neurological condition, and that the scenes which the delirious patient enacted might often refer to the specific incident that had triggered the onset of the condition. Theodor Meynert, professor of neurology at Vienna and a renowned brain anatomist, had thought enough of such confusional states to lend his own name to them ("Meynert's Amentia"), a move that led a disgruntled former student of his, Sigmund Freud, to rename them yet again ("acute hallucinatory confusion") in his own catalogue of nervous conditions. Meynert had stressed the wish-fulfillment aspect of such states and associated them accordingly with the mentation of childhood. Freud kept the wish-fulfillment hypothesis, but sought the context in a present erotic situation.

The truth is that physicians of that era knew both a lot more and a lot less about psychotic hysteria than today's clinicians. They knew more because they had far more direct experience. Nowadays, an incipient hysterical symptom, whether a strange pain, or a cramp, or a dizzy spell, is likely to lead to a trip to an internist or family physician. There the patient will be prescribed Valium—one of the most widely prescribed medicines in the United States today—or the like, and sent on his or her way. Those who are persistent enough to return a second and third time, and to insist in the face of a negative diagnostic work-up that their symptoms are getting worse, will eventually be sent off to a psychiatrist with the thought that obviously they are under a lot of stress. This unsympathetic regime, coupled with a widespread cultural dissemination of certain basic psychological principles, is sufficient to keep most cases from progressing very far along the hysterical path. It is rare nowadays for hysteric patients to reach the stage of delirium, and when they do, and are admitted to a psychiatric facility, interns and residents are rounded up from all around to see the syndrome in full flower. This on the basis that they may never be so lucky as to see such a case again.

At the turn of the century, however, matters were quite otherwise. The incipient symptom might lead straightaway to a trip to the local nerve specialist. There the patient would be interviewed with great curiosity and, depending on the doctor's specialty, a regime of treatment would be instituted that might consist of cold showers (properly dignified as "hydrotherapy"), electro-galvanic massage (with the current strong enough to leave welts), or a trip to a local spa (one the physician usually was personally connected with). If the condition worsened, more severe remedies might be tried, including, ultimately, ovariectomies and clitoridectomies. In the meantime, it was up to the family to provide for the patient as best they could. But what were parents or spouse and children to do when the condition had already been sanctioned by a nerve specialist? In such a climate, hysteria flourished. So, too, did scientific knowledge of it.

The basic syndrome had, of course, been known to the ancients. Classical Greek theory had it that the seat of the disease was the uterus (*hystera* in Greek), hence the name "hysteria," and the presumed cause was thought to be some sort of sexual or procreative frustration, for which the equally classical remedy of sexual intercourse might be prescribed. The Greeks knew, further, that a purely psychological cause might be sufficient, such as a secret passion that the patient would not reveal. The latter insight was subsequently amplified by the great medieval physician Avicenna for a related condition then prevalent in the Islamic world, "love sickness." As part of the examination, Avicenna would take the patient's pulse while inquiring if there were not perhaps a certain person that the patient had taken a fancy to. If the pulse quickened, the inquiry grew progressively more precise: did this person live in a certain city, a certain quarter, a certain street? And so on, until the identity of the secret love was revealed. At that point, to be sure, it was up to the families to see what could be arranged; only if marriage was out of the question did Avicenna institute other forms of treatment designed to strengthen the will.

The suspicion of concealed or frustrated eroticism continued to cling to hysteria—"the disease of nuns, virgins, and old maids"—almost down to the modern era, though each historical period speculated differently as to how best to conceptualize the physical mechanisms involved. In the mid-nineteenth century the work of two men, the ophthalmologist Richard Carter of London, and the French physician Paul Briquet, brought a sudden new clarity to the topic. Carter provided an entirely modern psychological portrait of the illness, a feature of which was his contention that the psychological motivations involved changed as the illness progressed. Briquet, meanwhile, put to rest the suspicions about sexual frustration by demonstrating that hysteria was far more common among Parisian prostitutes than among working girls in other professions. As to its causes, Briquet identified the "passions," and he was especially compelling as to the role of psychic trauma in fomenting the disease.

At the time of Spielrein's hospitalization, however, this clarity had been almost totally lost. The culprit, paradoxically, was an increase in scientific knowledge. For at the same time that Carter and Briquet were working out their psychological portraits of the illness, Louis Pasteur in France and Robert Koch in Germany were doing the far more important work of putting the final touches on the modern theory of disease. According to this new synthesis—we should pause to reflect on just how new it is—disease is caused by a disruption in the functioning of organs brought about by a specific pathogen, most often a bacterium or virus. Where the disease progressed to death, its impact upon the afflicted organs could be examined directly through postmortem anatomical examination. Otherwise, the physician could attempt to classify the disease according to the symptoms and clinical course, and then seek confirmation of his thesis by demonstrating through bacteriological study that a given pathogen was invariably present in such cases. The theory was both revolutionary and entirely sound. Moreover, since it provided a way of uniting all the relevant disciplines (clinical description, bacteriology, physiology, and postmortem anatomical examination), it almost instantly passed into universal acceptance. Koch and Pasteur ascended directly into the medical pantheon.

Unfortunately, applied to the great mass of psychiatric illnesses, the new synthesis was hopelessly premature. For in the vast majority of psychiatric ailments, excepting tertiary syphilis and a few dramatic neurological syndromes, postmortem examination could reveal no organic changes in the brain, the presumed seat of the illness. The search for pathogens was equally unavailing. To be sure, the study of the physiology of the nervous system began to make fitful if essential progress, as did knowledge of the localization of certain functions in the brain, but the only real consequence of these endeavors was that microscopic researches became part of a psychiatrist's training.

Thus it happened that in the last decades of the nineteenth century, in a well-intentioned effort to be scientific, official psychiatry went off in a hundred directions at once. Clinical syndromes multiplied as phy- sicians struggled to identify certain regular clusters of symptoms with little else to go on but direct observation. Psychiatric theorizing, meanwhile, entranced by the exciting discoveries being made concerning the nervous system, was increasingly preoccupied with extrapolating new explanations of mental disorder on the basis of a very rudimentary set of hypotheses about brain tracts, metabolic toxins, and the like—to the point where a few sharper minds realized that the whole field was degenerating into a kind of "brain mythology."

Of the many theories put forth in this period, two concern our story directly: the theory of hereditary degeneration and the theory of "functional" changes in the nervous system. The theory of hereditary degeneration was a kind of speculative psychiatric attempt to align the discipline with the new concepts of Darwinian evolution. Specifically, it was contended that in certain families hereditary taint would manifest itself in progressively more severe conditions over successive generations. Thus, in the first generation, one might find only such mild disorders as nervousness and a general psychological eccentricity (perhaps manifest in unusual religious ideas or else in an artistic bent). In the next generation, more severe illnesses would emerge, such as epilepsy or severe hysteria. In the third generation, these in turn would be replaced by psychosis and overt criminality. And so on, until the line died out. The theory strikes the modern reader as quite odd, even if upon a moment's reflection he or she will realize that it is based on a true-enough observation, namely that mental illness does indeed seem to run in families, with increasing pathology seen at least in some of them. Where we differ from the nineteenth-century view is in our predilection for attributing any progressive deterioration to psychological causes, and for seeing in bad parenting the causes of pathology in the next generation. At the turn of century, however, it seemed equally reasonable to assume that such psychological causes were supplemented by physical ones, that the familial protoplasm was deteriorating along with its mental health. And though sharper minds were beginning to object to this theory, too, its day was not yet done. Accordingly, one of the first duties of an admitting psychiatrist in a state psychiatric facility such as the Burghölzli was to take a family history.

The theory of hereditary degeneration also made its mark in fields other than psychiatry proper. For example, beginning with Krafft-Ebing's pioneering work *Psychopathia Sexualis,* it was regularly invoked as an explanatory variable in the literature on sexual deviancy. Then, too, it enjoyed a very definite cultural vogue as social critics used it as a basis for attacking what they saw as degenerate trends in literature and the arts. Max Nordau's enormously popular book *Degeneration* sought to portray any number of modern artists as variants on the criminal-genius type, with the notorious composer Richard Wagner as a prime example. But by far the most ominous development was the use of the degeneration idea to foster incipient theories of racial inferiority. This was a particularly sensitive matter for Jews, since it was then accepted as a simple medical fact by Jewish and Gentile physicians alike that rates of nervous illness were higher among Jews than among the other races of Europe.

The other prominent theory which concerns our story, and which would have been routinely applied to Spielrein's case, was the doctrine of "functional" nervous disorders. This category of illness was a direct outgrowth of the recalcitrant peculiarity that the brains of nervous sufferers showed no anatomical changes at postmortem examination. Thus, by the early 1880s, it had became fashionable to theorize about "functional" changes in the nervous system, i.e., nonstructural changes, as the cause of "nervous illness," or "neurosis" as it is now called. In trying to conceptualize how such functional change could arise, medical theories turned to the idea of a trauma: just as a magnet mysteriously loses its power of attraction if it is repeatedly struck by a hammer, so, too, it was thought that the nervous system might somehow alter its functioning in the face of trauma, whether external (such as being struck by a runaway carriage) or internal (in the form of an endogenous toxin such as might be produced by an overactive thyroid). It was readily understood that such a trauma might be sexual in nature, such as traumatic abuse in childhood, just as it was well understood that the physiological changes of puberty constituted a significant endogenous stressor that might evoke hysterical symptoms in the constitutionally predisposed. But such possible sexual causes were not especially privileged; the "functional" view, unlike that of earlier eras, understood that a wide range of precipitants might be sufficient to trigger hysteria. The real cause lay in the resulting alteration of the nervous system, itself only possible in the hereditarily predisposed.

Interestingly enough, roughly the same paradigm had also seemed to prove its worth, at least for a time, in the study of hypnotism. The juxtaposition of the two conditions, the hypnotic trance and hysterical "somnambulism," was largely the work of Jean-Martin Charcot.

Charcot had a legendary career. By the end of it, not only had he first identified all manner of valid neurological syndromes, including tabes dorsalis and poliomyelitis, but, having married into wealth and possessing a knack for sociability, he had also established his home as one of the most popular of all the salons of Paris. His Tuesday lectures at the Salpêtrière Hospital were attended not only by every foreign physician in town but also by the local Parisian literary and artistic elite. In the early 1880s, with Gallic confidence, Charcot declared that the study of structural neurological disorders, i.e., those confirmed by postmortem examination, was largely exhausted and he turned his attention to the then new category of functional disorders, hysteria being the prime example. For all its legendary success in the area of structural neurosis, however, Charcot's theory of disease was a throwback to an earlier era. Viewing neurological diseases as more or less species unto themselves, he sought to chart the degree of their manifestation in any given patient. This had worked well for an illness like polio, and Charcot did not hesitate to import it to the study of functional disorders. Thus, for hysteria, he described four stages in the hysterical attack, while for hypnotism he outlined three degrees of hypnotizability. Moreover, by mixing and matching symptoms from these two domains, Charcot thought he had discovered an essential connection between them based on symptomatic similarity. In his view, hysteria involved a constitutional weakness of the nervous system whose principal psychological effect was to render the patient amenable to spontaneous hypnotic states. The juxtaposition also worked the other way around, according to Charcot: only hysterics were truly susceptible to hypnosis. On this theoretical basis, illustrated with dramatic case material, Charcot in 1882 won recognition of the neurological reality of hypnotism from the French Academy of Sciences, the same august body which had twice before rejected the idea.

There was, however, a fatal problem with Charcot's theory—or, rather, with his praxis. The attending physicians who were responsible for preparing his case demonstrations were well aware of the theory, as were the patients themselves, largely working-class women who had found a second home of sorts in the Salpêtrière. Eager not to leave, and well coached by junior physicians eager not to disappoint, these patients, largely traumatized and largely female, quickly learned how to enact all that was expected of them at Grand Rounds. Duly performed were the three stages of the hypnotic trance along with the even more dramatic phenomena of the four stages of an hysterical attack. When Charcot touched one of them, say, in the ovary, she would promptly go into a swoon. This illustrated the power of the "hysterogenic zone." When he touched the spine with a metal rod, the paralysis that afflicted the right arm suddenly switched to the left. This was called *le transfert*. And so forth, all according to the latest neurological principles. Moreover, since the phenomena were accepted as genuine, it soon occurred to an elite group of inventive researchers that the alterations of perception entailed in some hysterical symptoms might offer a comparative basis for studying basic psychological principles. Thus was French experimental psychology born, with Charcot's hysterics serving as its laboratory frogs.

The corrective to this grand though persuasive folly appeared soon enough. In 1888, Hippolyte Bernheim of Nancy published the first of two important works in which he argued that hypnotism was but a special case of general human suggestibility. As a necessary corollary to this view, Bernheim maintained that just about anyone, not just hysterics, could be hypnotized. He argued further that the phenomena that people exhibited under the impact of suggestion, including the trance state itself, were just that, the effects of the suggestion, and had no independent neurological reality of their own. Bernheim had been drawn to the study of hypnotism partly for medical reasons—it offered a quick, effective remedy for certain nervous complaints—and partly because as a Jew he was concerned with a recent sensational murder case in Eastern Europe where a rabbi's son had testified that he had seen his father murder a Christian child to obtain blood for the Passover ritual. The charge of ritually murdering Christian children—the so-called "blood libel"—was a staple of anti-Semitism that dated back to the Middle Ages. Its reappearance in a well-publicized trial in the latter half of the nineteenth century was an ominous development indeed. As he studied the trial records, Bernheim realized that the prosecutors had been suggesting the needed testimony to the witness. Bernheim concluded, rightly, that if mere suggestion could be so gruesomely powerful in such highly charged circumstances, then it could also be the sole efficient factor underlying all of Charcot's recent work. In his book, which devoted chapter after chapter to the Salpêtrière, Bernheim pulled no punches.

The ensuing debate—Charcot died suddenly in 1893, just in time to be spared the full extent of his debacle—had both serious and comic aspects. From a theoretical point of view, it meant that the study of hysteria was once again open territory for fresh research efforts. If

Charcot's particular synthesis did not hold, it was still conceded that some alteration of the nervous system was involved, usually conceived of as inborn nervous hypersensitivity. From a more practical point of view, it meant that henceforth researchers would have to be extremely careful lest similar charges of using unwitting suggestion be lodged against themselves. In particular, this meant not relying too heavily on the self-reports of hysterical subjects, whose testimony was now scientifically suspect. But the real stir created by Bernheim lay in his assertion that anybody, not just hysterics, could be hypnotized. For German medicine had already grown comfortable with the idea that the extraordinary conditions Charcot was describing could occur only among the relatively inferior racial stock of the French. German physicians, therefore, rather than being reassured by Bernheim's contention that the Charcot phenomena were not genuine, now felt threatened by the prospect of the spectacular French symptoms spreading to their own home grounds. There thus arose in both the medical and the legal literature in Germany worries about a possible "psychical epidemic" if Bernheim's findings became widely disseminated to the populace. Nobody seems to have had the wit to notice that this medico-legal worry, which became quite widespread, was itself a psychical epidemic of sorts, though a discerning Belgian commentator, Joseph Delboeuf, did weigh in with the very pertinent observation that it had really been the French physicians who had shown great suggestibility, more so than their patients.

By the turn of the century, whether as a delayed aftereffect of these debates or for other reasons not yet fully understood, the phenomenology of hysteria had begun to change. The most dramatic forms, with their somnambulistic and delirious states, started to disappear from all parts of Europe. In this respect, Spielrein's delirium was part of the final crest of a once great wave. Her case was destined to be one of the last to be described in what had been a hitherto burgeoning literature.

Diagnosis is a matter of perception; it depends upon prior experience and upon theory. Spielrein's delirium was a familiar enough sight from both points of view. Numerous cases similar to hers had been well described in the literature, and though some suspicions remained as to just how seriously one ought to take the hallucinations and vehement emotional expressions, it was still considered good medicine to grant that the patient suffered from something. The prevailing view had it that the real disturbance lay in the hysteric constitution itself, conceived in terms of an inherited physiological hypersensitivity of the nervous system. Opinion varied on a wide variety of subsidiary matters, such as whether the condition could exist in men, or how best to conceive the psychological deficit brought about by the physical condition, or what etiological weight to assign to various environmental factors. Nonetheless, it was well understood that such hysterical deliria could arise and yet bode no more ill in terms of the ultimate prognosis than any of the other, more common manifestations of the hysteric constitution.

HOSPITAL TREATMENT

ANOTHER SOURCE of diagnostic misconception is the fact that Spielrein had to be hospitalized. In our day and age, such a radical step tends to be reserved for more serious illnesses. Thus, our imaginations tend to envision not only a grave condition in the patient but especially heroic efforts by her doctors. Here again, we easily misjudge the practice of an earlier era. In fact, hospitalization was often employed as a treatment for hysteria, especially in cases where delirium was manifest, precisely because it was well known that such symptoms tended to remit almost immediately once the patient had been separated from the family.

Charcot, whose theory had stressed the seemingly irremediable factor of hereditary taint, was nonetheless himself a great believer in hospitalization—as was his quondam disciple Pierre Janet, who at the time of Spielrein's admission was perhaps the foremost authority on hysteria in the world. On this issue (as, indeed, on other hypotheses of Charcot's) Janet supplied a subtle psychological rationale of his own. In his view, hospitalization was needed to isolate the patient from the family while ratifying the patient's sense of being ill. For in "the moral struggle" that arose around the symptoms, the family's reaction itself typically became pathogenic:

> The excess of the insistence causes an exaggeration of the resistance; the girl seems to understand that the least concession on her part would cause her to pass from the condition of a patient to that of a capricious child, and to this she will never consent.

In effect, it fell to the hospital to win the negotiation over symptoms after the family, and such local physicians as had been consulted, had failed. Of course, the patient might well recognize what was afoot and protest accordingly. Thus in 1893 Sigmund Freud found it politic, while writing up a similar case for admission to the Binswangers' private sanitorium in Kreuzlingen, to append the following grace note to the chart:

> I have promised her that the doctors there will be treating her equally humanely and lovingly as we do and will not believe that she is simulating or exaggerating. If one shows her interest, maybe something could be done for her.

The same year as Spielrein's hospitalization, the prominent Swiss neurologist and psychotherapist Paul Dubois of Bern published his magnum opus on the moral treatment of nervous disorders. Dubois was a radical who disbelieved in such standard notions as hereditary degeneration, and his treatment method, "persuasion," differed significantly from ordinary hypnotherapy. Nonetheless, he, too, favored hospitalization:

> I am accustomed to see these hysterical manifestations, especially the dramatic ones, cease during the first days of sojourn in a sanitorium, often from the first hour, under the sole influence of a change of moral atmosphere, without even giving myself the trouble to provoke the auto-suggestion of the cure. Sometimes, however, one must bring it about by conversation.

Other leading physicians were inclined to see the "conversation" as superfluous. Thus at Emil Kraepelin's hospital clinic in Munich, there existed no rooms set aside for a patient and a doctor to have a private talk. And in Paris, under Charcot's successors at the Salpêtrière, Joseph-Jules Déjerine and Joseph Babinski, the treatment of choice for hysteria was total isolation, which went so far as to amount almost to sensory deprivation: the patient's bed was surrounded by white sheets, and food was slipped in on a tray.

No one, however, stressed the therapeutic use of hospitalization for nervous conditions more than the American physician, and sometime novelist, Weir Mitchell. The Weir Mitchell Rest Cure, which achieved worldwide fame and was endorsed by Sigmund Freud among others, consisted of enforced bed rest, the isolation of the patient from friends and all lively diversions, and overfeeding. Mitchell uniformly prescribed overfeeding (thereby earning the sobriquet "Dr. Quiet and Dr.

Diet'') for all nervous conditions, on the theory that the enhanced nutrition had physiological as well as moral effects.

The real problem was not what to do with the patients while they were hospitalized, but the difficulties ensuing upon their release. The rapid remission of symptoms raised questions. Dubois addressed this issue:

> I have seen this false shame that patients feel in yielding to a psychotherapeutic influence not only hinder the cure but provoke relapses on their return to the family circle.... They experience a very natural repugnance to confessing to their neighbors and their friends the rapid cure of their old troubles. They fear that they will say to them: "What! You were cured in two months of this trouble which lasted for years, and that by psychotherapeutic measures! But then you were a 'malade imaginaire'; you could have cured yourself long ago if you had more energy. I could have told you that." There are patients who fear such judgement, and who voluntarily prolong their convalescence in order not to call forth these unkindly receptions.

For all the severity of their treatment regime, Déjerine and Babinski had no better strategy than to leave discharge up to the patient. In 1907, an American physician, A. A. Brill, visited the Salpêtrière, and found a woman who had undergone *traitement par isolement* a number of times: "She said that when she became bored and no longer enjoyed her isolation, she asked for her discharge, and the doctors were very *gentils* about it." Weir Mitchell's solution was to set a very definite duration ahead of time—two weeks in bed and no more, with light exercise then following. When one patient balked at rising from her cot at the appointed hour, Mitchell found a spirited remedy. If she would not get up, he announced, then he would join her, and he began to undress, a performance that sent the recalcitrant woman scrambling for her clothes and the exercise room.

Here, as with so many matters having to do with hysteria, and with nervous diseases generally, it was Pierre Janet who had worked out the most sophisticated treatment strategies. Once the newly hospitalized patient became accessible, Janet made a careful study of his or her case, writing down everything that was said and using a variety of other means, such as automatic writing, automatic talking, and hypnosis, whenever conscious recall was unavailing. In this way, Janet built up beautifully detailed case histories in which he was able to track how various constellations of split-off ideas—for Janet the hallmark of the syndrome—had been gradually built up over time. For treating specific dissociated ideas, such as the split-off memory of a traumatic incident, Janet would again employ hypnosis, this time as a vehicle for combatting the resulting symptom directly or else for literally undoing the traumatic memory, i.e., by suggesting that it had never happened. Thus for a patient whose symptoms ultimately traced back to a night in childhood where she had shared her bed with a girl whose face was horribly disfigured, Janet had the patient imagine, under hypnosis, that she was back in that scene but that the little girl's face was normal. Over the longer haul of a protracted hospitalization, however, Janet stressed rehabilitation, and he employed a variety of means such as work therapy, mental exercises, and specific instructions to undertake certain tasks, all of which were designed to rebuild the patient's moral strength, understood in terms of "mental energy." This regime of mental rehabilitation accorded well with Janet's theory that the underlying cause of hysteria was a constitutionally weakened nervous system, manifested in a tendency toward dissociated states. The net effect was to provide a reeducation toward life and thus prepare for the day of discharge.

A GYMNASIUM EDUCATION

JANET ONCE remarked that many patients were merely "acting" and that one should not believe "one-fourth" of what they say: "They try to impress you with their grandeur or their guilt, in which they themselves believe only half-heartedly or not at all." Spielrein's parents seem to have acted on similar advice, for they brought their daughter to Zurich expressly with the idea that as soon as her delirium cleared she could enroll herself at the prestigious medical school at the University of Zurich. Consideration of this somewhat startling plan ought by itself to make us rethink the significance of the presenting complaints, and of what was and was not unusual about the case.

Spielrein's preoccupation with defecation, especially during mealtimes, was not unusual. It was a commonplace symptom at the time and, indeed, there was another case of it at the same hospital within the next two years. Though Victorian mores have been blamed for too much in the genesis of hysteria, here they did play a decided role in shaping a certain common run of symptoms. Girls who had been inculcated with an ideal of femininity so celestial that it precluded even basic physical functions like eating, defecating, and perspiring tended to make just such things the topics of their preoccupations when their will to sublimate was otherwise breaking down. It was a simple enough psychic logic whereby a well-bred teenager might protest against the formality of a sit-down dinner with thoughts about where the food would soon be coming out again.

Similarly, Spielrein's visual hallucination of her father's hand about to strike her was not unprecedented. Such cases were common enough, and ever since Rousseau's descriptions in *The Confessions* of his youthful pleasure at being beaten, the connection with eroticism had been well understood. Krafft-Ebing had updated the scientific understanding of the connection in his monumental *Psychopathia Sexualis* with numerous cases such as that of a woman who derived voluptuous pleasure simply from imagining the blows of her "school-mistress' hand." Nor was intimate knowledge of such things confined to the medical world. Rudolph Binion, in his biography of Lou Andreas-Salomé, has described scenes of beating and defecation in her early childhood, scenes which for the grown woman were still vivid enough, and exciting enough, to be commemorated in a very private diary. And once again, though hysterics were in short supply at the Burghölzli hospital, yet another patient turned up in a few years' time with similar concerns about being struck by her father:

> Her father loved her, sexually; it struck her as a child that he, besides other evidence of tenderness, slapped her in a peculiar way on her nates, and indeed only in the absence of her mother.

Nor were Spielrein's "ill-concealed masturbation" and grand displays of disgust so unusual. As we shall see in a later chapter, there had been still one more patient with a virtually identical constellation of symptoms who had been treated at the Burghölzli two and a half years earlier.

The seeming crudity of Spielrein's privately enacted drama may strike today's reader as extreme. But here, too, the attending physicians would have had a ready avenue for understanding the case in a gentler fashion. It would have been noted that the young woman was Russian, and it was well known that hysteria could take rather uncivilized forms in that portion of the world. No less an authority than Krafft-Ebing was of the opinion that overt masochism was a congenital, and regularly self-confessed, sexual preference among Russian and Slavic women. Similarly, Albert Schrenck-Notzing, Krafft-Ebing's student and a pioneer in the use of hypnosis as a remedy for sexual idiosyncrasy, found some of what he described as his most intractable cases among his Russian patients. And even Jung as Spielrein's physician would appeal to her nationality when, five years later, he would apologize to a colleague, Sigmund Freud, who had commented on the peculiarities of her manner of expression. In explanation, Jung remarked simply that "Frl. [Fräulein] S. is a Russian, hence her awkwardness."

Yet, if many aspects of Spielrein's case were relatively unexceptional, some were quite unusual. To begin with, the very fact that she was a hysteric from a rich family made her stand out at that hospital. Hysterics from good families ordinarily went to private sanitoria, while the Burghölzli, though it had an affiliation with the University of Zurich, was a large cantonal facility, roughly akin to one of our state hospitals. Such hysterics as the Burghölzli did admit were uneducated and came largely from the lowest classes. Their numbers were relatively small compared with the other patient groups, such as the dements, tertiary syphilitics, and schizophrenics, that made up a state hospital's usual run of cases at that time. Thus, in the year 1904, of 276 new admissions to the Burghölzli, only twelve patients bore a diagnosis in any way entailing hysteria. Among those twelve, perhaps only Spielrein and one or two others came from sufficient wealth that they could afford "first-class" accommodations.

The fact that Spielrein was Russian also made her rare at the Burghölzli. Of the same 276 admissions in 1904, only five patients were Russians. That she was Jewish was likewise exceptional, for Jews were almost equally rare, constituting altogether nine of the total of 332 patients, old and new, who would be lodged at the hospital in 1904.

Spielrein's Russian background provided her with yet something else that was quite distinctive in her new milieu—a Gymnasium degree. As such she was the beneficiary of a liberal Czarist educational policy quite different from the one existing in Switzerland at the time. In Russia, women were allowed to attend a Gymnasium and thence a university. In Switzerland, a daughter from a rich family could retain private tutors in adolescence, and thereby acquire the ability to feel comfortable in intellectual conversation, but such preparation did not equip her to begin university studies. Only the Gymnasium degree or its equivalent allowed one to enroll at a Swiss university in a degree program. Thus, when the Zurich medical school had opened to women in the early 1890s, the first female graduate had been a Russian. Spielrein's educational background and her university prospects were something a local Swiss girl could not match.

Spielrein would have seemed to the admitting physicians not so much a grotesque as an exotic. Her delirium aside, she was educated, she came from a rich family, she had professional ambitions, and as a Russian Jew she was an outsider. We would like to know more about her family, and her background, but virtually the sole source of information we have on either comes from passing comments in a diary Spielrein kept during the years 1909–1911. Moreover, it is not possible to correlate this information, such as it is, with the anamnesis reported by the doctor in charge of her case. The same is true of the early childhood recollections which Spielrein herself later published in an article in 1912. Between the diary and the article, one can see that as a very small girl Spielrein had been an imaginative child, given over to fantasy and exciting games wherein an uncle would playfully terrorize her by pretending to be God and pretending to take her away with him. She in turn had then played the same game with her baby brother, Jean, reversing the roles. As well, like many children, she was preoccupied with the question of where babies came from and devised numerous strategies, including a kitchen-counter version of alchemy, for bringing this miracle to pass. In adolescence, Spielrein developed into a very serious young woman, prone to think herself unattractive and prone to withdraw on account of it, but an excellent student who kept herself near the top of her class. She pursued music recreationally, and various men in the privacy of her own longing. If the worsening symptoms of her physician's description interfered with her social life, it is not evident in her diary. Nor did her condition interfere with her blossoming intellectuality. In Gymnasium she wrote erudite papers on the history of religion and she otherwise kept herself intelligently abreast of political developments in Russia.

Spielrein's parents were cosmopolitan people who took their vacations not only in St. Petersburg but also in Paris, in Kolberg on the Baltic Sea, and by the shores of Lake Constance in Switzerland. They maintained a household in Rostov-on-Don, after Odessa the leading seaport on the Black Sea, complete with a nanny, or *babushka,* for the children. The father was a businessman, the mother a university graduate who had settled into an upper-class life-style full of travel and private intrigues. They were decidedly not in love, and Spielrein's mother competed with her adolescent daughter for the attentions of various men, including a Gymnasium teacher who had roused Spielrein to great displays of bashfulness. As well, the mother seems to have capitalized on her husband's name to extract a peculiar revenge against him. In German, ''Spielrein'' means ''play-pure'' and easily takes on sexual connotations. Having accepted Herr Spielrein's marriage proposal only grudgingly, Frau Spielrein then elected to have Sabina, the first of five children born to their union, raised in complete sexual ignorance. The logic of this policy was that the child should exist outside of the contaminated world of an unhappy marriage bed. Such was the clout that the Spielreins enjoyed locally in the boomtown of Rostov that Frau Spielrein was even able to have the Gymnasium curriculum changed so that her daughter would be spared having to learn about reproduction in biology classes. The fact that Herr Spielrein enjoyed giving his firstborn child an occasional slap on the behind may have been due to an understandable wish to break into the all-too-pure magic circle of mother and daughter. That his daughter understood these slaps erotically might have been at least partly in response to his fantasies about the matter.

SEX AND TRAUMA

ONE OTHER FACTOR made Spielrein's delirium potentially significant for Jung and the other Burghölzli physicians, though it had nothing to do with her personally. Early in 1904, several months before Spielrein's admission, there appeared Leopold Löwenfeld's latest work, *Psychic Obsessions,* which contained two important communications from Sigmund Freud. Eugen Bleuler, the Burghölzli director, promptly wrote a favorable review of the volume for the *Munich Medical Weekly* in April of 1904. In his review, Bleuler paused to give special praise to Freud.

Freud had first come to notice in the mid-1880s through his advocacy of a new drug, cocaine, as a treatment for the fatigue, impotence, and other symptoms characteristic of a then well-recognized neurosis, neurasthenia. Soon thereafter he had congenially translated into German two volumes of Charcot's, along with one of Bernheim's, and then followed in 1891 with an exceptional theoretical monograph of his own on the subject of aphasia. The monograph is still cited to this day in the neurological literature. He also had published a lesser-known series of papers on childhood paralyses.

But Freud really burst into the medical science of his day with his joint publication in 1895 of *Studies on Hysteria* with the distinguished Viennese internist and physiological researcher Josef Breuer. It was immediately recognized that Breuer and Freud's sensitive psychological portraits of their patients were at least the equal of Pierre Janet's published cases, and far superior to those of all other writers in the field. Their theory, meanwhile, was both accessible and entirely reasonable: hysteria, according to Breuer and Freud, arose from strangulated emotional experiences that, deprived of the normal avenues of discharge, manifested themselves anew in the symptoms. Breuer's and Freud's method of treatment, moreover, bore a uniquely rational relationship to their conception of the disorder: if the patient, usually under light hypnosis but sometimes even without it, could be brought to reexperience the affect that had been suppressed in the first instance, then the symptom would disappear. This method—named "cathartic therapy," somewhat imprecisely, after Aristotle's theory of the purgative value of viewing tragedy in the theater—was soon tried by a number of physicians in other cities, generally with a view to comparing it with more standard forms of hypnotism. Results were mixed, but not unpromising. As to the kind of psychic traumas that might cause strangulated affect, Breuer and Freud kept an open mind: in their most celebrated case, that of "Anna O.," the pathogen seems to have been the great strain of caring for a dying father, but in many other cases of hysteria the two authors did not hesitate to invoke as causal what Breuer termed the secrets of the marriage bed.

The following year, 1896, however, Freud went off on his own and staked his reputation on a radically more specific thesis, namely that the sole and sufficient cause of hysteria was a sexual trauma that had taken place in childhood. According to Freud, the symptoms of hysteria were produced by the repressed memory of the childhood assault. The startling novelty of this finding, Freud argued further, was derived from the fact that he had begun using a new, superior, nonhypnotic treatment method, which he called "psychoanalysis."

Freud's theory of 1896 is now known as "the seduction theory" and has lately enjoyed a renaissance in the minds of some contemporary observers. In fairness, it may justly be said that Freud was one of the first to recognize and describe in psychological terms the truly horrific, long-term impact that childhood sexual abuse can have. But this way of viewing the matter misses the essential point that Freud was trying to make at the time and that his contemporaries understood him to be making. For Freud was primarily interested in hysteria, not child abuse. The latter was of interest only because, in his view, it explained the former. By Freud's claim, repressed memories of childhood sexual abuse were the sole and efficient cause of every case of hysteria; all other theories were now out of date.

Understandably, Freud's claim raised epidemiological eyebrows. Hysteria was enormously widespread. It simply did not seem possible that child abuse could have occurred in every case. Krafft-Ebing, who well knew the realities of childhood molestation, chaired the meeting of the Vienna Society of Physicians when Freud first presented his new findings. Though otherwise well disposed toward Freud, Krafft-Ebing commented in the discussion that it all sounded "like a scientific fairy-tale." Some critics in the literature were harsher still, accusing Freud of having suggested the repressed memories of abuse to his patients. That Freud worked chiefly with hysterics, whose testimony was still thought suspect, made this charge all the more plausible, though to be sure Freud had also reported a similar etiological formula for obsessional neurosis.

Freud had since gone on to write a book on dream interpretation and a number of other papers, all of which were distinctive for their literary quality and for the ingenuity of their psychological analyses. Included in this output were two medical monographs published in 1901, *On Dreams* and *The Psychopathology of Everyday Life,* which had enjoyed relatively wide professional readership and largely positive critical comment. But, though he personally had changed his mind, his novel proposal on the etiology of hysteria was still his theory of record.

With the publication of Leopold Löwenfeld's book *Psychic Obsessions* in early 1904, that situation changed. In his book, Löwenfeld reported a personal letter from Freud announcing that his etiological views had undergone revision. Though still cognizant of the terrible impact of a childhood sexual trauma, Freud was now inclined to lend greater consideration to constitutional factors and to the role of fantasies at least insofar as obsessional neurosis was concerned. This of course left hysteria hanging, but the door was now opened. That Freud's letter was posted to Löwenfeld might have been due to the fact that in 1899 Löwenfeld had published the confession of one of Freud's former patients: "The patient told me with certainty that the infantile sexual scene which analysis had apparently uncovered was pure fantasy and had never really happened to him." Interestingly, the other communication from Freud in Löwenfeld's volume was a brief description of "Freud's Method of Psychoanalysis," written in the third person. Though the description was seriously deficient in important respects, it was the most comprehensive to date.

Löwenfeld's volume circulated among the Burghölzli physicians in the spring of 1904. Spielrein was admitted in August. She was a rare patient for that facility: a hysteric who was at once intelligent, well educated, and in the midst of a classical delirium—all in all, the perfect sort of person on whom to try out Freud's newest ideas.

CHAPTER 2

A Psychiatric Monastery

If I were to express briefly . . . my father's conception of schizophrenia, it would be this: He has a great tendency to sympathize with the schizophrenic patients and to share their fears and their worries. He is happy when he feels that something in a schizophrenic patient's mind responds to his attention. I believe that all his conceptions about schizophrenia have been due directly to this attitude. Both the basis and the results of his work with schizophrenic patients have been the conviction that it is worthwhile to give them individual interest and personal sympathy.

—Manfred Bleuler, 1931

―――――――

THE YOUNG RUSSIAN woman had, thanks to her delirium, landed in a very interesting milieu. The Burghölzli, under the stewardship of Eugen Bleuler, was then fast becoming the foremost psychiatric teaching hospital in the world, and was soon to eclipse even Emil Kraepelin's prestigious university clinic in Munich. Physicians from far and wide, including America, would shortly be arriving to train there.

All this would have been quite startling to anyone familiar with the Burghölzli's past. It had been set up more than four decades earlier to care for the insane of the canton of Zurich. Its founding was a source of great civic pride, and the celebrated novelist Gottfried Keller, then the poet laureate of the canton, had climbed to the top of the rafters during construction of the main building to read a poem about the new age dawning. Unfortunately, by decree of the cantonal council, the directorship of the institution had from the first been tied to the newly founded chair of psychiatry at the University of Zurich at a time when academic prestige was best won through researches into brain anatomy. Ordinarily, a professor of psychiatry at most European institutions could expect to have at his disposal a small university clinic where he would have a few short-term cases to use as teaching material. The Burghölzli was another matter altogether. Any man who signed on as professor of psychiatry at the University of Zurich found himself simultaneously entrusted with the care of more than a hundred patients, most of them incurable, for whom he was the chief medical officer. Making matters worse still were issues of language. At the time, any educated person could speak High German, but ordinary folk spoke Low German, and patients from the outlying areas around Zurich spoke a Swiss dialect all their own, one that no foreign physician could understand.

The situation was transparently unworkable right from the start. The great Wilhelm Griesinger, virtually the father of modern European psychiatry and then on the faculty of the Zurich Medical School, promptly departed for his native Germany rather than accept the dual appointment of professor of psychiatry and director of the Burghölzli. Thereafter, the chair was occupied by a parade of distinguished foreign microscopists, none of whom could speak the local dialect and all of whom quickly fled to posts in other cities in order to escape the onerous responsibility of running the asylum. The parade became self-sustaining as the prestige of the Zurich chair grew while the hospital deteriorated to the point where it was better known locally for the brothel situated on the far side of its grounds.

Things finally began to improve with the appointment in 1879 of Auguste Forel, a crusading polymath of international reputation, who restored order at the asylum while adding further luster to the Zurich chair. Forel was a Vaudois-Swiss of severe temperament. Lonely, isolated, and quite miserable as a child, he had found his salvation in studying ants, a hobby that led him to Darwinian evolution and thence to the study of the brain. By the time he ascended to the Zurich chair of psychiatry, he was an internationally known psychiatrist with a reputation second to none, as well as the world's leading authority on ants. The list of Forel's scientific accomplishments is staggering and includes the codiscovery of the neurone theory, the introduction of the first modern curriculum for psychiatry, and the successful propagation of hypnotism as a viable therapeutic method in the German-speaking medical world. That was merely in the world of medicine. In his native Switzerland, Forel was a fiery champion of numerous social causes, including the campaigns against prostitution and against alcohol.

At the Burghölzli, Forel did whatever needed to be done, from getting into fistfights with intruders on the hospital grounds (it once seemed sporting to have a picnic and watch the insane) to hypnotizing his night staff to sleep through the night but to awaken if an emergency arose. But even the redoubtable Forel eventually grew weary of the Burghölzli and opted for early retirement in 1898. Forel was determined that he would be succeeded by a psychiatrist who would continue to enforce his ban on all alcoholic beverages at the asylum. Thinking that his first choice as successor would be blocked by those members of the cantonal council who opposed him on this question (there was money to be made if alcohol was reintroduced), he came up with an alternate candidate whose views on the matter were not so strongly on record. Through this well-meant intrigue, the esteemed Zurich chair in psychiatry, by now the rival in prestige to the chairs of Berlin and Vienna, fell to a virtual unknown, Eugen Bleuler.

Bleuler hailed from the peasant village of Zollikon, outside Zurich, and had been its first citizen ever to attend medical school. In Zollikon, as in other rural areas in the canton, there was much grumbling about the Burghölzli, where the physicians could not even talk to the patients. This complaint had even greater urgency in Bleuler's home—his own sister was catatonic. Bleuler grew up with the dream of someday running the asylum, making him perhaps the only person who ever really wanted the job. He worked there as a young assistant under Forel, and he quickly demonstrated some of his chief's eclecticism, developing a theory of color perception, contributing to the field of aphasia studies (which led to an exchange of letters with Sigmund Freud in 1892), and experimenting with hypnotism. Then in 1886, taking twelve long-term patients with him, Bleuler departed to take over the canton's chronic-care facility, the Rheinau asylum. For most men, the Rheinau post would have been a stepping-stone, and a low one at that. Bleuler spent twelve happy years there. Not yet married, he made his charges his family, and both staff and patients literally called him "father." It was here that Bleuler developed his revolutionary notion that even the most severe conditions could sometimes be arrested if one developed a personal relationship with the patient.

At Rheinau, Bleuler also received some instructive lessons as to the value of reality-oriented tasks. When a typhoid epidemic broke out, he had no choice but to press some of his patients into service to care for the sick. To his surprise, these patients performed quite well, even admirably, only to slip back into their typical delusional and withdrawn condition once the crisis was past. Then there was a day when the firewood ran low and Bleuler needed to organize an expedition to chop down some trees. He carefully divided up the able-bodied men according to whether they were dangerous or not, then went out ahead to scout out the terrain. But the staff misunderstood his directions and in short order Bleuler found himself joined by all the most dangerous patients in the asylum, each of them brandishing an axe. The day passed without incident. These and similar episodes persuaded Bleuler that the challenge of dealing with reality could be therapeutic in itself. He began to experiment more forcefully along these lines, even going so far as to announce suddenly to an occasional patient, usually one long-mired in psychosis, that he was being discharged. Astonishingly, some of these surprise discharges worked.

In 1899, the year after he was appointed director at the Burghölzli, something happened that was to ensure Bleuler's reputation for posterity: the sixth edition of Emil Kraepelin's textbook came out. In this edition Kraepelin, basing himself on laboriously accumulated outcome statistics, further codified a diagnostic distinction that he had first proposed three years earlier. Specifically, he took two well-known syndromes, manic-depressive insanity and paranoia, and gave them new status by distinguishing them from a third condition, which he labeled "dementia praecox" (now known as "schizophrenia"). Included in the dementia praecox category were the previously distinct syndromes catatonia, hebephrenia, and paraphrenia, which had been separately introduced over the years on the basis of their distinctive clinical presentation. (Paraphrenia, for example, was said to involve well-systematized litigious and persecutory delusions without apparent intellectual deficit.) Kraepelin's synthesis was revolutionary. Each of his three basic groups, manic-depression, paranoia, and dementia praecox, not only showed distinct psychological symptoms, but they also had typically different courses and different outcomes. This was clinical medicine at its best. To be sure, no one knew what the causes of each syndrome were, but one now had a reasonable classification to work from. Kraepelin's text almost at once supplanted Krafft-Ebing's *Textbook of Insanity* as the leading psychiatric text of the day, and his system of classification remains the cornerstone of modern psychiatric nosology. But the new entity of dementia praecox, as Bleuler knew instantly, had been incorrectly described in one very important respect. According to Kraepelin, if the condition did not spontaneously remit early on, then the patient inevitably deteriorated over time. But from a decade at Rheinau, Bleuler knew that in fact it was possible to arrest the illness, sometimes even to reverse it, provided one established a personal rapport with the patient. This, in conjunction with setting the patient reality-oriented tasks, produced great improvement and, indeed, Bleuler had actually been discharging patients from Rheinau back to the community, something heretofore unheard of.

As Bleuler took over the Burghölzli, however, publicizing his discovery took back seat to the problem of running the asylum. Using the university's reputation as a lure, Bleuler transformed the Burghölzli into a psychiatric monastery. Recruiting young physicians from all over Switzerland, he used this added manpower to its best advantage. Patients got the first adequate staff coverage they had ever known, and his students got initiated into a kind of intensive psychological approach to severe mental illness that was completely unprecedented at the time.

In the absence of a definitive biography, it is difficult to get a clear picture of Bleuler's personality. Certainly, some of those who served under him, notably Ludwig Binswanger, later remembered him with great admiration and personal fondness. There were others, however, notably Carl Jung, who chafed under his rule and found him insufferable. In his writings, Bleuler shows himself to be a mixture of originality and caution, and the same seems to have been true of his person: he was capable of getting greatly excited by a new idea, only to be tortured by second thoughts thereafter. Bleuler's conception of science was stolid, conscientious, and in keeping with his character. For Bleuler, the only way to make progress was to check everything, avoid premature closure, and keep in contact with one's colleagues to compare results. Accordingly, though notoriously open-minded to the potential value of new developments, Bleuler was cautious in his intellectual commitments, very much a man who could not be pushed. Above all, he was dedicated to his job, sometimes excessively so. One story has it that early in his career as an institutional psychiatrist he came to the opinion that sleep was a waste of valuable time and proceeded to go without it for three days—until he collapsed of exhaustion. He was authoritarian to a degree, though not as much as the patriarchal culture of the time allowed. He regularly inspected the living quarters of all the Burghölzli staff, including the assistant physicians, yet when young Franz Riklin decided to grow grass between the floorboards of his apartment, Bleuler had the wit to grasp that the joke was on him. In short, Bleuler was an odd combination of somewhat overbearing chief medical officer and an intellectual gentleman. He was the sort of man who could give patriarchalism a good name.

Under his direction, the Burghölzli became a model teaching hospital. The patient was the center of everything. The attending assistant had to see all his patients twice a day and write down everything they said, whether he understood it or not. Three times a week the entire professional staff met for morning rounds. These were generally devoted to patient care, though the assistants were also made to report on new developments in the literature. Assistants were required to live in, abstinence from all alcoholic beverages was mandatory, and if one planned to stay out at night after ten, one had better get permission, and the key, from Bleuler or the first assistant.

Among the new developments in the field that Bleuler was eager to learn about was the use of experimental psychology to study the insane. In 1900, he dispatched a young assistant, Franz Riklin, to study in Kraepelin's psychological laboratory, the first ever to be attached to a psychiatric clinic. Experimental psychology was barely past its infancy. Prior to its birth, psychology had been a subdivision of philosophy, and the idea of subjecting psychological ideas to experimental validation had been a relatively daring innovation. William James of Harvard and Wilhelm Wundt of Leipzig, philosophers both, had tied for the honor of being the first to set up psychological laboratories at their universities. Kraepelin, though a psychiatrist by training, had studied under Wundt and come to the conclusion that the new experimental techniques might also be useful in psychiatry. Bleuler had come to the same conclusion. By dispatching Riklin to Kraepelin's clinic, he was announcing in effect that he intended to start his own laboratory.

At Kraepelin's clinic, under the tutelage of Gustav Aschaffenburg, Riklin learned of a new procedure called the association experiment. The procedure had the experimenter call out a list of words and the subject answer each in turn with the word or phrase that first came to mind. The procedure was a bit like our modern game "Password," only the subject was not trying to guess a correct answer, but only respond with whatever came into his head. Typically a list of stimulus words ran to a hundred, and a stopwatch was used to time how long it took the subject to respond to each. Afterward, the subject was asked to go through the list again and remember his or her responses. The procedure, sans stopwatch, had been originated thirty years earlier by the eclectic English genius Sir Francis Galton. Using himself as a subject, Galton had made three basic discoveries: first, that some of the associations elicited in this way were quite surprising, involving memories and sentiments one had not previously been thinking of; second, that many of these surprising associations stemmed from childhood; and third, that with continued administration of the test many of the associations kept recurring. In Berlin, Theodor Ziehen had picked up where Galton left off and made the experiment part of his research program into the general laws governing the association of ideas. Out of this came a novel system of psychology which featured, among other things, the idea of a "complex of feeling-toned ideas." Aschaffenburg, meanwhile, had begun sampling the test responses of normal subjects under varying conditions of fatigue and intoxication and comparing these with the records of dementia praecox patients, this on the basis of a widespread belief that an unidentified endogenous toxin might be the cause of that illness. Among other things, Aschaffenburg was able to show that the responses of the insane did indeed resemble those of intoxicated subjects: in both there was a predominance of "external" associations, i.e., associations based on rhyming, or other phonetic characteristics.

When Riklin returned to Zurich in the spring of 1901, Bleuler was at the train station to meet him. During the carriage ride back to the hospital, he excitedly told Riklin about a brilliant new assistant, an intellectual aristocrat and a man of extraordinary physical and mental energy, who had logged on during Riklin's absence—Carl Gustav Jung. That night, the three of them, Riklin, Bleuler, and Jung, stayed up late talking about the association experiment.

THE BASEL ARISTOCRAT

BLEULER CAME from a peasant village and had been only its second university graduate. By contrast, Jung came from a very distinguished family in the Swiss city of Basel, whose university had an ancient and honorable tradition and whose faculty had included Jakob Burckhardt and Friedrich Nietzsche. Jung was the firstborn and only son of the Reverend Paul Jung and Emilie Preiswerk. Paul Jung in turn was the son of the illustrious physician and Freemason Carl Gustav Jung the Elder, around whom numerous legends had already sprung, including one that identified him as an illegitimate son of Goethe. Carl Gustav the Elder had clearly been a formidable character. One story has it that when the woman he was courting turned down his proposal, he stormed off to the local tavern and asked the barmaid to marry him, which she did. When this woman died a few years later, Carl Gustav renewed his proposal to the first woman. She accepted speedily and Paul Jung was a late-born son of this delayed union. Emilie Preiswerk, meanwhile, was the daughter of an almost equally distinguished man, Samuel Preiswerk, theologian and Hebraist at Basel University, and one of the early champions of the idea that the Jews of Europe should have their own homeland.

Unfortunately, Paul and Emilie were members of what Henri Ellenberger has called "the sacrificed generation," born after their fathers had become impoverished. Paul had wanted to become a Hebraist himself, but for financial reasons became instead a country pastor after marrying his favorite professor's last-born daughter. Kindly, pedantic, inwardly defeated, he seems not to have known how to cope with his haughty and contentious wife or with his obstreperous son. From 1879 until his fatal illness of 1896, Paul served as pastor of Klein-Hüningen, a peasant village in the vicinity of Basel City, and as Protestant chaplain to the nearby Friedmatt Mental Hospital.

His wife came from a family steeped in spiritualism. Her own mother had had to do regular battle with the returning ghost of her husband's first wife. Emilie herself had been required as a child to sit behind her father while he composed his sermons—to keep the devil from insinuating himself into the text of the next day's address to the faithful. The marriage of Carl Gustav's parents was seriously troubled and the mother spent time outside the home as a patient in the Friedmatt Hospital.

Jung's childhood reminiscences are familiar to the many readers of his extraordinary memoirs, the first three chapters of which he composed at the very end of his life. His mother's hospitalization occurred when Jung was three; thereafter, as he later put it, "I always felt mistrustful when the word 'love' was spoken." At the age of four, Jung had a dream of a giant phallus enthroned in an underground cave, which awed and terrified him. His mother's warning in the dream—"That is the man-eater"—Jung associated with "Jesuits." At the age of six, Jung first became aware that his mother "consisted of two personalities." After nightfall she would speak in an altered voice and in flat contradiction to her ordinary conformist rebukes to the pastor's son. As Jung later remembered the utterances of his mother's second personality, they struck "to the core of my being."

The child was not well adapted to polite, or even juvenile, society. A lifelong friend, Albert Oeri, remembers his childhood impressions thus: "I had never come across such an asocial monster before." At about the age of eight, Jung developed choking fits—"the atmosphere in the house was beginning to become unbreathable"—which were alleviated by visions of a blue moon with golden angels. Also at this age, Jung took to playing a game with himself; he would sit on a stone and ask himself whether he was Jung or the stone: "The answer remained totally unclear and my uncertainty was accompanied by a feeling of curious and fascinating darkness." He began building fires in secret countryside caverns and persuaded neighboring peasant children to join him. When he was ten years old, he carved a small mannikin out of a ruler and hid it, together with a stone painted to look as if it were divided into an upper and a lower half, beneath the attic floorboards. For about a year thereafter, he ritually presented the tiny man with scrolls written in a secret language: "This possession of a secret had a very powerful influence on my character; I consider it the essential factor in my childhood."

At the age of eleven, Jung entered the Basel Gymnasium, his first real step outside the home and the world of the countryside. His new classmates—realizing that Jung, as a habitual miscreant, could not give a convincing account of himself in any case—took to blaming their own transgressions on him. Jung did not know how to escape this role. He adapted to it by rehearsing alibis for every possible occasion. His first years in Gymnasium were fairly miserable. On one occasion, a fellow schoolboy gave him a blow sufficiently strong to cause Jung to lose consciousness, which led him to be sent home for the day. Eager to escape the torments of his peers, Jung took to faking dizzy spells on every occasion. While resting at home on one of these occasions, he overheard his father talking to a friend in despairing tones: "The boy is interested in everything, but how will he ever earn his living?" Jung rallied, forced himself to overcome the dizzy spells, which by now had taken on a life of their own, and resumed his studies.

Understandably, he became preoccupied with the theme of identity. Off by himself on one occasion, he came to the following realization: "For a single moment I had the overwhelming impression of having just emerged from a dark cloud. I knew all at once: now I am myself!" But around this same time, while being reprimanded by an adult for having commandeered the man's rowboat, Jung first began to feel that he was really somebody else, in fact a man who had lived in the late eighteenth century. This became the basis for what Jung ever after called his "No. 2" personality. The historian Henri Ellenberger has indicated that the protoype was Goethe.

The central event of Jung's first year at Gymnasium, however, was a daydream. In it, he imagined God on a throne high above Basel Cathedral dropping an enormous turd on it that smashed it. This daydream, which Jung had spent two days trying unsuccessfully to ward off, was accompanied by a feeling of "relief," even bliss. The feeling of "grace" it entailed contrasted ever so strongly with the emptiness and disappointment Jung would subsequently feel during his first communion, mandatory for membership in the Swiss Reformed Church and a traditional rite of passage for German-Swiss youths.

One has to pause for a moment here, and put to one side the engaging prose of Jung's memoirs, to appreciate the vision. The Basel Cathedral, far from being a dark, imposing Gothic structure, is a charming, almost playful edifice—more a gingerbread house than a cathedral as conventionally conceived. There is colored tiling on the roof, and on one wall a statue of Saint George on his horse slaying a dragon who sits mounted on a separate ledge a few yards away. That anyone, let alone God, would want to destroy this structure with an enormous turd is a thought that deserves scrutiny. It goes beyond the adolescent protest of Spielrein's images of defecation while seated at the dinner table. It bespeaks Jung's upbringing that he spent two days trying to ward off the fantasy. But having given in to it, Jung became determined not to lose the possibility of the resulting bliss. Ever after, he considered his private, somewhat blasphemous revelation of a natural, amoral Godhead to be superior to the consolations of orthodox Christianity.

Jung kept his revelation to himself. As the requisite pre-communion catechism lessons with his father continued, they were colored on Carl Gustav's side by a pity bordering on contempt: "I could not plunge my dear and generous father . . . into that despair and sacrilege which were necessary for an experience of divine grace. Only God could do that. I had no right to; it would be inhuman." For his part, Paul Jung now lost his faith after reading Hippolyte Bernheim's book on suggestion in Sigmund Freud's translation. At the time, it was not atypical for a devout man to resist the encroachments of materialism by appealing to the ongoing possibilities of miracles, such as had been reported in previous centuries and even down to the present. As part of his program of debunking, however, Bernheim showed that it was possible to reinterpret many seemingly miraculous phenomena, such as the cures at Lourdes or the stigmata of various saints, as the result of autosuggestion. Nor was Paul Jung alone in his despair at this realization; many men were finding that the new psychological perspectives, sturdily anchored in materialist philosophies, constituted a grave challenge to the possibilities of faith.

The son, however, thought there well might be an opening in materialism for his own, more mystical beliefs. With his mother's connivance, Carl Gustav began to supplement the theological discussions with his father with secret readings in the elder Jung's library. From Biedermann, theologian at Basel University and inspiration for Nietzsche, Jung learned that God had historically been conceived by analogy from man's ego. From Goethe, by legend Jung's great-grandfather, Jung learned to personify evil as the devil and to suspect that through the devil's power one might gain access to the "mystery of the Mothers." From Krug's *General Dictionary of the Philosophical Sciences,* he learned how etymology could enter into theological debate as well as how arbitrary definitions might preordain its outcome. From secondary sources, Jung discovered that he had a particular affinity for Nietzsche, most especially for *Thus Spake Zarathustra.* But as Nietzsche had gone famously insane, and as the adolescent had good reason to fear for his own emotional stability, Jung decided it was too dangerous as yet to plunge directly into Nietzsche's texts. Nietzsche aside, Jung's secret readings apparently began to show in his demeanor. His Gymnasium classmates found a new nickname for the youth, who by this time had become quite imposing physically. They took to calling him "Father Abraham."

Jung had hoped to study science, but financial realities drove him in the same direction as they did so many similarly inclined students. In April 1895, he entered the medical school of Basel University on a scholarship. There he promptly joined the local chapter of the Zofingiaverein, a student drinking and literary society, but did not attend its meetings until he gave his own inaugural lecture, "The Border Zone of Exact Science," some eighteen months later. Thereafter, he distinguished himself by his intellectuality, his originality, and his ebullience. Albert Oeri checked the society's records in his old age:

> The minutes read, "Jung *vulgo* 'Barrel,' the pure spirit having gone to his head, urged that we debate hitherto unresolved philosophical questions. This was agreeable to all, more agreeable than might have been expected under our usual 'prevailing circumstances.' But 'Barrel' blithered endlessly, and that was dumb. Oeri, *vulgo* 'It,' likewise spiritually oiled, distorted in so far as such was still possible, these barreling thoughts . . ." At the next meeting, Jung succeeded in having the word "blithered," which he held to be too subjective, struck from the minutes and replaced by the word "talked."

Jung's addresses before the society were a mixture of science, philosophy, and occultism, and show him carrying his theological quarrels with his father into new domains. Specifically, Jung objected to the

reductionistic materialism of the age—"the Judaization of science"—
while appealing to various authorities in support of spiritualism, telepathy, and clairvoyance. As to the reality of these phenomena, Jung
had no doubt:

> In 1875, for the first time, paraffin molds were taken of hands
> that spontaneously materialized in space. . . . I myself have in my
> possession photographs of such phenomena, and anyone who would
> like to see them may do so at any time.

Contemporaneously with his Zofingia lectures Jung was himself
holding séances. Present were his mother; two female cousins, Luise
and Helene Preiswerk; and a fourth woman, Emmy Zinstag. The séances had begun with a strange event, whose reality Jung continued
to believe in for the rest of his life. Coming home one day, he found
his mother puzzling over a kitchen knife whose blade had mysteriously
shattered in two for no apparent reason. Both mother and son took
this as a portent of something to come, which turned out to be that
Cousin Helene could communicate with the spirits of the dead. Jung's
memoirs are full of similar such occurrences, of strange coincidences
and auguries of future events. Much later in his career he coined a
special term for the phenomenon, "synchronicity." Apparently, he
first began to believe in such coincidences at this time. In any event,
the séances began in 1895 and continued on and off for at least four
years. The teenaged Helene Preiswerk, who was in love with Jung,
served as the medium. None of the participants' fathers were told about
the sessions, which were held at nightfall in the Klein-Hüningen pres-
bytery that served as the Jung home. Jung's father's final illness and
death in January 1896 interrupted the meetings for over a year.

Over the course of the séances, the spiritualistic phenomena showed
a definite development. At first, in the three meetings of 1895, Helene
communicated with the grandfathers on both sides, Samuel Preiswerk
and Carl Gustav Jung the Elder. When the séances resumed in 1897,
Samuel Preiswerk reappeared and entrusted Helene with the mission
of bringing the Jews to Palestine and converting them to Christianity.
(In his lifetime Samuel Preiswerk had advocated only that Jews have
a homeland. In 1897, Basel was the host city for the First International
Zionist Congress.)

Subsequently, however, with the help of hypnotic trances induced
by Jung, Helene revealed a second personality in herself, named
"Ivenes." "Ivenes" possessed a ladylike poise and seriousness quite

in contrast to Helene's personality when awake. "Ivenes" was Jewish, and she had had numerous past lives; she had once been Goethe's mother, and in another incarnation his lover as well. Given Goethe's central role in Jung's own private romance of himself, it seems safe to say, with George Hogenson and with William Goodheart, that there was more going on in these sessions than met the eye.

Gradually, however, they got out of hand. Helene began increasingly to fall into trances apart from the séances and, according to Spielrein's later account, she went so far as to appear uninvited in Jung's bedroom one night dressed in a white robe. Meanwhile, her spiritualistic revelations deteriorated as less serious subpersonalities began crowding in with cosmological mumbo-jumbo obviously cribbed from Justinus Kerner's well-known book *The Seeress of Prevorst*. The last straw came when Jung unwisely invited some of his Basel University classmates in for a look at materialization phenomena and they, less enamored than he, quickly caught Helene cheating. Humiliated, Jung quit attending the séances.

Putting to one side the romance of the seventeenth-century "Ivenes," let us note that Jung's interest in séances and mediums was less eccentric than it may seem today. Though familiar spirits have been known in human society since time immemorial, the practice of having regular convocations with them without a self-confessed witch present—"spiritualism" was the term given to this new practice—had begun only in the year 1850, courtesy of the Fox sisters. These two women hailed from an upstate New York county so steeped in religious revivals that it was locally known as the "burnt-over" district, in reference to the great many times the fiery spirit of the Lord had manifested itself there. One of the sisters, Isabelle Fox, had a trick joint in her big toe which she could manipulate at will to provide a sharp knocking or rapping sound. This, plus a good deal of imagination and a certain empathic sensitivity, enabled the sisters to make a living by giving convincing demonstrations of communication with the dead, who obligingly would answer the questions of the living by seeming to rap the table invisibly in response, once for no and twice for yes. Unlike young Helene Preiswerk, the Fox sisters were never caught cheating. Spiritualism soon became a craze, in both America and Europe. In short order other practitioners appeared, almost all of them women, who outdid one another in the persuasiveness of their performances and in the elaborateness of their knowledge of what the beyond was like.

But as spiritualism spread, so did scientific curiosity about it. While some men exhausted themselves trying to prove the phenomena genuine, others more thoughtfully elected to make psychological studies of the mediums themselves. Pierre Janet had begun his career with such a study, but first honors in this area go to an Englishman, Frederic Myers, who in 1882 founded the distinguished London Society for Psychical Research. (An American branch was established soon afterward by William James.) Though romantic in temperament and mystical in belief, Myers was an enormously intelligent and perceptive man, a natural psychologist of great gifts. The minimalist position Myers adopted for himself was this: Even if one disbelieved in the authenticity of the phenomena, the romances that the mediums spontaneously produced in quasi-trance states sometimes showed great creativity and originality and were thus worthy of study for what they showed about the inner workings of the subconscious imagination. Since the mediums often had to make almost clairvoyantly astute guesses as to what responses the living wanted to hear from the recently departed, they were also worth studying for what they revealed about subliminal perception.

Thus, as Jung began to explore the literature on occultism for his lectures to his university classmates, he would have found himself in the company of some highly esteemed authors. Eventually, he made the shift from trying to prove the spiritualist phenomena real to deciding to study them psychologically. Pivotal in this transformation was the appearance in 1900 of Théodore Flournoy's celebrated study of the medium "Hélène Smith," *From India to Planet Mars*. Flournoy, like his close friend William James, was a pioneer philosopher-turned-psychologist of great perspicacity, and in "Hélène Smith" he had a marvelous subject to study, too marvelous as it turned out. When Flournoy's book became a runaway best-seller, the medium sued for a share of the royalties on the basis that, after all, this was her material. (Flournoy gallantly agreed to an accommodation.) Flournoy was inclined to believe in the genuineness of some of her claims, though he did offer the thought that, were he himself dead, he suspected he might have better things to do than traipse around the city of Geneva answering to the beck and call of every medium who summoned him hither. More important, however, Flournoy was able to show that many of the otherworldly scenes which she described in her séances could be found in earthly sources she had access to, though they had been transformed by her imagination. For the fact that she had no conscious recall of ever having been exposed to these sources, Flournoy originated the term "cryptomnesia." Jung was excited enough by

Flournoy's book that, though still a medical student, he wrote to Geneva offering his services as a German translator. Thereby he earned his first important rebuff as an adult. A busy man, Flournoy let Jung's letter sit on his desk for over six months before he answered it, by which time he already had a deal with a German publisher.

Though he had taken two different courses in psychiatry at the University of Basel, Jung's own account has it that his decision to enter this field came to him only late in his studies. Specifically, his decision was made, he tells us, when he read in the preface to Krafft-Ebing's *Textbook of Insanity* that it was a "subjective" field. Some sense of what excited Jung can be gleaned from considering what Krafft-Ebing actually wrote: "Owing to the peculiarity of this science and its state of incompleteness, textbooks on psychiatry present more or less prominently subjective features dependent upon the personality of their authors." In effect, Jung thought he had discovered a field tailor-made to his own gifts.

It is important to emphasize the almost Rabelaisian nature of those gifts. Jung had enormous powers of concentration, tremendous physical energy, and an abiding sense of the heroic importance of his own personal quest. Physically imposing, a robust man with a booming voice, Jung loved practical jokes and delighted in finding the chinks in the armor of the self-important and those in authority. There was also another side to Jung—indeed, several sides. He was endowed with intense sensitivity, not subject to his conscious control, which allowed him to make intuitive, empathic connections to the inner lives of other people. This sensitivity sometimes reached the point where he felt the need to protect himself from it, and in his personal relations Jung could alternate suddenly between excessive closeness and sudden flashes of hostility. He was afflicted as well with a kind of inner awkwardness, a sense of never being quite at ease with himself. This led him at times to conceal his feelings and at other times to compensate with arrogance. Finally, we should note that Jung was perennially attractive to women. Despite his imposing size and his general ebullience, he seems to have had the knack of seeming docilely dependent and worshipful in feminine company. Over the course of his long life, he never lacked for female companionship.

Entering the medical novitiate of the Burghölzli in December of 1900, Jung quickly showed himself to be a tireless worker and a voracious student of the literature. His first assignment for the thrice-weekly rounds was to report on Sigmund Freud's recent monograph *On Dreams*. (Jung found it psychologically strong, neurologically weak.) Over the next six months, Jung managed to read fifty-odd volumes of the *Allgemeine Zeitschrift für Psychiatrie*—"in order to acquaint myself with the psychiatric mentality." He also secretly compiled data on the family background and heredity of his colleagues, "and gained much instruction."

Under Bleuler's supervision, Jung wrote up, as his medical dissertation, a scientific account of the séances he had participated in. (At that time, a dissertation was required for the medical degree.) The result, published in 1902, was an important contribution to the growing psychopathological literature on occultism. In it, Jung showed himself extremely well versed in the French literature, including the works of Janet, Binet, Charcot, Richet, Azam, and Ribot, on hysteria, hypnotism, and dissociated states. Jung's own contribution to the analysis was to suggest, in a manner reminiscent of cases previously reported by Weir Mitchell and Azam, that the second personality represented by "Ivenes" was preferable to that of Helene:

> Speaking with her [as "Ivenes"], you had the impression of speaking with a much older person, who through numerous experiences had arrived at a state of calm composure. . . . Beside the obvious broadening of her whole personality, the continued existence of her ordinary character [as Helene] was all the more startling.

Put another way, in the Jewish "Ivenes" the medium had caught a subliminal glimpse of the adult personality that was awaiting her. What was striking about this claim in context was that Jung had otherwise stressed the girl's hereditary taint. Thus, ever so gingerly, he was implying that in some cases such "psychopathic inferiority," with its inborn hypersensitivity and tendency to dissociation, might bode well and not ill. Since Jung shared half of Helene's lineage, his hopeful surmises about the possibilities of a subliminal end run around hereditary taint would have applied to himself as well. Meanwhile, to avoid the ready charge that his use of hypnotism had skewed the data, Jung discreetly avoided mentioning the fact, making it seem instead that Helene's trances were entirely spontaneous.

As for the real Helene, she moved to Paris to pursue her trade as a dressmaker. It is said that Jung's dissertation, with its invocation of hereditary taint, had wrecked her chances of marrying. Not only had her identity been readily discernible in the small world of Basel, but the code name Jung used for her, "S.W.," was itself a final act of spite. Jung had lifted the name from the *Textbook of Insanity,* specifically from the case of another "S.W.," a seamstress who suffered from an "intensified feeling of self-importance, which found its expression in affected speech and grand airs, now and then attended with evidence of eroticism and coquetry."

Incidentally, it may be noted that though Freud's name came up very occasionally in Jung's dissertation with regard to specific psychological mechanisms, it did not appear in connection with sexuality. For example, Jung was perfectly capable of making the following assessment entirely on his own warrant:

> We shall not be wrong if we seek the main cause of this curious clinical picture in her budding sexuality. From this point of view the whole essence of Ivenes and her enormous family [in the romances] is nothing but a dream of sexual wish-fulfillment, which differs from the dream of a night only in that it is spread over months and years.

At the Burghölzli, Jung continued to pursue the study of hypnotism. His only other paper of 1902, "A Case of Hysterical Stupor in a Prisoner in Detention," besides making a foray into the then new subject of the "Ganser syndrome," shows him to be quite skillful as a hypnotist. His dissertation, meanwhile, drew largely favorable comment, including an appreciative review by Flournoy himself.

The year 1902 was a pivotal one for Jung, not only because it saw him finally qualified as a full physician but because during it he became engaged to his future wife. Emma Rauschenbach, the twenty-year-old daughter of an extremely wealthy Schaffhausen industrialist, had refused Jung's first offer. She did not want to be married to a "slave to an ideology." But she did not decline his second. She was pretty, sensitive, honest. As Fräulein Rauschenbach was rich, and Swiss marriage laws were still unreformed despite the efforts of Forel and others, Jung could also look forward to finally getting out of debt.

During the winter semester of 1902–1903, Jung took a sabbatical as part of the continuing education program at the Burghölzli. Bleuler sent him to Paris to attend Janet's lectures and also to meet with the great French psychologist Alfred Binet. Quite conceivably, Bleuler entertained hopes of getting a Zurich-Paris collaborative axis going. Interpretations vary as to what happened on this trip. One version has it that by making contact with the French, Jung prepared the way for the subsequent reception there of his work on the association experiment. Since in those days French opinion traveled directly to Boston through the correspondence of Pierre Janet and his colleagues with members of the Boston Psychopathological Society, this then helped ensure Jung's early recognition in America.

Another interpretation of the Paris visit has it that Jung simply botched matters. Jung did meet with Binet, who was perfectly willing to collaborate on the word association experiment. But Binet insisted that the protocols be taken in French, which put Jung at a serious disadvantage. Nothing came of the proposed collaboration. This was Jung's second important rebuff. Jung also sat in on Janet's lectures and met with him privately. But by this time Jung had already absorbed most of Janet's work, and whatever transpired between the two men personally—Jung later claimed it was an important moment in his own development—did not lead to further collaboration.

It is totally unknown what sort of report Jung turned in upon his return to Zurich, though the net effect was most certainly negative. Thereafter, though his own ideas were quite similar to Janet's in important respects, Bleuler completely omitted reference to the Frenchman in his own writings, a most uncharacteristic performance for the Burghölzli chief. Apart from his duties as an emissary, Jung used his holiday to enjoy himself and look in on his dressmaker cousin Helene. The couple spent several evenings together at the theater.

THE JEWESS COMPLEX

UPON HIS RETURN to the Burghölzli in 1903, Jung married Emma, who took up residence in his apartment at the hospital, and resumed his researches. In 1903 he published an interesting paper, "On Manic Mood Disorder," in which he stressed the impact of feelings in causing shifts in a chain of associations, and an even more interesting one, "On Simulated Insanity," in which he staked out his own position in the debate, now under way in earnest, over the authenticity of the Ganser syndrome. This is a mental condition that arises in prisoners awaiting trial and gives the appearance of malingering—Ganser patients give obviously wrong answers to even the most innocuous questions—though Jung made an eloquent case that it was actually a quasi-hysterical dissociated state. The immediate effect of the paper was that Jung quickly made a name for himself in the new science of criminology. But its real importance lay elsewhere.

Thus far, Jung, Riklin, and Bleuler had conceived of the word association experiment as a means of comparing normal and clinical populations. Bleuler's own theory was that in dementia praecox the normal associative bonds between related ideas were somehow weakened. This weakening of associative bonds made it impossible for the patient to maintain his ordinary sense of his own "I" and left him prey to unusual combinations of ideas, manifested in hallucinations and delusions, which would spring up in the pathologically tilled soil of his mind. The basic idea went back to Griesinger, but by specifying the presence of micro-splits in the chain of associations—"loose associations"—Bleuler introduced a new precision. On the basis of this conception, in a few years' time, Bleuler would rechristen dementia praecox with the label "schizophrenia," the name still used today. It was going to be no small matter to test Bleuler's idea, however—the methodological issues are very complex and a true experimental test was more than half a century away.

Obviously, the first order of business was to begin collecting a sample of normal associative responses to serve as a control group. Jung's wide reading in the literature of French experimental psychopathology had turned up an experimental variable that had heretofore escaped the notice of both Aschaffenburg and Ziehen—distraction. It was for this reason that in collecting their sample of normal responses Jung and Riklin routinely introduced various conditions of distraction as well as giving the association test under normal conditions and in a fatigue condition. The long-term goal was to compare normal associative responses under all these conditions with the associations given by dementia praecox patients.

In his paper "On Simulated Insanity" Jung described in passing the work being done at the Burghölzli with the word association experiment, while noting its connection with "the beautiful experiments conducted by Binet and Janet on automatization in states of distractibility." However, as Jung went on to present his analysis of the Ganser syndrome as an hysterical twilight state, itself understood as arising from a mixture of distractibility, suppressed guilt, and psychopathic predisposition, it suddenly struck him that he really ought to have administered the word association test to one of the patients under discussion to document the inner, self-generated distractibility.

This was a brand-new idea—using the test to detect the presence of a specific mental process with a particular ideational content in an individual patient—and in his next paper, coauthored with Riklin, Jung brought the idea to a set of revolutionary conclusions. "The Associations of Normal Subjects," published in four installments in Forel's and Vogt's *Archiv für Neurologie und Psychologie* over the course of 1904, is an intriguing document. Its ostensible purpose, stated at the outset, is merely to provide a statistical description of normal responses to the test—the task Bleuler assigned. But the apprentices have outstripped the master, and already in their second sample, "Educated Men," Jung and Riklin are pointing out the presence of internal distractions, caused by competing ideas, which sometimes interfere with normal responses. Soon the discussion of psychology begins to outstrip the reportage of results. Some of these distracting ideas have great emotional significance, argue Jung and Riklin, but have been "repressed." The existence of these repressed feeling-toned complexes of ideas—"complexes" for short—can be seen through various telltale indicators including lengthened response time, sudden shifts to unusual content, failures to remember the response subsequently, and a tendency to repeat responses (perseveration) every time the complex is stimulated. Moreover, as Jung and Riklin go on to point out, "the majority of complexes operative in the association experiments relate to direct or transposed sexuality."

By the time the authors reach Subject 19 in the "Educated Men" sample, they can no longer resist giving the reader a detailed analysis of a sample complex as it emerges on repeated administrations of the test given at intervals during 1902–1903. The subject is identified as a twenty-five-year-old physician who "had not yet outgrown adolescent internal conflict, and as he had had a strict Christian upbringing, his inclination for a Jewish girl worried him a great deal." The subject is almost certainly Jung, but it is not possible to make out the identity of his secret love, who is given the pseudonym "Alice Stern," unless one supposes that he was still thinking about "Ivenes." In any event, Jung's "Jewess complex" was now a matter of record for any who could pierce the thin layer of disguise in his account. Writing about oneself in this way was certainly not new—James had done it just two years before in his *Varieties of Religious Experience*—though, however briefly, Jung was going into fairly sensitive personal matters.

After Subject 19, the monograph runs a curious course. It never loses its ostensible organizational plan, that of presenting typical responses according to the type of subject, but more and more space is given to the exciting new endeavor of discovering repressed complexes. The monograph thus comes to mirror its subject matter as the discussion of complexes takes on a life of its own and unseats the authors' stated intentions. Perhaps Jung and Riklin were trying to seem as though they were still complying with Bleuler's instructions by not emphasizing their own novel ideas. The need for such a dutiful charade did not last long. Bleuler perfectly well understood the significance of what the two men had turned up and soon gave them their head to pursue the idea wherever it took them.

The discovery was both unprecedented and extraordinary. Jung and Riklin had provided an experimental demonstration of the dynamic efficacy of subconscious ideas. Beyond all doubt their subjects' responses were being influenced by emotional complexes of ideas at least some of which they had not consciously been thinking of beforehand. By the same token, Jung and Riklin had also invented the world's first projective test, one that could readily be adapted for discovering repressed complexes in both inpatient and outpatient settings. Up to this time, the study of emotions had been the despair of experimental psychology. Some had even concluded that laboratory work would forever be unable to shed much light on human passions. Here Jung and Riklin were studying not only emotions but unconscious emotions as well. In the bargain, they had found a method which was immediately adaptable to the clinical study of individual cases. Such was the magnitude of the discovery that the future academic careers of both men were already assured.

It might appear that Jung and Riklin's conception of repressed erotic complexes owed a great deal to Sigmund Freud. But one of the curiosities of "The Associations of Normal Subjects" was that Freud's name appeared in the text only twice, both times in trivial contexts. Jung later recalled this period of his life:

> Once, while I was in my laboratory and reflecting again upon these questions, the devil whispered to me that I would be justified in publishing the results of my experiments and my conclusions without mentioning Freud. After all, I had worked out my experiments long before I understood his work. But then I heard the voice of my second personality: "If you do a thing like that, as if you had no knowledge of Freud, it would be a piece of trickery. You cannot build your life upon a lie." With that, the question was settled. From then on I became an open partisan of Freud's and fought for him.

In fact, the question was not settled. "The Associations of Normal Subjects" ran to nearly two hundred pages and four installments before Freud's priority on the idea of repression was belatedly acknowledged in a footnote. The devil was doing more than whispering in Jung's ear; he was guiding his pen. Apparently, however, Jung had forgotten to let his partner in on his plans. In a lecture before the

Society of Swiss Physicians in the fall of 1904, duly abstracted for the *Psychiatrisch-neurologische Wochenschrift,* Riklin expressly noted that the distinguishing trait of the hysterical-reaction type on the test was that "the strong feeling-toned complex of ideas ('the complex') is repressed in the Breuer-Freud sense." Riklin's presentation, which was soon followed by a second paper appearing in the same weekly in February, made it clear where the two Swiss collaborators had gotten their understanding of repressed erotic complexes.

"SABINA S."

JUNG'S PAPER "On Simulated Insanity" had one other feature perhaps worth noting. Late in the paper, Jung brought up a case reported by Carl Fürstner in 1888. It involved a seventeen-year-old girl who upon reading Clemens Brentano's life of the "saint" Katharina Emmerich engaged in a hysterical reenactment. Brentano had devoted five years of his life to the cataleptic Fräulein Emmerich, and his two books on her mystic visions had attracted widespread attention, in particular among theologians. Fürstner's patient improved on the original. In Jung's words, she "staged an enormous swindle by passing herself off as a saint . . . and performed all sorts of miracles which fooled the doctors and officials and created a general sensation." Jung noted that the "purpose of the whole undertaking, apparently, was that she wanted to stay with a relative, who functioned as a priest." The name given to this girl by Fürstner, as reported by Jung, was "Sabina S."

The anecdote is odd and does not really belong in Jung's paper. But some several months after Jung's paper was published, by chance a second "Sabina S." appeared—Spielrein. As a believer in such portents, Jung undoubtedly noticed the coincidence. The way was thus prepared for Jung to see Spielrein as a revenant of his cousin Helene and to see in Spielrein's admission something potentially momentous for his own career. Helene, albeit in her role as "S.W.," had helped get Jung's career launched. Spielrein would help it take a new turn.

CHAPTER 3

Jung's Test Case

She was, so to speak, my test case, for which reason I remembered
her with special gratitude and affection. Since I knew from experience
that she would immediately relapse if I withdrew my support, I
prolonged the relationship over the years and in the end found myself
morally obliged, as it were, to devote a large measure of friendship
to her.

—Jung, letter to Freud, 4 June 1909

A T THE BURGHÖLZLI in early 1904, the resident expert on hysteria was not Jung but Riklin. It was Riklin who undertook to
examine the responses of a group of hysterics on the association experiment, and it was Riklin who had first interested himself in the new
methods of alleviating hysterical symptoms. As early as the end of 1901,
Riklin had attempted to replicate the findings of Breuer and Freud by
applying their "cathartic method"—the abreaction of trauma under
light hypnosis—to a Burghölzli patient named "Lina H."

"Lina H." suffered profound nausea and recurrent vomiting, and
no physical basis for these symptoms could be found. Riklin interviewed her under light hypnosis and over the course of six sessions
discovered multiple sexual traumas dating from her adolescence, including a rape by her uncle and an even earlier rape, at age twelve,
by her alcoholic father. At first, the findings in this case seemed to
augur well for the etiological significance of juvenile sexual traumas,
but Riklin noted that the abreaction of those scenes did *not* lead to a
cessation of the symptoms. Pursuing the investigation further, he then
discovered that "Lina H." was secretly masturbating at night. During
the masturbation she would visualize her father as he had been the
night he assaulted her. The next day she would be overcome with
remorse and disgust at herself, and it was these emotions that caused

her symptoms. Riklin's conclusion was thoroughly prescient: fantasies, not trauma, lay in back of it all. But though this finding was essentially in place by 1902, Riklin had thus far declined to publish it.

It was already plain to the doctors of the Burghölzli that Freud was on to something important in the explication of basic psychological processes, even if he had overstated his case with regard to the etiology of hysteria. Then, early in 1904, Löwenfeld's book came out containing not only Freud's second thoughts about the etiological significance of trauma but also the updated description of his treatment method. Its appearance gave Bleuler, in his review in the *Munich Medical Weekly*, occasion for this positive comment:

> Freud, in his studies on hysteria and on dreams, has shown us part of a new world, though by no means all of it. Our consciousness sees in its theater only the puppets; in the Freudian world, many of the strings that move the figures have been revealed.

For the sake of keeping the chronology clear, it is important to keep in mind these comments by Bleuler. As we shall see, they were to have important consequences in the faraway cities of Vienna and Berlin. The story of the institutionalization of psychoanalysis pivots on the Löwenfeld volume, and Bleuler's review, in more than one respect.

FREUD'S PSYCHOANALYTIC METHOD

THE DESCRIPTION of psychoanalysis in Löwenfeld's book was the most extensive description yet to appear. It was seriously overdue. And it was incomplete. Here we come to an oddity that, though it was widely commented on at the time, has almost entirely escaped scholarly notice since. One of the great curiosities of Freud's work during the period 1896–1904, noted by Löwenfeld and others, was that while he repeatedly based his claims on his new method of "psychoanalysis," he was forever begging off a detailed discussion of what exactly that method entailed. To be sure, there was no question but that Freud believed that an inquiry into the patient's history was needed, and that once the original trauma was discovered, and abreacted, a cessation of symptoms would ensue. Likewise it was clear that he readily broadened the inquiry to take stock of dreams, slips of the tongue, and chance ideas should these arise. But beyond that, Freud's procedure was obscure, at least in terms of its technical aspects.

In *Studies on Hysteria*, written with Breuer, the principal method of investigation had been questioning the patient closely about the history of a given symptom under hypnosis. But Freud had also described an alternative, the ''pressure technique.'' Instead of using hypnosis, he would press his hand on the recumbent patient's forehead and then, upon releasing the pressure, inquire closely about the first thought or image which next came into the patient's mind, all this in the context of an ongoing inquiry into the history and point of origin of a symptom. Allegedly, the next thought or image that occurred was invariably of great significance in understanding the psychological structure of the case. But, as should be immediately clear upon reflection, the memory or image that occurred to the patient was not ordinarily self-explanatory. How and where this piece fit into the puzzle of a complicated neurosis was a matter of interpretation. Freud demonstrated that his was a formidable interpretive machinery, and that he had many ways of considering a piece of data in relation to the symptom picture. He also had a good ear for when he was being misled. But the reliance on his interpretive skill, ultimately his deft handling of the ''resistance,'' finally left the usefulness of the pressure technique hanging.

In 1896, in ''Further Remarks on the Neuro-Psychoses of Defence,'' Freud referred back to the *Studies* while coining a new term for his method: ''There . . . some information is to be found about the laborious but completely reliable method of psycho-analysis used by me in making those investigations—investigations which also constitute a therapeutic procedure.'' And to the charge that he might be implanting the idea of pre-pubertal sexual trauma in his patients, Freud had this to say: ''[W]e may ask that no one should form too certain judgements in this obscure field until he has made use of the only method which can throw light on it—of psycho-analysis for the purpose of making conscious what has so far been unconscious.'' But neither here nor in a companion piece published the same year, ''The Aetiology of Hysteria,'' did he describe his method further—it could not even be discerned whether he still used pressure—beyond insisting that it entailed the recovery of the original trauma underlying the symptoms. In effect, Freud was claiming that his procedure was uniquely effective, but was relying on his findings to carry the point.

The evasiveness continued. In works such as ''The Psychical Mechanism of Forgetting,'' ''Screen Memories,'' and *The Psychopathology of Everyday Life,* Freud presented detailed reconstructions of the chains of associations underlying various symptomatic acts, while making it clear that his interpretive devices were derived from a therapeutic method he was otherwise employing with nervous patients. But that method had yet to be published. The lack was made official in *The Interpretation of Dreams:*

> If a pathological idea . . . can be traced back to the elements in the patient's mental life from which it originated, it simultaneously crumbles away and the patient is freed from it. Considering the impotence of our other therapeutic efforts and the puzzling nature of these disorders, I felt tempted to follow the path marked out by Breuer, in spite of every difficulty, till a complete explanation was reached. I shall have on another occasion to report at length upon the form taken by this procedure and the results of my labours.

In this context, it is unsurprising that Löwenfeld, an expert hypnotherapist who kept consistently up-to-date on all the latest developments in his field, finally petitioned Freud for a description of the therapeutic method. "Freud's Psycho-Analytic Procedure" in Löwenfeld's volume went far in terms of the mechanics involved: the patient lay on a couch, the analyst did not touch the patient or do anything else that would suggest a hypnotic induction, the patient was instructed not to suppress chance ideas, etc. But, writing in the third person, Freud insisted that there was yet a great deal more to know specifically with regard to the rules of interpretation:

> The details of this technique of interpretation or translation have not yet been published by Freud. According to indications he has given, they comprise a number of rules, reached empirically, of how the unconscious material may be reconstructed from the associations, directions on how to know what it means when the patient's ideas cease to flow, and experiences of the most important typical resistances that arise in the course of such treatments.

Here we have to pause to take stock of what was going on. Unless he was simply being disingenuous, Freud evidently believed that his procedure, including interpretive rules, could be systematized. But most of his recent publications had been based on self-observation, known to constitute methodologically shaky ground, and even in the face of criticism on just that point, Freud had thus far refrained from publishing a comprehensive, objective account of his method, though he continued to insist he had one.

Instead, Freud had reported any number of occasions where eliciting trains of associations had indeed seemed to clarify the unconscious motivations underlying various psychic phenomena, including nervous symptoms, dream images, and slips of the tongue. He had also argued, most prominently in *The Psychopathology of Everyday Life*, that it was a simple logical necessity that the unconscious motives behind these psychic phenomena would betray themselves in the associations called forth by the examiner's inquiry. In fact, Freud's self-assurance on this last point was misplaced. Associations are determined by the subject's frame of mind and current interpersonal context; no matter how revealing, they do not necessarily reflect what was operative in his or her mind on any prior occasion. But even if that consideration is set aside, Freud's reliance on associative chains to extend the realm of the physician's inquiry plainly required that one be able to identify the associations that were most relevant, also that one be able to translate these back into the language of motivation. What was called for, in other words, was a manual of interpretation. In the absence of such a manual, anyone seeking to utilize Freud's technique would be forced to rely purely on empathy and clinical intuition.

Beyond this, we also have to note another aspect of Freud's reticence. For reasons that simply cannot be fathomed, Freud had also failed to report that in one very important respect his method had undergone a significant change some years previously. In every publication to date, the Löwenfeld article included, Freud had consistently described the elicitation of the chance idea or "free" association (*Einfall* in German), in the context of an ongoing inquiry directed by the physician into the meaning of a specific symptom, slip of the tongue, dream symbol, or chance memory, all of it controlled and directed by the physician. That is to say, Freud had not yet reported the method, which he had been using for at least four years, where the patient, and not the doctor, sets the day's agenda.

SPIELREIN'S ANALYSIS

THE YEAR 1904 was a watershed for the new treatment method. In America, the Harvard neurologist James Jackson Putnam was trying his hand at psychoanalysis on the new ward for nervous patients at Massachusetts General Hospital. But Jackson's efforts were relatively primitive. Regarding technique, he seems to have thought the point of inquiring after associations was to distract the patient from the symptom (this sort of "side-tracking" was one of Dubois's techniques). Putnam's sense of psychology can best be summarized by the single notation he inserted into one of his patient's charts: "All nervous symptoms began 7 years ago after an *affaire de coeur.*'' At the Burghölzli, by contrast, a sophisticated approach was adopted at the outset. Jung and Riklin were fast becoming masters of the association experiment. Riklin had begun examining a sample of hysterics with the new method while Jung had started collecting the spontaneous associations of a dementia praecox patient to see what complexes they revealed. And Bleuler was composing an important volume, *Affectivity, Suggestibility, and Paranoia,* whose argument would depend in important parts on Freudian theories of symptom formation.

Spielrein was admitted in late August. Even assuming that her delirium cleared rapidly, this was the time of year when the hospital staff was regularly decimated as its physicians took turns satisfying their yearly military obligation. Not until mid-October would there have been sufficient staff coverage to allow Jung the luxury of offering this one patient one- to two-hour interviews every other day. Karl Abraham arrived at the Burghölzli to take up a post as an assistant in December of 1904. His subsequent account had it that Jung's analysis of Spielrein was definitely complete by the time of his arrival. Spielrein's analysis, then, took at most two months and may well have been considerably shorter.

The shortness of the analysis was consistent with its use as an investigatory technique, i.e., as something rather akin to an unstructured association experiment. The Breuer-Freud therapeutic strategy of abreacting the trauma, meanwhile, was thought suspect. In June 1905, Jung would again psychoanalyze a patient—his first known case after Spielrein—and when he subsequently wrote up his results, he deliberately soft-pedaled the idea of abreaction:

> The confession of her sinful thoughts may have given considerable relief to the patient. But it seems unlikely that the cure can be ascribed to their verbal expression or to the "abreaction." Pathological ideas can be definitely submerged only by a strong effort. People with obsessions and compulsions are weak; they are unable to keep their ideas in check. Treatment to increase their energy is therefore best for them. The best energy-cure, however, is to force the patients, with a certain ruthlessness, to unearth and expose to the light the images that consciousness finds intolerable. Not only is this a severe challenge for the patient's energy but also his consciousness begins to accept the existence of ideas hitherto repressed.

Raising the patient's energy level was Janet's rationale, confrontation with reality was Bleuler's, and combining the two of them to justify the Viennese procedure was, when Jung published it in 1906, a nice piece of diplomacy.

Jung's technique differed in another respect; he did not use a couch. Rather, he had Spielrein sit in a chair while he sat behind her. Or, at least, that is the method he reported for his second known psychoanalytic patient, the one seen in June of 1905. The variation seems never to have bothered Jung much. Freud had a couch handy for the simple reason that it was a standard piece of equipment for an outpatient neurologist, necessary for the administration of certain routine procedures such as electro-galvanic massage. But Jung was not a neurologist and he did not have experience dealing with reclining patients. As for the seating arrangement Jung chose, Janet had reported sitting out of sight of a celebrated patient, "Achilles," who was possessed by a devil, so as not to interrupt the man's dissociated state. Janet's example would have surely struck Jung owing to its resemblance to his mother's having to sit behind her father—to keep the devil out—while he composed his sermons. But perhaps Spielrein had something to do with it as well; she considered herself unattractive, disliked being looked at, and may have been more cooperative once her psychoanalyst agreed to sit out of sight.

At some point, then, in late October or early November 1904, Sabina Spielrein was sufficiently composed to volunteer for an experimental procedure designed to elucidate the pathological antecedents of her hysterical delirium. She sat in a chair; Jung sat behind her. He asked her to tell him the history of her nervous troubles, being careful to include any stray thoughts that came into her mind. At certain points, such as when an image appeared in the train of associations, Jung asked her to associate to that image with the next thought that came to her. He also would have been on the lookout for certain telltale "complex indicators." Should she hesitate, forget her train of thought, interject a literary quotation, gesture, or become symptomatic, he would have pressed her for the thought that had provoked the change. A given interview would have taken from one to two hours, and interviews would have been held as often as every other day. The entire procedure, as already noted, took no more than two months and quite possibly less.

What did Jung find? It is easier to say what he did not find—a sexual assault in childhood. Had such a thing turned up in Spielrein's responses, Jung would certainly have reported it, since the issue was very much up for discussion at this time. There is, however, no evidence for such a thing in any document we possess concerning Spielrein, nor is there any mention of such a finding in any of the descriptions of her case penned by Jung. But if not an assault, then what?

The mystery deepens when we consider that Jung utterly missed something of importance in the case—the fact that Spielrein's mother had kept her completely ignorant of the sexual facts of life. Spielrein's own later account is quite explicit on this point: she confronted this lacuna in her conscious awareness only after she enrolled at the university. Spielrein's account has it that as a child she had been tortured by thoughts of the Plague, which she personified as a tall, dark figure that would take her away with him. According to her own later analysis, behind this fantasy lay a fear, and knowledge, of sexual processes. By the time she entered the Burghölzli, Spielrein had long since forgotten this fantasy, but when she enrolled at the university nine months later, and began studying diseases in earnest, she had a foreboding sense that the subject matter was somehow familiar to her. It was then and only then that her deeply repressed knowledge of the sexual facts of life returned to her. It is important to be clear about the chronology here: Spielrein did not enroll at the university until April of 1905 and was not allowed to start attending classes until after her discharge in June. But Jung's "analysis" had already been completed the previous December.

That is more than a little surprising. Jung was an extremely sensitive clinician and a very tough interviewer. Further, the endless word association protocols should have sharpened his ear to the point where he would have been a natural at the new method. And yet he had missed an important fact about Spielrein's state of mind—she was consciously ignorant of what the procreative act was all about.

The answer to the riddle of Jung's oversight may be simpler than we imagine. Quite conceivably, Jung never got much further than analyzing the immediate content of Spielrein's delirium—her father's chastising hand. In the literature on sexual deviancy of the day, it was a commonplace observation that some men derived sexual pleasure from delivering blows to the "nates" and furthermore that some men— also some women—derived pleasure from receiving them. Once the aspect of sexual excitement was established, the rest of the case—displays of disgust coupled with "ill-concealed masturbation"—fell readily into line with Riklin's "Lina H." All that was truly different here was the (assumedly) inborn masochistic tendency—Freud was lately stressing constitutional factors, too—which mediated between the precipitating event and the sexual reverie. Indeed, it is likely that Jung elected to make Spielrein his test case precisely because her dynamics so closely resembled those of Riklin's earlier case. Once one grasped the masochistic element, Spielrein's delirium was almost self-explanatory: she was fantasizing being beaten by her father and feeling both sexual pleasure and a concomitant sense of disgust with herself as a result. The business of the psychoanalysis, in this context, was to determine what events in Spielrein's day-to-day existence served to trigger the delirium. Or to put it in terms derived from the word association experiment, the job at hand was to determine which stimuli provoked the erotic complex, such as it was. In terms of her history, similarly, one would want to know which scenes, perhaps redolent with other meanings, had precipitated worsenings of her hysteria.

Such a scenario (and the brevity of the treatment) might account for Jung's extraordinary oversight in the case. Conceivably, it might have been possible to uncover any number of instructive scenes, instances where masochistic fantasies were provoked, without its ever occurring to the doctor that the girl did not know how she was *supposed* to express her sexual feelings. Then, too, Jung may have been betrayed by his method as well. So long as it fell to him to set the agenda for each session, and direct the inquiry, Spielrein was free to remain happily silent on the matter of sexual knowledge on the basis that her doctor evidently felt it was not worth going into. And by her own subsequent account, Spielrein rather "liked" herself "in my innocence."

WORK THERAPY

BEYOND THE "energy-cure" of a brief psychoanalysis, Jung's therapeutic efforts with Spielrein seem to have been chiefly didactic. That is to say, he attempted to educate her about the mechanisms of dissociation by way of encouraging her to build up her level of concentration and self-control. Since his dissertation contained an excellent summary of the issues, he assigned it to her for her edification. She, in turn, grasped a parallel between herself and Helene Preiswerk:

> The girl was deeply rooted in him, and she was my prototype. It is also significant that right from the beginning of my therapy Dr. Jung let me read his dissertation, in which he described this S.W. Later on he would sometimes turn reflective when I said something to him: such and such a woman had spoken just this way. And it was always this girl.

Jung also appears to have assigned Spielrein another book out of his library, Joseph Grasset's 1902 volume, *Le Spiritisme devant la Science*. Grasset was a popularizer of the findings of French psychopathology with his own terminology. His "polygonal" psychology was constructed with "the personal, conscious, free and responsible ego" at its apex. Either at Jung's behest or by her own invention, Spielrein regularly went to bed imagining the image of a polygon while thinking of the various things she had to do the next day.

Beyond reeducation, Spielrein was also expected to participate in some form of work therapy, and, as she planned to enter medical school, she was assigned to help Jung and Riklin in the psychological laboratory. At this time, Jung was preparing a new contribution, "The Reaction-Time Ratio in the Association Experiment," which was to be a rigorous demonstration of his contention that increased reaction times were regularly associated with feeling-toned complexes. This paper was also to be Jung's *Habilitationsschrift*, the publication entitling him to teach at the university. Seeking subjects, Jung seems to have turned first of all to his wife. She is almost certainly "Subject No. 1" of the paper, described as "a married woman who placed herself at my disposal in a most co-operative manner and gave me all the information I could possibly need." According to Jung's analysis, the central complex for this subject involved her pregnancy and her fear that her husband might be losing interest in her. In any case, Spielrein also assisted:

> He gave me some work to do on his . . . paper, "The Reaction-Time Ratio in the Association Experiment." We had numerous discussions about it, and he said, "Minds such as yours help advance science. You must become a psychiatrist." I stress these things again and again so that you may see it was not just the usual doctor-patient relationship that brought us so close together. He was writing that paper while I was still in the mental hospital. At that period I told him once I had dreamed about his wife, who complained to me about him, saying he was so terribly dictatorial and that life with him was difficult. Even then he did not respond to this like a doctor, but sighed and said he had realized that living together was difficult, etc. I spoke of the equality or intellectual independence of women, whereupon he replied that I was an exception, but his wife was an ordinary woman and accordingly only interested in what interested her husband.

Jung and Spielrein became friends. He showed her various archaeological books he kept in his library, and they occasionally went on
walks together. Jung reported on one of these walks in passing in a
little paper, "On Cryptomnesia," published in 1905 in a popular Berlin
magazine, *The Future*. The topic, unconscious plagiarism, had been the
subject of a recent article there, and Jung saw a chance to report on
his own investigations, not only into "cryptomnesia" but on other
topics as well. The anecdote concerning Spielrein came amidst a discussion of hysteria and genius:

> Recently I had to treat a hysterical young lady who became ill
> chiefly because she had been brutally beaten by her father. Once,
> when we were out for a walk, this lady dropped her coat in the dust.
> I picked it up, and tried to get the dust off by beating it with my
> stick. The next moment the lady hurled herself upon me with violent
> defensive gestures and tore the cloak out of my hands. She said she
> couldn't stand the sight, it was quite unendurable to her. I at once
> guessed the connection and urged her to tell me the motives for her
> behavior. She was nonplussed, and could only say that it was ex-
> tremely unpleasant for her to see her cloak cleaned like that.

Incidentally, by this time Jung had reread Freud's book on dreams
and begun interpreting his own dreams. The "Cryptomnesia" paper
notes his reaction in passing: "Anyone who has read Freud's dream
analyses or, better still, has done some himself, will know how the
unconscious can bedevil the most innocent and decent-minded people
with sexual symbols whose lewdness is positively horrifying."

Whatever else might be said of Jung's treatment of Spielrein, it
quite clearly worked—for both of them. She enrolled at the University
of Zurich in April 1905, though she naïvely listed her address as the
Burghölzli, with the result that her papers were deemed incomplete
until she obtained a letter from Bleuler saying she was fit. She departed
the hospital on 1 June 1905. Jung, meanwhile, was named *Oberarzt*, i.e.,
second in command to Bleuler, in April, and in June he became as
well the head of a new outpatient department where ambulatory patients, including nervous cases, could be seen. Moreover, Jung also
became the head of the psychology laboratory as Riklin left the scene
to take over Bleuler's old post as *Direktor* of the Rheinau asylum. Riklin's new post constituted an important promotion, but in terms of
career paths, he had made a mistake by removing himself from the

psychology laboratory. Henceforth, Jung would have a clear field to direct the research as he pleased—and to put only his name on it. Thus it happened that Riklin's role in the pioneering experiments eventually came to be all but forgotten.

By mid-1905, Jung had got over the temptation to present his theory of complexes as entirely original, and his publications now began to make increasingly clear, and positive, comments about Freud's pioneering work in the area of repression and other topics. To be sure, Freud had recently published a paper (to be examined more closely in the next chapter), in which he had made Jung the veiled target of some surprising criticism. Specifically, Freud doubted that a "young" assistant at a hospital (in German, a *"jung"* assistant) could conceivably do a creditable job at analysis on the basis of what had so far been published about it. Jung undoubtedly knew about Freud's statement, but he responded only by taking another patient into analysis in June of 1905. It is important to make the preceding point explicit: Not only did Freud and Jung first become aware of each other through their publications, but by virtue of that fact these publications also became their initial mode of communication. What they were signaling to each other was that each man had a lively sense of his own property rights when it came to matters of theory and practice.

It is in this context that we should also take notice of a curious document that Spielrein later claimed to have in her possession: a letter, dated 25 September 1905, written by Jung describing her to Freud. Spielrein describes the letter as one

> . . . in which Dr. Jung describes me as a "highly intelligent and gifted person of greatest sensitivity." I was still a baby of 19 then, and ran around in very simple dresses and with a long, dangling braid, since I wanted to elevate my soul above my body. That explains why Jung went on, "Her character has a decidedly relentless and unreasonable aspect, and she lacks any sense of appropriateness and external manners, most of which must, of course, be attributed to Russian peculiarities."

What makes this letter remarkable is the date Spielrein gives: 25 September 1905. This would mean that it was written some nine months before Jung's and Freud's correspondence ultimately began—written, but apparently never sent. Perhaps Jung had set about writing to Freud about Spielrein's case, and then changed his mind. But this leaves obscure why Spielrein herself should have ended up in possession of the letter. A more likely scenario is that Spielrein was to have a consultation with Freud just before the fall semester got under way and Jung gave her the letter as an introduction. This was another indirect way for the two men to communicate, by referring patients. In effect, Jung's intention was to show off his handiwork, and, no doubt, he hoped to learn something as well. As Spielrein was now his friend as well as his former patient, he could expect to hear from her in detail what Freud had been like. Then, for reasons that can only be guessed at, the plan fell through. In any event, the letter places Spielrein, in her dual capacity as former patient and as fledgling medical student, at the center of the relationship between Jung and Freud—even before it had properly begun.

"CATTERINA H."

ONE OF THE more interesting cases seen in the Burghölzli in the second half of 1905 involved a second Russian student, also hysterical, who was examined by Riklin with the word-association experiment. According to Riklin's account, this twenty-year-old woman was like Spielrein in yet another way, for she was

> . . . able so to repress all sexual experiences, and that knowledge which everyone necessarily acquires in the course of growth, that she was over twenty without having any correct ideas on the subject, although she was a student. She even took part in a discussion on prostitution without really knowing what prostitution was.

"Catterina H." first developed hysterical symptoms when a boyfriend ("R.") killed himself after she had spurned his advances. To that trauma was soon added a second:

> Her condition was worsened by another circumstance. The patient was informed by a woman acquaintance, a midwifery student, about male sexuality and the sexual act, upon which the knowledge of the subject, hitherto repressed, entered completely into consciousness. She felt herself unhappy; mankind, hitherto idealized, became a beast; the idea that R. loved her sensually . . . troubled her terribly . . . . In slight twilight states she would often say, "I must go to his grave and ask him if he knew it." She hated mankind on

account of its sexual function, hated also her doctor, who she imagined was also like the rest; she could only esteem him when she saw him in attendance upon his patients and was then able to exclude the sexual image.

By contrast, we have no document describing what Spielrein did when she de-repressed her knowledge of sexuality. It may be guessed that, like "Catterina H.," she had a considerable reaction, and that it was the basis for Jung's later statement that she was prone to relapse if he withdrew his support. In any event, at some point in the year following her discharge and her matriculation at the Zurich medical school, Spielrein resumed seeing Jung on a regular basis—with scheduled appointments—rather more as an outpatient than as a friend and fledgling colleague, but with aspects of both.

Spielrein's heretofore sterling status as Jung's "test case" would have been at least slightly tarnished—for both of them—once they grasped what they had missed. That, I suspect, is what lies behind the following comments, which Spielrein appended to her later description of the unsent letter to Freud mentioning her "Russian peculiarities":

How else should the good man have spoken, when I wanted to see him poor rather than rich, since wealth destroys the soul; when I wanted to view everyone as a fine person and of course soon had to recognize that "it's all a swindle, all a comedy, people are all stupid and false," etc. Ability to view the world as an artist [does] would come only with age, with the awakening of the sexual component. Then unreasonableness makes way for "maidenliness." But at that time [September of 1905] Dr. Jung also failed to understand a number of things; before my very eyes he has undergone such great intellectual growth. I was in a position to follow his intellectual development step by step, and I learned a great deal not only from him but also from observing him.

CHAPTER 4

The Organic Untruthfulness
of Woman

It is thus possible for the person affected to declare a sexual desire to be an "extraneous body in her consciousness," a sensation which she *thinks* she detests, but which in reality has its origins in her own nature. The tremendous intensity with which she endeavors to suppress the desire (and which only serves to increase it) so that she may the more vehemently and indignantly reject the thought—these are the alterations which are seen in hysteria. And the chronic untruthfulness of woman becomes imbued with man's ethically negative valuation of sexuality. . . . Hysteria is the organic crisis of the organic untruthfulness of woman.

—Otto Weininger, 1903; phrase in quotes from Freud

—————

IN ZURICH, during the years 1904–1905, Jung was wrestling with the problem of repression, whose reality as a psychological phenomenon was being established by the word-association experiment. In Vienna, during the same two-year period, Sigmund Freud was struggling with the same problem and was poised to put the finishing touches on a daring new clinical synthesis in which sexual repression was a key component. But for a tangle of reasons, personal and professional, he was not free to use his own favorite biological explanation of how repression worked. What made matters more complicated during this period was that Freud now first began to learn of the important work being done at the Swiss hospital, work that made it all the more urgent for him to get his unpublished clinical theory into print.

To understand how Freud got himself into this predicament, we have to backtrack to 1897, when, only a year after he had broadcast it as the first fruit of his new method of "psychoanalysis," Freud realized that his etiological theory of childhood sexual trauma, the so-called seduction theory, was simply wrong. The realization was both embarrassing and liberating. It ushered in a period of profound professional isolation, but it also spurred Freud to new heights theoretically. Professionally, Freud simply withdrew: he ceased to offer his lecture course at the university, where he held a post as lecturer, and he likewise stopped making public presentations before medical gatherings. Compounding this situation was Freud's belief, which was likely correct, that his application for a titular professorship was being blocked for reasons of anti-Semitism. Turning inward to his roots, Freud responded by joining the local chapter of the B'nai B'rith and becoming active in its affairs.

Outside of an occasional lecture by "Brother Freud" at the B'nai B'rith, the only person to be kept continuously abreast of the new directions of Freud's theorizing during this time was his close friend and confidant Wilhelm Fliess. Fliess was a Berlin-based internist with an imposing reputation for therapeutic zeal who was then closing in on important biomedical theories of his own. The two men had been brought together some years earlier by their common interest in functional disorders of the nervous system, and it was Fliess who now heard of the marvelous clinical-psychological synthesis that Freud was putting together. Already in 1896 Freud had realized that his clinical method of investigating neurotic symptoms—eliciting associations and working backward to a repressed wish or memory—also seemed to work when applied to dreams. That dreams might reveal wishes, especially sexual wishes, was a well-known clinical verity at the time and had been duly noted by Charcot, Janet, Krafft-Ebing, and Schrenck-Notzing, among others. But that only applied to dreams whose content was unmistakably clear, such as a dream where a man's wife might be replaced in bed by a homosexual lover from his past. No one yet knew what to do with dreams that were fragmented and seemingly nonsensical (as the great run of dreams are in many people) except to assume that they were random neurological accidents, perhaps caused by bad digestion. To his delighted surprise, Freud seemed to have a method which could potentially make sense of these more obscure dreams.

During the next three years, roughly from 1897 to 1900, Freud gradually expanded his interpretive repertoire to include not only dreams but also slips of the tongue, bungled actions, the forgetting of names, and what he called "screen memories" (vivid but essentially counterfeit recollections from childhood). All these phenomena became roughly analogous to the subliminal mental processes which determined the formation of symptoms in nervous sufferers: they were products of a dynamic interplay between wishes and defenses against those wishes, with the interplay generating a half-conscious and half-intended result. It was this synthesis of disparate phenomena, all yielding to the same basic interpretive strategy, which was soon to make "Freudian" into a universal adjective. It was what Bleuler had in mind in 1904, when he wrote that "in the Freudian world" some of the strings that move the puppets of consciousness had been revealed.

Freud's stylistic gifts would prove to be an important factor in winning an audience for his psychological ideas. During the time he was putting his new psychological synthesis together, Freud served double duty as his own best subject for observation. He became, in effect, his own patient. Just this circumstance, which was otherwise methodologically suspect, then allowed Freud to adopt a disarmingly confessional mode in reporting his results. Since the theory called for wishes that one might want to repress, it fell to Freud to reveal just those aspects of his character that another person might wish to conceal. It was a paradoxical route to take, to use one's personal foibles as a vehicle for establishing scientific objectivity, and such are the stylistic demands of the enterprise that in the ninety years since Freud no writer has dared to repeat it. At the time, to be sure, there were a few keen-eyed critics who would have none of it and insisted that the methodological problems entailed in self-observation had not been solved. By far the more general reaction, however, was to find the presentation agreeable, even compelling. Moreover, in the years to come many readers would be pulled into the texts in a unique way, for, by virtue of Freud's example, they were being invited to examine their own mental processes.

While he was forging his general psychological synthesis, however, Freud was also radically revising his conception of sexuality, which he continued to believe was etiologically crucial for the formation of a neurosis. Prior to 1897, Freud had conceived of sexuality in essentially toxicological terms, as akin to the well-known intoxicants like cocaine or alcohol; further, he supposed that this putative "sexual chemical" became active only in puberty. Now, however, under the impact of some of Fliess's ideas and those of another Berlin physician turned sexual researcher, Albert Moll, Freud began to view sexuality in developmental and evolutionary terms. Just as the means of procreation had developed over the course of evolution, so, too, in the course of individual development, sexuality might first take one form and then another as the individual progressed from infancy to adulthood along the path that evolution had laid down for it.

A problem with this new developmental approach to sexuality, however, was that it wreaked havoc with Freud's existing theory of repression. In the *Studies on Hysteria* with Breuer, Freud had tentatively advanced an essentially commonsense version of how repression might work: the patient naturally suppresses and forgets things which he or she deems painful, shameful, disgusting, or immoral. In context, Freud's commonsense suggestion had been quite radical. In effect, he and Breuer were arguing that psychic conflict alone might be sufficient to bring about the "splits in consciousness" that typified hysteria and that had heretofore been assumed to reflect a neurological substrate. The following year, in his papers outlining the "seduction theory," Freud had addressed this issue by presenting a theory of repression that appealed to organic factors as well as psychological ones. This was the theory of "deferred action," according to which the mere fact of childhood sexual abuse, no matter how painful, was not sufficient in and of itself to cause neurosis; it was only when memories of such abuse became reawakened during puberty that they became neurotogenic. The two-step nature of the process was especially clear in Freud's portrait of obsessional neurosis: here the original childhood experiences, typically with a playmate, were not thought to have been traumatic in themselves; it was only their subsequent coloring with adolescent sexual energies that made them potent unconscious sources for the endless, often nonsensical self-reproaches that characterized the adult disorder. The beauty of the deferred-action theory was that it offered a plausible rationale for restricting the range of potentially pathogenic memories. By Freud's logic, only sexual and quasi-sexual memories could draw unto themselves the new sexual energies of adolescence and thus necessitate continuously ongoing repression. Other traumatic experiences might also have been repressed, but they would remain dormant without ever becoming activated again. They lacked the energic status, neurologically speaking, to do the kind of damage that could lead to a nervous illness.

Once Freud grasped the reality, and universality, of childhood sexual urges, however, this explanation no longer worked. If the child was already a sexual creature in the first place, which is what the new developmental conception demanded, then there was no biological reason why his or her memories of childhood sexual scenes should become newly problematical in puberty. Nor was there any logical basis for giving special consideration to sexual memories as opposed to all other traumatic occurrences. The problem might not have been apparent to a lesser mind, but such was Freud's systematic grasp of the issues that he realized the implications immediately. As he wrote to Fliess at the

time: "Now I have no idea of where I stand because I have not succeeded in gaining a theoretical understanding of repression and its
interplay of forces. . . . [T]he factor of a hereditary disposition regains
a sphere of influence from which I had made it my task to dislodge
it—in the interest of illuminating neurosis."

It was in this context that, in December 1897, at one of the periodic
get-togethers which the two men liked to call "Congresses," Fliess
suggested to Freud an alternative explanation of repression based on
his own researches into male and female cycles. According to Fliess's
still-preliminary findings, in both men and women there appeared to
be operative two different biorhythms, one a twenty-eight-day female
cycle, the other a twenty-three-day male cycle. Fliess's interest in these
cycles was primarily physiological; he hoped to be able to predict from
them the timing of various diseases, including nervous illnesses. But it
had struck Fliess that his research might have important psychological
corollaries.

Fliess's idea with regard to repression was quite simple. If, as his
research on cycles suggested, all organisms were fundamentally bisexual, then during the process of sexual maturation one half of the inborn
bisexual disposition must necessarily be suppressed by the other before
an adult sexual disposition could be achieved. A male animal must
suppress his female side, a female her male side. Yet, if this was true,
then it suggested that somewhere along the course of evolution a natural mechanism had been put in place which called for adolescence to
be a time not only of sexual flowering but also of sexual repression,
aimed at the other half of the original bisexual disposition. Further, it
suggested an important difference between childhood sexual experiences and adult ones, for any childhood scenes that occurred would
necessarily have taken place while the inborn bisexual disposition was
still operative; as a result, they would be colored by both female and
male sexual energies. Just this quality, however, would make them
problematic at the time of puberty, and continuously so thereafter. In
effect, bisexual theory rescued the deferred-action theory of repression
and made it consonant with the fact of childhood sexuality.

At first, Freud was unimpressed by Fliess's idea, but the more he
thought about it, the more reasonable it became. Indeed, Freud became frankly envious. Within a year's time, at yet another of their
"Congresses," Freud was excitedly telling Fliess of what he, Freud,
had recently figured out along these lines. When Fliess pointed out
that he had told Freud the exact same thing a year before, Freud
objected strenuously, only to realize afterward that his memory had

played a very bad trick on him. The lapse of memory was subsequently written up as an anecdote for *The Psychopathology of Everyday Life*, which Fliess read in manuscript. A little while afterward, Freud had a wish-fulfilling dream in which he laid out "before my friend a difficult and long sought-after theory of bisexuality." He also had a second dream, now known as the "Non Vixit" dream, whose interpretation hinged in part on a matter that was in dispute between two unidentified friends and involved a wish that one should die and leave the other in sole possession of it. Both dreams were included in *The Interpretation of Dreams*, which Fliess also read in manuscript.

Fliess began seriously to worry about the priority of his claim to the idea being maintained. This concern, combined with other tensions that had accumulated between the two men over the years, led to an extremely bad falling-out at a meeting in Achensee in August 1900. It is clear from Freud's follow-up letter after this meeting that the bisexual explanation of repression had been specifically at issue in their quarrel. The two men managed to continue their correspondence for a time—as an internist Fliess was a valuable interlocutor with regard to a mysterious, potentially grave illness that had recently overtaken Freud's sister-in-law, Minna Bernays—but their relationship was never the same afterwards.

HERR PROFESSOR FREUD

THE UPSHOT of the quarrel with Fliess was that there was a curious bifurcation in Freud's career in the early years of this century. Following the publication of his major psychological works, *The Interpretation of Dreams* in 1899, and *On Dreams* and *The Psychopathology of Everyday Life* in early 1901, Freud resumed his professional career in earnest. In March 1902, thanks to the lobbying of a wealthy former patient with the minister of education, Freud was finally awarded a titular professorship at the University of Vienna. This was an important, long-overdue honor. Among its perquisites was a new form of social salutation: henceforth Freud was to be addressed as "Herr Professor," his wife as "Frau Professor." In October 1902, his new title in hand, Freud resumed giving lectures at the university medical school, his first since 1898. The same month also saw the beginning of a weekly Wednesday night discussion group in Freud's waiting room involving himself, the physician Rudolf Reitler, two internists with journalistic credentials, Wilhelm Stekel and Alfred Adler, and a local nerve specialist, Max Kahane. The first evening's discussion was devoted to the psychology of cigar-smoking. Nor were Freud's efforts to interest his colleagues in his ideas confined to Vienna. A year later, for example, he took the liberty of writing to an anonymous Berlin reviewer of his dream book and, for his trouble, found himself in correspondence with the psychologist and prominent medical commentator Willy Hellpach, who was then preparing his own treatise on hysteria.

But if his academic career, long in self-imposed drydock, had been refitted and was now steaming forward again, Freud's publications were at an uncharacteristic standstill. He was as prolific as ever at his writing table; he just was not releasing the manuscripts. In February 1901, he completed a detailed account of one of his treatments (the "Dora" case), but first delayed its submission for Ziehen's medical monograph series and then retracted it altogether. He then began two other works, "Human Bisexuality" and "Forgetting and Repressing," neither of which ever saw the light of day. Yet another work, on the psychology of jokes, was finished in April of 1903, but it, too, was not submitted for publication. In short, apart from his communication on his method in Löwenfeld's volume early in 1904, Freud had published no new papers for the past three years.

The problem was the bisexual explanation of repression. Freud had come to believe that so far as the neuroses were concerned the theory was, as he wrote to Fliess, "indispensable." By 1900, if not sooner, he had made it a regular part of all his treatments. He also wrote the theory into *all* the aforementioned unpublished manuscripts. In sum, the theory had become a critical part of what he considered the "sexual organic foundation" of his theory of neurosis. To be sure, Freud was more than willing to cite his erstwhile friend, but just there things were still sticky. For Fliess did not want to be cited. In fact, Fliess did not want the theory out at all. Or at least he did not want it out until *he* could publish it, along with the rest of his ideas on bisexuality and biorhythms. Unfortunately for Freud, however, the empirical side of Fliess's theory involved the meticulous documentation of the physiological ramifications of twenty-three-day (male) and twenty-eight-day (female) cycles in both men and women, and collecting all the necessary data was going to take years. In the meantime, Freud was forced to wait.

Freud was thus in the frustrating position during the years 1901–1904 of knowing where his clinical theory was going—the direction was quite radical—but not being able to communicate it outside of a local circle of friends and patients.

He seems to have used the waiting period to solidify his persona.

By now, Freud had settled into a routine that he was to keep for decades to come. During the day, in the office adjoining his second-floor apartment, he saw patients, often for eight hours straight, stopping only to cross the hall for lunch and then for a walk before dinner. Weekday evenings were set aside for writing, except for Wednesdays, when the discussion group met in his waiting room, and Fridays, when he gave his lecture course. On Saturdays, Freud joined three longtime friends for a game of tarok at the B'nai B'rith. On Sundays, he kept up with his correspondence. Freud's wife, Martha Bernays, and her sister, Minna, ran the household in Freud's absence. Everything was arranged so that his work would not be disturbed, though the children had to be available for mealtimes, and there only family matters—no business and no psychoanalysis—were discussed.

Freud's self-presentation in this period of time is spoken for by nearly all who met him. Physically, he was only of average stature, if that, and there was something softly reticent, almost feminine, in his manner. He was not a man to command crowds; indeed, he seems never even to have been at home in the cafés that were the setting for so much of Viennese social life. But in venues where he was comfortable, Freud made an impression that was extraordinary and lasting: face to face, he was at once genial, gentlemanly, reasonable, well-read, tolerant, and almost mesmerizingly articulate. He was equally superb as a listener and he possessed a remarkable capacity to organize a thoughtfully systematic response on the spot. Moreover, as he was steeped in literature, in cultural history, and in virtually any other topic one wanted to bring up, there were few subjects that Freud could not somehow connect with his own theories—and vice versa. As an interrogator, Freud was doggedly insistent with patients, and he no longer suffered much if they failed to get better. But with new colleagues he had a definite knack for making personal revelation seem like a new kind of pleasant and essentially collaborative intellectual exercise, rather as though it were all so interesting how the laws of the psyche continually played themselves out, even in gentlemen—and ladies—such as ourselves.

A single anecdote may help here. In the fall of 1904, Bruno Goetz, a young poet and a student at the University of Vienna, consulted Freud because of persistent headaches. Freud took a brief history—Goetz was spending what little money he had on books—then engaged the young man in a long discussion of contemporary writers. At the end of the hour, Freud announced that he was writing a prescription for the headaches and after sealing it in an envelope sent Goetz on his way with the warning that psychoanalysis might not be good for poetry. When Goetz reached the street, he opened the envelope and found both Freud's assessment and his remedy. The headaches were caused not by neurosis but by hunger, and Freud had enclosed money for Goetz to buy a few good meals.

History would soon require of this man that he know how to be "Freud"—and, given the radically difficult nature of that task, the Herr Professor of 19 Berggasse had found as good a way of going about it as any.

SEX AND CHARACTER

BY THE BEGINNING of 1904 the situation between Freud and Fliess had become considerably more complicated, though Fliess was as yet unaware of what the complications were. The two men had managed a decorous meeting during Easter of 1903 on Freud's home ground in Vienna. But since their meeting two new books had appeared, one by Hermann Swoboda, the other by Otto Weininger. Both authors were Viennese, both authors had written about bisexuality, and both authors were personally acquainted with Freud. Of the two books, the one by Otto Weininger was by far the more important. Entitled *Sex and Character*, it had appeared in mid-1903, to little public notice. Then in October 1903, Weininger, a philosopher turned neurological camp follower, had killed himself. The Viennese newspapers picked up the story—young genius dies by his own hand—and with the added publicity, sales of the book began to skyrocket.

Sex and Character was an enormously readable book, though an endlessly infuriating one. Arguing from the biological premise that bisexuality was inherent in all living organisms, Weininger attempted to explain human character on the basis of relative mixtures of male and female components. In his view, all individuals could be arrayed along a hypothetical continuum of x parts masculinity and y parts femininity, with an increase in one component always coupled with a decrease in the other. Any number of puzzling psychological phenomena could be explained with this key. Thus, for example, sexual attraction, seemingly so mysterious a process, could be explained in terms of complementary ratios, a 3:4 feminine man being attracted to a 3:4 masculine woman, and so forth. Similarly, the phenomenology of hysteria could be explained by positing an unfortunate mixture of male and female elements, one which resulted in unsuccessful attempts to suppress sexual desire.

To get his hypothetical characterology to work, however, Weininger had to come up with ideal types of masculinity and femininity, since, by his definition of the problem, these were no longer identical with observed gender. And here his thesis rapidly became outrageous. Masculinity was equated with powers of intellectual discrimination and memory; with morality, will, and religion; with true love; with genius; and, finally, with the Aryan race. Femininity was equated with credulousness and forgetfulness; with amorality, impulsiveness, and irreligion; with sexual desire; with hysteria; and, predictably, with Judaism. Though Weininger finally concluded with a redemptive scheme whereby Jews and women might raise themselves up even as men and Aryans became reconciled to their bisexual nature, most of the 472 pages of his volume were taken up with laying out the basic polarity, with any number of memorable aphorisms along the way.

There was one problem in particular with this perversely fascinating book. The doctrine of bisexuality, including the law of sexual attraction and the explanation for repression in hysteria derived from it, was not, properly speaking, Weininger's intellectual property. These ideas were the brainchildren of Wilhelm Fliess. Nowhere in Weininger's book, however, was Fliess's name mentioned.

For his part, Freud was not entirely enamored of Weininger's portrait of repression—"the organic untruthfulness of woman"—even though it was very, very close to his own. But, most gratifyingly, Weininger had repeatedly cited him along with Breuer, Janet, and Forel's principal collaborator, Oskar Vogt, in his chapter on hysteria. Freud was thus being civilized in seeing to it that his own thoughts about the book—"the literary bomb of an intellectual anarchist"—appeared under a discreetly veiled attribution in Wilhelm Stekel's newspaper review.

AN OFFICIAL PSYCHIATRIST

IN APRIL 1904, something happened that ultimately broke the logjam of unpublished works sitting on Freud's writing table—and ended Freud's relationship with Fliess once and for all. Eugen Bleuler's review of Löwenfeld's book appeared. The review contained specific praise for Freud's psychological views. Favorable notice had scarcely been unknown to Freud until now, but this notice came from the sitting professor of psychiatry at the prestigious University of Zurich. Freud decided to seize the moment. He and his small group of Wednesday night regulars would start their own journal, they would solicit Fliess's participation, and with the prestige of the Zurich chair as the bait, Fliess could scarcely refuse. On 26 April 1904 Freud wrote to his erstwhile friend that a group of his "pupils" were planning a new journal:

> They will ask you to collaborate, and, anticipating them, I should like to ask you not to deny them your name and your contribution. They believe the time is right, because everywhere the signs of agreement with my views are increasing. I recently found an absolutely stunning recognition of my point of view in a book review in the *Münchener medizinische Wochenschrift* by an official psychiatrist, Bleuler, in Zurich. Just imagine, a full professor of psychiatry and my +++ studies of hysteria and the dream, which so far have been labeled disgusting. [The " +++ " mocks the custom of painting three crosses on farm dwellings to keep the devil away.]

But no sooner had Freud played his trump card than he tipped the rest of his hand. In the very next paragraph of his letter, Freud proceeded to ask Fliess if he had yet received a copy of Hermann Swoboda's new book on biorhythms. About the book, Freud wrote, "I am in more than one respect the intellectual originator, though I would not want to be its author."

Fliess already knew that Swoboda's new book, which also featured sexual cycles, contained a botched version of his own theories. He wrote back immediately to register his "regret" that Freud had been in any way involved in the book's genesis. But that was as nothing compared to what happened next. Two months later, Fliess got around to reading that new best-seller, *Sex and Character*. To his astonishment, he saw from a passage in it that Weininger and Swoboda had been close friends. To his further astonishment, he also saw that it contained his own theory of bisexuality, including the explanation of repression. And to his absolute astonishment, he grasped that between Swoboda and Weininger the essence of his own unpublished theory had now been pirated. Fliess was outraged.

Fliess set out for Vienna in mid-July of 1904. Freud, departing for his vacation two weeks earlier than usual, was not there to greet him. With no other recourse, Fliess finally wrote to Freud on 20 July accusing him of being the conduit for Weininger's theft. Freud wrote back on 23 July and related "everything I know about it": Swoboda had not been a pupil, but a patient; bisexuality came up in his treatment as it always does; Swoboda mentioned the idea to Weininger when he found the latter brooding about his sexual problems—"Whereupon Weininger clapped his hand to his forehead and rushed home to write his book." To be sure, Freud had helped Swoboda find a publisher, but that was no more than a good deed in a dark world and it had nothing to do with Weininger, whom Freud did not admit knowing at all. That regrettable misunderstanding out of the way, Freud then went on to say that he was just now finishing up a new work, *Three Essays on the Theory of Sexuality,* in which he would, as much as possible, try to avoid the topic of bisexuality though, in fact, it had to come up in a few places and how did Fliess want to be cited?

Fliess next went to their mutual friend Oskar Rie. There he found at least part of the truth: whatever else, Freud not only had met with Weininger personally but had also read through an early draft of Weininger's manuscript. Indeed, it turned out that the two men had specifically discussed Weininger's chapter on hysteria, which had been written especially to curry Freud's favor. Freud apparently had found the chapter garbled and unsatisfactory and he later claimed that he had urged Weininger not to publish it. That tidbit aside, however, Freud's behavior had been plainly indefensible. Fliess now wrote again to Freud, who this time had to confess his role. He still, however, found room for lecturing Fliess that ideas could not be "patented" and for insisting that "the harm done to you by Weininger is very slight, because no one will take his shoddy piece of work seriously." (The "shoddy piece of work" was fast becoming an international best-seller and would be translated into no less than sixteen foreign languages.) At the end of his letter, however, Freud suddenly turned urgent:

> I trust you will still be so kind as to help me out of my present predicament by reading the remarks on bisexuality in the proofs of my just completed "Essays on the Theory of Sexuality" and changing them to your satisfaction. It would be easier to postpone publication until you have surrendered your biology to the public. But I do not know when this will be. You will scarcely hurry for my sake. In the meantime I can do nothing, not even finish the [book on] *Jokes,* which in a crucial point is partially based on the theory of sexuality. . . .
>
> I ask you to reply to *this.*

The urgency had been there all along, but now there was a terrible complication. Would Fliess go public with his reproaches? Over six years had passed since Freud's last publication on hysteria, and in the intervening period he had completely revised his conception of the libido. But Freud still believed that the libido and its repression were the key to understanding all nervous complaints; indeed, the whole point of *Three Essays on the Theory of Sexuality* was to lay out a sexual-developmental scaffolding for Freud's revised theory of the neuroses. There can be no question—we have his repeated, explicit statements on this in the letters to Fliess—but that Freud had hitherto contemplated making the bisexual theory of repression a major part of this new synthesis. By July 1904, however, in the absence of any reassurance from the enraged Fliess, just that course of action would have been very ill-advised. For if Freud now went into print with the theory, and Fliess went public with charges of plagiarism, it would become readily apparent to the discerning reader just how much Freud had helped both Weininger and Swoboda. Freud's theory would thus be born in scandal and it would be that much more difficult for it to get a fair hearing on its merits.

A WIDESPREAD AND ERRONEOUS IMPRESSION

IN AUGUST 1904, while Freud was vacationing in Italy and Greece and considering how to amend his manuscripts, Spielrein was admitted to the Burghölzli in the midst of her delirium. A correspondence had already begun between Freud and the Burghölzli chief, Eugen Bleuler, and by the time Freud returned to Vienna in late September, Bleuler had given his permission to Carl Jung to undertake a trial of "psychoanalysis" with the young Russian patient. No doubt Bleuler apprised Freud of the trial. Both Bleuler and Jung assumed that the description Freud had published in the Löwenfeld volume was more or less adequate to their needs. But by Freud's lights, the Löwenfeld account was not adequate, for it did not include the rules for interpretation. Spielrein was scarcely the first patient to be psychoanalyzed outside of Vienna; similar attempts at replicating Freud's, and Breuer's, findings had been regularly made in recent years, with mixed results. But as the patient of record in Zurich, where the sitting professor of psychiatry was favorably disposed, Spielrein was unusually important.

Freud decided to protect himself. He scheduled a lecture, "On Psychotherapy," to be given at the Vienna Society of Physicians. The talk, presented on 12 December 1904, constituted Freud's first appearance before a professional body in eight years. It was a lyrical, but ultimately evasive lecture. Freud noted at the outset that his technique had not yet been communicated in a way that would "give medical readers . . . the directions necessary to enable them to carry though the treatment completely." Unfortunately, he could only "hint" at his method here. In fact, all that was really communicated about the method was that it constituted a "re-education in overcoming internal resistances" to sexuality. And, yet, Freud managed to make his failure in reporting into a line of defense:

> It seems to me that there is a widespread and erroneous impression among my colleagues that this technique of searching for the origins of an illness and removing its manifestations by that means is an easy one which can be practised off-hand, as it were. I conclude this from the fact that not one of all the people who show an interest in my therapy has ever asked me how I actually go about it. . . . Again, I am now and then astonished to hear that in this or that department of a hospital a young [in German, *jung*] assistant has received an order from his chief to undertake a "psychoanalysis" of a hysterical patient. I am sure he would not be allowed to examine an extirpated tumour unless he had convinced his chiefs that he was conversant with histological technique.

This, in effect, was Freud's review of Spielrein's initial round of treatment at Jung's hands. Since we don't know what Bleuler specifically communicated about Jung's "test case," we do not know just why Freud elected to dismiss the possibility that the "young assistant" might have done a creditable job.

It is worth pausing for a moment to consider the implications of Freud's stance. He had invented the new procedure, he had spent nearly ten years working with it, and at the very least he had had the opportunity to learn from his own mistakes. It was thus entirely reasonable for Freud to believe that nobody else could appreciate all the subtleties involved as well as he did. And by implication, that meant nobody else was quite in a position to make a fair test of how well the method worked. Just this situation, however, was terribly suspect from a scientific point of view. In science, any proposed "method" must be capable of being stated in formal terms. To be sure, as with Freud's own example of "histological technique," a procedure may be difficult to learn and its full acquisition may require considerable training. Moreover, there are some scientific procedures that are so extremely difficult that only a very few people ever master them completely.

Nonetheless, the method has to be capable of being formalized, at least in principle. Put another way, it must be capable of being set forth in a handbook, even if everyone agrees that the handbook is not quite adequate. A method that cannot be formalized is like a finding that cannot be replicated. However interesting it may be, it is not scientific.

Freud was completely aware of this requirement. So, too, were his contemporaries. Willy Hellpach, with whom Freud was still corresponding, would make the issue the basis for a telling comment two years later: "Though one may recognize that psychoanalysis in the hands of its creator ingeniously and fruitfully illuminates for us some obscure relationships, the treatment lacks the most important elements for it to become a 'method' and as such to show itself as better than or even on a par with old-style sympathetic observation." In short, if Freud was the only person who could do it, psychoanalysis was destined to remain an interesting curiosity. The best way to reply to this criticism was to publish a manual, one that included interpretive rules. And Freud still intended to do just that. In the meantime, however, he was content to take the position, as he did before the Society of Physicians, that for now the only way to learn the method was through direct personal instruction from him.

THE NEW DOCTRINE OF NERVOUS ILLNESS

THOUGH MY STORY concerns the development of the intellectual axis between Zurich and Vienna, I would be remiss if I fostered the impression that only in these two cities was important work going forward in the understanding and treatment of nervous disorders. The opposite was true; there was an international explosion of interest in these topics. In Switzerland alone, Ludwig Frank, Dumeng Bezzola, Roger Vittoz, Arthur Muthmann, and Paul Dubois were all independently developing their own distinctive treatment methods. Similarly in America, Boris Sidis, Morton Prince, James Jackson Putnam, and others were all experimenting with various ways of alleviating nervous complaints. Such was the general interest that at the international exposition in St. Louis in September of 1904, there was even a special section devoted to psychopathology. Adolf Meyer, an expatriate Swiss who had trained under Forel, chaired the event; Morton Prince and Pierre Janet were the guest speakers.

Medical opinion had moved far from the day when Charcot had linked hysteria with arthritis on the basis that both were hereditary and both involved painful cramps, and when Paul Möbius, a Berlin professor of electrotherapy, could make an important contribution simply by insisting that the hysterical attack involved an "idea." It had become clear to many thoughtful men that the way to make further progress in understanding hysteria and other nervous disorders was through psychology. That, in turn, meant clarifying the relationship of psychic factors to the organic substrate of the nervous system.

Accordingly, at this time there were a host of new works, each advancing a new synthesis. In 1902, Otto Gross, an assistant at Kraepelin's clinic and the son of Hanns Gross, the father of modern criminology, had published an important volume, *Die zerebrale Sekundarfunktion*. In it Gross combined the insights of the great brain anatomist Carl Wernicke with those of Kraepelin, Freud, and Janet to come up with a novel psychology of clinical types. In 1904 in Bern, DuBois's massive treatise *Les Psychonévroses et Leur Traitement Morale* appeared. The first nineteen chapters were devoted to a history of the evolution of the modern understanding of nervous complaints while the last sixteen were devoted to the treatment of individual nervous symptoms such as sleep disorders, intestinal problems, traumatic accidents, and the like. (DuBois was of two minds about sexual inquiry. On the one hand, he argued that "there is very little 'nervousness' in those who have no sexual disturbance," and that it was crucial to "get your patient to confess to you." On the other hand, he decried those physicians "who seem to take a lascivious pleasure in . . . putting indiscreet questions to their patients.") In early 1905, Auguste Forel weighed in with a massive work, *The Sexual Question,* which ran the gamut from the details of unicellular reproduction, complete with colored plates, through the role of erotic attraction in hypnotism, to the much-needed reform of contemporary sexual practices lest the white race get overtaken by the yellow one.

In short, it was an age that seemed to cry out for great syntheses—and for the geniuses who could provide them. The call was heard everywhere. In April 1905, a young man named Otto Rank asked his internist, Alfred Adler, if he might once again borrow that interesting book on the interpretation of dreams. By August, he was personally acquainted with the book's author. And by the end of 1905 he had submitted no less than three manuscripts for Freud's appraisal. The first manuscript, brief and personal, was a reanalysis of one of Freud's own dreams; contrary to what Freud had written, argued Rank, he did not want his sons to surpass him. The second was a study, *The*

Artist, which was published two years later, minus a section on bisexuality. And the third, never published, was entitled "The Essence of Judaism." In this work, a mixture of Weininger, Freud, and Nietzsche, Rank made the case that the "essence of Judaism" was "its stress on primitive sexuality," a trait which, in an age of sexual repression, qualified Jews to be the "physicians" to mankind.

It is in this context that we should understand Freud's three publications of 1905. The first, appearing early in the year, was entitled *Wit and Its Relation to the Unconscious.* Here, borrowing the psychology of the dream book, and some of its terms ("jokework" as opposed to "dreamwork"), Freud took his reader on an essentially untranslatable tour of *fin de siècle* humor, with a few Jewish jokes thrown in for good measure.

Published almost simultaneously with the joke book was *Three Essays on the Theory of Sexuality.* In the first essay, Freud reviewed the literature on sexual deviancy, taking pains to show that the idea of component instincts seemed to be required by the diversity of the phenomena, and finishing up with the radical claim that neurotic symptoms involved similarly perverse components which had undergone repression. In the second essay, Freud examined the operation of the component sexual instincts in infancy; the emphasis was on showing how through various combinations of constitutional endowment and infantile experience some of these components might become strengthened to the point where they could serve as the rudimentary organic basis for perverse activities or neurotic symptoms in the adult. In the third essay, the transformations of puberty were discussed. In health, all the infantile components were brought together around a single (genital) aim that focused on a single (heterosexual) object. Where, however, the road to adult sexual behavior was blocked for whatever reason, the upsurge of libido at this age would flow back into the old infantile channels and either perversion or neurosis would result.

In respect to the individual elements of Freud's picture of libidinal development, there was little that had not in one form or another already been discussed in the literature, including infantile sexuality. The one idea that was truly new was the claim that neurotic symptoms always involved a repressed infantile "perversion." Yet Freud presented absolutely no data on this point. It was then simply a matter of course in the literature of human sexuality to present extensive case material by way of documenting one's arguments. Krafft-Ebing, Moll, Havelock Ellis, Schrenck-Notzing, had all done so; Krafft-Ebing's enumerated cases ran literally into the hundreds. Yet, in making his claim, Freud said only that it was borne out by his experience with psycho-analysis over "the past 10 years." In short, the central thesis of the book depended on a kind of massive promissory note.

But if Freud had withheld the psychoanalytic data that would have lent some weight to his scheme, it was still quite clear in what direction he was heading. For in the middle essay on infantile sexuality, he carefully laid the groundwork for reinterpreting all the more common neurotic complaints. Amnesias, intestinal problems, enuresis, *globus hystericus*, examination anxiety, obsessions, even intellectual over-work—all these symptoms are mentioned as analogues of one or an-other facet of infantile sexual life. Indeed, one could almost say that the only common neurotic complaint that Freud had failed to interpret in infantile terms was "railway spine," but, surprisingly, that was there, too; it was connected, in Freud's scheme, with a child's sexual excitement during any kind of vigorous physical motion, like riding on a swing. Since neurotics no longer typically present with such focal complaints, this aspect of Freud's presentation tends to be lost on the modern reader; the passages are there, but one scans them without quite taking them in. At the time, however, it was commonplace for nervous sufferers to fix on a particular complaint, and texts such as Dubois's were organized accordingly. Thus what Freud was claim-ing—that a specific infantile-sexual analogue could be regularly identified behind each symptom—would have leapt out at the profes-sional reader with full force.

Yet for all their overwrought specificity, Freud's claims nonetheless entailed a major, indeed crucial, theoretical advance. Far from being just another popular-science account of the burgeoning field of sexual studies, *Three Essays on the Theory of Sexuality* was in fact the skeleton for what would become a full-fledged theory of emotional development suitable for use in outpatient psychotherapy. Nothing like this had quite existed before. There were theories of child development, but such theories did not help the clinician much, for as soon as the ques-tion of mental disease entered in, however one might conceptualize that term, there was no clear-cut way to distinguish between what was within the normal range and what was already a manifestation of the disease process.

Krafft-Ebing makes the pertinent comparison here. Contrary to what one might expect, Krafft-Ebing had quite a sophisticated grasp of the psychology of the people he studied. He wrote of how, "by a transference through association of ideas," the sexual attraction of part of the body could be displaced onto a fetish. He knew that a sexual act might depend on an "intervention of fancy," whereby, for example, an actual heterosexual partner might be replaced with an imagined homosexual one. He knew that the sexual feeling might be "repressed," leaving behind only a seemingly inexplicable perverse idea. He knew that certain "fancies" derive from "early youth" and do not lead to real satisfaction if acted out, since "the whole thing chiefly belongs to the realm of the imagination." He knew that a masochistic fantasy might be "latent," and yet remain the "unconscious motive" behind a fetish. He knew well of infantile masturbation, "erogenous zones" (including the anus), the sexual significance of sucking at the breast, and the role of shame, disgust, and moral education in inhibiting the libido.

What Krafft-Ebing did *not* know was where to draw the line between illness and health. More than once in his case histories, he traced the development of a perverse tendency back to childhood and even described its first operation in relation to another family member—and then backed off and marked down the infantile experience as an early manifestation of the hereditary degeneration that would become full-blown in adulthood. Thus all the very pertinent psychological insights failed to lead anywhere theoretically, nor did they offer any leverage therapeutically beyond establishing the diagnosis. The observations were all there, but the matter remained enigmatic.

In essence, Freud had found a solution by redrawing the line between normality and illness. In infancy, perversions are the norm; by themselves they bode neither good nor ill. It was only when some combination of factors, including constitution, early experience, and adult opportunity, were added that the infantile impulse became the basis for the adult aberration. It was an unappealing argument in one way, since it made all men and women potential perverts and/or neurotics, but it was clinically very powerful since now the clinician knew what to look for: not some mysterious hereditary degeneration read back into infancy, but an otherwise normal childhood experience that would bear a resemblance to the adult behavior (or in the case of neurosis, to the adult repressed fantasy). Moreover, it shifted the burden of the symptom back onto the patient. No longer excused by some untreatable hereditary burden, the patient could be told that as a child he or she wished this or that and as an adult was seeking to escape back to this (sexual) wish.

FREUD'S BOOK had other merits, most notably its style. It was free of any remarks about topics such as degeneracy and inferior races; it thus struck an appealingly cosmopolitan and essentially modern note. In effect, Freud was showing that one could enter into a scientific discussion of such issues as sexual constitution without getting bogged down in the usual distinctions then commonly made between blacks and whites, Jews and Aryans, Europeans and Asians. Besides being a contribution to civility, Freud's omission of this customary theme itself represented a theoretical advance. Race then constituted an important source of scientific mystification. So long as neurological and psychiatric theory reserved a place for racial differences as an important biological consideration, progress in understanding nervous complaints would be correspondingly retarded. Then, too, Freud's presentation was also free of the moralizing, fearfulness, and sentimentality that were then thought by other writers to be stylistic necessities when writing about sex. Sexuality had been an accepted scientific topic for more than twenty years, yet Freud managed to bring a new tone to the discussion.

All the considerable virtues of Freud's style, however, were not sufficient to carry Freud's argument, at least not so far as the staff at the Burghölzli was concerned. The sticking point was not the existence of sexual complexes—this was now accepted as a truism in Zurich— but Freud's more specific contention that behind every symptom lay a repressed infantile sexual tendency. The new assistant, Karl Abraham, was so unimpressed that he just ignored the work, instead continuing to search out sexual traumas in hysterics and dementia praecox patients. So did Riklin. Eugen Bleuler began observing his infant son Manfred more closely, but was otherwise unconvinced.

Carl Jung, meanwhile, was taking the high road. In April 1905, he contributed a review of Hellpach's new book on hysteria to a medical journal. He was critical of Hellpach's basic thesis, that hysterical mechanisms showed the impact of class and cultural factors, though he did recognize positively the support Hellpach gave Freud. Then, in June, Jung took over the newly created outpatient clinic and attempted his second known test of psychoanalysis. This second test case involved a woman troubled by insomnia and obsessive ruminations about death. His treatment description ought to be required reading for beginning candidates at analytic institutes. The woman wriggles uncomfortably in her chair; she is embarrassed; she claims this is only going to make her worse; she jumps up and starts to leave; "with gentle force" Jung makes her sit; there is a "long debate on the use and purpose of my method"; finally a single idea comes into her head but it is too "silly" to tell the doctor; another debate ensues; and then, amid protests that this is her last session, she starts to relate some passing thoughts which just happen to involve how she came to her knowledge of sexuality.

More interesting than the case was Jung's method, which entailed the elicitation of "free associations." Jung's instructions to the patient were "to tell me calmly everything that came into her mind, no matter what it was about." What is striking about this is that Jung had *already* taken a history of the symptoms, preparatory to administering the word-association experiment to the patient. In other words, the call for "free associations" was not part of a structured interview about symptoms. To the contrary, the situation had been deliberately unstructured and it was up to the patient to set the agenda. Jung's use of this unstructured format marked the first time it had ever been tried outside of Vienna. Presumably, Jung had learned of it from Bleuler, who would have heard of it directly from Freud.

In September 1905, Jung published a new paper on the word association experiment, "Experimental Observations on the Faculty of Memory." Here Jung seized on another facet of subjects' responses, their inability to remember previous answers on a follow-up administration, and showed how this, too, was regularly associated with the presence of complexes. That is to say that when a complex had been touched by a stimulus word it frequently happened that the subject would then forget what answer he or she had given. In essence, Jung had experimentally demonstrated the reality of repression as a psychological phenomenon and in his paper he went to some lengths to link his findings with Freud's as well as to mention Riklin's own separate contribution on the same subject. Also in September, Jung wrote but did not send that letter introducing Spielrein to Freud.

In October 1905, Jung began lecturing at the University of Zurich. In his inaugural address he chose to describe the typical complex of women:

> The woman's complex is, in essence, usually of an erotic nature (and I am using the word "erotic" in the nobler literary sense as opposed to the medical). It is concerned with love, even in apparently intellectual women, and is often particularly intense in the

latter, although it is only revealed in a negative way to the outside world. No woman who thinks scientifically will take amiss my revelation of this fact.

Jung's university demonstrations chiefly involved the word association experiment and hypnosis, though he continued to take an interest in psychoanalysis. In November, however, he went off in a new direction with "On the Psychological Diagnosis of Facts," wherein he endeavored to claim priority for discovering the incriminating possibilities of "feeling-toned complexes." The issue had come up because two German authors, Max Wertheimer and Julius Klein, publishing in Hanns Gross's criminology journal, had thought to use the association experiment as part of criminal interrogations. Jung then followed this very brief article with a more extensive one, "The Psychological Diagnosis of Evidence," wherein he described using the word association test to catch a domestic thief. In the process, he paused for a defense of his method—and Freud's:

> I repeat what I have already said elsewhere: The truth of this experiment is not obvious, it has to be tested; only someone who has used it repeatedly can judge it. Modern science should no longer recognize judgments *ex cathedra*. Everybody derided and criticized Freud's psychoanalysis, because they neither applied nor even understood the method, and yet it ranks among the greatest achievements of modern psychology.

What Jung had in mind here was equally the new forms of self-examination described in Freud's psychological works as well as the unstructured interview format that he was experimenting with at the outpatient clinic. The irony, however, was that Jung's ringing endorsement of "the method," the most glowing yet to appear in the German psychiatric literature, appeared just as Freud's procedure was about to become controversial as never before. For in the meantime, Freud's "Dora" case had finally appeared in print.

THE JEWEL CASE

IF THE *Three Essays* constituted a massive promissory note, then the "Dora" case, entitled *Fragment of an Analysis of a Case of Hysteria,* was meant to make good on the debt. Instead, it touched off a furor. Part of the problem was the style. The *Three Essays* was written in a dry, civilized tone, almost a little too abstract. The "Dora" case, on the other hand, had been written four years earlier and only recently revised. Its style was the style of the earlier period—gossipy, irreverent, almost eager to shock. (Freud had written Fliess at the time of its composition, "It is the subtlest thing I have written so far and will put people off more than usual.") Worse still, the content matter approached the lurid owing to the appalling state of Dora's family. Her father was syphilitic. Her mother, undoubtedly infected, busied herself cleaning and recleaning the house. There was a maid with an apparent interest in the child, but it was a cover for a very real interest in Dora's father. There was a neighboring family, the "K's," who befriended the girl. But Dora's father began having an affair with Mrs. K. At which point Mr. K. propositioned the fourteen-year-old Dora, more or less expecting that she would be payment for his not interfering in his wife's affair. Dora refused, became symptomatic, and, after several years of unsuccessful treatment by a host of nerve specialists, was brought by her father to an old acquaintance, Freud, to get fixed.

This is not a happy story in English at the end of the century. In German at the beginning of the century it was even worse. It played on all the typical family tensions of the time: the fear of contagion, the belief that all parental misdeeds were visited upon the children, the claustrophobic grip of patriarchal rule, the power of hysteria to upset a household already crippled by reciprocal guilt and hostility between generations, the use of female servants for the master's pleasure, the emotional abandonment of the children coupled with an obsessive concern for their health. In short, Freud had chosen an unusually prepotent domestic horror story for his first extended case history in the ten years since publication of the *Studies on Hysteria*.

In this context, what one would like to see is a therapeutic fairy tale: the kindly doctor cures the girl and she finds a young man to rescue her. And, indeed, at the very end Freud did suggest, mistakenly as it turned out, that after she left him, Dora found a suitable young knight. But there was no kindly doctor in this story. According to his own account, Freud had gone at her dreams with an almost inquisitorial determination to uncover her sexual secrets, while Dora had fended him off with all the tricks and impertinences that a determined young invalid could manage. In the end she quit on him. In Freud's view, that was her final act of revenge, since he was just then closing in on the cure. Freud's presentation of the treatment has continued to raise eyebrows down to our own day, and Dora has not lacked for contemporary defenders eager to improve on Freud's clinical detachment by showing her ever greater degrees of sympathy. However, as Hannah Decker has noted, in the end Freud did do Dora some good, far more good than any of the other nerve specialists who had treated her up to this time. She had gotten the opportunity to talk about some very important issues, and to reveal some terribly troubling secrets.

There were some stunners along the way. From a single sentence in a dream, Freud brought out the fact that she used to wet the bed. He then guessed, rightly, that it was secondary to masturbation. He further supposed that this secret explained her childhood antipathy to physicians, who might find out, and even her behavior with him—she was still playing secrets. From a chain of reasoning that involved her dreams and his theories, he correctly arrived at an understanding of "jewel case," a dream symbol, as standing for a variety of wishes and apprehensions pertaining to her genitals.

The book's value for the Burghölzli physicians would have been its glimpses into Freud's technique. As it happened, Freud explicitly and repeatedly stated that he could not pause to give all the technical rules that applied. His postscript reiterated the point: "I have in this paper entirely left out of the account the technique," a topic that "demands an entirely separate exposition." Which is to say that Freud had issued yet another promissory note on the question of his method. But, in point of fact, the book did contain a great deal of information about Freud's method, much of it never before in print.

To begin with, it was here that Freud first publicly announced that he "let the patient himself choose the subject of the day's work, and in that way I start out from whatever surface his unconscious happens to be presenting to his notice at the moment." This was the method of truly free associations: the patient set the agenda. Not that this meant the analyst was not active. Throughout the case description, Freud constantly took wide interpretive license, especially with regard to dream symbolism: ". . . I came to the conclusion that the idea had probably occurred to her . . . ," ". . . allows us to substitute 'box' for 'station' . . . ," ". . . I could not avoid supposing . . . ," ". . . a fact which I did not neglect to use against her." Nor was Dora allowed to correct him:

If this "No," instead of being regarded as the expression of an impartial judgement (of which, indeed, the patient is incapable), is ignored, and if work is continued, the first evidence soon begins to appear that in such a case "No" signifies the desired "Yes."

Freud was here describing the "spirit of contradiction" noted by Dubois. Dubois's way of handling it was to say to the patient, "You are one of those persons who say 'No' and mean 'Yes'," and then to add by way of sweetening the pill, "That is much better than the inverse fault." But Freud went even further, sometimes insisting that a given dream symbol stood for its opposite and refusing to be put off. And not only would he not take no for an answer, he wouldn't allow her to refuse Herr K.:

> "So you see that your love for Herr K. did not come to an end with the scene, but that (as I maintained) it has persisted down to the present day—though it is true that you are unconscious of it." And Dora disputed the fact no longer.

Years earlier, Adolf Strümpell, Möbius's colleague and office-mate, had complained about the aggressiveness of the inquiry into patients' private affairs in the *Studies on Hysteria* and had betrayed his underlying concern by using the word "penetration" in three consecutive sentences. Now it appeared that "penetration" had virtually become a technical rule.

The most important revelation from a technical standpoint, however, was neither the aggressiveness of the inquiry, nor even the device of truly free associations, but the elucidation of "transference" which took up the entire "Postscript" to the case. It had been well known that hysterical women often formed quasi-erotic attachments to their physicians. It was also well known, even if it was sometimes disputed, that hypnosis tended to foster an erotic fixation. Neither of these facts prevented medical men from engaging in hypnotic outpatient treatment, though they did conspire to make it necessary to adopt a high moral tone in writing about it, as if the personal probity of the physician were the only guarantee against untoward developments. The matter was made more complicated by two additional phenomena, both well known. The first was that certain patients fought the hypnosis tooth and nail; the technical term for this at the time was "resistance." The second complicating factor was that the typical hysterical attack, the very thing the hypnosis was being brought to bear on, often involved an erotic scene in which the patient might play multiple parts. Janet, in one celebrated case, had taken over one of the parts in such an enactment so as to make closer contact with the patient.

What Freud did in his "Postscript" was to reorganize these facts. He argued that the patient sought to reexperience old erotic situations in relation to the physician. Where these old experiences were essentially positive, compliance and suggestibility would be manifest. Where the old experiences were essentially negative, or else conflictual, negativity and resistance would be manifest. Thus, in order to manage a case successfully the physician had to be aware of these crosscurrents coming from the past; at the same time, these "transference" manifestations potentially provided valuable information about otherwise forgotten events. In short, an erotic drama was being played out, one that had approximately the same relation to the patient's previous love-life as the scene that a hysteric might play out in the middle of a delirium had had to a previous trauma. In Dora's case, for example, not only was Freud being apprehended in terms of her previous experiences with Herr K., but he was also being seen as a revenant of Frau K., whose emotional abandonment of Dora had been compounded by her imputations concerning the child's sexual curiosity. Freud's point was that besides being discussed, these previous relationships were also being covertly reenacted, sometimes with a change of roles, during the treatment.

This was genius. Moreover, it was extremely timely genius. By 1905, the movement in psychotherapy throughout Europe was away from outright hypnosis toward the use of suggestion (or "persuasion") in the waking state. At the same time, for reasons that have never been completely understood, the full-blown hysterical attack, with its traumatic reenactments, was rapidly disappearing as a typical symptom. The absence of both these things, hypnosis and the attack, was robbing psychotherapy of much of its drama and a good deal of the necessary information. With the doctrine of "transference" in hand, however, it became possible to see that the old erotic reenactments had not disappeared and, indeed, were still accessible to the discerning physician.

The "Dora" case was to be the great dividing line. For those who could grasp the idea of "transference," new vistas opened up. For virtually everybody else, the method seemed nearly pornographic. As Decker has noted, "The publication of the 'Dora analysis' did more to arouse enmity against Freud's method than had any other of Freud's writings up to that time." Indeed, even Freud seemed to have realized that he had made a mistake. It was almost fifteen years before he again made a woman the subject of a detailed case report.

Jung's attitude at the time can be assessed from his writings during the first half of 1906—he acted as if the "Dora" case simply didn't exist. And though he readily grasped the idea, and began employing it in his own treatments, he studiously avoided the term "transference." As for the altogether less objectionable *Three Essays on the Theory of Sexuality,* Jung elected to give that a wide berth for the time being, too.

But Jung was forced to notice one thing. For it was during this time that Spielrein de-repressed her knowledge of sexuality and, on that account, suffered a relapse of unknown proportions. Indeed, given that Riklin's "Catterina H." was doing the same thing, there would appear to have been a small epidemic of de-repression going on among Russian women in Zurich. But it was a most instructive epidemic. Just this phenomenon, the tendency of hysterical women to repress their knowledge of sexual processes, had been described by Freud in both the *Three Essays* and the "Dora" case.

THE WEININGER AFFAIR ERUPTS

As 1905 came to an end, two books went to press in Berlin. The first was Wilhelm Fliess's long-delayed *The Rhythm of Life.* It contained, among other things, data submitted by his old friend Freud in support of the theory of twenty-three- and twenty-eight-day male and female cycles. The other book was by a new friend of Fliess's named Richard Pfennig, a librarian who had already published a work on priority disputes. Entitled *Wilhelm Fliess and His Subsequent Discoverers: O. Weininger and H. Swoboda,* Pfennig's book described how Fliess's ideas had been stolen with the connivance of Sigmund Freud. For documentation, Pfennig excerpted from Freud's own letters to Fliess. The plagiarism was now out in the open.

Freud's response was basically to lie low, though he eventually did take steps locally by trying to interest the prominent Viennese journalist Karl Kraus in writing an article denouncing the "brutal" Fliess. Kraus refused. Weininger, of course, was dead. But Hermann Swoboda, the third party in the affair, was very much alive and he began preparing a lawsuit against Pfennig for libel. Unfortunately, that meant that the affair would continue to be before the public eye for yet another year.

The Weininger affair has drawn far too little attention in the secondary literature on Freud. Part of the problem is that it is hard for modern readers to take the disputed theory seriously. To be sure, our modern appreciation of the theory might be otherwise if we possessed a more sophisticated version of it put forth in Freud's own commanding prose. Yet it is just this exposition that we lack, for, contrary to what he had once intended to do, Freud never published his ideas on the subject. Apparently the taint of scandal derailed his plans.

Freud was a systematic thinker of the highest rank, yet the clinical theory that he advanced in his works of 1905 had an important logical hole in it. In both the "Dora" case and in the *Three Essays,* Freud had argued that in cases of nervous illness "the symptoms constitute the sexual activity of the patient." As a logical matter, however, this assertion demanded that sexual wishes be uniquely liable to repression, for in Freud's system it was only repressed wishes that could transform themselves into symptoms. Yet in neither the "Dora" case nor in the *Three Essays* had Freud presented a convincing rationale for why that should be the case, for why repression should be selectively aimed at sexual wishes, and most especially at childhood sexual wishes, as opposed to all others. Not only did Freud not use the bisexual explanation—the architecture of both works cries out for it—but he did not use any other systematic rationale either. And without such a rationale, there was no way of insisting a priori on a uniquely sexual etiology for nervous disorders. The claim had to be based solely on empirical findings and this was no small disadvantage to a theory that accepted as evidence only heretofore unconscious wishes that had been recovered through the use of a method which itself had not yet been fully reported. Freud's enterprise was still logically tenable, but it hung by the slenderest of inferential threads; the charge of suggestion hovered over it like an evil twin.

This was the theoretical ground upon which the Zurich-Vienna collaboration would be based. As a psychological phenomenon, the reality of repressed erotic complexes had been experimentally demonstrated. What remained was to interpret its theoretical significance.

Part Two

The New Doctrine of Nervous Health

Has not perhaps the gallant Viennese atmosphere—reminding one of Rococo culture—of which the extraordinary erotic refinement of Austrian women is a part, strongly turned the authors of *Studies on Hysteria,* and especially Freud, in a certain direction? The strong national differences in hysteria are well known. . . . [The sexual history of a Viennese married couple who recently consulted the author] illustrated once more what I had already known from hundreds of other experiences, but what one often forgets: what role the erotic, in all its expressions, had played for these good middle-class people—a role of which the average North German has not the least concept.

—Willy Hellpach, *Basics of a Psychology of Hysteria,* 1904

CHAPTER 5

The Rise of the Zurich School

It is a matter of complete indifference whether Freud's therapeutic results can also be obtained in other ways; also whether it is good or evil to talk to young and old women about their sexuality; or whether there is conversion, repression or abreaction in Freud's sense of the terms; or whether all or only a part of the enormous complex of diseases that we call neuroses are dependent on sexuality, etc. No matter what the definitive answers to these questions turn out to be, the significance of the new discoveries will in no way be reduced.

—Eugen Bleuler, 1907

JUNG'S ENTRY into the field of criminology brought to the attention of a wide audience that important work was being done at the Burghölzli, and the phrase "the Zurich school" came into circulation. In only a few years' time, however, "the Zurich school" ceased to refer to a particular school of thought with regard to the association experiment and began to refer to a brand of Freudianism. Zurich was about to become the international center for psychoanalysis. The reason for this, at least in part, was that Jung had his own methodological problems to cope with.

QUESTIONS OF METHOD

IT MUST BE understood that in the association experiment one had only the subject's response words to go on; it was readily possible to identify which of the subject's reactions were disturbed, but on the basis of the response words alone it was not usually clear what the disturbances were about. To get around this, Jung had from the start adopted the practice of interviewing his subjects immediately after the experiment about all their responses; by the beginning of 1905 he had shortened the interview to cover only the disturbed reactions.

. Just this aspect of Jung's procedure, the post-experiment interview, however, had drawn fire. At the time, German experimental psychology was committed methodologically to the technique of controlled self-observation using specially trained observers. Depending on the experiment, the training might be long and laborious; and a well-trained subject, capable of accurate introspection, was considered as valuable as any precision laboratory instrument. In such a climate, it could be readily argued against Jung's procedure that his subjects, untrained as they were, would not be able to recall accurately what had actually passed through their minds. The pioneering psychologist William Stern, who had earlier criticized Freud for basing his theories on the testimony of hysterics, now weighed in with a trenchant criticism of Jung's paper "The Reaction-Time Ratio."

By way of reply to this esteemed critic, Jung conceded in his 1905 paper, "The Psychological Diagnosis of Evidence," that his method was "difficult and dangerous." Indeed, in Jung's retelling, it had been for that reason that he had, in fact, used subjects "whose life and psychological make-up were known to me." But such a defense being of limited value for the future, Jung went on to argue that in general "a fair knowledge of certain aspects of psychopathology" was adequate protection against being misled by the faulty introspection of one's subjects. He identified these "certain aspects" as "the principles of Sigmund Freud's ingenious psychoanalysis." Then, to save himself the charge that he was trading another man's speculative approach for his own, he went on to argue that while Freud might be "a man of genius," his technique was "not an inimitable art, but a transferable and teachable method."

In his next important paper, "Psychoanalysis and Association Experiment," published in early 1906, Jung turned things around. Now he argued that psychoanalysis was an "art," a "rather difficult" one at that, "since the beginner easily loses courage and orientation when faced with the innumerable obstacles it entails." For that reason, Jung currently preferred to give the association experiment first, since the results then "served as signposts among the ever-changing fantasies that at every stage threatened to put the analyst on the wrong track." This innovation, argued Jung, was "useful for facilitating and shortening Freud's psychoanalysis." Jung had absorbed the interpretive style of the "Dora" case, but had found an alternative way of talking about the method:

. . . there is a particular way of thinking required for psychoanalysis, which aims at bringing symbols to light. . . . Thinking in symbols demands from us a new attitude, similar to starting to think in flights of ideas. These seem to be the reasons why Freud's method has only exceptionally been understood and even more rarely practised, so that there are actually only a few authors who appreciate Freud, theoretically or practically.

Jung's next important paper, "Association, Dream, and Hysterical Symptom," written in early 1906 and published in the fall of that year, was a tour de force in the art of combining information of different kinds. The subject of the paper was a patient treated during the last months of 1905, a woman with recurrent physical complaints of fever and sensations of heat. Physical preoccupations were, of course, typical for nervous sufferers at that time, and for this phenomenon Jung now coined the term "illness complex." In analyzing the illness complex of his patient, Jung reported data of three different kinds. First, he presented the results of six different administrations of the word association experiment; for the last of these he gave the follow-up interview as well. Second, he gave a series of nine dreams from a brief psychoanalysis, with associations and interpretations for each. Third, he reviewed the patient's history, using the data from the first two investigations to put the symptoms in a new perspective. Jung's handling of the woman's dream symbols was distinctive:

The blood and fire dreams seemed to me to be stereotyped expressions of the dream-life, as the heat-sensations were of the waking life . . . For the therapeutic purpose of setting her against these dreams . . . I said to the patient casually: "Blood is red, red means love, fire is red and hot, surely you know the song: No fire, no coal can burn as hot, etc. [i.e., "as a secret love no one must know"— Goethe]. Fire, too, means love."

Not surprisingly, the dreams began to change and Jung showed how the analysis and the dreams kept pace with one another. In effect, he and the patient's dreams were having a conversation. The key dream in the series was the fifth. The patient's account:

"I was outside and stood next to Miss L. We both saw that a house was on fire. Suddenly a white figure emerged from behind the house; we both got scared and exclaimed simultaneously: 'Lord Jesus!' "

In the paper, Jung demonstrated that the figure of Lord Jesus stood for himself through an interpretation of the unidentified "Miss L."

> Miss L. is a patient who has a crush on the author. She was, like the patient, taken ill because of an erotic complex. The patient therefore expresses through this person that she has fallen in love with the author. Thus the patient substituted the tender relationship with her [overprotective and infantilizing] mother, which is damaging to her energy, by the erotic relation to the doctor.

As it happened, this "transposition" did not last long, because Jung "ruthlessly destroyed her illusions" by pointing out that he was already married. Then the figure of the woman's brother began turning up in the dreams. But Jung could make no headway in divining whatever secret related to him. She then abandoned treatment and a month later Jung got a report "that she is just as bad as before and that she now grumbled about the hospital and the doctor, with indications that the doctor had only tried to find opportunities to make morally dangerous conversation with her."

Jung's conclusion about the case was twofold; first with regard to the dreams and their methodological value:

> Above all we see that the dreams completely confirm the complex revealed by the association tests. . . . The analysis of the dream images revealed the sexual complex, its transposition to the author, the disappointment and the patient's reversion to the mother [whose worries fostered the bodily preoccupations] and the resumption of a mysterious childhood relationship with the brother.

And then in regard to the treatment:

> The complex has an abnormal autonomy in hysteria and a tendency to an active separate existence, which reduces and replaces the constellating power of the ego-complex. . . .
>
> A purposive treatment of hysteria must therefore strengthen what has remained of the ego, and that is best achieved by introducing some new complex that liberates the ego from domination by the complex of the illness.

The idea that the "ego," the "I" (in German, *Ich*) of ordinary consciousness, was composed of a complex of personal associations dated back fifty years to Wilhelm Griesinger's great psychiatric text; so, too, did the conception of mental illness as being composed of an alternative set of ego-alien associations. (In Griesinger's phrasing, the onset of psychosis was experienced as the intrusion of a "Thou.") While most men of science remembered Griesinger chiefly for his dictum that mental disease was brain disease, Jung had followed Bleuler's lead in mining Griesinger's system for his insights into ego psychology, insights which could be readily adapted to the study of neurotic conditions. As for the "autonomy" of the complex in hysteria, both the term and the conception were derived from Janet. The idea was that in conditions of dissociation, the split-off ideas would not be tempered by the ordinary correctives of conscious reflection; they would thus become impervious to change—"fixed ideas"—and would take on a life of their own. Janet's conception, itself derived from Charcot, had proven its worth not only in the study of hysteria and in obsessional disorders, but had also lent itself well to the study of mediums. As for the term "illness complex," this was of course Jung's phrasing, but the basic idea was a commonplace one. Specifically, it was well known that certain nervous patients would become preoccupied with the idea that they had one or another incurable disease, from which belief no amount of medical counsel would dissuade them. The syndrome was thought in some circles to be especially common among eastern European Jews, but Jung makes no mention of this. Like Freud, though for different reasons, Jung had already essentially given up on the theory of hereditary degeneration, and without that mystifying notion to obscure his vision he saw no reason for including race as a factor in his theories.

In short, Jung had pooled together a number of conceptions from different sources and arrived at an attractive and accessible restatement of what he took to be Freud's position, namely that neurosis was psychologically determined. His own specific contribution lay in the therapeutic goal of seeking to provide the patient with a "new complex" that might tip the balance toward psychic health. In context, the "new complex" would seem to refer explicitly to Jung's intervention in the woman's dreams and her subsequent "transposition" to the doctor.

There was a problem here, which we do well to note. If "ruthless" disillusionment was to regularly accompany a stage in which "transposition" to the doctor had been deliberately encouraged, with the risk that its first form might be sexualized, then there were going to be some fairly unpleasant scenes between doctor and patient as a matter of course. A less sophisticated man might have supposed Jung's method called for leading a patient on with the promise of a flirtation only to disappoint her subsequently. Jung was tentatively clear that the therapeutic rapport ought be distinguished from sexual attraction:

> The patient was unable to reveal her innermost secret; the sexual compromise with myself had failed (apparently she could not find anything in me, apart from the sexual aspect, that would have been so valuable to her that she could have separated herself from her role as an invalid).

We must also pause to consider the emphasis on symbols. For Jung, as for Bleuler, symbols were the carriers of affective charges par excellence. The conception was Kantian in its comprehensiveness. In effect, Bleuler and Jung believed that Freud had discovered that there existed another level of mind with its own set of categorical a prioris, its own symbolical way of organizing experience. While the conscious mind operated within the Kantian categories of time, space, causality, etc., the unconscious mind operated symbolically, forging its affective meanings through a logic uniquely its own. The importance of Freud's work from this standpoint was that it opened a way to examine even grossly psychotic symptoms from a psychological perspective. Thus in Bleuler's monograph *Affectivity, Suggestibility, and Paranoia,* the role of Freudian mechanisms in symptom formation would be described not only in the symbolic productions of neurotic patients but in the delusions of paranoid patients as well.

Jung's use of "transposition" instead of "transference" was also important. Jung's term came from academic psychology. In the revolt initiated by Ziehen and William James against Wundtian elementalism, the revolt that would eventually lead to Gestalt psychology, it had been argued that there were formal properties in perception, immediately recognized by the mind, that were not reducible to the constituent parts. The proof of the assertion was that the formal qualities could be "transposed" to another medium entirely and still be recognized. A square made of pebbles on the beach could be identified as essentially the same as a square drawn with pen and ruler on parchment. A melody moved to a different key and played on different instruments was still heard as the same melody. And, going back to Jung, an erotic complex could still be recognized as such, no matter whether it took as its object the patient's brother, her doctor, or Jesus Christ. Indeed, just this transposability was what enabled one to penetrate the indistinctness of the symbolic veil, and later Jung would write to Freud of "thinking in analogies, which your analytical method trains so well." The emphasis on "analogies" had itself been borrowed from yet two more disciplines, philology and the study of mythology. In these linguistic disciplines, the method of analogy referred to the means whereby in prehistory concrete words had gradually taken on new, more abstract meanings—a process crucial both for the evolution of myths and for the most recent round of reinterpretations of their meaning. For Jung, the method of analogy was the mode of operation of the symbolizing mind. That was what Jung had in mind when he talked of psychoanalysis as requiring the skills of a "poet."

A DREAM

Jung was getting himself into the curious position, in early 1906, of strongly endorsing a procedure about which both he and his chief still entertained reservations. Jung may have hoped that the new sexual theory would fade as an older one had in an earlier period of Freud's writings. (In that case, Freud's "My Views on the Part Played by Sexuality in the Aetiology of the Neuroses," appearing in 1906 in a new edition of yet another volume by the prolific Löwenfeld, would have come as an unhappy surprise. Löwenfeld, incidentally, had done Freud a great favor by allowing this new communication to replace a chapter of his own on Freud's views. For that chapter, which now disappeared, had in previous editions contained the confession of one of Freud's former patients that his alleged childhood sexual trauma had been pure "fantasy.")

Jung's decision to endorse Freud's method so strongly deserves comment. Given the tenor of his own researches, Jung could scarcely have failed to see the parallels with Freud's work, but he could easily have followed Bleuler's lead and made it clear that he was reserving judgment on some issues. Instead, Jung went out of his way to praise strongly the one thing that Freud had explicitly stated had not yet been fully reported—the method. It was a bold step to take in any case, and in the climate change initiated by the "Dora" case, it was getting bolder day by day.

Here let us recall that on his own testimony Jung had since childhood felt himself to be inwardly divided, that beneath the external persona he showed the outside world he felt the stirrings of an entirely different soul. Originally, Jung had gone looking for this deeper self, which was linked in his mind to the figure of Goethe, via the study of the occult. Now, however, Jung found that he could use Freud's methods, most especially Freud's method of analyzing dreams, to do approximately the same thing—make contact with the other world within.

There was a great risk, however. For what Jung was looking for in his subconscious was a second self, a buried "ego-complex," to use his terminology. That there might be such a thing—a "subliminal self"—had long been postulated as a possibility by both the doyens of French psychopathology and by Frederic Myers and his followers in the London Society for Psychical Research. But just this element was missing in Freud's theory. Instead of primary and secondary egos, Freud talked only of primary and secondary processes; instead of subliminal selves, Freud postulated only unconscious sexual desires.

Jung's personal quest not only accelerated his espousal of psychoanalysis; it also complicated it. A sense of Jung's predicament can be gleaned from a dream he had in the spring of 1906:

> I saw horses being hoisted by thick cables to a great height. One of them, a powerful brown horse which was tied up with straps and was hoisted aloft like a package, struck me particularly. Suddenly the cable broke and the horse crashed to the street. I thought it must be dead. But it immediately leapt up again and galloped away. I noticed that the horse was dragging a heavy log along with it, and I wondered how it could advance so quickly. It was obviously frightened and might easily have caused an accident. Then a rider came up on a little horse and rode along slowly in front of the frightened horse, which moderated its pace somewhat. I still feared that the horse might run over the rider, when a cab came along and drove in front of the rider at the same pace, thus bringing the frightened horse to a still slower gait. I then thought now all is well, the danger is over.

Jung subsequently published the dream in his book *The Psychology of Dementia Praecox*. There, he would interpret the dream as follows: The unidentified dreamer was professionally ambitious and wanted to take a trip to America to further his career, but was prevented from doing so by the pregnancy of his wife; the horse stood for the dreamer, who was being hoisted to the top of his profession, but he preferred to gallop off on his own; the log referred to his college nickname, which was "Log" (though it was actually "Barrel," in joint reference to his build and his drinking); the horse with the little rider stood for the pregnant wife; and the cab was full of children, i.e., a large family aborning. Thus, at a deeper level, the prospect of too many children was said to provide a restraint on the sexually impetuous nature of the dreamer.

Jung later spelled out parts of what had been hidden in letters to Freud. There was a wish for a male child. The log did equal the penis, as one might suspect. And the wish for sexual restraint was ". . . merely a convenient screen pushed into the foreground and hiding an illegitimate sexual wish that had better not see the light of day." Jung did not tell Freud who the unknown object of that illegitimate sexual wish had been. To be noted is that yet another anecdote about Spielrein appeared in the same book and likely dated from the same period, that is, the first half of 1906:

> A certain young lady could not bear to see the dust beaten out of her cloak. This peculiar reaction could be traced back to her masochistic disposition. In her childhood her father frequently chastised her on the buttocks, thus causing sexual excitation. Consequently she reacted to anything remotely resembling chastisement with marked rage, which rapidly passed over into sexual excitement and masturbation. Once, when I said to her casually, "Well, you have to obey," she got into a state of marked sexual excitement.

It is tempting to suppose that Spielrein was the object of Jung's "illegitimate wish" if only because for both of them sexuality seemed to represent a force that was difficult to control once it was let loose. For Spielrein, sexuality was connected with rage and masochistic excitement. For Jung, sexuality was symbolized by a horse gone out of control.

The last point perhaps needs emphasis. Jung's dream spoke less of a sexual wish than it did of a near-panic: his horse was being chased by its log-barrel-penis and reassurance was needed all around. What was Jung frightened of? An infidelity, perhaps with Spielrein? Surely not. Zurich was a long way from Paris, but it was still a European city and the mechanics of handling an affair discreetly were scarcely unknown. (Forel's *The Sexual Question* would make no sense at all if we took Swiss Calvinism to have been the sole source of Swiss sexual mores.) If Jung merely wanted an affair, it could surely have been managed, though perhaps in the monastic atmosphere of the Burghölzli the mechanics of such a thing might have been thought-provoking.

Here we are back to the special nature of Jung's personal quest. At the time he had this dream, Jung was trying hard to come to terms with Freud's sexual theory in terms of its relevance to his own identity. The dream was as much a theoretical exploration—a kind of thought experiment—as it was a personal one. Sexuality was the one place Jung could not look for the origins of his "Personality No. 2" because sexuality was an exalted intoxication that disrespected the individual ego. Jung's behavior around the dream is further evidence of just how much Freud and his theories were on his mind. First he took an explicitly sexual interpretation of it to Bleuler, who told him not to publish it. But Jung was unwilling to abide by Bleuler's ruling. Then, he had his wife take down a new interpretation from dictation and in this way restrained himself for the published version. The first and third segments were thus enacted, Jung's breaking free from restraint and his finding it again. That left only the middle segment to enact and, in April of 1906, Jung took this step as well: he wrote to Freud. The risk of panic had been temporarily put aside: the horse was galloping off.

CONTACT

ALONG WITH his letter, which does not survive, Jung also sent Freud his newly published volume on the association experiment. Freud answered on 11 April 1906:

> Many thanks for sending me your *Diagnostic Association Studies,* which in my impatience I had already acquired. Of course your latest paper, "Psychoanalysis and Association Experiments," pleased me most, because in it you argue on the strength of your own experience that everything I have said about the hitherto unexplored fields of our discipline is true. I am confident that you will often be in a position to back me up, but I shall also gladly accept correction.

Freud's characterization of Jung's latest paper as confirming "everything" he himself had said may be partially excused by the graciousness it took not to say other things; that paper was the only one of this particular collection that properly treated of Freud's priority in connection with the repression concept in anything more than a footnote.

Revealingly, Freud did not mention *why* he had been so impatient to acquire the book. In point of fact, he had been invited to give a talk on the association experiment before a seminar of criminology students, and he was preparing to defend the relative superiority of his own method. The talk was not given until June, time enough for him to weigh the implications of the unsolicited gift from Jung, and the tone of the published version of Freud's lecture may be milder than originally contemplated. Freud began his talk by pointing out that "an exactly similar method" had been long practiced by himself, namely psychoanalysis. Then, basing himself on Jung's "The Psychological Diagnosis of Evidence," Freud went on to explain how three out of the four principal "complex indicators" of the Zurich school were contained within his own technique. As for the fourth indicator, "perseveration," Freud argued that it was irrelevant since he, Freud, let the patient stay on the disturbing topic rather than forcing him on to a new stimulus word. Freud's assertion that his method was superior to the word association experiment, like Jung's suggestion that the word association test might "facilitate and shorten" the conduct of analysis, is indicative of the sense of priority that both men had with respect to their own ideas. Jung's inner excitements notwithstanding, his relationship with Freud was from the very first marked by a certain natural competitiveness—on both sides.

In Zurich, not bothering to respond to Freud's thank-you note, and not knowing about his lecture, Jung settled down to his writing table for the difficult job of finishing *The Psychology of Dementia Praecox*. A. A. Brill later wrote of this book that it contained everything important yet written about that syndrome. In the first portion of the book, Jung presented a comprehensive overview of all current psychological theories bearing on the illness; in the second portion, he presented an analysis of the complexes evidenced in the associations of a chronic dementia praecox patient. Jung showed that even in the most fragmented delusions, one could see the impact of certain affective constellations. The psychotic patient might be able to hide from reality, but not from his or her complexes; these continued to manifest themselves in the affective tone of the delusions.

The name "Freud" appeared everywhere in the text. Among the prior contributions Jung noted positively in his literature review was Freud's 1896 case report of a paranoid woman. Jung also had particular praise for the "Aliquis" episode from *The Psychopathology of Everyday Life*, in which a failure of memory betrayed an illicit affair. Jung's authorities were many—Otto Gross also got special consideration—but it was Freud who won first honors and it was Freud who took up the heart of Jung's preface, written in July of 1906:

I can assure you that in the beginning I naturally entertained all the objections that are customarily made against Freud in the literature. But, I told myself, Freud could be refuted only by one who has made repeated use of the psychoanalytic method and who really investigates as Freud does; that is, by one who has made a long and patient study of everyday life, hysteria, and dreams from Freud's point of view. . . . Fairness to Freud, however, does not imply, as many fear, unqualified submission to a dogma; one can very well maintain an independent judgement. If I, for instance, acknowledge the complex mechanisms of dreams and hysteria, this does not mean that I attribute to the infantile sexual trauma the significance that Freud does. Still less does it mean that I place sexuality so predominantly in the foreground, or that I grant it the psychological universality which Freud, it seems, postulates in view of the admittedly enormous role which sexuality plays in the psyche. As for Freud's therapy, it is at best but one of several possible methods, and perhaps does not always offer in practice what one expects from it in theory. Nevertheless, all these things are the merest trifles compared with the psychological principles whose discovery is Freud's greatest merit; and to these the critics pay far too little attention.

Jung's endorsement was clear: he was accepting Freud's psychology, while still entertaining reservations about the sexual theory. Moreover, he was claiming the right to hold both opinions on the scientifically respectable basis that he himself had tried the new method, about which he also continued to hold reservations.

In July 1906, when Jung wrote his preface, the Freud-Fliess dispute was in the courts—Swoboda was suing Pfennig—and, much worse, in the newspapers. As it happened, Jung's book was destined to appear in print in December of 1906, the same month that a Berlin court, in very strong language, ruled against Swoboda and for Pfennig. As much as it ever would be, Freud's role in the plagiarism dispute was accepted as fact. Jung's favorable endorsement of Freud would come at a very good time.

TWO WARRING WORLDS

JUNG NEXT decided to take up the cudgels against the harshest critic of psychoanalysis yet to appear in academic psychiatry—Gustav Aschaffenburg, the man who had once taught Riklin the word association experiment. Now professor of criminology at Cologne, in 1906 Aschaffenburg became the first man to deliver a paper denouncing Freud at a regular psychiatric convention. By getting that report into print, he also became the first man to publish a paper devoted to demolishing Freud. And by responding in print, Jung became, in the train of firsts set off by Aschaffenburg, the first man to devote a paper solely to Freud's defense.

Aschaffenburg was pugnacious; he was also very astute, and his criticisms were incisive. Among his points were these: Freud did not present his case material in the accepted scientific manner, i.e., in terms of the number treated and their outcomes; the prolonged inquiry into sexual matters had a profound effect in steering the course of associations; the intense involvement with the patient coupled with a specific etiological hypothesis announced with conviction had a decidedly suggestive effect; traumatic hysteria was well understood and did not require a sexual explanation; the evil effects of masturbation, such as they might be, were due not to any toxic effects—this was then Freud's official view—but to the accompanying fantasies; and the fact that there was one plausible interpretation of a dream did not rule out the possible existence of other, perhaps even more appropriate, interpretations. Aschaffenburg presented all this in strong language. Taking the position that psychoanalysis was nothing more than an uncontrolled association experiment, he said it might be ignored as an aberration; it was only because men like Hellpach and Löwenfeld were now partially endorsing it that it was important to speak out against its dangers.

Jung's published reply to what he called Aschaffenburg's "moderate and cautious criticism" was rather thin on both conviction and argument. In particular, Jung tried to portray Freud's sexual theory as merely empirical in nature and he even tentatively suggested that owing to Freud's writings he might be attracting a "somewhat one-sided" collection of patients. Jung thus felt free to amend Freud's findings "with the consent of the author" to say: "An indefinitely large number of cases of hysteria derive from sexual roots." As for the psychoanalytic method, Jung again insisted that it had to be tried before one could criticize its results.

To be sure, Jung had no guarantee that Freud would back him up on the version of the theory he was advancing. And he had absolutely no warrant for implying that his amended version of Freud's results enjoyed the "consent of the author." It was time to write to Vienna again. Freud had made the task easier by sending along at summer's end an unsolicited volume of his own, a collection of his short papers on the neuroses. Remarkably, these papers, which largely dated from the late 1890s, had gone to press with little revision despite the fact that the whole basis of the sexual theory had changed since their inception.

Freud had simply arranged them in chronological sequence while portraying the changes in his views as the progression of an honest scientist who had stayed the course with a difficult topic. A single paper only was missing, the one on "Screen Memories." (Freud had likely suppressed it primarily because the alleged patient in it had been none other than himself; now that he was becoming better known his fiction stood to be readily discovered. Beyond that, the argument of the paper specifically allowed that infantile memories might be falsified, or even fabricated outright, during later developmental periods, especially adolescence. On both counts, then, the paper raised serious methodological issues and one might rightly wonder what a Stern or an Aschaffenburg or a Hellpach might have done with it.)

The gift of the volume of short papers was an important signal to Jung: evidently Freud would be more responsive than had Flournoy, Binet, and Janet in years past. But there was still the business of the reply to Aschaffenburg to get out of the way. Jung's thank-you letter of 5 October 1906 betrays his predicament:

Recently I conducted a lively correspondence with Aschaffenburg about your theory and espoused this standpoint, with which you, Professor, may not be entirely in agreement. What I can appreciate, and what has helped us here in our psychopathological work, are your psychological views, whereas I am still pretty far from understanding the therapy and the genesis of hysteria because our material on hysteria is rather meagre. That is to say your therapy seems to me to depend not merely on the affects released by abreaction but also on certain personal rapports, and it seems to me that though the genesis of hysteria is predominantly, it is not exclusively, sexual. I take the same view of your sexual theory. Harping exclusively on these delicate theoretical questions, Aschaffenburg forgets the essential thing, your psychology, from which psychiatry will one day be sure to reap inexhaustible rewards. I hope to send you soon a little book of mine, in which I approach dementia praecox and its psychology from your standpoint. In it I have also published the case that first drew Bleuler's attention to the existence of your principles, though at that time with vigorous resistance on his part. But, as you know, Bleuler is now completely converted.

It would not have escaped Freud's eye that, besides being more in agreement with Aschaffenburg than he admitted, Jung was also claiming credit for something that did not exist—Bleuler's complete conversion. Evidently the two senior physicians at the Burghölzli were not in close communication even if they lived and worked in the same building. Accordingly, Freud began his reply of 7 October 1906 by helping his young correspondent further down the path along which he was already strolling: "Your letter gave me great pleasure. I am especially gratified to learn that you have converted Bleuler." Freud then went on to take cognizance of the fact that Jung still kept his distance on the issue of sexuality, while adding hopefully, "I venture to hope that in the course of the years you will come closer to me than you now think possible." The rest of the letter was a call to arms: there was no use trying to reason with the critics; what they had here was "two warring worlds." To sweeten the pill, Freud got in a gibe at Aschaffenburg designed to whet Jung's appetite: ". . . he shows no understanding of the simplest symbolism . . . the importance of which any student of linguistics or folklore could impress on him if he is unwilling to take my word for it." Freud closed with a postscript: "My 'transference' ought completely to fill the gap in the mechanism of cure (your 'personal rapport')."

The two men were only five brief letters (three extant) in, and matters were already getting sticky and elusive at the same time. Jung's next letter, of 23 October 1906, avoided an open dispute on either sexuality or "transference," though Jung did allow that "one feels alarmed by the positivism of your presentation." Jung had other things on his mind:

> At the risk of boring you, I must abreact my most recent experience. I am currently treating an hysteric with your method. Difficult case, a 20-year-old Russian girl student, ill for 6 years.
>
> First trauma between the 3rd and 4th year. Saw her father spanking her older brother on the bare bottom. Powerful impression. Couldn't help thinking afterwards that she had defecated on her father's hand. From the 4th–7th year convulsive attempts to defecate on her own feet, in the following manner: she sat on the floor with one foot beneath her, pressed her heel against her anus and tried to defecate and at the same time to prevent defecation. Often retained the stool for 2 weeks in this way! Has no idea how she hit upon this peculiar business; says it was completely instinctive, and accompanied by blissfully shuddersome feelings. Later this phenomenon was superseded by vigorous masturbation.
>
> I should be extremely grateful if you would tell me in a few words what you think of this story.

Jung had resisted involving Spielrein in an abortive attempt to make contact with Freud a year earlier. Now, with a regular correspondence just barely under way, she was the first patient Jung brought up.

ANAL EROTICISM

SPIELREIN'S REMINISCENCES in Jung's office contrast strongly with a diary that she kept from this same period. In her diary, she reveals herself as serious, sober, and deeply committed to social change, especially as regards her native Russia. Her feelings about psychoanalysis are of a piece with these concerns: it needs to involve itself with the larger questions of society, and its principal value for the future might lay in its contribution to pedagogy. And yet in Jung's office, Spielrein was portraying a very different side of herself: she had once been a little girl who had connected spankings with defecation and both with sexual excitement. Herein lay the essential creativity of the new method. Between the unstructured nature of the interview situation and the openness to hearing about different kinds of childhood experiences it was possible to reflect in a new way on the origins of one's own personality.

Yet if the new method made possible a deeper form of self-revelation, it also demanded of the therapist that he know what to make of the new material. But as his letter to Freud reveals, Jung was rather at a loss before Spielrein the toddler, sitting on her heel. In effect, Spielrein had once again shown a deeper insight into Freudian theory than her doctor. In July, in finishing off his preface, Jung had explicitly doubted the importance of "infantile sexual trauma." Now in October, he was reporting one. More, given that the material was frankly anal-erotic, Spielrein seemed to be confirming one of the suppositions of the *Three Essays on the Theory of Sexuality*, namely that erotic pleasure involving the anal sphincters was a regular component of the sexual drive in early childhood. What had happened, apparently, was that with the de-repression of Spielrein's sexual knowledge there had come an after-shock, namely the further de-repression of her earliest childhood memories. This may have been helped along immeasurably by the fact that Spielrein had kept diaries from a young age. Conceivably, she may only recently have retrieved them from Rostov. In two years, she and Jung had gone from the delirium of her masturbatory phantasies to the delirium of her recollected infancy.

From the tone of Jung's letter, it would appear that he was considerably less comfortable with this material than his patient. Spielrein likely did not grasp the nerve she had hit. It must be recalled that a central event of Jung's own childhood was his vision of the cathedral of Basel being crushed by a giant turd dropped from an enthroned God on high. It was this vision, with its mixture of sacrilege, grace, and "indescribable relief," that gave Jung the confidence to resist his father's theology. Now it appeared that Jung might have overlooked something about the vision. If there was such a thing as childhood anal eroticism, and the girl appeared to be proof positive, then perhaps there was a root to his vision that he really ought to reconsider.

Matters may have been even worse than Jung was letting Freud know. For in Spielrein's childhood diaries there was more than just the retention of feces for the purposes of masturbation. There was a whole wish to be the Creator, to make the world over or at least to make over its parts alchemically. And there was a curious game played first with her uncle and then with her brother in which she was successively the terrified believer and then, with the brother, God himself. In short, her antics were not just infantile-sexual; they were also sacrilegious-erotic. There were some hair-raising possibilities here for Jung: her delirium might relate directly to his. But self-protectively, he told Freud only as much as would seem to fit the few brief passages on anal eroticism in *Three Essays on the Theory of Sexuality*.

If Jung was perplexed, Freud had every reason to be astonished. Thus far, Freud had been content to play along with the young lion of the Burghölzli, an obviously talented fellow, though a little less than honest, who seemed to want something, though exactly what was not clear. Freud could not have expected that Jung would suddenly turn up with this kind of case material. The problem was that the theory of anal eroticism was *nothing more* than a few brief passages in the *Three Essays on the Theory of Sexuality*. Though he had a theory that linked suppressed anal eroticism to adult character formation, Freud had never published any case material on the subject: indeed, there is no evidence that he even had any at this time.

Freud's next letter, dated 27 October 1906, was more cordial than before. He thanked Jung for the offprint of "Association, Dream, and Hysterical Symptom": "You certainly did not show too much reserve, and the 'transference,' the chief proof that the drive underlying the whole process is sexual in nature, seems to have become very clear to you." And when he went on to consider Jung's "most recent experience," he elected to use some of Jung's terms:

I am glad to hear that your Russian girl is a student; uneducated persons are at present too inaccessible for our purposes. The defecation story is nice and suggests numerous analogies. Perhaps you remember my contention in my *Theory of Sexuality* that even infants derive pleasure from the retention of faeces. The third to fourth year is the most significant period for those sexual activities. . . . The sight of a brother being spanked arouses a memory trace from the first to second year, or a fantasy transposed into that period. It is not unusual for babies to soil the hands of those who are carrying them. Why should that not have happened in her case? And this awakens a memory of her father's caresses during her infancy. Infantile fixation of the libido on the father—the typical choice of object; anal autoerotism. . . . Such people often show typical combinations of character traits. They are extremely neat, stingy, and obstinate, traits which are in a manner of speaking the sublimations of anal erotism. Cases like this based on a repressed perversion can be analyzed very satisfactorily.

This letter marked the first known instance when Freud wrote out the relation of infantile anal eroticism to the anal character type, but he passed it off as old hat. The trouble was that his anal character didn't sound a bit like Spielrein, even granted that Jung had left God and alchemy out. Spielrein was conflictually masochistic; the caresses she wanted and didn't want from Father were spankings. She was also intensely idealistic and her idealism was focused on Jung as the person who was going to pull her out of the anal-sexual morass. As well, she was bright and creative, but *not* terribly organized. In sum, she was hysterical, not compulsive; Russian, not German, Austrian, or Swiss; overproductive, not retentive or repressed; and mystical, not practical. Freud's analysis, with its great gift of the unpublished theory of the anal character, failed completely to capture the flavor of the difficult but likable girl Jung was dealing with. Accordingly, Jung let the matter drop. There would be no further mention of Spielrein in the correspondence for the next eight months.

But there would be a correspondence. Jung's asking for advice, in effect the first known request for analytic supervision, and Freud's reply concretized what had heretofore been only a possibility, namely that the two men could have a collaborative relationship through the mails. Moreover, if Freud had misstepped with regard to the one case Jung was most interested in, his seniority had nonetheless been granted.

In the letters that shot back and forth between Vienna and Zurich over the next two and a half months, the two men embarked on an intense and animated discussion of the relationship of dementia praecox to hysteria and of both to what Jung called the "instinct for the preservation of the species." Along with his letters Jung also sent his "Freud's Theory of Hysteria: A Reply to Aschaffenburg" and *The Psychology of Dementia Praecox*. These had to be got out of the way. Jung needed Freud's imprimatur for his endorsements, which for all their passion were equivocal on crucial points. Jung's awkwardness was compounded by his dream of the horse, the censored interpretation of which had run in the book on dementia praecox. Freud immediately spotted the dream as Jung's own, spotted too the undiscussed sexual symbolism, and Jung was forced to explain himself all over again. Throughout these early letters, Freud patiently kept insisting on the correctness of his own ideas and the aptness of his terminology.

The upshot was that Jung was so busy trying to ingratiate himself that he allowed himself to yield his position with regard to nomenclature. Jung was successful insofar as Freud became more and more interested in him; in December, Freud even invited Jung to visit him in Vienna the following spring. But Jung was unsuccessful insofar as he failed to hold fast to his own point of view; in the face of Freud's "positivism," Jung gave ground rapidly. In particular, Jung did not insist on a distinction between "rapport" and "transference." That left Freud free to claim their identity:

Transference provides the impulse necessary for understanding and translating the language of the ucs. [unconscious]; where it is lacking, the patient does not make the effort or does not listen when we submit our translation to him. Essentially, one might say, the cure is effected by love. And actually transference provides the most cogent, indeed, the only unassailable proof that neuroses are determined by the individual's love life.

Jung had heretofore been interested in how "rapport" could be used to give his outpatients "new complexes" in place of their old ones. As he weighed Freud's invitation in December of 1906 to visit Vienna the following spring, Jung was left to ponder the sexual redefinition of the rapport as it applied to his patients—and himself.

IN JANUARY of 1907, and again just before the end of February, Jung agreed to be a subject for experiments that Ludwig Binswanger was running for his medical dissertation, experiments which combined the word association test with an electro-galvanometer. In the process of helping young Binswanger out, Jung revealed that Spielrein was still very much on his mind.

A word about Binswanger, arguably the most brilliant among a very talented group of Burghölzli assistants. Binswanger came from a line of respected but open-minded psychiatrists; indeed, for the Binswangers, psychiatry was practically a family business. Binswanger senior ran the family asylum at Kreuzlingen, the Bellevue, which is where "Anna O." had been sent to recuperate from the first cathartic "cure." Ludwig's uncle Otto was the sitting professor of psychiatry at Jena, the man who had treated Nietzsche in his last years, and an acknowledged authority on any number of topics, including hysteria. It was a measure of how far the Burghölzli had risen that the scion of this family went there instead of to Kraepelin's nearby clinic in Munich to finish his training. And it was a measure of the relationship springing up between Jung and Binswanger that Jung volunteered to be his subject and thus took the risk of letting a man with Binswanger's family connections catch a glimpse into his own private life.

In the published account of Jung's associations, Binswanger found no less than eleven different complexes. The most important, in the sense that they produced the greatest disturbances in the reactions, were "the Goethe complex," about which Binswanger would say nothing further, a "philosophical complex," a "travel complex," Jung's wish to have a son, memories of his father's death, hypochondriacal ideas relating to the possibility of his own death, restlessness with his life at the asylum, and a "ruefulness complex." The "ruefulness complex" referred to Spielrein—we have this on her authority—though it was entangled with other complexes, most particularly with the wish to have a son and the wish to escape the Burghölzli.

Binswanger's published account of Jung's responses constitutes a psychological labyrinth for the historian. Jung, of course, is not identified as the subject, but his name does pop up repeatedly as the authority on the test itself. There is thus more than one Jung, as it were, in the paper. And this double, self-reflexive existence is likewise manifest in Jung's responses. For example, Jung gave the word "have" as a response five times—following the stimulus words "manners," "money," "child," "fame," and "family." At first glance, this amounts to an almost bored self-description. Jung had money, children (two girls), fame, family, and manners (unlike Spielrein, who was still running around in peasant dresses at this time). But, as Binswanger rightly pointed out in his article, the repetition of "have" constituted a perseveration, and so was a complex-indicator. In effect, Jung, an old hand at the experiment, was self-consciously making a bitter joke. He had all these things, but something else was on his mind.

Binswanger drew a veil over the meaning of those responses which concerned Spielrein directly. Some of them appear to refer to her masochistic bent—e.g., "threaten-hit"—while others seem to refer to her headstrong nature and Jung's difficulty in achieving a friendly yet sufficiently distant attitude toward her. The only response whose meaning is self-evident is "ruefulness-faithfulness"—Jung regrets his fidelity to his wife. Spielrein's own reaction upon reading Binswanger's paper some nine or ten months later focused on a different association, not noted by Binswanger: "child-have, cap-put on." The reference appears to be to contraception. Beyond this, the reader learns only that Jung was currently having dreams about Spielrein and that he was worried that she might have slandered him in some unstated way.

Binswanger discussed in detail Jung's wish to have a son. "Sex-determination" referred to this complex directly, while "box-bed" referred to his wife's most recent pregnancy. (The latter pair had appeared in her own protocol in the "Reaction-Time" paper.) Then there were the pairs "wall-star" and "star-house." We have Binswanger to thank for the second pair; he was struck by the first response and substituted "star" back into the list as an impromptu stimulus word to see what he would get; thus does the association experiment blend into psychoanalysis. Through a train of phonetic associations in the post-experiment interview involving "s" sounds, Jung arrived at the "Star of Bethlehem" and the thought of "Unto us a child is born."

Here, however, Binswanger left something out. Although he did mention that "star" was an association on a previous test (allegedly, the subject's sister-in-law had given that association on a test during the time of her own engagement), concealed beneath this was Jung's own previous reaction as Subject 19 of the "The Associations of Normal Subjects." There his complex involved a Jewish girl; her pseudonym in the published paper was "Alice Stern"—*Stern* meaning "star" in German—and the word "star" was prominent in the disturbed reactions. Now the word had cropped up again. Both Jung and Binswanger were thus aware that history was repeating itself.

As it happens, later in the paper, when Binswanger returned to the subject of Jung's "s" responses, he gave an additional illustration of the same mechanism in another subject who was identified only as a "female student." Binswanger gives but five responses for this subject:

11.	Young [*jung*]	old
12.	Ask	answer
13.	State	Russia
14.	Stubborn	-minded
15.	Stalk	talk

About the pair "young [*jung*]-old," Binswanger notes that there was an unusually long reaction time (twenty-four seconds) as well as a very strong deflection of the galvanometer. About the content he says only that "two strong complexes were aroused which were and are still important to her." The next pair, "ask-answer," also came after a long reaction time and was accompanied by a strong deflection; the response is said to reflect the subject's concern about an exam. Then, at the end of a very brief, noncommittal discussion of the remaining reactions, Binswanger abruptly refers the reader back to the earlier discussion of one of Jung's responses, specifically "divorce-avoid."

In all the literature on the word association experiment, this is the only place where the historian can be relatively confident he has come across Spielrein as a subject. Between the context and Binswanger's discretion, however, one learns less than one would like, Binswanger's suggestive juxtaposition of her responses with Jung's notwithstanding.

Freud also turns up in Binswanger's report. During the first week of January, Jung was accepting Freud's invitation to visit Vienna that spring. (At the end of February, the two men finalized the date.) Binswanger's first administration of the experiment thus caught a new complex aborning, Jung's "Vienna complex":

98. Vienna	Paris
100. Soon	yes

. . . he is contemplating a journey to Vienna as soon as the vacation begins; he can hardly wait. . . . Has a general feeling "something is soon going to happen." The strong deviation [of the galvanometer] points to the subject's need of new "sensations."

FREUD HAD evidently considered his invitation carefully. He had reported the publication of Jung's paper "Association, Dream, and Hysterical Symptom" to the Wednesday Night Meeting of his discussion group on 31 October 1906. That same night a crony, Eduard Hitschmann, presented a review of Bleuler's new book, *Affectivity, Suggestibility, and Paranoia*, a work which had repeatedly cited Freud's theories. In the discussion that followed, however, Freud made reference only to Bleuler's "half-hearted acceptance" of his own ideas while specifying that Bleuler "lacks any understanding of sexual matters." On 28 November 1906, to the same group of colleagues, Freud read Jung's letter of 26 November and noted that Jung had replied publicly to Aschaffenburg. From 12 December on, the meetings were cancelled. This gave Freud time to read Jung's dementia praecox book among other things (such as the verdict of the Berlin court against Swoboda) and to proffer his invitation.

The Wednesday Night Meetings resumed 23 January 1907, two weeks after Jung had signalled his intention to visit. But Jung was not the first visitor to set out from the Burghölzli. Max Eitingon was. Eitingon was independently wealthy, Jewish, and he had a reputation as a ladies' man. It is not known why Bleuler selected him as his emissary to Vienna; perhaps Eitingon had volunteered to pay his own way. In any event, the minutes of the Wednesday Night Meetings record the fact that on the nights of 23 January and 30 January, Max Eitingon was present in the official capacity of Bleuler's emissary. Bleuler had sent along a number of questions to be put up for discussion. The group treated Eitingon rather roughly. According to Rank's minutes, Freud himself was not above expressing irritation with one of the questions, which dealt with nonsexual factors in neurosis:

> The sexual component of psychic life has more bearing on the causation of the neuroses than all other factors. This assertion can be proven only in so far as any psychological processes can be proven. Mr. Eitingon's question betrays the theoretical disavowal which has not always been maintained by the Zurich School.

Other subjects also came up. Eitingon asked whether neuroses were more prevalent among Jews; those assembled answered, "Yes." Eitingon raised Jung's idea of substituting a new complex; Freud did not answer on point, but talked at length about transference, at one point repeating his *bon mot* "Our cures are cures of love." Freud also got in a criticism, an unfair one, of Jung's theory of a toxin specific to the complexes of dementia praecox. Adler, on the other hand, was willing to agree that a new complex could be introduced through treatment, but only in the form of a sublimated activity like "painting, music or psychology." The role of social class, Hellpach's thesis, came up. And so forth. It was not quite two warring worlds, but it was clear that the Viennese had their own set of concerns, and that they didn't consider they had anything to learn from their visitor. Indeed, they seem barely to have considered him educable. Not that Eitingon couldn't take care of himself. He accused one speaker of dealing in generalities, another of using the sexual theory as an all-purpose explanation, and to Adler he said that he found him "vague and incomprehensible."

It was all a calculated slap at Bleuler. In the two meetings, his ideas came up not even once. And the questions he had sent along were treated merely as pretexts for various sorts of posturing. We can only guess what sort of report Eitingon brought back with him. What makes the slap important was not its impact on the relationship between Bleuler and Freud. Bleuler was a methodical, intellectually honest man, and no amount of personal unpleasantness would keep him from endorsing theories that he otherwise thought were correct. What makes the slap important is what it indicates about Freud's private feelings about Jung. Whatever Jung's awkwardness in his letters, he had managed to persuade Freud that he might well be the man to champion Freud's cause. Accordingly, by the beginning of 1907, Freud had already decided that he no longer had to court Bleuler so assiduously. Jung, whom Freud had yet to meet, was already the man in whom Freud was investing his hopes.

CHAPTER 6

Jung and Freud

... modern European society ... *simultaneously* makes fun of the "old maid" and condemns the unmarried mother to infamy. This double-faced, putrescent "morality" is profoundly *immoral*, it is *radically evil*. It is moral and good to contest it with all our energy, to enter the lists on behalf of the right to free love, to "unmarried" motherhood. . . . Two million women [in Germany] in a condition of *compulsory* celibacy and—coercive marriage morality. It is merely necessary to place these two facts side by side, in order to display the complete ethical bankruptcy of our time in the province of sexual morality.

—Iwan Bloch, *The Sexual Life of Our Times in Its Relations to Modern Civilization*, 1906

I N 1903 Weininger had taken up "emancipated women" as a form of sexual deviancy second in importance only to homosexuality. By 1907, the climate had changed decisively. The Bund für Mutterschutz (Association for the Protection of Mothers) had been founded in Berlin in 1905 with a roster of distinguished academicians including Iwan Bloch, Willy Hellpach, Werner Sombart, Max Weber, and the prominent sexual researcher and leader of Berlin's homosexual community, Magnus Hirschfeld. Statistics on illegitimacy, prostitution, venereal disease, and the like were both available and shocking. Thus did the German-speaking world come to know in a new, scientific way what it had long known in private conversation: it was paying an awful price for insisting on monogamous marriage while making marriage utterly dependent on the economic prerogative of the male.

Iwan Bloch's massive—766 pages in the English translation—tome on contemporary sexual life, brought out in late 1906 though postdated to 1907, meant to bring an anthropological perspective to bear on the problem, though it was full of outraged polemic couched in terms consonant with the sensibility of the German-speaking world. It was not sufficient that a change in sexual practices be practical. Such a change had to be simultaneously moral, scientific, and compatible with high culture. Bloch saw fit to argue that it was "a simple evolutionary necessity that free love . . . will find its moral justification." And he made the following case with regard to culture:

> It would be an interesting task to collect statistics relating to such free unions, and the resulting "illegitimate" offspring, in the case of notable men and women! The marriage fanatics would be horrified! . . . It is my intention, as soon as possible, to represent in a brief work the role of free love in the history of civilization, and to adduce proofs that free love is very well compatible with a moral life. Who would venture to reproach with immorality a Bürger, a Jean Paul, a Gutzkow, a Karoline Schlegel, a George Sand, or even a Goethe?

In Vienna, the small group of internists and intellectuals that had gathered around Freud in the Wednesday Night Psychology Club stood in uneasy relation to this swell of sentiment in the German world. Though Jewish, they were scarcely outsiders; most of them hailed from established families, all of them save Rank were university-educated, and a few of them had already won local reputations as unusually capable physicians. In terms of professional standing, there was no obstacle to collaborating with members of the new north German movement, and in the years to come the group did indeed join forces with Magnus Hirschfeld to produce a survey questionnaire about sexual development.

The problem, rather, was the milieu. For in Vienna, there had grown up a tradition of elaborate public courtesy coupled with a self-confident hypocrisy in matters public and private. Such was the state of Viennese morals that Auguste Forel was decidedly shocked when he had visited for a semester during his student years, and Bloch saw fit to include in his book a whole section (including 100 case descriptions) devoted to the sad state of Viennese married life. It is not fair to argue that Viennese immorality was the only soil in which Freudianism could first take root, but it is fair, as Hanns Sachs has noted, to see a relation between Freud's ideas and the convenient double consciousness that was part and parcel of Viennese life. If official change in sexual mores came to the German world, it would come last to Vienna and, in a way, make the least sense there.

JUNG'S VISIT

JUNG AND his wife, with young Ludwig Binswanger in tow, arrived in Vienna the first weekend in March of 1907. Many years later, when he was an old man, Jung liked to recall his first meeting with Freud—"the first man of real importance I had encountered"—as an occasion when he sat down to listen and learn from his better. Thus does the graciousness of old age distort memory. Actually, Jung did most of the talking, at least at first. Ernest Jones had the good fortune to meet Jung in July of 1907 when the visit was still fresh in his memory:

> . . . Jung gave me a lively account of his first interview. He had very much to tell Freud and to ask him, and with intense animation he poured forth in a spate for three whole hours. Then the patient, absorbed listener interrupted him with the suggestion that they conduct their discussion more systematically. To Jung's great astonishment Freud proceeded to group the contents of the harangue under several precise headings that enabled them to spend the further hours in a more profitable give and take.

The two men continued this way into the night on Sunday, 3 March, not stopping until two o'clock in the morning, some thirteen hours in all. Freud later told Jones that Jung had the most sophisticated grasp of the neuroses of any man he'd met. Jung was almost equally awed:

> . . . in my experience up to that time, no one else could compare with him. There was nothing the least trivial in his attitude. I found him extremely intelligent, shrewd, and altogether remarkable. And yet my first impressions of him remained somewhat tangled; I could not make him out.
>
> What he said about his sexual theory impressed me. Nevertheless, his words could not remove my hesitations and doubts. I tried to advance these reservations of mine on several occasions, but each time he would attribute them to my lack of experience. Freud was right; in those days I had not enough experience to support my objections. I could see that his sexual theory was enormously important to him, both personally and philosophically.

On Monday, Jung returned for another meeting, this time with Binswanger at his side. Freud asked both men their dreams of the night before. He interpreted Jung's dream as involving a wish to "dethrone him and take his place," while in Binswanger's dream Freud detected a wish to marry his, Freud's, oldest daughter. The mood was congenial, and the quiet dignity of Herr Professor Freud showed to its best advantage. According to Binswanger:

> The easy-going, friendly atmosphere that marked our visit from the first day on can easily be seen in these [dream] interpretations. Freud's dislike of all formality and ceremony, his personal charm, simplicity, natural openness, and kindness, and not least his humour, left no room for constraint. And yet one could not for a moment deny the impression of greatness and dignity that emanated from him. To me it was a pleasure, albeit somewhat skeptical, to see the enthusiasm and confidence with which Freud responded to Jung, in whom he immediately saw his scientific "son and heir."

Freud had his two visitors attend a Wednesday Night Meeting of the Psychology Club on 6 March. Alfred Adler was given the job of presenting. It can scarcely have been accidental that the case Adler presented was a Russian student with, it turned out, anal erotic trends. Adler and Freud seemed to have worked it out ahead of time. Adler presented childhood memories in which the fellow was sensitive about the size of his penis, a fact which gave Adler the chance to bring in his own theory of organ inferiority as a contributing cause to neurosis. Next Adler related the patient's obsession with three numbers: 3, 7, and 49. Finally, he discussed the patient's "Jewish complex." Then, in the discussion, Freud gave his interpretation of the obsession: "3 may perhaps stand for the Christian penis; 7 the small and 49 the large Jewish penis." Further, without any obvious clues, Freud went on to talk about the patient's stinginess. Adler in turn confirmed Freud's surmises about the man's frugal character and then supplied new material on the patient's childhood incontinence. Which gave Freud the opportunity of arriving at a final remark; Rank's minutes:

> Professor Freud points out the connection of stinginess and lavishness with the stress on the anal zone. Such people are distinguished in later life by special characteristics: they are orderly, clean, and conscientious, stubborn and peculiar in money matters.
> Finally it should be pointed out that the contents of the symptoms have the nature of a compromise: It is as if the patient said, "I want

to be baptized—but the Jewish penis is still larger. (Thus I remain a Jew.)''

There was something for everyone here. Between Adler and Freud there was the byplay that Adler had gone the politically expedient route, taken by many Jews in this Catholic city, of getting baptized, while Freud had not. For Jung, there was a case of a Russian student who just happened to have anal-erotic traits. And for the rest of the group there was the sop about the larger Jewish penis. (It can scarcely have evaded anybody's notice that Jung and Binswanger were the first non-Jews ever to attend one of these meetings.)

Perhaps mindful of Eitingon's experience, Jung and Binswanger kept a low profile during the evening. Binswanger simply asked a question, while Jung talked a little about number responses on the association experiment, made a point of following Freud in praising Adler's theory of organ inferiority, but otherwise begged off, saying he was still attempting to scale the peak of Freud's theory. As Max Graf later recalled, it was plain to everyone how much Freud seemed to like his Swiss visitors, especially Jung. The feeling was mutual. Jung even in later life liked to talk about how "handsome" Freud was.

The feeling did not extend to Freud's group. Jung is said to have told Ernest Jones a few months later that it was a "pity" Freud had no followers of any weight and that he was surrounded by a "degenerate and Bohemian crowd." Most unfairly, the antagonism between Jung and the Vienna group has been laid—largely through Jones's handiwork—to some vaguely defined anti-Semitic streak in Jung. This just will not do. At the time of his first visit, Jung was still in the grip of what can best be described as his Jewish romance. He was positively attracted by the Jewishness of psychoanalysis, just as in his personal life he was powerfully attracted by Jewish women. If Jewish intellectuals were moving out ahead of traditional nineteenth-century European culture, Jung was ready to join them, though coming from another direction. Having early abandoned Swiss Calvinism, the faith he was raised in, Jung was without a church of his own; for him Judaism, like occultism, was an intriguing church next door. It was only logical that he should seek to make friends with the congregation by way of completing his own liberation from the religion that had manifestly failed his father. Indeed, in little more than two years' time, Spielrein would explicitly describe Jung's attitude toward Judaism in terms of "the drive to explore other possibilities through a new race, the drive to liberate himself from the paternal edicts."

To be sure, Jung's views later changed and he was willing to endorse positions that can only be characterized as anti-Semitic. But that unwholesome transformation was still some years away, and the events that it was predicated on had yet to happen. It was not a factor in Jung's dislike of the Viennese around Freud. For the record, Jung never mentioned the fact that Freud's group was Jewish, though he made no secret of his distaste for them. But then Jones, who *did* make a point of discussing their Jewishness, didn't like them, either. About Adler, Jones wrote that he was "sulky and pathetically eager for recognition." About Isidor Sadger that he was a "morose, pathetic figure, very like a specially uncouth bear." Hitschmann got off merely with "dry, witty, and somewhat cynical." "The egregious Stekel" received special treatment at length. And for the group as a whole, Jones wrote:

> The reader may perhaps gather that I was not highly impressed with the assembly. It seemed an unworthy accompaniment to Freud's genius, but in the Vienna of those days, so full of prejudice against him, it was hard to secure a pupil with a reputation to lose, so he had to take what he could get.

For that matter, Freud didn't much care for them. Following that Wednesday Night Meeting of 6 March, Freud, in Binswanger's words, "took me aside afterward and said, 'Well, now you have seen the gang.' " Binswanger's reaction to this comment was to note to himself that despite his relative isolation, Freud's social judgment had remained "keen."

About the special character of the relationship that sprang up between Freud and Jung much has been written. It was something like love. One could say that Freud needed an ideal son, while Jung needed an ideal father, and certainly they played at enacting these roles. That said, they were in many ways an unlikely match, differing in age, tradition, temperament, and in the specific cast of their ambitions. Moreover, it was not even established which man was currently the more important of the two. Freud had seniority, but Jung's meteoric rise to international prominence in the preceding two years had been impressive and unparalleled. Moreover, Jung's work did not suffer under the burden of controversy. Indeed, given that the two men were going into the same area—the articulation of unconscious mental processes—but doing so from quite different points of view, were a contemporary commentator asked to pick which of their viewpoints would be most likely to endure, he surely would have chosen Jung's. Not only did Jung's theory of complexes entail affects, a far less problematic idea than Freud's polymorphously perverse libido, but it had already generated an impressive record in empirical research. Freud's assets were scarcely negligible: a matchless gift for expression in the German language, a host of original observations, a daunting capacity for systematization, and a quietly indomitable belief in the correctness of his own ideas, to name but four. But, in the face of the ebullient visitor, the heir apparent to the Zurich chair, Freud's situation was essentially that of an assistant college professor whose very rich relatives have popped in for a visit—the trick in such circumstances is to keep one's composure, direct the conversation carefully, and not seem to lack for anything. Nor was it clear what Jung's plans were. Freud's interpretation of Jung's dream, that it betrayed Jung's wish to supplant him, had landed disarmingly close to the heart of the situation: Jung had already staked his own claims to be a pioneering depth psychologist and professionally he was free to do as he pleased in the future.

In short, there was plenty of room for wariness, for skepticism, for latent distrust—on both sides. Yet in person, between the two of them, all of this seemed to disappear beneath Freud's almost visible affection and Jung's sense that he had finally won recognition from a great man. Their coming together had been carefully rehearsed by each man in private, and neither was about to let the moment disappoint. It was a time to find out about each other, made easier by the happiness of finally having an other worth finding out about.

THE BILLINSKY ACCOUNT

ARGUABLY JUNG found out something else during his visit, something terribly disturbing and something that would change his life forever. But this is a story unto itself, since it involves a great secret that was kept for many, many years and then became a great open secret which, even after it was published, nobody would discuss.

In 1957, John Billinsky, Guiles Professor of Psychology and Clinical Studies at Andover Newton Theological School, paid Jung a visit at his home in Küsnacht outside Zurich. Billinsky had been following Jung's ideas since attending his Terry Lectures at Yale some twenty years earlier and enjoyed a personal friendship with Carl Meier, Jung's closest associate at that time. Jung had recently become embroiled in an ongoing dispute with a number of theologians, so he was perhaps more than usually eager to resume his acquaintance with the psychologist of the Andover Newton Theological School. Why Jung told Billinsky the following is anybody's guess:

> In 1907 I arrived with my young and happy wife in Vienna. Freud came to see us at the Hotel and brought some flowers for my wife. He was trying to be very considerate and at one point he said to me: "I am sorry that I can give you no real hospitality, I have nothing at home but an elderly wife." When my wife heard him say that she looked perturbed and embarrassed. At Freud's house that evening, during the dinner, I tried to talk to Freud and his wife about psychoanalysis and so on, but I soon discovered that Mrs. Freud knew absolutely nothing about what Freud was doing. There was a very superficial relationship between Freud and his wife. Soon I met Freud's wife's younger sister—she was very good-looking, and she not only knew enough about psychoanalysis, but also about everything that Freud was doing. I learned that Freud was in love with her and had sexual relations with her.

Further, Jung claimed to have learned of the affair not from Freud, but directly from Minna Bernays:

> When, a few days later [after arriving in Vienna], I was visiting Freud's laboratory, Freud's sister-in-law asked me if she could talk with me. She was very much bothered by her relationship with Freud and felt guilty about it. From her I learned that Freud was in love with her and that their relationship was indeed very intimate. It was a shocking discovery to me, and even now I can recall the agony I felt at the time.

Billinsky himself apparently felt something like agony hearing this. The interview went on for three hours; immediately after taking his leave he began making notes on it. But he did nothing with the notes for the next twelve years. Jung died in 1961. Then, in 1969, angered by a *Time* magazine article that saw fit to repeat unfavorable remarks made by Freud about Jung to Stanley Hall, the American psychologist, Billinsky decided to publish part of his interview.

And then nothing happened. Ellenberger's massive tome on the history of the psychology of the unconscious came out the following year without making any reference to Billinsky; perhaps it had already gone to press. The *Freud/Jung Letters* came out five years later; again no mention, despite the fact that Billinsky had offered the editors the use of all his notes. And in the enormous secondary literature that has sprung up since the publication of the letters, there are scarcely a dozen works which even mention Billinsky's report and almost none that credit it.

The report was easy to dismiss as improbable hearsay. It was said against the idea of a romance between Freud and his sister-in-law that it was impossible that such a thing could have existed and not have led to rumors in Vienna, against Jung that his memory was probably playing tricks on him (he was seventy-one when he gave the interview), and against Billinsky that it seemed most unlikely that he alone in the entire Western world should have been made privy to such a terrible secret. Billinsky himself simply let the matter drop, though he never retracted his statements. He died in 1983.

There are indeed problems with Billinsky's published account, but there are far more problems with the opposing views. To begin with, there *were* rumors in Vienna about Freud's sister-in-law; in fact, much later in life, Freud even upbraided a patient who was too readily disinclined to put any credence in such rumors. Certainly, Freud and Minna had frequent opportunity to turn the rumors into reality, often traveling alone together during the summer while Martha stayed with the children. Oskar Rie, family friend and physician to the Freud children, commented on what was readily observable to all who were close to the household: "For children, Freud went with Martha; for pleasure, he took Minna." Then, too, Jung's memory may have slipped a bit in his early seventies, but either the story is true or it is an outright lie—this is not the sort of thing a person misremembers. And, finally, Billinsky was *not* the only person Jung told. He told any number of people who subsequently went on record, including the great Harvard psychologist Henry Murray; an Italian journalist, Hugo Charteris; and an analyst in training, John Phillips.

Carl Meier was openly critical of Billinsky at the time of his first report and apparently pressed him to drop the matter. But, when he himself was interviewed by Gene Nameche the following year for the Jung Oral History Archive, he had this to say:

> Jung had hardly known him. He [Jung] made one of those blunders he very often made, because he was a very bad judge of human beings. He trusted this man Billinsky absolutely 100 percent the very first time he saw him. Billinsky came back from Jung and told me

a story of the type now released. I was convinced up to that moment that this story was only known to Toni Wolff and me—nobody else. . . . I would never think of publicizing a thing like this. What is the use? But apparently not so Billinsky.

Toni Wolff was a colleague and for nearly thirty years more or less openly Jung's mistress; she died in 1953. Meier's own status in the Jung world is unquestioned. It is perhaps worth adding that his obvious distaste for Billinsky's report—"What is the use?"—expresses the attitude of most Jungians. The time for quarreling is long past; nobody in the Jung camp wants to start it up again. The fact remains, however, that later in life Jung was giving out this story, first only to intimates whose absolute discretion he could count on, but then, in garrulous old age, to a number of people.

The idea that there was such a sexual involvement between Freud and Minna Bernays has recently received independent support from an entirely different direction. Peter Swales, on the basis of a careful reconstruction of Freud's activities and an unusually acute reading of Freud's letters and texts, has concluded that Freud was indeed passionately attracted to his sister-in-law during the late 1890s and that the passion was finally consummated during August and September of 1900. Swales's thesis is considered controversial. To be sure, there has never been any question but that Minna Bernays was an extremely important figure in Freud's life, serving a variety of roles from correspondent to secretary, from traveling companion to intellectual confidante. Her own chances for marriage lost through the death of her fiancé in 1886, she had joined the Freud household in 1895 to assist with her sister's sixth, last and unwanted, pregnancy. She then returned the following year and remained with the family the rest of her life. She was, so to speak, one of those two million women living in compulsory celibacy that Iwan Bloch was writing about. Where Swales has gone further than previous commentators is in demonstrating how Minna's proximity to Freud—they traveled alone together for the first time in July of 1898—can be meaningfully juxtaposed with various autobiographical comments concerning the distressing state of Freud's love life that are scattered throughout his writings during the years 1897 through 1901, when Freud completed his major psychological works while using himself as his own best subject.

The linchpin of Swales's argument involves two works that Freud wrote in the fall of 1900 immediately following his second vacation trip alone with Minna. In the first of these, *On Dreams*, Freud presented as a useful example one of his own dreams, the theme of which was his wish to have love "free of cost." In context, "free of cost" was both concrete and metaphorical, that is, it referred to money but it also stood for love free of "guilt." The provocation for the dream, Freud tells his reader, was that he had recently paid out a considerable sum of money for a member of his family. The same dream was also referred to explicitly in *The Psychopathology of Everyday Life,* where one learns that the money was paid out on behalf of a relative "absent for purposes of cure." It was clearly money laid out for Minna's six-week stay at a spa in Merano, which was ongoing at the time Freud wrote up his analysis of the dream and which had commenced immediately after her recent month-long holiday alone with Freud that summer. Very much to the point is Freud's comment that he cannot fully interpret the dream as it would cause "serious mischief in important directions."

Written contemporaneously with *On Dreams* was the "Aliquis" episode which forms Chapter 2 of *The Psychopathology of Everyday Life.* In it, Freud recounts how a misremembered quotation from Virgil—the word "Aliquis" was omitted—revealed the fear of a momentary traveling companion that his mistress might be pregnant. It is a lovely anecdote, quite brief and almost miraculously solved by the ingenious Freud—one of the principal delights of Freud's most delightful work. It has fallen to Swales, and to another researcher, Anthony Stadlen, to break the code of Freud's literary conceit: like the earlier paper on "Screen Memories," the "Aliquis" episode constitutes disguised autobiography. Not only do the imagined interlocutor's attitudes and situation fit exactly with Freud's own, but *every association* he gives in Freud's description can be convincingly traced to some event, person, or book with which Freud was personally familiar, this to the point where all the bounds of coincidence completely collapse.

I will not try to reproduce the Swales-Stadlen demonstration here. (Swales's contribution has been published only partially, Stadlen's not at all.) The demonstration requires too arduous an excursion into the minute details not only of Freud's writings and of his correspondence, but also of his reading habits, of his travels, and of his very special circumstances in the years 1897–1900. Nonetheless, in my view it will eventually become incontestable, once the Swales-Stadlen material is published and assimilated, that Freud not only entertained fantasies of a sexual encounter with Minna Bernays but that he had further fantasies—a month after she had taken her leave in the fall of 1900—specifically of her having gotten pregnant. To be sure, a person may fantasize about things that never happened. Accordingly, it remains conceivable that Freud was inwardly pondering the possible consequences of an imagined affair, not an actual one. Just here, however, Jung's later testimony would seem to tip the balance. Ultimately, of course, it is not in anyone's power to advance incontrovertible proof for the thesis. As Rosemary Dinnage has remarked in another connection, "Later generations who try to find out who did what to whom sexually are always on a losing wicket."

Part of the problem in taking the idea of an affair seriously is that it seems to throw our understanding of Freud's character into a completely new realm. I am not sure that this is the case. Minna Bernays had lost forever her chances for marriage, and once she had joined the household, there was no honorable way of then asking her to leave. The mores of that era demanded that she should stay. Freud's own situation was likely intolerable if we assume that he began to feel a tragic attraction to the new boarder, a woman whom he had long been close to and whose temperament was closer to his own than was his wife's. It is too little observed, in this context, that the exact theory Freud was espousing at the time that Jung met him bore a close relation to his own predicament. For Freud was then arguing that what he called a psycho-neurosis could only be triggered by a present erotic conflict. That is to say, while the predisposition to a neurosis might have arisen through some combination of sexual constitution and infantile experience, the actual condition in the adult could only be triggered by the presence of some current sexual frustration that was caused by internal conflict. Arguably, the theory aptly describes Freud's own situation from 1896 onward, though of course by itself this begs the question of whether the theory may have helped him to move from the temptation to the deed.

AN UPROAR OF COMPLEXES

AT FIRST, Jung did absolutely nothing with the new information, assuming that he had it. He told no one. Nor did he confront Freud with it. He finished out his week in Vienna and then he and Mrs. Jung went on to Budapest to rendezvous with the Leopold Steins. And from there, on to the seaside resort of Abbazia, where his "Jewess complex" resurfaced in the form of what he subsequently described to Freud as a "compulsive infatuation" with an unidentified woman. Then, back to the Burghölzli.

Perhaps Jung didn't know what to do. Perhaps he just wanted time to think it all over. It was already clear to Jung that Freud was a genius. As a genius, he was certainly entitled to the same freedoms as Goethe, Jean Paul, George Sand, and the others Iwan Bloch was planning to write his next book about. Had Freud been involved with any other woman, Jung probably wouldn't have given it another thought. No, the sticking point was that it was his wife's sister. That was incest. Incest did not fall within the new freedoms being invoked in the name of science, ethics, and high culture. Beyond the liberality traditionally accorded to genius, Freud was seemingly asking for an unusually dark dispensation. Did that relate somehow to the special insight into the mind that Freud was opening up?

Here we have to distinguish sharply between what the situation in the Freud household might have meant to Freud and what Jung might have made of it. Jung likely understood nothing of the prehistory of Freud's relation with either of the Bernays sisters, and his understanding of Freud's milieu was approximate at best. Freud's Jewishness may have played a part in Jung's attempts at rationalization, since it was then an item of faith in the dubious discipline of "racial science" that Jews were more inbred than Aryans. Indeed, the only question at the time was whether the frequency of marriage between close relatives was a cause of the high incidence of neurosis among Jews or, to the contrary, whether it helped keep their stock pure from contamination by other racial groups. Such debate is offensive to our ears, yet the fact is that at the time Jewish physicians no less than Gentile ones logged themselves in on both sides of the issue. As for the sexual habits of Jews, these were considered to be influenced by the same factors. Forel, in *The Sexual Question*, had this to say:

> The Jews, who have preserved their race in all climates and under all possible conditions of existence, furnish an object lesson. . . . The traits of their character are reflected in their sexual life. Their sexual appetites are generally strong and their love is distinguished by great family attachment. . . . They are not very jealous and are much addicted to concubinage, at the same time remaining affectionate to their wife and family.

But intrafamilial romance was scarcely thought to be a Jewish preoccupation only; it was a regular theme of contemporary German literature, to the point where Wagner had written it into his operas and young Otto Rank was currently collecting any number of examples for a massive tome, *The Motif of Incest in Literature and Legend*. Nor was this preoccupation thought obscene. Indeed, to face issues like incest was thought an indication of a writer's philosophical and psychological depth. Had not Schopenhauer written to Goethe:

> It is the courage of making a clean breast of it in face of every question that makes the philosopher. He must be like Sophocles' Oedipus, who, seeking enlightenment concerning his terrible fate, pursues his indefatigable enquiry, even when he divines that appalling horror awaits him in the answer. But most of us carry in our hearts the Jocasta, who begs Oedipus for God's sake not to enquire further; and we give way to her and that is the reason why philosophy stands where it does.

And did not Nietzsche proclaim in *The Birth of Tragedy:*

> Oedipus, his father's murderer, his mother's lover, solver of the Sphinx's riddle! What is the meaning of this triple fate? An ancient popular belief, especially strong in Persia, holds that a wise *magus* must be incestuously begotten. If we examine Oedipus . . . in the light of this Parsee belief, we may conclude that wherever soothsaying and magical powers have broken . . . the magic circle of nature, extreme unnaturalness—in this case incest—is the necessary antecedent, for how should man force nature to yield up her secrets but by successfully resisting her, that is to say, by unnatural acts?

The long-range problem for Jung would have been how to bring up this matter between himself and Freud. There was, however, no manual of etiquette for such a situation. Perhaps this was something that could be handled with "psychoanalytic frankness," to use a recent phrase of Freud's. But, then, there was no manual for psychoanalysis either. The short-range problem was not to let the month of March end without writing. Freud, as befitted the host, remained silent. On the last day of March, three full weeks later, Jung finally put pen to paper:

> You will doubtless have drawn your own conclusions from the prolongation of my reaction-time. Up till now I had a strong resistance to writing because until recently the complexes aroused in Vienna were still in an uproar. Only now have things settled down a bit, so that I hope to be able to write you a more or less sensible letter.

The most difficult item, your broadened conception of sexuality, has now been assimilated up to a point and tried out in a number of actual cases. In general I see that you are right.

And from there Jung went on to discuss, and partially dispute, Freud's ideas on auto-erotism as the basis for dementia praecox. Rather than ask Freud outright about his personal life, Jung had retreated back into theory. Perhaps he hoped to find some clarity there.

If Jung had hoped that the beginning of his letter constituted an invitation to discuss personal matters, Freud certainly didn't take it that way. His reply of 7 April 1907 began:

I am choosing different paper because I don't wish to feel cramped in speaking to you. Your visit was most delightful and gratifying; I should like to repeat in writing various things that I confided to you by word of mouth, in particular, that you have inspired me with confidence for the future, that I now realize that I am as replaceable as everyone else and that I could hope for no one better than yourself, as I have come to know you, to continue and complete my work. I am sure you will not abandon the work, you have gone into it too deeply and seen for yourself how exciting, how far-reaching, and how beautiful our subject is.

Freud went on to say that they would gain nothing by watering down the libido theory for the sake of public approval: "We cannot avoid resistances, why not face up to them from the start?" All in all, it was a most ingratiating letter and Jung took cognizance of that in his turn:

Many thanks for your long and exceedingly friendly letter! I only fear that you overestimate me and my powers. With your help I have come to see pretty deeply into things, but I am still far from seeing them *clearly*. Nevertheless I have the feeling of having made considerable inner progress since I got to know you personally; it seems to me that one can never quite understand your science unless one knows you in the flesh. Where so much still remains dark to us outsiders only faith can help; but the best and most effective faith is knowledge of your personality. Hence my visit to Vienna was a genuine confirmation.

After this renewed invitation for Freud to talk about himself, Jung went again into a theoretical discussion of dementia praecox, followed with gossip about Bleuler and others. There was one important additional item, however—Jung has been invited to give a talk, with Aschaffenburg as his opponent, at the coming First International Neurology Congress at Amsterdam. The topic would be "Modern Theories of Hysteria." In essence, Jung had been asked to defend Freud.

By return mail Freud brushed Jung in on the history of the invitation while again sticking to business:

> You see, my view of our relationship is shared by the world at large. Shortly before your visit, I was asked to give that report in Amsterdam. I declined in haste for fear that I might talk it over with you and let you persuade me to accept. Then we found more important things to talk about and the matter was forgotten. Now I am delighted to hear that you have been chosen.

At this point, Jung ceased making mention of both his visit and Freud's personality. Henceforth, for the next month and a half, the two men would talk shop. Theories, observations, and psychiatric politics soon swirled around one another in the mounting excitement of a deepening collaborative exchange. To be sure, Jung kept bringing up the work of other men in the field, often favorably, while Freud kept knocking them down, largely on the basis that they would not, or could not, accept the libido theory.

In late May, there was an abrupt change. Freud had been sending along theoretical remarks; now he sent a new work, his analysis of a popular novel, *Gradiva,* which had just come out as the first of a monograph series Freud was starting. Jung's response was more than enthusiastic:

> Your *Gradiva* is magnificent. I gulped it at one go. The clear exposition is beguiling, and I think one would have to be struck by the gods with sevenfold blindness not to see things now as they really are. But the hide-bound psychiatrists and psychologists are capable of anything! . . . Often I have to transport myself back to the time before the reformation of my psychological thinking, to re-experience the charges that were laid against you. I simply can't understand them any more. My thinking in those days seems to me not only intellectually wrong and defective but, what is worse, morally inferior, since it now looks like an immense dishonesty toward myself.

Delusions and Dreams in Jensen's Gradiva was so important to Jung that it incorrectly became part of the history of the work that it was written especially for him. It was not. It was written in the summer of 1906, after Freud had read the *Association Studies* but before the two men had begun corresponding in earnest. The work shows Freud handling the same material as Jung—erotic complexes and dreams—in a very stylish vein of his own.

The plot of the novel *Gradiva* involved an archaeologist with an obsessive desire, exacerbated by a dream, to find a woman with the same gait as a woman on a bas-relief dating from ancient times. Through pluck and insight, a young woman, Zoe Bertang, manages to cure the anthropologist of his obsession. The resolution of the story hinges on the fact that Zoe, a companion from childhood, is the real source of the delusion; it is she whom the anthropologist really loves. The climax of the novel involves her bringing the anthropologist to an awareness of this. In his analysis, Freud took the reader through the story pointing out its correspondence with psychoanalytic theories of the dream. He argued that the young heroine's devices were the same as those used in psychoanalysis. (It should be noted that this made the fictional Zoe Bertang the first woman psychoanalyst and the devices of a seduction, albeit a well-meaning one, equivalent to psychoanalytic technique.)

Freud's monograph, like the series it began, marked at once a continuation and a new departure. For Freud, the psychological analysis of literature and culture was an old habit and a ready diversion. In this respect, he was no different from Jung or Bleuler or any other educated man of the period, though of course he had a very distinctive viewpoint. Moreover, insofar as myths and works of fiction were like dreams, that is, creative products with an unconscious source, they seemed ready-made for psychoanalytic investigation. Yet here the methodological footing grew very slippery. With only a few exceptions, Freud's method of decoding dreams as reported in the dream book depended on eliciting the dreamer's associations. But exactly this was impossible with regard to myths and literature. Instead, one had to appeal to the essential reasonableness of the interpretation, no great obstacle for a writer of Freud's talent, but one that any number of his followers, beginning with Franz Riklin, would soon trip over. As for the monograph series itself, it was sponsored by Hugo Heller, prominent Viennese publisher and sometime participant in the Wednesday Night Psychology Club. Heller's confidence in Freud's editorial judgment was important, for it freed Freud from having to rely on the goodwill of Ziehen of Berlin and Löwenfeld of Munich, the editors of the two most popular existing medical monograph series.

The methodological risks inherent in this new form of cultural criticism were not readily apparent in *Gradiva*, though it did occur to Jung that perhaps it might be profitable to contact the author of the novel to see if he would provide biographical information. Apart from that suggestion, however, Jung's praise was uniformly lavish and he even added a thought of his own. In the story, the song of a canary in a cage sets the hero off on a journey to Italy, there to pursue, and resolve, his obsession. Jung seized on the bird to bring in a mythological angle:

> One question which you leave open, and which the critics may pick on, is this: why is the complex in Hanold repressed? Why doesn't he let himself be put on the right track by the song of the canary bird and other perceptions?
>
> The part played by the bird is equally diverting. Howsoever, for understandable reasons you have not pursued the meaning of this symbol any further. Do you know Steinthal's writings on the mythology of the bird?

Heymann Steinthal was one of the leading figures in the psychology of folklore and mythology. The bird reference alludes to various analogical resemblances between the Phoenix of legend, lightning, fire, the rubbing stick used in making fires, and the penis. Jung was suggesting that the bird was a disguised phallic symbol in the novel. What made this suggestion distinctive was that Jung had not gotten it from the novel itself, but from his readings in the psychology of myth. He was assuming that what worked for the primitive myth-making mind also necessarily worked for the unconscious.

Freud was grateful for the praise: ". . . a statement such as yours means more to me than the approval of a whole medical congress; for one thing it makes the approval of future congresses a certainty." As for Jung's suggestion, Freud was happy to keep Jung going in the direction he wanted him to go: "You are right. I have kept silent about the 'bird' for reasons well known to you, out of consideration for the publishers and public, or because of your mollifying influence, as you prefer." Freud went on to suggest that perhaps Jung might himself to make a contribution to the new monograph series and to let Jung in on a surprise: the next edition of *The Psychopathology of Everyday*

Life would contain several of Jung's anecdotes! The mention of the volume, in turn, gave Freud the opportunity to dispose of a delicate matter in the course of a fresh blast at his critics:

First they write as if we had never published a dream analysis, a case history, or an explanation of parapraxis; then, when the evidence is brought to their attention, they say: But that's no proof, that's arbitrary. Just try to show proof to someone who doesn't want to see it! Nothing can be done with logic, about which one might say what Gottfried von Strassburg, rather irreverently I think, says of the ordeal:

"that Christ in his great virtue

is as wavering as a sleeve in the wind"

But just let five or ten years pass and the analysis of "aliquis," which today is not regarded as cogent, will have become cogent, though nothing in it will have changed. There is no help for it but to go on working, avoid wasting too much energy in refutation, and let the fruitfulness of our views combat the sterility of those we are opposing. . . .

But all the same, don't worry, everything will work out all right. You will live to see the day, though I may not. . . . Every time we are ridiculed, I become more convinced than ever that we are in possession of a great idea. In the obituary you will some day write for me, don't forget to bear witness that I was never so much as ruffled by all the opposition.

Jung, and Bleuler before him, had previously singled out the "Aliquis" episode for public praise, so it was only natural for Freud to bring it up. Freud's reference to it becomes daring only if one has pierced the veil of Freud's fictionalization, but that requires that one have detailed information about Freud's habits some seven years earlier, and Jung did not. To be sure, Freud was providing Jung with one final clue. As Stadlen has discovered, the line of poetry quoted in Freud's letter deals with a scene from *Tristan* in which evasive testimony under oath goes unpunished by God (hence Christ is said to waver). The analogy to "Aliquis" is precise, for what makes the testimony evasive is not the content, but the fact that it involves a disguise: Tristan has been impersonating another man and Isolde's testimony hides the fact that the two characters are really one. In any event, if Jung had broken the code of Freud's disguise in the "Aliquis" episode, and connected it with his own conversation with Minna Bernays two and a half months earlier, he now gave no indication of it. Instead, in his letter of 30 May 1907 he went back to *Gradiva*, and after that to his own rather startling plans:

> In my entourage *Gradiva* is being read with delight. The women understand you by far the best and usually at once. Only the "psychologically" educated have blinkers before their eyes. . . .
>
> . . . My plan, which has Bleuler's vigorous support, is to affiliate to the Clinic a laboratory for psychology, as a more or less independent institute of which I would be appointed director. Then I would be independent, freed from the shackles of the Clinic, and able at last to work as I want. Once in this position, I would try to get the chair for psychiatry separated from the running of the Clinic. . . . As I have seen from my recent dreams, this change has its—for you—transparent "metapsychological-sexual" background, holding out the promise of pleasurable feelings galore. Anyone who knows your science has veritably eaten of the tree of paradise and become clairvoyant.

To be sure, Jung had most certainly *not* gotten Bleuler's approval for part two of his scheme—getting the chair of psychiatry reassigned. To put it bluntly, this part of his plan was treacherous insofar as Bleuler was concerned. It was also decidedly unrealistic since the cantonal authorities would never allow such a separation of functions. But that part of Jung's plan lay far in the future; the source of his current excitement at the prospect of finally escaping the walls of the Burghölzli plainly lay elsewhere.

Freud's reply is not extant. Jung found it encouraging: "The remark in your last letter that we can 'enjoy our riches' is admirable. I rejoice every day in *your* riches and live from the crumbs that fall from the rich man's table." By this time, Jung's excitement was carrying over into his clinical work, for his letter went on to give two case reports that were little more than sexual histories. In the midst of all this, Jung paused for a comment: "I'd like to make an amusing picture-book in this style, to be enjoyed only by those who have eaten of the tree of knowledge. The rest would go away empty-handed."

In context, it was just a passing remark. Freud pounced on it:

> A picture-book such as the one you are thinking of would be highly instructive. Above all, it would provide a general view of the

architectonics of the cases. . . . Do you already feel up to a serious struggle for the recognition of our new ideas? If so, the first thing to do would be to start a journal: "for psychopathology and psychoanalysis" you might call it, or more brazenly, just "for psychoanalysis." A publisher can surely be found; the editor can only be yourself, and I hope Bleuler will not decline to join me as a director. So far we have no one else. . . .

Doesn't it tempt you? Think it over!

It would take almost a year for the two men to finally put the suggestion into action, but this was the beginning of the first psychoanalytic journal ever—Jung's "picture-book." A journal specially devoted to psychoanalysis was a far more ambitious undertaking than Freud's newly launched monograph series. Not only would such a journal have to appear in regular issues, but it would have to compare favorably with the numerous existing journals devoted to neurology, psychopathology, hypnosis, sexual studies, and the like. Henceforth, Freud would continue to lobby Jung at every opportunity to begin such a journal.

There was a great irony attending Jung's almost instantaneous elevation to the position of scientific "son and heir," in Binswanger's phrase. There was nothing yet to inherit. Jung would soon discover what other favorite sons have learned to their chagrin: if he wanted one day to take over the family business, he would have to build it first. The personal relationship between himself and Freud was not the only order of business here. Freud also had very definite organizational plans—the journal was only the first item—and these were surprisingly ambitious. Indeed, even now, Freud was considering what he might do to reorganize the Wednesday Night Psychology Club into a more official organization that might be formally under his control. To put it simply, Freud saw in Jung something more than a friend.

Jung spent June keeping Freud informed about his cases. He wrote: "It is amusing to see how the female outpatients go about diagnosing each other's erotic complexes although they have no insight into their own." He was also making trips to other cities. In Geneva, he found that Claparède was already at work trying to absorb Freud. In Paris, he found Janet disappointingly ill-informed and Babinski's *traitement par isolement* "a very bad *blague.*" Jung's excitement at having "eaten of the tree of paradise" had begun to reach manic proportions. While in Paris, he struck up a conversation with an attractive German-American lady at a party and, out of the clear blue sky, suggested to her that her dislike of black coffee was related to a desire to get pregnant. His wife seems to have been alarmed by the breach of etiquette. She subsequently commented, "I am going to write a psychotherapeutic handbook for gentlemen."

Freud continued to be pleased with Jung's reports. He had been worried that the "Vienna complex might have to share the available cathexis with a Paris complex." In this, Freud had misread the signs: it was not Jung's theoretical allegiance that he should have been worried about; it was Jung's emotional stability.

FLIGHT OF IDEAS

JUNG'S LETTER of 6 July 1907 began, "Would you mind my boring you with some personal experiences?" It then launched into a most uncritical telling of the story of the German-American lady, the one who was told point-blank over coffee that she wanted to get pregnant. It closed with a nutty passage introduced like a stage show, "Now for a bit of historical mysticism!" The mysticism involved a series of analogies between Freud, Mesmer, and Gall (the founder of phrenology) on the one hand, and the various free cities of Germany on the other. In between the lady coffee drinker and the historical mysticism came two case reports. One involved a woman with pathetically deep concerns about her anus—"what a frightful tussle it was until the whole story was out." The other, surprisingly, involved Spielrein:

> An hysterical patient told me that a verse from a poem by Lermontov was continually going round in her head. The poem is about a prisoner whose sole companion is a bird in a cage. The prisoner is animated only by *one* wish: sometime in his life, as his noblest deed, to give some creature its freedom. He opens the cage and lets his beloved bird fly out. What is the patient's greatest wish? "Once in my life I would like to help someone to perfect freedom through psychoanalytic treatment." In her dreams she is condensed with me. She admits that actually her greatest wish is to have a child by me who would fulfill all her unfulfillable wishes. For that purpose I would naturally have to let "the bird out" first. (In Swiss-German we say: "Has your birdie whistled?")
>
> A pretty little chain, isn't it? Do you know Kaulbach's pornographic picture: "Who Buys Love-gods?" (Winged phalli looking like cocks, getting up to all sorts of monkey-tricks with the girls.)

Jung gave Freud no indication that this was the same patient whose childhood anal masturbation he had discussed in his letter of the previous October. (Though Adler's presentation during Jung's recent visit to Vienna had constituted a provocation to describe her case, Jung did not discuss Spielrein in all his many hours of conversations with Freud.) Jung also gave Freud no hint that this was the same patient featured in his "ruefulness-faithfulness" complex in Binswanger's paper on the galvanic reflex. Yet that paper was about to appear in Forel and Vogt's prestigious *Journal für Psychologie und Neurologie* and in the very same letter Jung flagged its appearance for Freud while making a joke of it: "You will then see that you too have absorbed the secrets of the galvanometer. Your associations are indeed excellent."

Plainly, Jung's excitement had passed all reasonable bounds. Freud's response was immediate:

> I am writing to you—briefly and in haste—in order to catch you before you leave and wish you a period of rest from mental effort. It will do you good.

Freud's letter went on to give his summer address and ask that Jung stay in touch over the vacation. It also inquired about a Dr. Abraham who had been writing. Jung had not known the Burghölzli first assistant had started his own correspondence with Freud. This information, coupled with Freud's express concern about Jung's state of mind, was sufficiently sobering that Jung did not write back for over a month. After giddiness, silence. And, luckily, three weeks of compulsory military service. When Jung finally did write again, he was full of apprehension about his upcoming Amsterdam address, i.e., the gladiatorial duel with Aschaffenburg on "Modern Theories of Hysteria," set for the first week in September.

Freud decided to encourage his wavering new friend. On 18 August he wrote:

> Don't despair . . . Your lecture in Amsterdam will be a milestone in history and after all it is largely for history that we work. What you call the hysterical element in your personality, your need to impress and influence people, the very quality that so eminently equips you to be a teacher and guide, will come into its own even if you make no concessions to the current fashions in opinion. And when you have injected your own personal leaven into the ferment-

ing mass of my ideas in still more generous measure, there will be no further difference between your achievement and mine.

Jung had been less than bold in his published reply to Aschaffenburg. Now, as he informed Freud by return post, he had the additional burden of having accepted the sexual theory: ". . . I have unpleasant presentiments, for it is no small thing to be defending *such* a position before *such* a public." In fact, Jung wanted to know from Freud just how important he thought sexuality was vis-à-vis the emotions in determining complexes. This topic—Freud baldly announced that ideas like Bleuler's "ego" and "affectivity" were so much "surface psychology"—took up the next round of letters. But with only two days remaining before Jung's address, Freud got off one last word of encouragement:

> Whether you have been or will be lucky or unlucky, I do not know; but now of all times I wish I were with you, taking pleasure in no longer being alone and, if you are in need of encouragement, telling you about my long years of honourable but painful solitude, which began after I cast my first glance into the new world, about the indifference and incomprehension of my closest friends, about the terrifying moments when I myself thought I had gone astray and was wondering how I might still make my misled life useful to my family, about my slowly growing conviction, which fastened itself to the interpretation of dreams as to a rock in a stormy sea, and about the serene certainty which finally took possession of me and bade me wait until a voice from the unknown multitude should answer mine. That voice was yours; for I know now that Bleuler also came to me through you. Thank you for that, and don't let anything shake your confidence, you will witness our triumph and share in it.

The Amsterdam Congress's section on "Modern Theories of Hysteria" on 4–5 September 1907 was not an august occasion. Jung bungled his address badly, mistiming the length of his speech, and became angry and flustered when the chairman insisted he stop after the allotted time. On the second day, during the discussion, Jung did not speak at all. Aschaffenburg for his part marred his participation with slips of the tongue which revealed his own conflicts about which side he should be on. Moreover, in his address he related with a great deal of self-righteousness how he had forbidden a patient under his care to discuss her sexual complexes. The other participants did not cover themselves with glory, either. Janet, easily the most prominent figure at the conference, had nothing more edifying to say about Freudian theory than that it sounded like a "bad joke."

In his follow-up reports on the occasion to Freud, Jung resorted to vitriol as a cover for his embarrassment over a poor showing. He would not send Freud a copy of his address as "it still needs a bit of polishing." Actually, the finished version, "The Freudian Theory of Hysteria," was reasonably argued and perhaps more forthright than Jung had been in person. It did repeat Jung's earlier, and unconvincing, sleight of hand whereby Freud's findings applied to "an indefinitely large number of cases of hysteria." Freud's method, meanwhile, was described essentially in terms of reeducation, with an explicit parallel made to Dubois's method of persuasion. Jung also continued to take the high road with regard to sexual symbolism:

> The public can forgive Freud least of all for his sexual symbolism. In my view he is really easiest to follow here, because this is just where mythology, expressing the fantasy-thinking of all races, has prepared the ground in the most instructive way. I would only mention the writings of Steinthal in the 1860's, which prove the existence of a widespread sexual symbolism in the mythological records and the history of language. I also recall the eroticism of our poets and their allegorical or symbolical expressions. No one who considers this material will be able to conceal from himself that there are uncommonly far-reaching and significant analogies between the Freudian symbolisms and the symbols of poetic fantasy in individuals and in whole nations.

For the most part, however, the lecture was composed of a review of Freud's development since the time of Breuer, culminating in a lucid restatement of the theory of the "Dora" case and of the *Three Essays*, both of which were explicitly discussed. And for good measure, Jung provided a case report, analyzed according to Freudian principles, which displayed all the theoretically significant hallmarks beginning with an infantile perversion. According to Jung's summary, the infantile fantasies returned in force in adolescence with disastrous consequences for the patient's attraction to a young man:

> When real sexual demands are made, requiring the transference of libido to the love-object, all the perverse fantasies are transferred to him. . . . Her libido exhausted itself in struggling against her

feelings of defence, which grew ever stronger, and which then produced the symptoms. Thus Freud can say that the symptoms represent nothing but the sexual activity of the patient.

It was probably bad tactics on Jung's part that for his case report he
had selected a woman with markedly primitive symptoms (anal masturbation, defecation and beating fantasies). And it was most surely
bad manners. For the woman was Spielrein, who was then about to
enter her third year of medical school. One can only imagine what she
felt when she found out. (She subsequently wrote a thoughtful, detailed
critique.)

Spielrein was still the patient Jung knew best and this by itself
might account for his using her in his address. Moreover, as we shall
see in the next chapter, the two had lately been very much at loggerheads over Jung's recent interpretations, so it is possible that an element of spite may have been involved. Jung's motives aside, however,
what stands out in retrospect is his circumspection. He described neither his initial treatment of the young woman nor any of his most
recent interventions. Matters were getting terribly complicated for
Jung, both professionally and personally. Here he was at an important,
nay historic, conference and he was reporting, most uncomfortably,
not his own ideas, but Freud's. And in making this report he was
abstracting the erotic history of a young woman who already meant a
good deal to him personally. Jung's Freudianism was dividing into a
public and a private version. Psychologically, Jung was nearly back to
where he had started, with an outer and inner self, and no easy way
to reconcile the two.

A JEW IN GERMANY

THE AMSTERDAM address, despite Jung's awkwardness and despite
the audience's reaction, was indeed a historic occasion, for it established Jung as Freud's most important ally. To Freud's credit as an
organizer, he knew immediately what Jung might be worth. While
Jung was speaking, Freud was busy dissolving and re-forming his own
Wednesday Night Psychology Club. Ostensibly this was merely a formality designed to allow people to withdraw gracefully if they so chose.
In actuality, it established that the society was Freud's to dissolve. It
was the first step in consolidating his control in preparation for more
detailed negotiations with the Zurich school.

Karl Abraham was the third member of the Zurich school, after Eitingon and Jung, to fashion his own personal connection with Freud. Abraham was not a likely candidate for psychoanalytic stardom. His first psychoanalytic paper, sent to Freud in June, was a well-intentioned effort to extend Freudian theory to dementia praecox patients, but unfortunate in that it made the mistake of endorsing the seduction theory. In the initial phase of their correspondence, Freud had tried to set him right about this, but had been too gentle in an effort to be gracious. The result was that Abraham's second analytic paper, just now going to press, would repeat the same mistake. Hardly an auspicious beginning. But Abraham had three things going for him: he was a Zurich-trained psychiatrist; he rather liked intramural politics; and he was willing to open up shop in Berlin. In early October, Abraham announced his plan in a letter to Freud:

> I intend to leave Zurich in about a month . . . The reasons are not far to seek. As a Jew in Germany and as a foreigner in Switzerland, I have not been promoted beyond a junior position in the past seven years. I shall therefore try to set up in practice in Berlin as a specialist for nervous and mental diseases. . . . You will already have guessed why I am writing to you. I should like to ask for your recommendation, should you ever have the opportunity of suggesting a doctor to undertake psychological treatment in Berlin. . . . I should . . . also like to ask your permission to turn to you for advice if necessary. I should be most beholden to you for your kind support in both these respects.

Freud's reply of 8 October 1907 showed that he understood the message:

> I quickly suppressed the first impulse of regret I felt on reading your letter. No harm can come to a young man like you from being forced into the open *au grand air,* and the fact that things will be more difficult for you as a Jew will have the effect, as it has with all of us, of bringing out the best of which you are capable. That you have my sympathy and best wishes in setting out on your new path is obvious, and if possible I should like to offer you more than that. If my close friendship with Dr. W. Fliess still existed, the way would be smoothed for you, but now unfortunately that road is completely blocked. During the past year I have repeatedly been in the position

of having to tell patients from Germany I was sorry I knew no-one
there to whom I could recommend them, but if such cases recur this
year I shall know what to do. If my reputation in Germany increases, it will certainly be useful to you, and if I may refer to you
as my pupil and follower—you do not seem to me to be a man
to be ashamed of that description—I shall be able to back you
vigorously.

The deal had been struck. The two would meet for the first time in
December of 1907. In private, Abraham continued to do battle with
Freud's ideas and with his own "resistances." But, as he would put it
in a letter to Eitingon, when Freud told him personally that he had
three grades of "followers" and that Abraham was of the highest grade
in that he accepted the libido theory, Abraham found the praise "very
gratifying." Perhaps equally important in the months ahead was the
fact that Abraham also knew how to respond in kind whenever Freud
sought to traffic in their mutual Jewishness.

Much has been written about Freud's own identity as a Jew. It is
a difficult, complex topic. Here, basing myself principally on the analysis of Dennis Klein, let me say only that there were two sides to it.
In Freud's youth, the heroes of Jewish schoolboys were the ministers
of the Austrian empire. The political allegiance was with the quiet
Parliamentary revolution of the Liberal party; the cultural allegiance
was with Germany; the ultimate goal socially was assimilation. In the
period of increased anti-Semitism that began in the late 1880s, Freud
only very gradually came to feel any loyalty to the new, noncosmo-
politan and unassimilated Jews streaming in from the eastern portion
of the Empire. But at the same time he still envisioned a career that
was international in scope, a career in which his Jewishness played no
role at all. It was only in 1897, when he believed that his professorship
was being blocked for anti-Semitic reasons, that Freud joined the B'nai
B'rith and turned inward toward his roots. Yet, when first Bleuler and
then Jung happened on the scene, Freud allowed his participation
with the B'nai B'rith to wane. Freud had not the time to be more deeply
involved, for one thing, and for another, he was again entertaining
ideas of an international career.

For Freud, Jung meant a new, Gentile friend but also old, assimi-
lative and cosmopolitan hopes. The moment Karl Abraham broke
ranks and offered his own covenant, these hopes took on the ambivalent underside inherent in Freud's double identity. While Jewish,

Abraham could not be confused with any of the "gang" in Vienna. He was a well-trained psychiatrist from the "Zurich school" and ready to make a go of it in Berlin, the very center of north German medicine. Freud did not find him personally all that congenial, and in correspondence he never romanced him the way he continued to court Jung, but then, that apparently wasn't necessary. Abraham thus potentially constituted a double complication for the Freud-Jung relationship. Insofar as he was Jewish, and more than willing to criticize his former Zurich colleagues for their Gentile "mysticism," he was inserting the issue of religious differences into the picture. Then, too, if he proved to be a success in Berlin, he would simultaneously complicate the organizational picture: Jung might be the "son and heir," but Abraham could well claim his own place in the line of succession— and in whatever formal institutions came into being.

There was, ominously, yet a third complication, more personal in nature. The fact was that Karl Abraham did not much like Carl Jung.

CHAPTER 7

The Science of Fairy Tales

In Psychiatry and the related sciences there has lately broken out a struggle for and against the Freudian theories. I count myself fortunate to be able, by means of such beautiful, inviting material as fairy tales, to bear a weapon in this conflict.

—Franz Riklin, *Wishfulfillment and Symbolism in Fairy-Tales*, 1907

FRANZ RIKLIN'S *Wishfulfillment and Symbolism in Fairy-Tales* appeared as the second number of Freud's *Papers on Applied Psychology* in early 1908. Riklin, who had his own correspondence going with Freud, was well known as Jung's collaborator and as director of the Rheinau asylum. Publishing Riklin's book represented a small but significant step forward for Freud. That said, Riklin's volume was quite slim, dubiously argued, and frankly apologetic about its shortcomings. The difficulty was that no matter how diligently Riklin applied himself to the scholarly literature on folktales—he was in personal communication with Otto Stoll, the Zurich folklorist—he ultimately had no interpretive rationale other than that "the human psyche . . . is always still a fairy poetess." Taking his cue from Freud's book on dreams, Riklin concentrated on ferreting out sexual symbols, but his justification for identifying them as such was the bald assertion, twice repeated, that their meaning was clear to "the initiated." The methodological problems inherent in applying psychoanalytic formulations to literature, problems which Freud had so skillfully evaded in *Gradiva*, had begun to show.

Riklin did have some instructive points to make. The star of the book was the familiar figure of the Frog Prince. Riklin interpreted him as a symbol of the ambivalence of the virgin toward male sexuality. That is to say, the animal side of sexuality, which invites loathing and disgust, was transformed in stories of this kind into an idealized love for a prince. Both repression and splitting into positive and negative images were involved. Moving outward from this theme, Riklin went on to discuss various disguises for the motifs of insemination and birth, and also various portrayals of infantile egoism, typically manifest in the form of antagonism toward the father. He also proffered an interpretation of the familiar sleeping potions of fairy tales as symbolic of romantic introversion wherein love makes one oblivious to the outside world. All this in context appeared at least plausible, and in singling out the Frog Prince for attention Riklin had tumbled to something enduring.

But, gradually, Riklin lost his way and the discussion degenerated into a phantasmagoria of ever wilder stories culled from cultures around the globe coupled with ever more tentative interpretations. Thus, a princess had her legs chopped off by a giant, and Riklin asked in parentheses, "Abasia [hysterical dizziness] dream motive?" A wicked minister, who was actually the heroine's father bent on incestuous designs, ended up confined to a chair with iron bands constricting his chest, and Riklin's parentheses grew more uncertain: "Anxiety? Bad conscience?" When a magic golden pike tore three nets, twice over, Riklin asked about the nets, "Symbol for the hymen?" Meanwhile, though Riklin didn't realize it, he undercut his use of Freudian dream theory by bringing in stories in which delightfully there was no disguise whatsoever regarding the incest motif. Freud's argument in the dream book had allowed that certain dream symbols were truly universal, but by far the bulk of Freud's interpretations had emphasized rather how symbols served the purposes of disguise and thus helped the dream-wish evade censorship. But what could possibly be disguised in a tale in which the princess married her father and both lived happily ever after?

Riklin's topic was enormously important. Mythology and folklore occupied a place of importance in German culture quite unlike anything in English. When German men of letters first freed themselves from Christianity, they turned to philosophizing for their moral justification. But for their aesthetic justification they turned to the Greeks, whom they profoundly misunderstood. A nativist reaction then ensued and the indigenous products of the German folk soul soon became celebrated while men like Herder and the brothers Grimm were elevated to the heights of literary greatness. The native German folktales and myths were cherished both for their intrinsic value and as the carrier of nationalistic hopes for a people politically fragmented until as late as 1870. Thus a mythological motif might serve as the inspiration for individual fantasy, as an emblem for nationalistic hopes, as the window dressing for the latest racist theory of Aryan supremacy, or as the raw material for a scholarly enterprise in the emerging fields of philology, mythological studies proper, or what was then called *Völkerpsychologie*, the study of national character as it had evolved over the ages. The study of mythology was a field where the highest level of intellectuality might comfortably coexist with the most deeply felt sentiments. It was likewise an area in which a new scholarly contribution might have immediate and wide-ranging impact on the general educated public.

Riklin's book touched off a stampede. Karl Abraham thought he saw a better way to proceed and managed to get his own *Dreams and Myth* into print the very next year as the fourth number of Freud's monograph series. (Jung's lecture to laymen about the new directions in psychiatry, *The Content of the Psychoses*, was the third number.) Rank weighed in immediately after with *The Myth of the Birth of the Hero*, number five in the series, and the race to be the first to offer the definitive psychoanalytic statement on mythology was on. Methodological caution was thrown to the winds—the topic was too important to wait.

THE SIEGFRIED COMPLEX

SPIELREIN, OF COURSE, knew Riklin from her days as a patient doing work-therapy in the psychology laboratory, and it is possible, even likely, that she learned of his study while it was still in progress. But her own interest in mythology lay not in psychoanalytic reinterpretations of it. Rather, as with many young people of that time and milieu, she found in myths and folktales emblems for her own deeper strivings.

As we have seen in the previous two chapters, in January 1907 and again in July, Spielrein had been the occasion for Jung's various ruminations about his own complexes and for his flights of fancy. Yet, properly speaking, we have thus far only heard Jung's side of the story. In fact, neither Jung's confessions to Binswanger in January, nor his giddy letter to Freud in July, at all capture the real flavor of Spielrein's emotional state nor of what she was confiding to him during this period. Accordingly, here let us backtrack and take in Spielrein's side of the story, so far as it can be known from her own retrospective accounts.

A decisive change occurred in Spielrein's spirits following her sessions with Jung in October 1906 in which they reviewed her childhood memories of her brother and her father, and her sitting on her heel. Putting her beating complex temporarily behind her, Spielrein began to envision for herself a career as a psychiatrist, as someone who could do for others what she felt Jung had done for her. Jung had become her hero and her model. Her "ego complex" having been strengthened through the therapeutic rapport, Spielrein's renewed self-confidence was paralleled by a change in her dreams. Siegfried appeared.

Siegfried is the greatest figure in Teutonic mythology, the child of the hero Siegmund by his sister Sieglinde, the slayer of the dragon Fafner, the rescuer of the fallen Valkyrie Brünnhilde—and the subject of so many widely varying folktales that a scholar might well ask which "Siegfried" Spielrein had in mind. Luckily, Spielrein subsequently made it clear, in a draft of a letter written in the late spring of 1909:

> It was Wagner who planted the demon in my soul with such terrifying clarity. I shall omit the metaphors, since you might laugh at the extravagance of my emotion. The whole world became a melody for me: the earth sang, the trees sang, and every twig on every tree.

Spielrein had long been musically inclined, and Wagner's operas had been among her favorites. In putting together his famous four-opera cycle, *The Ring of the Nibelungs,* which had premiered in Munich in 1869, Wagner had adapted the Siegfried legend to his own artistic purposes. In his version of the story, there is first an incestuous union between the twin brother and sister, Siegmund and Sieglinde, who are children of Wotan. Subsequently, at the instigation of his wife, Fricka, and against his own wishes, Wotan allows Siegmund to be killed, but Sieglinde is aided by Brünnhilde and escapes long enough to give birth to the love-child Siegfried. As a punishment, Brünnhilde loses her immortality and is placed in a deep sleep surrounded by a ring of fire, destined to become the lover of the first man who penetrates the flames. Siegfried is raised by the evil smith Mime, and grows up without knowing what fear is. In time, Siegfried slays both the dragon Fafner and the treacherous Mime; thereafter, he rescues the Valkyrie Brünn-hilde and they fall in love. In the final opera, however, he is be-witched by a potion to forget Brünnhilde, whom he delivers as a wife to Gunther, while he himself is murdered by the evil Hagen. All of this narrative is set against a rich cosmological and symbolic backdrop in which the three races of gods, dwarfs, and giants are equally en-snared in an accursed struggle for supremacy through possession of the Ring. The destinies of the various human heroes have from the begin-ning been enmeshed in this cosmological struggle. Thus, at the end, Siegfried's death and Brünnhilde's fury, which leads her ultimately to sacrifice herself so that she may be joined with Siegfried in death, set into motion the general destruction (Götterdämmerung) of the final opera, *Twilight of the Gods,* in which the corrupt old order finally per-ishes and a new age begins. Wagner's is a rich, psychologically com-plex tapestry, with the themes of incest and betrayal made palatable by their juxtaposition with innocence and the heroic. Throughout the opera the antinomies of duty versus true passion and of love versus power are invoked in ever more complex embodiments.

The impact of the saga for Spielrein seems to have resided in the fact that though Siegfried is a hero he is also essentially an orphan and an innocent, one who has needed the initial, self-sacrificial protection of a woman (Brünnhilde) whom he then subsequently rescues and loves, all this in the context of a general sense that the younger gen-eration, who are capable of true love, have been sacrificed by the gods, who are hypocritically bound by duty. Apart from an occasional men-tion in a diary Spielrein kept during the fall of 1910, there are two main sources of information about Spielrein's "Siegfried complex": letters she wrote to Jung in the years 1917–1919 and drafts of letters she wrote to an interested third party in May and June 1909. (At this time, letters were routinely copied over before being sent.) The lattermost account, chronologically the closest in time to the actual events, is the most vivid, but is unfortunately fragmentary. The following passage is typical:

> Thus Siegfried came into being; he was supposed to become the greatest genius, because Dr. Jung's image as a descendant of the gods floated before me, and from childhood on I had had a premo-nition that I was not destined for a mundane life. I felt flooded with energy, all nature spoke directly to me, one song after another took shape in me, one fairy tale after another.

The feeling that a great destiny awaited her was tied up in Spielrein's imagination with a sense that she must make an equally great "sacrifice." She was twenty-one years old at the time.

It scarcely required the new methods of psychoanalysis to interpret the essence of the sudden transformation. It had well been understood right along in the medical literature that with the upsurge of sexuality in puberty, especially in hysterical women, there was likely to occur a triad of exalted self-consciousness, religious preoccupations, and a yearning for self-sacrifice. It was also well known that all that was usually needed to resolve these superficially mysterious "symptoms" was that they attach themselves to a suitable young man. There would be sacrifice enough in having his children, he would himself take the place of the gods, and the temporary overflow of self-consciousness would give way, with maturity, to the poised, self-aware charms of a lady who knew her worth.

Accordingly, we don't really know how naïve Spielrein allowed herself to be when Wagner's Siegfried theme first rose from the unconscious orchestra, but she seems to have been clear enough that Jung was at the center of the complex. At the time, Spielrein was ambiguously both Jung's friend and his patient. Whichever, she did not fail to bring her new complex to his attention. Contrary to his published policy of ruthless disillusionment, he treated her gently:

> When I confessed this complex to Dr. Jung for the first time, he treated me with tenderest friendship, like a father, if you will. He admitted to me that from time to time he, too, had to consider such matters in connection with me (i.e., his affinity with me and the possible consequences), that such wishes are not alien to him, but the world happens to be arranged in such a way, etc., etc. This talk calmed me completely, since my *ambitia* was not wounded and the thought of his great love made me want to keep him perfectly "pure."

Though the onset of Spielrein's "Siegfried complex" cannot be dated precisely, it is likely that the above scene took place at the end of 1906 or the very beginning of 1907. That is to say, it was probably this scene, in which Jung reassured the young woman by confessing that he occasionally entertained similar thoughts while cautioning her about "possible consequences," that led to Jung's subsequently feeling "threatened" at the time of Binswanger's first experiment in January

1907. Upon reflection, Jung seems to have realized that he had said more than it was perhaps wise to say. In any case, his initial strategy seems to have been to encourage Spielrein to keep her love for her Siegfried perfectly pure; Jung was still acting on his stated principle that the therapeutic rapport should involve something more than mere sexual attraction.

There was, however, another important phenomenon entailed in Spielrein's "Siegfried complex," namely an ability to produce "prophetic dreams." It was, of course, a common folk belief, which dated to antiquity, that dreams could tell the future. Freud would no doubt smile at such a claim—he specifically contested the prophetic powers of dreams in *Gradiva*—but in the twist Spielrein gave things, psychological sophistication was no protection against her personal brand of mysticism. For besides telling the future, she could also tell the hidden complexes of other people, most especially Jung. For example, among her "prophetic" dreams were some which foretold the unveiling of Jung's own secret wish to have a son, wishes that he had so far kept from her but which he had indeed revealed to Binswanger.

To the modern reader, the evidence for Spielrein's clairvoyance is quite equivocal, but she manifestly believed in it. Once during this period Jung became irritated with her claims and challenged her to crack his diary; she opened it right at the page where he described his cousin the medium coming to his room at night dressed in a long white robe. Thereafter Jung himself seems to have been inclined to give it some credence. Spielrein wrote in another of the 1909 letter-drafts, "I was able to read Dr. Jung's thoughts both when he was nearby and *à distance,* and he could do the same with me." Reading thoughts at a distance was one of the things that had interested Jung in the occult back in his college days. In short, in its original incarnation, Spielrein's "Siegfried complex" seems to have been an innocent mixture of romanticism and idealization, tailored in such a way that it would capture Jung's attention. It was not destined to stay that way.

THE SEXUAL BASIS OF RAPPORT

IN THE AFTERMATH of his trip to Vienna in March of 1907, Jung began to investigate the sexual complexes of his patients with renewed seriousness. Jung's handling of Spielrein's "Siegfried complex" changed accordingly. Specifically, he began vigorously interpreting Siegfried as the child she wanted to give him; equally as vigorously, she resisted the imputation. As she much later put it:

Without your instruction I would have believed, like all laymen, that I was dreaming of Siegfried, since I am always dwelling on heroic fantasies, whether in conscious expressions or in the form of a "heroic psychic attitude." I am, and most especially always was, somewhat mystical in my leanings; I violently resisted the interpretation of Siegfried as a real child, *and on the basis of my mystical tendencies* I would have simply thought that a great and heroic destiny awaited me, that I had to sacrifice myself for the creation of something great. How else could I interpret those dreams in which my father or grandfather blessed me and said, "A great destiny awaits you, my child"?

Discussions about the real meaning of Siegfried continued throughout the late spring of 1907, a time when Jung was passing around his copy of *Gradiva*—"the women understand you by far the best"—and secretly plotting his escape from the Burghölzli, so as better to taste the fruit from Freud's "tree of paradise." The two, Jung and Spielrein, made an increasingly mad pair, with her continuing to insist upon her mystical destiny while he basked in his new sexual understanding of what she really wanted. Jung's inner reverie climaxed in the scene reported in his manic letter to Freud of 6 July 1907, wherein Spielrein's secret identification with him, her wish to set someone free through psychoanalysis, and her wish to have his son all swirled around in his imagination with images of "birdies" and pornographic "love-gods."

Spielrein's contribution to that occasion is lost, but from other documents we know that she most often dreamed of "Siegfried" in the form of symbols, such as a candle that Jung gave her or as a "book that grew with colossal speed," symbols which "only yielded 'Siegfried' as a real child upon being subjected to analysis." Sometimes, too, she herself appeared as Siegfried in disguise—"in her dreams she is merged with me"—while at other times, Siegfried was replaced altogether by "Aoles," a wandering "Aryan-Semitic minstrel."

The overall irony of the situation, in early July of 1907, was that Jung was sexualizing a situation which by Spielrein's lights was already well sublimated. Jung's wife was not the only person who wanted to write a "psychotherapeutic handbook for gentlemen."

AFTER THE publication of the Carotenuto documents in 1982, a second cache of Spielrein's personal and professional papers was discovered in the family archive of Edouard Claparède in Geneva. Included in this batch was a folio some twenty pages in length written in German in Spielrein's hand. It would appear to have been a journal of sorts except that, first, it regularly addresses itself to another person—Jung—and, second, it specifically identifies itself as a "letter" at one point and asks that Jung return it so that she may keep it for reference. It may be that we have here all or part of a "letter" alluded to in the following passage from the Carotenuto documents:

> That he could say such a thing to me, who had always been so proud, who had defended myself in letters against every impertinence (one even ran to 40 pages), who had finally simply been forced as a patient to confess my love for him and had warned him countless times against too thorough an analysis, lest the monster get in, since my conscious desires are much too compelling and demand fulfillment.

The folio is divided into three parts. From internal evidence, the third part was not written until the spring of 1908, while the first two parts appear to have been written during her summer vacation in 1907. What we are dealing with in the first two parts, then, are Spielrein's own contemporaneous reflections during the summer of 1907 while Jung was preparing for his Amsterdam address. It is an extremely important document.

The folio begins dramatically. In an almost epigrammatic introduction entitled "Two Speakers," Spielrein puts the reader on notice, in prose more polished than anything that will follow, that the journal constitutes an inner psychological dialogue that represents a continuation internally of her recent talks with Jung. Part One proper begins with the impressive title "The Theory of Transformation and its Corollaries." It contains Spielrein's answer to the point of view Jung had lately been pushing in her therapy. All mental life, in her Herbartian view, is governed by two fundamental tendencies: the power of persistence of the complexes and the instinct of transformation. The latter, which subsumes the sexual instinct but is not identical with it, seeks to transform the complex by attracting to it new meanings. In what are the journal's most difficult passages, Spielrein attempts to interrelate the instinct for transformation to "the instinct for species preservation." She is a mixture of Janet, Bleuler, and received medical wisdom. Every complex strives to realize itself, in her view, strives to become autonomous. One naturally seeks to discover similar complexes in other people since this leads to a feeling of having objectified the complex and thus of having gained mastery over it. However, sharing complexes also leads to a feeling of sympathy between the two people and this, in turn, since it entails an implicit feeling of similarity, can generate sexual attraction. Explicitly, she states that this sort of unintended attraction can occur between a doctor and patient.

About sexuality itself, however, Spielrein has a further observation, one worthy of Schopenhauer: since it operates at the level of the species and depends only on a racial similarity or identification, sexuality, unlike love, is ultimately antagonistic to the differentiated individual. For this reason it is felt to be something "demonic" and "destructive." Accordingly, sexuality is typically accompanied by its own resistances as the individual seeks to preserve what he has achieved by way of differentiation. The resistances can be seen even in children who do not yet know to what the sexual feeling will lead. Still, one can distinguish this sense of the demonic or destructive from the wish to make a great "sacrifice" for the sake of a cause so often seen in young people—here Spielrein is taking issue with received medical wisdom—for the latter entails the instinct for transformation as well. Even in the act of copulation, moreover, part of the sexual instinct is still necessarily repressed, held at bay by those fragments of the complexes transformed in the intimate relationship; otherwise, she asserts, the sexual act would degenerate into murder and martyrdom. Here, to be sure, we have a revival of a personal theme—beating fantasies and masochistic excitement—but Spielrein's prose gives little hint of it.

Part Two continues the discussion, and Spielrein's vigorous German only grows stonger. The dissolution of a complex through empathic sharing (with attendant sexual attraction) is but one of the avenues open to the instinct for transformation. Others are "art" and "science," both ways of objectifying complexes; art in particular allows complexes "to express themselves to the utmost." Spielrein insists, however, that the common denominator between art and intimacy is the instinct for transformation, for refashioning the complexes, and not sexuality *per se*. Thus, for example, she says that she no longer loves Jung "in the ideal way" and that "this state is worse than death." She despairs about getting him to understand her: "I have to take an extreme position in regard to you, because you don't admit the possibility of a non-sexual transformation in your enthusiasm for your new theories.''

The following passage forms the conclusion to the second part and clearly addresses itself to the struggle that had lately been going on in their sessions:

> Understand me well; when undertaking to treat hysteria, it's necessary to consider two different things:
>
> No. 1: Do it in such a way that the psychosexual component . . . of the Ego transforms itself (this could be by means of art or through simple [ab]reaction—as you wish); the component would find itself weakened thereby like a phonographic record running down. Furthermore, the feeling having been fulfilled, the psyche doesn't exhaust itself in resistances.
>
> No. 2: More often than it seems, wouldn't it be necessary to hinder the stimulation of the psychosexual component as much as possible. . . . It is dangerous to pay too much attention to the [sexual] complex, to feed it with new representations; an artist can live only in that way—yet even for him there are limits which are beyond his powers. . . .
>
> What concerns me is that with the interruption of my studies my family has put me fully back in the complex again. My desolation is again without limits. Will I get out of it safe and sound?

By this time, her parents were advising Spielrein to take some time off from school. She herself, showing the same insight as Janet and Charcot had before her, knew that she had to get back out of the family if she was to again recover.

A RELIGIOUS CRUSH

JUNG'S UNSTEADINESS at the Amsterdam Congress takes on new meaning in light of Spielrein's "Transformation Journal." The featured patient was, at the time, in open rebellion against the treatment. More, she was bringing to bear a very sophisticated psychological rationale drawn from the best contemporary theory had to offer. Indeed, her position resembled nothing so much as the theory Jung himself had held scarcely a year earlier. Yet, ultimately Spielrein did return to Zurich for the fall semester and she also resumed seeing him. And for his part, Jung continued his correspondence with Freud, while mulling over various organizational ideas of his own.

In historical retrospect, the most one can claim for Spielrein at this particular time is that she was the occasion, and scarcely the only one, for Jung's new style of interpretation. She was not the cause of it. Where Spielrein differed from the other female outpatients was in her intuitive capacity to grasp what was going on in Jung and in her intellectual ability to frame her "resistances" in terms of theory. In this respect, she was tailor-made for Jung as he continued to explore the range of the new interpretive style. But that Jung viewed her case in an altered way, and seemed to enjoy himself while doing it, depended as much on his new friendship with Freud and its relation to his own continuing self-exploration as it did on the unique qualities of the young woman. Indeed, it was in his letters to Vienna that Jung's psychoanalytically transformed second self chiefly put in its appearances.

In his second post-Amsterdam letter, of 11 September 1907, Jung expressed "a long cherished and constantly repressed wish"—to have a photograph of Freud. In his next letter, of 25 September 1907, he expressed his ambivalence toward Eitingon, who had since parlayed his unfortunate visit nine months earlier into a summer excursion with Freud in Florence and Rome; Jung declared Eitingon an "impotent gasbag," but on reflection had to admit that he envied the expatriate Russian his "uninhibited abreaction of the polygamous instinct." In the same letter, Jung also mentioned Otto Gross, assistant at Kraepelin's clinic and son of the criminologist Hanns Gross, and perhaps the only pro-Freudian at the Amsterdam Congress who had acquitted himself well. Gross's views were distinctive. Like Spielrein, he seemed to think that, once made conscious, sexual desires tended to demand expression; unlike Spielrein, he didn't think this such a bad thing. Jung disagreed:

> Dr. Gross tells me that he puts a quick stop to the transference by turning people into sexual immoralists. He says the transference to the analyst and its persistent fixation are mere monogamy symbols and as such symptomatic of repression. The truly healthy state for the neurotic is sexual immorality. Hence he associates you with Nietzsche. It seems to me, however, that sexual repression is a very important and indispensable civilizing factor, even if pathogenic for many inferior people. . . . I feel Gross is going along too far with the vogue for the sexual short-circuit, which is neither intelligent,

nor in good taste, but merely convenient, and therefore anything but a civilizing factor.

Jung's letters also reported on the meetings of a newly founded "Freudian Society of Physicians" in Zurich. Ernest Jones, a young British neurologist who had trailed Jung back to the Burghölzli from Amsterdam, sat in on the second meeting, which Bleuler kicked off with some "priceless doggerel" aimed at Freud's critics, leading Constantin von Monakow, professor of neurology at the University of Zurich, to shrivel in his seat. Afterward, Jones teased von Monakow: "If only his respectable colleagues knew about it [his attendance] they would say he might as well climb the Brocken to attend a Witches' Sabbath."

Jung also continued to report to Freud on patients. His letter of 10 October 1907 asked for supervision about one of them:

> I would like to ask your sage advice about something else. A lady, cured of obsessional neurosis, is making me the object of her sexual fantasies, which she admits are excessive and a torment to her. She realizes that the role I play in her fantasies is morbid, and therefore wants to cut loose from me and repress them. What's to be done? Should I continue the treatment, which on her own admission gives her voluptuous pleasure, or should I discharge her? All this must be sickeningly familiar to you; what do you do in such cases?

Freud's reply, unhappily, does not survive. The case might or might not be Spielrein. Spielrein had resumed her medical studies, but about the only thing we can infer for certain about her relationship to Jung in the fall of 1907 is that she was still talking to him—with no fee charged. That said, the following anecdote from one of her later letter-drafts, with its telltale mention of Freud's visage, may well date from this time:

> For a long time our souls were profoundly akin: for instance, we never discussed Wagner, and then one day I come to him and say that what distinguishes Wagner from previous composers is that his music is profoundly psychological: the moment a certain emotive note occurs, its matching melody appears, and just as the emotive note at first rumbles dimly in the depths when the appropriate situation is evoked, so, too, in Wagner the melody first appears almost unrecognizably among the others, then emerges in full clarity, only

to blend and merge with the others later on, etc. Wagner's music is "plastic music." I liked *Das Rheingold* best, I say. Dr. Jung's eyes fill with tears. "I will show you, I am just writing the very same thing." Now he tells me how Freud sometimes moved him to tears when they thought along the same lines this way. He found . . . [Freud's] face enormously likeable, particularly around the ears, etc. . . . He [Jung], too, always liked *Rheingold* best.

By the end of October, there were even more revelations in Jung's letters to Vienna. Freud had complained about Jung's tardiness in correspondence. Jung defended himself by citing his work load, but he also noted his "self-preservation complex":

Actually—and I confess this to you with a struggle—I have a boundless admiration for you both as a man and a researcher, and I bear you no conscious grudge. So the self-preservation complex does not come from there; it is rather that my veneration for you has something of the character of a "religious" crush. Though it does not really bother me, I still feel it is disgusting and ridiculous because of its undeniable erotic undertone. This abominable feeling comes from the fact that as a boy I was the victim of a sexual assault by a man I once worshipped.

For the record, the "assault" happened in Jung's adolescence, when he was already of fairly imposing size; it was therefore more in the manner of a seduction. In his letter, Jung went on to say how the transferential reactions of his colleagues now struck him as "downright disgusting," singling out Bleuler for special abuse. In his next letter, of 2 November 1907, he stated that he was suffering "all the agonies of a patient in analysis" and went on to speak of a dream he had had while in Vienna that Freud was a very frail old man. Jung proceeded to analyze the dream as a defense against *"your +++ dangerousness!,"* the crosses to ward off the Devil having been borrowed from an earlier letter of Freud's, before going back to Jensen (the author of *Gradiva*) as a topic, invoking, again with emphasis, the *"theme of brother-sister love."* Next he announced his election to the American Society for Psychical Research and confessed that he was again dabbling in "spookery": "Here too your discoveries are brilliantly confirmed."

In short, Jung was still alternately basking in and wrestling with the new sexual vision, and in Freud he had a confidant with whom he could be as unreserved as he could himself manage.

A. A. BRILL was lucky enough to gain the post of Burghölzli assistant left open by Karl Abraham's departure in November of 1907. At his first Grand Rounds, Brill was astonished to see how rapidly the attending physicians disposed of an odd symptom in a post-menopausal woman, i.e., her staining her bedsheet with red wine, which was readily interpreted in terms of her wish that her period would return. Brill was impressed with both the psychological emphasis and the openness with which sexuality was talked about. He was also struck by the general milieu and subsequently wrote the most vivid account we possess of what life was then like at that institution:

> In the hospital the spirit of Freud hovered over everything. Our conversation at meals was frequently punctuated with the word "complex," the special meaning of which was created at that time. No one could make a slip of any kind without immediately being called on to evoke free associations to explain it. It did not matter that women were present—wives and female voluntary interns—who might have curbed the frankness usually produced by free associations. The women were just as keen to discover the concealed mechanisms as their husbands. There was also a Psychoanalytic Circle, which met every month. Some of those who attended were far from agreeing with our views; but despite Jung's occasional impulsive intolerance, the meetings were very fruitful and successful in disseminating Freud's theories.

Like everyone else, Brill was impressed with Jung's "enthusiasm and brilliance." Jung was a doctrinal lion:

> Jung was at that time the most ardent Freudian. . . . Jung brooked no disagreement with Freud's views; impulsive and bright, he refused to see the other side. Anyone who dared doubt what was certainly then new and revolutionary immediately aroused his anger.

The disconcerting paradox was that the more Jung beat the Burghölzli bushes for Freud, the less personal reassurance he got out of him. There is a distinct shift in the tone of the extant Freud-Jung correspondence in the last two months of 1907. In the next letter after confessing his "religious crush" to Freud, Jung, on 8 November 1907, invited Freud to visit him over Christmas, this while reassuring Freud that he had regained his composure: "My old religiosity had secretly found in you a compensating factor which I had to come to terms with eventually, and I was able to do so only by telling you about it." To which Freud replied on 15 November 1907: "What you say of your inner developments sounds reassuring; a transference on a religious basis would strike me as most disastrous; it could end only in apostasy...." At this point Jung, as though trying to prove his worth, wrote that he was brokering the idea of holding a "Congress of Freudian followers" with Sándor Ferenczi, Leopold Stein, and the visiting Jones. It is not clear who first had the idea, but it clearly fell to Jung to organize it and he began to call for papers. Jung also entered into secret negotiations with Claparède and Morton Prince about founding a psychoanalytic journal, to be published either conjointly or amalgamated with Prince's year-old *Journal of Abnormal Psychology*. Freud duly took note of Jung's "magnificent plans," but in the end he did not come to Zurich for Christmas and, worse still, his holiday greetings came along with the unhappy news that Karl Abraham had just visited him in Vienna. The chill did not last long. In his letter of 25 January 1908, Jung was back to open affection:

> I have a sin to confess: I have had your photograph enlarged. It looks marvelous. A few of our circle have acquired copies. So, like it or not, you have stepped into many a quiet study!

If Jung meant to keep his personal relationship with Freud exclusive, he might as well have been commanding the historical tides. On 2 February, Freud had two more visitors to report, Sándor Ferenczi and Leopold Stein, the Hungarian contingent at the Burghölzli.

Jung was silent the first two weeks of February of 1908. His letter of 15 February apologized for it, pleading an attack of the flu, but Jung also wrote mysteriously that "a complex connected with my family played the very devil with me." The rest of his letter was all business; among other things, the plans for the journal were not going well. Now Freud became solicitous. His letter of 17 February addressed Jung simply as "Dear friend." In German, opening and closing salutations are governed by an elaborate etiquette and for that reason are essentially untranslatable. The change in the form of address from "Dear friend and colleague" to "Dear friend"—Freud remarked on it in the body

of the letter as well—was an unmistakable overture for greater intimacy. But at the same time Freud sounded a very peculiar note. After
discussing preparations for Jung's coming Congress for Freudian Psychology, to be held at Salzburg, Freud relaxed into the following theoretical remarks:

> At last I come to science. I have been in contact with a few
> paranoia cases in my practice and can tell you a secret. . . . I have
> regularly encountered a detachment of libido from a homosexual
> component which until then had been normally and moderately
> cathected. . . . My one-time friend Fliess developed a dreadful case
> of paranoia after throwing off his affection for me, which was un-
> doubtedly considerable. I owe this idea to him, i.e., to his behav-
> iour. One must try to learn something from every experience. . . .
> Altogether I have a good many budding and incomplete ideas to tell
> you about. Too bad that we shall not be exactly undisturbed in
> Salzburg!

Everything was wrong with this. First of all, though Jung could not
predict how it was going to go, Freud was announcing that he intended
to write up a theory about paranoia, thus crossing over into what had
heretofore been Jung's and Bleuler's territory, the psychoses. Proposing a policy of "intellectual communism," Freud had already shared
some of his thoughts on the subject with Jung over a year earlier, but
had then let the subject drop after Jung had diplomatically expressed
his dissent by seeming to get everything muddled. Now Freud was
resuming the initiative. Then there was the equation of paranoia with
a split-off homosexual component; whether Freud meant to do so or
not, this stepped rather heavily on the toes of Jung's "religious crush."
That it came in the same letter which began with the "Dear friend"
salutation was potentially bewildering for Jung, all the more so since
there was in fact something like a paranoid streak in Jung himself. We
should note, too, the mention of Fliess and the great peculiarity of a
man theorizing about a former friend to a current one. What Freud
had in mind here was Fliess's conviction that Freud had wanted to kill
him at the time of their next-to-last meeting at Achensee in 1900. To
be sure, Freud's dream book, which Fliess had read in manuscript
many months before that meeting, had made explicit mention of a wish
that Fliess should die (and thus leave Freud in sole possession of bisexuality theory). In the charged atmosphere of the meeting at Achensee,

Fliess, who was physically quite a small man, had apparently found Freud's invitation to go hiking on a dangerous mountain trail nothing less than sinister. It is not clear how much of the story Jung knew, but he certainly knew that he was trying to replace Fliess as Freud's special friend.

Jung found a gracious way to reply to what had been a very mixed message:

> I thank you with all my heart for this token of your confidence [i.e., the salutation]. The undeserved gift of your friendship is one of the high points in my life which I cannot celebrate with big words. The reference to Fliess—surely not accidental—and your relationship with him impels me to ask you to let me enjoy your friendship not as one between equals but as that of father and son. This distance appears to me fitting and natural. Moreover it alone, so it seems to me, strikes a note that would prevent misunderstandings and enable two hard-headed people to exist alongside one another in an easy and unstrained relationship.

It was Freud's turn to feel confused. As far as he knew, Jung had had a rotten relationship with his own father. In explicating his associations for Binswanger's experiment, Jung had talked only about his father's death, not about any great filial bond between the two of them. (In point of fact, there was none.) Be that as it may, the damage was now done. Henceforth, confessions of affection, filial or otherwise, did not recur in the letters between the two men for the next six months.

What they did instead was to begin swapping "paranoia formulas" as they jockeyed for position vis-à-vis what had once been the Zurich school's special domain. To be sure, the jockeying had its Alphonse and Gaston aspect as each man pressed for his own viewpoint only while seeming to agree with and echo what the other man said. Jung began right away. In the very same letter, after saying that he had been able to "confirm" Freud's views "many times over," he went on to propose a distinctive psychological rationale for distinguishing paranoia from hysteria in which "libido" was only a secondary factor. Yet, if Jung had reason to feel pleased with both sides of his reply to the "Dear friend" letter, he also had reason to feel a little lonelier than before. Thus, after posting his letter, he went off to Jena to visit young Binswanger and his important uncle Otto. Just to remind Freud of his connections, he found the time to mail a postcard from Jena signed by himself and Binswanger junior as "Jung and Jünger" ["Young and Younger"; alternatively, "Jung and Disciple"].

Freud was both gracious and wary in reply: "You really are the only one capable of making an original contribution; except perhaps for O[tto] Gross, but unfortunately his health is poor." Freud also knew, however, that Karl Abraham had decided to speak at the Salzburg Congress, now two months away, on the psychosexual differences between hysteria and dementia praecox. Abraham, the third and highest degree of "follower," already accepted Freud's contention that dementia praecox could be interpreted in terms of "auto-eroticism." Freud saved the news of Abraham's planned talk for his next letter. Jung took cognizance of it on 11 March 1908; "Of course the devil had to put a spoke in my wheel with that lecture of colleague Abraham's; I can hear you chuckling." There were as well other matters connected with the congress to discuss. Jung wanted Freud to lecture about one of his cases and to make the hotel arrangements. Freud wanted Jung to get Bleuler to chair the meeting—Jung never even asked him—and also to see both Jung's Amsterdam lecture and a recent joint paper with Bleuler on the aetiology of dementia praecox, before they all met. Freud got his wish in regard to the papers, but was disappointed with both articles and let Jung know. Jung finally was becoming desperate. On 18 April 1908, but one week before the congress, he wrote:

> Your last letter upset me. I have read a lot between the lines. I don't doubt that if only I could *talk* with you we could come to a basic understanding. Writing is a poor substitute for speech.

Jung had been gradually discovering that a friendship at a distance was not necessarily all that friendly. Insofar as Jung had wanted to enjoy an exclusive relationship with Freud, his hopes were doomed from the start. It was inevitable that other physicians, including other Burghölzli physicians, would eventually make their own pilgrimages to Vienna, and equally inevitable that at least some of these pilgrims would also become Freud's friends. Ferenczi, for example, had initially found Freud's ideas to be nothing short of disgusting and had only gradually seen some profit in them. Nonetheless when he met Freud in person in February 1908, he found him to be an arresting figure and rapidly developed his own equivalent of a religious crush; a lifelong friendship thus began. All this Jung simply had to accept. But Jung was gradually discovering something else as well, something not a little disconcerting, namely that one's stock with Freud potentially rose and fell by degrees depending on the extent of one's theoretical agreement. Jung had been able to manage the pressure fairly comfortably so long as it was contained within a private dialogue. Now, however, that dialogue was being triangulated by other dialogues.

Most uncomfortably for Jung, psychoanalysis had begun to acquire a political dimension. The coming Congress for Freudian Psychology, scheduled for Salzburg on 27 April, represented Jung's chance to once more get back out in front of the field.

ANALYSIS TERMINABLE

IF JUNG'S relationship with Freud was becoming strained, his relationship with Spielrein was totally disintegrating. Jung had continued to see her for weekly sessions in which he behaved with an almost sadistic therapeutic correctness, probing the meanings of her "Siegfried" dreams while steadfastly refusing to discuss any of his own feelings. Her humiliation had grown accordingly. The intolerable situation now came to its logical crisis point: between them they decided to call off any further attempts at "psychoanalysis." Yet her feelings were scarcely spent. In search of a private abreaction she returned to her "Transformation Journal" for the first time since the previous summer, to write the third and final portion of this document. This third section, composed in the early spring of 1908, explodes with furious recriminations, coupled with confessions of passion. It begins:

Don't act on the first impulse—my principle is sound. I am certainly tired at this hour but calm, I believe. Yesterday's conversation seems to me like a bad dream that does not cease to oppress me. Yes! This is the moment to react! Must I act on my pride? Play the woman, righteous and offended? That would seem to be lying to myself and to you. Ah! If only all my being were of one mind! And in spite of everything it is dreadful to me to hear you speak to me so. At the same time, you must take into account that my "unconscious" wants nothing that your unconscious refuses. The way things are, I can (or rather must) be frank and you can't. And the fact that I abuse this frankness is a source of constant reproach to me, but how can I do otherwise? The complexity of the situation makes me adopt the unnatural role of the man and you the feminine role. I am far from taking what has been said as final; I understand that you must resist, but I also understand that your resistances excite me. I am also quite aware that if everything depended on me, then I would resist desperately. . . . Oh you! If you knew how dear you are to me without the least thought of the child. Isn't the wish to have a little boy by you merely the wish to possess you at least in a little form. . . . Yes, if there were an affectionate link that united you to me! But you seek to smother every strong feeling in regard to me. The consequence is that you are only tact and lies.

Spielrein goes on in her recriminations to say that as a consequence of his posture Jung's own unconscious has had to make use of detours. By giving her Binswanger's paper to read—probably meant as an antidote to the recently published Amsterdam lecture—he has in effect admitted his own desires, most especially his wish to have a son with her. And in the conversation they had yesterday he was able to break the silence only by bringing up his cousin the medium, as though that story should be a moral lesson to her. Does he expect her to believe what he tries to make others believe? He dares to speak of how refined "S.W.'' 's unconscious was; the truth of the matter is that it is *his* unconscious he's speaking of—the girl represents him, not herself. She mocks him, again bringing up the confessions in the Binswanger experiment: is this how he would cross the flames to rescue his Brünnhilde?

She frankly misses their old relationship:

Before you could converse with me about the most abstract subjects, you would show me different things in the laboratory, would have me at your place and show me paintings or ancient books; now everything which doesn't have a close connection with the sexual complex, you call "making speeches" . . .

She agrees with him that further therapy is out of the question:

I don't feel very much at ease talking to you like this and yet, what to do? It's impossible for me to let you defend yourself before me while humiliating me. For me this is infinitely more dreadful than if it were necessary for me to die for you to have peace. What must I do? I agree with you completely that we should never talk together about the unconscious.

From here Spielrein goes on to speak of her own bad conscience, and yet scarcely has she done so than she complains that Jung's wife borrows Jung from her as much as the other way around. The journal closes with thoughts of the child:

> . . . *we either decide not to touch on such subjects or if we do decide to touch on them I will have to react as required by your remarks.* My wishes cannot naturally change following a conversation because conscious reflection for too long necessarily has its effects. But my wish has never been formulated as: "I want to have a little boy by you." Because that would mean above all: "I agree to renounce you forever." And that seems possible only in the isolated moments when I feel profoundly offended by you; it's then that the desire to have your child dominates completely. But otherwise I cannot do it and that is why I myself put up so great a resistance to the complex. I am usually taken with fear that our relationship would not be as nice as if it were a totally disinterested friendship. But at the same time there are moments when the fact I'll never have a child by you seems abominable. When the time comes when I must definitely take leave of you . . . then I don't know . . .

From the letter-drafts of June 1909, we know that Spielrein's spirits had lifted considerably by the end of April 1908. For whatever reason, she was once again in the exaltation of the "Siegfried complex" and was understandably delighted by her ability to foretell not only the dates of her exams but also what they would cover.

By that time, Jung was at Salzburg for the long-awaited Congress for Freudian Psychology. Afterward Jung went to Munich to see the architect who was building his new house at Küsnacht, a ferryboat ride from Zurich. The money for this handsome dwelling was provided by his wife's dowry, though in accordance with the very same laws that Forel had railed against, the money was largely at Jung's disposal.

By the end of April something else was certain. Emma Jung was pregnant again—with Franz Jung, the first boy who would be born to this family.

THE CONGRESS FOR FREUDIAN PSYCHOLOGY

HISTORY HAS subsequently called it the First International Congress for Psychoanalysis. It was held in Salzburg on 27 April 1908 at the Hotel Bristol. Forty-two people went. Jung, Bleuler, Riklin, and Eitingon attended from Zurich. Edouard Claparède of Geneva was the lone participant from French Switzerland. A. A. Brill upheld America's honor as its sole representative. From England, Ernest Jones brought along his friend, the prominent surgeon Wilfred Trotter. Karl Abraham was the only participant from Berlin. Vienna came in force with twenty-one participants. Stein and Ferenczi represented Hungary. Löwenfeld came from Munich, as did Otto Gross. There were two women in attendance, Frau Dr. Sophie Erismann of Zurich, a physician herself and married to a noted internist, and Otto Gross's wife, Frieda, who was there to keep an eye on her husband.

It was not a sterling occasion for Carl Jung. First of all, for his talk in the afternoon session, he took the opportunity to present his rather mad version of the toxin theory of dementia praecox. The idea that some form of endogenous toxin, presumably the result of faulty metabolism, was the cause of this illness was widely held, and Kraepelin even supposed that the as-yet-unidentified toxin might be related to sexual processes. Jung's divergence from the prevailing psychiatric consensus was based on his own research into complexes. Specifically, he proposed that the putative toxin was produced by the activity of a particularly severe complex. This amounted to saying that certain thoughts, or at least certain feelings, were metabolically dangerous. In fairness to Jung, it should be pointed out that any psychosomatic theory of psychosis must sooner or later jump the great divide between mental and physical processes. At Salzburg, however, the audience was not willing to take this particular leap.

Karl Abraham, meanwhile, in his talk, "The Psychosexual Differences Between Hysteria and Dementia Praecox," proposed just the theory that Freud had been trying to plant with both men right along, the theory of auto-eroticism. Jung and Bleuler had already demonstrated in a general way what Brill had lately learned at the Burghölzli Grand Rounds regarding the woman who spilled wine on her bedsheets, namely that sexual complexes could determine specific symptoms. Where the theory of auto-eroticism went much further was in supposing that a specific functional alteration of the libido, a turning in upon itself, was the necessary and sufficient cause of dementia praecox and of all the striking alterations of consciousness and ultimate intellectual deterioration that came with it. A bold claim, indeed, and yet no empirical way of testing it was advanced. In effect, here as with mythology, the appeal was to the essential reasonableness of the idea.

In one sense, what was going on here was a situation not unknown in the history of science, namely that a set of hypotheses that appear to be conceptually fruitful in one area are rapidly applied to other areas to see what they will yield. Yet, in another sense, matters were subtly shifting in the direction of what would prove to be a problematic enterprise. Both logically and scientifically, Freud's endeavor ultimately held together on the basis that it was possible to demonstrate that the recovery of sexual traumas, or of repressed sexual wishes, led to the elimination of symptoms, and ultimately of the neurosis itself. But, at Salzburg, no one supposed that a similar demonstration would soon be forthcoming with regard to dementia praecox (i.e., our "schizophrenia"). The intractable, treatment-refractory facts were known; Abraham's speculative reinterpretation of their significance in terms of libido theory was just that—an interpretation. Its comparative superiority to Jung's equally speculative toxic-complex theory lay solely in its terminological and conceptual consonance with Freud's theory of the neuroses. Theory was becoming subtly divorced from empirical test; almost imperceptibly, psychoanalysis was becoming a *Weltanschauung*.

To make matters worse, Abraham had originally heard of the theory of auto-eroticism from Jung during his days at the Burghölzli. Having thus stockpiled fuel enough for a good quarrel between Zurich and Vienna, Abraham also supplied the match: his address neglected to cite the work of either Bleuler or Jung in the whole area.

Not enough has been said about Abraham's tactics in this regard. According to Jones, Abraham was already complaining in private conversation about the "unscientific and mystical" tendencies of the Swiss, while suggesting that they would not long stay the course with an explicitly materialistic theory like Freud's. Intellectually, Abraham did have at least half a point to make here, but he consistently seasoned his remarks with his accumulated personal resentments. Well aware of Riklin's monograph in progress on fairy tales, he had begun his own study, *Dreams and Myth,* and had managed to mail it off to Freud, along with his opinion that Riklin's study was inferior, before the Salzburg congress, Freud's first chance to meet Riklin. (At the congress Riklin, a last-minute replacement for Morton Prince, spoke on the topic "Some Problems of Myth Interpretation.") In private conversation with Jones at Salzburg, Abraham whispered, "Do you think Jung can escape the anti-Semitism of a certain type of German?" (Jones, to his credit, replied with Edmund Burke's dictum: "I do not know the method of indicting the whole nation.") As for Bleuler, Abraham had raised him as a psychological problem during his first meeting with Freud. No Zuricher was safe.

Freud was not unaware of what was going on. For example, Abraham was told in mid-February of 1908 to look out for the publication in March of the paper "Character and Anal Eroticism." This gave Abraham the chance to convey the news, in his letter to Freud of 4 April 1908, that the theory therein "fits a case of hysteria analysed by Jung with which you will be acquainted from his description." Abraham, who would have known Spielrein from her hospital days, and who would have well known that hers was the case in the published version of the Amsterdam address, thus told Freud what he wanted to know and what he did not want to have to ask Jung.

Twice in the months immediately after the Salzburg congress Freud would be obliged to put Abraham in his place vis-à-vis Jung just for the sake of keeping the peace. Peace did not keep him from then encouraging Abraham to work on the "Soma" myth and to see in it the solution to the "toxin" question: the magical drink of the ancient Persians and the dreaded toxin of dementia praecox were both to be viewed as varieties of a hypothesized sexual chemical in the brain. In the great scheme of things, the Burghölzli-trained and Berlin-based Abraham was strategically positioned to cut off the lines of conceptual retreat for the Zurich school. Abraham relished the job; Salzburg was his coming-out party.

At Salzburg, Jung didn't get to see as much of Freud as he would have liked because, out of the clear blue sky, Freud's half-brother Emmanuel, seventy-four years old, showed up unexpectedly at the banquet following the meeting, thus tieing up Freud for the rest of the evening and the next morning. That gave Jung rather more time to meet the rest of the Viennese, who, according to Jones, were even at this early date saying privately that Jung would not stay with psychoanalysis long. All in all, it was a less than edifying occasion. Wilfred Trotter, exposed for the first time to the level of discourse among the Viennese, consoled himself in a grumpy aside to Jones that he was the only person there who knew how to cut off a leg.

Of course, Jung did get to hear Freud lecture—for four and a half hours. Before the congress, Freud had intimated to Jung that he might speak on "Transformations in the (Conception and) Technique of Psychoanalysis," but Jung had persuaded him instead to present case material. To be sure, if one examines Freud's comments to his own little Wednesday Night group during the course of the previous year, what he had to say about "technique" was not likely to gladden the hearts of the Zurich school. First, Freud was of the opinion that the association experiment was vastly inferior to psychoanalysis and was only useful as a teaching device. Second, in his view there was no room for mixing the experiment with psychoanalysis proper as Jung, and lately Stekel, had done. Third, psychoanalysis did not primarily seek to discover complexes; its proper business was to remove resistances. Fourth, psychoanalysis was not possible with dementia praecox patients; all that could be done was to use what had been learned from neurotic patients as a guideline to the symptoms and then confront the psychotic patient directly. The upshot of all these qualifications, if they had been pooled into a single trenchant presentation, would have been that whatever Jung had so far been writing about, it wasn't psychoanalysis.

But Freud had a real problem here quite apart from the politics of holding together his various disparate supporters. As he himself had admitted in the Wednesday Night discussion of 27 November 1907, "Associations as well as free thoughts yield much chaff." How then did the analyst decide which associations, or free thoughts, were important? Did not analytic "technique" depend on what the analyst chose to respond to? In the absence of any rule for distinguishing analytic wheat from chaff, did not the analyst's selectivity lead to the situation that Aschaffenburg complained of, and lately the influential Moll as well, namely that the analyst was shaping the material in support of the very theories that the analysis was meant to demonstrate? It was precisely here that the work of the Zurich investigators was potentially crucial, for they could claim to have identified specific empirical indicators as to when an association, or a free thought, was disturbed.

No doubt Freud balked at the thought of hooking up an electrogalvanic machine alongside the couch or of holding a stopwatch in his cigar hand. No doubt, too, he was right in supposing that treatment had to adopt a more free and easygoing approach than the demands of immediate experimental validation would permit. But the fact remains that the experiments going on in Zurich had enormous bearing on the scientific status of psychoanalysis as a method of investigation.

In any case, seated at the head of a long table in the conference hotel room at Salzburg, Freud opened the conference not with schematic remarks about technique, but with an extended case presentation—the case of the "Rat Man." This patient's symptom was worthy of Dostoyevsky. He feared that an exotic torture, by which rats were forced to eat their way into the anus of the victim, would be applied both to the lady he was courting and to his late father unless he returned a small sum of money to a fellow officer who had paid it out for him at a village post office while they had been on maneuvers. When it developed that, in fact, the officer had not advanced any money on his behalf, thus making the compulsion impossible to fulfill, the fear became overwhelming and ostensibly irremediable.

The "Rat Man" was blessed, so to speak, with an illness whose time was ripe. Interest in this syndrome, which was characterized by compulsive thoughts, doubts, absurd rituals, and the like, was currently quite high. Under a variety of labels—compulsion neurosis, psychasthenia, *folie du doute,* obsessional neurosis—it had already attracted the theoretical attentions of Löwenfeld, Janet, and others. It would indeed be a coup for psychoanalysis if it could shed new light on this condition, so far removed in its phenomenology from hysteria and the usual run of anxiety states. Luckily, the "Rat Man" was also blessed with an unusual ability to make use of the psychoanalytic method for the purpose of disassembling his obsessional formula. Henri Ellenberger has written that great psychotherapists require great patients. Breuer's "Anna O.," the featured case in *Studies on Hysteria,* had been such a patient. So, too, in her own way, was Spielrein. In the person of the "Rat Man," Freud had yet one more such great patient. The wordplay of free associations seemed just the ticket for this man; he took to it as to the manner born, and between his intelligence and his dawning conviction that something could indeed be done for him, he proved to be an enormously productive patient. His productivity in turn enabled Freud, always at his best when considering the secret language of symptoms, to dissect the obsessional formula and show how it had been built up, piece by piece, almost phrase by phrase, from the ground of the patient's unresolved childhood ambivalence toward a loved but entirely too punitive father. (In the published version, and perhaps also at Salzburg, Freud improved somewhat on the actual case record so that his interventions could stand in sterling, nonsuggestive juxtaposition with the patient's spontaneous self-revelation.) All in all, it was a stunning demonstration of the method and a matchless psychological study in its own right, well worth the four and a half hours' time spent on it. Nothing like it existed anywhere in the vast literature on obsessional neurosis.

With case material like this Freud could afford to be generous, even magnanimous, and he seems to have used the occasion to make one overture after another to the Swiss. For a close reading of the published case shows Freud using the language of the Zurich school to a degree that was never again to be repeated. He spoke of a "splitting of the personality," of "repressed complexes," of "diversion of . . . attention," and even of "complex sensitiveness." He also talked about unconscious "symbolism" and about the "perfect analogy" between a transference fantasy and an earlier event. At one point, he even had some fun with this game of making the crew from Zurich comfortable; Freud described the scene in which his patient first heard of using rats to torture people thus:

> It was almost as though Fate, when the captain told him his story, had been putting him through an association-test; she had called out a "complex stimulus-word," and he had reacted to it with his obsessional idea.

Freud's diplomacy was not idle. Following the afternoon session, he closeted himself with the various members of the Zurich school; Abraham, Ferenczi, Brill, and Jones were present, as were the Swiss, but from his own party, Freud brought along only young Otto Rank. The twenty-odd remaining members of the Viennese contingent were left to mill about the lobby and wonder what was afoot. When the meeting broke, there was an important announcement. It had been decided to start a periodical, a biannual yearbook, for psychoanalysis and related researches. Jung was to be the editor; Freud and Bleuler would be co-directors.

Beneath all the social awkwardness and petty sniping of the conference, the important thing had happened. Freud had persuaded the Swiss that psychoanalysis was an open science, that it was still producing new and sturdy findings, and that between the assembled they had enough qualified contributors to make their own journal. They did not have to wait for Morton Prince or anyone else to come aboard. By meeting with members of the Zurich school privately, moreover, Freud made it clear that he personally was ready to rise above any lingering Viennese parochialism. Bleuler's willingness to lend his name to the new venture, meanwhile, was in keeping with his role of patriarch of the Zurich school. As for Jung, he was more than just the logical first choice as editor—his participation was plainly indispensable to the viability of the new enterprise. Jung did not get the personal chat with Freud he sought at Salzburg, but he did get this recognition of his preeminence and it was enough for him to take on the post of editor.

And the excluded Viennese? For them there was nothing, save the hope that Jung might deem their own submissions worthy for inclusion in the new yearbook. Stunned, they spent the banquet that followed swapping remarks about the Zurich "Siegfried," as they took to calling Jung with an uncanny contempt.

OTTO GROSS AT THE BURGHÖLZLI

THE CENTRAL theme of Freud's case presentation, ambivalence toward the father, had had special relevance to at least one member of the audience—Otto Gross. For at this time Gross was in no little conflict with his own father, Hanns Gross, professor at Graz and a force in European sociology. Alarmed at his son's behavior, which was passing beyond eccentricity into his own special area of competency, outright criminality, Gross senior had been trying for months, for everyone's protection, to get his son committed to a hospital. To that end he had written to both Jung and Freud, who, in turn, had been discussing the problem between themselves in their letters immediately prior to the congress. The original plan had called for Jung to escort Gross junior from Salzburg back to the Burghölzli, but Jung had ducked that unhappy assignment.

Jung did not evade Gross for long. Less than a week after his return to Zurich, Jung received from Freud the certificate officially committing Otto Gross to the Burghölzli. Graciously, Freud promised to take Gross off Jung's hands in October—five full months hence. Meanwhile, Freud had two new visitors to attend to, Ernest Jones and A. A. Brill, yet two more men trained in Zurich, who were in Vienna for their first visit with the inventor of psychoanalysis.

Ernest Jones had met Otto Gross at the Amsterdam Congress and then again during a stay in Munich. Jones later described him as "the nearest approach to the romantic idea of a genius I have ever met. . . . Such penetrating powers of divining the inner thoughts of others I was never to see again." An extremely brilliant man, Gross never lacked for influential followers throughout his short life. His novel psychiatric and psychological theories were debated by the best intellects of his day. He had a special appeal to writers and appeared as a character in a half-dozen different novels. In Munich, he split his time between Kraepelin's clinic, where he had one of the prized assistantships, and the cafés of the Schwabing district, Munich's answer to Greenwich Village, where he conducted impromptu psychoanalyses into the night.

Central to Gross's adherence to Freudian principles was his belief that here lay a practical method for cultural revolution. Gross wanted a world where monogamy did not exist, where all patriarchal authority had been overthrown, and where communal living and self-exploration would guide each individual to his own artistic heights. At Salzburg, Gross had wanted to talk about the "cultural perspectives" of psychoanalysis, earning this reproach from Freud: "We are doctors, and doctors we remain."

But it was not his views that got Gross into trouble; it was his insistence on living out his fairy tale. To begin with, he was a charter member of The Great Unwashed. Then, in 1906, there had been a disturbing incident where he had given a patient, who was perhaps his lover as well, the poison that was the means of her suicide. In 1907, his wife, Frieda, had given birth to his son; so did Else Jaffe, who was married to someone else. More recently, there had been a local controversy in Munich concerning his treatment of a young woman whose family had subsequently hospitalized her to get her away from him. Then, too, there was Gross's plan to sue his chief, Kraepelin, for malpractice on the basis that he did not offer psychoanalysis at the clinic, a plan from which Ernest Jones dissuaded him. And all along there had been marathon group discussions in which clothes were stripped off along with defenses. By the time of his forcible admission to the Burghölzli during the second week of May 1908, moreover, Gross was addicted to both cocaine and morphine. To be sure, the erosion of Gross's personality had only just begun and his intellect and his charm were still intact. It could have been said about him as it was once said of Lord Byron: he was mad, bad, and dangerous to know.

Gross and Jung hit it off famously right from the start. Jung had been starved for intellectual companionship, and under the circumstances Gross could not have hoped for a more attentive and responsive physician. Beyond hailing from very similar professional backgrounds, the two men were temperamentally and intellectually compatible, enough so that Jung did not hesitate to think of Gross as his psychic "twin brother." Thus, while his correspondence with Freud following the conference was taken up with various business matters pertaining to the planned journal, also with a discussion of colleague Abraham's behavior, Jung's primary emotional energies went into his plan to analyze, and cure, this most important new inpatient.

At first things went swimmingly. Gross voluntarily reduced his drug intake while Jung devoted every free hour and then some to the care of this intriguing man. At one point they stayed up analyzing continuously for twelve hours; at the end, as Jung later confided to Jones, both of them sat stuporously "like nodding automata." But it was not only the analysis of Gross that kept them up. With charm, insight, and professional courtesy to play on, Gross was able to turn the tables so that what transpired was equally an analysis of Jung. In a letter in late May, Jung described the novel procedure to Freud:

> I have let everything drop and have spent all my available time, day and night, on Gross, pushing on with his analysis. . . . Whenever I got stuck, he analyzed me. In this way my own psychic health has benefited. . . . He is an extraordinarily decent fellow with whom you can hit it off at once provided you can get your own complexes out of the way. Today is my first day of rest; I finished the analysis yesterday. . . . The analysis has yielded all sorts of scientifically valuable results which we shall try to formulate soon.

In his various replies to Jung's reports over the next two weeks, Freud allowed that it would be a fine thing if a collaboration grew up between the two men. However, as the man who had essentially introduced cocaine to Europe, and as someone with extensive personal experience with the drug, Freud knew well the gravity of Gross's situation. As regards the treatment, he tried gently to caution Jung on a number of points—the analysis was too brief, the concurrent use of drugs was masking the resistance—but in the face of Jung's insistently sanguine view, he finally acceded to the idea that perhaps things had indeed gone as well as Jung claimed: "Still, I have never had a patient like Gross; with him one ought to be able to see straight to the heart of the matter." Three weeks later, however, Jung had a different version to report: all the therapeutic insights had been lost, nothing permanent had been achieved, and in fact, left unguarded the day before in the yard, Gross had jumped over the hospital wall and disappeared. Jung attempted to cover up his embarrassing failure with the self-protective assessment that Gross was really suffering from dementia praecox, hence the failure of the treatment to stick. This allowed Freud once more to launch into theoretical remarks about his views on paranoia and dementia praecox, a development which Jung finally responded to by proposing that Freud visit him at the Burghölzli in September. Implicit in Jung's invitation was the thought that they might thereby have the chance to examine some patients together—and compare observations. As for Gross, Freud wrote: "He is addicted and can only do great harm to our cause."

Following Gross's escape, Jung continued to get reports as to his fate. For a time Gross was quite paranoid, but then he managed to pull himself together and write a paper in the fall which Jung found not at all bad. And so it went with Gross, in and out of trouble, for another five years, until once again Gross senior managed to get him hospitalized, this time in Vienna.

As for Jung, matters went quite differently. Soon his embarrassment about the affair took second seat to Freud's embarrassment about Stekel's new book, which, owing to an interpolation by Freud, blurred the distinction between hysteria and anxiety neurosis and thus made it appear that all neuroses could be cured by sexual activity. Jung did not hesitate to pounce on this Viennese version of Gross's philosophy, and Freud had to concede Jung's points as their correspondence drifted into the summer doldrums. During his August vacation, Freud wrote that he was pondering a new direction for his theory: "One thing and another have turned my thoughts to mythology and I am beginning to suspect that myth and neurosis have a common core." The "one thing and another" were Abraham's study of myths and dreams, Rank's *The Myth of the Birth of the Hero,* and two papers by Freud himself on children's sexual development, all of which were awaiting a final round of editing.

THE SIGNIFICANCE OF THE FATHER

THERE WERE two immediate consequences of the Gross affair in Zurich. The first was theoretical. Regaining his composure, Jung began writing up "The Significance of the Father in the Destiny of the Individual" and finished it in time to include it in the very first volume of the new journal. In the paper, Jung discreetly credited "an analysis carried out conjointly with Dr. Otto Gross" as his inspiration. Beyond containing a distillation of some of Gross's own ideas, it was, for any of the "initiated," plainly an analysis of Gross's character; that said, it also had application to Jung's own psyche, though this was less apparent. The paper began with a preliminary nod to the Freudian theory of regression:

> A man disillusioned in love falls back, as a substitute, upon some sentimental friendship, masturbation, or false religiosity; if he is a neurotic he regresses still further back to the childhood relationships he has never quite forsaken, and to which even the normal person is fettered by more than one chain—the relationship to father and mother.

Citing the recent 1907 paper of his student Emma Fürst, Jung argued that "reaction-types" on the association experiment tend to run in families and that this psychic legacy predetermines the subsequent neurotic regression. In other words, the neurotic fails at his life tasks, especially the erotic ones, because he approaches the conflict with the emotional attitudes acquired from his parents rather than relying on his own. Arguing on the basis of experimental data and from his own clinical experiences, Jung suggested tentatively that the father typically appeared to be decisive in shaping the reaction-type of his children. He then presented four lucid case histories demonstrating the point; in each, it was transparent that the individual never succeeded in going beyond the attachment to the father and thus forever addressed life with the attitudes formed by that relationship. In his discussion section, Jung argued that the attachment was essentially if secretly sexual:

The infantile attitude, it is evident, is nothing but infantile sexuality. If we now survey all the far-reaching possibilities of the infantile constellation, we are obliged to say that *in essence our life's fate is identical with the fate of our sexuality.*

From here Jung moved into a Nietzschean digression on the history of religion, "the history of the fantasy systems of whole peoples and epochs," where he detected an alternating cycle between periods dominated by versions of the father—"Jehova" was the model—and periods where prophets and reformers achieved a more perfect sublimation by identifying themselves with the divinity. Then he picked up the theme of "fate" again:

Like everything that has fallen into the unconscious, the infantile situation still sends up dim, premonitory feelings, feelings of being secretly guided by otherworldly feelings.

These are the roots of the first religious sublimations. In the place of the father with his constellating virtues and faults there appears on the one hand an altogether sublime deity, and on the other hand the devil, who in modern times has been largely whittled away by the realization of one's own moral responsibility. Sublime love is attributed to the former, low sexuality to the latter.

The finished paper was brief, cogent, topical, and brilliant. As well, it announced a new approach to the problem that had been hovering about the Burghölzli ever since Riklin began his work on fairy tales: how to get into mythology from a psychoanalytic perspective. The secret was not to look at individual myths, but to look at a succession of them. For the succession ought to show the same pattern of progressive differentiation from parental authority that took place in the psychological differentiation of each generation.

Amazingly, it also worked the other way around. For the model also suggested what to do with the rare case, like Spielrein's and also perhaps Jung's, where there seemed to be a natural talent for accessing the deeper, mythologically informed strata of the unconscious. Once one was face-to-face with the archetypal father image, be he Jehova or Wotan, the task was to move forward to an independent mythic (and, implicitly, libidinal) heroism of one's own—to Jesus or Siegfried or whomever. For Jung, this theoretical opening not only possessed an unassailable logic but also offered the opportunity to make sense of some unusual clinical data at his disposal. His central problem, all of a sudden, was not how to proceed, but with whom to proceed. For with the loss of Gross, Jung was, as he complained to Freud in early September, largely without a decent intellectual companion.

THE DEVIL WHISPERED

THERE WAS in Zurich one other immediate consequence of the Gross affair, more personal in nature. It was subsequently described by Spielrein in the letter-drafts written in the late spring of 1909:

> I told him [Jung] how my exams had gone, but was deeply depressed that he displayed no pleasure at hearing I was capable of doing good work after all and was now an official candidate for the medical degree. I was ashamed of having believed in any prophecies and told myself: not only does he not love me, I am not even a good acquaintance, whose welfare matters to him. He wanted to show me we were complete strangers to each other, and it is humiliating if I now go to see him. But I decided to go the following Friday, but to act completely professional. The devil whispered other things to me, but I no longer believed them. I sat there waiting in deep depression. Now he arrives, beaming with pleasure, and tells me with strong emotion about Gross, about the great insight he has just received

(i.e., about polygamy); he no longer wants to suppress his feeling for me, he admitted that I was his first, dearest friend, etc., etc. (his wife of course excepted), and that he wanted to tell me everything about himself. So once more this most curious coincidence that the devil so unexpectedly turned out to be right.

CHAPTER 8

Sexual and Psychological Researches

Thus at that time I learned a very great deal: much that was of scientific value, but something of practical importance as well— namely, that it was impossible for a "general practitioner" to treat a case of that kind without bringing his activities and mode of life completely to an end. I vowed at the time that I would *not* go through such an ordeal again.

—Josef Breuer describing his cathartic treatment of "Anna O." in a letter of 21 November 1907 to Auguste Forel

T HE COMPLEX WEB in which Jung was entangling himself was destined to become still more tangled. The next complication for Jung's career as a Freudian appeared in the person of Auguste Forel, professor emeritus of the University of Zurich, former head of the Burghölzli, and still a force in international psychiatry. In the fall of 1907, apprehensive over the recent developments at the Burghölzli, Forel had written to Josef Breuer, dean of Vienna's internists and an acquaintance since Forel's student days, to find out how psychoanalysis had gotten started. It was Breuer who had first interested Freud in hysteria about twenty-five years earlier by telling him of the case of "Anna O." Their subsequent joint publication, *Studies on Hysteria*, had been predicated on Breuer's finally agreeing to publish the case of this remarkable, and remarkably ill, woman. In reply to Forel, Breuer was discreet. Contrary to what the published account implied, "Anna O.," who likely had a neurological illness in addition to hysteria, had not completely recovered. This was something Forel potentially knew already from the Binswangers, whose asylum at Kreuzlingen had become "Anna O." 's residence following the supposed cure. Beyond that, "Anna O." had also developed a fantasy pregnancy during the course of Breuer's treatment, announcing in a delirious enactment of childbirth that Herr Doktor's baby was coming. Even in the face of this event, Breuer had not quit his patient. He abandoned his daily sessions with her only some months later when his wife, despairing over the amount of time her husband was devoting to the young heiress, had made a suicide gesture.

Breuer did not fill in Forel on any of the above details, but he did indicate that the treatment was indeed extremely arduous, which was why he subsequently referred his nervous cases to his younger neurologist-colleague, Freud. Breuer and Freud had since become estranged, to the point where Freud publicly snubbed his former mentor on the street, but in his letter to Forel, Breuer allowed only that Freud perhaps went out of his way "to shock the bourgeoisie." Otherwise, Breuer resolutely defended the new sexual findings: "I confess that the plunging into sexuality in theory and practice is not to my taste. But what have my taste and my feeling about what is seemly and what unseemly to do with the question of what is true?"

Forel did not stop with Breuer; he began polling various Swiss physicians of his acquaintance who were experimenting with one form or another of the "cathartic" method. And his private opinions were growing sharper, to the point where the Swiss psychotherapist Bezzola, who used free associations as a means of *inducing* a hypnotic trance, protested in reply to one of Forel's letters that Jung and Bleuler were serious men and that "pigs" was not the right word to use for them.

The best answer to a principled doubter like Forel would be to swamp him with case reports, and cures, but this required a journal willing to publish the very different kind of case report that was at the heart of the new science. To be sure, Freud could readily place his papers in periodicals like Hirschfeld's *Zeitschrift für Sexualwissenschaft* and Marcuse's *Sexual-Probleme*, but only when he had a general contribution to make, such as his earlier paper "The Sexual Enlightenment of Children" or his recent "Civilized Sexual Ethics and Modern Nervous Illness." Such journals were scarcely the place to elaborate a new treatment method. The psychological journals, meanwhile, were also available to Freud and his colleagues, but here the sexual emphasis was sure to draw fire, and rebuttals, from other contributors.

The Yearbook for Psychoanalytic and Psychopathological Researches was ostensibly Jung's project, both in inspiration and in terms of the ultimate responsibility. Nonetheless, it was Freud who found the publisher,

Freud who got the galleys first, and Freud who had the last word on everything. He redid the title—to give it a better ring. He redesigned the masthead—so that he could appear as "Prof. Dr. S. Freud." And he rewrote the declaration of editorial intent that began the first volume—blurring beyond recognition the distinction between the Zurich school and his own Vienna group.

The first half-volume of the *Jahrbuch* did not finally appear until late February of 1909, but in its specialized way, it made a splendid beginning. There were five papers in all: Freud's case of "Little Hans," Jung's paper on the significance of the father, Abraham's paper on marriages between close relatives, a case analysis by young Binswanger, and a discussion of the relation between epilepsy and hysteria by Alphonse Maeder, a French Swiss attached to the Binswanger asylum. The sexual doctrines were everywhere, but from beginning to end the volume had the look and feel of a regular scientific periodical. Freud wrote of the first half-issue to Jung, "You have revenged yourself brilliantly for Amsterdam."

Freud had a special problem with regard to the *Jahrbuch*. As it was to be the scientific calling card for psychoanalysis, it was important that its contributors show an appreciation for the sensibilities of a wider professional audience, and that they be comfortable with all the regular trappings of scientific style from footnotes to literature reviews. This was no problem for Freud personally. Nor was it a problem for the Zurichers, trained as they were by Bleuler to keep abreast of the contemporary literature. But it was an enormous problem for most of Freud's Viennese, who had grown all too accustomed to the manifest truth of their own views and whose prior training was largely in internal medicine. With characteristic prescience, Freud had set his little group to work preparing literature reviews and brief case reports even before Salzburg. But it was going to be a while before they caught up to the Swiss, and the first *Jahrbuch* issues would be dominated by men trained in Switzerland. (Karl Abraham even complained about this, only to be told, pointedly, that he himself counted as a member of the Zurich school.)

LETTERS TO A FRIEND

JUNG HAD a somewhat different problem with regard to the *Jahrbuch*, one that he did not grasp right away. He was shortly going to appear in print as editor-in-chief of this new enterprise; it thus behooved him, now more than ever, to be quite clear in his own mind just where he stood on the general issues, and most specifically on the issue that Forel was privately complaining about, namely the propriety of a prolonged sexual inquiry. For that reason it was exactly the wrong time to be having secret meetings with a former patient. The meetings between Jung and Spielrein that began in June 1908 took place in different locales: his office, her apartment, the countryside. These meetings involved a risk that the editor-in-chief of the new *Jahrbuch* simply could not afford.

No letters from Spielrein to Jung survive for 1908, but several letters from Jung to her are extant from the summer and early fall of that year and they are terribly important for capturing the flavor of their liaison. There are certain things, of course, that no sensible, even minimally discreet person dares to put in a letter. But the change in their relationship had begun when Jung decided at last to share with her his own feelings, and both parties felt free to continue their discussions of each other's psychology through the mails. Indeed, their letters, and presumably their conversation as well, were as much about psychological matters as about other things. Yet psychological confessions in their own way are as revealing as any others. Despite his manifest efforts at discretion, Jung's letters are plainly compromising.

Save for a few passages previously excerpted by Carotenuto, Jung's letters to Spielrein over the years have been published only in the German edition of Carotenuto's book. Actual inspection of the documents makes one thing vivid in a way difficult to anticipate. In his description of them, Carotenuto has noted that among the thirty-four extant letters from Jung to Spielrein are four undated visiting cards. One of these is inscribed "Dr. Med. C. G. Jung—Küsnacht—Zurich" and dates from mid-1909 at the earliest, and more probably from the fall of 1910. The other three, however, are not inscribed; moreover, each of them announces a time and a place for a meeting. Seeing them, one grasps that they were not sent through the mails but left in Spielrein's box personally by Jung; he had come calling at her apartment to arrange a meeting.

The first dated letter is Jung's note of 20 June 1908, which places it three days after Otto Gross jumped over a wall of the Burghölzli. In it, Jung tells Spielrein that "you have vigorously taken my unconscious into your hands with your saucy letters" and announces a time and a place where they can meet so that they can be alone and "find a clear way out from the turmoil we are in." Jung's next letter, dated 30 June, begins "My dear friend" instead of "My dear Miss," and thereafter this form of address alternates with "My Dear." In his letter, Jung talks of how lucky he would be to find in her a "strong spirit who does not get bogged down in sentimentality, but whose real and innermost reason for living is freedom and independence." He also writes, "You cannot imagine how much it means to me to have hopes of loving a person whom I must not condemn, and who does not condemn herself, to being smothered in the banality of habit." The letter ends by noting that they will meet Friday at the usual time, i.e., the time of Spielrein's official appointment. The next extant letter, of 4 July, is written in the same vein: Jung says their talk of the day before has had an especially absolving effect and says that his faith in her makes up for "many disappointments." He feels "calmer and freer" and talks hopefully of their being able to avoid getting stuck in sentimentality. He suggests a rendezvous in Rapperswill.

A man having an affair is always busy. He can't be reached, he doesn't return calls, he falls behind in correspondence, and there is always someplace else he has to be. Being interminably busy is of course useful in explaining one's whereabouts; it is also useful in keeping the demands of the lover at bay. Jung's next two notes, of 6 July and 22 July, have this flavor. Both are quite short, both suggest he is pressed for time just now, and both give Spielrein only the briefest of slots when she may meet him. The tone suggests that Jung had begun to weigh the extent of his indiscretion, though by the same token, he clearly was not prepared to break off from her completely. Then, too, he had lately learned that Freud would be coming to visit in two months' time, though whether this was a chastening thought is impossible to know.

In August, Spielrein returned to Russia for a vacation. Jung did not hear from her for over a week and he began to worry. Finally, a letter arrived and he quickly wrote back, on 12 August 1908, to confess his darkening state of mind. He complained that the previous week he had been "somewhat hysterical," even staying in bed for a day because of a cold, and that his mood kept "shifting volcanically from grey to gold." He had been very happy to hear from her; her letter was a "beam of light" and calmed him. He made it quite clear that he was afraid of her recent silence, afraid, as he put it, that "the devil had gotten his hand in." Apparently, Spielrein had in her most recent letter intimated that she had discussed their friendship with her parents, for Jung also wrote that he admired the "generous spirit" of her parents, especially of her mother, since women are usually more conservative. Apparently, too, Spielrein had announced that she had decided to give up wearing peasant dresses and to become more ladylike in other ways; Jung's letter applauds this change in no uncertain terms.

Jung was reflecting more deeply on his situation by this time. In the same letter, he cautioned Spielrein about a Fräulein Gincburg, yet one more Russian medical student who was also his patient, who had moved into the neighborhood of her quarters back in Zurich. He wrote of his mounting worry, phrasing himself in such a way as to make Spielrein conscious of her duty to avoid scandal. Carotenuto has excerpted the following from the 12 August 1908 letter:

> I notice how much more attached I am to you than I should have ever thought. I happen to be terribly suspicious and always think others want to exploit me and lord it over me. It is only with great difficulty that I can actually master that belief in man's natural goodness which I so often proclaim. Which certainly does not apply to my feelings for you!

Jung's next extant letter to her, of 2 September 1908, is brief and bids her to return soon to Zurich. The next letter after that, of 28 September 1908, is incomplete. The portion that survives speaks glowingly of Freud's recent visit. Before, he only admired Freud; now, as he put it to Spielrein, Jung found himself genuinely fond of him. Jung went on to talk of Freud's experience of life and his ability to see into people. But to this praise, which suggests at least the possibility that Jung had sought Freud's counsel about his own life, Jung added the curious admission that Spielrein had been right all along. Plainly, Freud's character was something that Spielrein and Jung had already been discussing among themselves. From there, Jung announced his impending leave for military service and then asked her if she was calm and what she thought of her fate. He added that he worries about her sometimes "because of the" . . . The second page is missing.

FREUD AT THE BURGHÖLZLI

IF WE TAKE matters from Freud's point of view, perhaps the most disturbing aspect of the Jung-Gross misalliance had been their decision to analyze each other. Given the fact that Jung and Gross were arguably the two most experienced analysts outside of Vienna, Freud was going to have to live with the results of their experiment, results that Jung was intending to publish in the first half-issue of the *Jahrbuch*. It now occurred to Freud that he might usefully emulate Jung's example, and forestall any future experiments of this kind, by making himself available for personal consultation. During the summer of 1908, while Jung was in Zurich, Abraham was in Berlin, and Ernest Jones was shuttling back and forth all over the globe, Sándor Ferenczi was summering with Freud at the Berchtesgaden resort. There he worked up an important paper on "Introjection and Transference" under Freud's watchful eye while also discussing his own personal foibles—arguably, the first training analysis. And for those who wanted to follow in Ferenczi's footsteps, it soon became clear that the summer months offered the best opportunity. Thus in the evolving world of psychoanalytic politics did August vacations become as important as congresses. Ferenczi's paper, meanwhile, contained a trenchant reexamination of the idea of the therapeutic rapport, that central concept in the treatment philosophy of the Zurich school, in terms of the libido theory. Freud persuaded Ferenczi to delay its submission to Jung, however, on the basis that he wanted to write his own companion piece, a general exposition of his method. Such an exposition was, of course, long overdue. Nonetheless, it had to be put off just a while longer, owing to the press of manuscripts for the *Papers on Applied Psychology* monograph series.

Jung was next on Freud's vacation agenda. Jung's invitation to visit had been proffered in June amidst a renewed and somewhat touchy discussion of paranoia and dementia praecox. Freud had accepted with alacrity: "Why, of course! We're not living in different centuries, not even on different continents. Why shouldn't we get together to discuss a matter of such importance to both of us?" To Abraham, Freud termed the planned visit a "tour of inspection," while to Jung, he wrote on 13 August 1908 that it would be a chance "to demolish the resentment that is bound to accumulate in the course of a year between two persons who demand a good deal of each other." Freud also announced to Jung that he wanted to win "a few personal concessions" with regard to both theory and politics:

> My selfish purpose, which I frankly confess, is to persuade you to continue and complete my work by applying to psychoses what I have begun with neuroses. With your strong and independent character, with your Germanic blood which enables you to command

the sympathy of the public more readily than I, you seem better fitted than anyone to carry out this mission. Besides, I'm fond of you; but I have learned to subordinate that factor.

Jung was delighted that Freud was coming—and coming expressly to see him, not Bleuler. (About his chief, Jung wrote, "Prof. Bleuler has nothing against your visit, how much he has for it no one knows, least of all himself.") Beyond the chance to examine some patients together, and perhaps finally to get some closure on their differing views of the psychoses, Jung was also eager for the personal contact absent at Salzburg. He had a lot to tell Freud: "I am looking forward so much to talking with you again in peace, for since I saw you in Vienna very, very many things have changed, much is new and further progress has been made."

In September, Freud traveled to England, then Berlin (where he did not see Abraham), and then stopped at the Burghölzli from the seventeenth through the twenty-first. Freud's five-day stopover in Zurich has attracted little attention in most histories of the Freud-Jung relationship, partially because firsthand accounts are lacking, and partially because in a relationship that ultimately turned stormy, it was a quiescent, even pacific interlude. Yet, it was terribly important for what it meant to Jung personally. As we now know from Jung's letter to Spielrein of 28 September 1908, Jung found a whole new affection for Freud as a result of their five days together. Moreover, during the visit, to Jung's delight and with his connivance, Freud mixed the charm with some hardball in Bleuler's direction: he pointedly slighted Bleuler by not calling on him once, even though he stayed at Jung's flat at the hospital which was directly above Bleuler's. (The slight worked: Bleuler, forever the gentleman, gave Jung time off to attend to his visitor and then promptly made his own pilgrimage to Vienna with his wife the following month to reestablish friendly communication. The Bleulers' visit went well, as Freud grasped that they were being very kind—"insofar as his unapproachability and her affectation permit," as he put it to Abraham.)

During Freud's five days in Zurich, he and Jung spent up to eight hours a day walking and talking. We know only a little of what they talked about. Jung gave Freud a tour of the wards and introduced him to the featured patient in his book on dementia praecox. Still pushing the toxin theory, Jung made the point that the fragmentation of her language was altogether unlike anything seen in the neuroses. (Freud, once he was back in Vienna, promptly dug up a counter-instance of language fragmentation in the productions of an obsessional neurotic.) Jung also came up with the very interesting paradox that dementia praecox patients try to cure themselves by becoming hysterical, while "in analysis we guide hysteria patients along the road" to dementia praecox. What he apparently meant by the latter remark was that by investigating fantasies, and making the patients take them seriously and sexually, analysis raised the complexes to delusional intensity before dissolving them. It is likely that Spielrein's mythological neurosis came up at this point, but perhaps not the exact manner in which she and Jung were currently resolving it. Jung also discussed his relations with his wife, who was now nearly seven months pregnant, and who returned from vacationing with the children in the middle of Freud's visit. As well, the two men discussed Jung's "star complex," i.e., his wish to have a son as revealed by Binswanger's experiment. After the visit Jung wrote to thank Freud, saying that the visit "has done me so much good" that he was resolved to pay a return visit to Vienna the following spring. Apparently this view of things was shared by Emma Jung, for she wrote not one but two thank-you letters.

Freud's view of the visit stressed the bottom line. In July, Abraham had warned that a "secession" was going on in Zurich, that people there were saying that "Freud seems to be an idea that has been superseded," and that Jung had "been reverting to his former spiritualistic inclinations." To that, Freud had replied that there was "a personal liking" between himself and Jung and that in any case Jung was already in too deep: "Moreover, he can hardly back out, he could not repudiate his past even if he wanted to, and the *Jahrbuch,* of which he is the editor, is a tie not to be broken." Reporting to Abraham two days after the visit, Freud had turned frankly optimistic:

> I am glad to say that you were only partly right, that is to say, only about Bleuler. As for Jung, he has overcome his vacillation, adheres unreservedly to the cause, and also will continue to work energetically on the dementia praecox question on our lines. That is highly gratifying to me, and I hope it will be pleasing to you also. But nothing will come of Bleuler, his defection is imminent, and his relations with Jung are strained to the breaking-point. Jung is giving up his position as physician but remains head of the laboratory and will work completely independently of Bleuler.

Freud went on to say that he had prepared the ground for a reconciliation between Jung and Abraham, noting that Jung had evinced a "high regard" for Abraham's scientific work and also that Jung felt that certain unnamed others had put the wrong idea into Abraham's head about himself. The peace lasted two months.

THE BIRTH OF "SIEGFRIED"

SPIELREIN ARRIVED back in Zurich in early October for the start of the fall semester. It is not known if she saw Jung before he left for his military service during the last two weeks of October. During November, they presumably did resume meeting, if only under the cover of her regular Friday appointment time. Jung was now terribly busy with the *Jahrbuch* manuscripts, plus a paper on dreams he was writing at Binet's specific request—this was important recognition—as well as with running both the lab and the outpatient clinic.

November was a fateful month in other ways. Auguste Forel had been privately drumming up antagonism against the new Freudian trends at the Burghölzli for over a year. Now he went public with his reservations. In a brief but well-conceived survey of the contemporary state of psychotherapy, Forel lamented the lack of coordination between different practitioners and called for a new international organization of all psychotherapists and hypnotists. In an ironical twist, he actually paused to praise Breuer and Freud, though he lamented the fact that Freud, like Dubois of Bern, had subsequently abandoned the use of hypnosis. Where Forel drew the line was in the constant search for sexual complexes; in his view this only fostered pathological development by encouraging the further fabrication of new complexes. Though Jung was not specifically named, there was no question but that he was the target of the criticism, a case of the son paying for the sins of the father. Forel's paper, which signaled that the lines of battle were starting to form in Switzerland, came out at the start of November. Freud promptly brought it to Jung's attention: "Forel's attacks are chiefly on you, probably out of ignorance."

Not to be outdone in martyrdom, Karl Abraham soon instigated his own clash with the established authorities. Speaking before the Berlin Association of Psychiatrists and Nerve-Specialists on 10 November, Abraham presented his paper on "Intermarriage Between Relatives and Neurosis." The essence of his argument was to reverse the time-honored observation of degeneration theorists that marriage between relatives resulted in neuroses in the offspring; according to Abraham, it was a hallmark of neurotic development to seek quasi-incestuous relationships because in this way the dependent ties of childhood were least compromised: Neurosis led to intermarriage, not the other way around. The argument, a good one, had a double personal significance for Abraham. His wife's uncle, the prominent professor of neurology Hermann Oppenheim, who was present, had already gone into print upholding the prevailing view that intermarriage among close relatives was especially common among Jews and a cause of their high rates of neurosis. Abraham was thus proclaiming his professional independence. He was also, in a manner of speaking, breaking his ties to his personal past, for the family tree he used as his chief example was none other than his own. In any event, the discussion that followed his presentation was characterized by Abraham to Freud in extremely colorful terms—"I stood in lonely opposition to the well-attended gathering"—leading Freud to write to Jung in equally colorful terms: "I hear from Abraham that he has survived his first battle in Berlin. He is on dangerous ground in that advance outpost."

Actually, the meeting was not nearly so acrimonious as Abraham made out. Henri Ellenberger has reviewed the published minutes, and only Ziehen, professor of psychiatry at the University of Berlin, seems to have been truly outspoken. (It *had* gone down hard to hear that C. F. Meyer, the celebrated novelist, had had an attraction to his sister, but that was a most minor point, even if Abraham elected to leave it in the subsequent version published in the *Jahrbuch.*) Abraham's own true assessment of the evening may be gauged from the fact that he went back to the same association for another presentation within the year. Still, even if we grant that a delight in self-dramatization had distorted Abraham's report to Freud, Theodor Ziehen was a very important figure in German psychiatry—his own work with the association experiment had prefigured Jung's—and thus an important new enemy.

Then there was the figure of von Monakow, Zurich's own resident professor of neurology. Von Monakow had been attending the meetings of the Zurich Freudian Society, where he had been made to feel as uncomfortable as Swiss manners would allow. Now he retaliated by cofounding with Dubois a new Swiss Association for Neurology. According to Jung, "every last hillbilly in our fair land" was invited, including Otto Veraguth, the Zurich experimental psychologist who had originated the use of the galvanometer in connection with the word association experiment. (Jung wrote of Veraguth's participation, "the only thing he understood on the entire programme was the dinner.")

Jung's reaction to these events was one of ostensible unconcern. A characteristic passage from his letters to Freud during the month of November:

> *Magna est vis veritatis tuae et praevalebit!* [Great is your truth and it will prevail—a paraphrase from the Vulgate, Appendix, 3 Esdras 4:41] . . . Nothing is more detestable than to blow the horn of instant public acclaim and settle down on densely populated ground. Hence I am delighted by the vigorous opposition we provoke. Obviously there are plenty more waiting to make fools of themselves. Even Forel still has a chance to do so at the eleventh hour. For some time now I have noticed the gentle zephyrs of prudery blowing across from America, for which Morton Prince seems to have a quite special organ. Everyone is terribly afraid for his practice, everyone is waiting to play a dirty trick on someone else.

But there was something else coming to pass that Jung could not be unconcerned about. On 27 November, Emma Jung began her confinement. Four days later, Franz Jung, the first boy, was born. Freud had written in anticipation of the event that he hoped "the star" had finally risen over the Jung home. Jung wrote back after the birth on 3 December:

> You can imagine our joy. The birth went off normally, mother and child are doing well. Too bad we aren't peasants any more, otherwise I could say: Now that I have a son I can depart in peace. A great deal more could be said on this complex theme.

To which Freud, knowledgeable about the literary allusion if not the "complex" one, replied on 11 December:

> I must say, your regret at being unable to play the ideal hero-father ("My father begot me and died") struck me as very premature. The child will find you indispensable as a father for many years, first in a positive, then in a negative sense!

The line "My father begot me and died" is from Wagner's *Siegfried,* Act 2, scene 3; it is spoken by Siegfried to Brünnhilde. Freud, either on the basis of his September talks with Jung or else his general literacy, had correctly contextualized the import of Jung's statement about departing in peace—"Siegfried" had been born, the hero without a father. Yet, Jung did not want to die. But he didn't want to do what he had to do, either. By this time, Emma Jung knew of Spielrein's existence as a patient in whom her husband was taking an extraordinary interest.

THE END OF THE AFFAIR

THE LAST extant letter from Jung to Spielrein for the year 1908 is dated 4 December, is incomplete, and is utterly desperate in tone: he has not treated her professionally, he begs her to not revenge herself on him, he must meet with her immediately—in her apartment, where they will be freer—and he needs her help badly since his work is endangered. Throughout the letter Jung makes himself out to be the vulnerable party and he even recalls a childhood incident when he was rescued from death. One should understand this tone in reading the excerpts already published by Carotenuto:

> I am looking for a person who can love without punishing, imprisoning and draining the other person; I am seeking this as yet unrealized type who will manage to separate love from social advantage or disadvantage, so that love may always be an end unto itself, not just a means for achieving another end. . . . It is my misfortune that my life means nothing to me without the joy of love, of tempestuous, eternally changing love. . . . Return to me, in this moment of my need, some of the love and guilt and altruism which I was able to give you at the time of your illness. Now it is I who am ill.

It is not a love letter. At one point, Jung announces that he pities the girl who falls in love with him, for "faithfulness" is not in his nature: "Therefore when one is already married it is better to commit the lie only once and to pay the price for it than to repeat the experience again and again, again to lie and again to disappoint."

From the letter one can guess that they had just met, but two days after little Franz's birth, and had had a dramatic confrontation. We have no other account to rely on, so we cannot be sure what happened, but the most likely scenario would seem to be that Jung had tried, unsuccessfully, to get rid of her. Paradoxically, however, the single most pressing motive leading Jung to break with her was equally well served by placating her in whatever way she would accept. For the one thing Jung could not afford was a public scandal.

No mention of any of this occurs in the letters to Freud. Jung's letter of 15 December announced that it had been written in haste and evaded any discussion of family matters, but his next letter, of 21 December, was leisurely and confident, and thereafter the extant correspondence is entirely taken up with politics and, in Freud's phrase, the coming "birth of Jung's *Jahrbuch,* as everyone will call it." The letters are full of high spirits. For example, at one point Freud wrote that "if I am Moses, then you are Joshua who will take possession of the promised land of psychiatry, which I shall only be able to glimpse from afar." Jung, for his part, settled down to various clinical anecdotes along with some charming vignettes of how his little daughter Agathli interpreted the mechanics of the recent birth. It would appear that Jung had gotten everything squared away at home.

But Jung had not stopped meeting with Spielrein. It was left for his wife to take the necessary step. In mid-January of 1909, Spielrein's mother received an anonymous letter saying that she should save her daughter. Frau Spielrein, as mothers will, promptly wrote to Jung saying that having saved her daughter once, he should not ruin her now. Jung replied to Frau Spielrein thus:

> I moved from being her doctor to being her friend when I ceased to push my own feelings into the background. I could drop my role as doctor the more easily because I did not feel professionally obligated, for I never charged a fee. This latter clearly establishes the limits imposed upon a doctor. You do understand, of course, that a man and a girl cannot possibly continue indefinitely to have friendly dealings with one another without the likelihood that something more may enter the relationship. For what would restrain the two from drawing the consequences of their love? A *doctor* and his *patient,* on the other hand, can talk of the most intimate matters for as long as they like, and the patient may expect her doctor to give her all the love and concern she requires. But the doctor knows his limits and will never cross them, for he is *paid* for his troubles. That imposes the necessary restraints on him.

Jung ended by announcing, "My fee is 10 francs per consultation," while hoping that Mrs. Spielrein would choose "the prosaic solution."

Since the publication of the Carotenuto documents, Jung's initial reply to Frau Spielrein has become infamous for its callousness and its apparent opportunism. But we must remind ourselves what Jung's situation was. The *Jahrbuch* was due out in scarcely more than a month, the issue of the sexual inquiry was polarizing Swiss medicine, Herr and Frau Spielrein were important people, and their daughter was by no means ready or willing to end her secret meetings with her ''Siegfried.'' Having botched the middle-game, Jung was faced with an impossible end-game. Try as he might, he had not found a way of placating Spielrein in a way that she could accept, except by continuing to see her. Now he had to worry about the political ramifications for his fellow Freudians if his secret meetings should be discovered. ''Ten francs per consultation'' can be seen as a weak man's way of trying to save his colleagues, if not himself.

Two more rounds of secret letters were then exchanged between Jung and Spielrein's mother before Jung, still without explanation to Spielrein herself, suddenly declined to visit her and asked instead that she come for the regular appointment hour. Jung's second letter to Frau Spielrein bears quoting, since while it admits much it does contain an apparent denial:

> I have always told your daughter that a sexual relationship was out of the question and that my actions were intended to express my feelings of friendship. When this occurred, I happened to be in a very gentle and compassionate mood, and I wanted to give your daughter convincing proof of my trust, my friendship, in order to liberate her inwardly. That turned out to be a grave mistake, which I greatly regret. . . .

Spielrein, offended by the mysterious turn in Jung's behavior but thinking it spoke only of his inner turmoil, stayed away for three consecutive appointments. Perhaps she was still remembering the good effect the scene in early December had had and thought to worry him again. After three weeks she relented. At the time she finally appeared at his office, she still did not know of the correspondence between Jung and her mother, but she had just heard of another female patient who claimed that Jung had led her on, then rebuffed her. To Spielrein's amazement, Jung, now set in the only course open to him, confronted her along the lines of his defense to her parents: he had been too good to her, she wanted too much, her symptoms were her unfulfilled desires, etc. He proposed to her that they get down to work analyzing all this. As she later recorded it, "... he gave me a long sermon about all he had done for me and was still doing, that ... well, what it all added up to is that he is just my doctor again."

This was on Friday, 26 February 1909. In response to Jung's lecture, Spielrein did what any sane person might do under similar circumstances. She attacked him, drew blood, then ran out.

SPOOKERY

SPIELREIN'S ASSAULT and subsequent disappearance left Jung too petrified with fear of what would happen next to notify Vienna. Perhaps, like Gross, he would now be viewed as someone who "can only do great harm to our cause." Making matters worse, the first volume of the *Jahrbuch* had just come out, its masthead making Jung an official representative of Freudianism. The young woman was in a position— she had Jung's letters—of doing incalculable harm, not only to Jung personally, but also to psychoanalysis as a whole, most certainly in Switzerland and quite possibly in the rest of the German-speaking world as well.

Jung had already begun hedging his bets. In January and February of 1909, he had begun courting the favor of some new colleagues, most notably the Zurich pastor Oskar Pfister, and the Basel philosopher and schoolteacher Paul Häberlin. At the same time, he also began downplaying the sexual inquiry as a technical device while distancing himself from Freud's nomenclature. In a remarkable letter of 25 February 1909 written to Ernest Jones the day before Spielrein attacked him, Jung announced that each of Freud's basic psychological concepts—"repression" was but one example—could be reinterpreted, and renamed, in line with basic, functional biological considerations. As for the sexual inquiry, Jung frankly advocated caution to Jones, who had just moved to a new post in Toronto: "Both with students and patients I get on further by not making the theme of sexuality so prominent."

When the *Jahrbuch* had been been out for ten days and there was still no word from Jung, Freud finally telegrammed an urgent inquiry. Jung wired back and then responded at length on 7 March 1909. After piling one excuse upon another for his prolonged silence, he let Freud know that there was potentially trouble ahead, but he was still too scared to tell the truth:

> The last and worst straw is that a complex is playing Old Harry with me: a woman patient, whom years ago I pulled out of a very

sticky neurosis with unstinting devotion, has violated my confidence and my friendship in the most mortifying way imaginable. She has kicked up a vile scandal solely because I denied myself the pleasure of giving her a child. I have always acted the gentleman towards her, but before the bar of my rather too sensitive conscience I nevertheless don't feel clean, and that is what hurts the most because my intentions were always honourable. But you know how it is— the devil can use even the best of things for the fabrication of filth. Meanwhile I have learnt an unspeakable amount of marital wisdom, for until now I had a totally inadequate idea of my polygamous components despite all self-analysis. Now I know where and how the devil can be laid by the heels.

Jung did not elaborate on the situation further, except metaphorically; he mentioned "the buffetings fate has given me" and added that he looked forward to visiting Vienna ten days hence and "to recuperating from all my batterings."

In reply, Freud had important news of his own: he had just been invited by Stanley Hall to speak at Clark University in America the following fall under circumstances that he could afford. Hall had previously invited Freud at the end of December, but, over Jung's protests, Freud had declined for financial reasons. In the matter of America, Jung was prescient; he understood that the prestige accruing from such an invitation was worth almost any investment. There was the example of Janet to go on, and more recently, Kraepelin had received the extraordinary fee of 50,000 marks for a single consultation in California. By March of 1909, Freud had finally accepted Jung's logic, along with Hall's renewed invitation.

Only after discussing the invitation to America did Freud take up Jung's troubles. By a fateful coincidence, Freud had just recently heard from a visiting physician, Arthur Muthmann of Munich, of another Zurich patient who claimed to have been Jung's mistress. Understandably, Freud assumed that this improbable charge was the source of scandal that Jung was worrying about. Hysterical accusations against doctors were nothing new and Freud saw no particular threat from them to the new specialty of psychoanalysis: "To be slandered and scorched by the love with which we operate—such are the perils of our trade, which we are certainly not going to abandon on their account."

To be sure, Jung's two-week silence had been bothersome; it called to mind the dwindling correspondence with Fliess some years earlier, and in his letter Freud went on to mention his sensitivity on this point—

"traumatic hyperaesthesia." The old complex, Fliess—a journal—collaboration—disaster, was still active. But what had been perhaps even more alarming about Jung's letter was the unexpected and strangely sincere-sounding talk about "filth" and "the devil." Here Freud took a reasonable guess. In January, Jung had mentioned his new friend Pastor Pfister in striking terms: "Oddly enough, I find this mixture of medicine and theology to my liking." Pfister had in the meantime himself written to Freud, and his thoroughly Christian outlook on psychoanalysis had proved unnerving but not completely indigestible. Freud now guessed that Pfister had reinfected Jung with the old religion bug, something that should be squelched forthwith. Thus it happened that Freud's reply to Jung's letter hinting at a potential scandal took aim not at any indiscretion, real or imagined, but at Jung's high-toned phrases:

> And another thing: "In league with the Devil and yet you fear fire?'" Your grandfather [Goethe] said something like that. I bring up this quotation because you definitely lapse into the theological style in relating this experience. The same thing happened to me in a letter to Pfister—I borrowed every conceivable metaphor from the flame-fire-pyre etc. complex. I couldn't help myself, respect for theology had nailed me to this quotation (!): "One way or the other, the Jew will be burned." I was still so unaccustomed to being on good terms with Protestant theologians.

It was almost comical: depending on what Spielrein did, Jung might be ruined, and yet here he and Freud were discussing his "theological style." But Freud was indeed on to something—the smell of the pyre was faint but not imagined—even if he could not guess where it would go.

Jung's reply of II March could have been only partially reassuring:

> I must answer you at once. Your kind words have relieved me and comforted me. You may rest assured, not only now but for the future, that nothing Fliess-like is going to happen. . . . Except for moments of infatuation my affection is lasting and reliable. It's just that for the past fortnight the devil has been tormenting me in the shape of neurotic ingratitude. But I shall not be unfaithful to ΨA on that account. On the contrary, I am learning from it how to do better in the future. You mustn't take on about my "theological"

style, I just felt that way. Now and then, I admit, the devil does strike a chill into my—on the whole—blameless heart.

Lord knows what Freud, still short of the requisite information, made of this. Jung was obviously glad to hear that Freud worried about losing him, but his letter also betrayed unfathomable second thoughts— "neurotic ingratitude"—about psychoanalysis. And the "devil" was still on board. Indeed, Jung's letter went on to mention his recent discovery of E. T. A. Hoffmann's novel *The Devil's Elixirs*, which depicts the Faustian adventures of one Brother Medardus, a renegade Capuchin monk who, intoxicated by a strange elixir, leaves the monastery and goes into the world disguised as a nobleman. Medardus's adventures, in Hoffmann's telling, are a nightmare of secret guilt and of the humiliation that comes of being discovered. Pursued by an evil double, and caught in a web of strange coincidences, the monk falls into one temptation after another, into lust, incest, murder, and madness, before he finds repentance and ultimate redemption. *The Devil's Elixirs* was later destined to have a lasting impact on Jung's thought, but, more important, its relevance to his current situation—waiting to be unmasked for his secret sins—was truly uncanny. As it was, to Freud Jung allowed only that he was thinking of doing an essay on Hoffmann's book for Freud's monograph series, this on the basis that the book contained a "whole tangle of neurotic problems . . . all palpably real," and that "a good deal of my 'theology' evidently comes from there."

Something was indeed wrong; the portents were beginning to mount up. The next thing to happen was that Jung's visit to Vienna, scheduled for the nineteenth of March, was delayed a week, ostensibly for professional reasons. At the same time, however, Jung found time to visit Häberlin in Basel. Jung had the poor grace to mention the visit to Freud in his letter of 21 March:

> Lately I visited Häberlin. He is a far-sighted fellow with an unforeseeable future. . . . He was born in the same village as I, he the son of a schoolteacher, I of a parson. Now we meet again in this field. He tops Pfister by a head in psychological acuity and biological knowledge. Nor does he lack a certain mystical streak, on which account I set special store by him, since it guarantees a deepening of thought beyond the ordinary and a grasp of far-reaching syntheses.

Much was happening, and happening very fast. Jung had previously submitted his Burghölzli resignation to Bleuler in January but had thoughtfully delayed his departure until the end of March when the work load proved unusually heavy. Now his departure was overdue and a celebratory vacation, to include Vienna, had already been planned. Meanwhile, the new family house at Küsnacht, outside of Zurich, which had been five years in the planning, was almost finished. Jung was going to be on his own professionally. The dalliance with Spielrein had ended just in time so far as these important moves in Jung's personal and professional life were concerned, but until he knew what revenge, if any, she planned, it behooved him to continue to hedge his bets in terms of his career.

It was on this unsteady ground that Jung elected to meet Freud. The historical record has it that Carl and Emma Jung were in Vienna for a second time from Thursday, 25 March, to Tuesday, 30 March, 1909. Nothing is known about this visit, save what can be learned from the letters that Freud and Jung exchanged immediately afterward and from the following passage in Jung's memoirs describing their last night's conversation together:

> It interested me to hear Freud's views on precognition and on parapsychology in general. When I visited him in Vienna in 1909 I asked him what he thought of these matters. Because of his materialistic prejudice, he rejected this entire complex of questions as nonsensical, and did so in terms of so shallow a positivism that I had difficulty in checking the sharp retort on the tip of my tongue. . . .
> When Freud was going on this way, I had a curious sensation. It was as if my diaphragm were made of iron and were becoming red-hot—a glowing vault. And at that moment there was such a loud report in the bookcase, which stood right next to us, that we both started up in alarm, fearing the thing was going to topple over on us. I said to Freud: "There, that is an example of a so-called catalytic exteriorization phenomenon."
> "Oh come," he exclaimed. "That is sheer bosh."
> "It is not," I replied. "You are mistaken, Herr Professor. And to prove my point I now predict that in a moment there will be another such loud report!" Sure enough, no sooner had I said the words than the same detonation went off in the bookcase. To this day I do not know what gave me this certainty. But I knew beyond all doubt that the report would come again. Freud only stared aghast at me.

"Catalytic exteriorization phenomenon"—the phrase was worthy of Jung's college days, when he was all occultism. In effect, colleague Abraham had been proved right about the Swiss tendency to mysticism, only the bookcase, most disconcertingly, seemed to be taking Jung's side in the matter. As for Jung's feeling of a red-hot, glowing vault—Freud later thought it a pregnancy fantasy—the depth of his resentment was plainly beginning to show.

The intellectual stakes were as serious as the emotional ones. Intellectually, Jung was about to become more closely acquainted with a man he had long revered, the great Geneva psychologist Théodore Flournoy. And Jung already knew that Flournoy, though no lightweight scientifically, made room in his description of the unconscious for latently spiritual and progressive tendencies. Indeed, in a recent paper on that subject, Flournoy had explicitly cited a passage from Jung's book on dementia praecox in support of his formulation.

Emotionally, the still unresolved, and to Freud undescribed, crisis with Spielrein seemingly had pushed Jung to the limits of human experience. Distraught, he was making his own entry into the potentially ever-present human side-world of premonition and strange coincidence. In a way this was where Jung always had wanted to be, though not in these circumstances. That he was prepared to defend this change in his sensibilities face-to-face with Freud speaks to his integrity. But by the same token it availed him little in the one direction that mattered most. For he did not yet know, neither cognitively nor precognitively, what Spielrein was going to do.

Following the visit to Freud, the Jungs vacationed in Italy. There Jung had a "great dream" in two parts, which he subsequently reported to a seminar in 1925 and later published, in a somewhat prettified version, in his memoirs. In the first part of the dream, Jung encountered Freud as an aging, disgruntled Imperial Austrian customs official. In the second part, Jung encountered a twelfth-century Crusader going about during the noon hour tumult of a modern Italian city. As the account in Jung's memoirs makes clear, the contrast between the two figures was emblematic of an incipient difference in the views of the unconscious held by himself and Freud. Whereas Freud, the customs official, was content with snooping about for human contraband, for the evidence of man's all-too-human limitations, he, Jung, was looking for a numinous element in man's psychic depths, looking for something that would give meaning to life. But beyond that, there was a strong resemblance between the two figures, for, as Jung made clear to his 1925 seminar, they were both "dead," but they seemed not to know it.

The darker version of the dream given at the 1925 seminar more accurately captures Jung's mood at the time he dreamed it. And the sense of dread comes through even more clearly when we grasp that the dream images were undoubtedly informed by two speeches taken from Hoffmann's *The Devil's Elixirs*. Both speeches in the novel specifically carry the weight of admonitions—they are part of the consistently painful and frequently uncanny education which Brother Medardus is undergoing as a result of his sins. In the first speech, he is lectured to about the limits of consciousness, which is compared to "the miserable activity of some pettifogging toll-keeper, or customs-officer . . . who sets up a pokey little office in his mind and says, whenever any goods are to be sent out: 'Oh, no! Export prohibited. They must remain here.' " In this way, the passage goes on to say, man is blocked from the "heavenly city" of the spiritual world. This was more or less Freud's position, as Jung saw it. The second speech is an extended diatribe against the position of modern nobility, who cling to their lineage from ancient knights even as they are increasingly marginal in modern society: "This may well explain their tactless behavior . . . , the product of a deep despair that the triviality of their past glory will be exposed to the knowing gaze of the wise, and their insufficiencies held up to ridicule." This was more or less Jung's own situation. And, as his dream of bad conscience told him, the difference between himself and Freud might not matter much: they were both "dead," even if they did not yet know it.

Jung was deeply worried, and therefore deeply cautious. In his first follow-up letter to Freud, which he began on 2 April 1909 but did not finish till Easter Monday, 12 April 1909, he apologized for his "spookery," in part because of a resemblance to Fliess (who had built himself a notable reputation for his uncanny medical predictions). He also made mention of his recent dream, but elected not to describe it. All in all, however, Jung was still heaven-bent on his new direction and his letter was principally concerned with recounting fresh clinical material in support of it. In the process he dredged up a favorite term of Morton Prince's, "psychosynthesis":

I had the feeling that under it all there must be some quite special complex, a universal one having to do with the prospective tendencies in man. If there is a "psychoanalysis" there must also be a "psychosynthesis" which creates future events according to the same laws. (I see I am writing rather as if I had a flight of ideas.) . . .

That last evening with you has, most happily, freed me inwardly from the oppressive sense of your paternal authority. My unconscious celebrated this impression with a great dream which has preoccupied me for some days and which I have just finished analysing. I hope I am now rid of all unnecessary encumbrances. Your cause must and will prosper . . .

Jung's erratic behavior—before, during, and immediately after his visit with Freud—made sense if one understood the horrible bind he was in. But from the point of view of Vienna, Jung was behaving quite oddly, and for very mysterious reasons at that. Freud rose to the occasion. His letter in reply to Jung's strange missive of 2/12 April was a masterpiece of warmth and skeptical toleration rendered all the more magnanimous by being set against an initial display of hurt feelings:

> It is strange that on the very same evening when I formally adopted you as eldest son and anointed you—*in partibus infidelium*—as my successor and crown prince, you should have divested me of my paternal dignity, which divesting seems to have given you as much pleasure as I, on the contrary, derived from the investiture of your person. Now I am afraid of falling back into the father role with you if I tell you how I feel about the poltergeist business.

The phrase *"in partibus infidelium,"* literally "in the lands of the unbelievers," was an ecclesiastical title denoting the rank of bishop without a diocese, i.e., as a missionary. Freud went on in gentle fashion to say that though the creaking in the bookcase had continued since Jung left, his own credulity had "vanished with the magic of your presence":

> . . . I confront the despiritualized furniture as the poet confronted undeified Nature after the gods of Greece had passed away. Accordingly, I put on my fatherly horned-rimmed spectacles and warn my dear son to keep a cool head, for it is better not to understand something than make such great sacrifices to understanding. I also shake my wise head over psychosynthesis and think: Yes, that's how the young people are, the only places they really enjoy visiting are those they can visit without us, to which we with our short breath and weary legs cannot follow them.

And then, playing the penitent grown wise, Freud told Jung the story of his trip to Greece in 1904 when he was plagued by a recurrence of the numbers 61 and 62, which seemed to foretell the age of his own death. Genially, he then analyzed this superstitious preoccupation, explained its connection to the numerology of his former friend Fliess, and remarked on "the specifically Jewish nature of my mysticism." The letter was a masterpiece and it had its effect. Jung responded docilely, "I have not gone over to any system yet and shall also guard against putting my trust in those spooks."

Freud's position was clear enough. With the *Jahrbuch* now before the public view, he was not about to lose his influence over its editor and certainly not on the eve of a trip to America, where thanks to the word association test Jung's reputation was already established. If that meant indulging Jung's strange mood, it could all be managed. As for Jung, we do him a disservice if we do not keep in mind that the new turn in his thought had many antecedents. In 1906 he had argued that it was necessary to provide patients with a new complex so that their energy might be marshalled to deal with the life tasks of the present and the future. And in 1902, he had suggested that the subliminal romances of his mediumistic cousin were simultaneously attempts to bypass her psychopathic ego and prepare for her adult life. But let us also note that what he was now arguing—that the complex, instead of merely repeating its infantile-sexual and incestuous past, might also transform itself and begin to organize the future—was nothing other than what Spielrein had been insisting on in her Transformation Journal some ten months before their liaison began.

To summarize, in March and April of 1909, while his most recent set of theories lay smashed on the rocks of his most recent experiences with Spielrein, experiences whose consequences he could no longer control, Jung privately began toying with a revised interpretation of the unconscious, one that emphasized its "prospective" potentials while appealing to broadly based functional biological principles. In one sense a return to earlier ideas, Jung's new views offered him a potential escape hatch politically. If things went badly, and he was forced to recant his Freudianism, he could yet find his audience elsewhere in the international community of psychopathologists and psychotherapists. Beyond these considerations, Jung's new views also offered an interpretive stance from which to examine at least some of his recent experiences with Spielrein, such as their reading each other's thoughts at a distance, and perhaps also to mollify at least some of the pangs of his "rather too sensitive conscience."

PERSONS WHO have been betrayed in love are fearsome even to themselves. It may be that no loss is worse than the loss of a true love. Betrayal makes that loss lethal. It does not help matters that true love, perhaps always but most certainly when it is adulterous, partakes of the demonic. The only true solution is to turn to another love, but just this, save for a momentary pretense, is impossible. In the meantime, no deed is so extreme that it might not happen.

As her letter-drafts of June of 1909 make clear, Spielrein was thoroughly beside herself. Immediately after her angry last encounter with Jung, she left Zurich for the countryside to recoup her senses. Subsequently, her mother, then her father, came to Zurich to watch over her. Her mother tried to meet privately with Jung, but he insisted that any interview take place at the Burghölzli during office hours.

Spielrein's continued stay at the university was imperiled and she managed to keep up with only one course, histology, though she did continue her work at the university medical clinic. Finally, in May, she resolved to face Jung. She went to his lecture, but, standing in the back, she more resembled an apparition than a student, and with all eyes on her, she fled. At the end of May, she conceived one last hope. Putting pen to paper, she wrote to a man she didn't know:

Dear Professor Freud:

I would be most grateful to you if you would grant me a brief audience! It has to do with something of greatest importance to me which you would probably be interested to hear about.

If it were possible, I should like to ask that you inform me of a convenient time somewhat in advance, since I am an intern at the hospital here and therefore would have to arrange for someone to substitute for me during my absence.

Perhaps you expect me to be a brazen seeker after fame who plans to bring you some wretched "earth-shaking" scholarly paper or something of the sort.

No, that is not what leads me to you. You, too, have made me feel awkward.

Freud's response was immediate. He received the letter on 3 June; the same day, he mailed it off to Jung with the following inquiry:

Weird! What is she? A busybody, a chatterbox, or a paranoiac? If you know anything about the writer or have some opinion in the matter, would you kindly send me a short wire, but otherwise you must *not* go into any trouble. If I don't hear from you, I shall assume you know nothing.

Jung's telegram is missing; whatever it said, it allowed Freud to write back to Spielrein on 4 June 1909 politely asking her to state her business before she undertook to come to Vienna. The same day Jung followed up his telegram with a letter of explanation to Freud; the letter does not do him a lot of credit:

At the moment I don't know what more to say. Spielrein is the person I wrote you about. She was published in abbreviated form in my Amsterdam lecture of blessed memory. She was, so to speak, my test case, for which reason I remembered her with special gratitude and affection. Since I knew from experience that she would immediately relapse if I withdrew my support, I prolonged the relationship over the years and in the end found myself morally obliged, as it were, to devote a large measure of friendship to her, until I saw that an unintended wheel had started turning, whereupon I finally broke with her. She was, of course, systematically planning my seduction, which I considered inopportune. Now she is seeking revenge. Lately she has been spreading a rumour that I shall soon get a divorce from my wife and marry a certain girl student, which has thrown not a few of my colleagues into a flutter. . . . Like Gross, she is a case of fight-the-father, which in the name of all that's wonderful I was trying to cure *gratissime* (!) with untold tons of patience, even abusing our friendship for that purpose. On top of that, naturally, an amiable complex had to throw an outsize monkey-wrench into the works. As I have indicated before, my first visit to Vienna had a very long aftermath, first the compulsive infatuation in Abbazia [with an unknown woman], then the Jewess popped up in another form, in the shape of my patient. Now of course the whole bag of tricks lies there quite clearly before my eyes. During the whole business Gross' notions flitted about a bit too much in my head.

Freud elected not to read any menace in the allusion to Jung's first visit to Vienna, for the tone of his return letter of 7 June was thoroughly bemused. He let Jung know that he had this new, ill-conceived correspondence under control, having written Spielrein in the meantime as though the matter concerned himself and not Jung. Then, addressing himself to Jung's chagrin, he went on to admit that he himself had "come very close to it a number of times and had a narrow escape." He had grasped that Jung's trouble had grown out of his use of psychoanalysis and he forgave all:

> I believe that only grim necessities weighing on my work, and the fact that I was ten years older than yourself when I came to ΨA, have saved me from similar experiences. But no lasting harm is done. They help us to develop the thick skin we need and to dominate "countertransference," which is after all a permanent problem for us. . . .
>
> The way these women manage to charm us with every conceivable psychic perfection until they have attained their purpose is one of nature's greatest spectacles.

Jung had said as much as he ever intended to say and he was enormously relieved by Freud's reply. Indeed, he was moved to contrition: ". . . it is too stupid that I of all people, your 'son' and 'heir,' should squander your heritage so heedlessly, as though I had known nothing of all these things." Beyond gratitude, something else had happened to make Jung suddenly want to pick up the mantle of "son and heir" which for the previous two months he had been trying to cast off—the very same week, he, too, had been invited by Stanley Hall to lecture at the Clark University congress in America three months hence. Such are the ironies created by an inconstant course: no sooner had Jung become deeply troubled by his association with psychoanalysis than it granted his long-unfulfilled wish, the chance for an American audience. So, he and Freud were to be allies after all.

Freud, of course, was delighted to hear that Jung would be going to America with him and Ferenczi, who had invited himself, and further news of Spielrein was relegated to the fifth paragraph of his next letter, of 18 June 1909:

> Fräulein Spielrein had admitted in her second letter that her business has to do with you; apart from that, she has not disclosed her intentions. My reply was ever so wise and penetrating; I made it appear as though the most tenuous of clues had enabled me Sherlock Holmes–like to guess the situation (which of course was none

too difficult after your communication) and suggested a more appropriate procedure, something endopsychic as it were. Whether it will be effective, I don't know. But now I must entreat you, don't go too far in the direction of contrition and reaction. Remember Lassalle's fine sentence about the chemist whose test tube had cracked: "With a slight frown over the resistance of matter, he gets on with his work." In view of the kind of matter we work with, it will never be possible to avoid little laboratory explosions. Maybe we didn't slant the test tube enough, or we heated it too quickly. In this way we learn what part of the danger lies in the matter and what part in our way of handling it.

Freud's second letter to Spielrein has survived. It is kindly but noncommittal. He makes it clear that Dr. Jung is his friend and colleague and that before he will judge him he will obey "the old legal dictum: *audiatur et altera pars.*" The "something endopsychic" which he recommended to her was the following:

From the enclosures you sent with your letter, I rather gather that you used to be close friends, and it is not difficult to infer from the present situation that this is no longer so. Did that friendship perhaps arise from some medical consultation, and did his readiness to help a person in mental distress perhaps kindle your sympathy? I am tempted to think so, for I know of many similar instances. But I know nothing of how and through whose fault it came to grief, and do not want to pass judgment on that. Still, if on the basis of the above assumptions I might be permitted to address a word to you, then I would urge you to ask yourself whether the feelings that have outlived this close relationship are not best suppressed and eradicated, from your own psyche I mean, and without external intervention and the involvement of third persons.

Along with his letter, Freud returned to Spielrein some enclosures she had sent, presumably Jung's letters to her mother. Nevertheless, he held on to her letter itself, and offered it to Jung, saying he could send it "whenever you like." Jung had been playing Faust, so Freud adopted the role of Mephistopheles: on the one hand, he would chase away this unwanted Gretchen, but, on the other, he would wait to see just how curious Jung would allow himself to be about her disclosures. Both men had misjudged the character of the girl. She was moved by Freud's letter—"He loves him! What if he could understand all this?"—not put off as she was supposed to be. Thus inspired, on 10 June she began writing out the history of her relationship with Jung. Through this pen-and-paper abreaction she began to regain her composure, and by 19 June, she was sufficiently steadied to confront Jung directly after one of his lectures. Jung was surprised to find out that she was *not* the source of rumors about an impending divorce from his wife. Spielrein was surprised to find out that he was pretending that the whole attraction to her had been a spin-off from some alleged attraction toward Freud's daughter. Both parties wanted peace. He wanted her continued silence. She had conditions. They reconciled, and parted.

Jung had been pretending, both to Freud and to her parents, that her difficulties were the result of her neurosis acting up; her distraught state had only made that diagnosis seem more credible. Thus, the first of her conditions was to require Jung, as the price of peace, to retract his earlier statements. Undoubtedly, he was obliged to write something to her parents, but no documentary evidence on this survives. What we do know is that she also obliged him to write to Freud—she'd grasped the import of "something endopsychic"—and confess his culpability. Jung's follow-up letter to Freud, of 21 June 1909, was a guilty admission of everything except intercourse. Especially, Jung regretted the letters to Spielrein's mother—"a piece of knavery which I very reluctantly confess to you as my father." As for Spielrein's current state of mind, Jung wrote: "[S]he has freed herself from the transference in the best and nicest way and has suffered no relapse (apart from a paroxysm of weeping after the separation)." Jung rounded out his confession by asking Freud—no doubt also in line with Spielrein's demands—to write to her informing her of his "perfect honesty."

Jung had behaved badly and Spielrein was perhaps entitled to this bit of revenge. Freud did his part, on 24 June 1909, as gracefully as possible, by writing her to say, "the fact that I was wrong and that the lapse has to be blamed on the man and not the woman, as my young friend admits, satisfies my need to hold women in high esteem." But more than mere spite was animating Spielrein. The entries in her pen-and-paper abreaction of the relationship bear dates after 19 June, the day of the reconciliation. And what was making this ongoing confession possible was the thought that there was someone out there who might understand it all—Freud. The reason for getting Jung to admit the truth to Freud was so that she might keep writing to him! Freud was the one person to whom it was safe to confess: he was Jung's friend, he understood psychoanalysis, and he lived outside Zurich. On 30 June, Spielrein answered Freud's letter, which, in truth, had needed no reply.

We don't know what Spielrein's letter of 30 June actually contained, but we do know what she had imagined sending. In this book, we have been relying on the "letter-drafts of 1909" right along as a source of information about her evolving relationship with Jung over the years. But we have done little to characterize the real flavor of this document, and nothing to specify its further significance. Begun by Spielrein on 10 June, but not finished until the end of the month, the document is vivid, impassioned, and chaotic: fresh emotional outbursts alternate with periods of momentary calm, and the story line, such as it is, constantly fragments into details whose meaning cannot always be deciphered. It is meant to be a personal defense and a chronicle of all the ins and outs of Spielrein's entire relationship with Jung. Their work together in the psychology lab, Binswanger's experiment, the mediumistic cousin "S.W.," "Siegfried," prophetic dreams, reading thoughts at a distance, Otto Gross, their mutual mythic and latently incestuous dreams—all this is described and more, including repeated mysterious references to their having had "poetry" together. But beyond their impassioned and chaotic quality, here we must ask the reader to consider this document in an entirely different aspect. For the fact is that these are all drafts of a single long letter *written and sent to Freud* in late June of 1909.

One may well imagine Jung's chagrin. His whole secret career as sorcerer's apprentice was within Spielrein's ken, and his recent interest in "spookery" potentially stood in a very different light, depending on what she said about "Siegfried" and prospective dreams. And certainly, Freud did grasp some of what had happened. But Jung was saved from greater embarrassment by Spielrein's incoherence. Still profoundly distressed, she was unable to pull her story into a straightforward narrative. Freud commented to Jung about her final, long and unsolicited letter:

> Amazingly awkward—is she a foreigner by any chance?—or very inhibited, hard to read and hard to understand. All I can gather from it is that the matter means a great deal to her and that she is very much in earnest. Don't fault yourself for drawing me into it; it was not your doing but hers. And the matter has ended in a

manner satisfactory to all. You have been oscillating, as I see, between the extremes of Bleuler and Gross.

And there, save for one final thank-you from Jung to Freud in a letter of 10/13 July, the Spielrein affair ended. Or seemed to. Thanks to her disorganization of the moment, Freud's very civilized sexual morality, and Jung's mistaken belief that she would shortly be leaving Zurich for the University of Heidelberg, the storm had come and gone and everything was still left standing. Freud and Jung were still allied with each other, the papers for the second half-issue of the *Jahrbuch* were being assembled for November publication, and Stanley Hall was waiting for his distinguished visitors in Massachusetts.

POETRY

FREUD WAS not the last person to be mystified by Spielrein's unsolicited letter of 30 June 1909. Modern readers, too, find it very tough going, at least in the only form available to us, the "letter-drafts" published by Carotenuto. To begin with, Spielrein repeatedly rides off on tangents that have meaning only to her. Furthermore, even when she sticks to the topic of her secret meetings with Jung, a certain maidenly modesty intervenes in her account like a dogged literary chaperone trying to avoid the worst. Consider the following passage:

> To suffer this disdain at the hands of a person whom one loved more than anything in the world for four, five years, to whom one gave the most beautiful part of one's soul, to whom one sacrificed one's maidenly pride, allowing oneself to be kissed, etc., for the first and perhaps the last time in my life, because when he began my treatment I was nothing but a naïve child . . .

It would be nice to know, just once for the record, what "etc." covered. In the following passage, the "etc." is joined by a code word, "poetry," which recurs throughout the letter-drafts:

> Four and a half years ago Dr. Jung was my doctor, then he became my friend and finally my "poet," i.e., my beloved. Eventually he came to me and things went as they usually do with "poetry." He preached polygamy; his wife was supposed to have no objection, etc., etc.

In the above instance, "poetry" seems to be straightforward. But then what to do with the following passage, which suggests that she and Jung backed off at the prospect of a possible pregnancy:

I begged him ever so many times not to provoke my "ambitia" with various probings, because otherwise I would be forced to discover similar complexes in him. Finally, when the inescapable had happened, and when at the very outset I observed anxiety and deep depression in him, I renounced everything; he knows that. His profoundly sensitive soul was more important to me than anything else; from then on I always refused the "consequences." My love for him transcended our affinity until he could stand it no longer and wanted "poetry." For many reasons I could not and did not want to resist. But when he asked me how I pictured what would happen next (because of the "consequences"), I said that first love has no desires, that I had nothing in mind and did not want to go beyond a kiss, which I could also do without, if need be. And now he claims he was too kind to me, that I want sexual involvement with him because of that, something he, of course, never wanted, etc.

All of these passages bear close scrutiny—there are others like them in the letter-drafts and also in Spielrein's 1910 diary entries—for while on first reading they seem to be describing an illicit affair pure and simple, they always stop short of an unambiguous statement of what happened. It was this ambiguity that prompted Rosemary Dinnage's comment quoted earlier, "Later generations who try to find out who did what to whom sexually are always on a losing wicket." For myself, I find it at least plausible that the two stopped short of intercourse. As an indication to the contrary, though, I have to note the reaction of the two when they were caught out. Clearly, in their own minds, they had sinned.

It has occurred to many a modern reader, as it no doubt occurred at the time to Freud, that the whole matter would be a great deal clearer if we knew what "poetry" meant. In the two passages immediately above, it would seem clearly to indicate lovemaking. But in subsequent diary entries from the fall of 1910, Spielrein once again talks of having "poetry" with Jung in contexts in which actual intercourse would have been almost certainly out of the question. The editor of the Carotenuto documents was mindful of the ambiguity; in a footnote he concedes, "For 'poetry' we must surmise a metaphorical significance known only to Jung and Sabina." Then, betraying his own suspicions, he promptly provides a similar usage from literature where it indicates "the act of physical possession."

Actually the place to look for "poetry" is not in the literature of the day—we know surprisingly little of Spielrein's extracurricular reading habits in any case—but in the medical texts. Within those texts, moreover, the first place to look is Spielrein's own subsequent publications. And, indeed, in her medical dissertation, "On the Psychological Content of a Case of Schizophrenia (Dementia Praecox)," the term crops up repeatedly, along with "art" and "religion," explicitly as a synonym for both love and sexuality, as in the formula "Poetry = Love." The matter is much more complicated, however, than this straightforward usage would seem to imply. The woman whom Spielrein studied was a chronic dementia praecox patient at the Burghölzli, a woman caught up in a frighteningly fragmented world in which sexuality seemingly permeated everything. But her sexuality was purely an affair of the imagination, "autistic" in Bleuler's phrase, "auto-erotic" in Freud's. In context, Spielrein's explication of "poetry" was meant to elucidate some bizarre statements by the patient to the effect that she was powerless to keep her imagination from being overwhelmed by sexual fantasies. Given that the woman's speech was a veritable word-salad, however, the meaning of "poetry" was not at all self-evident. Spielrein had to figure it out. The question is where she got her key.

Again, the place to look is the literature on medical psychology. Krafft-Ebing seems to have started the tradition on "poetry." In his introductory chapter to *Psychopathia Sexualis* he had repeatedly brought up the topic of "poetry" as the literary form which best lent itself to sexual reverie. Thereafter he occasionally allowed "poetry" a purely metaphorical existence in his text, as when he wrote of the "poetry" of the symbolic act of subjection.

Independently, the researchers of the Zurich school had discovered that citations from poetry were regularly a complex indicator. It thus came naturally to them to employ poetry as a metaphor for unconscious fantasies generally. Riklin had written that the unconscious was "still always a fairy poetess," while Jung had maintained that the practice of psychoanalysis required the skills of a "poet."

But in all likelihood it was neither from Krafft-Ebing nor from the Zurich school that Spielrein derived her key. Rather, she got it from Forel's 1905 volume, *The Sexual Question.* Working within the tradition of Krafft-Ebing, Forel devoted a whole chapter of his book to the subject of sexual influences over poetry and the arts, this with an eye to distinguishing legitimate influences as opposed to the pornographic. Of interest to a young woman worried about "consequences," the chapter closes with a discussion of the aesthetics of contraception, including the thought that "the poetry of love does not suffer much from their use." A similar metaphorical usage also crops up several times in Forel's chapter on the role of suggestion in erotic attraction, where for example he writes of "the poetry of amorous intoxication."

With respect to Spielrein, the question of Forel's influence is relatively clear-cut: not only did he and his book figure extremely prominently in the delusions of the patient Spielrein later reported, but his views also inform the protests of Spielrein's Transformation Journal. The sequence appears to be this. Sometime after her discharge from the hospital in 1905 but before she began the Transformation Journal in mid-1907, Spielrein came across Forel's book. There she found a discussion of legitimate versus pornographic erotic influences in the arts which squared with her own incipient ideas about sublimation and "transformation," ideas which were then used to fend off Jung's interpretation that "Siegfried" represented her wish for his son. She also found in Forel the metaphorical use of "poetry" to describe "amorous intoxication," which a year later captured her feelings for Jung, and perhaps his for her, when their "poetry" began. Then, sometime after the breakup, she made the acquaintance of a chronic patient of the Burghölzli who spoke of "poetry," "art," and "Forel." The solution to the riddle of the patient's delusions seemingly lay out in the open.

The secret meetings had been about "poetry." They had been about the strange turn of imagination that can arise when a sexual attraction asserts itself. As Spielrein put it, "we could sit in speechless ecstasy for hours." But, we do well to understand that this imaginative turn was likely given a psychoanalytic cast as well. In this context, we should note the strange confession in the letter-drafts that Spielrein regularly identified Jung with both her father and her younger brother, with the latter also substituting for Jung in her dreams, while Jung regularly identified her with his mother. These identifications, I would suggest, not only constituted an interpretation of their shared "Siegfried" fantasy, but also sometimes alternated with it in the rapture of their mutual entrancement. Interpretation had been a prelude to fantasy, and both, by degrees, had begun to blend with lived experience.

Such a development was hardly without precedents. In the realm of enacted psychoanalytic fantasy, Otto Gross was still proudly living out his antipatriarchal daydream, and his call for "polygamy" amounted to nothing more or less than winning away from the fathers all the mothers and daughters who were brave enough to come. And if Jung took his cue from Gross, Spielrein could take hers from Wagner, who had celebrated brother-sister incest and made it one of the emotional high points of the *Ring* cycle. Nor was love between brother and sister the only motif at stake here. For when Spielrein was not otherwise being Brünnhilde she was implicitly personifying "Sieglinde," Siegfried's mother. Thus "Siegfried" stood simultaneously for the son she would give Jung and for Jung himself, with Spielrein in the role of the protective, self-sacrificing mother. By the same token, by being both Siegfried to her Brünnhilde and Siegmund to her Sieglinde, Jung was fathering himself through her.

In short, "poetry" was Spielrein's word for what happens when a couple, both enamored of mysticism, move backward from it to a sexual realization—and keep psychoanalyzing. Analysis and fantasy, incest and myth, had started to merge into each other. Freud may certainly be excused by history if he failed to grasp what the young woman was going on about.

THE ANALYSIS OF DREAMS

How important, finally, had Spielrein been to Jung and how important was her precipitous loss? In these matters, a person sometimes knows only afterward. Assuming that he had ever really been in love with the young woman, Jung had proved himself a coward, even if in the end there was no other course he could realistically have taken. But beyond both his loss and whatever self-recriminations may have haunted him, the most important aspect of the Spielrein affair was the change it occasioned in his relationship with Freud. For Jung had been quite earnest in trying to broaden both his theoretical outlook and the professional audience to which he was addressing himself. Even now, he was making plans to attend the Sixth International Congress on Experimental Psychology, called by Claparède and Flournoy for Geneva in August. His personal resentment—"neurotic ingratitude"—toward Freud had been no less real. To be sure, Freud had stood by him in the crisis and that counted for a great deal. Yet, gratitude was a mantle that a man like Jung could only chafe under, and Freud's various patronizing remarks during the preceding few months could not have gone down easily. Professionally, the two men were still aligned on the masthead of the *Jahrbuch*—"a tie not to be broken"— but their personal relationship, so crucial to Jung's early enthusiasm, was decisively altered.

As Jung surveyed his situation vis-à-vis Freud in the wake of the Spielrein affair, the one fact that would have mattered above all else was this—Freud had Spielrein's last letter. Freud had not offered to send it to him, and Jung, having declined to see her earlier letter, did not volunteer that he was curious to see this one. Nor did he dare ask Spielrein herself. Which meant that he did not know exactly what Freud knew about him beyond the summary appraisal that he had been "oscillating . . . between the extremes of Bleuler and Gross." Jung had long felt himself divided between a public and a private self, and his psychoanalytic transformation had equally had its public and private sides. Now, in some side drawer of Freud's desk, the two sides had finally come together—in the worst possible way. It was a very uncomfortable position to be in.

Jung's distress could only have been aggravated by his private knowledge of the situation in the Freud household. Whatever license he had taken was ultimately less scandalous than what he took to be Freud's more serious transgression. Yet any self-justifying attempt to confront Freud on the point would have been both unseemly and without issue. Lacking proof, Jung would have the short end anyway. To be sure, at the height of the crisis he had written to Freud suggestively that "my first visit to Vienna had a very long aftermath." But Freud had not read any malice in the allusion and had most certainly not taken the bait. Now, in the wake of the final resolution of the Spielrein affair, the galling reality was that the best Jung could do would be to content himself with veiled innuendo. Here the documentary record is decidedly meager, but there is a distinct suggestion that Jung may have done just that.

To begin with, there is a very curious passage in Spielrein's letter-drafts of June 1909 having to do with Freud's daughter. In their critical meeting of reconciliation of 19 June, Jung had pretended to Spielrein that his feelings toward her were a transference from Sophie Freud, to whom he now surprisingly, and most improbably, claimed to have been attracted during his first visit to Vienna. There is no hint in any other extant documents of any such attraction on Jung's part and Spielrein herself manifestly disbelieved it. Nevertheless, in her ramblings to Freud she saw fit to address the issue:

At the time Dr. Jung met your daughter, we were already such good friends that Dr. Jung could admit to me without further ado that he had met your daughter, who had impressed him as a very pretty and intelligent girl. With my acute sense for such things, Frl. Freud did not cause me the slightest jealousy. . . . The person who stood in my way was Prof. Freud himself. He displayed certain peculiarities of character which I recognized at once, because they are also present in me, completely suppressed, and so I thought that Dr. Jung must be repelled by you, and if you become disgusting to him, I will, too. I even prophesied . . .

The next page is missing. The caesura may well be more provocative than the missing page was and, let us remind ourselves, we have no way of knowing if any of this was actually included in the final unsolicited letter to Freud. There is little to go on here, the only certainties being that she and Jung had previously discussed Freud's character and that whatever Jung said had worried Spielrein in regard to herself.

Johann Jakob Honegger, Jr., was a young student, the same age as Spielrein, who was at this time training under Jung at the Burghölzli. In mid-June he sent off to Freud an unsolicited letter of his own containing a youthful attempt at analyzing the master. (Jung mentioned the effort to Freud in his letter of 21 June 1909, indicating that it was sent off a few days earlier, i.e., at the height of the Spielrein crisis.) The analysis must have been harmless enough, or else Freud would not have mentioned its existence to Oskar Pfister in July: "Honegger has fathomed me well; the sample shows that the young man has a gift for psycho-analysis." Since Honegger's letter has never been recovered, the matter is left there by history. It was assumed that another neophyte enthusiast had sent along an analysis based on the autobiographical portions of Freud's writings just as Otto Rank had done in 1904. Recently, however, the French psychoanalyst François Roustang has noted what should have been obvious all along: whatever Honegger had written had first been discussed with Jung—it was thus as much *Jung's* analysis, based on his personal acquaintance with Freud, as it was anything that Honegger had divined from reading the autobiographical portions of the dream book or *The Psychopathology of Everyday Life*.

Thus, in whatever veiled form, there came out of Zurich in the early summer of 1909 Jung's "analysis" of Freud's character, most definitely from Honegger's pen and quite possibly from Spielrein's as well. There also came in Freud's mail a short article on dream interpretation that Jung had written up the previous fall for Binet's *L'Année Psychologique*.

"The Analysis of Dreams" is a brief, lyrical piece, Jung at his stylistic best. Jung takes as his point of departure an imagined dream that Faust's Gretchen might have had, a dream of a faraway king who was endlessly faithful. Thus, Jung points out, would a present wish (that Faust be faithful) be gratified in a disguised form. Jung goes on amiably to explain how he would deal with a Gretchen in analysis, uncovering her love affair, her secret pregnancy, her disappointment, etc. Then another dream, also about disappointed love, is briefly described in the article. The central figure in the dream is Pope Pius X, the first association is to a Moslem sheikh ("a kind of Pope") known to the dreamer from his travels, and the first level of interpretation is to the idea that "I am celibate like the Pope, but I would like to have many wives like the Moslem." One would have to recognize Jung as the dreamer, and to know that parodies of religion, replete with mocking and self-mocking references to playing the "Pope," were a feature of the correspondence with Vienna, before one would suspect that Freud lay behind the figure of the Moslem sheikh. Jung's article had been written the first week of November in 1908. Freud got the offprint—"the surprising gift of your article"—in mid-July of 1909.

Jung would not leave well enough alone. He had already made a bad mistake: by severing his ties with the Burghölzli, he had left Bleuler's protection and sacrificed his own independent institutional base. (Jung's dream of being made head of the psychology lab, and thereafter ascending to the psychiatry chair, had predictably come to naught.) Now he was making another bad mistake: role models being an easy target for a bad conscience, Jung was raising Freud's character as an issue. (It is at least possible that the dalliance with Spielrein had been partially modeled according to Jung's understanding of Freud's situation, for at one point Jung had tried, astonishingly, to introduce Spielrein into his own household.) No doubt Jung still needed to make sense of the Spielrein debacle and this meant rethinking things through from the beginning, but, bad manners aside, the answer he sought ultimately lay in his own character and his own philosophy, not Freud's. As it was, he was burning his bridges at both ends.

Perhaps Jung thought he had other options. He had signed on as a member of the Swiss reception committee for the Sixth International Congress on Experimental Psychology at Geneva at the beginning of

August, chaired by Flournoy, who distinguished the occasion with a call for resuming the scientific study of mediums and for a new initiative in the psychology of religion. Amalgamated with this congress was another, the First International Congress on Pedagogy; pedagogy was a topic that had begun to occupy Jung's attention, thanks in part to his observations of his daughter's reactions to the birth of her baby brother. Yet, in the end, Jung seems not to have attended either conference, though sometime in this period he did find time for a private visit with Flournoy. Instead, he spent the first five days of August in Munich, visiting Kraepelin's clinic and proselytizing among the assistants there. Then came a trip to Basel, to visit his mother and look in on Häberlin, before he set out for Bremen to rendezvous with Freud and Ferenczi for the sail aboard the *George Washington* of the North German Lloyd Line to America.

And what of Spielrein during this time? She spent August and September on vacation with her parents in Berlin and Kolberg. A few pages survive from a diary she began at this time and they reveal a woman, still quite young, touchingly trying to come to terms with her situation when not otherwise reflecting on the "psychology of so-called modest girls, to which category I also belong." She confesses to feelings of "gruesome loneliness," of "yearning for love," and of a "fear of emotional atrophy." But she also confides to her diary that she likes to look at herself naked to the waist in the mirror with the window curtains left slightly opened:

> . . . it's so nice when someone admires me; down to the waist I am not embarrassed; I took pleasure in having the contours of a grown woman, I was happy that my skin is soft, my curves lovely and well developed. Even if I have a very ordinary face, I can still be attractive. What can be more beautiful than a healthy young girl, if she is 'maidenly'?

As for Jung, she pleads with Fate that she be able to keep his friendship—"Allow me to be his guardian angel, his spirit of inspiration"—even while she was being counseled more practically:

> Mother says it is impossible for my friend and me to remain friends once we have given each other our love. A man cannot sustain pure friendship in the long run. If I am nice to him—he will want love.

As ONE MIGHT expect, Jung did not make an altogether gracious traveling companion. He, Ferenczi, and Freud assembled at Bremen on 20 August. Over dinner, Jung was coaxed into a glass of wine—symbolic emancipation from the abstinence so dear to Forel and Bleuler and required of all Burghölzli physicians. But, then Jung went off on a long harangue over the recent discovery of perfectly preserved skeletons in the town, a discovery which Jung got confused with peat-bog mummies dug up in Belgium a while before. (Peat-bog mummies were, and remain, of great archaeological interest because a great deal of information can be discerned about the people's style of life, also about the exact manner of their death.) Freud wanted Jung to get off this topic. Jung persisted. Freud fainted.

The cause of Freud's faint remains mysterious. It has been said that Freud suspected Jung of having a death wish against himself. Perhaps. To be sure, after a long day's railroad journey, a pointless harangue from a younger colleague one is accustomed to having greater control over would seem difficult in any circumstances. Whether that harangue was made more intolerable by other misgivings about Jung's recent behavior, is difficult to say.

Meanwhile, Stanley Hall was waiting in America to hear all about the new doctrines of nervous health.

Part Three

The Movement

Finally, to judge by my own experience, the strict application of the "psycho-analytic" method in all its thoroughness is very difficult, and implies a degree of skill which few physicians can attain, if not the possession of personal characteristics of an unusual sort. It is an unfortunate function of Freud's analytic method, as he himself points out, that it makes necessary as a rule the establishment of a relation of dependence of the patient upon the physician which it may, in the end, be difficult to get rid of. Janet long ago called attention to the same necessity in relation to analogous methods adopted by him, and indeed every one who has dealt much with the treatment of neurotic patients must have noticed the same tendency. This is an evil which must be accepted if it cannot be avoided, but when the physician is fully imbued with the belief in the sexual origins of the patient's illnesses he must, by virtue of the closeness of this relationship, be in a position to impress his view, unconsciously, upon his patients, and might easily draw from them an acquiescence and endorsement which would not in reality be as spontaneous as it seemed.

—James Jackson Putnam, 1906, reporting on the first use of
psychoanalysis at Massachusetts General Hospital,
in the *Journal of Abnormal Psychology*

CHAPTER 9

America and the Core Complex

> Our own soul is full in all its parts of faint hints . . . , dim and
> scarcely audible murmurs of a great and prolonged life, hot, intense,
> richly dight [adorned] with incident and detail that is no more; a
> slight automatism, perhaps, being the sole relic of the most central
> experiences of many generations, a fleeting fancy all that survives of
> ages of toil and blood, . . . Yet these psychophores, whatever they
> are, are wax to receive and marble to retain. Thus soul is truly
> telepathic only to its own past . . . never of a future state.
>
> —G. Stanley Hall, 1904, *Adolescence*

F ROM A EUROPEAN perspective, America was a land of potentially fabulous professional opportunity. Yet, the American sensibility was in some ways hard to fathom. American reviews of Freud's
works had ranged from soberly appreciative to wildly dismissive. Ernest Jones had written Freud from his new post in Toronto not to push
the sexual doctrines too hard during his visit. Freud found the advice
contemptible, but also unenlightening. He had set sail without preparing any lectures.

On shipboard, the omens were mixed. Freud was delighted to find
his cabin steward reading *The Psychopathology of Everyday Life,* a positive
sign, but his personal relation with Jung was strained as never before.
Then, too, Freud's digestion gave out, and he developed urinary difficulties and severe intestinal complaints. The symptoms stayed with
him a long time thereafter and he came to refer to the condition off-
handedly as his "American colitis." For his part, Jung ungallantly
took the symptoms as evidence that Freud himself had a "neurosis."
The omens were mixed for Jung as well. He had looked forward to
having the heir to the McCormick fortune, who'd already consulted
him once in Zurich, on board during the crossing. Instead, he found
William Stern, the psychologist and fellow Clark invitee whose criti-

cisms of the association experiment had first led Jung to embrace psychoanalysis four years before.

The general apprehension over what to expect did not bring Freud and Jung any closer. As their ship sailed into New York harbor, Freud turned to Jung and remarked about how surprised the Americans would be to hear what they had to tell them. Jung made a comment about how ambitious Freud was. Freud replied that he was the only man who wasn't ambitious. To which Jung answered grumpily that that was still something—to be the only one.

The genial A. A. Brill was there to greet them in New York, which helped matters, and between various sight-seeing expeditions to Chinatown and elsewhere, the time passed rapidly. Jung and Freud did take a few hours out for a private chat in Central Park. Jung apparently had something on his mind concerning the differences between Jews and Christians that he wanted to ventilate. Freud was up to the discussion and the occasion passed without incident.

From New York, the four men, Jung, Freud, Ferenczi, and Brill, made their way by steamer to Fall River, then took a train to Boston and then another train out to Worcester for the congress. Their host, Stanley Hall, proved to be as hospitable as he was distinguished. Ernest Jones soon turned up with an important new acquaintance in tow, the Harvard neurologist James Jackson Putnam. The psychoanalytic contingent now ostensibly numbered six, though Jones was still hedging on the depth of his affiliation and Putnam was an unknown quantity. Privately, Ferenczi and Freud began to map out Freud's talks. Jung kept his own counsel.

The tensions between Freud and Jung were not to disappear. Indeed, in only a few weeks' time, on the voyage back to Europe, there would be another confrontation. Yet the significance of these tensions, for both men, was temporarily to recede in importance in the face of a surprising transformation. At the Clark congress, Freud and Jung discovered that they were—Freud and Jung.

FIRST OFFICIAL RECOGNITION

THE MAN inadvertently responsible for this metamorphosis was G. Stanley Hall. In a heroic age of American intellectualism, G. Stanley Hall cut a perfectly splendid figure all his own. Born in 1844 to a Massachusetts farmer, who wanted Hall to take over the farm, and his Congregationalist wife, who wanted Hall to enter the ministry, Hall finally found his career in the physiological psychology being taught

by William James at Harvard. Hall rapidly became James's most important student and, in time, his principal rival for American preeminence in the new discipline. In 1887, Hall founded the *American Journal
of Psychology,* the first such journal on this continent. Subsequently, in
1889, he became the first president of Clark University in eastern
Massachusetts. Taking his journal with him, he arrived in Worcester
with dreams of creating a first-class research institution that would
combine graduate and undergraduate training on the European
model. It was not to be. Within a few years the University of Chicago, itself newly founded (in 1891) with Rockefeller money, had pirated away Hall's best faculty, while in 1890, James finally published
his *Principles of Psychology.* Hall was left with mountains of worthless
notes for his own text, the endless fund-raising chores that are a
university president's lot, and renewed doubts about his own psychological makeup. He responded by coming to question the masculine,
achievement orientation of American culture. In time, in the privacy
of his study, "maternal nurturance, emotional spontaneity, aesthetic
responsiveness, and mythopoeic creativity" were combined into a
new ethos.

The fruit of Hall's meditations, published in 1904, was a monumental two-volume study, *Adolescence, Its Psychology and Its Relations to
Physiology, Anthropology, Sociology, Sex, Crime, Religion and Education,* a work
which covered just about every subject under the sun including, literally, the sun and the moon. (Adolescent girls tend to disrobe and lose
themselves in fantasy during a full moon, Hall's questionnaire research
showed.) From the teaching of science to high school students—
something akin to nature-worship was recommended—to the theories
of Breuer and Freud—said to shed "sad new light upon the peculiar
vulnerability of early adolescence in girls"—Hall had an opinion on
everything. His basic rationale for these far-flung discussions derived
from a novel methodological approach to the issues of development.
As did many thinkers of his age, Hall accepted as given the Phylogenetic Law promulgated by the great German champion of Darwinism,
Ernst Haeckel, which held that ontogeny recapitulates phylogeny (in
the course of development an individual of a species recapitulates the
evolution of the species as a whole). Accordingly, Hall believed that
the study of man's cultural evolution would throw light on the laws of
personality development, since the individual was bound to repeat the
steps taken by the race. Specifically, he thought that during adolescence, psychological remnants from past ages—"psychophores"—
became newly active. (Today, the putative "phylogenetic" match

between evolutionary and developmental sequences has no scientific standing and the term "phyletic" is preferred.)

Hall coined the term "genetic psychology" for his approach and believed that both the term and the outlook were original with him. To be sure, in Germany, Wilhelm Wundt had recently turned his attentions to a similar area—*Völkerpsychologie*—and had independently hit on the term "genetic psychology" to cover his investigations. Wundt's idea was that the psychology of the *Volk* ("people") was logically prior to the psychology of the individual. The history of the *Volk*, therefore, and by extension, the cultural history of mankind, was the proper terrain for studying the progressive development of consciousness. The evolution of the motif of the hero as it appeared in myths and folktales, for example, was said to reflect the historical emergence of individual self-consciousness; this progression, in turn, necessarily found its echo in a child's coming to full self-awareness during the course of growing up.

In line with his phylogenetic approach, Hall thought it appropriate to take the reader of *Adolescence* on a tour of ancient religions and their cumulative progress from religions of the Great Mother through phallic cults to the culmination of Christianity and its altruistic redefinition of love. The sequence, in Hall's view, was repeated in the development of the adolescent's ability to love: it too moves away from maternal influences through an aggressive phallicism before it reaches the mature stage of altruistic love, of self-sacrifice for the good of the next generation.

Jung was greatly impressed by Hall's phylogenetic speculations. Hall's countrymen were impressed by his constant recourse to the topic of sexuality. *Adolescence* was shot through with discussions of sexuality, for it was sexuality, in Hall's view, which fueled the adolescent's spontaneous exploration of the inherited potentials. To be sure, Hall's was a high-minded sexuality, ultimately reconciled with Christian ethics and artistic achievement, the very motor of spiritual progress. In an officially sympathetic review, the psychologist Edward Thorndike wrote justly of the reader's predicament in the face of *Adolescence* that "one must combine his memories of medical textbooks, erotic poetry and inspirational preaching." Privately, however, Thorndike characterized the book as "chock full of errors, masturbation and Jesus."

But it was as a purely practical man that G. Stanley Hall made his biggest contribution to history. Still doggedly pursuing funds and recognition for Clark University, Hall had decided to repeat the ploy he used for the school's tenth anniversary on the occasion of its twentieth—an international congress devoted to the latest developments in the social sciences. From the breadth of his own reading—he even owned a copy of the *Jahrbuch*—Hall had come to know the work of every innovative theorist in all the relevant disciplines and he rounded up an exceptionally interesting roster of speakers that included Franz Boas, E. B. Titchener, William Stern, and, of course, Freud and Jung. Hall also rounded up an audience to listen to them that was almost equally distinguished.

We remember William James for his philosophy, but it was as a pioneering "physiological psychologist" that he was needed at the Clark congress to meet the European visitors. James's distinctive career had first begun to take shape during a visit to the Bicêtre Hospital in Paris when he had a near-religious experience contemplating a "green faced idiot." At Harvard, he subsequently became interested in that new branch of philosophy, psychology, and even set up an informal laboratory for psychological experimentation, thus placing himself in a virtual tie with Wilhelm Wundt for the honor of being the first person in the world to do so. In 1896, James had delivered six talks on "Exceptional Mental States" for the Lowell Lecture Series, talks which were later cannibalized for the 1902 Gifford Lectures on the "Varieties of Religious Experience." In the earlier Lowell Lectures, which have been miraculously reconstructed by Eugene Taylor, James demonstrated that he was thoroughly up-to-date with the European literature on the psychology of the neuroses, including the *Studies on Hysteria* by Breuer and Freud, then out for only a year.

James Jackson Putnam, James's close friend and holder of the first American chair in neurology, also at Harvard, was another who was called out to meet the European visitors. Putnam had been experimenting with Freud's treatment methods since 1904 and was a regular participant in the roundtable discussions held at the home of Boston neurologist Morton Prince. Prince, too, was important. In 1906, he had founded the *Journal of Abnormal Psychology,* which from the outset ran featured pieces by both Janet and Jung. Also in 1906, Prince had published his influential study of a multiple personality, *The Dissociation of a Personality.* Some months prior to the Clark congress, Prince had introduced Putnam to a young physician down from Toronto who was staying with him, Ernest Jones. Putnam, a unique mixture of Yankee uprightness and Hegelian metaphysics, had lately begun to see in Freud's works a full-blown theory of character development that could be used therapeutically to foster ethical reform. Jones, for his part, could see in Putnam an extraordinarily important acquaintance, the bellwether of what Americans would and would not accept.

An hour's train ride to the west of Boston lay the city of Worcester, home of Clark University and of the Worcester State Asylum, Massachusetts's primary facility for the insane. Its previous director had been Adolf Meyer, an expatriate Swiss who had studied under Forel and under J. J. Honegger, Sr., the father of Jung's newest assistant. At the Worcester State Asylum, Meyer had opened up his wards to James's seminar students from Harvard and to the young men from Stanley Hall's new university. Meyer's reputation had originally been made in brain anatomy, but in recent years he had begun to pioneer a novel theory whereby "biological reaction-type" could be used to clarify both the onset and the form of adult psychoses. This led him to take an interest both in Freud's theories and in the results of the association experiment. In 1902, Meyer left Worcester to take over the jewel of the New York State asylum system, the Psychiatric Institute on Ward's Island. From there he had subsequently dispatched Frederick Peterson, A. A. Brill, and August Hoch to Zurich to study the new methods under Bleuler and Jung.

In 1909, Meyer returned to Worcester in the dual role of auditor and speaker at the Clark congress. His invitation to speak was scarcely undeserved. Kraepelin's revolutionary psychiatric nosology of 1896 had stressed both the unforeseen, and therefore especially tragic, onset of schizophrenia as well as its slow, deteriorating course. In this context, Eugen Bleuler's essential contribution lay in his immediate recognition that deterioration was not inevitable. For his part, Meyer had discovered that the onset was not entirely unpredictable. Today, the term "premorbid personality" is preferred to "biological reaction-type," but this change in terminology ought not to blind us to the fact that in 1909, between Kraepelin, Bleuler, Meyer, and Jung, the modern theory of schizophrenia was essentially at hand.

We could go quite a bit further in surveying the American scene and its far-flung connections with the best in European psychiatry and neurology. Suffice it to say that perhaps only in little Switzerland was there such widespread interest and sophistication in the areas of medical psychology and psychotherapy. And within America, the New York area notwithstanding, sophistication was at its height along the Boston-Worcester axis. In particular, there was enormous curiosity about both psychoanalysis and the experimental demonstration of "complexes."

Meyer gave voice to the general sentiment when he paused in his own presentation to take cognizance of the two visitors:

> We owe to our European guests, Professor Freud and Dr. Jung, the demonstration that what is at work in the centre of the stage is a complex or group of complexes consisting of insufficiently balanced experiences in various ways modified by symbolism. Their ingenious interpretations have made possible a remarkable clearing up of many otherwise perplexing products of morbid fancy, in ways the discussion of which, no doubt, I had better leave to their lectures.

Of course, the American character lent its own particular coloration to the interest in medical psychology. For example, the American interpretation of "neurasthenia"—an American, George Beard, had first named the syndrome in 1856—stressed the role of the rapid pace of modern life in overtaxing the nervous system. This was in contrast to the European view which tended to emphasize rather the role of heredity and decadent living. Likewise, the American approach to psychotherapy betrayed the optimism typical of the national character. Thus, in Boston at this time the dominant therapeutic school was the Emmanuel Movement, a loose-knit alliance of physicians and clergymen which operated literally out of church basements. Finally, it should be noted that in America, as in England, a sense of propriety reigned about sexual matters which, while it did not prevent serious men of high moral character like G. Stanley Hall from publishing, did create an occasional awkward scene. The following year, for example, Morton Prince would accept a manuscript from A. A. Brill for the *Journal of Abnormal Psychology* while asking for one single word to be taken out—the word was "sexual."

I stress the sophistication of the Clark audience, because I think it explains to a large extent the remarkable success enjoyed by the two European visitors. Contrary to what Freud had imagined, the Americans weren't at all surprised by what he and Jung had to tell them. This was what the Americans had been waiting for and they were enthralled. Amidst a whole gang of luminaries, Freud and Jung stole the show.

Freud and Jung seemed able to capitalize on every opportunity. As if by some prearrangement of fate, in a free moment, Hall, Putnam, and James produced a medium they had been puzzling over for months. It took the two savants from Europe no time at all to extract a confession from the young girl that her mediumship was a fraud designed to attract the attentions of a young man. At another point, the lectures were disrupted by the anarchist Emma Goldman, who had to be escorted from the hall. Freud wove her presence into the day's lecture: whereas Janet held that dissociated ideas continued silently off by themselves, he held that they were noisy interlopers, always seeking to regain admission to the auditorium of consciousness, and that it was only through an ongoing effort at repression that they were kept out. Jung, too, took advantage of what there was to work with. He had his association work to present—Americans had taken a keen interest in it from the outset—but he also managed to capitalize on the American interest in child development by a charming talk on how his daughter had reacted to the birth of her little brother and had gradually worked out a theory to explain it all.

There was even publicity. A full-page story ran in the *Boston Evening Transcript* with the catchy subhead, "The Emmanuel Movement Will Die." The story pretended to be an expanded interview with Freud, but actually, beyond one or two introductory remarks including the prophecy concerning the Emmanuel Movement, the "interview" was nothing more than an unacknowledged English translation of the 1905 paper by Freud about his method. (That paper, it will be recalled, had been written by Freud as a means of self-protection when he heard that a trial of psychoanalysis was being made at the Burghölzli with a then unknown patient by a "young" physician.) The perpetrator of this fraud is unknown, but one may reasonably suspect Stanley Hall, who wanted publicity and was otherwise in a position to be sensitized to the fear of Boston's neurologists that they were losing their nervous patients to the clergy of the Emmanuel Movement.

The man most responsible for the success of the American trip, however, was, ironically, the absent Pierre Janet. For once Janet's theories had been thoroughly absorbed, there was no further way to advance except to consider what Freud had to offer. Janet had taken as his clinical touchstone the phenomenon of multiple personality and had used this model to explain all manner of hysterical symptoms in terms of dissociated parts of the personality. But, having started off from a doctrine of psychic splits, Janet was at an apparent loss to go further and his observations were reduced to specifying with ever-increasing acuity where the splits lay. Hereditary weakness and moral degeneration remained the explanatory foundation of the theory. And

Janet's therapies, constrained by his concepts, remained chiefly focused on strengthening the overall integrity of the personality. It was, indeed, an advance to recognize that streaming across the various mental cleavages were currents of wishing ("libido" in Freud's view) and counter-wishing ("repression") whose vicissitudes lent meaning and coherence to the various mental states. It now became possible to recognize the essential continuity in a patient's productions. The wish that had been escorted out of consciousness was still trying to regain admission and it would regularly take advantage of altered states of consciousness, be they dreams, compulsions, or hysterical twilight states, to do so. Much of Janet's admittedly remarkable data could be usefully reinterpreted in the new scheme. Conflict, not constitution, lay in back of it all. Moreover, the new theory satisfied the environmentalist and developmental biases of the Americans. It also seemed to offer more optimistic prospects for therapy and ultimately for the ethical reform of the individual.

In short, to an audience well versed in Janet, as the American audience was, Freud was a revelation. His five lectures were modest and largely oriented to depicting psychoanalysis as a treatment method. As was his habit before new audiences, Freud began his account of "The Origins of Psychoanalysis" with Breuer's treatment of "Anna O." Then, with acknowledgments to Charcot and Janet, he described how his own experience with patients gradually led him to his current theory—"the fruit of an unprejudiced examination of the facts." On the question of infantile sexuality, he was careful to invoke Havelock Ellis and others. He also made mention of the "complex" doctrine of the Zurich school along the way, and, if he did not write this element in later, he made pointed reference to the ethical dimensions of mind as well as to the possibilities of "sublimation."

Stanley Hall was so impressed that he began to consider that psychoanalysis might constitute an entire domain unto itself within psychology and he at once commandeered Freud's lectures for a special commemorative issue of his journal. James Jackson Putnam insisted that the visitors spend a few days with him at his family's retreat in the Adirondacks. And Ernest Jones, who had been very carefully hedging his bets, was left with the special bitterness that a basically smart man feels when he realizes that he has miscalculated badly. (Freud's parting remark to Jones was that he hoped Jones would stay with them: "You will find it worthwhile.")

But perhaps the person most profoundly affected by Freud's lectures was Freud himself. Here, to an audience far, far superior to any he had ever commanded in Europe, he proposed himself as a scientist and a therapist who had made important empirical discoveries, and they responded with adulation. So successful were his talks, Jung's too, that the two men were selected for the special honor of receiving honorary degrees at the closing ceremonies. Jones records that Freud was "visibly moved" by the proceedings. Freud announced to the Clark gathering that "This is the first official recognition of our endeavors." Jung wrote to his wife the day after the ceremonies, "Freud is in seventh heaven, and I am glad with all my heart to see him so. . . ."

Following the congress, Freud, Ferenczi, and Jung went off with Putnam to the Adirondacks to stay at the Putnam summer campgrounds. Putnam proved an amiable if somewhat credulous host. At one point, he and Freud discussed the case of a young man suffering from severe agoraphobia whom Freud had examined. It had emerged that the youth had an unusually severe and demanding father, which led Freud to conclude that the youth's symptom was a means of compelling the father once more to take control over his life. Putnam asked about possible interventions and Freud replied cheerily, "Kill his father." Legend has it that it took Freud some time to persuade Putnam that he had in fact not recommended this form of therapy to the patient.

We should not close our account of the American visit without mentioning the decorations. A neighboring woman completed the gracious American reception by thoughtfully bedecking the cabins of the Putnam camp with German banners—thus were an Austrian, a Hungarian, and a Swiss made to feel at home.

THE MANUAL FOR PSYCHOANALYSIS

IN ESSENCE, at this time, Freud's theories constituted a kind of vision with regard to nervous health and nervous illness whose value had been proved in some cases, but whose overall empirical foundation had yet to be rigorously demonstrated. William James, for one, remained skeptical. James recognized that if medical psychology were going to make further progress, it would have to go Freud's way, at least for a while. Apparently he mentioned this feeling to Ernest Jones, who quotes him as saying, "The future of psychology belongs to your work." But James, no stranger to the data and with a keener epistemological eye than most, also saw difficulties. To his great friend, the Geneva psychologist Théodore Flournoy, James wrote:

I hope that Freud and his pupils will push their ideas to their utmost limits, so that we may learn what they are. They can't fail to throw light on human nature, but I confess that he made on me personally the impression of a man obsessed with fixed ideas. I can make nothing in my own case with his dream theories, and obviously "symbolism" is a most dangerous method.

James's comment was astute. For even granting that the elucidation of the symbolic elements in psychological symptoms had been a significant contribution—Meyer had specifically praised Jung and Freud for the innovation in his talk—the question remained as to where one drew the line on this kind of interpretation. How was one to distinguish between an appropriate interpretation and a tendentious one? Sometimes the symbolism was clear, as in the hysteric patient Bleuler had reported in his 1906 book *Affectivity, Suggestibility, and Paranoia,* who crushed rose petals against her temple while in a quasi-trance state. The act commemorated the suicide of her boyfriend, who had put a pistol to his head. But not all symptoms so easily gave up their secrets; Spielrein and Jung, for example, had argued long and hard about the meaning of "Siegfried" for over a year. That a patient might ultimately acquiesce in any given symbolic interpretation, moreover, did not by itself constitute a sturdy scientific warrant. The possibility remained that this was merely in response to suggestion. The physician's own belief in the correctness of the interpretation, it went without saying, was even less warrant.

The general methodological problems posed by suggestion, and by the physician's own auto-suggestion, were long known on both sides of the Atlantic. The prominent Berlin sexual researcher Albert Moll had recently raised them yet again, with specific reference to Freudian interpretation, in his important new book, *The Sexual Life of the Child*:

It is true that Freud and his followers report cases which they regard as proving their thesis. But I am by no means satisfied with these clinical histories. They rather produce the impression that much in the alleged histories has been introduced by the suggestive questioning of the examiner, or that sufficient care has not been taken to guard against illusions of memory. The impression produced in my mind is that the theory of Freud and his followers suffices to account for the clinical histories, not that the clinical histories suffice to prove the truth of the theory. Freud endeavors to establish his theory by the aid of psycho-analysis. But this involves so many arbitrary interpretations, that it is impossible to speak of proof in any strict sense of the term. Dreams are interpreted symbolically at will, and other definite objects are arbitrarily assumed to be symbolic representatives of the genital organs. I detect the principal source of fallacy in this arbitrary interpretation of alleged symbolism.

The only way to answer critics like Moll was to make the rules of interpretation explicit, so that the interpretive caprice of any individual therapist might be checked against independent judgments. Freud was aware of the requirement and he had repeatedly promised to publish a manual on the rules of interpretation. Just this, however, had lately been proving difficult to do. The extant Freud-Jung letters for the year previous to the Clark congress tell the story of Freud's dawning realization that he had promised more than he could easily deliver. In a letter to Jung of 8 November 1908, Freud had announced: "I have started work on a paper. The title—'A General Exposition of the Psychoanalytic Method'—tells all. It is getting ahead very slowly. . . ." Freud's plan of the moment was to have this essay round out a second volume of collected papers. Freud next made reference to the effort two months later, in a letter to Jung of 30 December 1908, once more giving as the title "General Exposition of the Psychoanalytic Method." By January of 1909, however, he was confiding to Jung concerning "my article on Methodology," that "I am having trouble finishing [it]." And by June of 1909, he was informing Jung that he had decided to postpone completion of the paper on method until the following year.

In short, at the time of the Clark congress there was still no manual for psychoanalysis. To some extent, Freud attempted to make good on the general methodological lack in his talks by explaining some of his more recent innovations such as free associations and transference. But what Freud had to say on those subjects was not sufficient to account for his interpretations. As Morton Prince would demonstrate in a year's time in his own monograph-length study of dreams, if one were not looking for the Freudian symbols one would not find them—even when they were there.

THE CORE COMPLEX

PARADOXICALLY, at the time of the Clark congress the interpretive range of psychoanalysis was increasing in a most remarkable way. For during the previous nine months, Freud had introduced a new concept into the literature of psychoanalysis—the "core (or "nuclear") complex." This *Kerncomplex* was to be a sort of all-purpose explanatory principle. Not only was it to be manifest in every case of neurosis, but it was also to be detectable in the original form of all myths (as opposed to later variants which might be considerably disguised and/or re-worked). It was, in a sense, to be the single forgotten dream of mankind, the universal basis for what James in his 1896 lectures had called, following Frederic Myers, "the subliminal self."

Two developments within psychoanalysis had made the idea of a *Kerncomplex* timely, if not exactly inevitable: the advent of the Zurich school with its doctrine of complexes and the burgeoning area of psychoanalytic investigations of myth. The trouble with the doctrine of complexes, from Freud's very systematic point of view, had been its thoroughgoing eclecticism. Jung and his associates might have demonstrated that "erotic complexes" were statistically the most frequent complexes among normal subjects, and in hysteric subjects the most important clinically, but they also allowed such things as "career complexes" and "injury complexes" into their analyses. Freud himself had gone a little way down this path in the 1907 re-edition of *The Psychopathology of Everyday Life,* where he made mention of a "personal complex," a "professional complex," and a "family complex." And in his personal correspondence he did not hesitate to use the term as a kind of shorthand as, for example, when he made mention of his "money complex" in a letter to Jung. But the tendency was for complexes to multiply geometrically. Binswanger, let us recall, had found in Jung's own protocol evidence for no less than eleven different complexes, including one he labeled a "philosophy complex" and another which might well have been called a "death/father complex."

Freud had taken a tentative first step toward restoring order in a 1908 paper, "Creative Writers and Daydreaming," where, without mentioning complexes *per se,* he had suggested how varying motivations might be reduced to a single sexual core. Professional ambition, for example, might well be in the service of impressing a particular lady. More disturbing than the proliferation of complexes, however, was the fact that there seemed to be experimental proof that any and

all of these complexes could be subject to repression. Freud's contention, dating back to the later stages of his collaboration with Breuer,
had been that it was specifically sexual feelings that occasioned repression. Jung had, in effect, proved Breuer's assertion to the contrary,
namely that any troublesome emotion might be suppressed.

A great deal was potentially at stake here. Freud's theory of record
was the one published in the 1905 book on sex. It not only called for
repression to operate with special pathogenic significance against sexual wishes as opposed to all others, it also called for each neurotic
symptom to have as its core a repressed infantile sexual wish, generally
of a perverse nature. But, owing to Fliess's untimely departure from
the fold and the concomitant loss of the theory of bisexuality, the theory of repression had a gaping hole in it. As Freud would comment to
his fellow Viennese in November of 1909 (during a discussion of the
core complex), "The entire theory of the neuroses is incomplete as
long as no light has been shed on the organic core of repression." And
while Freud was not above asserting that his psychoanalytic method
was superior to the association test as an investigatory technique—the
assertion was made official in his third Clark lecture—the actual conduct of analysis did little to bear out his theory as opposed to Jung's.
As memories, even repressed memories, are typically organized around
feelings, it had not proved difficult in analytic practice to locate the
kinds of repressed emotional complexes that Jung had described. It
had proved much harder, however, to find the sort of repressed infantile perversions which Freud's more specific theory called for. This did
not of itself disprove Freud's contention—maybe infantile perversions
were very deeply repressed indeed—but it did not support it, either.

The second development that had made the short-cut of a "core
complex" attractive was the newly opened possibility of investigating
ancient mythology from a psychoanalytic perspective. Riklin's excursion into fairy tales had created an important conundrum. The prize
here was that analyses of mythological material seemed at the time to
have special authority as glimpses into the soul. Whether one conceived of the terrain in terms of ancient religions, folktales, or some
other aspect of *Völkerpsychologie,* any psychological system that claimed
to universal validity had perforce to stake a proprietary claim in this
general area. The requirement, which was widely and deeply felt at
the time, applied equally well to theories of the unconscious mind.
Ever since Flournoy's pioneering work on the medium "Hélène
Smith" in 1900, if not before, the world of medical psychology had

become accustomed to thinking of the "mythopoeic" function of the subliminal self. It would indeed have been a coup for Freud if he could have demonstrated that his psychology penetrated yet more deeply into the mythopoeic mind. It would to the contrary prove an enormous embarrassment if all his followers' contributions proved to be as undisciplined as Riklin's. When an indeterminate number of complexes was juxtaposed against an indeterminate number of fairy tales, the result was known to be interpretive chaos. Nor had the threat of a woolly eclecticism ended with Riklin—by the end of 1909, if not before, Wilhelm Stekel was known to be interested in "symbolism."

One possible way out from the mythological thickets was already at hand. Folklorists, advancing fast from Adalbert Kuhn's pioneering work in the mid-nineteenth century, had convincingly shown the existence of a number of core myths and folktales, which had, through dissemination, given rise to countless variants, often quite dissimilar on the surface, spread across different cultures. The existence of these core myths, further, had been discovered in part through philological researches, i.e., through the investigation of common linguistic roots. Freud had already made a place for linguistic roots as a collateral basis for interpreting symbols in his dream book. This was a safe bet, in one sense, since philology had also shown that a great many word-stems had originally had explicitly sexual meanings. But now the temptation existed to go one very large step further. Not only could the appeal be made to the sexual roots of linguistic word-stems, but perhaps a plenary judgment could be won whereby the core myths of the folklorists were themselves shown to have had a definable sexual origin. That is to say, beneath the core myths, perhaps psychoanalysis could find a core complex.

THE SOLVER OF RIDDLES

IT IS POSSIBLE in retrospect to read the passage in Freud's dream book analyzing Sophocles' *Oedipus Rex* as already flirting with the possibility of a "core complex," but such a reading conflates Freud's general cultural program of 1900 with the more specific doctrine that only became relevant in the years 1908–1910. The figure of Oedipus, "the solver of riddles," had enormous significance for Freud personally as a hero-motif. It is recorded that on the occasion of his fiftieth birthday in the spring of 1906, when his small band of supporters had presented him with a medallion of himself inscribed with an epithet from Sophocles—"Who divined the famed riddle [of the Sphinx] and was a man most mighty"—Freud became faint, overwhelmed by the uncanny coincidence that he had long fantasized such an honor. Sophocles' dramatization of the Oedipus myth was important, too, in the wider world of German literature and philosophy during the second half of the nineteenth century, as Peter Rudnytsky has recently shown in great detail. But Oedipus was not yet, by any means, a "core complex," though he did stand as Freud's personal totem for the universality of childhood incestuous wishes.

Thus far, Oedipus had tentatively made his way only into a very occasional remark in the wider analytic literature. Riklin in his 1908 monograph had made a single excited reference in parentheses—"(Oedipus Saga!)"—while discussing infantile egoism. The same year, Ferenczi in a paper on impotence had noted about a patient that he was "a typical personification of the Oedipus myth, the general human significance of which has been revealed by Freud's discoveries." But, even in the analytic literature, the Oedipus legend was slow to take root. Abraham authored a paper for the first *Jahrbuch* on marriage between close relatives without so much as a mention of Oedipus. And Jung in the same *Jahrbuch* issue discussed at length the theme of the son's revolt against the father, again without even so much as a mention of Sophocles'—and Freud's—hero.

To put it another way, before Oedipus—or any other theme—could be enshrined as the core complex, the idea that there was such a thing as a core complex had to be established. Though Freud had been privately brokering the idea to his fellow Viennese for some time, the first Jung had heard of it was the offhand remark in Freud's letter of 13 August 1908: "One thing and another have turned my thoughts to mythology and I am beginning to suspect that myth and neurosis have a common core." The "one thing and another" was four manuscripts that Freud was then working on simultaneously. The first was Karl Abraham's *Dreams and Myth* for Freud's *Applied Psychology* series. Abraham had indeed improved, as he had promised, on the efforts of his erstwhile colleague Riklin. After an extended methodological excursus, in which he explicitly recognized that one lacked any associations to mythological symbols, Abraham argued, partially on the basis of Freud's dream book, that certain symbols were "typical" and therefore readily interpretable. Thus justified, Abraham proceeded to give a psychoanalytic rendering of the Prometheus myth, which had already been analyzed down into its core version by the folklorists. (Abraham's interpretation had it that what was being stolen from the gods was the mystery of male potency.)

The second manuscript, also for the *Applied Psychology* series, was Otto Rank's *Myth of the Birth of the Hero.* Rank had collected a large number of ancient myths and legends all describing the miraculous circumstances surrounding the births of various heroes. The story of the infant Moses being floated down the Nile in a basket may be taken by the reader as prototypical of Rank's collection of tales: there was typically a difficulty with the conception, an early separation from the natural parents followed by an adoption, and then, after a series of adventures, an ultimate confrontation and/or reconciliation with the natural father. The births of Sargon, Karna, Oedipus, Paris, Telephus, Perseus, Gilgamesh, Cyrus, Tristan, Romulus, Hercules, Jesus, Siegfried, and Lohengrin were all discussed in their turn. The case for reducing these disparate stories to a single motif, let it be noted, was derived principally from the writings of the folklorists, with only a very reasonable dash of the new psychology thrown in.

The Myth of the Birth of the Hero was published under Rank's name in the spring of 1909, but during the Wednesday Night Meeting devoted to its thesis on 25 November 1908, it became clear to all who the real progenitor was, and it was Freud who rose to defend it:

> These myths are a combination of two opposing motifs, both of which are subordinate to the main theme of the individual's vindication through the hero. The two motifs are: (1) gratitude and tender feelings toward the parents, and (2) rebellion against the father. Here, however, the conflict with the father has its origin not in sexual rivalry for the mother, but in the father's concealment of the facts about the sexual processes connected with birth.

We do well to note that last sentence. Hostility toward the father, in Freud's account, had its roots in the father's concealment of the facts about the sexual processes connected with birth—at least as far as these myths were concerned. The decisive point was that the myths typically describe miraculous events surrounding the birth of the hero, and in those events Freud believed he could detect the telltale evidence of infantile theories about where babies come from.

Here we come to a new theme, infantile sexual researches, and to the third of the four manuscripts Freud had been working on when he wrote Jung. "On the Sexual Theories of Children" appeared in a

Berlin sexology journal in December of 1908 and it introduced the exact term "core complex" for the first time. Ostensibly, the paper was concerned with an important social issue: sexual education. In keeping with his enlightened stance generally, Freud pointedly took issue with the child-rearing practices of the era, which dictated that children should be regularly mystified on the subject of how their baby brothers and sisters came into the world. Auguste Forel later provided, in his memoirs, a vivid picture of the usual state of affairs:

> Shortly after . . . my younger sister was born. The matter had been carefully kept a secret from me. When the midwife appeared in the house, and everybody began to hurry to and fro, I could not understand what was happening, and why I was made to sit in a little anteroom through which everybody came and went. This confused me terribly; also I felt annoyed by all the usual mystification, accompanied by giggling and laughing. It was only on the following morning that I learned of the event, although I could arrive at no solution of the riddle of what had really happened. . . .
>
> After my sister was born I soon perceived that men and women were differently made, and in spite of the careful secrecy observed by my parents I attempted to obtain information on the subject. It is incredibly mistaken of parents to conceal sexual relations from children as they were commonly concealed in those days, instead of telling them the truth, quietly and seriously; of course, without any admixture of eroticism and frivolity. But as we know they used to do precisely the contrary. . . .

Where Freud went insightfully beyond the protests of Forel, Moll, and others who concerned themselves with this issue was in his consideration of the fantasies such practices might evoke in the child. Not only did the child continue his investigations into the topics of sexuality and procreation, according to Freud, but this sometimes led to secret and quite fantastic theories, theories which might then continue unconsciously into adulthood. In his paper, Freud went on to spell out some of these fantasy-theories with great specificity, and for his warrant he invoked, among other methods of data collection, "the inferences and constructions . . . which result from the psycho-analysis of neurotics." With regard to this method of investigation, he volunteered: "I can only give an assurance that those who know and practise the psychoanalytic technique acquire an extensive confidence in its findings."

The promissory notes with regard to method were continuing. So, too, was the broadening of the interpretive range. Not only did Freud draw an analogy between these infantile sexual theories and the content of folktales, he also made the general issue surprisingly crucial for psychological development as a whole:

> . . . from the time of this first deception and rebuff they [children] nourish a mistrust against adults and have the suspicion of there being something forbidden which is being withheld from them by the "grown-ups," and . . . they consequently hide their further researches under a cloak of secrecy. With this, however, the child also experiences the first occasion for a "psychical conflict" . . . Such a psychical conflict may soon turn into a "psychical dissociation." The set of views which are bound up with being "good," but also with a cessation of reflection, become the dominant and conscious views; while the other set, for which the child's work of research has meanwhile obtained fresh evidence, but which are not supposed to count, become the suppressed and "unconscious" ones. The nuclear complex of a neurosis is in this way brought into being.

It may seem surprising to the reader that children's sexual researches should be accorded such a prominent role in this first official formulation of the idea of the core complex, but the fact is that in every subsequent discussion of the core complex during the years 1909–1910 Freud explicitly reinvoked the same theme. The problem was repression. No longer able to derive repression from bisexuality, Freud was turning to social processes for an explanation, specifically to the conflict between parents and children over sharing sexual information. Freud might have preferred an organic explanation for why sexual processes were uniquely liable to be repressed, but for the time being he was willing to rely on a social-environmental one.

The culmination of Freud's initial efforts to establish the idea of a core complex lay in the fourth manuscript he had been working on, the case of "Little Hans," which then appeared in the first *Jahrbuch.* "Hans" was Herbert Graf, son of the musicologist Max Graf, whom Freud had early recruited for his circle. In his third year, little Herbert had begun to evidence curiosity in sexual processes and in this capacity had put in a cameo appearance in the paper "On the Sexual Theories of Children." In his fourth year, little Herbert developed a frightful phobia of horses and thus became the subject of the first published analysis of a child. It was Max Graf who actually performed the "analysis," which consisted of questioning the child as closely as he would allow. Freud hung in the background advising the father and only on one occasion actually meeting with the child. The text is accordingly split between the father's own charming account, reproduced verbatim, and Freud's glosses. One feature of Freud's remarks was his defense of their young informant against the supposition, lately advanced all over again by Moll, that the early manifestation of a child's sexual inclinations was a mark of hereditary degeneration.

Method was again an issue. Freud's passing comments in the case on his psychoanalytic procedure were extensive, but they did little to answer his critics of that time. He appears to have been aware of Moll's charge that he influenced the data, as indicated by his taking pains to point out that he deliberately withheld certain formulations from the father, thus guaranteeing the authenticity of the child's productions. And yet, Freud also argued that at times the interpretation must precede the data, that the patient's fantasies rise to the surface only when they have been anticipated by the therapist's comments. That, plainly, let the element of suggestion back in. In seeming recognition of the point, Freud thereupon argued that psychoanalysis was *not* primarily a scientific research procedure so much as it was a form of therapy. Yet, even this characterization was belied by the manifest tenor of Freud's remarks. He was clearly less interested in the little boy's therapeutic progress than he was in tracking down each tiny detail of the phobia and fitting them into his overall interpretive schema.

The net result of Freud's handling of the issues of method in the case could only be a sharpening of the division between his followers and his critics. Moreover, as sometimes happens in such collaborations and to the detriment of all didactic purpose, it was the child who stole the show. In the person of little Herbert, who was alternately gallant and demure in pressing his affections on the women who had caught his fancy, the movement had found perhaps the most engaging spokesman for the doctrine of infantile sexuality it would ever command. Herbert was engaging in other ways, too. Besides a remission of symptoms, the chief consequence of his "analysis" was, in Freud's report, "that he got on to rather familiar terms with his father, as the latter reported with some amusement." Herbert could be critically minded as well. During his lone consultation with Freud, he was told that long before he was born Freud had told his father that a little boy would come into the world who would be afraid of his father even though he loved him. Afterward, on the way home, Herbert, sounding a little like William James, remarked to his father, "Does the Professor talk to God, as he can tell all that beforehand?".

The case was a scientific watershed. Between them, the three collaborators, little Herbert, his father, and Freud, had tumbled to a great discovery, one that properly speaking belonged to developmental psychology. There is indeed among well-adjusted children raised in modern society a normal period of development that entirely deserves the name "Oedipal stage." During this stage, roughly between the ages of four and six, children regularly construct fantasies and daydreams in which subliminal erotic and rivalrous wishes toward their parents are clearly manifest—once one knows to look for them. Moreover, when these wishes, which in health usually appear only in derivative forms, are heated up by the family milieu—Herbert's mother not infrequently took him into her bed—the child ordinarily develops a phobia, inside of which a private symbolism encodes the conflicted desires. Far from being a "degenerate" youngster, little Herbert was entirely typical, both in his wishes and in the kind of symptom he developed when these got to be too much for him. In any listing of the "great patients" of psychoanalysis in Ellenberger's terms, little Herbert, with his charm and his self-confessed "nonsense" about the horses, deserves a special place.

Freud's personal preoccupation with Oedipus had hit scientific pay dirt. Other commentators had anecdotally noted both amatory and jealous feelings in the occasional child, but nobody had heretofore supposed that such feelings might be more or less universal, nor that they would ordinarily manifest themselves in unconscious and symbolic ways—and then seemingly disappear. Yet Freud was not entirely content with his discovery. Even supposing that one could extrapolate the general phenomenon from a single case, a universal stage in childhood by itself did nothing to distinguish health from neurosis. Nor did it necessarily clarify the mechanisms governing the formation of the core myths. As he had written to Jung on 11 December 1908, Freud intended that the "Little Hans" case should embody the new doctrine, but it had left many questions unanswered: "I am so obsessed by the idea of a nuclear complex such is at the heart of the case of Little Herbert that I cannot make any headway." The actual text, however, was considerably more confident. In places, Freud argued that "Hans" was really a "little Oedipus," who wished to supplant his father and have his mother all to himself. But Freud supplemented this formulation by arguing that Hans's rivalrous feelings toward his father also had roots in Hans's curiosity about where babies came from, which question Freud compared to the "riddle of the Sphinx":

> He [the father] not only prevented his being in bed with his mother, but also kept him from the knowledge he was thirsting for. He was putting Hans at a disadvantage in both directions, and was obviously doing so for his own benefit.

In the last sentence of the work, Freud made it explicit that the nuclear complex was nearly at hand:

> I am therefore tempted to claim for this neurosis of childhood the significance of being a type and a model, and to suppose that the multiplicity of the phenomena of repression exhibited by neuroses and the abundance of their pathogenic material does not prevent their being derived from a very limited number of processes concerned with identical ideational complexes.

THE RETURN OF THE HERO

FOLLOWING THE vacation with Putnam in the Adirondacks, Freud, Jung, and Ferenczi returned by train to New York and embarked on the *Kaiser Wilhelm der Grosse* for the voyage home. On board, the three took turns analyzing one another's dreams. This became the occasion for yet another confrontation with Jung, but by the end of the voyage, Freud was seemingly left with the feeling that all questions concerning his own personal life had been put to rest. As he wrote to Jung afterward, "Now I hope that all the petty unpleasantness will soon go out of our memories of America and that only our surprisingly grand and beautiful impressions will remain."

The party disembarked at Bremen on 29 September. Freud and Ferenczi took their leave of Jung and together journeyed first to Hamburg and then to Berlin, where they took time out to investigate a local seeress. Abraham, more docile than ever, was there to greet them. He apparently had drawn his own conclusions about the American trip and the changed circumstances it occasioned and was determined not to fall out of favor. To Jung, Freud wrote that he found Abraham "pleasant and affectionate and not at all paranoid; I was almost ashamed in front of Ferenczi for having turned against him recently." Abraham even gallantly rode for an hour and a half with Freud on the train heading back toward Vienna. The Viennese, too, were on their best behavior. They held an evening reception on 12 October to welcome the returning hero. The high point of the evening was an impromptu case report by Stekel about a "beastly non-paying patient"—himself—made phobic by the master's absence. Freud himself was regenerated by the trip. He had very much enjoyed going about with men twenty years his junior and afterward made reference to this period as "the Indian summer of my eroticism." He even shaved his beard and, thus shorn, posed for a portrait. Soon, however, Freud's patients began returning to treatment, the Wednesday Night Meetings reconvened, the beard grew back, and it was business as usual. All in all, Freud's busy schedule left him precious little time for what he described to Jung as "my many, absolutely necessary scientific projects."

At his writing table Freud was a combination of conservator and innovator. The galleys of the "Rat Man" case, now long overdue, were corrected in October. The analysis of the case, which stressed ambivalent feelings toward the father, had occupied almost five hours at the Salzburg congress and was too well known to change now. Still, the core complex managed to pop up in a footnote: "The nuclear complex . . . comprises the child's earliest impulses alike tender and hostile, toward its parents and brothers and sisters after its curiosity has been awakened—usually by the arrival of a new baby brother or sister." A second edition of *Three Essays on the Theory of Sexuality* came out in December. It, too, was changed only in an occasional footnote. There was still no sign of the "nuclear complex" per se, though there was a new footnote on the sexual researches of children, and another on Isidor Sadger's discovery of a relationship between narcissism and homosexuality. In between these projects came the written version of the five Clark lectures for a commemorative issue of the *American Journal of Psychology*. The fourth lecture was finished and sent off to Stanley Hall at the end of November. It contained at its end a brief but unequivocal statement of the new program:

> The feelings which are aroused in these relations between parents and children and . . . between brothers and sisters are not only of a positive or affectionate kind but also of a negative or hostile one. The complex which is thus formed is doomed to early repression; but it continues to exercise a great and lasting influence from the unconscious. It is to be suspected that, together with its extensions,

it constitutes the *nuclear complex* of every neurosis, and we may expect to find it no less actively at work in other regions of mental life. The myth of King Oedipus, who killed his father and took his mother to wife, reveals, with little modification, the infantile wish, which is later opposed and repudiated by the *barrier against incest*. . . .

During the time when the child is dominated by the still unre- pressed nuclear complex, an important part of his intellectual activ- ity is brought into the service of his sexual interests. He begins to enquire where babies come from . . . The fact of this childish re- search itself, as well as the different infantile sexual theories that it brings to light, remain of importance in determining the formation of the child's character and the content of any later neurotic illness.

Away from the writing table, Freud continued lobbying for the core complex. In October, he announced to his fellow Viennese during a case discussion: "In general, neuroses are much more centered than we thought. In this case too it is the typical problem, the same story as has been disclosed in Oedipus and in little Hans." The following month, during a discussion of pediatrics, he elaborated a three-tier developmental scheme of nuclear complex–childhood neurosis–adult neurosis. This, though Freud did not say so, made the uncovering of the core complex part of the proper conduct of an analysis. (The pre- vious May, Freud had been explicit on this point in a letter to Binswanger.)

Meanwhile, Freud kept up his researches into "archaeology." In October, he began consulting regularly with a Gymnasium classics teacher, one David Ernst Oppenheim, in the apparent hope of round- ing out his own layman's knowledge of mythology and philology. He learned, for example, that "Oedipus" means "swollen foot," which on his own warrant he read simply as "erection." In his letters to Jung during October and November, Freud made it plain that my- thology was much on his mind. He welcomed Jung's going into this area—"A little less loneliness"—while pushing his own tentative syn- thesis—"I hope you will soon come to agree with me that in all like- lihood mythology centers on the same nuclear complex as the neuroses." In the service of sharing his viewpoint, and shaping Jung's, he twice shared his translation of Oedipus as "erection" and three times he strongly directed Jung's attention—in October and again in November and yet one more time in December—to the 1908 paper on children's sexual researches. By November, Freud was also busy re-

reading Jung's "Significance of the Father in the Destiny of the Individual" and had arranged for his university seminar to engage in a critical discussion of it.

But, by far the most important new topic of October and November was Leonardo da Vinci. By mid-November there was a draft of a paper. On 1 December, Freud was presenting it to the Wednesday Night group. (He found the locals insufficiently appreciative.) Freud continued to work on it in the months that followed, allowing the long-overdue paper on "general method" to be discarded indefinitely along with a newer paper on "faulty interpretive technique." Another piece, "On a Special Kind of Choice of Object Made by Men," also was postponed to make way for Leonardo. Even the researches into mythology were allowed to lapse, save for a singularly untaxing contribution, written in February, on "The Antithetical Sense of Primal Words." The study of Leonardo, meanwhile, was completed in March, its galleys corrected in April, and Jung had his copy of *Leonardo da Vinci and a Memory of His Childhood*, the seventh number in Freud's *Applied Psychology* monograph series, in May.

THE ROMANCE OF LEONARDO DA VINCI

FREUD'S MONOGRAPH began by taking stock of several of Leonardo's character traits: he was an indefatigable scientific researcher; he had difficulty finishing his paintings; he was sexually inactive as an adult, though he had a fatherly fondness for young boys; and his most famous canvas, the *Mona Lisa*, suggests a great and mysterious secret. Freud utilized a number of accounts to produce this portrait, but he relied chiefly on the prior historical research of the Russian novelist Dmitri Merejkowski. (Freud, in response to a publisher's request in 1907, had listed Merejkowski's *The Romance of Leonardo da Vinci* among his ten favorite books.)

Following his general portrait of the man, Freud went on to introduce a peculiar childhood memory of Leonardo's of a "vulture" brushing its tail feathers in his mouth. And now proceeded one of the great deductive feats in psychoanalytic literature. With little else to go on, Freud began discussing the symbolism of the "vulture" and linked it to ancient Egyptian mythology, where it was frequently used to indicate the figure of the mother (the same word, *mut*, being used for both "mother" and "vulture" apparently). Careful to keep his inferential footing steady, Freud then argued that Leonardo's "memory" was a screen memory fabricated later in life and that the artist had some familiarity with Egyptian symbolism. It was from this precipice that the text leapt into a daring reconstruction: the original "vulture" was Leonardo's natural mother, who overstimulated him sexually in infancy before Leonardo was shipped off to his father and stepmother sometime between the ages of three and five. The memory of the "vulture," in other words, was a screen memory which both depicted and concealed the early overstimulation.

The consequences of this overstimulation and subsequent separation were multiple, and Freud proceeded to gather in all the threads of his earlier description of Leonardo's character. Leonardo's love object was split—there were two mothers, a sexual one who was lost and an adoptive one. These two mothers appeared separately in the canvas *Madonna and Child with St. Anne,* argued Freud, after the smile of the *Mona Lisa* had awakened the memory of the earlier one. Leonardo's failure to assume an adult sexual identity reflected his continuing attachment to this overstimulating mother and, as well, his failure to identify with his father. In line with the newly inserted footnote in the second edition of the book on sex, Freud now spelled out the narcissistic nature of homosexuality—the adult male loves boys, both as a way of staying faithful to his mother and as a way of identifying with her love for him. In Leonardo's case, Freud argued, the homosexuality was sublimated artistically. Sublimated, too, were his childish sexual researches. Indeed, argued Freud, it is here that we find the source of Leonardo's inexhaustible scientific interests—and of his genius generally. Unlike most people, Leonardo did not suffer the crippling effects of an early thwarting of his sexual curiosity. He learned to sublimate it in the form of researches on nature (itself symbolic of the "mother").

It was a tour de force. Freud had entered into the relatively new and already controversial medico-literary genre of "pathography" and had come out with a fascinating and sympathetic account of a great man. Naturally, the sexual aspects of Freud's portrait drew yet another round of criticism—his old friend Löwenfeld was among those who objected—but in the small world of psychoanalysis it was gobbled up. Jung proclaimed, "The transition to mythology grows out of this essay from inner necessity, actually it is the first essay of yours with whose inner development I felt perfectly in tune from the start." Pfister even made an additional contribution: he discovered hidden in Leonardo's painting of *Madonna and Child with St. Anne* the outline of a vulture—plain as day once one knew to look for it! Pfister published his finding in 1913 and Freud added it to his own text as a footnote to the 1919 re-edition. (Jung, too, found a vulture, but in a different place and less convincingly drawn.)

There was, however, a problem, one that might have raised methodological alarums had it been known at the time. "Vulture" is a mistranslation. It is not to be found in Leonardo's notebooks. Indeed, it is to be found only in the German translation of Merejkowski's novel. Merejkowski's original Russian has it not as "vulture" but as "kite," which, indeed, is the word which actually appears in Leonardo's notebooks. Which means that Leonardo's childhood memory involved a "kite," not a "vulture." And for the record, "kite" appears to be unconnected to mother-symbolism in the mythology of ancient Egypt or any place else. In short, no "vulture," no "*mut,*" no mother.

There was, interestingly, no "Oedipus," either. Owing to the nature of his materials, Freud elected to leave that theme out altogether. By this time, the specific phrase "the Oedipus complex" had finally appeared in print. The honor of being the first to have used it in a published work went to Sándor Ferenczi, whose much-revised paper "Introjection and Transference" had appeared in November in the second issue of the *Jahrbuch* with the exact term. Ernest Jones was the first to use it in English in "The Oedipus Complex as an Explanation of Hamlet's Mystery," which ran in the January issue of Hall's *American Journal of Psychology.* Freud himself finally used the phrase "Oedipus complex" for the first time in a short paper on the psychology of love-life, "On a Special Type of Choice of Object Made by Men." This manuscript finally arrived in Zurich in June of 1910. In it, Freud described the passion of certain men for women of fallen reputation. Typically the man's passion is based on his belief that he can rescue the woman from depravity, and it only intensifies his ardor if the interests of another man are injured in the process. In examining the syndrome, Freud succinctly described the contribution of the "Oedipus complex," but only after he had once again brought in the theme of infantile sexual research. (In rescuing the harlot, the adult neurotic is undoing the child's disillusioning discovery that his mother is herself a fallen woman.)

THE AMERICAN TRIP, like the Spielrein crisis which had immediately preceded it, had more than one effect, each very important in its own way, each registering differently in different quarters. The first of the effects of the American tour was the enhancement of Freud's sense of his own stature as a theorist of the human condition. Just as Freud's identification with Oedipus as the "solver of riddles" had heretofore taken the specific form of his image of himself as the "discoverer" of infantile sexuality, so, too, his romance of Leonardo, that thoroughly splendid scientist-artist of another age, now revealed as a sublimated sexual researcher, almost certainly reflected the still-warm afterglow of Freud's own triumph at Clark. But more important than this afterglow was Freud's renewed attempts to articulate a definitive version of the core complex and to enlist Jung in that effort. In fact, Freud was still almost a year away from arriving at his final formulation of the core complex—he would add a phylogenetic rationale—and several years away from publishing it. Thus, for the time being, the concept still appeared to be an open one and there was room for other investigators to imagine making their own contributions to its delineation.

In terms of consulting-room realities, the effect of the doctrine of the core complex was to diminish the relative importance of the patient's present erotic conflict as the immediate precipitant of a neurosis in favor of an increased emphasis on childhood determinants. The ultimate importance of the idea, however, lay elsewhere and can be stated succinctly. It was the pivot upon which psychoanalytic theory turned from being an essentially clinical doctrine of nervous illness to being a general theory of human mind and culture. And it formed the conceptual terrain upon which the tensions between Freud and Jung were played out.

CHAPTER 10

The House with Two Skulls

Time here is so frightfully filled up. Yesterday Freud and I spent several hours walking in Central Park and talked at length about the sociological problems of psychoanalysis. He is as clever as ever and extremely touchy; he does not like other sorts of ideas to come up, and, I might add, he is usually right. He certainly has the most well-thought-out and unmitigatedly biological point of view one could imagine nowadays. We spoke a good deal about Jews and Aryans, and one of my dreams offered a clear image of the difference. But one can't really go very deep into anything here, because the general hustle and bustle is so overwhelming. Those few quiet hours in the park did me good, though.

—Jung, letter to Emma Jung, 31 August 1909

T HE SECOND GREAT consequence of the American triumph was that it enhanced Jung's sense of *his* stature as a unique theorist of the human condition. As his behavior prior to Clark had already demonstrated, Jung, though he was still committed to libido theory, was becoming theoretically restless. He also had begun courting the friendship of other men such as Flournoy and William James. Flournoy had already come to an astute appraisal of Freud's place in the history of ideas. In later life, Jung remembered Flournoy as someone who "spoke most intelligently of Freud, pointing out Freud's adherence to the antireligious age of enlightenment." As for James, Jung found time for his own private discussion with the American at Clark. They discussed the occult, the psychology of religion, and how a theorist's "personal equation" might affect his theory.

Jung's lectures at Clark only hinted at his restlessness. His first lecture, concerned with the word association experiment, was principally concerned with methodological issues, though here and there he noted the similarity of his findings with some of Freud's clinical concepts. Jung's second lecture, "The Family Constellation," took up Emma Fürst's finding that complexes and reaction-types tend to run in families, but rather than derive this from the persistence of infantile sexual dependence, as he had previously done, Jung attributed it to a general emotional contagion within the home. Moreover, in a move that would have pleased Stanley Hall, Jung went on to make adolescence the crucial developmental stage for it was then that the child had to accomplish the difficult step of separation from the family.

Jung's third lecture, "Psychic Conflicts in a Child," complicated matters by adding an entirely new element—"introversion." The child featured in the lecture, Jung's daughter, referred to by another name, turned inward to fantasy when she faced a difficult situation, namely the birth of her baby brother. At first glance, her "introversion" was entirely analogous to the inward-turning "depression" of the adolescent in the previous lecture. Indeed, there was the same telltale tendency to "poetry":

> Here we meet with an important new feature in the little one's life; reveries, the first stirrings of poetry, moods of an elegaic strain— all of them things which are usually to be met with only at a later phase of life, at a time when the youth or maiden is preparing to sever the family tie, to step forth into life as an independent person, but is still inwardly held back by aching feelings of homesickness for the warmth of the family hearth. . . . To approximate the psychology of a four-year-old to that of the boy or girl approaching puberty may at first sight seem paradoxical; the affinity lies, however, not in the age but in the mechanism. The elegaic reveries express the fact that part of the love which formerly belonged, and should belong, to a real object, is now *introverted,* that is, it is turned inwards into the subject and there produces an increased fantasy activity.

In a side-comment, however, Jung argued that there was a potentially adaptive aspect to introversion:

> When life comes up against an obstacle, so that no adaptation can be achieved and the transference of libido to reality is suspended, then an introversion takes place. That is to say, instead of the libido working towards reality there is an increased fantasy activity which aims at removing the obstacle, or at least removing it in fantasy, and this may in time lead to a practical solution.

Jung also noted the archaic nature of the little girl's productions and he equated them with "the poetry of fairytale, whose magic is felt even by the adult." Thus Jung here assented to the "poetry of fairytale," whereas earlier he had equated adolescent "poetic fancies" with a resistance to life. Evidently, Jung was still of two minds about "poetry." Archaic in nature, it might alternately lead one out from the family constellation, or back toward it. In the latter case, it could become the source of "resistance" in adult life. In the former case, however, there was another possible outcome to the process of "introversion," namely that the temporary turning inward might be followed by a creative new adaptation.

A THEORETICAL DREAM

DURING THE voyage home, Jung continued to muse on the differences in philosophical tradition between himself and Freud: ". . . I had the impression that Freud's intellectual history began with Büchner, Moleschott, Du Bois-Reymond, and Darwin." Then he had an important dream. The action of the dream was quite simple. In it, Jung found himself on the second floor of a building in a room decorated with fine old pieces in the rococo style. He thought to himself pleasantly that this might be his own house and, eager to explore it, he descended to the ground floor. The ground floor turned out to be rather dark and to have medieval furnishings. Next Jung toured the cellar, which dated from Roman antiquity, and finally, a sub-basement. There he found pottery, bones, and two skulls, all dating from prehistoric times.

Jung saw the house as representing his own psyche and its historical development. The second floor represented his education in the philosophies of the eighteenth and nineteenth centuries: the works of Kant, of Schopenhauer, and Krug's *Dictionary of the Philosophical Sciences* came to mind. The first floor represented their Christian forerunners, the scholastics; the floor was dark, as Jung's memoirs tell us, because since Darwin the medieval God had been lost. The basement, with its Roman wall, invoked an even earlier historical period; it also recalled Jung's own preadolescent love for archaeology. Finally, the sub-basement: not only was the earliest prehistory indicated, but also Jung's interest in paleontology while at medical school. In short, the dream presented a visual *Bildungsroman*—Jung's own intellectual development in four floors.

What was so remarkable about all this? The layout of the building did not follow the chronology of Jung's own life. The prehistorical level, the sub-basement, was out of order; it should have come at the top, as the most recent area of interest. Instead it came at the bottom. Similarly, as a childhood acquisition medieval theology should have come before the classical archaeology of late adolescence, not afterward. If the house did indeed represent Jung's own consciousness, then the message of the dream was that *consciousness was arranged on the basis of cultural and phylogenetic history, not on the personal past.* The layout of the house thus stood in marked contrast to Freud's theory:

> Certain questions had been much on my mind during the days preceding this dream. They were: On what premises is Freudian psychology founded? To what category of human thought does it belong? What is the relationship of its almost exclusive personalism to general historical assumptions? My dream was giving me the answer. It obviously pointed to the foundations of cultural history—a history of successive layers of consciousness. My dream thus constituted a kind of structural diagram of the human psyche. . . .

Jung's misgivings about Freud, however, were not solely theoretical; there was also a personal dimension. It is not altogether surprising, then, that this very same dream of the house with two skulls became the occasion for a very sharply pointed remark. Dream interpretation was one of the principal forms of amusement as Freud, Jung, and Ferenczi sailed back toward Europe. The pastime, however, was potentially dangerous, given the underlying tensions. These tensions finally came to a head when Freud refused to give his associations with regard to one of his own dreams. The incident has been discreetly described in Jung's memoirs:

> Freud had a dream—I would not think it right to air the problem it involved. I interpreted it as best I could, but added that a great deal more could be said about it if he would supply me with some additional details from his private life. Freud's response to these words was a curious look—a look of utmost suspicion. Then he said, "But I cannot risk my authority!" At that moment he lost it altogether. That sentence burned itself into my memory; and in it the end of our relationship was already foreshadowed. Freud was placing personal authority above truth.

It would help matters if we knew what Freud's dreams had been about. Jung later told Jones only that Freud's dreams had been "mostly concerned with cares for the future of his family and of his work." However, to Billinsky, in 1957, he went considerably further, in the process adopting a posture of near-arrogance:

> On the [American] trip Freud had some dreams that bothered him very much. The dreams were about the triangle—Freud, his wife, and wife's sister. Freud did not know that I knew about the triangle. And so when Freud told me about the dream in which his wife and her sister played important parts, I asked him to tell me some of his personal associations with the dream. He looked at me and said, "I could tell you more but I can't risk my authority." That of course finished my attempt to deal with his dreams. On that trip he developed severe neuroses and I had to do limited analysis with him. He had psychosomatic troubles and had for instance to urinate about every half an hour. I suggested to Freud that he should have complete analysis, but he rebelled against that because he would have to deal with problems that were closely related to his theories. If he would have tried to consciously understand the triangle he would have been much, much better off.

The dream interpretation did not stop there, however. All that had stopped was Jung's asking for Freud's associations. Jung took advantage of the continuing opportunity to relate to Freud his own dream of the previous April, where Freud had appeared as a "dead" customs official. Jung's motive seems to have been half spite and half curiosity, for he still had not figured out what to make of the formula whereby someone could be dead but not know it. Freud, however, didn't know what to make of it, either. Jung next related his more recent dream of the house with two skulls in the sub-basement. Freud readily volunteered the thought that there were two people Jung wanted dead and buried two basements down, and then asked Jung for *his* associations.

Late in life, shortly before his death, Jung penned two different accounts of his reply, one in his memoirs and the other in a paper written contemporaneously on dream interpretation. In both places, Jung insisted that Freud was looking for evidence of death wishes against himself. In both places, Jung said that he had no such death wishes. In both places, Jung admits that he lied in giving his answer. And in both places, he justified his lie by saying that the difference in their backgrounds guaranteed that Freud would be unable to interpret the dream correctly. In the paper on dream interpretation, Jung wrote that he withheld his real associations to the two skulls, for he was afraid Freud ". . . would have dismissed it as a mere attempt to escape from a problem that was really his own." But only in his memoirs did Jung report what he actually said: "My wife and my sister-in-law."

It is difficult not to hear this as anything but a veiled reference to the Freud household. Jung himself said about Freud's reaction:

> I was quite aware that my conduct was not above reproach, but *à la guerre, comme à la guerre!* It would have been impossible for me to afford him [Freud] any insight into my mental world. The gulf between it and his was too great. In fact, Freud seemed greatly relieved by my reply.

There is a persisting ambiguity about the shipboard confrontation. Jung's association—"my wife and my sister-in-law"—begs to be heard as a challenge. Yet, Freud manifestly did not hear it that way. Instead, according to Jung, he was "relieved," almost as if the whole issue had been laid to rest in a manner befitting gentlemen who do not discuss personal matters. Moreover, Jung's conduct in the immediate aftermath seems to have been more diplomatic than ever. In his first letter to Vienna after disembarking Jung wrote almost wistfully, "On the journey back to Switzerland I never stopped analysing dreams and discovered some priceless jokes. A pity there's no time for this now." And Jung's next letter sounded positively grateful: "The analysis on the way home has done me a lot of good." Yet, only three years later, Jung was remembering these same sessions with great bitterness. Apparently, at the time, with the Clark triumph still fresh in both their memories, Jung had concealed his true feelings, acting the docile disciple while inwardly accumulating resentment and a secret sense of superiority, both of which finally exploded in December of 1912.

JUNG'S ODYSSEY

JUNG DISEMBARKED at Bremen and took his leave of Freud and Ferenczi on 29 September 1909. His follow-up letter to Freud spoke of his eagerness to get started on the next phase of his career: "I am feeling in top form and have become much more reasonable than you might suppose." Once he was reensconced in the new house in Küsnacht, Jung took up the tangled threads of both his personal life and his professional career in earnest. In his own home, he began analyzing his wife's dreams. Professionally, he became a whirlwind of activity.

Jung's professional activities were diverse. In addition to taking on private patients and resuming his university lectures, he began a private seminar on psychoanalysis in his home for a group of doctors. Included in the seminar were two Americans: Trigant Burrow, who soon undertook to go into analysis with Jung, an analysis which was sometimes conducted aboard Jung's sailboat; and August Hoch, who was slated to take over Adolf Meyer's prestigious post as head of New York's Psychiatric Institute. At the same time, Jung undertook to write up six lectures on mental disturbances in children, which were to be delivered in January and February of the new year. All through this period, Jung continued to write reviews of the recent psychiatric literature for the *Bulletin of Swiss Physicians.*

The fall of 1909 was a critical time in Swiss medical politics and here, too, Jung made his indefatigable presence felt. Auguste Forel was energetically recruiting members for his International Society for Medical Psychology and Psychotherapy. (Trigant Burrow was pleased and honored when Forel, very much the great man, approached him during a Zurich reception and solicited his participation in the new group.) Freud and Jung were, of course, invited to join—the invitations were awaiting them upon their return—and Jung at first refused but, after some consultation with Vienna, made the arrangements for both of them in mid-November. The move paid immediate dividends at the Winter Meeting of Swiss Psychiatrists held later that month in Zurich. Three of the papers, by Bleuler, Ludwig Frank, and Alphonse Maeder, were slated to be on psychoanalytic topics. Early in the meeting, Forel rose to attack von Monakow, by now an avowed enemy of psychoanalysis, for founding with Dubois a rival organization of Swiss neurologists. Jung rose to take Forel's side and "Monakow & Co. lay on the floor totally isolated." Then, in the discussion that followed the psychoanalytic presentations, Forel returned the favor by siding with the speakers even though he maintained reservations about the doctrine of infantile sexuality. As Jung wrote to Freud in celebration of his diplomacy, "Your (that is, our) cause is *winning all along the line....*" Jung's lectures on child psychology in January and February of the new year further capitalized on this strategic victory. The lectures provided a common forum for propagandizing psychiatrists, educators, and the Zurich clergy. (The latter group, owing to Oskar Pfister's pugnacious espousal of the new doctrines, had lately become embroiled in a heated controversy over Freud's theories.)

But the whole time that Jung was forging ahead with his career, he was spending all his free time in his library reading books on mythology and ancient history. It was an obsession. Freud heard about it as early as 14 October: "Archaeology or rather mythology has got me in its grip, it's a mine of marvelous material." Early in his researches Jung followed the path taken by Stanley Hall and concentrated on tracking down the ancient religions of phallic worship. In his letter of 8 November 1909, he commented to Freud, "Rich lodes open up for the phylogenetic basis of the theory of neurosis." In his letter of 15 November 1909, Jung took the theme of phallicism directly into incest with the mother, along the way using Freud's terminology for the first time: "For me there is no longer any doubt what the oldest and most natural myths are trying to say. They speak quite 'naturally' of the nuclear complex of neurosis." But, by the end of November, Jung had gone beyond phallicism. His letter of 30 November 1909 announced, "Only the great, that is the *epic*, gods seem to be phallic." There was yet a more archaic streak in ancient mythology, he wrote Freud, which he labeled "elemental." The same letter also contained the following telltale appeal:

> I often wish I had you near me. So many things to ask you. For instance I should like to pump you sometime for a definition of libido. So far I haven't come up with anything satisfactory.

Moreover, Jung now made his phylogenetic leanings explicit:

> I feel more and more that a thorough understanding of the psyche (if possible at all) will only come through history or with its help. . . . For this reason antiquity now appears to me in a new and significant light. What we now find in the individual psyche—in compressed, stunted, or one-sidedly differentiated form—may be seen spread out in all its fullness in times past. Happy the man who can read these signs!

The letter brought a testy reaction from Vienna. In his reply of 19 December 1909, Freud suggested that for the definition of "libido" Jung could consult the "first sentence" of *Three Essays on the Theory of*

Sexuality. Within the limits of a studied tolerance, Freud spoke of the need for "a prolonged face-to-face discussion, amid creaking of the wall and furniture if you will. . . ."

Jung continued undaunted on his path during December: "I am turning over and over in my mind the problem of antiquity. It's a hard nut! Without a doubt there's a lot of infantile sexuality in it, but that is not all." The same letter of 25 December 1909 also announced that Jung had given one piece of his research, that dealing with reality loss in schizophrenia and its relation to mythological forms of thinking, to his assistant Honegger to work on. Jung next announced, in a letter of 30 January 1910, that he had just given a lecture on "Symbolism" in which he made the case that the forms of individual fantasy were "mythologically typical." Unfortunately, as he told Freud, "The supporting material is rather thin." Some idea of Jung's state of mind during the preceding month of January can be gleaned from what follows in the letter:

> During the time I didn't write to you [seventeen days] I was plagued by complexes, and I detest wailing letters. This time it was not I who was duped by the devil but my wife, who lent an ear to the evil spirit and staged a number of jealous scenes, groundlessly. At first my objectivity got out of joint (rule 1 of psychoanalysis: principles of Freudian psychology apply to everyone except the analyzer) but afterwards snapped back again, whereupon my wife also straightened herself out brilliantly. Analysis of one's spouse is one of the more difficult things unless mutual freedom is assured. The prerequisite for a good marriage, it seems to me, is the license to be unfaithful. I in my turn have learnt a great deal. The main point always comes last: my wife is pregnant again, by design and after mature reflection.

Whatever the devil had been whispering to Emma Jung, it likely did not concern Spielrein, who was hard at work as a student assistant at the Burghölzli trying to write a medical dissertation. However, Jung had already taken on a new patient, Toni Wolff, who was later to assist him, a year and some months hence, in his library. Fräulein Wolff was the youngest daughter of a wealthy family from Zurich, half-Jewish, and at the time in the midst of a terrible depression, perhaps with psychotic features, brought on by the death of her father. She was also, as later events bore out, a woman of considerable determination and intelligence. Jung's treatment of her earned him the gratitude of her family—it has been rumored that he saved her from the asylum—and thus cleared the way for their later, and ultimately intimate, association. From the available data, however, it appears that the initial round of therapy ended with all decorousness still intact. If it was Fräulein Wolff who worried Mrs. Jung, then it was with reason, but the actuality still lay very far in the future.

Freud and Jung were now entering into consequential discussions about the upcoming Psychoanalytic Congress at Nuremberg at the end of March, which Jung was calling in line with a tentative resolution that had been agreed upon at the Salzburg meeting two years before. The plans the two men were making for the Nuremberg congress reflected their changed appraisals of who they were: not only had the two men decided to stay together despite their differences, but they had decided to institutionalize their partnership. Henceforth, their correspondence was preoccupied with the congress and its aftermath, with the result that Jung's letters temporarily dry up as a source of information about his studies. Instead, Jung contented himself with passing references to the extent of his absorption. On 20 February 1910, he wrote of "the Walpurgis Nights of my unconscious." On 6 April, he spoke of "the overflowing delights of mythology, which I always reserve as dessert for the evening." And on 17 April, he told Freud, "At present I am pursuing my mythological dreams with almost autoerotic pleasure, dropping only meagre hints to my friends." The only exception to this pattern was the letter of 2 March which explicated further the content of the January lecture on "Symbolism":

> I explained there that "logical" thinking is thinking *in words,* which like discourse is directed outwards. "Analogical" or fantasy thinking is emotionally toned, pictorial and wordless, not discourse but an inner-directed rumination on materials belonging to the past. Logical thinking is "verbal thinking." Analogical thinking is archaic, unconscious, not put into words and hardly formulable in words.

Of all the diverse material Jung was weaving into the tapestry of his reflections, the most important was a little essay written by a Miss Frank Miller, entitled "Some Instances of Subconscious Creative Imagination." Frank Miller, named after her father, was a poetess and lecturer who had briefly studied under Flournoy in Geneva. The point of her essay was to demonstrate that some poems and fantasies that had come to her already composed while she was not fully conscious could be shown to obey known psychological laws, and thus had not a hint of the miraculous about them. In this way, she hoped to provide Flournoy with ammunition against the claims of occultists. What her essay provided Jung was the case material he had so sorely lacked in his January lecture. He has described what happened. We pick him up in the midst of his researches:

> I read like mad, and worked with feverish interest through a mountain of mythological material, then through the Gnostic writers, and ended in total confusion. . . .
>
> In the midst of these studies I came upon the fantasies of a young American altogether unknown to me, Miss Miller. The material had been published by my revered and fatherly friend, Théodore Flournoy, in the *Archives de Psychologie* (Geneva). I was immediately struck by the mythological character of the fantasies. They operated like a catalyst upon the stored-up and still disorderly ideas within me.

Miss Miller's paper began with a description of her own "nervous temperament," giving instances of how she was readily prone to both suggestion and auto-suggestion. Then she described the first poem, entitled "Glory to God," which came to her in a dream. She immediately dispelled the romance of its creation by describing how it clearly derived from literature that was familiar to her, including certain passages in the Book of Job and Milton's *Paradise Lost*. The second poem, "The Moth and the Sun," also had a religious cast to it. It came to her while she was in a hypnagogic state, i.e., half-asleep but still capable of self-reflection. Here, too, though with somewhat less self-assurance, she analyzed the poem in terms of her prior experiences. Finally, she presented "Chiwantopel," a hypnagogic drama that played itself out spontaneously in her mind. The drama features a long soliloquy of an Aztec warrior, whose name forms the title, in which he laments how he has never found a woman who will understand him. Then a little serpent appears and kills both Chiwantopel and his horse. In her analysis, Miss Miller recalled being fascinated by the Aztec ruins in childhood. Among literary models for Chiwantopel, she listed Shakespeare's Brutus, Samuel Johnson's Prince of Abyssinia, and, with special emphasis on his lament for Brünnhilde, Wagner's Siegfried.

SEXUALITY DESTROYS ITSELF

USING THE Miller fantasies as a scaffolding for his reflections about the phylogenetic basis of neurosis, Jung prepared a lengthy and important talk for the spring meeting of Swiss psychiatrists held in the city of Herisau on 16 May 1910. The text of Jung's Herisau lecture has been lost, but its essentials can be readily reconstructed. Jung began with the Freudian approach to symbolism in dreams and gradually worked his way into his ideas about the two kinds of thinking. Whereas rational thought, upon which science depends, proceeds verbally and has a definite direction, there exists in all of us a different kind of thinking, which uses images and symbols, that we retreat to in fantasies and daydreams. In this second kind of thinking our own wishes take precedence. Further, the images themselves often express the nature of the wish directly, so that for instance certain sexual wishes are often represented in terms of typical symbols such as a bull or a snake. These typical symbols derive from the phylogenetic experience of mankind. In dreams, these libido symbols emerge most clearly, as a kind of inventory of the dreamer's current psychic state, since the dreamer regresses to an archaic mode of self-expression. Dreams thus reverse the course of human history. In human history, we see a progression from symbolic forms of thought to more rational, verbal, and materialistic thought. This progression has been part and parcel of a progressive conquest of the primitive forms of sexual expression, a conquest that once had absolute survival value in periods of decadence and overpopulation, but which now results in unneeded repression of the sexual, archaic side of the psyche.

The unfortunate consequences of this repression can be seen in cases of modern nervousness, for which Miss Miller stands as an excellent example. We see in her first dream, "Glory to God," an ostensibly religious theme, but we find that immediately preceding it were various erotic impressions during the day. When we further investigate the symbolic structure of the poem, we find that the image of God derives from the figure of the father. Miss Miller is naturally unaware of this deeper element as the incest barrier blocks it from consciousness. So, her first example sets the stage: she tells us that she yearns for the paradise lost of sexuality, her childhood, when the father-God was not merely a moral force but an affectionate, sensual one as well.

Miss Miller's second poem again shows archaic and sexual roots of which she is unaware. Ostensibly "The Moth and the Sun" reflects a Christian's all-consuming love of God, but, drawing out the implications of her own scanty associations, we see rather a state of introversion taking hold. The sun that Miss Miller's ego flies toward is her own introverted sexuality. She is unable to escape the magic orbit of her father. Accordingly, a real drama, which Miss Miller knows nothing of, for all her sophistication, is unfolding in her account.

The hypnagogic drama of Chiwantopel contains the resolution of that drama. The Aztec hero Chiwantopel represents the dreamer's ego, his horse the dreamer's libido. We can hear in Chiwantopel's long lament the sufferings of introversion. The drama ends badly. The snake that emerges to kill both Chiwantopel and his horse is itself a libido symbol. That it attacks the horse as well indicates that there is a conflict contained within the sexual drive itself, specifically between the backward-looking incestuous tie (the snake) and the forward-going procreative urge (the horse). This same motif we find repeatedly in the ancient world, most vividly in the iconography of ancient Mithraism, a mystery religion that competed with Christianity in the early centuries A.D. Mithraic statuary repeatedly shows one sexual symbol devouring another. There is thus a conflict in the heart of sexuality: one part of it is set against the other and in the balance hangs the individual's adult adjustment. Jung summarized the inherent conflict with the maxim: "Sexuality destroys itself." The incestuous component of libido must be sacrificed, so that man's procreative force may be set free. It is only when this is accomplished through the voluntary self-sacrifice by the hero-god of part of his original sexual unity that true vitality can be achieved. In the case of Chiwantopel, however, we see the opposite outcome. Here the incestuous libido wins out, the hero dies, and the state of introversion continues. Ostensibly, Miss Miller has submitted her manuscript as an aid to science. Unconsciously, however, she has made a plea to be rescued from a deepening introversion that will gradually take her further into fantasy and ultimately into dementia praecox, where finally all ties to reality will be done away with as her mind becomes trapped in its archaic and symbolic layers.

Jung records in his letter to Freud that his lecture "aroused great applause." Well it might have—this was a masterly example of something which Jung, like Stekel, was extraordinarily good at, namely intuiting the meaning of symbols with very little else to go on. To predict a breakdown in someone so ostensibly viable as Miss Miller was a bold step. To make such a prediction creditable to a hall full of psychiatrists on the basis of mythological parallels was a tour de force. Even Freud appears to have been a little cowed by it all, for his comments on the manuscript included the admission that he had rather neglected symbolism in his dream book, an oversight, he told Jung, which Stekel was in the process of correcting.

Freud did have a few objections. To begin with, as John Forrester has noted, Freud disliked the contrast in the two ways of thinking between the symbolic and the verbal. In fact, Freud promptly undertook to write his own parallel paper, "Formulations Concerning Two Principles of Mental Functioning," where he would set forth his own prejudices on the subject. By way of forestalling Jung's ire, Freud informed him of the new project in his letter of 19 June 1910 with the admonition: ". . . don't accuse me of plagiarism, though there may be some temptation to." Freud then explained, "I conceived and wrote it two days before the arrival of your 'Symbolism' . . ." In August, however, Freud produced a different version of events for Jung. Writing from Italy, Freud admitted that the "Two Principles" paper was still unfinished; indeed, it was "tormenting" him "like a blocked bowel movement."

Freud's urge to get his own differing ideas about the reality principle and the pleasure principle into print was symptomatic of a new dimension that was opening up in the Freud-Jung relationship. The issue was not so much one of outright competition—appropriately muted, that had always been there—as of mutual assimilation. Freud had lately appropriated Jung's term, the "complex," for his own theory of the "core complex," in the process subtly altering its meaning. Similarly, Jung was now presenting his phylogenetic romance of self-sacrifice as a contribution specifically to "libido" theory, in the process implicitly enlarging that term to include something more than infantile sexuality. Paul Stepansky has written of the Freud-Jung relationship that at the beginning of it they had agreed to disagree. Paradoxically, just this was getting harder to do. Instead of having two different theories the two men were beginning to espouse two different versions of the same theory.

Freud had other criticisms of the Herisau talk as well. He disliked Jung's tendency to interpret Miss Miller's first dream directly. In his view, Jung had neglected the role of censorship and thus lost the thread of her unconscious purpose. Further, Freud was not so sure about the easy equation between dreams and ancient myths, especially as Jung seemed to imply that modern dreams were the residue of the ancient modes of thought: "This would be more apt if the ancients, who lived in mythology, had not also had dreams." Finally, and most predictably, Freud found Jung's statement "Sexuality destroys itself" a hopeless muddle. For Freud, the motif of self-sacrifice was a projection of repression, in which the conscious ego regretfully sacrificed its vigorous drives—"Basically, a part of the castration complex."

The last comment led to one of the most important exchanges in the entire extant correspondence. Jung responded on 26 June 1910 with a three-page discussion of the role of the self-sacrificial Hero in mediating between the two streams of libido. According to Jung, the Hero's role was to overcome the incestuous stream in the libido through symbolic self-sacrifice so that procreation could go forward: "Hence the comforting and truly dithyrambic outcome of the self-sacrifice: and *yet* we shall be fruitful again." By comparison with Mithraism, Christianity's version of self-sacrifice appeared as a kind of sublimated necrophilia: "The Christian identifies with the self-conqueror, eats his way right back into his dead body, propagates himself only furtively and on sufferance, without inner conviction." Jung's letter made it clear that he now intended to expand his talk and include in it a lengthy consideration of the self-sacrificial Hero as an intermediary stage in the phylogenetic evolution of libido symbolism over the millennia. Freud was perhaps dazzled by the virulence of Jung's remarks on Christianity; his reply of 5 July 1910 characterized Jung's as "a good letter full of important ideas," while adding that he now expected Jung to provide "ample proof" of his assertions. Moreover, any good that Freud's cautionary comments of late June might have done had already been undercut the month before by the arrival in Zurich of *Leonardo da Vinci and a Memory of His Childhood*. For in analyzing Leonardo's screen memory, Freud, too, had turned to mythological symbolism for a key piece of his puzzle. This was essentially the identical procedure Jung had employed in the Herisau talk.

A final methodological comment is in order. Jung had long been fascinated by the stream of inner visual imagery, both in himself and in other people, and his personal preoccupation in this regard had stood him in good stead scientifically. For the human mind does indeed appear to rely on two different modes of processing information—research into the phenomenon is still going on—and with his distinction between the "two kinds of thinking" Jung had given a preliminary description of it. But Jung's reliance on the iconography of Mithraism for his mythological analogue to the motif of self-sacrifice was problematic, even if it escaped comment at the time. The fact was that the devotees of this religion left behind *no* written texts, so that their imagery remains wholly a matter of interpretation. Jung's assessment of Miss Miller's personality, meanwhile, though certainly plausible, remained necessarily speculative, as did his prediction that she was headed for a schizophrenic breakdown. In fact, some years afterward Miss Miller did have a very brief hospitalization, but, as Sonu Shamdasani has shown, her actual clinical condition did not bear out Jung's prediction.

In short, his contribution to the psychology of thought notwithstanding, Jung had not escaped the basic methodological problems attending the idea of the core complex. Try as he might, Jung had no way either of piercing the veil of Mithraic symbolism or of going beyond Miss Miller's limited revelations about herself, except to weld them together via his own associations, with these not recognized as such. The coherence of Jung's talk ultimately depended on a phylogenetic recasting of the core complex: if there was a basic universal sexual constellation operative at a given stage in development, then perforce there had to be a stage in human prehistory when that constellation had been formed. But instead of providing a constraint on Jung's theorizing, the phylogenetic angle had only doubled his interpretive license. The net result was a clinical prediction that was, in fact, wrong.

Even if he had failed to escape the methodological snares of the core complex, Jung had managed to get his own theoretical house temporarily in order. With his distinction between the two different kinds of libido, one infantile, incestuous, and backward looking, the other adolescent, procreative, and forward looking, he had arrived at a version of the psychoanalytic vision he could live with. And this was important because, thanks to the Nuremberg congress at the end of March, he had lately allowed himself to become the main figurehead of the psychoanalytic movement.

Arguably, there was yet another dimension to the Herisau talk. For, in retrospect, it is possible to view the Herisau talk as a delayed expression of ambivalence regarding the Spielrein debacle. Just as Jung had initially turned to "psychosynthesis" in panic over what she might reveal, he had turned back to mythology once the coast was clear. And while the "autoerotic delights" of his library researches were his chief recompense for the loss of her company, the theme of the "procreative libido" with its teleological and adaptive aspects potentially enabled him to reincorporate into his personality some of the exhilaration he had felt being her "Siegfried." Or so I would argue. The issues were the same, but the whole matter had been displaced back into antiquity, into man's racial past. Assuming that the affair was still on his mind, Jung could now take safety in supposing that he had only been doing research into psychological issues—"psychophores"—that had been handed down phylogenetically over the millennia. Certainly, the moral lesson he derived therefrom—the Hero must sacrifice his incestuous attachments—was not without personal application.

CHAPTER 11

The International
Psychoanalytic Association

Our psychology is a science that can at most be accused of having
discovered the dynamite terrorists work with. What the moralist and
general practitioner do with it is none of our business, and we have
no intention of interfering. Plenty of unqualified persons are sure to
push their way in and commit the greatest follies, but that too does
not concern us. Our aim is simply and solely scientific knowledge,
and we do not have to bother with the uproar it has provoked. If
religion and morality are blown to pieces in the process, so much the
worse for them for not having more stamina.

— "Marginal Notes on Wittels, *The Sexual Need*,"
Jung, 1910

B Y THE TIME of their exchange on the Herisau lecture, Freud
and Jung had other, pressing matters to worry about. At the
Nuremberg congress held on 30–31 March 1910, they had founded the
International Psychoanalytic Association.

Ernest Jones later claimed he had been party to a discussion of
forming an official organization during the Clark congress, but the
extant correspondences tell quite a different story. To begin with, there
is no mention at all of such a plan in the letters between Jones and
Freud in the months prior to the Nuremberg congress. The extant
Freud-Jung letters, meanwhile, make it clear that though Jung was
expected to call another meeting like the one held in Salzburg two years
before, neither a specific date nor a specific agenda had been selected.
Moreover, the available documents indicate that Freud was initially
concerned less with forming his own organization than in allying himself and his adherents with one or more existing organizations. In this
connection, he had asked Alfred Adler to prepare a memorandum on

whether psychoanalysts should enroll themselves in the Social Democratic party.

The first known reference to a specific organization for psychoanalysis occurs in Freud's letter to Ferenczi of 1 January 1910. Freud also asked Ferenczi to consider whether an organization of this kind might need stricter internal discipline than was usual for a scientific society. The following day, Freud wrote to Jung to suggest that much had changed since the Salzburg meeting and that the coming congress might usefully "be devoted to other tasks such as organization." Even so, Jung continued to behave as though he were only calling another scientific meeting like the one two years earlier, and initially his biggest priority was to get Freud to lecture again on case material. It was not until early February of 1910 that Jung first heard from Freud the news that Ferenczi would be lecturing about "organization and propaganda" and would shortly be contacting him directly about it. Moreover, nowhere in his subsequent letters to Freud does Jung acknowledge that he knows he is to be made president of the planned association. Indeed, Jung was so cavalier about the proposed organization that one may well wonder if he even knew what his role in it was supposed to be. One of Freud's letters, a mere three weeks before the congress, is missing, but from Jung's startled reply—"How could you have been so mistaken in me?"—we can surmise that Freud finally called him to task for his coy ways and asked him point-blank: Did he want to be president for life or not?

That Jung was so silent about it in his letters to Freud suggests that he considered forming an official psychoanalytic association a less drastic step than it turned out to be. Which brings us to the obvious question: What did Freud and Jung feel they would gain by this step? Surveying their letters for the six months between the American visit and the March congress, one sees that they were principally concerned with the low quality of psychoanalytic publications and secondarily concerned with the poor tactics being used by their camp followers in medical politics.

Again and again the topic of the low quality of psychoanalytic publications came up in their letters in the fall of 1909. Freud was furious with Binswanger for what he elected to hear as a condescending tone in Binswanger's latest publication. Both men were concerned with a critical discussion of psychoanalysis being prepared by Bleuler. (Jung had the happy thought that if Bleuler were allowed to print it in the *Jahrbuch,* he would be forced to restrain his pen.) Riklin had finished a manuscript on Goethe's "Confessions of a Beautiful Soul," but Freud found it "so dull and colourless that I hesitate to include it in the *Papers.*" And that was just the usually reliable Swiss. The Viennese were, if anything, worse. Stekel, who had not allowed any changes in his most recent *Jahrbuch* piece on dreams, had recently topped that performance with a paper on obsessions that Freud found "absolutely frivolous and faulty in method." As for Isidor Sadger, the other prolific Viennese, Freud was hopeful Jung could keep him out of the *Jahrbuch* altogether: "Sadger's writing is insufferable, he would only mess up our nice book." In Freud's opinion, Adler was "the only one who can be accepted without censorship, though not without criticism."

Initially, Freud and Jung planned to vent their displeasure in a special review section in the *Jahrbuch.* The first targets of this review section were to be Bleuler and Stekel. The review section was Jung's idea, but Freud seconded it strongly:

> I suggest that you and I share the work on this critical section, you will rap the Viennese on the knuckles and I the Zurich people when they start producing versions of their own. These reviews must be the expression of our very personal convictions; this is an attempt at literary dictatorship, but our people are unreliable and need discipline.

That was in November of 1909, shortly after the Clark congress. By the following March, the two men had decided to make their "literary dictatorship" explicit. We naturally tend to view the fledgling International Association in terms of what it has become, a professional organization chiefly concerned with training and certification. Certainly part of the attraction of forming such an organization was that it would help make psychoanalysis appear to be a legitimate medical specialty. But the animus for the association was at least equally literary. What Freud wanted to control was the appearance of both scientific and polemical papers by his followers in journals other than the *Jahrbuch.* The office of the president was to be the clearinghouse for all such papers. That is, they would have to first receive the president's imprimatur before they could go out. This is what was entailed in the codicil in Ferenczi's proposal on organization stating that the president was to have responsibility over all "external matters." Given that Jung was Freud's candidate for the office of the president, and that the *Jahrbuch* was already in Jung's hands, the effect was to give Jung complete control over all psychoanalytic publications. Between his two jobs,

Jung could serve as official spokesman against the critics while having the clout internally to raise the scientific quality of psychoanalytic writing. As for Freud, by officially moving the seat of psychoanalysis to Zurich he could hope to capitalize on the prestige of the Zurich school, and on the institutional resources that Jung and Bleuler commanded. It seems never to have occurred to Jung, or to Freud, or to Ferenczi, how the arrangement would appear to their fellow analysts.

In historical retrospect, the decision to found the International Psychoanalytic Association, and to anchor it on the personal prestige of the two principals, Freud and Jung, can only be called rash. To be sure, the organization, or rather the skeleton that was left of it some years later, proved useful, perhaps even decisive, in propagating psychoanalysis in the period after the First World War. From this perspective, one could say that Freud was unusually farsighted. But the immediate consequences of the decision were unfortunate, very nearly ruinous, and before the following summer was out, both Freud and Jung would agree that they had acted precipitously and were now paying the price.

Whatever judgment we come to about the two men's actions, we should keep in mind that it was indeed a time for international movements in general. Forel had just banded Europe's psychotherapists together in a new group. An apothecary named Knapp was forming a new international ethical fraternity (another organization which Freud considered aligning psychoanalysis with). And the Darwinian biologist Ernst Haeckel had started what amounted to a new religion ("Monism") based on his theories, with the result that Haeckel Bunds were springing up all over the continent. (The Catholic church, more than a little concerned, had quickly countered with *Thomisten Bunden,* named of course for the great scholastic saint, and in short order yet another network, the Kepler Bunds, had been started by those who sought a middle way between the Haeckelians and the Catholics.) All this was in addition to the various organizations for sexual reform centered in Germany, numerous European youth groups, the abstinence movement headed by Forel, Bleuler, and Kraepelin, and, of course, the burgeoning professional societies in psychiatry, neurology, experimental psychology, and pedagogy. Indeed, in this climate of diverse organizational activity, it was not always clear where the lines of division lay, and one of the problems the psychoanalysts failed to resolve was to decide exactly what kind of group they wanted to be.

Freud's group got off to a very bad start. Even the countdown went badly. To begin with, the three collaborators (Jung, Ferenczi, and Freud) decided on total secrecy. The handout describing the association's proposed bylaws, which was to be distributed during Ferenczi's talk, bears the mark of a Nuremberg printshop. Apparently it was run off the morning of the first day of the congress. Freud himself arrived at Nuremberg several hours early for the express purpose of meeting Abraham, who had come down from Berlin. The best guess is that this is when Abraham was told. From all other available correspondence, there is absolutely no evidence that any other participant was let in on the plan. The secrecy constituted very bad tactics. When the Viennese saw what was afoot, they readily guessed that the three visitors to America were in cahoots.

Then there was the problem of marshalling the Swiss. Ferenczi's bylaws called for Zurich to be the permanent seat of the association. Perhaps Freud meant to surprise the Swiss. In the event, they surprised him. First of all, Bleuler, still a most important patron of the movement, decided to spend the last week of March having elective surgery rather than attending the Nuremberg congress. Then there was the business of Max Isserlin, an assistant at Kraepelin's clinic, who wanted to attend as a silent auditor. Isserlin had been following the development of psychoanalysis with interest and was at the time preparing a critical but respectful paper about it. But his private views were occasionally much sharper, and Jung had heard of him through the network of students passing back and forth between Munich and Zurich. Isserlin would not have been exactly welcome in any case, but in light of the specific character of the congress, Freud decided that it would be best simply to refuse him admission. This was a most unusual step for a scientific congress, treating an assistant at the Munich clinic as though he were a crank. Kraepelin was understandably furious. Jung considered it all a "bad joke," but the joke was going to have important repercussions—Kraepelin began to wonder publicly what was going on at the Burghölzli and he personally tore into Bleuler the next time they met—and it would have been wise for Jung to start the damage control immediately. Then at the last moment, Jung decided he could not refuse a consultation in America with the McCormick heir. Instead of seeing to the final preparations, and warning Bleuler that Kraepelin might be coming to town for something more than a consultation, Jung dashed back to the United States and left it to Mrs. Jung and young Honegger to make the final arrangements. Jung's disappearance on the eve of his coronation—the steamer for the return voyage was due to dock but one day before the congress began—was not welcome news to Freud. Next, Pfister wrote to say that he wasn't coming, either. Freud became anxious:

> I still have not got over your not coming to Nuremberg. Bleuler is not coming either, and Jung is in America, so that I am trembling about his return. What will happen if my Zurichers desert me?

Jung did make it back in time, but Freud's troubles were only just beginning. His own keynote address, "On the Future Prospects of Psychoanalytic Therapy," was perhaps the most militant thing he ever wrote, and he clearly meant it to rally the troops to the cause. It seems to have succeeded, however, through a kind of deferred action, only in galvanizing the response to Ferenczi's subsequent proposal on organization. Once they heard the Hungarian speak, those assembled grasped what Freud's subtext had been and what the overall plan looked like. Among Freud's points was the claim that the practice of psychoanalysis would become easier in the future as the prestige of psychoanalysis increased, for then the analyst would acquire greater suggestive authority in the eyes of his patients. In short, the association would make treatment easier. This good news was balanced by a warning that henceforth a self-analysis was to be required of one and all— "Anyone who fails to produce results in a self-analysis of this kind may at once give up any idea of being able to treat patients by analysis." In short, the association was going to have internal discipline. Freud closed by speaking of the cultural mission of psychoanalysis. In short, the association was to be a movement:

> I should therefore like to let you go with the assurance that in treating your patients psychoanalytically you are doing your duty in more senses than one. You are not merely working in the service of science, by making use of the one and only opportunity for discovering the secrets of the neuroses; you are not only giving your patients the most efficacious remedy for their sufferings that is available to-day; you are contributing your share to the enlightenment of the community from which we expect to achieve the most radical prophylaxis against neurotic disorders along the indirect path of social authority.

Ferenczi's talk on organization was scheduled for the afternoon of the first day. The discussion that followed it was so acrimonious that the meeting had to be adjourned, with decisions postponed for the next day. It is said that for a basically sweet man, Ferenczi had a terribly dictatorial streak and that on this occasion it was too much in evidence. Perhaps, but it is hard to see how any tone, no matter how conciliatory, could have rescued the text of his address. He began by dividing the history of psychoanalysis into two periods, the "heroic age," when Freud had to meet all attacks "entirely alone," and a second period, "heralded by the appearance of Jung and the 'Zurichers.' " Where this left men like Adler and Stekel, who had been on hand for the last eight years, was anybody's guess. Then, on the basis that "guerrilla warfare" was no longer practical, and that their lack of organization to date was a handicap, Ferenczi went on to imagine what a psychoanalytic organization should look like. As analysts, they were of course all aware that every group reproduced the dynamics of the family, that every president was a father, that the other officials were the older children, and that the rank and file were the younger children seeking to oust the older ones. But, as analysts, they should also know that they could not hope to escape these dynamics in themselves altogether. Therefore, their association should make use of the "family organization" self-consciously:

> It would be a family in which the father enjoyed no dogmatic authority, but only that to which he was entitled by reason of his abilities and labours. His pronouncements would not be followed blindly, as if they were divine revelations, but, like everything else, would be subject to thoroughgoing criticism, which he would accept, not with the absurd superiority of the paterfamilias, but with the attention that it deserved.
>
> Moreover, the older and younger children united in this association would accept being told the truth to their face, however bitter and sobering it might be, without childish sensitivity and vindictiveness.

Next came Ferenczi's concrete proposals, handsomely printed out that very morning. From the accounts of other participants, we know that orally Ferenczi made the following additional elaborations: Jung was to be president for life, with full authority over "external matters" (including all publications outside the *Jahrbuch*) and the right to disbar any member who violated the rules. In effect, not only was Jung being handed the whole organization, but he was also being given the right to curtail any member as he saw fit and, if he chose, to tell the Viennese what he thought of them ". . . to their face, however bitter and sobering it might be.'' Fritz Wittels has described the scene that followed:

It can readily be imagined that the unsuspecting Viennese ("We had no anticipation of such an onslaught") were utterly dismayed by these proposals. I doubt if powers so absolute have ever been entrusted to any one except the heads of certain Roman Catholic orders. . . .

Freud behaved like the Old Man of the primitive horde—was simultaneously ruthless and simple-minded. When he perceived that his Viennese pupils were up in arms, and that they were determined to resist Ferenczi's proposal with all their might (this determination was especially conspicuous in the cases of Adler and Stekel, whose interests were more closely touched than those of the others), he postponed the vote until the next sitting. The three years' struggle within the psychoanalytic camp had begun, the unedifying struggle that was to end in three great secessions. . . .

On the afternoon of this memorable day, the Viennese analysts had a private meeting in the Grand Hotel at Nuremberg to discuss the outrageous situation. Of a sudden, Freud, who had not been invited to attend, put in an appearance. Never before had I seen him so greatly excited. He said: "Most of you are Jews, and therefore incompetent to win friends for the new teaching. Jews must be content with the modest role of preparing the ground. It is absolutely essential that I should form ties in the world of general science. I am getting on in years, and am weary of being perpetually attacked. We are all in danger." Seizing his coat by the lapels, he said: "They won't even leave me a coat to my back. The Swiss will save us— will save me, and all of you as well."

It was an impossible situation. The Viennese would not budge, but they could do nothing on their own without Freud. Their whole claim to outrank the Swiss depended—Stekel's passionate address to the floor had stressed this—on their claim to have been the first at Freud's side. A compromise was worked out. Jung was given the presidency, but only for two years. Riklin was made secretary. The official seat of the association was to be the city where the president resided. Thus, Zurich was to be the seat of the association for now, but not necessarily permanently. There was to be no censorship.

The fight was just beginning. Adler and Stekel caucused between themselves after Freud left and decided to test the "no censorship" clause immediately. At the next day's session, Stekel sprang the announcement that the two were starting their own journal, the *Zentralblatt für Psychoanalyse*. Apparently, they also took whatever opportunities presented themselves to be rude to Jung personally.

Freud spent the day after the congress with Jung. In search of a diversion, they visited the nearby town of Rothenburg, home to the world's largest collection of medieval torture devices. Years earlier Freud had been unable to interest Fliess in witches and their confessions, and in that connection he doubtless was moved to reminisce about the various turns a man's fortunes can take. On Jung's side, it was probably here that he mentioned to Freud that he should really have a look at Daniel Paul Schreber's book, *Memoirs of My Nervous Illness*. A jurist, Schreber had risen to the high court of Saxony, only to be felled by insanity. In his book, Schreber described his experiences as though they contained important religious revelations, thus ensuring that his work would become a psychiatric classic. No hard information survives concerning this outing, but Freud and Jung seem to have parted each other's company with a renewed sense of their shared destiny.

When Freud returned to Vienna, he discovered the mood was still hot. The locals accused him of being the author of Ferenczi's proposal, and he did not deny it. There were hurt feelings; Freud had to explain his favoring Zurich. Nonetheless, despite the heat, Freud was in rare form. Having officially moved the center of the movement out of Vienna, at least for the time being, he was willing to make further concessions on paper to the locals. In short order, Adler became president of the Vienna society, Stekel vice-president. Freud also moved that the group take cognizance of its new status by finding an appropriate meeting place. It need no longer meet in his waiting room but could and should reserve a proper hall. Freud even offered to withdraw altogether from any official position, at which point sentiment shifted and he was made "Scientific Chairman." Freud wrote to Jung that he was satisfied with "the outcome of my statesmanship," as well he might have been because in the ensuing scramble of titles, he managed to end up as "Director" of the new *Zentralblatt*, and thus titularly above the editors, Stekel and Adler, an arrangement which belied their actual bargain. (Freud managed to persuade the two that his name on the masthead was being insisted on by a potential publisher. Over coffee, the three agreed to a de facto equality: each of them would have veto power over all contributions.)

Wittels's pithy observation that the "three years' struggle within the psychoanalytic camp had begun" needs to be qualified; the struggle initially had a good deal of foolishness about it. The immediate consequence of the Nuremberg decisions was that the Vienna group became transformed into something of a debating society with everyone self-importantly pushing his or her own "discoveries" forward. The competition had perhaps always been there, but the formalities of being an officially constituted body brought it strongly to the surface. For his part, Freud liked to imagine that he detected an increase in industriousness and sober thinking, but he balanced his pleasure with a seeming disdain for the organizational pretensions of the locals. This created the misleading impression that nothing serious was in the offing. Hanns Sachs later remembered Freud opening the annual business meeting of the Vienna group in the years that followed with the comment, "Today we must play high school fraternity." But, in point of fact, Freud took the new high school politics very seriously. He was just biding his time.

But this covers only the local problems of the Viennese. In the larger world the new association was a dramatic bust. Simply put, people would not join the International Psychoanalytic Association. In Berlin, Marcinowski, who had lectured at Nuremberg, "energetically protested against belonging." Frau Dr. Sophie Erismann, a Zurich regular—on paper, the first woman psychoanalyst—disappeared without explanation after attending the congress. Ludwig Frank, a fence-sitter with nominal ties to the Zurich group, now ostentatiously withdrew his affiliation, complaining that Freud had slighted him personally at Nuremberg. (Freud had. When Frank had introduced himself, Freud had replied, simply, that he knew all about him.) Eitingon, no fence-sitter but a man of independent means, saw no reason to join. Muthmann, an early champion whose "courage" had already been vouched for by Freud, also would not join. Wilhelm Strohmayer, *Privatdozent* for psychiatry and neurology at Jena, refused to let himself be listed on the masthead of the *Zentralblatt,* though he subsequently did allow himself two years' official membership in the Berlin group. Löwenfeld, Freud's personal friend and critic, had been willing to lecture at Nuremberg on hypnotherapy. Perhaps Freud had not expected otherwise, but Löwenfeld did not join the association. Wittels himself dropped out of the Vienna group during the summer of 1910 after a confrontation with Freud over whether he could publish his novel in which the central character was based on Karl Kraus, the prominent journalist with whom Wittels was connected through a love triangle. Hans Maier, Jung's successor as second-in-command at the Burghölzli and a friend of Binswanger's since childhood, would not join. Binswanger did join, but no one else associated with his illustrious family would, and he himself continued to entertain reservations about what in private he called Freud's "empire." As Jung put it, speaking of the association, "It seems to give people the horrors."

Most important, Eugen Bleuler would not join. The barring of Isserlin, an unusual step, had had important ramifications. Jung and Freud had no hope of courting favor with Kraepelin, and they had rather enjoyed this slap at one of his assistants, but they had indulged themselves without considering the position that this put Bleuler in. And, as Bleuler went, so went the Burghölzli. With the exception of Jan Nelken, the assistants there, now led by Maier, all refused to join, though they continued to sit in at local meetings. Jung, with Freud's blessing, tried to put a stop to this quasi-revolt by insisting on official membership, but this was voted down.

Bleuler's absence left the Zurich group essentially and inexorably leaderless. Pfister was the obvious second choice to be president of the Zurich society—Jung and Riklin were barred by virtue of their central posts—but Binswanger, who had to worry about the flow of referrals to his private asylum in Kreuzlingen, opposed Pfister on the grounds that he was not a medical man. Alphonse Maeder of Geneva was a good compromise choice, if and when he ever left his assistant's post at Kreuzlingen and settled permanently in Zurich. In the meantime Binswanger, whom Jung was beginning to distrust and whom Freud had accused of intellectual slumming some months earlier, was more or less in command. It was not quite chaos, but it was close. Adding to the complications was the fact that tensions between the Swiss and the Viennese were at new heights. The Viennese distrusted Jung more than ever, while on the Swiss side, Jung, Maeder, and Binswanger all flatly refused to publish anything in Adler's and Stekel's *Zentralblatt*. Bleuler's feeling about Stekel was so strong that he listed him as a separate reason for refusing to join the association. As he put it to Jung, "[O]ne didn't want to sit down with everybody."

Jung had no knack whatsoever for conciliation, nor for shepherding the faithful. Central direction was utterly lacking. The *Correspondenzblatt*, the official organ of communication between the presidency and the local societies, stumbled along for six haphazard issues before dying a young death. Business details Jung passed along to Riklin. But Riklin was even less organized; he didn't even answer letters. At one point the Viennese, who needed a copy of the international charter in order to register with the local Austrian authorities, so despaired of getting an answer out of Zurich that they entertained the possibility of going off on their own, at least on paper. And the propaganda value of having such an international organization was entirely lost. The truth was that without Bleuler's name on the rolls, an omission that was certain to draw unwanted attention, the association was reluctant to publish its own membership list.

For all this, neither intellectual respect nor an improvement in professional etiquette was gained. It was correctly perceived by outsiders that this was something more than an ordinary scientific society, and the phrase "the psychoanalytic movement" came into currency with a quite different ring to it than Freud would have hoped for. The wrong note had already been struck by Fritz Wittels the year before with his polemical *The Sexual Need,* which was nothing less than a call for widespread sexual reform based on Freud's teachings. And it was soon to be struck again by Jung in an alarmingly fanatical review of Wittels's book slated to appear in the *Jahrbuch* in August. But the first person to use the exact phrase derogatorily was Willy Hellpach of Berlin, whom Freud had courted for years. Writing in *Der Tag* in June, Hellpach predicted "the inevitable collapse of the Freudian movement." The month before, however, Alfred Hoche, professor of psychiatry at Freiburg, speaking before the Congress for South-West German Psychiatrists in Baden-Baden, had already found a better phrase. Hoche entitled his talk "A Psychic Epidemic Among Physicians." The phrase echoed essentially similar phrases that had been used some years before to decry the propagation of hypnotism. Adjusting himself to the vagaries of the present situation, Hoche defined a "psychic epidemic" as "the transmission of specific representations of a compelling power in a great number of heads, resulting in the loss of judgment and lucidity." To great applause, he scolded the Freudians for their superior attitudes, their jargon, their intolerance, their proselytizing, their credulity, and their fantastic overvaluation of their own contribution. Hoche went on to list as the causes of this epidemic a lack of historical sense and philosophical education as well as the thanklessness of treating nervous patients.

Perhaps the worst moment in a long summer came at the first congress of Forel's new International Society for Medical Psychology and Psychotherapy in early August. The young Freudians in attendance (the peripatetic Ernest Jones prominent among them) seemed ready to attack anybody who did not mention the name of Freud, to the point where Forel finally got up to protest, and Oskar Vogt, Forel's friend and coeditor of the *Journal für Psychologie und Neurologie,* was moved to the following denunciation:

> I object that a man like myself who has collected his own dreams since the age of sixteen and has investigated the problems under discussion here since 1894, that is, almost as long as Freud has done and longer than any of his disciples, should be refused the right to discuss these questions by any Freudian.

On 10 August, Freud wrote Jung from Holland:

> Maybe I am to blame, but it is easy to find explanations after the event, and the outcome could not have been foreseen. All the same, when I look at the situation objectively, I believe I went ahead too fast. I overestimated the public's understanding of the significance of ΨA [psychoanalysis], I shouldn't have been in such a hurry about founding the I. A. My impatience to see you in the right place and my chafing under the pressure of my own responsibility also had something to do with it. To tell the truth, we should have done nothing at all. As it is, the first months of your reign, my dear son and successor, have not turned out brilliantly.

Freud's disappointment, however, fazed Jung not at all:

> I heartily agree that we went ahead too fast. Even among the "favourably disposed" there are far too many who haven't the faintest idea of what ΨA is really about and especially of its historical significance. My ear is now cocked at our adversaries: they are saying some remarkable things which ought to open our eyes in several ways. All these mutterings about sectarianism, mysticism, arcane jargon, initiation, etc. mean something. Even the deep-rooted outrage, the moral indignation can only be aimed at something gripping, that has all the trappings of a religion.

Jung's secular religiosity then evolved into a charming apocalypse:

> Moreover ΨA is too great a truth to be publicly acknowledged as yet. Generously adulterated extracts and thin dilutions of it should first be handed around. Also the necessary proof has not yet been

furnished that it wasn't you who discovered ΨA but Plato, Thomas Aquinas and Kant, with Kuno Fischer [prominent philosopher and literary critic] and Wundt thrown in. Then Hoche will be called to a chair of ΨA in Berlin and Aschaffenburg to one in Munich. Thereupon the Golden Age will dawn. After the first 1000 years ΨA will be discovered anew in Paris, whereupon England will take up the opposition for another 500 years and in the end will have understood nothing.

Freud was charmed. To Ferenczi he wrote on 14 August 1910, "Yesterday I got an epistle from Jung which showed him to be at the top of his form and in full possession of those qualities that justified his election."

Freud had good reason for taking heart: For whatever else had gone wrong with the International Association, one very important thing had gone right: he had secured Jung as the official president of his movement. Here we must remark briefly on Freud's continued attachment to Jung. Peter Homans, following John Gedo, has suggested that it bore all the hallmarks of what is now called a narcissistic transference, i.e., that Freud loved Jung as a means of completing his own sense of self. How this attachment looked at the time, or at least how it looked in Switzerland, can be partially gleaned from an account given fifty years later by Alphonse Mæder:

> . . . he [Freud] regarded the coming together with Jung as something redeeming. He made Jung his "dauphin" [crown prince], as we say. He did not want a Jew. He was glad that he [Jung] wasn't a Jew. . . . In some ways he did not think highly of all his pupils, in character and also in creativity. He did notice that Jung was a genius-type, you see, he had strength and was healthy. I mean, if you looked at those Viennese, they all looked like decrepit, strange people. No one had anything fresh . . . and that [health in Jung] made Freud happy.

How things looked to the Viennese can be gauged from the following passage from Wittels's account. We pick up Wittels as he discusses the relation between Freud, Ferenczi, and Jung:

> The three travellers took vows of mutual fidelity, agreeing to join forces in the defence of the doctrine against all danger. One of these

dangers was that with which every scientific doctrine is threatened as soon as it becomes popular—the danger of vulgarisation and misunderstanding. Another risk seemed especially imminent to Jung, who was afraid of the trend of some of Freud's Viennese disciples . . . afraid of the Viennese far-fetched interpretations. Freud, though he must have known the whole-souled devotion of his Viennese disciples, was at this time markedly drawn to Jung. His face beamed whenever he spoke of Jung: "This is my beloved son, in whom I am well pleased."

In short, the principal virtue of the founding of the International Association was that for the present it seemed to have brought Freud and Jung closer together again. As Freud put it on 24 September 1910, "I send you kind regards and an expression of my certainty that nothing can befall our cause as long as the understanding between you and me remains unclouded."

There was one other, perhaps intended, benefit arising from the founding of the International Psychoanalytic Association. Now, it became possible for young physicians to imagine joining this organization, to imagine receiving further training in this new specialty, to imagine, in other words, becoming psychoanalysts. And thus it happened, even as the "three years' struggle" within psychoanalysis was beginning to get under way, a host of talented newcomers, almost all of them quite young and accordingly quite impressionable, slowly began to log themselves in as candidates for membership in the local societies. Between 1909 and 1911, a new generation—Hanns Sachs, Viktor Tausk, Theodore Reik, to name an outstanding few—made its debut.

A NEW ERA

IN ZURICH, at the end of August, Sabina Spielrein took an important step in joining the next generation of psychoanalysts. For the past year, Eugen Bleuler had been supervising her dissertation, a psychoanalytic investigation into a chronic dementia praecox patient. But Bleuler had not joined the new association, nor had he yet found time to read Spielrein's first draft. So, during a summer lull, Spielrein decided to approach Jung:

> Despair gave me courage. I ran to my friend, with whom I had not wanted to speak for a long time. For a good while I found no

words, until I was finally able to tell him of my desperate situation and ask him to read my dissertation, if for no other reason than that he figures in it. He laughed at Prof. Bleuler as an analyst and said surely I had not come to make fun of a person whom I liked so much. We arranged that in September, I would ask for my dissertation back from Prof. Bleuler and send it to my friend. . . .

The most important outcome of our discussion was that we both loved each other fervently again. My friend said we would always have to be careful not to fall in love again; we would always be dangerous to each other. He admitted to me that so far he knew no female who could replace me. It was as if he had a necklace in which all his other admirers were—pearls, and I—the medallion. At the beginning he was annoyed that I had not sent my paper to him long before, that I did not trust him, etc. Then he became more and more intense. At the end he pressed my hands to his heart several times and said this should mark the beginning of a new era.

CHAPTER 12

The Spiritual
Trend in Psychoanalysis

Finally, I want to emphasize the enormous importance of "description by the opposite," which was discovered by Freud, for the development of delusions. A particularly important instance of this is the description of sexual activity by death symbolism. The reason for this phenomenon is, as I see it, within the character of the sexual act itself, or, to put it more clearly, in the two antagonistic components of sexuality.

—Spielrein, 1911,
"On the Psychological Content of a Case of
Schizophrenia (Dementia Praecox)"

T HE DISSERTATION which Spielrein sent Jung at the beginning of September, "On the Psychological Content of a Case of Schizophrenia (Dementia Praecox)," was subseqently published in the *Jahrbuch* in 1911. It constitutes the only extant document bearing on her activities between her wistful reflections in her diary in the summer of 1909 and her excited diary entry in August of 1910 announcing that "a new era" was about to begin between her and Jung.

The patient Spielrein had elected to study was a well-educated but unusually hostile and strikingly fragmented woman, preoccupied with death and dissolution, whose communications were all but utterly incomprehensible. Nonetheless, Spielrein was able to decode much of what she had to say. For example, her published discussion of the patient's "Catholicizing" complex was both lucid and persuasive. The woman was Protestant, her philandering husband Catholic and the more sexual of the two. Thus, her having been "Catholicized" was a reference to her being overwhelmed by unwelcome sexual ideas. That complex led through "mythological experiments," which concerned the "birth of mankind," to the "Sistine experiments," which involved both hallucinated punishments for and denial of sexual desire. The "Sistine experiments" in turn brought about various "transformations" of the patient's body in which the battle between sexual desire and sexual resistance was fought out at the level of bodily protoplasm. Similarly, ideas concerning "poetry" and "art (painting)" came into play as synonyms for "religion," i.e., as various ways of envisioning sexual contact in the context of a love relationship.

Apart from sexual theme-hunting, Spielrein displayed a lively knack for deciphering her patient on the basis of a kind of commonsense cross-referencing of her delusions. For example, there were numerous references to Auguste Forel: one of the patient's central delusions was that she had a little "Forel" inside of her; "Sistine Question" was a reworking of *The Sexual Question;* Forel was the leader of the abstinence movement, hence the numerous references to alcohol; and so forth.

Jung also turned up repeatedly in the dissertation; the patient seemingly never tired of talking about him. One of her more prominent delusions, noted in the mental-status exam at the dissertation's outset, directly involved him. The patient stated repeatedly that she had been "flogged through Basel." Spielrein astutely picked up all the threads of this complex. Basel was the city Jung grew up in. Being "flogged" was related to various rituals of Carnival Time, in particular the *Schnitzelbank,* a kind of roast where the guest is ridiculed, and also to a form of running the gauntlet, both of which the patient explicitly mentioned. The underlying situation was that Jung had previously administered the word association test to this patient—the procedure calls for one examiner loudly to call out the stimulus word at the subject while a colleague measures the reaction-time—and the patient understood that her own complexes were being revealed and felt humiliated. Beyond this, she also felt that the test constituted a sexual assault on her.

Elsewhere the patient made various complimentary remarks about Jung. For example, she volunteered that his happy-go-lucky and witty character caused everyone to follow him around with their love. At another point, perhaps punning on Spielrein's name, the patient commented ironically on Jung's background: "Dr. J.'s father is a minister—he has a pure education. . . ." But perhaps the most incisive of these various portrayals was the following: "Dr. J. who has prostituted me is a friend of the Mormons—he wants to get divorced once a year."

If Spielrein enjoyed including these various gibes, she nowhere let on. Her tone was serious, even grave, throughout. And her conclusions were strikingly novel, for she had found an incisive way of linking

Freudian theories of defense with the phenomenology of dementia praecox:

> In general, the schizophrenic likes to use vague and abstract terms and this for a good reason. . . . The less sharply circumscribed a term is, the less it means something distinct and concrete and the more it can contain. I have the impression that a symbol in general is generated through the striving of a complex for multiplication, for dissolution into the overall system of [collective] thought. . . . By this means the complex loses its personal character for the schizophrenic.

As for the patient's persistent preoccupation with images of death, disease, dirt, and dissolution, Spielrein connected them to the threats to the differentiated ego inherent in sexual fusion. These threats were potentially felt by everyone, but in schizophrenia, where the ego was already embattled, they led straightaway to delusions. In these delusions, Spielrein argued, one could see the operation of "two antagonistic components" in the sexual drive, a dissolving (and thus destructive) component and a transforming one.

But Spielrein was not the only person in Zurich for whom these themes had personal import. Jung had independently come to consider that sexuality might have two different streams and that therein lay the key to motifs of death and rebirth. There now came in his mail a dissertation from his former lover in which a fairly similar model of the libido was used to explicate "death symbolism." Which brings us to the crux of the matter: having discovered a patient who herself mixed sexuality with religion, who spoke of "art" and "poetry" and loved "Dr. J.," Spielrein had succeeded in distancing herself from her own complexes by locating them in another. Her dissertation signaled to Jung that she was no longer the naïve girl of their dalliance, but a young professional woman who could, if she chose, take an appropriate distance on things while sacrificing none of her intuitive ability to plumb the psychological depths.

THE BENT UMBRELLA

IT WAS JUNG'S turn to feel ambivalent. He responded to the receipt of the dissertation with two letters, the second of which reached Spielrein on 13 September 1910. And while his first letter had allowed that "many passages" in her paper "had thrown him into raptures," his second was a good deal cooler—"he is miffed that everywhere I omit his name, as if intentionally, do not cite his works, and in the end even make fun of him."

The first time Spielrein actually met with Jung in the fall of 1910 was on Tuesday, 20 September. Her diary describes how difficult the occasion was for her:

> I explained to him as well as I could that I like him but cannot help it that my proud nature resists his excessive power over me. Everything went off peacefully. He suggested that I work through the dissertation with him, so that it can be accepted by the *Jahrbuch.* He said that the case was so interesting that I would be accepted into the Psychoanalytic Society. After some hesitation (because of the psychic torment I would undergo in his presence), I agreed. So this wish, too, which seemed so utterly unrealizeable, can also be fulfilled, and yet my unsated heart contracts painfully, for the main thing is missing, and this main thing is love. Oh, again this "What to do?" I hardly believe that I could love anyone the way I love my friend. I fear my life is ruined.

Spielrein's situation was further complicated by the fact that she knew all too well that she was not Jung's only admirer. Her own diary expressly describes Fräulein Aptekmann's concurrent infatuation. As well, we know from Jung's letter to Freud of 8 September 1910 and from Freud's reply of 24/26 September 1910, that two other ladies, Maria Moltzer of Zurich and Martha Böddinghaus of Munich, were currently at loggerheads with each other over Jung. All Jung confided to Freud, who once again had been called in to mediate through the mails, was that "Between the two ladies there is naturally a loving jealousy over me."

The next meeting between Jung and Spielrein apparently took place on Saturday, 24 September. Putting up, in her words, an unconscious "resistance" to her friend, Spielrein had arrived late for the ferry to Küsnacht. In a mad dash from the trolley to catch it, she had skinned her knee, torn her skirt, and "bent my umbrella." The umbrella in particular galled her, as she had only recently had a dream "that my mother's umbrella was already old, and mine, on the contrary, new and elegant." Her mother, it should be noted, had been her triumphant rival with regard to two of her suitors during her Gymnasium years. The broken umbrella was thus a reproach to Spielrein that her own current love interest was not going all that well, either. Jung was not sympathetic, at least not initially:

> He laughed at my accident with the trolley and said I should not go about fulfilling "anxiety desires." I laughed, too . . . Oh how all this annoyed me! To be one among the many who languish for him, and in return receive his kind gaze, a few friendly words. To gaze up at him and rush to fulfill his every wish, so as not to bring down his wrath upon oneself! For if one once fails to take his vanity into account—one must do bitter penance: he assumes a frigid, official tone, and who suffers from that? Not he, of course: a slight annoyance can be banished with work; love for one woman can be replaced by love for another; and then one is also sure that this one woman will finally be humiliated and she will be the one to endure tormented days and sleepless nights, the silly little girl.

Embarrassment and wounded pride aside, however, the meeting went reasonably well: "We discussed so many interesting issues. He suggested that I publish my second study along with his and Dr. Honegger's; he found the linkage 'sexual instinct–death instinct' well worth working out." With regard to the "death instinct"—her phrase—Spielrein had in mind the theory of Élie Metchnikoff, an expatriate Russian who had risen to the head of the prestigious Pasteur Institute in Paris and in 1907 had won the Nobel Prize. In several works, beginning with the popular 1903 treatise *The Nature of Man,* Metchnikoff had speculated that there might be a natural wish to die that would become evident at the end of a long life. In effect, Spielrein was supposing that this putative "death instinct" was in reality an expression of a sexual wish for dissolution.

The following Tuesday, however, found Spielrein once again mortified. She arrived for her appointment on 27 September quite on time, only to be turned away from the house without explanation. It was not until evening that she learned the reason for the slight: that morning Jung's wife had given birth to a little girl. The broken appointment was made good on Thursday, 29 September. It is clear from the diary entry made the next day that something dramatic happened, for Spielrein's mood was completely altered: "Yes, my dear, good friend. I love you and you love me. The thing I was longing for only recently has been fulfilled: he revealed his love almost too clearly."

We were supposed to sit down to work. Instead we discussed sexual instinct–death instinct, the portrayal of second thoughts in the form of death, the theories of dementia praecox, and the world of our ancestors. We talked on and on. My friend listened to me with rapture, then showed me his paper, not yet printed, and a letter to Prof. Freud and Freud's reply. He showed it to me because he was deeply stirred by the parallels in our thinking and feeling. He told me that seeing this worries him, because that is how I make him fall in love with me. I saw almost too well what I mean to him. It gave me the greatest satisfaction. "So I am not one among the many, but one who is unique, for certainly no girl can understand him as I can, none could surprise him this way with an independently developed system of thought that is completely analogous to his own. He resisted, he did not want to love me. Now he must, because our souls are deeply akin, because even when we are apart our joint work unites us." Yes, as I said, one can easily suppress one's erotic feelings in return for this beautiful, noble friendship. He urged me to write my new study on the death instinct, but I said that I first wanted to finish the one I am working on. Tomorrow I shall see him again, and we have resolved to keep to the task at hand. For now my only wish is that we may remain "friends" tomorrow.

By "tomorrow" the reader should understand Saturday, 1 October. Jung had previously scheduled a bicycle trip through the south of Switzerland and northern Italy for 1–14 October. He had delayed its start for only one or two additional days to monitor his wife's recovery from childbirth.

THE WORLD OF OUR ANCESTORS

JUNG WAS undoubtedly pleased to be seeing Spielrein again—the "medallion" in the necklace of his admirers—but he had other reasons for taking on this returning prodigal, reasons having to do with his new official position as president of the International Psychoanalytic Association. Jung saw his post as giving him both license and warrant to guide the further development of psychoanalytic theory. In Jung's dawning appreciation, Spielrein's contributions might fit in very well with his current plans. During the meeting of 29 September, Jung was bringing Spielrein up-to-date.

The unpublished "paper" which Jung showed Spielrein on 29 September was the manuscript of the Herisau talk; the two letters were almost certainly Jung's three-page letter of 26 June 1910, in which he sought to defend his ideas on the self-sacrificial hero, and Freud's reply of 5 July 1910, which described Jung's effort as "a good letter full of important ideas" while reserving final judgment until after Jung had provided "ample proof." In the interim, however, Jung had come to see that the themes of death and rebirth could be traced to myths more ancient still—myths of the sun-hero. Indeed, it may be said that the story of the sun-hero's death, his journey through the Underworld, and his ultimate resurrection was the most widespread in the ancient world. Usually the saga was modeled astrologically, with the hero represented by the sun, which sets in the Western seas, journeys beneath the ocean during the night, and rises reborn in the East at dawn. Often, the sun-hero was accompanied by a companion with whom he had to struggle at some point. Often, too, the sun-hero's consort was a moon-goddess who was said to entice him to his doom. Finally, many of these sagas depicted the sun-hero as ultimately returning with some great boon for mankind. For Jung, the whole saga was readily interpretable in terms of introversion, with the dangerous moon-goddess in particular as a symbol for the regressively charged inner image of the mother from whom the hero had to free himself.

Sometime between June and September, Jung had decided to expand his analysis of the third Miller fantasy to take into account the journey of the sun-hero. This, chronologically and analytically, was where Spielrein came in. In Jung's excited misapprehension, Spielrein had clarified the essential interconnection of symbols of death and rebirth—"transformation," in her language—and their relation to incestuous sexuality. Then there was the mythological angle. For Spielrein, mythic symbolism attracted her patient because it was the perfect realm for dissociation. Her emphasis was on the formal properties of myth as a kind of depersonalized and collective thought. Jung had pioneered this line of inquiry (thinking in "analogies"), but in the past year he had added a new claim, namely that the persistence of "mythologically typical" symbols in the unconscious reflected the fact that such forms of thought had been *phylogenetically inherited*.

This additional constraint had two important ramifications in Jung's nascent system, one moral, the other diagnostic. On the moral plane, it meant that whereas sacrifice had been a crucial element in ancient religion, there must be in each of us a phylogenetically acquired motif for the self-sacrifice needed to escape the snares of incestuous or resistant libido. On the diagnostic plane, the theory of the phylogenetic inheritance of mythic ideas implied that the more regressed a patient was, the more likely he or she was to be tapping the phylogenetically acquired level of mythological thought. The phenomenology of schizophrenia thus held a special relevance for Jung's theory, for here it ought to be possible to confirm or disconfirm his prediction. It had been specifically Honegger's job to find the confirming data on this point and it was this that Honegger lectured on at Nuremberg. Since Nuremberg, Jung had discovered similar data on his own. Contemporaneously with his September discussions with Spielrein, Jung had unearthed a mythic system in an ambulatory schizophrenic outpatient, and in a letter to Freud the same day as the meeting with Spielrein on 29 September, he excitedly described his discovery:

> I think my conjecture that the Miller fantasies really add up to a redemption mystery can be proved to the hilt. Only the other day a so-called Dem. praec. patient, whom I have almost set on her feet again, came out with a really grand, hitherto anxiously guarded moon-fantasy which is a redemption mystery composed entirely of liturgical imagery.

In the months that followed, at Jung's urging, Spielrein wrote into her dissertation some mythic parallels to her patient's delusions which she had hitherto been unaware of. The intrusion of the new interpretive rubric did not alter the dissertation much; but it did have an important historical consequence: Spielrein ended up being the first to go into print with data supporting Jung's phylogenetic contention with regard to schizophrenia.

Stepping back from the intellectual niceties of their conversation, we ought to note, too, that everything that was being discussed, from "second thoughts in the form of death" to the patient's assertions about "Dr. J." to the "world of our ancestors," contained personal referents of enormous significance for both Spielrein and Jung. What in one vein was merely a line of interpretation in another vein constituted a worldview which at this moment in time only the two of them shared. In this private ideology all human history going back to Adam and Eve could be boiled down to an essential conflict at the very heart of sexual desire, a conflict between dissolution and transformation that lived on in the present, even if it clothed itself with ancient motifs summoned up from the depths of the unconscious. The manifest intellectuality of their conversation notwithstanding, the two were once again inching their way perilously close to "poetry."

Jung was leaving town for two weeks to bicycle through the north of Italy with a physician friend down from Munich, Wolf Stockmayer. Apparently he thought it best to disillusion his young protégée before leaving. Spielrein's diary entry for 9 October, after Jung had left Zurich, speaks of finding some other father for her unborn baby "Siegfried." It also speaks of taking cyanide if that should fail to happen.

THE WORLD OF OUR ANCESTORS—A DREAM

Jung's bicycle expedition was fraught with significance, even before he began it. In planning the trip, he had made a special point of avoiding the city of Rome, this in apparent imitation of Freud's "Rome neurosis." (During the late 1890s, Freud, though an inveterate traveler, had developed a phobia of sorts with regard to visiting the Eternal City.) In a letter to Freud of 11 August 1911 describing his planned itinerary, Jung wrote: "Rome in particular is not yet permitted to me, but it draws nearer and I even look forward to it at odd moments."

Rome aside, the trip was almost a splendid success. In Verona, Jung found a strikingly suggestive statue of Priapus which Stockmayer photographed for him. The statue depicts a snake biting the god's penis, while Priapus looks on with a smile and points to the snake. For Jung, this was reminiscent of his contentions about the iconography of Mithraism—one libido symbol attacks another. Jung also found in Verona some ancient mystic inscriptions which he felt he could readily decode in terms of his most recent theories. Jung thus was entitled to feel that he was making his way splendidly into the heart of ancient paganism. As well, he may have enjoyed retracing some of the route taken by his "ancestor" and predecessor in Italian travels, Goethe. On the way back, however, something happened which completely dashed Jung's confidence. In Arona, on the shores of Lake Maggiore, Jung had a very disturbing dream:

> In the dream I was in an assemblage of distinguished spirits of earlier centuries . . . The conversation was conducted in Latin. A gentleman with a long, curly wig addressed me and asked a difficult question, the gist of which I could no longer recall after I woke up. I understood him, but did not have a sufficient command of the

language to answer him in Latin. I felt so profoundly humiliated by this that the emotion awakened me.

At the very moment of awakening I thought of the book I was then working on . . . and had such intense inferiority feelings about the unanswered question that I immediately took the train home in order to get back to work. It would have been impossible for me to continue the bicycle trip and lose another three days. I had to work, to find the answer.

Jung had had a very special variety of that commonplace anxiety-dream, the "examination dream." Contemporaneously, Freud and Stekel were both writing about such "examination dreams" and, in general, interpreting them in terms of doubts about one's manhood. Leaving aside the possibility of a sexual interpretation, Jung's dream would appear to concern his sense of mastery over his work. He was overwhelmed by what Janet called a *"sens d'incomplètude,"* that telltale sense of not being a whole person which indicates a failure to operate at one's full capacity for self-reflection. In fact, at this time Jung was indeed on the verge of completely losing his critical distance from his manuscript. In the months to come he would fall headlong into the trap of taking what was really his modern-day interpretive stance and reading it back into the ancient material. Jung's own gloss, however, which is dispersed in several separate passages in his memoirs, has it that the dream in Arona suggested to him that there was some kind of survival after death. He connected it with a recurring dream he had had shortly after his father's death in 1896. That dream, in which his father asked to return home and seemed not to know that he was dead, had first raised in Jung's mind the possibility that there might be survival beyond the grave. Jung's gloss thus implicitly bespeaks a revival in his earlier interest in occultism.

One would like to be able to interpret the dream still further, but in the absence of any further clarification from Jung himself, the best one can do is to try to locate the dream in its historical context. At the beginning of the decade, before Freud had entered so strongly upon the scene, Myers, Flournoy, and James had ranked preeminent, along with Janet, as investigators of the subliminal world. In their texts, unlike Freud's, the unconscious potentially contained marvelous things like telepathy and spiritual revelation. Granted this very recent past, Jung's dream would seem to indicate a wish to return to that literature and rescue some unnamed formula or phenomenon which had lately been eclipsed, most likely by giving it a new rendering in psychoanalytic terms.

But the more specific context of Jung's current situation deserves attention, too, and just there Jung's later gloss provides almost no illumination whatsoever. For Jung's most recent area of interest had been phylogenetic inheritance, not mediums, and while one might suppose that inherited ideas did indeed constitute a kind of one-way conversation with the dead, it is not immediately clear how one could derive from inherited ideas the kind of two-way conversation with a "spiritual forefather" that Jung's dream seemed to indicate was possible. Let us take leave of the Arona dream simply by noting that, according to Jung's own account, his current research was specifically implicated. Some revision in his theory was called for: "I had to work, to find the answer."

"SIEGFRIED" LIVES

JUNG ARRIVED back in Zurich on 16 October. On 20 October, he wrote to Freud with a new tone of urgency: "Since term time is starting up again, I am working under high pressure at my mythological studies; in term time there is too much distraction. What I sent you will be completely reworked on the basis of further studies which reached into the most impenetrable obscurities of philosophy." But from here forward a curious, and unprecedented, silence began to permeate the correspondence. After having kept Freud thoroughly informed about his work for the previous year, far better informed than Freud kept him, Jung simply stopped discussing it. To be sure, the two men were preoccupied at this time in their letters with the ongoing problem of how to recruit the recalcitrant Eugen Bleuler, whose membership in the International Psychoanalytic Association they considered a practical necessity. And in connection with a fresh initiative to that end, Freud announced in his next letter of 23 October a tentative plan to come to Zurich during the Christmas holidays. He and Jung thus would have an opportunity for personal discussion. (In the intervening months, the plan changed, and the Christmas get-together was ultimately held in Munich.)

In the meantime, Jung kept his ideas to himself. In his letter of 13 December 1910 Jung did inform Freud of his intention to break his manuscript into two parts and publish them in successive half-issues of the *Jahrbuch*. The analysis of the first two Miller fantasies, which would include Jung's ideas on "The Two Kinds of Thinking," was ticketed for the next issue. But the remainder of the manuscript was growing rapidly, and in his letter of 13 December Jung elected to be frankly mysterious about what it contained:

> The earlier lecture I sent you has been vastly expanded. Moreover the second half, the so-called drama of Chiwantopel, has proved to be so rich in archaeological material that I haven't yet been able to put everything in order. . . . It seems to me that this time I have hit the mark, or nearly so, as the material is falling into a surprising pattern. Too much shouldn't be revealed yet. But be prepared for some strange things the like of which you have never yet heard from me.

Jung presented a synopsis of his new views on 16 December to the Zurich Psychoanalytic Society and in his letter of 23 December 1910 he reported the occasion to Freud:

> I lectured at the ΨA Society on my forthcoming opus. The theologians were deeply impressed, especially Pfister. The spiritual trend in ΨA now taking shape in Zurich seems to me much more promising than the Bleuler-Adler attempts to squeeze everything into biology (biophysics).

The only other extant documentary source dating from this time that bears on Jung's new direction is Spielrein's diary. It is not an inconsiderable asset, given that she was arguably Jung's closest collaborator at the time, Honegger having taken a post at the Rheinau asylum. Moreover, exactly here, Spielrein's diary takes an extraordinary turn. In the next entry after Jung's return to Zurich, dated 18 October, Spielrein's private discourse changed dramatically. She began by resurrecting her old dream of "Siegfried," but in only a few sentences she mysteriously shifted gears and suddenly she was talking about a "higher calling":

> Should I tell everything in order? "Oh, Guardian Spirit, may my yearning be divine in origin!" I had to exclaim in the words of my friend last night, for this was what robbed me of my night's rest, the thought that I might be one of the many, that my accomplishments might not surpass the ordinary, and my "higher calling" might be a ridiculous dream which I must now pay for. The question is, where does this need to believe in a higher calling originate, this

need so firmly rooted in me? It may be in part inherited from my father, but we know—or, rather, those who accept the role played by the father in the individual psyche know—that the father must have an *analogon* in the mother who chooses him. And that is how it was: my great-grandfather and my grandfather were both rabbis, and therefore—God's elect.

And from here, the diary launches into an extended discussion of first her maternal great-grandfather—"Many stories were told about his prophetic abilities"—and then her maternal grandfather, who in her description appears to have been a remarkable man in his own right. This grandfather had in his youth loved the daughter of a Christian physician. The same pattern, Spielrein observes, happened with his own daughter, her mother, who also fell in love with a Christian only to end up marrying a Jew. And now the diary shifts to talking about Spielrein herself and how as a teenager she had been religious and as well had been torn between two friends—one Christian and one Jewish.

The next entry for the following day, 19 October, continues in the same unusual vein and runs on for the equivalent of nine printed pages. In this entry, Spielrein developed further the antithesis of Jew-Christian as it has applied in her own life. In fact, the diary describes four successive pairs of friends in which one was Christian, the other Jewish. The discussion culminates with "pair No. 4 . . . the present masculine pair":

The Christian in it—my friend; he is a doctor, married. Other elements, such as the strong religious sense and the sense of calling, are things of which he possesses more than enough, for his father was a minister! At the time our poetry began, he had two girls, and the potentiality for a boy within him, which my unconscious ferreted out at the appropriate time in "prophetic dreams." He told me that he loved Jewish women, that he wanted to love a dark Jewish girl. So in him, too, the urge to remain faithful to his religion and culture, as well as the drive to explore other possibilities through a new race, the drive to liberate himself from the paternal edicts through an unbelieving Jewess. His friend is Prof. Freud—a Jew, old *pater-familias*. . . . Here, too, the Christian is the "son" of the Jew. The latter is older and more independent. But at the same time my friend is my little son, so that *volens-nolens* we are married to Prof. Freud.

But here, after a few sentences devoted to Freud's daughter, Spielrein finally lost her composure and the reader of her diary suddenly discovers that the whole, lengthy exercise has been an attempt to resolve her "Siegfried complex":

> . . . I intend to cling to my belief that a great destiny awaits me. And now, what course will events take? I just played the piano. There is so much fire and so much love in me! *I feel the unshakable conviction: Siegfried lives, lives, lives!* No one can rob me of that certainty but my own death.

MYTHOLOGICAL IDEAS

BY ITSELF, Spielrein's diary entry for 18–19 October 1910 is nearly impenetrable. All one can tell for certain is that the issue of religious affiliation has somehow been raised in her mind and that she is trying to synthesize for herself the relation between Judaism and Christianity as it has applied in her own life. Beyond this, she appears to be trying to reconcile her belief in "Siegfried" with the idea of a "higher calling," a notion which has somehow figured in her most recent conversations with Jung. Arguably, however, we possess yet another account of those conversations, one composed much later. Let me begin by noting that Jung was admirably frank about his memoirs. They were not meant as an historical record; they were meant to present an account of his life as seen through his own personal myth. That said, let me direct the reader's attention to the following anecdote which occurs in the memoirs' fourth chapter, "Psychiatric Activities." It occurs several pages after a detailed description of the same ambulatory schizophrenic whose "redemption" fantasy Jung had described to Freud in his letter of 29 September 1910. Between that patient and the anecdote below there intervenes in the memoirs an ambling discussion of "method" and of "the unconscious identification of doctor and patient" which, Jung tells his reader, ". . . can lead to parapsychological phenomena." The anecdote at issue begins with some general remarks:

> I never try to convert a patient to anything, and never exercise any compulsion. What matters most to me is that the patient should reach his own view of things. Under my treatment a pagan becomes a pagan and a Christian a Christian, a Jew a Jew, according to what his destiny prescribes for him.

I well recall the case of a Jewish woman who had lost her faith. It began with a dream of mine in which a young girl, unknown to me, came to me as a patient. She outlined her case to me, and while she was talking, I thought, "I don't understand her at all. I don't understand what it is all about." But suddenly it occurred to me that she must have an unusual father complex. That was the dream.

For the next day I had down in my appointment book a consultation for four o'clock. A young woman appeared. She was Jewish, daughter of a wealthy banker, pretty, chic, and highly intelligent. She had already undergone an analysis, but the doctor acquired a transference to her and finally begged her not to come to him any more, for if she did, it would mean the destruction of his marriage.

The girl had been suffering for years from a severe anxiety neurosis, which this experience naturally worsened. I began with an anamnesis, but could discover nothing special. She was a well-adapted, Westernized Jewess, enlightened down to her bones. At first I could not understand what her trouble was. Suddenly my dream occurred to me, and I thought, "Good Lord, so this is the little girl of my dream." Since, however, I could detect not a trace of a father complex in her, I asked her, as I am in the habit of doing in such cases, about her grandfather. For a brief moment she closed her eyes, and I realized at once that here lay the heart of the problem. I therefore asked her to tell me about this grandfather, and learned that he had been a rabbi and had belonged to a Jewish sect. "Do you mean the Chasidim?" I asked. She said yes. I pursued my questioning. "If he was a rabbi, was he by any chance a zaddik?" "Yes," she replied, "it is said that he was a kind of saint and also possessed second sight. But that is all nonsense. There is no such thing!"

With that I had concluded the anamnesis and understood the history of her neurosis. I explained to her "Now I am going to tell you something that you may not be able to accept. Your grandfather was a zaddik. Your father became an apostate to the Jewish faith. He betrayed the secret and turned his back on God. And you have your neurosis because the fear of God has got into you." That struck her like a bolt of lightning.

The following night I had another dream. A reception was taking place in my house, and behold, this girl was there too. She came up to me and asked, "Haven't you got an umbrella? It is raining so hard." I actually found an umbrella, fumbled around with it to open it, and was on the point of giving it to her. But what happened instead? I handed it to her on my knees, as if she were a goddess.

I told this dream to her, and in a week the neurosis had vanished. The dream had showed me that she was not just a superficial little girl, but that beneath the surface were the makings of a saint. She had no mythological ideas, and therefore the most essential feature of her nature could find no way to express itself. All her conscious activity was directed toward flirtation, clothes, and sex, because she knew of nothing else. In reality she was a child of God whose destiny was to fulfill his secret will. I had to awaken mythological and religious ideas in her, for she belonged to that class of human beings of whom spiritual activity is demanded. Thus her life took on a meaning, and no trace of neurosis was left.

In this case I had applied no "method," but had sensed the presence of the numen. My explaining this to her had accomplished the cure. Method did not matter here; what mattered was the "fear of God."

This was Spielrein. The doctor who had previously "acquired a transference to her" was Jung himself. Jung could scarcely undertake a new analysis here; he was still trying to undo the results of the first one. Spielrein, of course, had plenty of mythological ideas, but she had come to understand them, thanks to Jung's previous analysis, as expressions of unconscious sexual wishes. The need for a corrective conversation would have become ever so clear by the time of their first meeting following Jung's return to Zurich, when he had discovered how utterly distraught she had been in his absence. In effect, he responded by encouraging her to think of "Siegfried" as emblematic of an ancestral and spiritual wisdom within, rather than merely as frustrated sexual longing. (However Jung phrased matters, it is plain from her diary that Spielrein embraced the new interpretation.) Jung's follow-up dream the next night of the umbrella, meanwhile, would have referred back to her chagrin and humiliation over the "bent umbrella" incident in late September. Given that her chagrin had been compounded by a feeling that she was "just one among the many," and by his lofty amusement at her embarrassment, we can readily appreciate the healing effect of Jung's telling her of a dream in which he got down on his knees to give her an undamaged umbrella. In effect, he was making amends by saying he had misjudged her true worth. As for his invocation of her grandfather the zaddik, this is plainly reflected in her excited ruminations about her family tree. (Incidentally, Jung's account emphasizes the paternal grandfather, while on the contrary Spielrein's diary focuses on her maternal grandfather and—the more important of the two—great-grandfather. But in this connection, one should note the telltale statement in her diary (above) that the maternal line echoes the spiritual potentials of the paternal one, that "the father must have an *analogon* in the mother who chooses him." Plainly, she is adapting herself to the specifics of Jung's intervention, while overlooking the fact that he is slightly misinformed about her lineage.)

The fact that Jung elected to include the anecdote in his memoirs many, many years later tells us that it was very important to him. With the better knowledge that the woman was Spielrein, we can grasp why, I think. She had been his psychoanalytic "test case." As well, she had been the occasion for his own descent into the depths of incestuous sexual fantasy. Who better, then, for him to try out his new "spiritual" perspective on? That his innovation of awakening "mythological and religious ideas" seemed to work with her was a very, very important confirmation that, his *"sens d'incomplètude"* notwithstanding, he was on the right track. In effect, Spielrein was now Jung's "test case" all over again.

THE SACRIFICE

SPIELREIN'S RECEPTIVITY to Jung's new interpretive stance seems to have complicated their rapport without weakening it. The next entry in Spielrein's diary, a brief note for 24 October, laments: "The two of us love each other as much as it is possible to love. If only he were free!" The following entry, for 9 November, is rather more excited still:

> Since yesterday, when I saw him, reason has abandoned me again. Reason! Is there any such thing? Can one even be reasonable when one loves this way? Describe calmly what happened? What he said to me? Yes, the stronger poetry probably occurred a week ago Tuesday [1 November]. He said then that he loves me because of the remarkable parallelism in our thoughts; sometimes I can predict his thoughts to him; he told me that he loves me more for my magnificent proud character, but he also told me that he would never marry me because he harbors within himself a great philistine who craves narrow limits and the typical Swiss style.

The entry concludes with the words: "Adieu, my little son! Fare thee well!"

Spielrein's next entry comes seventeen days later, on 26 November. She speaks of her father, who has come to stay with her as she prepares for her final exams, and of her determination not to go back with him to Russia afterward. She also worries that Jung may steal her idea on the "death instinct." The occasion, apparently, was a review Jung planned to write on a public presentation on "ambivalence" that would be given the next day by Bleuler at the winter meeting of Swiss Psychiatrists taking place in Bern. Bleuler had already sent Jung a written version of his talk, and Jung was planning to write a very harsh critique for the next *Jahrbuch*. (The essence of Jung's blast was that Bleuler had neglected established psychoanalytic views of sexuality and the defenses against it.) Bleuler, as a director of the *Jahrbuch*, was ultimately given the chance to submit a reply to Jung's comments; this, too, ran in the issue. Since his discussion of these matters with Bleuler in October, however, Jung had realized that Spielrein's theory of two components (destructive/dissolving and transforming) within sexuality made an attractive addition to his critique of Bleuler's views on ambivalence. But Jung's eagerness only made the young woman wary, and she called a halt. Thus, neither the critique of Bleuler nor Part 1 of Jung's monograph contain any mention of Spielrein's idea on the death instinct.

After this entry, Spielrein's diary wobbles back and forth between romance and the practical exigencies of her final exams, with the themes sometimes sharing space in the same passage:

> My friend said in parting that I will write an excellent exam because at present I am in league with the devil. May that be true. My friend and I had the tenderest "poetry" last Wednesday. What will come of that? Make something good of it, Fate, and let me love him nobly. A long ecstatic kiss in parting, my beloved little son!

Spielrein took her finals, eight in all, on four successive days, 16–19 January 1911. She received top honors in psychiatry. Apparently she left Zurich the evening of her last exam; a diary entry for 19 January says simply:

> "He is gone, and 'tis good thus."
> Good at least that my parents are now happy. "Ah, yes, what will happen now?"

Spielrein's dissertation was formally filed with the university authorities on 11 February. Her diary resumes some time later in February with an undated entry that speaks in almost religious terms about her fate and her sense of defiance. "Siegfried" was still very much on her mind and she was ready to "sacrifice" everything to keep him:

> I remain defiant, because I have something noble and great to create and am not made for everyday routine. This is the life-or-death struggle. If there is a God-Father, may he hear me now: no pain is unbearable to me, no sacrifice too great, if only I can fulfill my sacred calling! "He must be a hero"; for it is your will and "the will of my father Wotan."

The idea of "sacrifice" recurs in the next fragment—there is another break in the diary—as Spielrein discusses what was apparently an apparition she had just seen. We pick her up as the diary resumes on 27 February immediately after the missing page or pages, indicated by brackets:

> [. . .] could hear, when the apparition vanished. It is very unfortunate because as the descendant of several generations of religious men I believe in the prophetic powers of my unconscious. One can actually get so close to this "God" that one can speak with Him and learn what He wishes, that is, what is the most useful outlet for the total energy of countless generations, which one calls individuals. So what do you wish, God? . . .
>
> Is it a premonition of my end, or is this pain a sacrifice of the sort every great work requires?

With the thought of putting herself in the "hands of the divine," Spielrein let the entry end and went to bed hoping to have yet another of her prophetic dreams. When she awoke she wrote the following: "Either the gods are too weary and therefore not very productive, or my conscious mind is too critical to take in anything of beauty, but I can hardly believe in the prophetic truth of my last dream." In her dream her baby brother was ill—there was an explicit criticism of Jung for failing to diagnose the problem correctly—and in the midst of a glum description of how her parents seemed unconcerned with the problem, the extant diary suddenly breaks off, in the midst of the entry for 28 February 1911, not to resume again for almost a whole year.

The documentary significance of this portion of Spielrein's diary, from October of 1910 till February of 1911, can be boiled down to two surprising, completely unexpected historical facts. The first time Jung actually tried out his new spiritual perspective in practice, it had been specifically in the service of trying to alleviate Spielrein's still painful "Siegfried complex." And once Spielrein was no longer in his company, the ameliorative effect began to diminish, though it did not disappear completely.

THE MAN FOR THE FUTURE

BY THE TIME Spielrein had her dream of her baby brother, Jung's position as president of the new International Association had been greatly enhanced owing to two meetings at the Park Hotel in Munich. The first meeting was between Freud and Eugen Bleuler. In his letters to Freud during the fall of 1910, Eugen Bleuler had made his position regarding the new association consistently clear. He objected to the association's sectarian quality, especially to its intolerance toward responsible critics like Isserlin. Bleuler insisted, quite rightly, that open discussion was essential to science, but he struck an emotional note as well: "If I want to remain true to myself, I cannot go along. I regret it very much; I am the one who loses." When it emerged that Bleuler was longing for a private talk with Freud, a rendezvous at the Park Hotel in Munich was set up for Christmas Day.

Just prior to the meeting, Freud and Bleuler both published important papers addressing the situation. Bleuler's essay "Freud's Psychoanalysis: Defense and Critical Remarks" ran in the *Jahrbuch*. Freud commented about it to Jung: ". . . it is amazing how he works off his misbehavior in private dealings, which enables him to stand up very well in his public activity. I believe the piece will be enormously helpful." Freud's own piece, "On 'Wild' Psycho-Analysis," had appeared in the new Adler-Stekel *Zentralblatt*. Ostensibly, it concerned a technical point. Beginning with an anecdote of a nervous patient who had been told by her physician that the cause of her anxiety was her lack of sexual satisfaction, Freud went on to warn against the dangers of premature interpretation. Although he thought that the advice had conceivably done the woman some good, this was not psychoanalysis in Freud's view since no attention had been paid to the woman's inner resistances. Going further, he argued that such interventions should not be undertaken by people who were not specifically trained in "conformance to certain *technical rules* of psychoanalysis." Unfortunately, those rules could not "yet be learnt from books," but only "from those who are already proficient in it." It was just this situation, according to Freud, that had necessitated the founding of the new association:

> Neither I myself nor my friends and co-workers find it agreeable to claim a monopoly in this way in the use of a medical technique. But in the face of dangers to patients and to the cause of psycho-analysis which are inherent in the practice that can be foreseen of "wild" psycho-analysis, we have had no other choice. In the spring of 1910, we founded an International Psycho-Analytic Association, to which its members declare their adherence by the publication of their names, in order to be able to repudiate responsibility for what is done by those who do not belong to us and yet call their medical procedure "psycho-analysis."

The essay was the first communication from Freud since 1905 specifically concerned with the "technical rules" of his method. As a practical matter, the lengthy wait for the long-promised manual of psychoanalysis had come to an end—for good. So long as no manual existed, Freud could reasonably declare psychoanalysis a closed shop.

Freud and Bleuler spent Christmas Day together. The two men were of the same generation and in person each could supply what the other needed for a meeting of minds to take place. To Binswanger, Freud wrote afterward: "After his Defense of my ΨA I could only be frank and cordial with him, and he did not make things difficult for me. . . ." To Ferenczi, Freud wrote: ". . . he is only a poor devil like ourselves and in need of a little love, a fact which has perhaps been neglected in certain quarters that matter to him. It is almost certain that he will join the Zurich Society and then the division there will be healed." Bleuler did in fact join two weeks later.

Jung arrived at the Park Hotel the next day. Initially, he and Freud had kept their own rendezvous a secret but in the end they decided that this would be counterproductive should Bleuler found out about it. They had a lot to talk about. Jung promised to "discover and maintain the correct attitude toward Bleuler," as Freud put it to Binswanger. In his turn, Freud sought Jung's counsel about how to deal with Alfred Adler, currently the president of the Vienna society. Adler had lately come to believe that distortions of character, inculcated during childhood and involving an overweening attempt to be "masculine" at the expense of such "feminine" qualities as dependency and submissiveness, were the real forces at work behind neurosis. In November, a resolution had been passed in the Vienna society that Adler's new viewpoint be debated in relation to libido theory. Freud had promptly had the resolution amended so that the topic of repression was to be the focal point. Fortunately or unfortunately, the prospect of a full discussion had begun to stimulate Adler's sense of his own originality. Just as Freud and Jung had discovered they were Freud and Jung at the Clark congress, Adler was discovering he was Adler as he prepared for the forthcoming debates.

Of late, Jung had seen a parallel between Bleuler and Adler as officious nuisances who failed to appreciate the full interpretive significance of libido theory. But Freud instead insisted on an analogy between Adler and Wilhelm Fliess—"the same paranoia"—and in recent months had repeatedly described Adler in these insidiously clinical terms. As a topic, paranoia was on Freud's mind for yet another reason. He had brought with him to Munich his just-finished analysis of the memoirs of the mad jurist Daniel Paul Schreber, in which he made the case that Schreber's symptoms could best be understood as an outbreak of paranoia based upon repressed homosexual feelings. This formula, as Jung well knew, was said to have been discovered during Freud's rupture with Fliess. There was, in effect, a triple equation at stake here, Schreber = Fliess = Adler (= Paranoid). Freud even confided to Jung that he found the continued recurrence of the motif in his own life distressing. We know that he and Jung discussed Adler at Munich, but we don't know specifically what was said. As for Freud's analysis of the Schreber case, few clinical studies by Freud have been subject to so much modern rebuttal as this one, but Jung enjoyed it tremendously when he got around to reading it two months later.

Unlike Freud, Jung had not brought his current manuscript with him—he begged off at the last moment—but he did discuss his interpretation of the sun-hero motif as a saga depicting the ego's descent into the wellsprings of the libido through the incest barrier. He also seems to have discussed his Arona dream, and along with it his revived interest in spiritual forefathers, for he got the following reaction:

> I can still recall vividly how Freud said to me, "My dear Jung, promise me never to abandon the sexual theory. This is the most essential thing of all. You see, we must make a dogma of it, an unshakable bulwark." He said that to me with great emotion, in the

tone of a father saying, "And promise this one thing, my dear son; that you will go to church every Sunday." In some astonishment I asked him, "A bulwark—against what?" To which he replied, "Against the black tide of mud"—and here he hesitated for a moment, then added—"of occultism."

In his memoirs, Jung recalled his response: "After a few stammering attempts at my part, the conversation came to an end. I was bewildered and embarrassed."

But these recollections only partially capture the occasion. Freud was then in ill health. He had made a point of mentioning his physical condition in his last letter before the meeting—"Don't be dismayed if you do not find me in the best of health"—and then again in his first letter afterward. The cause of Freud's complaints—"strange headaches . . . lapses of memory"—turned out to be a small gas leak in his study, but until it was discovered a few weeks later, Freud had resigned himself to an arteriosclerotic decline. Indeed, at the Park Hotel, he and Jung made tentative plans for an emergency visit by Jung to Vienna in the weeks immediately ahead in the event Freud's health declined further. Moreover, the whole tenor of their extended discussion was predicated on the fact that Jung was president of the International Association. Freud may have been giving Jung fatherly instruction, and cautioning him in various ways, most especially concerning Bleuler and about going too far in his mythological studies; but, more important, he was consulting with him and asking his advice, and was in the end glad once again to enjoy the energy and ebullience of his designated successor. The two men spent very little time at all exploring the darker implications of their situation. Together, face to face, it all made sense.

After the meeting, Jung wrote to Freud, "I still owe you a mountain of thanks for Munich." Freud replied by remembering "the refreshing hours in Munich" and the "benefit" he received from them. To Ferenczi, Freud wrote of his meeting with Jung: "He was magnificent and did me a power of good. . . . I am more than ever convinced that he is the man for the future."

CHAPTER 13

The Dying and Resurgent God

This immortal saying [taken from *Faust*]: "Part of a power that would / Alone work evil, but engenders good." This demonic force, whose very essence is destruction (evil) and at the same time is the creative force, since out of the destruction (of two individuals) a new one arises. That is in fact the sexual drive, which is by nature a destructive drive, an exterminating drive for the individual, and for that reason, in my opinion, must overcome such great resistance in everyone; but to prove this here would take too much of your time.

—Spielrein, letter-drafts, 1909

I N THE SPRING OF 1911, working all by herself in Munich, Sabina Spielrein essentially solved the conceptual problem posed by sexual repression. Spielrein had enrolled for a semester's worth of courses in art history at the University of Munich, but she had continued to meditate on psychoanalytic theory and in the midst of writing up her study on the "death instinct" she suddenly realized that she had a very different contribution to make, one that in another age might have guaranteed her reputation. Her theory showed why repression tended to operate specifically and inevitably against sexual wishes as distinct from all other wishes. The secret lay in how one defined sexuality. Freud continued to define it in terms of discharge and pleasure; just this definition made it difficult to conceive why it should be so regularly repressed. Spielrein, by contrast, realized that sexuality could be characterized in quite different terms—as seeking fusion rather than pleasure—and that once it was so conceptualized the problem of sexual repression virtually solved itself. By any standard, hers was a remarkable insight, even if no one yet knew about it. In the long view of history, perhaps the more remarkable fact was that Spielrein had essentially hit on the solution several years earlier—and didn't know it.

The basic formula can be found both in her Transformation Journal and in the letter-drafts of 1909 (see above).

SEX AND DEATH

SPIELREIN'S SOLUTION had all the elegance of a new theorem in mathematics or physics. In Spielrein's conception, there were only two instincts of note: the instinct for self-preservation and the instinct for species-preservation (sexuality). As well, there were only two psychic structures: the ego and the unconscious. The ego (the "I" of ordinary consciousness) necessarily ran on energy provided by the instinct for self-preservation: the ego sought to maintain its own individuality and to fight off anything that would enforce unwanted change upon it. In its manner of psychical representation, furthermore, the ego dealt in purely personal experience, i.e., in experiences in which there was always implicit reference to the "I" of the experiencing individual. The unconscious, to the contrary, cared nothing in Spielrein's system for the uniqueness of the individual. It was, rather, collective, both in its aims and in its method of representation. It dealt in impersonal, communal symbols. And it sought to enforce aims which, like Schopenhauer's blind "Will," were entirely indifferent to the fate of the individual. In Spielrein's system, the energy of the unconscious consistently and exclusively came from sexuality (given its altogether conventional definition as the instinct for species-preservation). In effect, the unconscious was that part of the psyche where racial aims (directed toward the continuation of the race) were given preference over individual aims. Consciousness, by contrast, was that realm of the mind where the "I" had succeeded in differentiating itself out from the unconscious.

The system is extremely simple, but it yields a surprising result. If one grants that sexuality is always concerned with racial or species-wide aims (procreation), then it follows that sexuality will, in cases where there is a divergence, seek to override the ego's unique prerogatives. Sexuality "wants" (by teleological metaphor) children, and is ready to dissolve the ego in the act of sexual fusion to get them. Similarly, when one shifts to the hypothetical terrain of "sublimation," sexuality "wants" new artistic creations which the race can share. Sexuality does not care what this new creation "costs" the individual (another metaphor, "economic" in the French tradition). Thus, from the standpoint of the ego, sexuality contains an implicit threat of dissolution. As the species-wide aims of sexuality make themselves felt, they come into conflict with the purely personal motives of the individual "I." Accordingly, and this is the main point, *against sexuality the ego always responds with an attitude of resistance.* Psychically, this means that sexual desire will always be accompanied by defense reactions—expressed most often by the inner evocation of images of death and destruction—which represent the protest of the "I" against its dissolution.

Spielrein's was an amazingly correct idea, taken from a Freudian viewpoint. This was true even for the finer points of her system. For one thing, she took for granted the Freudian postulate that artistic creation involved "sublimated" sexuality. For another, she accepted the ubiquity of incestuous sexual attachments in infancy. Indeed, here, she had an additional comment to make. The reason why these incestuous attachments were universal and why they were so often revived in transferences was because family members were the most racially similar to one another. The degree of the ego's dissolution was therefore less severe in an incestuous attachment than it was in a nonincestuous attachment. According to Spielrein's terminology, incestuous attachments felt less "destructive."

There were a whole host of applications here. Spielrein herself was principally preoccupied with using her system to explicate, brilliantly, the emotional phenomena that accompany the progressive loss of the ego in schizophrenia. But there were an enormous number of things which Spielrein could have said which she didn't. For one thing, she had shed essential light on what Freud, writing to Pfister in March of 1909, had called "the indissoluble connection between sex and death." This "indissoluble connection" had long been known to the poets and playwrights of Romanticism, and it had lately begun to attract attention within the psychoanalytic movement. In March 1911, to take only the outstanding example, just at the time Spielrein was at work on her own paper, there appeared Wilhelm Stekel's *The Language of Dreams,* which devoted a whole chapter to the subject.

But Spielrein's solution was even more generally applicable. For throughout the published case histories of psychoanalysis to date, from the hallucinations of death's-heads in the case of "Anna O." to "Dora's" dream of being saved from fire, from Jung's second analytic case (first published) with her fear of contaminating others to Binswanger's "Irma," who feared poisoning, *symbols of death, disease, and destruction had been paramount in the clinical phenomenology of the neuroses as explicated by psychoanalysis.* Indeed, in a sense, Spielrein had cut right to the symptomatic heart of hysteria—its tendency to mimic other diseases—and had seen there not dissimulation, but a natural symbolic equivalence.

SPIELREIN KNEW what she had accomplished. The published version of her paper, "Destruction as a Cause of Coming into Being," begins by highlighting the problem of repression and asking rhetorically why it should be brought to bear upon sexuality even in childhood (when "consequences" are still unknown). Moreover, she had also arrived at her own critique of her mentor's views. The third section of her paper, "Life and Death in Mythology," would cover many of Jung's themes while coming to somewhat different conclusions. To begin with, Jung's all-important distinction between incestuous and procreative applications of the libido had no standing in Spielrein's system. For her, sexuality was a uniform drive and incestuous objects were chosen for exactly the same unconscious reasons that procreative objects were chosen. She accepted incestuous sexuality without demurrer. In this respect, she was more "Freudian" than Jung. Secondly, for Spielrein "destruction" was *always* part of sexuality, not just in cases of introversion but in all interpersonal sexual behavior. Spielrein's system also differed in its interpretation of "sacrifice." For Spielrein "sacrifice" was without moral connotations. It was, rather, the price that had to be paid in the loss of individuality before sexuality could go forward with its aims. Put simply, "sacrifice" was the price exacted by the "destructive" aspect of the libido.

In short, in Spielrein's system the three principal items which Jung was currently inventorying under introversion—fantasies of death, incestuous transferences, the need for sacrifice—were held to be universally true of sexuality, introverted or not. She did not disagree with Jung's portrait of the psychological structure of introversion so much as she disagreed that interpersonal sexual behavior was any different.

To be sure, Spielrein did not construct her system with an eye to contradicting Jung. Which brings us to an irony attending Spielrein's text. The entire time she was working on it, she was trying to square her endeavor with Jung's latest interpretation of her "Siegfried ideal" as standing for her "heroic destiny." Indeed, in a very real sense to her, her "Siegfried ideal" was incarnated, albeit in sublimated form, in the very act of writing this important paper. Hence the irony: the paper was written as part of an attempt to live out her "Siegfried ideal," but its very logic forced her into an altered interpretation of the meaning of "Siegfried."

Spielrein's analysis of "Siegfried" would come midway through the third and final section of her published paper. The section would begin with some observations about Adam and Eve in the Garden. Spielrein took it for granted that their sin was sexual, that by eating of the Tree of Life (sexuality) they had unleashed the destructive component of sexuality upon themselves. Their sin must henceforth be atoned for, hence the subsequent emergence of the Christ figure, who sacrifices himself upon the Cross and thus satisfies the destructive component of sexuality. In further pursuit of this idea Spielrein brought up a number of legends in which Christ's cross is fashioned out of remnants of the original Tree of Life. From here, however, she moved to a new, meteorological motif: Christ redeems mankind in the same sense that the sun god redeems the earth, i.e., by analogy to the coming of spring which redeems suffering nature from winter. And abruptly in the text, Siegfried and Brünnhilde make their appearance:

> In the Nibelungen myth, Siegfried and Brünnhilde replace the sun and earth. Brünnhilde (earth) who is in a state of hibernation gets redeemed by the conquering light of Siegfried (the sun) as he cuts through her armor (ice crust) with his sword and thus fertilizes her. . . . It is important that Siegfried fertilizes his mother in Brünnhilde. Siegfried's mother as we know is Sieglinde, but Brünnhilde is her sister and she loves what Sieglinde loves, namely Siegmund. Accordingly, she feels herself to be in Sieglinde's role; Sieglinde thus becomes her "wish personality" in terms of her sexuality. By saving Siegfried she saves her own wish-child. The correctness of this assertion, that Brünnhilde is the mother of Siegfried, is shown by the work of Dr. Graf [*The Lohengrin Saga* in Freud's monograph series]. Like Eve, Brünnhilde acts against the law of the father and like Eve's being expelled from paradise, she is expelled from the kingdom of the gods. The act of disobeying the law ... also brings Brünnhilde the death-like sleep out of which she is redeemed by Siegfried's Spring sun. That a longing for death is more often a longing to die in the lover is also seen in Wagner.

And now the extant text excerpts Brünnhilde's dying lament from Wagner's opera. Following that there is a detour into another Wagner opera, *The Flying Dutchman,* before Spielrein pauses for an interim summary:

> Wagner's heroes have in common that, like Siegfried and Brünnhilde, they sacrifice themselves for their love and die, typical of saviour-types. The similarities between the Nordic Siegfried and the

Eastern Christ are striking. Christ is also a savior-type who sacrifices himself for mankind. Siegfried is the sun god and his lover the mother earth; Christ is also the sun god. Christ dies at the tree of life; he is pinned to it and hangs on it like its fruit. And like fruit Christ dies off and comes into the mother earth as a seed.

Next, the text returns to Adam and Eve, and Spielrein concludes that God's punishment for their sin is precisely that he has made sexuality in part "destructive." To avoid that punishment, and to appease God, sacrifice is necessary, and this leads Spielrein, in the rest of this section of her paper, to consider various sacrificial rituals, Christian and Semitic, while being careful to spell out their relation to fertility.

This part of Spielrein's paper, published in mid-1912, strikes the modern reader as entirely problematical. Even at the time of its publication, the lucidity of this section was questioned. Let us keep ourselves to the essential point: she had interpreted the Siegfried legend as an incestuous union between mother (or at least a wish-mother) and son in which the son ultimately dies in order to rescue the mother and make her fertile. This must have been painful, given the reality of her own situation. Jung had not risked death nor even social ostracism on her behalf, nor had she become fertile. If anyone were in danger of dying it was the unborn "Siegfried" inside her.

Spielrein stayed in Munich through the spring semester. In July she made contact with Leonhard Seif, who had recently founded the Munich Psychoanalytic Society, and let him in on what she was working on. Then in August she moved to Vienna. It was in Vienna that Spielrein finished the third section of her manuscript containing her interpretation of the Siegfried legend. She sent off the completed draft of the entire paper to Jung for the next *Jahrbuch* along with a touching cover letter that began: "Receive now the product of our love, the project which is your little son Siegfried." Jung wrote back on 8 August 1911 to say that he had not been able to read the paper through to the end as he was busy with Seif, who was visiting from Munich. But Jung had already arrived at a "provisional judgment" of her work:

I am surprised by the abundance of very good ideas which anticipate some of my comments. But it is good that others see things the way I do. Your idea is courageous, far-reaching, and philosophical. The *Jahrbuch* therefore will hardly be the right place to publish it. Either you make it into a small book or we should try to put the work in Freud's series.

Jung's self-confident, matter-of-fact tone bespoke his emotional disengagement: for better or worse, Spielrein was now out of his life and he had no desire to change matters. In this respect, his reinterpretation the previous fall of "Siegfried" as standing for her heroic destiny, and for the self-sacrifice that was necessary for her to achieve it, had helped *him* to let go of her as much as it may have helped her to reconcile herself to losing him. But Jung was now erring on the side of keeping too much of a distance. In only a few months' time, he would deeply regret not having read her new paper more carefully.

As of June, Spielrein was officially graduated as a physician from the University of Zurich. As well, her medical dissertation was appearing in the current *Jahrbuch,* which finally came out in mid-August. Her career thus having been officially launched, she made plans to attend the upcoming Psychoanalytic Congress, which would be held in Weimar at the end of September. Since she had not yet attached herself to the Vienna group, she was planning to go as a member of the Zurich contingent. Jung blankly took cognizance of her intentions in his next letter, and suggested that she write to Karl Abraham, who was in charge of making the local arrangements.

THE MYTHOLOGY OF EVERYDAY LIFE

WHILE SPIELREIN prepared for her career, her mentor was inwardly foundering. Something terrible was happening with the second half of Jung's monograph "Transformations and Symbols of the Libido." His truly horrific difficulties were all the more puzzling in light of his manifest success with the first half, which was sent off to the printers in mid-February and which would appear side by side with Spielrein's dissertation in the *Jahrbuch* in August. It was the first half, after all, which had the burden of demonstrating that modern fantasies were analogous to ancient mythological motifs and, further, that this resemblance allowed one to interpret certain typical fantasies—the first two Miller fantasies in the present instance—even in the absence of sufficient biographical information or associations. When one considers that Jung also wanted to use this section of his monograph to introduce his nascent ideas about intellectual history and the growth of rational, scientific thought, while at the same time preparing the ground for his contentions about sacrifice and the two streams within the libido, it is easy to imagine him stumbling at the outset. Yet, even today, Part 1 of Jung's work makes rewarding reading. Jung had half a masterpiece here and he seemed to know it from the first page. The English translation is flawed, but even so, it captures some of the flavor of what was basically a stylistic triumph. Here is how the translator, Beatrice Hinkle, rendered Jung's beginning:

Anyone who can read Freud's "Interpretation of the Dream" without scientific rebellion at the newness and apparently unjustified daring of its analytic presentation, and without moral indignation at the astonishing nudity of the dream interpretation . . . will surely be deeply impressed at that place where Freud calls to mind the fact that an individual psychologic conflict, namely, the Incest Phantasy, is the essential root of that powerful ancient dramatic material, the Oedipus legend. The impression made by this simple reference may be likened to that wholly peculiar feeling which arises in us if, for example, in the noise and tumult of a modern street we should come across an ancient relic—the Corinthian capital of a walled-in column, or a fragment of inscription. Just a moment ago we were given over to the noisy ephemeral life of the present, when something very far away and strange appears to us, which turns our attention to things of another order; a glimpse away from the incoherent multiplicity of the present to a higher coherence in history.

Virtually the whole of Jung's program was already implied here, yet the impression was agreeable—very clearly Freudian, but high-minded and relatively untendentious. To be sure, in the pages that followed, Jung would cite with approval Burckhardt's maxim that what Oedipus was for the Greek soul, the figure of Faust was for the German soul. And it would be Faust, not Oedipus, to whom Jung returned repeatedly in the text. The central motif was clearly Faustian: casting aside the constraints of Christianity, Jung meant to make a descent into the depths of the soul, there to find the roots of man's being in the symbols of the libido which had been handed down from ancient times, and so to find redemption despite his own genial psychoanalytic pact with the devil.

To that end, midway through Part 1, Jung paused for a look at the potentially adaptive aspects of introversion. In his discussion of the first Miller fantasy, Jung argued that some of his own patients had had dreams that anticipated subsequent developments either in their lives or in their treatment, and in this connection he mentioned, almost in passing, Maeterlinck's concept of the "prospective potency of subliminal combinations." The attached footnote, which in the *Jahrbuch* ran at the bottom of the page, went much, much further:

This time I shall hardly be spared the reproach of mysticism. . . . Psychoanalysis works backwards like the science of history. . . . In so far as to-morrow is already contained in to-day, and all the threads of the future are in place, so a more profound knowledge of the past might render possible a more or less far-reaching and certain knowledge of the future. . . . But just so little as the science of history concerns itself with the combinations for the future, which is the function of politics, so little, also, are the psychological combinations for the future the object of analysis; they would be much more the object of an infinitely refined psychological synthesis, which attempts to follow the natural current of the libido. This we cannot do, but possibly this might happen in the unconscious, and it appears as if from time to time, in certain cases, significant fragments of this process come to light, at least in dreams. From this comes the prophetic significance of the dream long claimed by superstition.

The maladaptive aspects of introversion, meanwhile, emerged during the discussion of Miss Miller's second fantasy, "The Moth and the Sun":

> The passionate longing, that is to say, the libido, has its two sides; it is power which beautifies everything, and which under other circumstances destroys everything. . . . A woman who gives herself up to passion, particularly under the present-day condition of culture, experiences the destructive side only too soon. . . .
>
> To be fruitful means, indeed, to destroy one's self, because with the rise of the succeeding generation the previous one has passed beyond its highest point; thus our descendants are our most dangerous enemies, whom we cannot overcome, for they will outlive us, and, therefore, without fail, will take the power from our enfeebled hands. The anxiety in the face of the erotic fate is wholly understandable, for there is something immeasureable therein. Fate usually hides unknown dangers, and the perpetual hesitation of the neurotic to venture upon life is easily explained by his desire to be allowed to stand still, so as not to take part in the dangerous battle of life. *Whoever renounces the chance to experience must stifle in himself the wish for it, and, therefore, commits a sort of self-murder.* From this the death phantasies which readily accompany the renunciation of the erotic wish are made clear.

The passage, which inconsistently found "death" both in sexuality and in renunciation, had obvious biographical significance for Jung, containing as it did references to both the old warnings to Spielrein about "consequences" and to Jung's own feelings upon the birth of his first son.

After the above passage, Jung paused for a look at the Book of Job and Byron's poem "Heaven and Earth" (both cited by Miss Miller as among her associations), before finally closing Part 1 with the dramatic pronouncement that Miss Miller awaited the resurrection of her libido, if only it could be freed from the introverted state:

> The prophetic visions of [Byron's] Japhet have almost prophetic meaning for our poetess; with the death of the moth in the light, evil is once more laid aside; the complex has once again, even if in a censored form, expressed itself. With that, however, the problem is not solved; all sorrow and every longing begins again from the beginning but there is "Promise in the Air"—the premonition of the Redeemer, of the "Well-beloved," of the Sun-hero . . . the life of hope from race to race, the image of the libido.

To anyone who was familiar with Jung's sources and his inclinations, it was not too hard to guess where Jung was planning to go in Part 2. The key inspiration was Flournoy's 1908 paper on "Anti-Suicidal Teleological Automatisms." In that paper, Flournoy presented instances where persons contemplating suicide had last-minute visions persuading them of the meaning and value of life. From Flournoy's point of view, these visions were plainly purposeful—the goal was to preserve life—and this bespoke a teleological component in the unconscious mind, i.e., a force with prospective and adaptive potentials. In essence, what Jung was getting ready to argue was that as Miss Miller descended deeper into her introverted state, there would arise a symbol, completely analogous to one of Flournoy's teleological hallucinations, which would show her the way out of it.

The journey had been well begun, Jung's path was clear, the end was already in sight—and in the early months of 1911 the whole expedition went completely off the rails.

THE TERRIBLE thing that was happening to Part 2 of Jung's manuscript in the spring of 1911 was that it was becoming totally unreadable.
Long passages, ranging upward of twenty pages apiece, were being
almost randomly inserted into the text, passages which were rambling
where they were not irrelevant, impenetrable where they were not rambling, and grotesque where they were comprehensible. Worse, such
was their length and the frequency of their intrusion, the passages all
but drowned out the other material. It was a catastrophe without
parallel in Jung's stylistic career to date.

The theologian and contemporary psychoanalytic commentator Peter Homans has applied himself to the original version of "Transformations and Symbols." In lieu of torturing the reader with some
examples from the text itself, let me quote Homans's admirably trenchant and altogether accurate summary:

> In effect it simply uses the libido theory and the Miller fantasies
> as stimuli for a full-scale, grandiose foray into the myths, rituals,
> symbolism, and practices of Judaic, Hellenic, Eastern, and primitive
> cultures. . . .
>
> It presents the reader with a multiple series of free associations
> and flights of ideas in which one image or thought leads to another,
> and this to another, for pages on end. . . . It is, in short, a record
> of Jung's own fantasies, not an interpretation of the myths and sym-
> bols of the past.

Much later in life, Jung gave the book a thorough revision—and a
new foreword in which he frankly apologized to his readers for his
original transgressions, which he termed "the sins of my youth":

> I have never felt happy about this book, much less satisfied with
> it: it was written at top speed, amid the rush and press of my medical
> practice, without regard to time or method. I had to fling my ma-
> terial hastily together, just as I found it. There was no opportunity
> to let my thoughts mature. The whole thing came upon me like a
> landslide that cannot be stopped.

This judgment, nearly as severe as Homans's, represents the verdict of a more mature Jung, certainly. But, even at the time, Jung

seems to have realized that his fantasy life had become inextricably entangled in the ancient materials he was studying and that the resulting reverie was beginning to escape the bounds of the interpretive framework that was meant to contain it. If one consults his letters to Freud over the first six months of 1911, one sees that Jung not only continued the policy of evasion, begun the previous November, but also that he was increasingly tentative and apologetic about his progress. A confession of self-doubt in January was followed in February by the very tentative announcements that he was "very busy with the incest problem" and that "Something should come of it." By March, Jung was writing of ". . . a parallel investigation of incestuous fantasy in relation to 'creative' fantasy. Once my thoughts have matured I must seek your advice. I am still brooding on it." By May, he had plainly fallen back into reverie, which now included both occultism and astrology, but he had the wit to ask Freud's forbearance:

> Please don't worry about my wanderings in these infinitudes. I shall return laden with rich booty for our knowledge of the human psyche. For a while longer I must intoxicate myself on magic perfumes in order to fathom the secrets that lie hidden in the abysses of the unconscious.

THE DESTRUCTIVE MOTHER

THE ERUPTION of reverie in Jung's text was all the more curious when one realizes that there was no pressing obligation for Jung to go into the long excursus about the sun-hero and his descent into the Underworld, which excursus was the occasion for Jung's losing control over his materials. All that Part 2 needed to do was interpret the third Miller fantasy, and Miss Miller's hero "Chiwantopel" doesn't make any such descent into the Underworld—he and his horse simply get bitten by a serpent, symbolic of incestuous libido, and die. After this, to be sure, they are swallowed up by the earth, but that, for Miss Miller, is the end. No journey beneath the earth ensues, no confrontation with a moon goddess, no subsequent winning of any treasure, and most certainly no resurrection to a new life. Jung did not need the problematic material, he was incipiently aware that it was problematic, and yet he went on anyway. Why?

Though he was charismatic and unapologetically domineering in his public life, Jung continued to consult with a more sensitive inner self in the safety of his private reflection. Reverie constituted a temptation for this particular man beyond what it poses for most people. Moreover, there existed a treacherous homology between Jung's own intellectual quest and the very thing his study was lately concerned with, namely the journey of the sun-hero. For Jung as analyst was intent on penetrating the incest barrier—conceived as a barrier to self-knowledge—and making contact with the deepest libidinal wellsprings of the mind. But this was more or less the same endeavor that the myths of the sun-hero described, at least in Jung's psychoanalytically informed reading. The narrative of the sun-hero's journey, then, readily became substitutive for Jung's own critical exegesis; the more he lost himself in the former, the more he escaped from the intellectual difficulties attending the latter.

That said, and mindful of all the brave sentiments about the saga of the sun-hero constituting a redemption mystery, it must be observed that Jung's reverie was really very little concerned with any ultimate ascent. Instead, what occupied him was the *descent*. And in the course of the descent, what further occupied him was the regressively charged image of the incestuous mother, that gorgon who would keep the hero trapped in the Underworld. All interpretive roads constantly led back to her, identified as the "destructive" or "terrible" mother. Tree symbolism ultimately signified the son's yearning to be reunited with her. The same with fish symbolism. The same with serpent symbolism. Themes of dismemberment signified her destructive powers. Themes of death and rebirth signified the son's ambivalent yearning to be reborn through her. The dragon was a symbol for her. And so forth.

The "destructive mother" rules in this text: all interpretations ultimately have reference to her malevolent charms. To be sure, Jung postulates that there are two mothers. That is to say, in states of introversion, the mother imago gets split and there is a "dual-mother" image. Further, in Jung's view, the other side of the dual-mother takes the form of a positive, life-enhancing image, an "eternal feminine" to lead us on. But there is precious little said about this side of things in the text. Instead, again and again, the text tarries on the subject of the "destructive mother," rather as though Jung simply cannot tear himself away.

The result is that even as reverie the text is unsatisfactory. It was a gloomy, almost lurid excursion that Jung was making. Barbara Hannah, Jung's disciple and later his most sympathetic biographer, once had occasion to mention to him that of all his works, "Transformations and Symbols" was unique in that it was the only one which caused her to feel despair rather than hope, confusion rather than clarity. To this

Jung is said to have replied, "How extraordinary, for I was in a bad depression myself all the time I was writing it." Hannah was a participant in the seminar Jung gave in 1925 where he reconstructed his own theoretical development. She remembers his remarks thus:

> He was haunted by bad dreams, and it still took him a few years to see that the book . . . could be taken as *himself,* as a picture of his own psychic condition, and that an analysis of the book, even at the time, would have led to an analysis of his own unconscious processes. He used to explain that the two kinds of thinking (with which the book opens) could be defined as intellectual or directed thinking and fantastic thinking. At the time he felt the latter to be completely impure, almost a kind of incestuous intercourse with the unconscious that was immoral from an intellectual point of view.

The feeling of "incestuous intercourse" does indeed hang over the text like an unhappy haze.

There are several possible explanations for Jung's preoccupation with the figure of the incestuous and therefore destructive mother. On one level, Jung's mother, she of the two personalities, would seem to be implicated. That he tarried long around the figure of the destructive mother accords well with his statements in his memoirs that he found his mother's second personality to be the more compelling. Jung's own subsequent explanation to his 1925 seminar, however, focused instead on the figure of Miss Miller: "She took over my fantasy and became stage director to it, if one interprets the book subjectively." There would thus appear to be a double movement here, with Jung's reverie first surrendering to Miss Miller's lead, and then, at a deeper level, to his mother's (in her Stygian manifestation). The feminine does not always lead us on; sometimes it leads us back.

As persuasive as such an interpretation may be at first glance, it is not altogether adequate. Jung's interest in fantastic thinking had preceded by several months his first acquaintance with the Miller fantasies. What Miss Miller had initially provided was some sorely needed case material around which to organize the topic. She began not as stage director, but as lab specimen. Furthermore, Jung began adding the "destructive mother" to his text almost a year after his first acquaintance with Miss Miller.

A piece of the puzzle is missing in these accounts. The piece is Spielrein. If we hear hers as the voice of female authority which Jung was alternately succumbing to and protesting against in his libidinal reverie, matters become rapidly clearer. For what she was arguing *in her text* was that there was no real difference between a longing for a real woman and an introverted and incestuous desire for the mother—behind both lay the same all-powerful instinct for species-preservation. Nor did she see that a feeling of dread, ultimately a fear of dissolution and death, was any obstacle to love. It was merely the price demanded by the destructive component of the libido. As for "transformation" in her system, it was accomplished by surrender. In short, while Jung was describing an inner confrontation with a maternal image felt to be "destructive," Spielrein was explicitly arguing for "destruction" as a necessary part of love. The two texts, his and hers, adjoin each other like severed halves of a forgotten conversation.

There was indeed a personal, and quite contemporary, reason why Jung's reverie did not escape the overexcited Underworld ruled by the "destructive mother." Let us look at that reverie one last time. He descends into an Underworld of fantasy and there finds himself confronted by a woman who would hold him fast if she could, a woman who confronts him maliciously with exquisitely regressive temptations, a woman with ready access to his own fantasy life, a woman who is as comfortable being his fantasied mother as being his eternal consort, a woman who can experience him both as lover and as the son he would sire in her, a woman who tells him that all sexual attraction involves destruction, a woman who holds him at fault if he cannot experience this as transformation, a woman who in the end positively dares him to be "Siegfried." Behind the image of the "destructive mother" of Jung's reverie, I submit, stands the unabashed authoress of "Destruction as a Cause of Coming into Being."

"SIEGFRIED" LIVES

GRANTED THE intimate, and finally not so secret, symmetry between his and her points of view, it would have been a great disappointment if Jung's reverie, as expressed in his text, had not somehow found a way of including the figure of Siegfried, especially as his lament for Brünnhilde had figured as one of Miss Miller's own associations. Jung's analysis is all of a piece, though it is interrupted by some twenty-five pages of interpolations having to do with various digressive symbolic equivalences. Some sample passages:

It is a well-recognized fact that Brünnhilde, the Valkyrie, gives protection to the birth (incestuous) of Siegfried, but while Sieglinde is the human mother, Brünnhilde has the role of "spiritual mother" (mother-imago); however, unlike Hera towards Hercules, she is not a pursuer, but benevolent. This sin, in which she is an accomplice by reason of the help she renders, is the reason for her banishment by Wotan. The strange birth of Siegfried from the sister-wife distinguishes him as Horus, as the *reborn son,* a reincarnation of the retreating Osiris—Wotan.

* * *

Brünnhilde's sin is the favoring of Siegfried, but behind this lies incest: this is projected into the brother-sister relation of Siegmund and Sieglinde; in reality, and archaically expressed, Wotan, the father, has entered into his self-created daughter, in order to rejuvenate himself.

* * *

We can now answer the question as to the significance of Siegfried's longing for Brünnhilde. It is the striving of the libido *away from the mother towards the mother.* This paradoxical sentence may be translated as follows: as long as the libido is satisfied merely with phantasies, it moves in itself, in its own depths, in the mother. . . . Only the overcoming of the obstacles of reality brings the deliverance from the mother, who is the continuous and inexhaustible source of life for the creator, but death for the cowardly, timid and sluggish.

Jung's interpretation comes near the end of his next-to-last chapter, though it carries over into the very beginning of his concluding chapter, "The Sacrifice." From its location in the text it would thus appear that the Siegfried analysis was meant to be the capstone of Jung's long night of reverie and the prelude to the ascending movement of his final conclusion. As it had been in life, in the conversations with Spielrein in late October of 1910, the Siegfried legend would be the point of departure for Jung's bold new theory of "sacrifice" as a phylogenetically acquired moral imperative, a symbolic archway through which one could gain access to the "total energy of countless generations."

THE REALITY PRINCIPLE

THE FIRST few months of 1911 were a surprisingly trying time personally for Jung. With Spielrein's departure from Zurich in January, he was once more at a loss for decent intellectual companionship, not to say inspiration. There were also the ongoing problems locally with the Zurich group. Bleuler had joined but had declined the presidency. Moreover, he would not compel his Burghölzli assistants to accept official membership. In short order, he and Jung were again locking horns. Then there came in the mail a submission for the *Jahrbuch* by an ingenious Viennese newcomer, Herbert Silberer, in which he described a variation on fantasies of returning to the womb, namely fantasies of returning to the father's genitals prior to conception. Bleuler howled at the thought that his name would run over "Spermatozoa Dreams," but Jung could not really see what his problem was. Once more, Freud had to be called in to mediate.

Meanwhile, at the beginning of March, there had come the surprising news that Alfred Adler had been removed as president of the Vienna Society. Jung declared himself "flabbergasted" to Freud, but having long heard that Adler was "paranoid," he did not pursue the matter much further. Adler's clinical innovations, combined with his aggressive intellectuality and his resentment at having forever to stand in Freud's shadow, lent just enough verisimilitude to Freud's characterization to make it almost credible. (That other "paranoid," Wilhelm Fliess, still one of Berlin's most noted internists, had just recently made Karl Abraham's acquaintance—and had turned out to be quite normal.) The just-concluded debates on Adler's theories had been less than edifying. In December, Freud had justified the new association in terms of the need to develop competence in the technique of psychoanalysis. But inside the Vienna association a different standard had been applied. Instead of an examination of cases, or a comparison of therapeutic results, Adler was essentially denounced for abandoning the libido theory and thus weakening the movement. Wittels was not there, but he had Stekel as an informant: "The Freudian adepts made a mass attack on Adler, an attack almost unexampled for its ferocity even in the fiercely contested field of psychoanalytic controversy." Max Graf, father of "Little Hans," later recalled the debates thus: "There was an atmosphere of the foundation of a religion in that room." Following the removal of Adler, Graf adds, Freud reigned "as head of a church." To Jung, however, Freud presented the change in leadership—Stekel had resigned the vice-presidency in support of his beleaguered colleague—as part of his overall plan to continue moving the center of psychoanalysis westward to Zurich. To Binswanger, he went even further: "When the empire I founded is orphaned, it is Jung alone who must inherit the whole thing." In fact, the removal of Adler significantly strengthened Jung's position as president, though at some cost to the integrity of the movement. The International Association was not quite a year old and already there had been something like a heresy trial.

Finally, in mid-March came the belated appearance of the galleys of Freud's paper "Formulations on the Two Principles of Mental Functioning." In context, Freud's short paper reads like nothing so much as an attempt to steal Jung's thunder. All of the themes of Part I of Jung's work—phantasy, religion, science, art, the role of reality, sexuality as a force in fixation and regression—are brought up in this paper, but given Freud's own special twist. For Freud here introduced his notion that the "reality principle" was a secondary elaboration of an original "pleasure principle." The novelty of Jung's own ideas was sure to be at least partially eclipsed by these alternative notions with their differing terminology. (It did indeed happen this way. Most modern analysts are thoroughly familiar with Freud's paper; few have even heard of, let alone read, "The Two Kinds of Thinking.") Worse still was the fact that Freud's version let back in the old Abraham-Jung dispute about whether schizophrenia was a sexual disease. And worst of all was Freud's concluding observation. While discussing the distortions brought about by repression, Freud brought in a single dream:

A man who had once nursed his father through a long and painful mortal illness, told me in the months following his father's death he had repeatedly dreamt that *his father was alive once more and that he was talking to him in his usual way. But he felt it exceedingly painful that his father had really died, only without knowing it.* The only way of understanding this apparently nonsensical dream is by adding "as the dreamer wished" or "in consequence of his wish" after the words "that his father had really died," and by further adding "that he [the dreamer] wished it" to the last words. The dream thought then runs: it was a painful memory for him that he had been obliged to wish for his father's death (as a release) while he was still alive, and how terrible it would have been if his father had any suspicion of it! What we have here is thus the familiar case of self-reproach after the loss of someone loved, and in this instance the self-reproach went back to the infantile significance of death-wishes against the father.

This was Jung's dream. It had occurred repeatedly following his father's death in 1896. It is not altogether clear what precipitated

Freud's going into print with it. (Freud doubled his indiscretion by adding it to the third edition of the dream book.) Perhaps Freud had finally seen the relevance of this dream to the dream of himself as the customs official wherein he, too, was "dead" but did not know it. Or perhaps his lapse in psychoanalytic etiquette may have been provoked by a lingering dismay over Jung's Arona dream. But, in any case, the implication in Freud's text was that he had not heretofore shared his interpretation of the dream with the man who had dreamt it. For immediately after the above passage, Freud abruptly summed up by apologizing for the "deficiencies of this short paper" and then ended ominously with the following cryptic remark:

In these few remarks on the psychical consequences of adaptation to the reality-principle I have been obliged to adumbrate views which I should have preferred for the present to withhold and whose jus-tification will certainly require no small effort. But I hope it will not escape the notice of the benevolent readers how in these pages too the dominance of the reality-principle is beginning.

Freud's paper was already set in type. Jung took cognizance of it gamely in his letter of 19 March 1911:

I have taken your "pleasure and reality principle" to heart and have had to adopt your terminology for the time being. "Pleasure and reality principle" is indeed an excellent term with a wide range of application. My only regret is that I was not in possession of this point of view earlier.

With Bleuler still fuming, Spielrein gone, and Freud submitting his dream to public scrutiny, Jung was increasingly on his own emotion-ally. Jung next attempted to befriend Alphonse Maeder, who had just relocated in Zurich from Kreuzlingen. Maeder was very grateful for the show of support but he was wary of being submerged beneath Jung's overbearing manner, and kept a polite distance. At the time Maeder was working on a new approach to the theory of dream for-mation. The theory was based on an idea earlier launched into print by Edouard Claparède of Geneva. Claparède, borrowing from the psy-chologist Karl Groos's ideas about the "functional" nature of chil-dren's play—play prepares for adulthood by exercising skills which are still rudimentary—had proposed "functional" explanations for such things as hysteria and sleep. Maeder wondered if Claparède's and Groos's ideas might not make a worthy supplement to Freud's with respect to the subject of dreams. For Freud, the "purpose" of dreaming was simply to maintain sleep by discharging internal stimuli which would otherwise cause the dreamer to awake. What Maeder supposed was that in addition to this function, dreaming might also have the purpose of preparing the dreamer for the tasks of the following day. In this way, dreams would be entirely analogous to children's play.

In March, Maeder began corresponding with Freud about his idea. The result was that Maeder was pestering Freud about the purpose of dreams only a month after Jung had himself pressed for a change in the third edition of the dream book, which was going to press. Jung had wanted a thorough analysis of one of Freud's own dreams emphasizing the sexual element and its infantile, presumably incestuous, roots. That indeed constituted a glaring lack in the original, as Ellenberger has noted, but Freud was understandably not in a mood to oblige. His reply to Jung's request stopped short of being indignant, but it very clearly drew the line: "I simply cannot expose any more of my nakedness to the reader." That shortly thereafter another Swiss was writing to him again on the purpose of dreams might well have struck Freud as something of a dare, one bordering on bad taste.

If Maeder made a not altogether satisfactory companion, there was always the hope that young Honegger, lately stationed at the Rheinau asylum, might yet pull himself together, clear up the business of his fiancée, finish his dissertation, and return to Zurich as Jung's assistant in an office practice. But now came the most terrible development of all: on 28 March 1911, on the eve of his scheduled departure for his annual military obligation, Honegger killed himself with a lethal injection of morphine. It was, obviously, a personal disaster for Jung. The problem of Honegger's suicide has never been totally solved, despite the insightful investigations of Hans Walser. That Jung was deeply shaken is clear from his letters to Freud after the event. Jung struggled to turn the matter into a medical problem—and into a medical mistake. Honegger must have had a secret fantasy system, in Jung's guilty self-recriminations, and Jung had failed to detect its presence.

Introversion, and death, now wore the face of someone he knew. Jung could no longer really stand it. Though his letters to Freud continued to make an occasional reference to his manuscript in the months that followed, these increasingly involved astrology and/or the occult. With regard to the former, we should note that Toni Wolff, who is known to have done library research for Jung in connection with Part 2 of his monograph, was herself an amateur astrologer able to make star charts. Wolff was a former patient; now she was a research assistant. No doubt, entirely within the bounds of propriety, she offered companionship. In any case, at the time of Honegger's death, Jung turned away from his manuscript toward several new projects, thus leaving the reverie of the destructive mother intact and unedited.

NEW PATHS IN PSYCHOLOGY

THE FIRST of Jung's new projects was a popular piece on psychoanalysis, "New Paths in Psychology," promised to a local literary volume, *Raschers Jahrbuch*. The piece gave Jung a chance to reflect on his career to date, but Jung also found time to engage in a general polemic about the alienation of man's natural instincts in modern urban society. At the time, there was a widespread reaction against modernity under way in German culture generally. In effect, Jung was only giving a psychoanalytic cast to the general tendency to romanticize and idealize the rural and pastoral world which European civilization was leaving irrevocably behind. As he put it to Freud in a letter of 8 May 1911: "I am trying to be popular again—not to my advantage, as you will see."

But Jung's piece had yet another side to it. There was a long discussion on the problem of the hysteric constitution and its relation to trauma which led in the course of a case description to a summary statement that only a present erotic conflict was sufficient to provoke a neurosis. Jung did allow that in the face of a present erotic conflict, regression ensued and on that account infantile elements came into play in the unconscious. But he also pointed out that the unconscious contained something more than just infantile memories: "As the latest researches of the Zurich School have shown, besides the infantile reminiscences there are also 'race memories' extending far beyond the limits of the individual." The statement was remarkable insofar as with Honegger's death, the "Zurich School" had only two spokesmen on this question besides himself—Spielrein and Jan Nelken, the only Burghölzli assistant to officially enroll with the Zurich Psychoanalytic Society. Evidently, Jung was counting fairly heavily on Spielrein's dissertation, or rather on his interpolations into her dissertation, to help carry the day. In any case, now that he was putting the general claim—racial memories in the unconscious—down on paper for the benefit of

Zurich literary circles, Jung realized that perhaps he had best inform Freud as to what was coming. Accordingly in his letter of 12 June 1911, Jung wrote:

> Everything I am doing now revolves round the contents and forms of unconscious fantasies. I think I've already got some really fine results. You will see that this investigation is the necessary preliminary work for the psychology of Dem. praec. Spielrein's case is proof of that (it's in the *Jahrbuch*).

This was the first mention of Spielrein in the two men's correspondence since July 1909. Freud took notice of the announcement in his reply: "I gather that you have great surprises in store for me in the *Jahrbuch*. I shall read it attentively in Karlsbad." There were other things in "New Paths in Psychology" that would have been even more interesting to Freud had he known about them. For while the article noted that "by no means everything has been published that relates to the technique of a deep analysis," which was of course true, it went on to hint that the therapeutic process might pivot on "the mystery of self-sacrifice" in the service of providing the patient with a "working philosophy of life."

Jung also wrote a second paper, a report on a child analysis which he would deliver in person at the next International Congress of Pedagogy called by Claparède and secheduled for the second week of August in Brussels. The case, which concerned an eleven-year-old girl with a school phobia and, it emerged, a crush on her teacher, was actually analyzed by Maria Moltzer with Jung supervising. More important than Jung's glosses on the girl's behavior, or even on her motives, was what he had to say about the "contents and forms" of her fantasies. For the past three years, it had been accepted psychoanalytic wisdom that the resemblance between children's frequently fantastic theories as to where babies come from and the content of folktales and mythology, where babies pop out from ovens or from under lily pads with startling regularity, was evidence that the latter had been influenced by the former. Jung now realized that the whole formula could just as easily be turned on its head. When, in the absence of better information, the child went to concoct a theory of where babies came from, he or she fell back into reverie and in that reverie unconscious race memories from the dawn of mankind floated up as hypotheses. *That* was why children's theories resembled folktales. Since the Clark congress, Jung had been trying to anchor his reflections on libidinal development on a phylogenetic, evolutionary basis, as opposed to the personal-historical past. Now, he had a reasonable argument for carrying this shift of interpretive emphasis into childhood.

Prior to his August trip to Brussels, Jung also made time for separate trips to Stuttgart and Berlin seeking adherents—and for a blistering review of Morton Prince's new book. Prince was a personal friend of Ernest Jones, and had nearly lectured at the first Psychoanalytic Congess. But he could not find sexual wishes in the dreams of his patients and in 1910 went out of his way to say so in a monograph devoted to the subject, *The Mechanism and Interpretation of Dreams.* Freud had promptly dissociated himself from any further cooperation with Prince—"an arrogant ass who would be conspicuous even in our menagerie"—but as president of the International Association, Jung felt moved to an official reply. Jung's review was too strident by half. It was the stridency of a poor winner. In this particular deal Jung held all the trump cards. He was able to take the very same dreams of Prince's patient and demonstrate again and again that they were loaded to the gills with sexual symbolism—even that much of it was transferentially related to her doctor.

Jung's demolition of Prince was but one instance of a general trend that was beginning to make itself felt. From the first months of 1911 onward, psychoanalysis made steady institutional progress in both America and Europe. Not only could the movement advertise itself in any number of influential texts, but the high quality of some of its adherents, including men like Eugen Bleuler and James Jackson Putnam, guaranteed a respectful hearing in which its inherent superiority over rival therapeutic schools could be made manifest. Here let us remind ourselves of some of the essentials of the Freudian contribution in its historical context. These included: the studied openness toward the possibility of sexual and erotic factors in ostensibly nonsexual disorders; the demystification brought about by excluding racial and hereditary issues from both diagnosis and treatment; the consistent application of a developmental perspective; the therapeutic use of dreams to make the patient take responsibility for his wishes; the use of information derived from multiple contexts, including the treatment itself, to establish the continuity of a patient's productions across apparent psychic "splits"; the investigation of symptoms for their possible symbolic content; the nonjudgmental attitude of investigation taken toward childhood sexual experiences and fantasies; the understanding that establishing therapeutic rapport did not preclude discussion of the treatment relationship, including the patient's fantasies about the therapist; the close attention paid to idiosyncrasies in the patient's use of language as a potential clue to underlying motivations; and the open-ended nature of the interview format.

The relative superiority of the psychoanalytic vision had a double import for Jung's career. On the one hand, it gave him the support he needed to continue playing the role of psychiatric heretic in forums such as the Brussels Congress or the pages of the *Raschers Jahrbuch*. On the other hand, it had begun to generate a host of new associates. Psychoanalysis had reached that stage of institutional development where a theory becomes a kind of language. Jung and Freud increasingly kept themselves in the company of people who spoke that language more or less fluently—or were eager to learn it. Opposition was still encountered, but the vulnerable early days of the association seemed to be over. Jung had begun to enjoy being president of the International Association; his manuscript continued to go unattended.

THE CLAN GATHERS

THE THIRD Psychoanalytic Congress, held at Weimar, the city of Goethe, on 21–22 September 1911, would represent the high-water mark of the early history of the psychoanalytic movement. As congresses are first of all a matter of a guest-list, it was merciful news that in June Alfred Adler, who had continued to sit at meetings in stony silence, finally resigned as a member of the Vienna society. Freud commented to Jung: "A few rather useless members will probably follow his example." Three, in fact, did; they were all, like Adler, Socialists. A week later, on 20 June, six other Viennese signed a manifesto declaring their partiality to Adler but their wish to continue as members of Freud's group.

Wilhelm Stekel, surprisingly, survived the Adler affair. The chronicle of Stekel's rehabilitation—the only word for it—during the first half of 1911 constitutes one of the most surprising turnarounds in the whole of the extant Freud-Jung correspondence, exceeded only by the more protracted rehabilitation the previous year of Ernest Jones. It had already become clear to the discerning that Stekel was capable of falsifying case material, even fabricating it outright, in the pursuit of interpretive elegance. Nonetheless, he had been enough of a diplomat to maintain his line of communication to Freud at a crucial time, with the result that when Adler also resigned from the *Zentralblatt,* Stekel was left in charge.

The third week of August, the spring half-issue of the *Jahrbuch* finally came out. It was the fifth in the *Jahrbuch*'s brief but distinguished existence. It contained Freud's Schreber case, also his paper "Two Principles of Mental Functioning," Part I of Jung's "Transformations and Symbols," Spielrein's dissertation, a communication from Bleuler on infantile sexuality, Jung's critique of Bleuler's theory of "Schizophrenic Negativism," Bleuler's reply to Jung's critique, and Jung's review of Prince, as well as contributions from Maeder, Rank, Ferenczi, Binswanger, Pfister, and a newcomer named Heinrich Bertschinger. But while it was unquestionably the most impressive issue to date, it was also true that all the small tensions within the psychoanalytic camp were beginning to show, like so many tiny fault-lines in a large and richly but haphazardly decorated vase. Freud acknowledged receipt of the volume in his letter to Jung of 20 August 1911 and took advantage of the occasion to fire a friendly shot over Jung's bow:

> Since my mental powers revived, I have been working in a field where you will be surprised to meet me. I have unearthed strange and uncanny things and will be almost obliged *not* to discuss them with you. But you are too shrewd not to guess what I am up to when I add that I am dying to read your "Transformations and Symb. of the Lib."

This surprise announcement caught Jung off guard. In fact, Freud had begun work on a new project, *Totem and Taboo,* which would contain his own thoughts about ancient religion. Freud had conceived the endeavor but six weeks after his meeting with Jung in Munich at Christmastime, and his animus can perhaps best be summarized in terms of Jung's work. Where Jung had been concentrating on myths involving a son and a mother—Isis and Osiris may be taken as representative—Freud had begun to wonder about the missing figure of the father. More specifically, he had begun to suspect that the absence of the father in these myths bespoke a later corruption of the mythological record. He guessed that at a deeper stratum in the cultural archive one might find evidence for a primal father—and for a primal murder by the son. If that was the case, then one would have reason not only for supposing that an Oedipal motif had once been central, but also for arguing that its very repression had been handed down phylogenetically. Instead of an awareness of the original psychic situation, all that was left was a vague feeling of reverence, the residue of remorse for the forgotten parricide. And here we can begin to see the significance of Freud's discussion of Jung's dream at the end of the little paper announcing the "reality principle." In Freud's view, Jung's dream silently repressed the wish to kill the father. No doubt, Freud also conceived that Jung was potentially prone to the same oversight in regard to his selection of mythological materials.

It is worth pausing to observe a temperamental difference between Freud and Jung that was beginning to be reflected in their theories. Jung's nascent modifications of libido theory, and most especially his phylogenetic romance of the sun-hero, bespoke his inner wish to become whole within himself. In this respect, Jung's basic orientation toward the idea of the unconscious had changed little over the preceding ten years. Jung seems always to have wanted an "unconscious" that he could talk to, one that might counsel and guide him, even help him heal the divisions in his personality. Freud, on the other hand, sought no such personal relation with the inner world. Fundamentally, he appears always to have wanted an "unconscious" that he could examine like an arcane text, one that required deciphering and exegesis. Even in the face of dreams that read like jokes, Freud's delight lay more in the act of decoding than in deriving personal counsel. Jung's sun-hero moved much too freely across the incest barrier, conceived of as a barrier to self-knowledge, to suit Freud's taste. Freud preferred to guess at what might be hidden in mythology, at what might be repressed. The aesthetics of such a putative blind spot, devoutly handed down from one generation to the next, appealed to him in a way that it would never appeal to Jung.

Jung responded to Freud's gnomic pronouncement nine days later. He encouraged Freud to read his own essay with an open mind— "unleash your associations and/or fantasies"—while hoping that "your embargo on discussion will be lifted during your stay here." Meanwhile, final preparations had to be made for the Congress. Putnam was due in Zurich the second week of September, and Jung encouraged Freud to join them no later than the 15th so that the three might have sufficient time together prior to the trip to Weimar. As for the Zurich delegation to the Congress, Jung happily reported that the "feminine element" would be well represented: "Sister Moltzer, Dr. Hinkle-Eastwick (an old American charmer), Frl. Dr. Spielrein (!), then a new discovery of mine, Frl. Antonia Wolff, a remarkable intellect with excellent feeling for religion and philosophy, and last but not least my wife."

As it happened, Spielrein did not attend. At the last moment, she came down with a sore ankle and elected to stick it out in her Vienna *Pension*. Meanwhile, in his final extant letter before the Congress, Freud acknowledged Jung's entourage while venting his own prejudices about female psychology: "We Viennese have nothing to compare with the charming ladies you are bringing from Zurich. Our only lady doctor is participating like a true masochist in the Adler revolt and is unlikely to be present." More important, in the same letter Freud reported on his "first reading" of Jung's paper and in the process dispelled some of the mystery surrounding his own: "So you too are aware that the Oedipus complex is at the root of religious feeling. Bravo! What evidence I have to contribute can be told in five minutes."

Freud arrived in Küsnacht early on the morning of the 16th and stayed for four days. According to Jones, "There were of course seminars, visitors, and receptions, so it was by no means a pure holiday." For her part, Mrs. Jung felt that her husband and her visitor should have found rather more time to discuss their respective projects and was worried when they didn't. During his stay, Freud did find time to spend six hours analyzing the other guest, James Jackson Putnam. All that is known about this analysis is that at one point Freud suggested to the overly scrupulous Putnam, who as yet knew nothing of the *Totem* project, that inwardly he was still compensating for parricidal wishes from his childhood.

On the 19th of June, the Jungs, Freud, Putnam, and Maeder took the day's train up to Weimar. Bleuler and the rest of the Zurich contingent arrived the next day. The Third International Psychoanalytic Congress began on the 21st. James Jackson Putnam's appearance on the dais to inaugurate the proceedings constituted the emotional highpoint of the whole occasion. Putnam was a man of deeply philosophical bent, and his views were sufficiently complex that only those steeped in American Hegelianism were truly apt to make them out. Like Jung, Putnam believed that the conduct of psychoanalysis needed to be informed by a deeper philosophical understanding. Even more extraordinary was the fact that Putnam thought that a person's spiritual progress through analysis could be meaningfully related to myths of the sun-hero. He thus made the same connection Jung did. Interestingly, however, Putnam did it by bypassing libido theory altogether. Instead he argued that it was of the very essence of consciousness, itself a manifestation of an intrinsically creative and moral energy in the universe, that it constantly went out from itself to its object, only to return inward again in self-reflection. This primordial going out and returning, according to Putnam, was manifest both in the instincts of infancy and in mythology.

For his talk, Freud presented a very brief "Postscript" to the Schreber case. Noting that Schreber had been mentioned by both Jung and Spielrein in their recent *Jahrbuch* contributions, Freud went on to announce that certain aspects of the case made a good jumping-off point for the psychoanalytic study of religious practices, in particular totemism. Jung had two presentations to make, one in his official capacity as president, the other as theorist. The former was all confidence and statistics—so many new societies, so many new members, etc. The other was more tentative. He discussed the resemblance between certain primitive motifs of crucifixion on a tree and the delusions of a woman patient at the Burghölzli. Another member of the Zurich school, Jan Nelken, followed up with a second paper to the same general point, namely that ancient religious motifs and contemporary delusions had much in common. And then there was Spielrein's recently published dissertation. At Weimar, Jung gallantly upheld her presence in spirit by distributing offprints of her dissertation, then promptly made amends to himself by beginning a long letter scolding her for succumbing to a psychosomatic pretext instead of coming to the Congress.

Overall, it was a splendid affair. Everyone, save Adler and Spielrein, was there. A group photograph was taken immortalizing the occasion. (The women from Zurich were joined in the first row before the cameraman by Poul Bjerre's current lover, the redoubtable Lou Andreas-Salomé. Everyone else looked supremely distinguished, except Jung, who looked uncomfortable—as indeed he was, since, standing to Freud's immediate left, he thoughtfully crouched so as not to tower over the Master.) The presentations were of as high a quality as the photograph. On the floor of the Congress, Jung was in fine form. Jones reports that at one point someone unnamed (quite possibly Jones himself) remarked to Freud about the coarseness of Jung's jokes. To which Freud responded tartly, "It's a healthy coarseness." Putnam, meanwhile, took time out to compliment Freud on the high quality of his followers. To which Freud replied, "They have learned to tolerate a piece of reality."

Immediately after leaving the congress, Jung finished his lecturing letter to Spielrein. Freud stayed on an extra day at Weimar to meet privately with Karl Abraham. The topic was *Totem and Taboo*.

Part Four

Intimate Matters

All criticisms coming from without and all inner scientific differences do not so much harm what Freud brought forth, as does his infelicitous tendency to drive one-sidedness to absurdity. It is depressing to see such a movement work upon its own annihilation. For it can never be denied that it was first through the ideas which came from this direction, that psychotherapy was able to lift itself up to importance and become a general life-factor. Freud with one stroke has given the study of soul-life such breadth and such surety, that we have obtained a foundation upon which to build for all time. One may be never so bitter against him for the blunders he has made— yet no one can carry out a single simple treatment without making use of some thing he discovered. It devolves upon those who will take the scientific inheritance after him to see to it that all his daring ingenious ideas are followed out with every conceivable freedom from prejudice.

—Poul Bjerre, *The History and Practice of Psychoanalysis,* 1916

CHAPTER 14

On Transformation

I allow myself to write to you so openly and frankly since after long reflection about myself I have removed all the bitterness that still existed in my heart toward you. In truth this bitterness did not emanate from your dissertation—there is nothing there that is unpleasant for me—but from the inner anguish I suffered because of you—and you because of me. I truly wish you happiness from the bottom of my heart and will always think of you with such a feeling. But never forget that under no circumstance should you ever allow yourself to shrink back from an immediate goal which your heart views as true and beautiful. Every time this will involve a sacrifice of egoism, pride, and stubbornness and will appear to you as if you are losing yourself in the process. But only through this mysterious self-sacrifice will you win yourself in a new, beautiful form and thereby become a blessing and a source of happiness for other people. Therefore you should not under any circumstances have renounced your visit to the Congress.

—Letter from Jung to Spielrein, 21/22 September 1911

WHEN SPIELREIN canceled out from the Weimar congress at the last minute, it occurred to Jung that her presence in Vienna might constitute an important complication in his life. He was more than a little discomforted. Thus, for all the fine sentiments of his letter to her, begun while he was still in Weimar, he most ungallantly declined to send her a letter of recommendation, which is what she had asked for. Jung left it up to her to get herself situated:

Freud will certainly accept you. He has spoken of your dissertation several times, proof that you have made an impression on him. You don't need my recommendation but approach him as a great master and rabbi, and all will be well.

AT THE BEGINNING of October Jung went off to St. Gallen for four weeks' military duty. This gave him time to consider anew his options—and his manuscript. Over the years, Jung had been intermittently tempted by the idea of broadening the dynamic and motivational basis of psychoanalytic theory above and beyond sexuality. Putnam's Weimar address had revived the temptation. Then, too, with Honegger's death, it now fell to Jung to work out the relevance of his phylogenetic theories for dementia praecox.

Fueling his reflections was the happenstance that Jung had recently hit on a very nice approach to an anthropological fact of no small psychoanalytic importance. According to then current anthropological wisdom, the typical means for making fire among many primitive peoples involved rubbing two pieces of wood together, not in the modern boy-scout fashion, but by moving one stick, the rubbing-stick or "borer," back and forth along a groove in a small plank lying flat on the ground. The resemblance to coitus was unmistakable. It now occurred to Jung that this method of making fire was most improbable on the face of it: if one had never seen it work, one would never set out to make fire this way. The only conceivable explanation for the phenomenon was that primitives had first done it because it was pleasurable, i.e., because it symbolized coitus. Only after they had begun doing it did they realize that the rubbing-stick became quite hot, hot enough to ignite wood shavings. Jung might have noted to himself with pleasure that Karl Abraham had missed this line of analysis in his lengthy examination of the Prometheus legend, *Dreams and Myth*.

Now as Jung contemplated the dynamics of primitive discovery and pondered how he was going to incorporate the theory of phylogenetic regression in schizophrenia into his work, it began to dawn on him that the two problems were related. For what the primitive achieved by way of increased reality-contact, the schizophrenic lost by way of regression. In the former a sexual symbol became desexualized while in the latter a nonsexual function—reality-testing—became sexualized and thereby dysfunctional.

This was a heady brew already, but Jung had yet another concept to which he had decided to commit himself more strongly—the prospective function of certain symbols. Maeder, currently Jung's principal ally in Zurich, had by now worked his idea of the "functional" analysis of dreams up into a full-blown theory of the prospective significance of dream symbols. A Viennese newcomer, Herbert Silberer, seemed to be advancing independently along the same path in his ongoing work on hypnagogic imagery (images that form when one is only half-asleep). At least some hypnagogic images, Silberer argued, were not principally sexual but "anagogic," which is to say that they had a functional resemblance to an intellectual problem and constituted a rudimentary, and symbolic, attempt at framing a solution.

It thus occurred to Jung that sexuality might best be considered the joker in the deck of evolution with some more general force, such as Henri Bergson's *élan vital,* animating the rest of the cards. On the one hand, sexuality might engage objects in the environment via various symbolic equivalences, in the process suggesting new adaptations. Religious symbols in particular seemed to serve as a kind of holding-pen for these emanations of unemployed libido. On the other hand, in cases of regression, earlier stages of thought (sexualized but only because the corresponding desexualized form of adaptation had not yet been reached) might come to the fore as the individual accessed phylogenetically deeper levels of the mind. In short, it was all a matter of energy transformations, one in which both progression and regression typically were accomplished through temporary effluxes of sexuality.

The foregoing may be less than clear to the modern reader and, no doubt, in October of 1911 it was not altogether clear to Jung either. But one thing was clear: there was absolutely no chance that Freud was going to like a theory in which sexuality was incorporated within a new, generalized concept of psychic energy. Indeed, Jung had specifically broached the subject of broadening the "libido" concept some two years earlier, and if he had any illusions as to where Freud stood, he had only to go to his desk and retrieve Freud's testy letter of 19 December 1909.

It was a potentially radical step for another reason. Part 1 of Jung's text was already in print and some two hundred pages of Part 2 had already been committed to paper. The new viewpoint, if Jung were to adopt it, would call for major revisions. It would not be hard to square the new idea of energy transformations with the idea that certain dreams were best understood as symbolic communications from the unconscious rather than as mere wish-fulfillments. But it would be terribly difficult, both conceptually and editorially, to integrate these ideas with the old distinction between incestuous and procreative libido. In fact, a major overhaul of the existing manuscript would have to be made. Yet, on balance, such a revision might be preferable to staying the old course. For the theory of incestuous and procreative libido now began to look quite different than it had only six or nine months before.

The existing text of Part 2 of "Transformations and Symbols" scarcely constituted an autobiography, and, unless one had intimate knowledge of Jung's own fantasy life, there could be no way of knowing that a covert self-analysis was indeed going on there. So long as the whole set of issues was joined on the field of mythology, Jung was safe—provided Spielrein was safely in tow. She, and she alone, was in a position to provide the biographical key to the whole endeavor. But, from the moment she begged off attending the Weimar congress, it was clear that she was *not* safely in tow. Jung had no way of knowing if she would continue to hold fast to the interpretations of the previous fall. Hence his long, lecturing letter from Weimar on the subject of "self-sacrifice." He was reminding her of where they had ended up in terms of understanding "Siegfried." Of course, Jung had no particular reason to suppose that she would recant. And even less reason to suppose that she would be indiscreet about their personal relationship. Yet, it was an uncomfortable situation to be in, and Jung had not prepared himself for it.

It now occurred to Jung that he had read Spielrein's new paper on "Destruction" far too cursorily. As she was sure to be seen as his protégée, whatever she wrote was certain to be read in juxtaposition with *his* theories. Just this might turn out to be problematical. By the same token, however, a close reading of her text might be the best guide in deciding how far he should go in revising his. Jung wrote to her from St. Gallen and asked if he could have her manuscript back again.

THE NEWCOMER

JUNG'S RENEWED curiosity about Spielrein's manuscript was the first ripple in what would soon become a small eddy of worry stirred up by her presence in Vienna. Spielrein was the first full-fledged member of the Zurich school to relocate to Vienna and take up full-time residence there. Psychoanalysis was evolving quite differently in the two cities. Though there was a modicum of traffic between them, no one heretofore had been completely clear about the full extent of the difference. Spielrein potentially changed that. As a close associate of both Bleuler and Jung, she knew the Zurich milieu intimately and was thoroughly conversant with all the latest Swiss theories. Moreover, as someone who had gone from a hospitalized teenager to a graduate of the University of Zurich Medical School and a contributor to the *Jahrbuch,* in her own person Spielrein embodied the therapeutic philosophy of the Zurich school at its best. Both messenger and message, then, Spielrein potentially constituted an important communication sent from the one city to the other.

There was a problem, however. With so little shared context between the two cities, there was no easy way to read the message. Indeed, there was no way even to know ahead of time how important or worrisome the message might be. Understandably, the people for whom it mattered most would soon begin making guesses. Initially, they would all guess wrong. Spielrein herself went guilelessly ahead with her own agenda, oblivious to the chain reaction of worry she was about to provoke. She had two goals: she wanted to continue her training as a psychoanalyst and she wanted to win recognition for her new theory of repression. To that end, in the early evening of 11 October 1911, she set out to enroll herself as a member in the Vienna Psychoanalytic Society.

Gone were the days when the Vienna Psychoanalytic Society had met around a long table in Freud's waiting room amidst cigar smoke and spittoons. Gone, too, were the days when candidates for membership might spend their inaugural addresses describing their own sexual histories. To be sure, when Frau Dr. Margarete Hilferding had been proposed as the first woman member of the group in April of 1910, a spirited debate broke out as to whether women *could* be members. Isidor Sadger managed to round up two other members who were willing to vote against women members on principle, and, though Hilferding squeaked through by the barest of margins, the group's chairman, Adler at the time, took cognizance of the three votes against the idea and agreed that in the future caution would have to be exercised. Sabina Spielrein was the second woman to apply for membership in the Vienna Psychoanalytic Society.

11 October marked the first Wednesday Night Meeting for the fall semester of 1911. As was usual, the first meeting was held not in the lecture hall rented from the *Doktor Kollegium,* but in a café, this evening the Café Arkaden. Left to her own devices, Spielrein somehow found her way there and walked right into one of the uglier scenes of the early history of psychoanalysis. It was on this evening that Freud completed his campaign against Alfred Adler. Adler and three "worth-

less followers'' had already resigned from the society the previous June. Since then, they had started their own little group, the Society for Free Psychoanalysis. There were, however, six remaining individuals who, while they considered Adler's expulsion unjust, and attended meetings of his group, nonetheless wished to continue as members of the Vienna society. On the evening of 11 October, Freud put into motion his plan— he had discussed it with Jung at Weimar—for driving out this remnant of the ''Adler gang.''

The minutes for the meeting are skimpy, but the outline of what happened is plain. Speaking for the executive board, Freud announced a sudden change of policy, whereby membership in Adler's group would henceforth be held ''incompatible'' with membership in the official society. The six were being told, in effect, to renounce Adler or leave. One by one, Freud's loyalists spoke for the new rule, as did Freud himself, speaking personally this time. Karl Furtmüller, a philosopher by training and a political activist, spoke for the Adlerians, if that's what they were. A man of integrity, Furtmüller was not about to be dictated to. Stekel was alone in trying to postpone a decision in the hope that some mediation might prove possible. In the heat of the moment, Furtmüller demanded an official vote. The motion passed eleven to five. At which point, Furtmüller announced his own resignation and that of five other members, including that ''true masochist,'' Frau Dr. Margarete Hilferding, the society's first woman member. Thus came into being two separate societies, with no official contact with each other. It was bitter. As Paul Roazen reports the reminiscences of Hanns Sachs's wife: ''The feud broke up longstanding friendships. Wives stopped speaking to each other, and couples disliked being seated near one another at dinner parties.''

What Spielrein made of it all is unknown—as is also what she made of a resolution introduced by Isidor Sadger early in the evening's proceedings. Sadger proposed that henceforth less than a quarter of the membership would be needed to block a new member, with three nays being his idea of a sufficient number. Sadger, of course, had led the fight against Hilferding a year and a half earlier. Since there wasn't any discussion of Sadger's motion, nor of its rationale, it is entirely likely that the new woman member from Zurich failed to grasp that she specifically had been its target. In any case, Freud immediately tabled Sadger's motion and argued that since ''the applicants are known to a large number of the members,'' which was scarcely true in Spielrein's case, the balloting should take place immediately. Thus spoken for by the chairman, the three candidates were admitted unanimously. Freud called the roll in a letter to Jung the next day: August Stärcke of Holland, Jan Van Emden of Leiden, ". . . and Sabina Spielrein who turned up unexpectedly."

Spielrein was aboard. In the general socializing that followed the expulsion of the Adler gang, she took the opportunity to seek out Freud personally. Presumably she approached him as a "great master and rabbi," as Jung had instructed her to, but all we know of the interchange is what Freud volunteered to Jung: "She said I didn't look malicious, as she imagined I would."

His recent visit to Zurich was still much on Freud's mind, and his correspondence with Jung was still more important than any happenings with the locals. Two days later, on Friday, 13 October, Freud found time for a second letter to Jung about some intricate theoretical matters. Most important was his mention of the doctrine of the phylogenetic inheritance of ideas, "which unfortunately will soon become undeniable." Freud did not mention the use he himself was planning to make of it. Freud closed with the thought that "It's a pity we can only work together in such technical matters." Jung wrote back four days later on 17 October. In his letter, he revealed for the first time his view that "the so-called 'early memories of childhood' are not individual memories at all but phylogenetic ones." Ordinarily, this would have brought a howl from Vienna, or at least a query. But Jung's letter, which would have arrived on Wednesday, 18 October, was not the only one of note in Freud's mail that day.

LETTERS TO A FRIEND

EMMA JUNG had been worried about her husband. She had sensed that something was wrong, though she did not connect this with Spielrein. While Jung was on military duty in St. Gallen, Mrs. Jung decided it was a good time to write to Sándor Ferenczi, whom she knew from his days at the Burghölzli, saying that she felt something was amiss between Carl and Professor Freud. It had something to do with Carl's work on the libido theory, she thought, but also something to do with Freud's "authority." She asked Ferenczi for advice and begged him not to tell Freud of her concerns.

Ferenczi, eager to help but not at all eager to keep such a confidence, promptly mailed her letter to Vienna along with his own surmises about why Freud might perhaps have shown too much reserve lately toward his

Zurich son and heir. Ferenczi's letter arrived on 18 October. Freud wrote back immediately instructing Ferenczi to have Mrs. Jung write to him directly. As to the nature of Mrs. Jung's concerns, Freud was explicit. Ferenczi should "strike" all references to theoretical matters and instead ask her what she meant by "authority."

That evening at the Wednesday Night Meeting, Viktor Tausk, a jurist turned analyst, presented a philosophical analysis of selected analytic topics. Except for some sharp remarks from Stekel, who disliked Tausk intensely, it was a most desultory evening. Spielrein did not speak. Freud commented grumpily on the evening in his letter of 20 October 1911 to Jung, who was still in St. Gallen: "You see how petty one becomes when one is reduced to such company as I am here in the Vienna Society. Last Wednesday it was again brought home to me how much of the most elementary educational work remains to be done."

Meanwhile, Ferenczi, who had been there for the original shipboard confrontation between Jung and Freud on the way home from America, had done exactly the opposite of what he had been instructed to do. To be sure, he wrote Mrs. Jung and asked her to write Freud directly. But he told her to bring up Carl's theories and to leave "authority" out of it. Plausibly, if perhaps disingenuously, Ferenczi explained his actions to Freud in a letter of 21 October 1911 by saying that he had misread Freud's instructions, mistaking "strike" as "stress."

At the Wednesday Night Meeting of 25 October, Ludwig Klages presented on the "Psychology of Handwriting." Klages had formerly been a crony of Otto Gross's on the Schwabing café circuit in Munich. As well, he had his own eclectic philosophy built around a personal interpretation of the myth of the sun-hero. But his pioneering work on handwriting analysis was built on a concept of character utterly alien to the Viennese. Again the discussion foundered. Again Spielrein did not speak. Freud decided he would have to do something about the reticence of the newest member. He dropped her a solicitous note two days later, apologizing for the poor showing of the society of late and encouraging her to feel welcome. In short order, Jung received an urgent request from her. She needed her manuscript back, for she had been asked to present her ideas at an upcoming Wednesday Night Meeting! Jung wrote back at once:

> My Dear,
> Under the circumstances I must return your work immediately which I much regret since I still am not finished with it. . . . *Please*

send me the work right back when you have made the necessary use of it. . . .

My dear, you must not think that I have certain resistances against you. I only am waiting for a few days of rest and calm to enable me to read your work again without interruption. As long as I am always disturbed when I attempt this, I will never come to a clear, final understanding of it. I am sorry that you worried needlessly. I apologize for this. . . .

Your news from Vienna is interesting—and saddening. Stekel is a dreamer and unscientific. Klages may have gotten a good impression, but why does he go to Vienna? Except for Freud, Rank, and Sachs(?), little there is serious. Please don't betray me.

There was no Wednesday Night Meeting on 1 November. All Saints' Day was a legal holiday in Vienna and the *Doktor Kollegium* was closed, as were the city's post offices. The next day, two letters arrived for Freud. The first was from Jung, whose military duty was almost over:

A few words in haste to apologize for not having answered your last letter. The last 10 days of duty have completely worn me out. . . . I return to Zurich early tomorrow morning. To my immense surprise I am being replaced by Lieut. Binswanger, S. ΨA [parody of S.J., Society of Jesus]. He sends greetings. Once I am out of the brutalities of military life I shall write you a sensible letter. One just can't think here.

The other letter was from Emma Jung:

Dear Professor Freud,

I don't really know how I am summoning the courage to write you this letter, but am certain it is not from presumption; rather I am following the voice of my unconscious, which I have so often found was right and which I hope will not lead me astray this time.

Since your visit I have been tormented by the idea that your relation with my husband is not altogether as it should be, and since it definitely ought not to be like this I want to try to do whatever is in my power. I do not know whether I am deceiving myself when I think you are somehow not quite in agreement with "Transformations of Libido." You didn't speak of it at all and yet I think it would do you both so much good if you got down to a thorough discussion. Or is it something else? If so, please tell me what, dear Herr Professor; for I cannot bear to see you so resigned . . .

Please do not take my action as officiousness and do not count me among the women who, you once told me, always spoil your friendships. My husband naturally knows nothing of this letter and I beg you not to hold him responsible for it or to let any kind of unpleasant effect it may have glance off on him.

The mention of women who spoiled Freud's friendships, incidentally, had reference to, among other people, Ida Bondy, Fliess's wife.

Freud's reply to Mrs. Jung has not survived, though he seems to have asked her in a reassuring way why she should worry so unnecessarily about matters like theory. His next letter to her husband meanwhile was cheerful—"I am glad you are home again and no longer playing soldiers, which is after all a silly profession"—when it was not busy being bemused at his own difficulties:

My psychology of religion is giving me a good deal of trouble; I have little pleasure in working and constant *douleurs d'enfantement* [labor pains]; in short, I feel rather gloomy and I am not quite well physically either. Old age is not an empty delusion. A morose *senex* deserves to be shot without remorse.

Jung's reply to Freud of 6 November 1911 was all official business, though he did mention that Part 2 of his manuscript was still not finished and, indeed, would have to be postponed for yet one more *Jahrbuch* issue, the current one being too full already.

In the same post with Jung's letter came another from his wife:

Your nice kind letter has relieved me of anxious doubts, for I was afraid that in the end I had done something stupid. Now I am naturally very glad and thank you with all my heart for your friendly reception of my letter and particularly for the good will you show to all of us.

. . . If I talked about "Symbols" it was chiefly because I knew how eagerly Carl was waiting for your opinion; he had often said he was sure you would not approve of it, and for that reason was awaiting your verdict with some trepidation. Of course this was only a residue of the father (or mother) complex which is probably being resolved in this book; for actually Carl, if he holds something to be right, would have no need to worry about anybody else's opinion. So perhaps it is all to the good that you did not react at once so as not to reinforce this father-son relationship.

By this point in time, Jung was seriously considering a complete over-haul of "Symbols," father complex or no.

At the Wednesday Night Meeting of 8 November 1911, two speakers, Stekel and J. Rheinhold, took turns presenting "On the Supposed Timelessness of the Unconscious." Though Stekel had some perceptive remarks to make about how neurotics relate to time, the combined presentation was more than a little murky and it did not augur a lively discussion period. Either Spielrein was intrigued by the topic of time-lessness in the unconscious or enough had happened in the previous two weeks to buck up her courage, for according to Rank's minutes the young Fräulein Doktor from Zurich was the very first to speak during the discussion:

> Dr. Spielrein prefaces her comments by saying that she can con-sider these matters only from the standpoint of her school [i.e., the Zurich school]. . . .
> The reason why infantile experiences have such an influence and thus tend to stir up complexes lies in the fact that these experiences proceed along phylogenetic pathways, as shown by the play of chil-dren (Groos), the perversions (inversion, bisexuality), infantile the-ories of sex, and the regression to ideas of that sort in dementia praecox.
> The unconscious takes away from an event the character of being in the present and transforms it into an event that is not tied to any particular time. . . . In sublimation, too, a recent desire is trans-formed into a phylogenetic one.

The remarks were lucid, succinct, and on point: a promising young career had officially been launched. In person, Spielrein seems to have made an even better impression than she does in the historical record. The next two speakers, Viktor Tausk and Paul Federn, took explicit cognizance of her remarks in their own. Moreover, three speakers later, Gaston Rosenstein also expressly echoed one of her points in his re-marks—about phylogenetic pathways shaping fantasies.

Freud seems to have been in a relatively expansive mood himself that evening. His remarks take up more than two pages of the published minutes and show him to be following through on his sense of "how much of the most elementary educational work remains to be done." Among the things Freud responded to was the sudden clarity with which Spielrein's invocation of the phylogenetic inheritance of unconscious fantasy had galvanized the meeting. He had all but officially conceded the point in his letter to Jung three weeks earlier, but here it was running riot—time to add a few cautionary points derived from his recent study of the anthropological works of Sir James Frazer. As well, the idea that sublimation as a process might also be derived from phylogenetic memory was quite unorthodox. This is what Freud said on the subject:

> The interpretation of children's play by Groos (Spielrein) is flat: it is not a matter of preparation for life but of applications of wish-fulfillment. . . .
>
> The possibilities of association prove to be the basis for all magic; if an individual arrives at these associations, he is bound to produce the self-same superstition that his forefathers produced. As long as it is possible for us to explain these things by an analysis of psychic phenomena, we are not justified in coming to the conclusion that a store of memories has been carried along phylogenetically. What remains unexplained, after this analysis of the psychic phenomena of regression, may then be regarded as phylogenetic memory.
>
> Sublimation is not a process that makes use of the unconscious (Spielrein), but one that occurs precisely with the help of the potential of the conscious component.

A little later in his remarks, Freud mentioned more favorably another of Spielrein's points, about the unconscious not knowing time, in rounding out his portrayal of the unconscious as a system.

Freud's qualification of the theory of the phylogenetic inheritance of ideas fell short of a general dismissal, and Spielrein's only cause for chagrin was that he had not previously ventured this caveat at either of the last two psychoanalytic congresses, when members of the Zurich school had essentially presented the same basic idea. Perhaps Freud had just now thought of it. But his remarks on children's play and sublimation were another matter altogether. Evidently the tenets of psychoanalysis were going to be somewhat different here in Vienna than they had been in Zurich. Spielrein promptly wrote off to Zurich asking for clarification. No doubt, too, she also wrote to ask where her manuscript was, for Jung still had not returned it.

Jung's excuse was that he had misplaced her address. As for the manuscript, he finally let go of it on Monday, 13 November:

> I pray you to send me the work again as soon as possible. In the second part of my work (Have I sent you the first part separately?) I have referred to your ideas. I would like to do the same with your newer work. So that a harmony may arise.

Meanwhile, Freud had penned his own letter to Jung. The letter, dated Sunday, 12 November 1911, was clearly intended to be reassuring on every count. First some *Jahrbuch* matters involving Stekel and Silberer were gracefully cleared out of the way. Next, Spielrein's first contribution to a discussion earlier that week was noted gently: "At the last meeting Fräulein Spielrein spoke up for the first time; she was very intelligent and methodical." Then, hedging against the chance that the anxiety in Zurich had anything to do with the Fräulein Doktor's presence in Vienna, Freud promptly undercut it by jumping to the subject of another visitor from Zurich who was visiting in Vienna, A. Storfer. The point was that Storfer, too, had once been hospitalized at the Burghölzli—A. A. Brill had done the treatment and then published the case—and, like Spielrein, had since joined the movement in another capacity. The implication was that in matters having to do with former patients who turned up in other roles, medical discretion would of course continue to be honored. Finally, after all these reassuring items, Freud got down to the thing Emma Jung had been worried about, Carl's book. The tone was permissive, almost loving, though the reader looking carefully for irony can find that, too:

> The reading for my psychology of religion is going slowly. One of the nicest works I have read (again) is that of a well-known author on the "Transformations and Symbols of the Libido." In it many things are so well-expressed that they seem to have taken on definitive form and in this form impress themselves on the memory. Sometimes I have a feeling that his horizon has been too narrowed by Christianity. And sometimes he seems to be more above the material than in it. But it is the best thing this promising author has written, up to now, though he will do still better. . . .
>
> Not least, I am delighted by the many points of agreement with

things I have already said or would *like* to say. Since you yourself are this author, I shall continue and make an admission: it is a torment to me to think, when I conceive an idea now and then, that I may be taking something away from you. . . . Why in God's name did I allow myself to follow you into this field? You must give me some suggestions. But probably my tunnels will be far more subterranean than your shafts and we shall pass each other by, but every time I rise to the surface I shall be able to greet you. "Greetings" is a good cue to end this long letter. I need only add a "heartfelt," addressed also to your wife and children.

But that was not the only letter Freud sent off to Zurich; the other was somewhat harsher, at least if we judge from Mrs. Jung's reply, which was written Tuesday, 14 November:

You were really annoyed by my letter, weren't you? I was too, and now I am cured of my megalomania and am wondering why the devil the unconscious had to make you, of all people, the victim of this madness. And here I must confess, very reluctantly, that you are right: my last letter, specially the tone of it, was really directed to the father-imago. . . .

. . . I do not mean at all that Carl should set no store by your opinion; it goes without saying that one recognizes an authority, and if one cannot it is only a sign of over-compensated insecurity. . . . Lately Carl has been analysing his attitude to his work and has discovered some resistances to it. I had connected these misgivings about Part II with his constant worry over what you would say about it, etc. . . . Now it appears that this fear of your opinion was only a pretext for not going on with the self-analysis which this work in fact means. I realize that I have projected something from my immediate neighborhood into distant Vienna and am vexed that it is always the nearest thing that one sees worst. . . .

Please write nothing of this to Carl; things are going badly enough with me as it is.

The subject of "authority" had finally come up—apparently Freud had found a way of asking about it in his letter—but it did not bring the enlightenment which Freud may have hoped for. In any case, it was now plain to Mrs. Jung that she was bungling things. It is plain to anyone who reads her plaintive second and third letters that she was

more than a little depressed. And it was plain to Freud that, whatever
the causes of Mrs. Jung's depression, he was not going to find out
what he wanted to know by continuing to write her behind her husband's back.

SEX AND DEATH

AT THE WEDNESDAY Night Meeting of 15 November, Theodore Reik
presented on the relation of sexuality to death. Though Reik was a
relative newcomer, the topic was an old one and it had come up repeatedly in the Wednesday Night Meetings over the years, with the
result that many of the older members, most especially Stekel and
Freud, had long since worked out their own idiosyncratic views as to
such things as a "life instinct" and a "death instinct" and whether
they had any part to play in neurotic anxiety.

Reik tried for a broad-based synthesis. His presentation was extremely eclectic, touching on everything from Christianity to the Hindu
goddess of destruction, Kali, from Fliess's famous maxim that all anxiety constituted a fear of death to the phenomenon of "one-day flies"
which die after procreating, from syphilis to the sadomasochistic fantasies of sex criminals. The discussion which followed was extremely
animated and even more wide-ranging. Federn, Tausk, Sadger, Sachs,
Eduard Hitschmann, and Rosenstein all spoke before Spielrein was
finally recognized:

> Spielrein has dealt with many of the problems discussed today in
> a work that has already been completed (Destruction as the Cause
> of Coming into Being). She has discussed the fear of the dissolution
> of the ego or the fear of the transformation into a different person-
> ality . . . The biological relationship, as well as death fantasies as
> punishment for incestuous fantasies, are also taken up there.
> Thoughts about death are contained in the sexual instinct itself; it
> is only that in one instance the life components are given emphasis,
> in another the death components . . .

Stekel spoke next after Spielrein, and then Freud took the floor. He
began by going through his theory of neurotic anxiety. In effect, he
was taking the precautionary step of reminding the group, and informing the newcomer, what the chairman's position was. Then he spoke
on children's reactions to death and linked this to their inability to

master their own ambivalence in the course of mourning. And, finally, he touched on the subject of Christianity, mildly criticizing an argument in Jung's latest work which Federn had brought up.

Freud's were the remarks of an increasingly perplexed man. For that morning there had arrived not only Mrs. Jung's third letter (above), but her husband's reply to his own long, reassuring letter of 12 November. Jung was full of wary compliments:

> You are a dangerous rival—if one has to speak of rivalry. Yet I think it has to be this way, for a natural development cannot be halted, nor should one try to halt it. Our personal differences will make our work different. You dig up the precious stones, but I have the "degree of extension."

Jung was also full of various editorial matters, including complaints from the *Jahrbuch*'s publisher that some articles were just too long. He defended his judgment while delicately broaching a new topic: "But papers like Spielrein's are worth including. Perhaps you will give me your views." With regard to his own work, however, Jung was ready to announce something important, something that seemed to go well beyond the "self-analysis" his wife was talking about:

> In my second part I have got down to a fundamental discussion of the libido theory. That passage in your Schreber analysis where you ran into the libido problem (loss of libido = loss of reality) is one of the points where our mental paths cross. In my view the concept of libido as set forth in the *Three Essays* needs to be supplemented by the genetic factor to make it applicable to Dem. praec.

Jung had decided to take the fateful step. He was going to revise his theory.

Freud replied the next day. But his letter of 16 November 1911 was, as it announced in its first sentence, "Strictly business," and it made no mention of Jung's "genetic" revision of the libido theory. Among the business matters was the following: "Spielrein's paper certainly belongs in the *Jahrbuch* and nowhere else." In effect, the two men had now taken cognizance of Spielrein's paper and had agreed that it, at least, was not an issue between them, though in fact Freud had not read it yet.

On Wednesday evening, 22 November, the Vienna society had the first of a planned series of discussions on masturbation, discussions which were intended to appear as a separate volume. Spielrein did not speak, perhaps because the topic was potentially embarrassing. Masturbation had figured prominently in her own case description, used by Jung in "The Freudian Theory of Hysteria," and she may have worried that if she were not sufficiently detached in her comments, she might inadvertently bring that unhappy fact of her history to mind. Besides this, she was scheduled to speak the following week. She may simply have been preoccupied with preparing her own talk.

The post from Zurich next brought something for Spielrein: a letter from Jung of 24 November 1911, which sought to answer her query as to the differences between Zurich and Vienna. On the matter of phylogenetic inheritance, Jung predicted (accurately but with misplaced confidence) that Freud would soon come around to his position. But he warned that the basic differences between Zurich and Vienna were going to become even more evident once he had published Part 2 of his study. That, incidentally, was coming along well: "I am writing in my own style now." More generally, according to Jung, the Viennese tended to see neurosis as the result of sexual deprivation, while in Zurich it was the conflict that was emphasized. Swearing her to secrecy, Jung related an anecdote wherein Freud had commented about a philanderer that the man was not really entitled to have a neurosis. To be sure, Freud was too much of a scientist to keep to such a view, Jung added, but "Out of such an attitude was Stekel born."

Jung had several reasons to be pleased with his current progress on Part 2. What he had decided to do was to insert three new chapters into the beginning of it which would contain the broadened libido theory. And, certainly, his prose style was reviving: the interpolated chapters, though extremely difficult, are far more lucid than anything that comes after them in the rest of the text. But, perhaps more importantly, though he was necessarily gearing up for a quarrel down the road with Freud, Jung had avoided something far worse. Now, no matter what Spielrein might do with her paper, his own theory would be sufficiently different that it would be safe from any unwanted comparisons—and from any revelations concerning their private mythology.

The same day that Spielrein heard from Jung, Freud heard again from Mrs. Jung:

> Heartfelt thanks for your letter. Please don't worry, I am not always as despondent as I was in my last letter. . . . Usually I am quite at one with my fate and see very well how lucky I am, but

from time to time I am tormented by the conflict about how I can hold my own against Carl. I find I have no friends, all the people who associate with us really only want to see Carl, except for a few boring and to me quite uninteresting persons.

Naturally the women are all in love with him, and with the men I am instantly cordoned off as the wife of the father or friend. Yet I have a strong need for people and Carl too says I should stop concentrating on him and the children, but what on earth am I to do? What with my strong tendency to autoerotism it is very difficult, but also objectively it is difficult because I can never compete with Carl. In order to emphasize this I usually have to talk extra stupidly when in company.

I do my best to get transferences and if they don't turn out as I wished I am always very depressed. You will now understand why I felt so bad at the thought that I had lost your favour, and I was also afraid Carl might notice something. At any rate he now knows about the exchange of letters, as he was astonished to see one of your letters addressed to me; but I have revealed only a little of their content. Will you advise me, dear Herr Professor, and if necessary dress me down a bit?

More than eighty years later, Mrs. Jung still commands the reader's sympathy. If she was not the brilliant, mysterious consort her husband might have preferred to accompany him on his excursions into the psychoanalytic netherworlds, all available evidence indicates she was likable, down-to-earth, earnest, devoted. Even her bungled attempts at diplomacy bespeak the sincerity with which she kept her husband's interests at heart.

What Freud made of her fourth letter is unknown. He might well have reflected on his own offhand comment to Carl a month earlier about Oskar Pfister's impending divorce: "ΨA is beginning to shape destinies." In any case, there was obviously going to be little profit in busying himself further in Jung's domestic affairs. Jung now knew of the correspondence, and besides, Mrs. Jung's value as an informant had proved to be quite limited, though one point seemed to have been settled. Most mercifully, the "authority" business had come to naught. That seemed to leave only the new "genetic theory" of the libido to worry about. And Freud had already begun to prepare himself in that regard. Freud was surely consoling in his reply to Mrs. Jung's last letter, but whatever he said, his letter effectively ended the exchange.

Soon thereafter, she began to consult with Leonhard Seif of Munich about her difficulty in getting "transferences."

Freud's own troubles, however, like Jung's, were just beginning. Mrs. Jung's last letter had arrived Monday, 27 November. The next day, Tuesday, 28 November, Freud received a letter from Eugen Bleuler announcing that he was resigning from the Zurich Psychoanalytic Society. The bombshell announcement was completely in keeping with the position that the consistent Bleuler had espoused right along, namely that any scientific society necessarily had to open its meetings to all qualified professionals and to allow free discussion. The previous March, Bleuler had all but predicted that it would come to this. At the time he had spoken in clear, forceful terms about what was happening to psychoanalysis:

> This "who is not for us is against us," this "all or nothing" is in my opinion necessary for religious sects and useful for political parties. There I can understand the principle as such, but for science I consider it harmful. . . .
>
> I do not believe that the Association is served by such intransigency. This is not a "Weltanschauung" . . .

Bleuler hoped that he and Freud could still be friends: "I venture to hope that in view of what has happened you will regard this resignation as a self-evident and necessary step, and above all that it will not affect our personal relations in any way." That was on Tuesday. Sabina Spielrein spoke before the Vienna Psychoanalytic Society on Wednesday, 29 November.

ON TRANSFORMATION

FOR HER PRESENTATION, "On Transformation," Spielrein elected to use the extremely difficult third part of her essay. Perhaps she had been impressed by the local tendency to bring in literary analogues. Or, perhaps someone had suggested to her that it might be nice to hear her thoughts about mythology. Complicating matters further, Spielrein's announcement about her paper two weeks earlier during Reik's presentation on sex and death had somewhat queered the society's expectations. For the discussion that evening had gradually come to focus on sadomasochism as holding the key to certain forms of neurotic anxiety and thence to Reik's topic. In that context, it had appeared that her own upcoming talk had to do with certain philosophical and phenomenological aspects of sadomasochism. Of course, that impression would have been readily dispelled early in her presentation of 29 November. The problem was that it did not make it clear what her theory *was* about. The report on her presentation, as it appears in Rank's minutes:

Taking as her point of departure the question of whether a normal death instinct exists in man [Metchnikoff], Dr. Spielrein endeavors to prove that the component of death is contained in the sexual instinct itself; inherent in that instinct is at the same time a destructive component which is indispensable to the process of coming into existence. The fact that we do not customarily take note of this tendency toward self-destruction is explained in terms of Jung's scheme, according to which two opposing components are the root of all volition; and it is always by very little that one of them prevails. Thus, it usually seems to us that the instinct for becoming prevails; yet, on the basis of a slight shift in the other direction, we see in the sexual instinct only a destructive force.

In numerous mythological conceptions the need for destruction is even directly expressed: death is the way in which any transition to another state is conceived. In neurosis, too, there invariably exists a conflict, which consists in the dissonance between these two components of sexuality.

The mythological concepts of life and death are then pursued into the symbolics of earth and water. The tree of knowledge is shown in its dual role as symbol of death and symbol of genesis, in which role it makes its appearance once again as the wood of Christ's cross. The tree of life is also thought of as the bridge over the water, which is a procreative primeval force like earth.

These relationships are then pursued in the Siegfried myth and the legend of the Flying Dutchman; in this connection it is pointed out that it is in the manner of Freud's savior type that Wagner's heroes love, in that they sacrifice themselves and die. In this sense, Christ, too, is a savior type who sacrifices himself for mankind. . . .

These relationships prove to be analogous throughout the worlds of man, animal, and plant. For the instinct of propagation requires the destruction of [i.e., inherent in] the sexual instinct. Man has a need to come into existence and to perish; therefore to folk consciousness, eternal life appears as a burden. (The Flying Dutchman;

Glaukos.) Only sacrifice is capable of redeeming because it contains both components: one appropriates the component of coming into being and gives up to sacrifice that of destruction. . . .

Destruction is thus the cause of coming into being; the old mold must be destroyed for the new to take shape. . . . True, death in itself is quite horrifying, but in the service of the sexual instinct it is the saving grace.

Some exegesis is in order here. First of all, let us note that Spielrein had been explicit that hers was *not* a theory of a "death instinct" *per se*, i.e., as something distinct from sexuality. Then, too, we should note that somewhere in the course of this presentation, Spielrein brought up the relation of repression to the destructive component of sexuality; the ensuing discussion makes this evident, even if Rank elected not to record the point. On a different subject, her mention of a "savior type" was derived from Freud's essay "A Special Type of Choice of Object Made by Men," where he depicted a kind of man who seeks to rescue a fallen woman. It was *not* a feature of Freud's portrait of this type that they also seek to sacrifice themselves in this endeavor. This feature Spielrein had read into Freud's essay. That Siegfried might be a "savior" type in Freud's terms was not implausible, but that Christ had also been such a type was sure to have struck the chairman as quite curious. Her further argument that sacrifice in general was derived from the sexual instinct, specifically that it was a means of discharging its destructive component, represented an attempt to square her theory with Jung's. Again, it would have struck the chairman curious that "sacrifice" was such a prominent theme.

But perhaps the most curious of all Spielrein's points was her initial one about "Jung's scheme, according to which two opposing components are the root of all volition." Conceivably, Spielrein was thinking of some remark Jung may have made somewhere along the way about a balance between incestuous and procreative libido in line with the theory in the Herisau lecture. But, as Spielrein actually stated it, she was attributing to Jung what was actually Eugen Bleuler's more general theory of "ambivalence," derived from Darwin, namely that there was an intrinsic balance between every emotion and its opposite. Exactly one year earlier to the day, Jung had written Freud a letter positively blasting Bleuler's theory as nothing less than a "biological straitjacket." And, in the interim, Jung had gone into print expressly attacking Bleuler's idea. Now it appeared as though he had simultaneously been preaching the very same idea to his protégée—and claiming it as his own innovation. In short, Spielrein's talk presented a number of interpretive difficulties for her audience, most especially for Freud, who could have reasonably counted himself the most knowledgeable in terms of his prior acquaintance with the tenets of the Zurich school.

Sachs was the first to speak during the discussion; he took as his principal target what he termed Jung's theory of ambivalence. Tausk spoke next. He was delighted at the philosophical tenor of the presentation and he found her view "that resistance to sexuality stems from the destructive element . . . a valuable one."

And then the discussion went completely awry. The next four speakers—Federn, Rosenstein, Rheinhold, and Stekel—all took Spielrein's paper as a pretext for restating their own various positions on the subject of life instincts, death instincts, and the problems of neurotic anxiety. Josef Friedjung followed by decrying the metaphysical tone of the discussion and announcing that he saw "this presentation as an attempt to find a scientific consolation for the fear of death." Frau Dr. Stegmann, there as a guest and the only other woman present, followed Friedjung. For a moment, Spielrein could have only been grateful that somebody in the room had nearly understood her:

> Dr. (Mrs.) Stegmann remarks that during the course of the discussion the term "life" was not always used in the same sense; one must keep separate the personal and the universal (cosmic) life. The death wish makes its appearance as the wish to give oneself to the universe. The fear of love is fear of the death of one's own personality. Love is indeed to be regarded as a transition from the small individual to the great cosmic life.

Next Tausk, a hypersensitive man, sought to reply to what he took as Friedjung's attack on him. Then Stegmann, in tune with his wife's remarks if nothing else, brought in the great psychophysicist and mystic Gustav Fechner: "According to him [Fechner], dying means to man nothing but entering into the universe, into the state of the world soul. It was on the basis of Fechner's ideas that Nietzsche developed his ideas of the superman."

Freud waited till the end to speak. He first addressed himself to some incidental points which had come up during the discussion. And then, most surprisingly, he addressed himself not to Spielrein, but to her mentor. His comments had all the hallmarks of a prepared text:

The presentation itself provides the opportunity for a critique of Jung because in his recent mythological studies he also uses any mythological material whatsoever, of which there is an abundance in its present version, without selection. Now, mythological material can be used in this way only when it appears in its original form and not in its derivatives.

So much for Jung's "degree of extension." Freud continued:

The material [of myths] has been transmitted to us in a state that does not permit us to make use of it for the solution of our problems. On the contrary, it must first be subjected to psychoanalytic elucidation. Freud takes the Book of Genesis as one example of an especially strong distortion, and demonstrates this in detail.

We know from a subsequent letter what this demonstration "in detail" was about; the point, a most surprising one, had to do with whether there were one or two trees in the Garden of Eden. Freud continued:

The question of whether our psychological hypothesis that the instincts represent incompletely subdued astatic pairs [*sic*] may be applied also in the case of sexuality—an idea that is acceptable— must be decided by way of individual psychological investigations. In contradistinction to our psychological point of view, however, the speaker attempted to base the theory of instincts on biological presuppositions (such as the preservation of species).

Freud was evidently unsure of whose "biological straitjacket" was at issue here, Jung's or Bleuler's, but he was going to have at it nonetheless.

Freud had never before spoken of Jung so sharply, certainly never before the locals who, indeed, had long had to bear up under Freud's fawning attitude toward the hated interloper. Now suddenly they were hearing Freud criticize the Zurich "Siegfried," as they called him. It must have caused quite a stir. Spielrein seems to have picked this up, because she asked for the floor again, rather as though she were afraid she had said something wrong:

Spielrein, in her concluding words, expresses regret that as a result of her failure to take into consideration the fundamental chapters of her work, "Destruction as the cause of coming into being," a conceptual confusion has impaired the discussion. In her view, the sexual instinct is a particular case of the drive for transformation. In speaking of conflict, she referred to the personal ego, and not to the cosmic ego. Whether death wishes are directed against oneself or against another person depends on the preponderance of either the masochistic or the sadistic component. The desire to be consumed is a normal tendency; among women, it is often expressed as a fantasy of destruction.

These remarks, unfortunately, would have done little to clarify her ideas for this particular audience and even less would they have damped down the buzz occasioned by Freud's extended criticism of Jung. Her invocation of a "drive for transformation," in particular, would only have added to the general perplexity her presentation had caused.

From the perspective of the young Fräulein Doktor, it must have been a terribly disappointing evening. Not only had she utterly failed to win recognition for her new theory, a bitter enough disappointment in itself, but there was the further disconcerting realization—she surely sensed the emotions of the moment—that her new milieu was not at all well disposed toward her old mentors.

THE COLLAPSE OF THE ZURICH SCHOOL

JUNG'S NEXT LETTER to Freud arrived on Thursday, 30 November, the day after Spielrein's talk and two days after Bleuler's letter of resignation. The tone was that of a man who has been overtaken by events. Initially, Jung had nothing better to do than to apologize for the harried tone of his previous letter:

> I very much hope that the symptoms of my late ill humour have not had any bad aftereffects. I was furious because of something that had happened in my working arrangements. But I won't bother you with that . . .

What this change was can only be surmised. It is known that Toni Wolff, the "discovery" who had attended the Weimar congress, did some research work in Jung's library for "Transformations." It is also known that this arrangement was interrupted at some point and that, in fact, it was Mrs. Jung herself who ultimately helped Jung finish up the project. Perhaps this was the change in his "working arrangements" which had made Jung so furious, i.e., Emma Jung had insisted that this particular assistant had to go. If so, Mrs. Jung had found a new sense of resolve.

Jung's letter then went on about this and that—he had managed to avoid the prospect of analyzing Pfister's wife, for one thing—only to break off and resume again with news that the winter meetings of the Society of Swiss Psychiatrists had just been held over the weekend and that there was a good deal to say about this. Jung was even proud of the fact that five of the seven lectures were on psychoanalysis, including lectures by himself, Riklin, and Maeder. And then the letter, like the developments it had to report, went rapidly to pieces.

The tensions within the Zurich Psychoanalytic Society had never been really resolved. To begin with, the medical establishment, including Bleuler and Binswanger, viewed the practice of psychoanalysis by laymen such as Pfister with skepticism. Ellenberger, relying on the memoirs of Hans Blüher, has suggested that at this time there was a widespread resentment within the German-speaking medical community against the wildfire spread of psychoanalytic ideas to a larger community of artists, writers, and other avant-garde intellectuals of suspect commitments. Pastor Pfister, though a man of piety and great integrity, was pugnacious and outspoken and hence an easy target for those among the Swiss psychiatrists, prominent among them Ludwig Frank, who objected to the rise of psychoanalysis in their midst. Further complicating matters was the ambiguous position of the Burghölzli assistants, led by Hans Maier, who still refused to officially join the Zurich society although, in accordance with the policy laid down over Jung's objections, they continued to attend the meetings. It fell to Alphonse Maeder, who currently reigned as the compromise choice as president, to do something about Maier.

It was with this set of internal splits that the psychoanalysts had prepared to participate in the winter meetings of the Swiss psychiatrists. Trouble arose even before the meeting. The non-analysts, reading the roster of proposed speakers, became concerned about what sort of meeting this would be. They even worried that a larger-than-usual lecture hall had been rented so that the analysts could pack it with their own invitees. They went to Bleuler with their concerns, who then went to Riklin, who, as was his wont, did nothing. Making matters worse, Jung decided, perhaps in imitation of Freud's final purge of the Adler "gang," that now was the time for a showdown with Maier. Jung took the matter up with Maeder, who promptly took it up directly with Maier, who then went to Bleuler.

The net result was disaster on both fronts. Bleuler finally had had enough and quit. Meanwhile, at the winter meeting, Jung had counted his chickens a bit too soon and had left early the second day. Jung doubtless had much on his mind, but his early departure was a tactical mistake. For after he left, Frank reintroduced his motion that the next meeting of the Swiss psychiatrists should be held jointly with Forel and Vogt's International Society for Medical Psychology and Psychotherapy, which, as it happened, had chosen Zurich for its third annual congress scheduled for the following fall. The motion carried. Forel and Vogt's group, it should be noted, had already successfully resisted the pressure tactics of Ernest Jones and others at their previous two congresses.

With the loss of Bleuler and Maier, the Zurich society had lost all official connection with the people who ran the Burghölzli. The upshot was that in no time at all people like Binswanger would be sending assistants to train there without even bothering to route them through Jung. Meanwhile, with the Society of Swiss Psychiatrists rebelling against their domination, the psychoanalysts had lost their natural recruiting ground. What had been so carefully and painstakingly put together over the previous five years had fallen to pieces in a single weekend.

It would seem that the collapse of the Zurich school would have loomed large in Freud's response to Jung's news. And, indeed, it did. Freud's reply of 30 November 1911 rings with his determination to fight to the end. Bleuler will fall between two stools. Maier must go. They would someday settle accounts with Vogt. There was hope for Pfister after all. But, after a page, the letter then moved on to other topics, topics which also seem to have been equally on Freud's mind:

Here nothing much has happened. The meetings have been going quite well . . . Fräulein Spielrein read a chapter from her paper yesterday (I almost write the *ihrer* [her] with a capital "i" [*Ihrer*, your]), and it was followed by an illuminating discussion. I have hit on a few objections to your [*Ihrer*] (this time I mean it) method of dealing with mythology, and I brought them up in the discussion with the little girl. I must say she is rather nice and I am beginning to understand. What troubles me most is that Fräulein Spielrein wants to subordinate the psychological material to *bio*logical considerations; this dependency is no more acceptable than a dependency on philosophy, physiology, or brain anatomy. ΨA *farà da se* [goes by itself].

If Jung did not feel the chill already, he was not paying attention. But the letter got colder still. Next Freud reported on his own work on totemism, saying once again that it was giving him difficulties. He added: "I read between the lines of your last letter that you have no great desire for interim reports on my work, and you are probably right. But I had to make the offer." Freud's "offer," let it be said, had been as much "between the lines" as any putative refusal on Jung's part. And, if one were to begin reading between the lines in these letters, what sense was one to make of the statement that Fräulein Spielrein wanted to "subordinate the psychological material to *biol*ogical considerations"? Freud went on to query Jung directly:

> I should be very much interested in knowing what you mean by an extension of the concept of the libido to make it applicable to Dem. pr. I am afraid there is a misunderstanding between us, the same sort of thing as when you once said in an article that to my way of thinking libido is identical with any kind of desire, whereas in reality I hold very simply that there are two basic drives and that only the power behind the sexual drive can be termed libido.

Freud had been doing his homework. The reference was to "The Freudian Theory of Hysteria." That paper constituted Jung's historic Amsterdam address, so Freud had plenty of reason to be familiar with it. But, as it happens, it was also the place where Spielrein's case history had been described. If Freud had gone looking for her case, he had found there not only the business about "any kind of desire," but also in a footnote the exact phrase "preservation of the species" which had offended him during her recent presentation. It may still have not been completely clear how it all fit together, but plainly Freud had rounded up a good number of the pieces. Freud's letter of 30 November 1911 broke off with the pleasant-sounding but in context altogether ominous remark: "This letter must yield to the pressure of time, though I could go on chatting with you about a good many things."

For his reply, penned on 11 December, Jung pulled out a brand-new letterhead: across the top in bold black script was printed "Internationale Psychoanalytische Vereinigung" (International Psychoanalytic Association); beneath this imposing banner, in smaller script, was printed on one side "Dr. C. G. Jung, President" and on the other "Küsnach [*sic*]-Zurich." The text of Jung's letter began with an apology for the delay in his response—he had kept Freud waiting more than a week—before making explicit mention of the new stationery: "You will see from the letter-head in what manner I have replied to Bleuler's resignation." As if Bleuler were the subject principally on Jung's mind.

Four paragraphs later, amidst various *Jahrbuch* matters, Jung took up the subject of Spielrein's ill-fated presentation twelve days earlier:

> I'll gladly take Spielrein's new paper for the first number of *Jahrbuch* 1912. It demands a great deal of revision, but then the little girl has always been very demanding with me. However she's worth it. I am glad you don't think badly of her.
>
> So far as possible I shall take note of your objections to my method of dealing with mythology. I should be grateful for some detailed remarks so that I can turn your criticism to account in my second part. I know, of course, that Spielrein operates too much with biology. But she didn't learn that from me, it is home-grown. If ever I adduce similar arguments I do so *faute de mieux*. . . . Naturally I don't know how far Spielrein has gone in her new paper.
>
> . . . I have now put together all the thoughts on the libido concept that have come to me over the years, and devoted a chapter to them in my second part. . . . The essential point is that I try to replace the descriptive concept of libido by a *genetic* one. Such a concept covers not only the recent-sexual libido but all those forms of it which have long since split off into organized activities. A wee bit of biology was unavoidable here.

Jung was following through on his plan, distancing himself from Spielrein's theory while steeling himself for a theoretical dispute with Freud. In the interim, Spielrein had sent back her manuscript, and the same day Jung also sent off a letter to her which began: "My Dear, Do not get too depressed. Your work will be in the *Jahrbuch* where Professor Freud so desires. I *congratulate* you *on your success*." He went on to tell her that though the current issue was already complete, she would be appearing in the next one, alongside her former Zurich colleagues S. Grebelskaja and Nelken. The letter was brief and totally unconcerned. Seemingly Jung had nothing better to say to her than that now it had fallen to him to review Stekel's book on dreams, though in his postscript, he added with belated sensitivity: "Freud has spoken very positively about you to me."

FOR PURELY SCIENTIFIC REASONS

THAT FREUD used the occasion of her talk for a prepared criticism of Jung does not mean he was neglecting Spielrein in other ways. The minutes of the Vienna Psychoanalytic Society chart her participation during the month of December. The meeting of 6 December, a week after her own presentation, had been devoted to a second group discussion of masturbation. Once more, she did not speak on this topic. The following week's presentation on 13 December, however, was devoted to the subject of "Feeling for Nature," and the discussion had wandered into such areas as "art," "ambivalence," and, once again, "preservation of the species." That Spielrein did not speak on this occasion suggests that she was still recovering her composure after her own ill-fated presentation. By the evening of 20 December, however, she was sufficiently composed to speak, finally, during the third group discussion on masturbation. Her remarks on that occasion, about children's sexual researches, parental deceit, and the consequent symptoms of lying and inventing fairy tales, were lucid and to the point. Plainly, by 20 December, the young doctor had begun to feel better about herself and more comfortable with her new surroundings—and fully recovered from the debacle of 29 November.

A few days after the meeting of 20 December, Spielrein left Vienna for a two-week holiday in her native Rostov. It is quite possible that a letter from Jung, dated 23 December 1911, missed her. Jung's letter is noteworthy because he advised her to have Freud read through her manuscript before mailing it back to Zurich. The next *Jahrbuch* deadline, he informed her brusquely, was 31 January 1912. As for her query about how to give a lecture on child psychology, she should look up his third Clark lecture. The letter closed cryptically: "Prof. Freud in his letter spoke very flatteringly about you. I congratulate you on this success, even though I would wish you other successes much more." Jung was coming to his own conclusions as to her shifting loyalties.

While in Rostov, Spielrein lectured on child psychology to a warm reception at the local university. A single diary entry for 7 January 1912, penned immediately after her return to Vienna, noted the fact and then went on to describe her new situation in confident terms: "Prof. Freud, of whom I have become very fond, thinks highly of me and tells everyone about my 'magnificent article' and he is also very sweet to me personally.'' Spielrein's diary entry also noted that she was currently treating two nonpaying patients. At least one of these patients, and most likely both of them, had been referred by Freud himself—a most significant vote of confidence. (At that time, paying patients were in very short supply. Spielrein, however, was financially independent and would have been only too pleased to take on nonpaying referrals.) Given that Spielrein had just returned to Vienna after a two-week absence, it is clear that this change in her fortunes had occurred back in December before her holiday.

But if the evidence indicates that Freud had sought Spielrein out and taken her under his wing more or less contemporaneously with his challenging letter to Jung of 30 November 1911 which closed with the thought that he ''could go on chatting . . . about a good many things,'' the question remains as to what she and Freud might have been talking about. Here I would draw the reader's attention to the following statement by Spielrein, which occurs in a letter to Jung written almost exactly six years later: ''[O]nce I brought Freud a piece of analysis which I had already deciphered: the notion (in my dreams) that I could give a lecture as interesting as one by Freud or Jung; but the same symbolism also revealed fulfillment of the wish to create a great Aryan-Semitic hero. Freud not only agreed with this interpretation; he also found the analysis most interesting and profound.'' Yet another letter to Jung from January of 1918 appears to describe the same incident:

> Once, when for purely scientific reasons I showed Freud the analysis of one of my ''Siegfried dreams,'' he expressed his pleasure at how successfully I had done the interpretation, and then added: ''You could have the child, you know, if you wanted it, but what a waste of your talents, etc.'' These simple words exerted a tremendous influence on me.

Both accounts are inconclusive with regard to the date of this conversation. To be sure, the mention in the first account of her wish to give a lecture as good as one by Freud or Jung would seem to be in reference to her upcoming talk on child psychology over the holidays. And in the second account Spielrein goes on to mention that the conversation with Freud occurred at a time ''when I was not even close to him,'' a description that would seem to place the event some weeks before her departure for Rostov.

In short, there is reason to suppose that sometime in late November or early December of 1911, Spielrein and Freud had a private conversation about one of her "Siegfried" dreams, and her analysis thereof, which conversation revived her spirits considerably. But "Siegfried" had multiple meanings. Not only did he stand for the love-child she might give Jung, one who was to be "a great Aryan-Semitic hero," but he also stood for Spielrein's own spiritual and heroic destiny, one that required her to "sacrifice" herself. Indeed, it was this latter way of interpreting "Siegfried" that led naturally to his becoming a symbol of her professional ambitions, including such things as her wish to "give a lecture as interesting as one by Freud or Jung." Assuming that Spielrein shared both ways of interpreting "Siegfried" to Freud sometime in December of 1911, the effect would have been profoundly disquieting. Freud already knew that "Siegfried" stood for Jung's love-child, had known it since her last letter in June of 1909. But the alternative interpretation as a spiritual symbol, an interpretation which Jung had endorsed in the fall of 1910, would have caught him completely by surprise.

The Spielrein documents have been available for more than ten years now. And it has occurred to many people that Spielrein's becoming personally acquainted with Freud may have had important ramifications in his relations with Jung. But heretofore, the suspicions of most commentators have fallen on her having once been Jung's lover, as though Freud might have looked askance on Jung's having gotten involved with a patient. This is improbable. Jung was scarcely the only person to become involved with a patient. Gross's exploits were legendary, Stekel had long enjoyed a reputation as a "seducer," Jones was paying blackmail money to a former patient, and even good Pastor Pfister was lately being entranced by one of his charges. Indeed, the most extraordinary entanglement was Ferenczi's, the amiable Hungarian having taken into analysis the daughter of the woman he was having an affair with and then fallen in love with the girl. Freud in fact was then currently seeing the younger woman at Ferenczi's request in an attempt to help rescue the situation. That Spielrein had once been Jung's lover would have disturbed Freud not at all. But that "Siegfried," the very symbol of their union, could have been subsequently reinterpreted as indicative of a spiritual striving from within would have been shocking. Such an interpretation turned psychoanalytic theory on its head. In the bargain it would have smacked of what, from Freud's point of view, was the worst sort of hypocrisy, sexual hypocrisy masked by religious claptrap.

The foregoing is a reconstruction. What is certain is that in December of 1911 there occurred a very definite, and unprecedented, shift in Freud's attitude toward Jung. The candle of Freud's affection for his Swiss colleague, which had long burned so indomitably, went out.

IMPRESSED·BY YOUR STATIONERY

FREUD WAITED almost a week before he responded to Jung's letter of 11 December 1911 confessing to a "wee bit of biology." His reply of 17 December 1911 began by accepting Jung's conceit about his "International Psychoanalytic Association" letterhead:

> I am very much impressed by your stationery. Opposition is strengthening the ties between us. Maybe Bleuler will treat us better than before, now that he has become an outsider. That would in keeping with his ambivalence, i.e., his compulsive character.
> I am all in favour of your attacking the libido question and I myself am expecting much light from your efforts.

After these sentiments, Freud's letter drifted about for a few more paragraphs, before coming once again to the subject of Spielrein's presentation:

> You have asked for an example of my objections to the most obvious method of exploiting mythology. I shall give you the example I used in the debate. Fräulein Spielrein had cited the Genesis story of the apple as an instance of woman seducing man. But in all likelihood the myth of Genesis is a wretched, tendentious distortion devised by an apprentice priest, who as we now know stupidly wove two independent sources into a single narrative (as in a dream). It is not impossible that there are two sacred trees because he found *one* tree in each of two sources. There is something very strange and singular about the creation of Eve.—Rank recently called my attention to the fact that the Bible story may quite well have reversed the original myth. Then everything would be clear; Eve would be Adam's mother, and we should be dealing with the well-known motif of mother-incest, the punishment for which, etc. Equally strange is the motif of the woman giving the man an agent of fruitfulness (pomegranate) to eat. But if the story is reversed, we again have something familiar. The man giving the woman a fruit to eat is an old marriage rite . . . Consequently I hold that the surface versions of myths cannot be used uncritically for comparison with our

ΨAtical findings. We must find our way back to their latent, original forms by a comparative method that eliminates the distortions they have undergone in the course of their history. The little Spielrein girl has a very good head and I can corroborate the fact that she is very demanding.

With regard to the composition of Genesis, Freud was of course on firm exegetical grounds: as was then well known, the extant text is composed of two different versions deriving from different historical periods. Freud's other textual caveat was also sound, though it constituted no great methodological breakthrough. Jung had repeatedly shown himself to be entirely aware of the problems of variants and distortions when he had first begun his project over two years earlier. Freud was of course entitled to his opinion that whatever Jung's initial awareness of the problem he had nonetheless run afoul of it in Part 1 of his study. Then again, Freud's own interpretation of Genesis was quite extraordinarily tendentious, going well beyond anything that an informed exegetical analysis of the biblical text could support.

There is a far more disturbing way to read the analysis of Genesis in Freud's letter of 17 December 1911—as allegory. Then indeed it would make sense. The "wretched, tendentious distortion devised by an apprentice priest" would be none other than Jung's theory of the two streams of the libido which Jung "stupidly wove" together "as in a dream." In contrast, it was Freud's contention that there was only one "tree" and only one libido. And at bottom, the insinuation would seem to be, behind Jung's revisions there was the familiar motif of "mother-incest" and the consequent fear of death for that crime. Nor had the woman seduced the man—Jung had once claimed this about Spielrein—but rather it was the other way around. What was needed, to clear up all these mysteries, was to go back to the "latent, original forms by a comparative method that eliminates the distortions they have undergone in the course of their history."

If Freud's letter of 17 December 1911 was allegorical, it bespoke a more intimate knowledge of the evolution of Jung's theory in relation to Spielrein than Freud had previously possessed. It is not known whether Jung ever responded to this letter.

GREAT IS DIANA OF THE EPHESIANS

WRITTEN CONTEMPORANEOUSLY with the letter to Jung were two articles by Freud for the December issue of the *Zentralblatt*, which came out in January. The first paper, ironically, was on the technique of dream interpretation. Freud's point was that the analysis of any given dream should not be pursued so exhaustively that it interfered with the patient's freedom to bring in new material. Though the resemblance was surely coincidental, the same formula would appear to have described how Freud planned to deal with Spielrein: rather than press her further he would wait patiently until she told him more. The other article by Freud was a very short piece entitled "Great is Diana of the Ephesians." In the course of his reading in the psychology of religion, Freud had come across an interesting story about the city of Ephesus in a work by the French historian Sartiaux. In the *Zentralblatt*, Freud simply reported the historical facts.

The ancient city of Ephesus in Asia Minor—"for the exploration of whose ruins, incidentally, our Austrian archaeology has to be thanked"—had been conquered by the Greeks in the eighth century B.C. The Greeks discovered there a local cult of an ancient mother-goddess, Oupis, and identified her with Diana from their homeland. Several magnificent temples to Diana were built over the ensuing centuries and Ephesus became a kind of ancient Lourdes. In about A.D. 54, the apostle Paul spent several years there. In the face of persecution, Paul founded his own Christian community. But, as Freud's account goes on:

> Paul was too strict a Jew to allow the old deity to survive under another name, to re-baptize her, as the Ionic conquerors had done with the goddess Oupis. So it was that the pious artisans and artists of the city became uneasy about their goddess as well as about their earnings. They revolted, and, with endless repeated cries of "Great is Diana of the Ephesians," streamed through the main street. . . .
>
> The church founded by Paul at Ephesus did not long remain faithful to him. It came under the influence of a man named John, whose personality has set the critics some hard problems. He may have been the author of the Apocalypse, which teems with invectives against Saint Paul. . . . [W]hen John went to Ephesus, Mary accompanied him. Accordingly, alongside of the church of the apostle in Ephesus, there was built the first basilica in honour of the new mother-goddess of the Christians. . . . Now once again the city had its great goddess, and, apart from her name, there was little change. The goldsmiths, too, recovered their work of making models of the temple and images of the goddess for new pilgrims. . . .
>
> Then came the conquest of the city by Islam, and finally its ruin

and abandonment . . . But even then the great goddess of Ephesus had not abandoned her claims. In our own days she appeared as a saintly virgin to a pious German girl, Katharina Emmerich, at Dülmen. She described to her her journey to Ephesus, the furnishings of the house in which she had lived there and in which she had died, the shape of her bed, and so on. And both the house and the bed were in fact found, exactly as the virgin had described them, and they are once more the goal of the pilgrimages of the faithful.

It is a nice story: first Oupis, then Diana, finally the Madonna, yet always Ephesus had its mother-goddess. But, we may ask, what was the point? *Freud made no additional comment whatsoever.* The distinguished historian Henri Ellenberger has come to his own conclusions:

> Why did Freud publish this archaeological anecdote? One need not be well versed in hermeneutics to guess its allegorical meaning. Freud (Saint Paul) promoted a new teaching, and because of opposition to him, gathered a group of faithful disciples who became the object of violent persecutions because his teachings threatened certain interests. A disciple John (Jung) came to him, who at first was his ally but then introduced mystical tendencies, took his disciples away from him and organized a dissident community, which gratified anew the "Merchants of the Temple."

To Ellenberger's reading let us add an odd coincidence. Years before, Jung had published a synopsis of a case report wherein an hysterical girl had fraudulently imitated Katharina Emmerich; the patient's name had been given as "Sabina S."

IDENTITY, THEORY, AND POLITICS

THE MOST ominous feature of Freud's little essay was the contrast that it drew between Paul, as "too strict a Jew" to tolerate dissimulation, and John, as a renegade Christian disciple. Part of the beauty of the psychoanalytic system of explanation, considered purely from a scientific perspective, was that it allowed one to dispense with hereditary degeneration and thus with race as a factor in pathogenesis. Freud had, in effect, substituted sexuality in place of hereditary degeneration in the prevailing paradigm, and by making this new variable into a universal, one that basically varied on the basis of individual experience, he had effectively excluded the concept of race from the discussion. To repeat, this was an important scientific advance. From a purely philosophical standpoint, moreover, the theory had the further feature that it seemed to offer a materialistic basis for reinterpreting religious symbolism. As an inveterate foe of religion, Freud had taken repeated advantage of this opportunity. But these features of psychoanalysis also had their rhetorical drawbacks. In an age very much afflicted with racial and religious prejudice, it could opportunistically be argued *against* psychoanalysis that it was essentially a Jewish mode of explanation, one that reflected uniquely Jewish preoccupations. And, in fact, variations of such a charge did crop up from time to time. For example, the Berlin neurologist Hermann Oppenheim, though Jewish himself and the uncle of Karl Abraham's wife, was privately of the opinion that psychoanalysis was only fit for what Oppenheim saw as a degraded class of Eastern, Slavic Jews then streaming into Berlin.

From the first it had been of great political importance to Freud that Jung was a Gentile. His impassioned defense of Jung to his fellow Viennese at the Nuremberg congress had stressed the issue: "Most of you are Jews and therefore incompetent to win friends for the new teaching. . . . The Swiss will save us—will save me and all of you as well." Later that same month, at a Hamburg medical conference, a certain Alfred Saenger had denounced psychoanalytic theories of anal eroticism as grotesque, while insisting that it was fortunate that the north German population was far less sensuous than Vienna's. Taking cognizance of Saenger's remarks in a letter to Ferenczi, Freud had made his overall strategy explicit:

> There one hears just the argument I tried to avoid by making Zurich the center. Viennese sensuality is not to be found anywhere else! Between the lines you can read further that we Viennese are not only swine, but also Jews. But that does not appear in print.

Similarly, in a letter to Abraham, Freud had defended his courtship of Jung on the grounds that "Our Aryan comrades are really completely indispensable to us, otherwise psychoanalysis would succumb to anti-Semitism."

Freud's strategy had indeed worked. With Jung as president and Zurich as the international center for the movement, the allegedly Jewish character of psychoanalysis had not become a salient issue. Now, however, depending on how one heard Spielrein's revelations, both public and private, it appeared possible that Jung might be secretly experimenting with a Christianized version of psychoanalysis. The Jew-Aryan distinction thus was potentially raised all over again, this time within psychoanalysis itself. Moreover, Jung had the full weight of his office to throw behind his ideas. In this context, the import of Freud's essay seems to have been that if it came to it, he was ready for the challenge.

As disturbing as the political implications of Freud's essay were, they were as nothing compared to the import that it had in regard to Freud's personal feeling toward Jung. Let us recall that Freud's own identity as a Jew had two distinct strands in it, one proud and militant, the other cosmopolitan and assimilated. In his personal feeling for Jung, in particular, Freud seems to have been living out vicariously the cosmopolitan and assimilated side of his own identity. Paradoxically, Freud's identification with Jung had actually become more deeply rooted when Karl Abraham happened along. For with Abraham, Freud was free to live out the other, indomitably Jewish, side of his identity. With Jung, Freud plotted the rise of the International; with Abraham, he gave free rein to all his suspicions about Aryans, Christians, and the Swiss. The pressure of holding in tandem these two respective sides of Freud's identity had told in the relationship between Abraham and Jung. They quickly became rivals, each deeply suspicious of the other. But, whatever Freud was ready to say and write to Abraham, his deeper passion, as Abraham gradually realized to his chagrin, had always lain with Jung. In an important sense, Freud had never experienced Jung in the terms he regularly used in his relationship with Abraham. For Freud, Jung was not a Christian, nor an Aryan, nor even a Swiss—he was himself as he wished he had been when he was Jung's age.

This is the proper backdrop for understanding the enormous significance both of Freud's letter of 17 December 1911 and of "Great is Diana of the Ephesians." The issue of Christian versus Jew had explicitly been raised in Freud's mind. And for the first time, I submit, Freud began to experience Jung as Aryan and wholly other, as something completely outside the scope of his own personality. The longstanding identification, the sense of participating in Jung's personality, had given way to an incipient sense of strangeness and alienation. Here let me hasten to add that while there were significant differences between the two men, these differences in reality had little to do with their being Jewish or Christian. But now, when so many things were going undiscussed between them, the issue of Christian versus Jew could not be resolved or even properly discussed. And once that issue could not be resolved, nothing could be resolved.

The relationship between Freud and Jung had lost its originating foundation. Spielrein had innocently played the decisive role in fomenting this change. The message sent from Zurich to Vienna, the message that was her person, had finally been read. Or at least inspected. Spielrein was not in control of the drama she was unleashing, and the lines she had spoken had been prepared for her by Jung. Yet she had brought the house down. Had she meant to revenge herself on the two men, she could not have done a better job.

SWISS STYLE AND ART

As if to confirm Freud's darkest misgivings, there arrived in his mail at the very end of December the offprint of Jung's latest contribution, "New Paths in Psychology," which had just appeared in *Raschers Jahrbuch für Schweizer Art und Kunst* (Yearbook for Swiss Style and Art). This essay, it will be remembered, not only spoke of certain unnamed innovations in the technique of psychoanalysis but also marked Jung's first foray into social criticism. In it, Jung had contrasted the simple life of the peasant with the helter-skelter, and repressed, life of the city. But Freud was most curious about where it had run:

> Your little piece from Rascher's *Jahrbuch* has arrived as a New Year's greeting. It is a powerful, roughshod thing which, I hope, will make its way with the readers. But who is Rascher? A publisher? And his *Jahrbuch*? Is it something on the order of the old calendars with articles to edify and inspire us for a new year about which we know nothing?

As it happened, Freud had guessed correctly. Rascher was indeed a publisher—he would soon take over Jung's works—and his *Jahrbuch* was indeed an end-of-the-year collection of edifying articles on all manner of popular topics "of a specifically Swiss character." But that fact should not lead us to disregard Freud's query. The point was that Jung's "New Paths" (*"Neue Bahnen"*) had taken its title from a popular Austrian novel of the same name. And *Neue Bahnen* the novel had been but one of series of novels in the "blood and soil" tradition—also known as *Provinzkunst* ("Province Art")—which glorified the folkways of the peasant and condemned the corrupting influence of the modern city. In Austria, a good deal of this literature was blatantly anti-Semitic. In Vienna, moreover, this sort of literature typically ran in a journal entitled *Der Kyffhäuser* (after a mountain by that name which figured in the nationalistic myth of a legendary German king, Barbarossa.) And *Der Kyffhäuser* had been expressly founded with the specific aim of advancing the German nationalist movement of that notorious right-wing Austrian parliamentarian and egregious anti-Semite, Georg von Schönerer. That was why Freud was asking Jung about what sort of journal he'd elected to publish in. Anything now seemed possible.

CHAPTER 15

The Death of a Friendship

The whole idea of dementia praecox originates with Kraepelin. Almost exclusively to his work we also owe the grouping and description of the separate symptoms. It would be too tedious to acknowledge our debt to him in each and every instance, and I hope that this remark will serve for all subsequent omissions. An important aspect of the attempt to advance and enlarge the concepts of psychopathology is nothing less than the application of Freud's ideas to dementia praecox. I feel certain that every reader realizes how greatly we are indebted to this author, without my mentioning his name at each appropriate point of the discussion. Also, I wish to thank my co-workers in Burghölzli of whom I mention only Riklin, Abraham, and particularly Jung. It would be impossible to state precisely who contributed this or that idea or observation.

—Eugen Bleuler, *Dementia Praecox, or the Group of Schizophrenias*, 1911

T HE INTEGRATION of psychoanalysis with orthodox psychiatry received official sanction with the publication in June 1911 of Eugen Bleuler's long-awaited masterpiece *Dementia Praecox, or the Group of Schizophrenias*, in Gustav Aschaffenburg's series of medical handbooks. Shortly thereafter, during the fall Congress of German Psychiatrists at Stuttgart, Ludwig Binswanger was inspired by a speech by Hugo Liepmann on "The Significance of Wernicke for Clinical Psychiatry" to think of writing his own parallel essay to be entitled "The Significance of Freud for Clinical Psychiatry." With the Binswanger family name on it, such an appreciation might well have its own impact in psychiatric circles. Binswanger apprised Vienna of his plans during the fall—a nice counterpoint to the other letters coming out of Switzerland—but caught Freud in a distrustful mood: "Perhaps you need to justify a certain reserve that you impose upon yourself at present vis-à-vis the Association." The collapse of the Zurich school four days later, however, made Binswanger potentially more important, and by the end of December, Freud was adopting a less disaffected tone. Binswanger later summarized Freud's end-of-the-year greetings:

In his last letter of that year, dated December 26, 1911, he [Freud] thanked me for my Christmas greetings, "which, as it happens, are the only ones from our circle," conveyed his good wishes to me, my family, and my clinic for 1912, and voiced his confidence that I would live to see the recognition of psychoanalysis and rejoice over the fact that in my youth I belonged to the rebels. (In this he was quite right.) "Don't worry about me; I cannot even wish to be *that old.*" Then he returned to the "vexing events in Zurich": "But I know Bl. too well to hold Jung responsible for them. I fared no better with Breuer: I was willing to be grateful but he did not want me to."

The thought that Freud's gratitude to Josef Breuer went unavailing deserves comment. It was Freud who pulled away from Breuer, not the other way around. Moreover, at the time of Freud's letter to Binswanger, Breuer's seventieth birthday was then less than three weeks away and a foundation was being set up in his honor. The subscription totaled 58,125 crowns and the list of contributors included the names of the foremost scientists, writers, and artists of Vienna. But, as Henri Ellenberger has noted, Freud's name is absent from the list.

The parallel between Breuer and Bleuler threw into high relief the great change in Freud's circumstances. Following the break with Breuer, Freud had promulgated the seduction theory while claiming that it was his new method of psychoanalysis that had led him to this discovery. The quick collapse of the theory had then led straightaway to a period of profound professional isolation. By contrast, as he surveyed the scene at the end of 1911, Freud would have realized that he was now a "man of property," so to speak. There were two journals devoted solely to psychoanalysis, with a third, titled *Imago*, about to be born. There was the International Association, comprising no less than six branch societies, and there was the satisfaction of knowing that even if his theories were still held controversial, knowledge of them was spreading like wildfire. All of this was testimony to what Jung had been worth—and was *still* worth—and to the impossibility of going backward to the days when the local B'nai B'rith had been Freud's only audience.

The issue for Freud was how to keep Jung in tow while curbing the Zuricher's tendencies toward promulgating a different brand of psychoanalytic theory. Given the enormous power Jung had within the association, however, and given that internationally Jung's reputation was equal to his own, the only real leverage Freud had was the emotional capital he had accumulated over the years of their collaboration. Appealing to Jung's sense of personal loyalty had been successful in the past, but such appeals had been both easier and more palatable when Freud was still in the grip of his infatuation for his younger, more ebullient colleague. During the first months of 1912, Freud tried to determine what his attitude should be. In a letter to Ferenczi of 23 January 1912, Freud described himself as a "sentimental donkey" in regard to Jung. In a follow-up letter to Ferenczi of 2 February 1912, Freud was still hopeful that their mutual interests would keep himself and Jung together even in the absence of an intimate relationship. By now Freud was feeling hurt: "Do *I* always have to be right, always have to be the better one?"

The issue for Jung was how to reconstruct his psychoanalytic identity to accommodate his new theories while working within the existing institutional arrangement. It was a daunting proposition in any case, but Freud's possessiveness, coupled with Spielrein's capacity to do harm if she chose, made it unspeakably difficult from an emotional standpoint. In the first months of 1912, Jung reacted by becoming increasingly remote, not only from Freud and Spielrein but also from his Zurich colleagues. He rationalized this by telling himself that he was concentrating his energies on his work. In little more than half a year's time, Jung would belatedly realize where his interests lay, and, almost despite himself, would begin to take up the twin causes of theoretical pluralism and clinical relevance as the best ways of justifying his innovations. But temperamentally he was no less autocratic than Freud, nor was he less persuaded of the unique value of his own particular perspective. For the time being, he was more interested in personal vindication than in anything else.

HER DUTY

WHILE FREUD's letters to Binswanger grew friendlier, and his letters to Ferenczi more wistful, his letters to Jung began to focus on a patient known to history as "Frau C." in the Freud/Jung letters and as "Frau H." in the Freud/Pfister correspondence. She hailed from Zurich—by herself a significant part of the traffic linking the two cities—and she had been in and out of treatment with Freud since 1908. Over the years Freud had spoken of her, "my chief tormenter," in consistently disparaging terms in his letters to Jung. In November of 1912, unhappy with her progress, Frau C. decided to have a consultation with Pfister, after which she mysteriously failed to return to Vienna. Freud had mentioned her disappearance in his elliptical letter to Jung of 17 December 1911: "Of course she is right, because she is beyond any possibility of therapy, but it is still her duty to sacrifice herself to science."

Instead of returning to Vienna, Frau C. consulted with Jung, who elected not to mention this fact to Freud. To Jung, she complained that Freud was remote and uncaring. Jung responded by agreeing with her and by providing a demonstration of his own concern, then sent her on her way. The result was that at the end of the year she rematerialized in Vienna telling tales out of the Zurich school. In his letter of 31 December 1911, Freud commented to Jung:

> Frau C. has told me all sorts of things about you and Pfister if you can call the hints she drops "telling"; I gather that neither of you has yet acquired the necessary objectivity in your practice, that you still get involved, giving a good deal of yourselves and expecting the patient to give something in return. Permit me, speaking as the venerable old master, to say that this technique is invariably ill-advised and that it is best to remain reserved and purely receptive. We must never let our poor neurotics drive us crazy. I believe an article on "counter-transference" is sorely needed; of course we could not publish it, we should have to circulate copies among ourselves.

Freud's letter went on to suggest that "The problem with you younger men seems to be a lack of understanding in dealing with your father-complexes."

Jung's letter of explanation, dated 2 January 1912, was delayed in the mails and did not arrive in Vienna for almost a week, which made it two weeks since Freud had last heard from his president. Freud's reply was cool. He was unmoved by Jung's apology concerning Frau C.—"What you write about the Frau C. incident almost makes me feel sorry"—and openly irritated by Jung's silence—"I have been racking my brains for a fortnight, wondering why I have received no answer from you. . . ." In the meantime, Jung had written two more letters, both of which crossed with Freud's. In his letter of 9 January 1911, Jung adopted a less repentant attitude with regard to the Frau C. affair:

For me the cardinal rule is that the analyst himself must possess the freedom which the patient has to acquire in his turn, otherwise the analyst will either have to play possum or, as you say, be driven crazy. I think it is far more a question of our different ways of living than of any disagreement in principle.

What Freud made of this is unknown. Meanwhile, Jung's other letter, of 10 January 1912, was brief and businesslike, though it did get around to answering Freud's earlier query about Rascher's *Jahrbuch*.

In the past, whenever Freud had had one of his periodic irritable outbursts, Jung had responded with an immediate apology and/or an attempt to set the record straight. This time was going to be different. Jung again lapsed into silence. It was yet another two weeks before he next wrote to Freud.

Part of what was preoccupying Jung was that a firestorm of criticism was breaking loose on the cultural page of the Zurich daily paper, the *Neue Zürcher Zeitung*. The controversy had been touched off by a presentation on psychoanalysis at the local Kepler Bund in early December. The appearance two weeks later of Jung's "New Paths," with its cries for sexual reform, had only added fuel to the fire. Ellenberger has chronicled the ensuing debate in great detail. Among the less edifying points raised was the thought that it was no accident that psychoanalysis had originated in half-Slavic Vienna. Among the more sweeping charges was that as a method of treatment psychoanalysis was false, unscientific, and morally dangerous. Jung's own contributions to the debate were more surly than effective, and it was not he but Auguste Forel who brought the newspaper discussion to a close. Forel's initial contribution was relatively moderate, but his final verdict, delivered 1 February, was damning: "I must definitely declare that lucid researchers fully agree with . . . [the] condemnation of the one-sidedness of the Freudian school, its sanctifying sexual church, its infant sexuality, its Talmudic-exegetic-theological interpretations." From there, the debate relocated temporarily to the pages of a local literary journal, where Jung defended the psychoanalytic method in terms of his broadened conception of libido, and then finally ended up in a pastoral journal, where Adolf Keller, another pastor turned psychoanalyst, defended the Zurich brand of psychoanalysis in terms of its sensitivity to moral, religious, social, and pedagogical issues.

Freud first heard of the Zurich firestorm not from Jung, but from yet another patient. Jung's belated letter of 23 January 1912 complaining that the analysts had been victims of public "blackmail" did little to soothe the "venerable old master," as Jung had called Freud in "New Paths." Nor did Jung's apology for his two-week silence—"I am not giving out any libido, it's all going into my work"—work any great magic. Freud's reply of 24 January 1912 was immediate, brief, and totally uninterested. "I have no desire to intrude on your concentration . . . ," it began and for all intents and purposes ended.

In the meantime, Freud had submitted two more papers on technique for the *Zentralblatt*. The first of these was "The Dynamics of Transference." Its chief impetus was to link Jung's notion of "introversion" with the idea of an unconscious positive transference, itself reconceptualized as a manifestation of resistance. The old rationale—"the cure is effected by love"—was significantly qualified. Only the patient's conscious love for the physician abetted the treatment; a secret, unconscious love, by contrast, was said to perpetuate the illness. The second paper was "Recommendations to Physicians Practising Psychoanalysis." Among the things Freud recommended that the physician *not* do were to volunteer information about himself, encourage the patient to learn new ways of sublimating, or give the patient psychoanalytic articles and books to read. Jung, over the years, had experimented with all these devices. But, by this late date, the coming confrontation would not be over matters of method; it would be over mythology. And Jung had come to the point of decision. As his letter of 23 January 1912 noted, he had begun work on "The Sacrifice," the final chapter of his manuscript.

Meanwhile, Freud was true to his word. While the debate in Zurich continued to rage, and Jung desperately wrestled with his manuscript, not a word from Freud. The silence must have been deafening. In principle, it was still Jung's turn to write and finally, in mid-February, he dropped a "quick word" to Vienna, his first to Freud in three weeks. Jung tried to be brave about his situation: he was having "grisly fights with the hydra of mythological fantasy"; in Zurich, psychoanalysis was "the talk of the town"; his wife was fine and "working conscientiously at etymology." It read like the letter of a distracted man, as indeed Jung was, for in the meantime, he had gotten a very mixed message from Spielrein.

THOUGH SHE was back in Vienna, Spielrein was not present at the Wednesday Night Meetings for 10 and 17 January. Presumably, she was concentrating her energies on finishing her manuscript in time for the *Jahrbuch* deadline. She did finally resume her attendance on Wednesday, 24 January, catching the Fourth Group Discussion on Masturbation on 24 January, where she offered the thought that "a woman in love identifies herself with her lover's place." (Freud during the discussion offered the thought that castration anxiety might have phylogenetic roots.) Four days later, on 28 January, a diary entry noted that she had just sent off the completed work to Jung and concluded with the uncomplicated thought: "Now I want to be happy!"

But along with her *magnum opus,* Spielrein also sent the manuscript of a brand-new paper, "Contributions to the Understanding of a Child's Soul," which besides describing two recent consultations with children also contained a lengthy analysis of her own childhood memories. Plainly at this time Spielrein envisioned making a specialty of the psychoanalytic treatment of children, and her remarks before the Wednesday Night Meetings in the months ahead would increasingly concern child psychology. (It was an obvious niche for her as the Vienna society's only woman member, males being barred from this line of work by a deep-seated social taboo.) Unfortunately for Jung, Spielrein's interpretations were uniformly couched in terms of a conventional understanding of libido theory. This was especially true regarding her own case. Though she chronicled the various religious and alchemical fantasies that had occupied her as a small child, also her fears of the plague, in the end she concluded that these were all erotically based. Beneath everything lay the fearful sexual fantasies of a small child. It was a remarkable piece of self-analysis, but her conclusion would have been most unwelcome from Jung's point of view, for he was just then preparing to argue in his concluding chapter that the sexual fantasies of infancy were best understood symbolically, as a manifestation of an archaic phylogenetic heritage, and not literally. It would have been readily apparent to Jung that this most important protégée, whom he was already beginning to distrust, was assimilating herself to the local psychoanalytic idiom. This at a time when men like himself and Keller were finding it convenient to distinguish their brand of psychoanalysis from the Viennese kind.

There are only three more extant entries in Spielrein's diary, two for February of 1912 and one last one in July. The two for February are crucial. In her entry of 17 February, Spielrein noted that Jung had acknowledged receipt of her packet in a letter of 5 February. Jung's letter had been so cryptic—"I hereby confirm the receipt of both your manuscripts"—and so formal—she was addressed as "Dear Colleague"—that Spielrein had become angry. Apparently she wrote back telling Jung so, and for her trouble received another curt reply. In her diary Spielrein wrote:

> Today there was another unpleasantness. I could take no more.
> I wrapped my collar protector around my neck and with ecstasy saw
> myself released from this wretched existence. . . . Oh, because of a
> man who has smashed my whole life, or perhaps I am lying, because
> if anyone were around who resembled him and who were mine, I
> should be madly happy!

The other crucial diary entry comes five days later and describes a dream of the night before. In the dream, Fräulein Aptekmann, whose infatuation with Jung had earned Spielrein's self-confident pity back in October of 1910, announces that Jung has been made director of the Burghölzli. Spielrein responds indignantly that, no, Bleuler is still the director. To which Fräulein Aptekmann replies that now Bleuler is only allowed to go down to the coal cellar. Spielrein analyzes the dream forthwith: the reference to coal is taken from a line of Goethe's: "No ashes, no coal can burn with such glow / as a secretive love / of which no one must know." "Cellar" entails womb symbolism. And "Bleuler" stands for "Freud." Thus:

> Further analysis superfluous. Now Prof. Freud is the one who
> causes me to glow: if Dr. J. were also the director, his love would
> leave one cold (Frl. A.).

Jung had made a mistake. His protégée could rightly claim to have solved the problem of sexual repression, and desperate for recognition of this fact, the one thing so far denied her in Vienna, she had turned one last time to him. But already suspicious as to where her loyalties lay, Jung missed the opportunity and in the process reopened the old wounds.

There was a double tragedy here. Neither Jung's brusqueness nor her sudden shift of affection constituted an adequate summation of their feelings toward each other. The rift opening between them would in the years ahead prove more painful, and more difficult to resolve, than either party anticipated. Beyond that, Jung's failure to take a timely interest in her ideas meant that he was doing his part to undercut the reception of her theory. The loss would eventually rebound in his direction. If one consults Spielrein's published paper closely, it reads like nothing so much as an attempt to mediate between the two theoretical worlds of Zurich and Vienna.

THE HORROR OF INCEST

JUNG'S HARASSED letter to Freud of mid-February had been only his second in five weeks; Freud's reply of 18 February took this in stride:

> I was very glad to receive a letter from you. I am not fond of breaking habits and find no triumph in it. Wrenched out of the habit, I no longer remember what I have told you, and besides, I still want to be considerate of your work.

Next there were various publishing matters to catch up on. The Swedish hypnotherapist Poul Bjerre, who was allied with the Zurich group, had contributed a piece to the *Jahrbuch* as part of a campaign to substantiate Freud's theory of paranoia. Jung had shifted the burden of editing it onto Freud, who now reported his displeasure: "I have edited Bjerre's piece of confusion and delivered it to the printer. It is not very pleasant to have to publish such muddles." Next came a real barb: "I am inclosing a prospectus of *Imago* . . . I should have been glad to see your name figure prominently in this journal and the *Zentralblatt*, but instead you hide behind your religious-libidinal cloud." And after the barb, a warning of sorts: "It seems to me that you are still giving me too much precedence. In my paper on the Horror of Incest I have stressed, to your satisfaction, I hope, the part played by you and your followers in the development of ΨA."

"The Horror of Incest" was the first of the four essays constituting *Totem and Taboo;* it was slated to run in the inaugural issue of *Imago*. Freud's work, like the journal that would publish it, was going forward fitfully. Jung would not be alone in this field. The title of this first essay reflected the anthropological facts—Frazer's primitives did indeed demonstrate a horror of incest—so it is questionable whether one should also take it as a veiled reference to Jung's latest theoretical turnaround. In the *Imago* version, Spielrein was listed among Jung's "followers," though her name was subsequently struck from the book version which appeared later.

Jung thought he detected something untoward. He replied a week later:

> I think I am not wrong in suspecting that you rather resent my remissness as a correspondent. In this regard my behavior is indeed a little irresponsible, as I have allowed all my libido to disappear into my work. On the other hand I don't think you need have any apprehensions about my protracted and invisible sojourn in the "religious-libidinal cloud." I would willingly tell you what is going on up there if only I knew how to set it down in a letter. Essentially, it is an elaboration of all the problems that arise out of the mother-incest libido, or rather, the libido-cathected mother imago. . . . So please do forbear with me a while longer. I shall bring all sorts of wonderful things with me *ad gloriam* ΨA.

Freud wrote back on 29 February; his disaffection was beginning to show:

> What you say about my resentment of your tendency to neglect our correspondence warrants more thorough ΨA elucidation. There can be no doubt that I was a demanding correspondent, nor can I deny that I awaited your letters with great impatience and answered them promptly. I disregarded your earlier signs of reluctance. This time it struck me as more serious . . . I took myself in hand and quickly turned off my excess libido. I was sorry to do so, yet glad to see how quickly I managed it. Since then I have become undemanding and not to be feared. As we know, irresponsibility is not a concept compatible with depth psychology.

Freud then went on to turn Jung's new letterhead against him. Jung's letter had described the situation in Zurich, and about the only positive thing Jung could report was that they had founded a psychoanalytic association for the patients! (Riklin, who went unnamed, had edged Jung out for the chairmanship of the new group.) Accordingly, the rest of Freud's reply was devoted to the shambles that the International Association had become: no contact between groups; only one presidential *Bulletin* (in the *Zentralblatt*) since the last congress; no plans made for the next congress; and still not one word out of the association's secretary, Riklin. Freud's mood about it all is spoken for by the fact that while it was still Jung's mandate from the previous congress to schedule the next one within a year's time, he, Freud, would just as soon skip it.

Jung was not slow on the uptake. "Your letter has made me pensive," his reply of 3 March 1912 began. He went on to fend off Freud's various organizational complaints as best he could before taking up the subject of his flagging correspondence:

> I have not kept up a lively correspondence during these last weeks because I wanted if possible to write *no letters at all,* simply in order to gain time for my work and not in order to give *you* a demonstration of ostentatious neglect. Or can it be that you mistrust me? Experience shows how groundless this is. Of course I have opinions which are not yours about the ultimate truths of ΨA—though even this is not certain, for one cannot discuss everything under the sun by letter. . . . I would never have sided with you in the first place had not heresy run in my blood.

At last, Jung's cards were on the table—sort of. His letter ended with eight lines from Nietzsche's *Zarathustra* extolling the need of the student to strike out on his own.

Jung would never be Freud's equal at the art of letter-writing. Freud's reply of 5 March 1912 was a masterpiece of irritation:

> Why so "pensive" when the situation is so simple? I have pointed out to you that the Association cannot prosper when the president loses interest in it over a period of months, especially when he has so unreliable an assistant as our friend Riklin. You seem to recognize that I am right, which disposes of one point. You make it clear to me that you don't wish to write to me at present, and I reply that I am trying to make the privation easy for myself. Isn't that my right? Isn't it a necessary act of self-defense? . . .
>
> You speak of the need for intellectual independence and quote Nietzsche in support of your view. I am in full agreement. But if a third party were to read this passage, he would ask when I had tried to tyrannize you intellectually, and I should have to say: I don't know. I don't believe I ever did. Adler, it is true, made similar complaints, but I am convinced that his neurosis was speaking for him. . . .

Why, I repeat, should you be so "pensive"? Do you think I
am looking for someone else capable of being at once my friend,
my helper and my heir, or that I expect to find another so soon?

Jung decided to get out of this conversation. His reply of 10 March
1912 thanked Freud for "your kindly letter" and renounced any intention of "imitating Adler." The rest was mostly gossip about other
people. There were only two items of importance. First, Part 2 of
"Transformations" was finally done: "I have finished my work except
the addenda." "Finished" was hardly the right word here. Jung had
just given up and sent off what he had. The reverie of the Destructive
Mother was still intact, changed only by the presence of an occasional
interpolation; as for the rest of the manuscript, Jung simply assembled
the pieces and hoped for the best. The other item of importance was
that he had begun editing "Destruction as a Cause of Coming into
Being": "I'm afraid I shall have to trim it quite a bit. This always
takes me an awfully long time."

Freud waited ten days before writing a reply. The silence was perhaps less deafening than before—his work finished, Jung was now resigned to his situation. Jung's own later account had it that "I knew
in advance that its publication would cost me my friendship with
Freud."

JESUS AND NICODEMUS

GIVEN THE circumstances under which Jung composed the last chapter of his work "The Sacrifice," it would have been fitting if it clarified
his disagreements with Freud, and fitting, too, if it synthesized Jung's
various different interpretations of his far-flung material. In fact, it did
both, but it did so in a way that was hopelessly obscure and offensive
in the bargain.

Let us recall that Part 2 of "Transformations" originally had nothing more to do than interpret the third of Miss Miller's fantasies, the
saga of "Chiwantopel." The last chapter in turn needed only to interpret Chiwantopel's death. The preceding three chapters have prepared
the reader for the denouement: the death of Chiwantopel symbolizes
Miss Miller's deepening introversion, the regressive triumph of her
incestuous longings. But this way of viewing her symbolism, already
formulated at the time of the Herisau lecture, was not what Jung now
wanted to argue. Meanwhile, in the three new chapters inserted into
the beginning of Part 2, Jung had postulated that sexual fantasies rep-

resented streams from an original pool of undifferentiated psychic energy. The symbols contained in these fantasies might point the way to new adaptations to reality.

Astonishingly, in "The Sacrifice," Jung now applied *both* interpretations to the death of Chiwantopel. No sooner did he describe the "phantastic self-oblivion" that would result from Miss Miller's retreat from the "individual erotic conflict," than he reversed his field and gave the alternative interpretation: the death of Chiwantopel constituted a message of prospective import sent from Miss Miller's unconscious telling her that she must sacrifice her infantilism if she wished to go forward in life.

> It is not to be forgotten that the *sexual phantasies of the neurotic and the exquisite sexual language of dreams* are regressive phenomena. The sexuality of the unconscious is not what it seems to be; *it is merely a symbol;* it is a thought bright as day, clear as sunlight, a decision, a step forward to every goal of life—but expressed in the unreal sexual language of the unconscious, and in the thought form of an earlier stage; a resurrection, so to speak, of earlier modes of adaptation.

Interpretively speaking, this left Miss Miller in the lurch: Was she going crazy or had she just come to an important realization? Earlier in Part 2, Jung had cited Jesus' speech to Nicodemus from the New Testament—"Marvel not that I said unto thee, Ye must be born again"—as an example of how religious imagery makes symbolic use of incestuous fantasy as a means of redirecting the libido. Jung now returned to this point when, after an eighteen-page digression on the mad poet Hölderlin, he finally got around to squaring his accounts with his heroine:

> . . . I take it to be a wise counsel which the unconscious gives our author, to sacrifice the infantile hero. This sacrifice is best accomplished, as is shown by the most obvious meaning, through a complete devotion to life, in which all the libido unconsciously bound up in familial bonds must be brought outside into human contact. . . . That such a step implies the solution or, at least, the energetic treatment of the individual sexual problem is obvious, for unless this is done the unemployed libido will inexorably remain fixed in the incestuous bond, and will prevent individual freedom in essential matters. Let us keep in mind that Christ's teaching sepa-

rates man from his family without consideration, and in the talk with Nicodemus we saw the specific endeavor of Christ to procure activation of the incest libido. Both tendencies serve the same goal— the liberation of man; the Jew from his extraordinary fixation to the family, which does not imply higher development, but greater weakness and more uncontrolled incestuous feeling, [and which] produced the compensation of the compulsory ceremonial of the cult and the religious fear of the incomprehensible Jehovah. When man, terrified by no laws and no furious fanatics or prophets, allows his incestuous libido full play, and does not liberate it for higher purposes, then he is under the influence of unconscious compulsion. . . . His unconscious incestuous libido, which thus is applied in its most primitive form, fixes the man, as regards his love type, in a corresponding primitive stage, the stage of ungovernableness and surrender to the emotions. Such was the psychologic situation of the passing antiquity, and the Redeemer and Physician of that time was he who endeavored to educate man to the sublimation of the incestuous libido.

The passage is clear enough by itself, but for the psychoanalytically initiated it contained a further implication. Jung's reference to "his love type" echoed Freud's usage in "A Special Type of Choice of Object Made by Men," where the specific phrase "the Oedipus complex" had been introduced for the first time. In essence, Jung was implying that enduring Oedipal fixations reflected a particular form of family organization—that of Jews. Which was unconscionable, even if Jung displaced his construction back into "passing antiquity."

As regards Christianity, vis-à-vis Mithraism, meanwhile, Jung was reversing himself. Toward the end of "The Sacrifice" he made this explicit:

The comparison of the Mithraic and the Christian sacrifice plainly shows wherein lies the superiority of the Christian symbol; it is the frank admission that not only are the lower wishes to be sacrificed, but the whole personality. The Christian symbol demands complete devotion; it compels a veritable self-sacrifice to a higher purpose . . .

It might be supposed that the foregoing passages would have caught Freud's eye when they were published and, indeed, there is some reason to believe that they did. But, fortunately or unfortunately, their impact was very much diluted—one can easily read right by them without noticing—by virtue of the extraordinary indigestibility of the chapter as a whole. Simply put, "The Sacrifice" was nearly unreadable. All the flaws in the preceding chapters—the endless digressions, the lack of a consistent avenue of attack, the uncertainty of the goal—turned up in this chapter, too. For example, between the two foregoing passages on Christianity, there intervened in the text an extensive and unwieldy discussion of primitive incest symbols and the incestuous fantasies of children, both of which were reinterpreted as indicative of a continuing struggle for adaptation. Yet, as to what that struggle ultimately might entail, Jung was content to speak obscurely about an inherent conflict between the "will for life and [the will] for death."

An even greater obstacle for the reader was Jung's less than lucid handling of his two primary distinctions concerning the libido. In essence, as regards actual behavior, Jung continued to hold to the old distinction between incestuous and procreative libido. But, as regards symbols and fantasies, the new distinction between sexual and nonsexual applications applied. When adaptation to reality is blocked, surplus energy flows off into sexual imagery in an attempt to find an alternative adaptation. The resulting imagery might be sexual, but its deeper meaning is otherwise. In short, the two different sets of distinctions applied at different logical levels. But nowhere in "The Sacrifice" did Jung make this explicit. And without this key, any reader who came fresh to the concluding chapter was guaranteed to get utterly lost.

The result was that when Part 2 of "Transformations and Symbols" finally appeared the following September, not one of Jung's contemporaries, Freud included, fully understood it. On a theoretical level, Jung may have imagined he was being quite daring. In reality, he had succeeded only in being obscure. Nor was his work destined to end his friendship with Freud, as he had imagined. The friendship did not last that long.

HER OWN COMPLEXES

NOWHERE IN "The Sacrifice" (nor anywhere else in "Transformations") was Spielrein's "Destruction" paper cited. As his letter to Freud of 10 March 1912 indicates, Jung had finished his manuscript before finally sitting down to edit her paper. Apparently he felt entitled to rest on his own priority. By 18 March, however, he was writing her a most surprising letter. He had just now begun to realize, he told her, the "incredible parallels" between their two works. Heretofore, he claimed, he had always misread her title, reading "distinction" as opposed to "destruction." Now, however, he had gotten the correct reading: "One wants not only the ascent but also the descent and the end. . . . I, too, speak about it at length." Jung then went on to observe that Stekel, whose *Language of Dreams* is cited in "The Sacrifice," had already said it all.

Spielrein's reply has been lost. On the evidence of Jung's next letter, it is fair to say she exploded. "Once more you get yourself unnecessarily excited," Jung wrote back in his letter of 25 March 1912, adding:

> When I said that there were "uncanny" similarities, you once again took this much too literally. I meant this as a compliment . . . the priority is yours. . . . The death wish was clear to you much earlier than to me. Understandably! . . . I have expressed myself in my work so differently that no one will think you have gotten it from me.

Jung's letter went to observe that they had unconsciously "swallowed" part of each other's souls, as though the similarity of their works were due to telepathy. But this "secret penetration of thoughts," Jung warned her, was "not for the public." Jung concluded by saying that he was glad she was there in Vienna to defend him, as his new work was likely to be misunderstood. "Represent me to Freud," Jung added, quite oblivious to the possibility that this letter might be no more acceptable to the Fräulein Doktor than his last one.

In the meantime, in response to Jung's recent query, Freud had written Jung to give his own appraisal of her thesis:

> As for Spielrein's paper, I know only the one chapter that she read at the Society. She is very bright; there is meaning in everything she says; her destructive drive is not much to my liking, because I believe it is personally conditioned. She seems abnormally ambivalent.

In context, "ambivalent" meant combining love and hate. Significantly, Freud's letter went on to invoke "ambivalence" in a different context: "My paper on Taboo is coming along slowly. The conclusion has long been known to me. The source of taboo and hence also of conscience is ambivalence."

Spielrein's truly remarkable theory was on the verge of becoming a dead issue. Jung had lately misread her as describing a "death wish." And Freud had misconstrued her as speaking of her own characterological tendencies. Neither man took the time to grasp what she had accomplished. Yet where was psychoanalytic theory going to go if not in her direction? However one cut it, some theory of the ego in relation to the problematic nature of sexual desire was an utter necessity, and once this step was taken, the further problem of explaining the specifics of sexual repression practically necessitated the postulate that the ego reacts ambivalently to the dissolution inherent in sexual fusion. As if in implicit testimony to the inevitability of her thesis, at the very next meeting of the Vienna Psychoanalytic Society, on 27 March 1912, Viktor Tausk lectured on "Sexuality and the Ego."

In Tausk, Spielrein had at last found an ally. His remarks were essentially consonant with her theory—with one exception. As Tausk reviewed the two sets of instincts, those of self-preservation and those of procreation, and their differing impact upon the ego, he gradually came to focus on the phenomenon of sadism as representing a special case, in which the two might be combined. By focusing on sadism, Tausk had in effect given a masculine cast to his portrait of the ego. Once his own thesis was absorbed, Spielrein's would be retrospectively construed as describing a feminine and thus, in the local idiom, masochistic version of the same situation. Nonetheless, the similarities were striking, as Spielrein herself noted in her remarks:

> The problem of why the individual defends himself against sexuality can be approached on the basis of the fact that the sexual instinct is bipolar: it contains one component that calls for the dissolution of the ego. In asserting that the ego is dissolved during the sexual act, Tausk is saying the same thing. Klages' opinion that every strong affect bears the tendency toward ego dissolution is advocated also by the present speaker . . . Every psychic reaction has a tendency toward dissolution of the ego into its phylogenetic past; the second factor is that of projection and adaptation to the present.

Spielrein's remarks on adaptation and phylogenetic regression involved the finer points of her theory and perhaps were not fully understood by the audience. But the rest of her comments were completely clear. Spielrein had tried one last time to make it explicit that her theory involved an explanation of the problem of repression.

Stekel spoke next, then Freud. Freud's remarks involved ideas which he would later return to in his own writings concerning narcissism and the phylogeny of repression. About Spielrein's thesis, Freud had only this to say: "Dr. Spielrein was right in stating that the problem of sadomasochism is identical with that of the instinct of destruction." For anyone who had read Freud's letter to Jung six days earlier—"She seems abnormally ambivalent"—the import of this statement would have been obvious. "Ambivalence" was the cause of any and all problematic feelings toward sexuality. In the context of the discussion, however, the import of Freud's statement was not at all obvious. Freud could just as easily have been heard as saying that he supported the idea that sadomasochistic phenomena represented an attempt to bind the degree of ego dissolution, to structuralize a universally present complication of sexual desire. Which is what Spielrein was arguing. Spielrein spoke a second time during the discussion, but she did not clarify her own position in this regard, nor did she ask Freud for a clarification of his. She evidently had not grasped the full implications of his way of phrasing matters. Her theory was being dismissed; she seems not to have realized it.

Sometimes when a person is not being heard, it is appropriate to blame him or her. Perhaps he or she is speaking obscurely; perhaps he is claiming too much; perhaps she is speaking rather too personally. And one can, perhaps, charge Spielrein on all three counts. But, on balance, her inability to win recognition for her insight into repression was not her fault; it was Freud's and Jung's. Preoccupied with their own theories, and with each other, the two men simply did not pause even to take in the ideas of this junior colleague let alone to lend a helping hand in finding a more felicitous expression for her thought. More ominously still, both men privately justified their disregard by implicitly casting her once more into the role of patient, as though that role somehow precluded a person from having a voice or a vision of his or her own. It was and remains a damning comment on how psychoanalysis was evolving that so unfair a rhetorical maneuver, one so at odds with the essential genius of the new therapeutic method, came so easily to hand. In the great race between Freud and Jung to systematize psychoanalytic theory, to codify it once and for all, a simpler truth was lost sight of: Sometimes a person is not heard because she is not listened to.

The meeting of 27 March, when Tausk spoke, is the last for which we have any record of Spielrein's participation. Here the documentary record suddenly grows unaccountably skimpy, with only minimal minutes extant for the meetings of 3 April and 17 April. There seems to have been no meeting on 10 April, perhaps owing to Freud's absence—he was visiting with Ferenczi. Sometime during this period, most likely during the third week of April, Spielrein left Vienna for Berlin. (A letter from Stekel followed after her, complaining that she had not called on him once during her stay in Vienna. What was the cause, Stekel asked, "Phobia or Jungianism?") Her reasons for the change of residence are unknown. Also unknown is when she met one Paul Scheftel, whom she was to marry in two months' time. And about Scheftel all that is known is that he was Jewish, handsome, a physician, and a somewhat difficult personality.

Spielrein was also about to disappear from the Freud-Jung correspondence. Jung had finished editing her paper just before going off on vacation. His letter of 1 April 1912 to Freud mentioned the fact while pealing the death knell for any serious consideration of her thesis. In his letter, Jung elected to concentrate on the third part of her essay, the part containing her analysis of "Siegfried" and the part which Freud had already criticized:

I was working on Spielrein's paper just before my departure. One must say: *desinat in piscem mulier formosa superne* ["What at the top is a lovely woman ends below in a fish"—Horace]. After a very promising start the continuation and end trail off dismally. Particularly the "Life and Death in Mythology" chapter needed extensive cutting as it contained gross errors and, worse still, faulty, one-sided interpretations. She has read too little and has fallen flat in this paper because it is not thorough enough. One must say by way of excuse that she has brought her problem to bear on an aspect of mythology that bristles with riddles. Besides that her paper is heavily over-weighted with her own complexes. My criticism should be administered to the little authoress in *refracta dosi* only, please, if at all. I shall be writing to her myself before long.

During his vacation in early April, Jung visited the town of Ravenna and there, in the company of his wife, meditated long on the stained-glass windows of the chapel above the tomb of Galla Placidia, a woman who had lived in the fifth century. In his memoirs, Jung later wrote: "Her tomb seemed to me a final legacy through which I might reach her personality. Her fate and her whole being were vivid presences to me." On its own, the passage is quite opaque, but for the reader who has familiarized himself with the workings of Jung's ongoing romance with past lives, the meaning is fairly clear. Just as Jung himself was a reincarnation of Goethe, Spielrein was now being retrospectively viewed as a reincarnation of Galla Placidia. It was a strange way to mourn a woman—putting her centuries into the past—but Jung was comfortable with it.

Jung's vacation gave both him and Freud a welcome excuse not to write. The silence was not broken again until Freud finally wrote on 21 April. Amid other desultory comments, Freud made one final mention of Spielrein. It was the last time her name would ever appear in the Freud-Jung correspondence: "Spielrein, to whom I was glad not to mention your criticism, came to say good-bye a few days ago and discussed certain intimate matters with me." Freud's phrasing was so casual and offhand that one would not think anything was afoot. In point of fact, Spielrein had consulted Freud for a specific purpose. She wanted to go into analysis with him the following fall. Her reason for seeking analysis was to resolve her feelings for Jung, the man who had "smashed my whole life." How the two parties came to this decision, which still needed to be finalized before October, and how they felt about it are both unknown. What is known is that Freud never mentioned the plan to Jung; judging from the extant documents, neither did Spielrein. In any event, the mention of Spielrein was not the only item with quietly ominous import in Freud's letter of 21 April. "My correspondence with Binswanger has revived," Freud noted, adding, "what I had interpreted as flagging interest might better have been explained by illness and an operation."

THE KREUZLINGEN GESTURE

DURING THE first week of March, Binswanger had undergone an emergency appendectomy, during which the surgeon discovered and removed a cancerous tumor. Binswanger's life had been spared by the fortunate timing of his appendicitis attack, but no one knew it. For the best medical wisdom of the time held that surgery was an ineffective remedy for this kind of cancer and that it invariably progressed toward death. Thus, Binswanger mistakenly thought he was going to die and he had asked Freud to keep his secret.

There was more going on than met the eye, however. Binswanger intended to use his last days to work on his new project, "The Significance of Freud for Clinical Psychiatry," and Freud had offered full cooperation. More to the point, Freud had asked if he might not come for a visit sometime soon. And the list of topics for such a personal meeting was expanding. Jung had been added to the agenda, though, as Binswanger later recalled it, Freud was not altogether pessimistic about the current situation: "Although no longer as satisfied with Jung as he had been, Freud nevertheless still hoped for a 'painless end to the whole disturbance.'" Like Spielrein's proposed analysis, the proposed visit was not mentioned to Jung, despite the fact that Kreuzlingen, where Binswanger lived, was but forty miles from Zurich.

Jung next wrote Freud on 27 April. His letter was friendly, if uninformative. At the end of it, he thanked Freud for an offprint of "The Horror of Incest" while adding that, as it happened, he was working on the same problem: "The tremendous role of the mother in mythology has a significance far outweighing the biological incest problem—a significance that amounts to pure fantasy." Jung's cavalier, oh-by-the-way style misled Freud not at all, and in his reply, which is missing, Freud finally asked Jung what his game was.

Jung was a changed man. Currently, he was writing up lectures entitled "The Theory of Psychoanalysis" for an upcoming appearance scheduled at Fordham University in America in September. "The Sacrifice" had been Jung's Rubicon. As he drafted the Fordham lectures, he made no bones about how his position differed from Freud's. Nor was Jung as upset by this as he had been in the past. Judging from the prose style of the Fordham lectures, which are clear and surprisingly persuasive, Jung had found a new degree of inner peace. (In historical retrospect, it scarcely seems credible that these lectures could have been begun but one week after "Transformations and Symbols" was finished. No doubt the topic helped; away from the difficulties and the temptations of explaining ancient mythology, Jung's thought suddenly became lucid again.)

All of this helps explain why in his next letter to Freud, dated 8 May 1912, Jung was uncontrite and elected to go into even greater detail about his revised conception of the incest taboo. Jung's idea had multiple roots, both clinical and personal, but in his letter Jung elected to concentrate on the anthropological aspects of his idea. This was easily the least accessible side of his argument, and Freud wrote back quickly to tell him so: "It will surely come as no surprise to you that your conception of incest is still unclear to me."

Two days later, Freud wrote again to Binswanger. Though the visit to Kreuzlingen had been left up in the air because of the illness of

Freud's seventy-seven-year-old mother, he was now able to report confidently that he would be arriving on Saturday, 25 May. He was glad Binswanger was going forward with his paper and he looked forward to a personal conversation "about that which is close to our hearts, about Bleuler, Jung, and the general world situation."

Jung, meanwhile, tried one more time. In a letter to Freud of 17 May 1912, he not only restated the argument on anthropological grounds but also added in a clinical parallel: "Just as *cum grano salis* it doesn't matter whether a sexual trauma really occurred or not, or was a mere fantasy, it is psychologically quite immaterial whether an incest barrier really existed or not, since it is essentially a question of later development whether or not the so-called problem of incest will become of apparent importance."

It was, in a way, all quite peculiar. Ostensibly the two men were conducting an erudite colloquy on the highly specialized topic of the psychoanalytic interpretation of primitive mythology. In reality, they were touching on a subject with deep personal and professional implications for both of them. The topic was incest. Left unmentioned, however, were both Jung's suspicions about the Freud household and Freud's knowledge of how Jung's new interpretive scheme had originated in reaction to his involvement with Spielrein. Of course, this way of talking, more precisely of not talking, about personal matters had become standard practice between the two men since the voyage home from America more than two and a half years before. But there was clearly some limit as to how long such a non-conversation could continue. In his next letter, Freud broke the tension—and terminated the conversation once and for all.

Freud would be leaving Vienna for Kreuzlingen on Friday, 24 May. The day before leaving he penned the decisive letter to Jung. It amounts to a psychoanalytic declaration of war:

> In the libido question, I finally see at what point your conception differs from mine. (I am referring, of course, to incest, but I am thinking of your heralded modifications in the concept of the libido.) What I still fail to understand is why you have abandoned the older view and what other origins and motivation the prohibition of incest can have. Naturally I don't expect you to explain this difficult matter more fully in letters; I shall be patient until you publish your ideas on the subject.
>
> I value your letter for the warning it contains, and the reminder

of my first big error, when I mistook fantasies for realities. I shall be careful and keep my eyes open every step of the way.

But if we now set reason aside and attune the machine to pleasure, I own to a strong antipathy towards your innovation.

The phrase "attune the machine to pleasure" invoked the relatively new terminology of "Two Principles of Mental Functioning," which had ended with Freud's reinterpretation of Jung's 1896 dream as concealing a wish to kill his father. From there Freud's letter went on to make two points: he disliked the "regressive character" of Jung's innovation, and he especially disliked what he termed a "disastrous similarity to a theorem of Adler's." In connection with Adler, he added: "In light of your hints, I have no doubt your derivation of the incestuous libido will be different. But there is a certain resemblance."

Freud's polemical agenda was clear. Of course, it was conceivable that Jung might miss the subtlety of the reference to "Two Principles of Mental Functioning." As if to forestall just such a possibility, immediately after bringing up Adler, Freud promptly went back and made the reference explicit: "But I repeat: I recognize that these objections are determined by the pleasure principle."

Freud's letter ended quietly—with the news that he was coming to town but would not be seeing Jung:

I shall be closer to you geographically during the Whitsun weekend. On the evening of the 24th I shall be leaving for Constance to see Binswanger. I am planning to be back on the following Tuesday. The time is so short that I shall not be able to do more.

The visit to Binswanger, from whom Jung lately felt estranged, had been presented as a *fait accompli*. Despite Freud's later protests to the contrary, Jung clearly was not welcome to join them. The subject of this slap in the face, soon dubbed the "Kreuzlingen gesture," shortly became a matter of failing recollections and subsequently of revisions of historical fact. We should pause to take in three points. First, it is quite clear that the subject of Jung was explicitly on the agenda for the meeting with Binswanger. Second, the announcement came in a letter which was otherwise a declaration of war. Third, the letter arrived the same day Freud did.

It took Jung two weeks to absorb the blow. His letter of 8 June 1912 took cognizance of the changed state of affairs:

On the question of incest, I am grieved to see what powerful affects you have mobilized for your counter-offensive against my suggestions. . . . The parallel with Adler is a bitter pill; I swallow it without a murmur. Evidently this is my fate. There is nothing to be done about it, for my reasons are overwhelming. I set out with the idea of corroborating the old view of incest, but was obliged to see that things are different from what I expected. . . .

The fact that you felt no need to see me during your visit to Kreuzlingen must, I suppose, be attributed to your displeasure at my development of the libido theory. I hope we shall be able to come to an understanding on controversial points later on. It seems I shall have to go my own way for some time to come. But you know how obstinate we Swiss are.

Freud responded by feigning injured innocence. In his letter of 13 June 1912 he ventured a tortured account of his visit, suggesting that while it would have been an "imposition" to ask Jung to spend his holiday weekend traveling, he nonetheless would have been "pleased if you yourself had thought of it." He found Jung's hurt incomprehensible: "Your remark pains me because it shows that you do not feel sure of me." Yet Freud's account was disingenuous. In his letter, Freud stated that the visit had been up in the air owing to an illness in his family and added, "When I saw that it would be possible, I wrote to you . . . ," thus implying that he acted as quickly as he could. The historical record is otherwise: he had confirmed his reservation on 16 May, then waited a full week to inform Jung.

As for Jung's theoretical innovations, Freud was waiting to become better informed:

About the libido question, we shall see. The nature of the change you have made is not quite clear to me and I know nothing of its motivation. Once I am better informed. I shall surely be able to switch to objectivity, precisely because I am well aware of my bias. Even if we cannot come to terms immediately, there is no reason to suppose that this scientific difference will detract from our personal relations.

Freud surely did not expect to become "better informed" from Jung personally. The following day, Freud wrote to Spielrein. He began by noting that one of her patients had come by to see him to thank him for the referral—"I, too, was very gratified." Next, Freud sought to dispense with the issue of Spielrein's priority on the phylogenetic inheritance of ideas by pointing out that Abraham (writing under his own editorial supervision) had already made the basic point in his *Dreams and Myth*. Nonetheless, he told her, in the future he would "have to amend my praises of Jung in your and A's [Abraham's] favor." Apparently Spielrein had written to Jung on the subject of his tensions with Freud in the interim, for Freud's letter then closed by thanking her for her efforts in that direction, while pursuing their plan to analyze her:

> I look forward as October approaches to receiving your decision about coming to Vienna in order to break your dependence on Jung. I am most grateful for your clever words to Jung: there is no lack of others who are at pains to widen these chinks into a breach.

From the last clause, it is clear that Freud had begun to speak more openly of his disaffection with Jung to his intimates.

"YOU, SIR . . ."

BINSWANGER'S OPINION was that Jung was indispensable for the International Association. Binswanger also felt that Jung had the unhappy knack of first befriending people and then alienating them. As Freud reflected on his situation in the early summer of 1912, he had reason to see that Binswanger was right—on both counts. He also had reason to see that, his antipathies aside, the situation was not comparable to the one with Adler. Jung had only promised to go his own way theoretically; nothing yet was in print.

Yet, if a display of hurt feelings no longer had any impact on Jung, there were others among whom Freud's burgeoning disappointment still had effect. Ernest Jones had come to Vienna in mid-June for the purpose of getting his common-law wife into treatment with Freud to resolve her morphine addiction, her long-standing hysteria, and her attachment to himself. To his surprise, Jones found that Freud's attitude toward Jung was altogether different from what it had been nine months earlier at Weimar. Jones began making the most of a very special opportunity. Privately with Rank and Ferenczi, he broached the idea of forming an elite group around Freud to protect him from further disappointments.

In early July, Freud wrote to thank Pfister for a recent intervention with Alphonse Maeder, the nominal head of the Zurich society, and to issue the following blast at Jung, one tailor-made to raise questions:

> It is a pity that you did not meet or speak to Jung. You could have told him from me that he is at perfect liberty to develop views divergent from mine, and that I ask him to do so without a bad conscience.

Word of this letter would almost certainly have gotten back to Jung, and probably represents the provocation for Jung's letter of 18 July 1912, his first since Freud's tortured explanation of his visit to Binswanger more than a month earlier:

> Until now I didn't know what to say to your last letter. Now I can only say: I understand the Kreuzlingen gesture. Whether your policy is the right one will become apparent from the success or failure of my future work. I have always kept my distance, and this will guard against any imitation of Adler's disloyalty.

To Ernest Jones, who had since left Vienna, Freud wrote that Jung's note could not "but be construed as a formal disavowal of our hitherto friendly relations." To Ferenczi, he went further. He sent along Jung's letter as evidence that Jung's neurosis was acting up—Binswanger also got a copy—while adding that his efforts at uniting "Jews and Goyim" in the service of psychoanalysis were becoming undone: "They separate like oil and water."

At the end of July, Jones wrote to Freud informing him of the conversation with Rank and Ferenczi, this in the context of Jones's tentative appraisal that Jung was abdicating his responsibilities. Freud wrote back immediately, on 1 August, to second the idea of forming a core group. Freud wanted the group to be "strictly secret." Meanwhile, Jung informed Freud that Bleuler would be editing the next *Jahrbuch* issue while he, Jung, was in America. Jung also made it plain that his upcoming Fordham lectures would feature his revised interpretation of the incest question and, in view of that fact, he offered to put his presidency up for discussion at the next congress.

In Freud's letters to his other correspondents, the theme of Jews versus Christians became increasingly overt. To Rank, in July, Freud wrote in terms of his having tried to unite "Jews and anti-Semites [*sic*] on the soil of ΨA." In August, Freud wrote Spielrein again:

So you are a married woman now, and as far as I am concerned that means that you are half cured of your neurotic dependence on Jung. Otherwise you would not have decided to get married. The other half still remains; the question is what is to be done about that.

My wish is for you to be cured completely. I must confess, after the event, that your fantasy about the birth of the Saviour to a mixed union did not appeal to me at all. The Lord, in that anti-Semitic period, had him born from the superior Jewish race. But I know that these are my prejudices.

We had agreed that you would let me know before 1 Oct. whether you still intend to drive out the tyrant by psychoanalysis with me. Today I would like to put in a word or two about that decision. I imagine that the man of whom you say so many nice things has rights as well. . . . Meanwhile, it might happen that someone else will turn up who will have more rights than both the old and the new man put together. At this stage, it is best for analysis to take a back seat.

Freud had already decided he could spare himself having to hear anything further about "Siegfried." The plan to form a secret core group was gaining momentum. The Committee, as it was later called, was to consist of Rank, Sachs, Ferenczi, Jones, and, if the others agreed, Karl Abraham.

Abraham was relatively late sensing the change in Freud's attitude. Having unsuccessfully resisted Jung's domination of the movement for so long, he had given up trying. More than perhaps anyone except Binswanger, Abraham had benefitted from recent attempts to forge a rapprochement between psychoanalysis and official psychiatry and he was in no mood to disturb the peace. Thus, while the more politically astute of Freud's followers were lining up to capitalize on the situation, Abraham had still been writing hopeful letters from Berlin suggesting that it could all be worked out. And Freud, after having for so long waved the flag of their Jewishness in his letters to Abraham, now discreetly volunteered no more than that Jung had taken unacceptable liberties.

In early September, while Jung was on his way to America to give his Fordham lectures, Jones managed to get early pageproofs of "Transformations and Symbols" from Leonhard Seif. These he promptly handed over to Freud along with his own comments. Emma

Jung did the same, though her reasons for keeping Freud abreast of her husband's work were of course quite different. In October, Jones traveled to Zurich and discussed Jung's manuscript with Seif and Maeder. Acting in a statesmanlike way, Jones thought perhaps the situation could still be rescued.

Once he read "The Sacrifice," Freud was in a position to demand further clarification from Zurich. But now the problem was that after a summer of almost total silence, Jung was in America and could not be reached. So Freud decided on the next best thing. He would write to Alphonse Maeder to see if he could bait him into a more damaging discussion. Some time in the early fall, Freud received a further communication from Maeder that allowed him to strike. He mentioned the effort in his letter to Ferenczi of 20 October 1912: "I have answered Maeder's letter as sharply and as honestly as possible, and am curious to see what effect it will have."

Poor Maeder. His own paper on the prospective function of dreams, though presented at the ill-fated Winter Meeting of Swiss Psychiatrists the previous November, still lay in Jung's desk drawer awaiting publication. Whatever Freud knew about it, he had learned either from his correspondence with Maeder himself or from whatever he guessed about its contents from Jung's works. Now, out of the blue, Maeder got a very startling letter. It was from Freud and it began: "You, sir, are an anti-Semite."

CHAPTER 16

The Rest Is Silence

I know that your ideal is an ethical one and that you live by it. Jones tells me that you really would like to envisage analysts as perfect human beings, but we are far from that. I continually have to calm down my own personal irritations and must protect myself from those I arouse in others. After the disgraceful defection [*sic*] of Adler, a gifted thinker but a malicious paranoiac, I am now in trouble with our friend, Jung, who apparently has not outgrown his own neurosis. And yet I hope that Jung will remain loyal to our cause in its entirety; nor has my feeling for him been greatly diminished. Solely our personal intimacy has suffered.

This does not argue, I believe, against the efficacy of psychoanalysis. Rather, it shows that we use it on other people's personalities rather than on our own. . . .

—Freud, letter of 20 August 1912 to James Jackson Putnam

FREUD'S LETTER to James Jackson Putnam of 20 August 1912 accurately reflected the predicament that both Freud and Jung now faced. Some accounting had to be made—their close personal friendship was too well known for its demise to escape comment—but that posed problems, all the more so since there was initially no shortage of would-be peacemakers. The two men could not pretend still to be friends, yet neither one of them was really free to say what the matter was. Apart from a pair of paragraphs in Jung's "Transformations and Symbols," all that Freud knew about Jung's new Christianized version of psychoanalysis he had learned from Spielrein. Freud was unwilling to reveal either the source or the substance of these confidences. Nor could there conceivably be any profit in raising the distinction between Jew and Christian in public. As Freud had written to Maeder, it was important that the Viennese and the Swiss not get caught up in this, that they not "tear each other to pieces." As for

Jung, he could scarcely broadcast his unconfirmable suspicions about the Freud household, nor about how that situation might be affecting Freud's theory. Even less could Jung reveal the personal sources of his own theoretical turnaround. Such things, as Jung had belatedly written Spielrein, were not for the public.

The two men evolved different ways of coping with the situation. Following Jones's and Abraham's lead, Freud began casting around for evidence that Jung was neglecting his duties as president of the International Association in favor of promoting his own career, this while otherwise vaguely asserting that Jung's "neurosis" was acting up. Freud's politicking with his correspondents was designed to bring pressure to bear on Jung from within the psychoanalytic movement. In effect, Freud was hopeful that Jung could be held by the bounds of institutional loyalty and by the necessity of maintaining some sort of continuity with his previous views.

Jung, by contrast, was intent on broadcasting his emerging scientific differences with Freud to a larger community of interested professionals. Jung's politicking was designed to bring pressure upon Freud to open up the psychoanalytic paradigm by appealing to empirical evidence, on the one hand, and by demonstrating that a broadened conception of psychoanalysis increased the points of contact with the work of other researchers. In effect, Jung was hopeful that once couched in the more neutral terms of a purely scientific disagreement, the differences between himself and Freud would become less personally contentious and more easily managed. Jung's strategy was intellectually respectable, but emotionally risky in that he could not really hope to find outside the movement the same degree of intimate support that he had once found inside it. Freud could count on the camaraderie of the planned secret Committee. Jung would more or less have to go it alone.

And so the two men entered the fall of 1912 with different strategies and different audiences in mind. The situation was ripe for escalation, with Jung's courtship of a wider audience seeming to justify the self-promotion charge, while Freud's reliance on personal insinuation and internal political pressure left Jung's scientific challenges hanging. But that was as nothing compared to the unresolved personal situation: however much they might be resolved to maintain a degree of professional decorum, both men were in an emotionally volatile state.

SPEAKING BEFORE an audience of colleagues at the Academy of Medicine in New York, Jung gave the clinical essentials of his new view while pointedly comparing it with older conceptions. Noting that Freud began with the theory of early sexual trauma, but then abandoned it on empirical grounds, Jung made a parallel case for now going beyond the theory of fixation on early fantasies. With a nod toward Freud as a "sincere empiricist," and an admission that the existence of these fantasies was predicated largely on data gathered from the use of psychoanalysis with adults, Jung proceeded to argue that though such fantasies were certainly present in neurotics they were also present in normal people. The determinative factor for neurosis, then, must be looked for elsewhere, specifically in the precipitating factors in the patient's current life. In passing, Jung observed that Adler had come to a similar view, and he closed by arguing that his own revised conception of normal personality development in relation to the neuroses offered a means of reconciling certain of Freud's views with Janet's.

There was a subtext here, but it was not immediately apparent. Jung's address to the Academy of Medicine also broached the subject of his revised conception of libido, in which a general kind of psychic energy might take on a sexual cast in cases of regression. With that conception as his backdrop, his discussion of precipitating events was necessarily broad. Essentially, however, he was returning to the old theory, strongly propounded in the "Dora" case and the *Three Essays on Sexuality,* but eclipsed thereafter by the doctrine of the core complex, namely that the onset of a psycho-neurosis was caused by a present erotic conflict. What Jung believed about Freud, but was not saying, was that the triangle with Martha and Minna Bernays was the source of Freud's recurrent physical complaints. Jung also believed that Freud's failure to deal with the triangle was skewing Freud's theories by causing him to become blind to the critical role of current life events. None of this, of course, could be said, but Jung did volunteer to A. A. Brill in private conversation the thought that Freud himself had a "neurosis."

There was another subtext as well, also not apparent. Jung's own misadventure with Spielrein had left him feeling both threatened and exhilarated. In some ways, his whole intellectual saga since that time was predicated on the attempt to recapture the sense of exhilaration while escaping the sensed dangers of the incestuous fantasy that had first brought it into being. In Jung's defense, it should be added that some of the formulations he had come to in the course of that quest did indeed have clinical weight. For example, it is simply the case that in a variety of conditions, ranging from schizophrenia proper to what is now called narcissistic personality disorder, an upsurge of uncontrolled sexual desire often reflects a failure of current personality integration far more directly than it bespeaks the emergence of long-suppressed wishes. The intellectual merit of Jung's position, however, did not by itself cancel the fact that it was emotionally laden. One is entitled to imagine, then, that the address at the Academy of Medicine, rather in the manner of an extended, personally administered association experiment, brought forth no little amount of emotion from the speaker. Consider, for example, the following passage, which is the sharpest in terms of its formal disagreement with Freud:

> I am unable to vindicate any particular strength to incestuous desires in childhood as little as in primitive humanity. I even do not seek the reason for regression in primary incestuous desires or any other sexual desires. I must say that a purely sexual etiology of neurosis seems to me much too narrow. I base this criticism not upon any prejudice against sexuality, but upon an intimate acquaintance with the whole problem. Nobody can say of myself that I did not adopt Freud's working hypothesis. I found it works to a certain extent, but not always and everywhere.

James Jackson Putnam managed to catch Jung's lecture, and between that and a personal chat afterward, he came to a quick assessment of Jung's position, both intellectually and emotionally. He reported on the occasion to Ernest Jones:

> What Dr. Jung said, in effect, was that while he still held to the importance of the psychoanalytic technique, he had come to rate the infantile fixations as of far less importance than formerly as an etiological factor, and, indeed, as I understood him, as an almost negligible factor in most cases . . .
> He seems to me a strong but egotistic man (if I may say this in complete confidence), and to be under the necessity of accentuating any peculiarity of his own position for his own personal satisfaction. I cannot think that any serious breach would be occasioned by this present movement on his part.

It ought not to escape notice that Putnam was concerned with whether Jung's views presaged his intent to break with the movement. It was already in the air, apparently, that Jung planned to go his own way. Such was the bind facing Freud's former "son and heir": if he left, he was disloyal; if he stayed, he was dishonest. Ernest Jones, meanwhile, hastened to inform Freud of Putnam's report, while suggesting that in Putnam's view Jung was acting somewhat strangely.

More important than Jung's address at the Academy of Medicine were his nine lectures at Fordham University where he had the opportunity to spell out his new views in detail. Jung's Fordham lectures are remembered more for what people said about them than what they contain. It would no doubt surprise many to hear that Jung announced for the first time that the "Oedipus complex" was universal in development and was also the "core complex" in the neuroses. Jung also coined a new phrase, the "Elektra complex," for the female version of the same basic constellation. Then, too, Jung demonstrated his virtuosity as a clinician by proceeding to analyze three different cases along exquisitely sexual lines. The surprises continue for anyone who bothers to read the lectures.

Like Freud, but with different specifics in mind, Jung attempted to anchor his clinical interpretations in an overall theory of the functioning of desire in personality. Unlike Freud, Jung argued for an enlarged view of the libido derived from evolutionary considerations. Whereas in simpler organisms, the work of procreation is achieved by producing an enormous amount of offspring, in more advanced organisms procreation entails a whole host of secondary behaviors, such as nesting and child-rearing, which no longer have an explicitly sexual coloring. In effect, then, the original unity of the libido has been lost, with much of it drained off into these secondary, nonsexual adaptations. But Freud had already demonstrated that, both in childhood and in neurosis, it is possible for these secondary functions to become reinvested with sexual sensations. Why should we not combine these observations under a more general law of the conservation of psychic energy? Where energy is blocked in one area, it will spill over into another, sometimes taking on a sexual cast, at other times losing it.

With this broad "genetic conception" of the libido as his backdrop, Jung went on to argue for a specific developmental scheme based on the relative weight accorded to the sexual instinct at each stage. First, there is a "presexual stage," roughly from ages one to three, where sexual sensations take a back seat to the instinct of nutrition as the organism concentrates on its maturation and development. Then in middle childhood, beginning somewhere between ages three and five, there is an efflorescence of sexuality which readily attaches itself to the parents. The consequence of this is that the "Oedipus complex" is universal in human development, universal but undeterminative. Whether a person becomes normal or neurotic depends on the outcome of a third state of development, that of adolescence. Here the primary task is to go out into the world and find new sexual objects. Where this goes awry, the libido turns back onto the incestuous objects of the Oedipal phase and neurosis arises.

Jung's developmental scheme in turn provided the backdrop for his clinical theory. In analysis, Jung argued, we are typically dealing with mental products caused by regression. Where the patient fails to master his or her current life task, the energy needed for that task is displaced onto the sexual sphere and from there retreats backward to the incestuous objects of the Oedipal phase. But the resulting efflorescence of incestuous fantasies has to be understood as the consequence of regression, not as its cause. And the proper conduct of analysis should entail directing the patient back to the current life conflict, not in developing ad nauseam the full range of his or her incestuous fantasies. Without a proper understanding of regression, Jung warns, the analyst will inadvertently find him or herself in the untenable, and untherapeutic, position of encouraging the very thing that needs to stop, namely the regressive production of incestuous fantasies.

All in all, this was an interpretive scheme of considerable clinical power. It left room for the unearthing of Freud's core complex, but it also addressed itself to the problematics of regression, dependency, and unconscious collusion between patient and analyst as factors which would derail treatment when they were not squarely addressed. In his lectures, Jung demonstrated the clinical relevance of his ideas by applying his scheme to his case material, along the way making pertinent comments about the evolution of psychoanalytic theory in general. To be sure, there were aspects to Jung's thought that would be controversial in any age. For example, between the Oedipal stage and the stage of adolescence, Jung interposed an intermediary stage of renunciation, whose inner logic was said to be best represented by the "Christian symbol" of "sacrifice." (The "Viennese," Jung noted with implicit scorn, referred to the same stage under the "ambiguous name" of the "castration complex.") Then, too, there were various claims made about the prospective function of certain symbols, the part played by

phylogenetically inherited myths in abetting development, and the relation of psychoanalytic treatment to the institution of confession that
many might find objectionable, if not irrelevant. That Jung had carefully tailored his position with a view to placating his Swiss critics is
undeniable. But by emphasizing development and adaptation as independent factors in psychic life, and by allowing for a multiplicity of
intersections between these factors and sexuality, he had indeed broadened, and to some extent refined, the psychoanalytic vision.

The English version of Jung's lectures, grandly entitled "The Theory of Psychoanalysis," was serialized in *The Psychoanalytic Review*. This
was a new journal founded by William Alanson White and Smith Ely
Jelliffe, the man who had invited Jung to lecture at Fordham. It was
the first journal devoted exclusively to the subject of psychoanalysis
ever to be published in the United States. Not only had Jung stolen a
march on everyone else by getting himself into the inaugural issues,
but he used the opportunity to write a preface that was little more than
a calling card for his own views. Meanwhile, for a separate German
edition, Jung penned a second preface shortly after his return to Zurich
in which he announced that these lectures contained his mature criticisms of Freud, criticisms which he had been a long time coming to
and which he had hitherto withheld. With an air of almost imperial
disdain for the very notion, Jung specifically added that his new views
did not signify a "schism" within the psychoanalytic movement: "Such
schisms can only exist in matters of faith." He also took note of Alfred
Adler's latest work, *The Nervous Character*, saying that he had only recently read it and was surprised to find that he and Adler agreed on
many points. Almost despite himself, Jung was gradually becoming
the champion of theoretical pluralism within psychoanalysis.

By the time Jung added these various attempts at self-promotion,
he had already been forcefully apprised by Freud that his Fordham
talks would not find favor. Jung had not written to Vienna once during
his entire trip, but immediately after returning home he sent off an olive
branch of sorts on 11 November 1912. Jung's agenda was entirely clear.
Freud would no doubt disagree with him, but this was no cause for an
open break. All Jung wanted was a cessation of psychoanalytic hostili-
ties—in other words, no more insinuations about his own complexes. We
pick up Jung as he is describing his still unpublished lectures:

> I found that my version of ΨA won over many people who until
> now had been put off by the problem of sexuality in neurosis. As

soon as I have an offprint, I shall take pleasure in sending you a copy of my lectures in the hope that you will gradually come to accept certain innovations already hinted at in my libido paper. I feel no need to let you down provided you can take an objective view of our common endeavors. I regret it very much if you think that the modifications in question have been prompted solely by resistances to you. Your Kreuzlingen gesture has dealt me a lasting wound. I prefer a direct confrontation. . . . I hope this letter will make it plain that I feel no need at all to break off personal relations with you. I do not identify you with a point of doctrine. I have always tried to play fair with you and shall continue to do so no matter how our personal relations turn out. Obviously I would prefer to be on friendly terms with you, to whom I owe so much, but I want your objective judgment and no feelings of resentment. . . . I can only assure you that there is no resistance on my side, unless it be my refusal to be treated like a fool riddled with complexes. I think I have objective reasons for my views.

Freud's reply of 14 November was quick and icy. His letter began with a coldly formal salutation which had never before been used in the correspondence—"Dear Dr. Jung." The first paragraph was no better:

I greet you on your return from America, no longer as affectionately as on the last occasion in Nuremburg [i.e., following Jung's last trip, in 1910]—you have successfully broken me of that habit—but still with considerable sympathy, interest, and satisfaction at your personal success. . . . You have reduced a good deal of resistance with your modifications, but I shouldn't advise you to enter this in the credit column because, as you know, the farther you remove yourself from what is new in ΨA, the more certain you will be of applause and the less resistance you will meet.

The rest of Freud's letter continued in this vein of unamused disdain. Freud admitted to feeling the "same need to continue our collaboration," but found "your harping on the 'Kreuzlingen gesture' both incomprehensible and insulting." And did Jung know that Adler, who had been to Zurich during Jung's absence for the meeting of Forel's Society for Medical Psychology and Psychotherapy, was reporting that he found the Zurich people in "a panic flight from sexuality," but was "unable to prevent them from making use of his ideas"?

Freud's agenda, too, was clear: he was reserving the right to make the comparison with Adler and to draw the obvious conclusions. In this situation, there was nothing for Jung to do but once more offer to resign, and by return post he again proposed putting the issue of his presidency to a vote at the next congress. Jung's readiness to clarify the institutional situation had no doubt been affected by another development. For in the meantime, he had had a visit from Maeder, who was still perplexed by Freud's letter charging him with being an "anti-Semite."

While Jung was out of town, Maeder had taken it upon himself to respond to Freud's letter, which he saw not only as an attack upon himself but also on the Swiss analysts generally. Protesting that his first love had been Jewish, and that many of his friends were Jews, Maeder had gone on to say that it nonetheless seemed to him fitting that a Jew had discovered psychoanalysis: "I am convinced that ΨA had to be discovered by a Semite, that the Semitic spirit is particularly suited for analysis." Maeder added that he felt the Christian spirit was particularly suited for unearthing the prospective potentials within the unconscious and for taking advantage of the phantasy of rebirth as a vehicle for bringing about personality change. In effect, Maeder had unwittingly confirmed Spielrein's equally unguarded testimony on this point: the prospective interpretation of symbols such as "Siegfried" did indeed have as part of its intellectual context a putative distinction between Jewish and Christian psychology. But Maeder had not been privy to Spielrein's confidences, nor had he thought this the crucial issue. Accordingly, he did not stop there. He went on to say that the tactics of the psychoanalysts had been adversely affected by the "Semitic spirit": "Most of the analysts and especially the colleagues from Vienna have reacted against the opponents with a negative father complex containing unmistakably Semitic features." Beyond that, he drew Freud's attention to the prospectus for *Imago* in which the idea of replacing organized religion was specifically broached. Then again, Maeder felt that Freud himself had transcended the Semitic spirit in his own recent writings. He also felt that the two traditions, Christian and Semitic, could usefully serve as checks against each other within psychoanalysis.

In short, Maeder's were the kind of views that should never see the light of day. But Maeder remained perplexed as to why his own theory of the prospective function of dreams, which had still not appeared in print, should automatically be considered to represent a peculiarly Christian view. In his perplexity, he went to Jung shortly after the latter's return to Zurich. Jung's response was immediate and decisive: Maeder should let the issue drop and he, Jung, would straighten things out.

THE TROUBLE WITH STEKEL

ONE CAN only wonder how things would have worked out between Freud and Jung if matters had been left entirely to their correspondence. But, most unexpectedly, they had a face-to-face meeting, once more at the Park Hotel in Munich, on 24 November 1912. The meeting came about because of an unusual situation which had arisen in regard to Stekel's *Zentralblatt*.

It was Stekel's turn to get the axe, though this time theory was not an issue. At the very last Wednesday Night Meeting of the spring semester in 1912, an unusually bitter quarrel had broken out between Stekel and Viktor Tausk. The two men had hated each other for as long as Tausk had been associated with the Viennese group, but this last quarrel apparently—there are no minutes—set a new standard for overt hostility. Sometime over the course of the summer, Freud had an inspiration: he would appoint Tausk to be the book reviewer for the *Zentralblatt*. Perhaps Freud hoped the move would irritate Stekel into resigning. At the very least, Tausk could serve as Freud's watchdog over the enterprise.

Freud had miscalculated. It will be recalled that the compromise negotiated after the Nuremberg congress had given the right of veto to all three principals in the enterprise. Adler, of course, was now gone from the scene, but Stekel had not forgotten what the rules were. And if he could veto an article, he could veto an appointment. He calmly announced that no book review by Tausk would appear in his journal. That gave Freud the provocation he thought he needed. Early in the fall of 1912, he wrote an official letter in his capacity as director to J. F. Bergmann, the publisher, demanding Stekel's removal as editor. And at the meeting of the Vienna society of 9 October, he had Sachs announce in the name of the society's executive board that Stekel had in fact been removed. However, there was a problem. Bergmann also remembered what the rules were and informed Freud that Stekel was within his rights and that he, Freud, was out of line. Stekel was still the editor as far as Bergmann was concerned.

Freud was caught completely off guard. He felt betrayed by both men and thereafter spread the rumor that Stekel had treacherously entered into a "secret contract" with Bergmann. The truth appears to have been simpler. Since the Weimar congress, the *Zentralblatt* had been charged with carrying the *Bulletin,* that ill-conceived presidential news-letter which Jung hardly ever bothered with. As part of this arrange-ment, a subscription to the *Zentralblatt* was prepaid for all European members by the International Association. Freud had assumed that by making the *Zentralblatt* into an official organ of the association, he, or at least Jung, had gained jurisdiction over it. But Stekel had considered the same possibility, and before agreeing to the new arrangement had taken the precaution of conferring with Bergmann about whether this altered their prior understanding. Bergmann didn't think so. That was the whole of Stekel's "treachery."

In any case, having embarrassed himself with Sachs's premature announcement, Freud was more determined than ever. Next he con-fronted Stekel in his office and personally demanded his resignation from both the *Zentralblatt* and the association. Stekel was ready for this, too. Freud spoke to him of the harm he was doing the cause—the familiar charge—and of how he, Freud, was tired of defending him to everyone else. Stekel was capable of a great simplicity, especially in the service of his self-admiration, and he calmly inquired who it was Freud had in mind. Freud shot back the name of Jung. Adler had apparently been told the same thing and had responded with an indig-nant letter to Zurich demanding an explanation. Stekel not only did not rise to the bait but got off a timely barb of his own. He would be practicing psychoanalysis, he responded, long after Jung had deserted the movement. In the end, Stekel was willing to resign from the local society—he did not like quarrels and had no appetite for repeating Adler's gloomy ploy of attending meetings in silence—but not from the *Zentralblatt.* Journalism had become his calling.

Stekel's farewell meeting with Freud had been surprisingly amica-ble, but on the matter of the *Zentralblatt,* Freud could not be appeased. If Stekel wouldn't quit, then *he* would—and take all of Stekel's con-tributors with him. By the time Jung returned from America, Freud had already formed a new journal of his own, the *Zeitschrift,* which was slated to begin publication in January of 1913. Stekel seems to have been ready for this, too. To Ernest Jones, Stekel got off the following friendly warning on 12 October 1912:

You will learn sooner or later that from time to time Freud has to sacrifice a friend. He only has use for people who confirm. Pagodas who say Yes. Your hour too will come, once you arrive at an independent opinion. The next sacrifice is Jung and this friendship already has a hypocritical undercurrent.

Stekel's sunny confidence in the face of Freud's maneuvers reflected the financial facts: the yearly contract between the International Association and the *Zentralblatt* had just been renewed, thus committing the International Association to another twelve months of subsidy. Besides which, the association was still officially connected with the now discredited journal. By the time of Jung's return from America, Freud had already obtained resolutions from the various branch societies endorsing his new journal. But the contract with Bergmann remained in force—and it was up to Jung to find a way to get out of it.

It was a heaven-sent opportunity for Jung to demonstrate his loyalty, and he seized the chance. On his own authority, Jung hastily convened a council of the presidents of the local societies to resolve the situation. The meeting was slated for the Park Hotel in Munich for 24 November. Actually attending were Freud, Abraham, Seif, Jones, Jung, Riklin, and a Dutchman, Johan van Ophuijsen, who was currently secretary of the Zurich society. Jones arrived late, in part owing to Jung's having misdated the occasion in his invitation. When Jones showed Jung the invitation, Jung's astonishment was such that Jones realized it had been an honest mistake—a slip of the pen—but even so, Jones later thought to mention it to Freud, who commented grumpily, "A gentleman should not do such things even unconsciously."

Jung kicked off the 9:00 a.m. meeting by announcing that Freud's proposals should be accepted forthwith without discussion. But Freud insisted on telling his side of the story and proceeded to do so. Seif later recalled that Freud seemed agitated during his talk. Jung then took the lead in reassuring Freud that the association backed him to the hilt. After Freud's proposals passed, the group took up the subject of the next congress and agreed that dream interpretation would be the topic. Maeder would speak for the Swiss, Rank for the Viennese.

It must all have been strangely edifying. Though an air of tension hung over the meeting, Freud and Jung were working hand in glove to resolve two very ticklish situations and doing it very efficiently. Seemingly the organization had never functioned better. Afterward, the two principals went off for a two-hour walk before lunch, leaving everyone else to sit around and wonder which way the wind was really blowing. As they departed, Seif heard Freud complaining to Jung that he had never inquired about his ill mother the previous spring. The illness of the mother had figured in Freud's version of the Kreuzlingen visit. Seif did not necessarily know this, but he did think to himself that Freud was taking rather a paternalistic air, as though Jung were guilty about being insensitive toward his spiritual grandmother.

No doubt during their walk Freud and Jung reminisced about their last meeting at the Park Hotel nearly two years earlier. And the "Kreuzlingen gesture" certainly did come up. There was potentially a good deal to discuss about that, ranging from the illness of Freud's mother to Binswanger's great secret (his seemingly terminal cancer), from Freud's delayed announcement of the visit to the fact that Jung had actually been out of town when Freud's letter had arrived. All that is known for certain is that eventually Jung allowed that perhaps he'd failed to check the date of Freud's letter upon his return. In short, it was all a big misunderstanding. Beyond that, sometime during the talk Jung volunteered the thought that he always had trouble feeling independent when he worked too closely with another man. The best guess is that this came up in the context of an apology about his dwindling correspondence with Freud the previous winter, when, as he put it at the time, all his libido was going to his work. In effect, Jung was shouldering the blame for their estrangement by appealing to a personal idiosyncrasy.

The upshot of it all was that the two men rejoined the group with their difficulties seemingly resolved. Yet, no sooner had lunch begun than Freud began upbraiding Riklin for having failed even to cite him in his most recent publication. Riklin replied that Freud's contribution was so well known that such citations were not necessary. Next, the subject of Karl Abraham's recent essay on the ancient Egyptian ruler Amenhotep came up. Amenhotep, generally credited as the originator of monotheism, had as part of his reforms erased his father's name from public monuments. Freud used this to support his thesis that Amenhotep harbored parricidal wishes. Jung hastened to disagree. Actually, Jung argued, it was all a good deal more complicated than that, since in his own lifetime Amenhotep's father had been considered a god, as had his father before him, and eliminating the old god's name was part and parcel of consolidating the new religion. Here Freud interjected the thought that all this reminded him of the Swiss, and their failure to cite his name in their psychoanalytic publications. Jung now jumped in to defend Riklin and his countrymen by saying that Freud was so well known, etc., etc. But Freud would not let go of the issue and Ernest Jones later remembered thinking that he was taking it all a bit too personally. Then Jung resumed talking about Amenhotep, his tone less apologetic than before: "The story may be crude and even brutal, but it's true to nature. For the father already has a name, whereas the son must go out and make one for himself." To this Freud replied, "Fine, then, that may be true for ancient times, but not necessarily in this instance." After this, Freud fell silent, while Jung continued expounding on Amenhotep. Then Freud fell off his chair in a dead faint.

Jung rushed to the fallen Freud. Jung later recalled what happened next:

> I picked him up, carried him into the next room, and laid him on a sofa. As I was carrying him, he half came to, and I shall never forget the look he cast at me. In his weakness he looked at me as if I were his father.

Not only did Freud look at Jung this way, he said something as well. As Jones later recollected the occasion, Freud looked up at Jung and said—"How sweet it must be to die!"

There was, of course, no question of continuing the discussion, as all eyes were solicitously turned on the fallen Master. Somehow or other, Freud regained his composure. He attributed his reaction to having slept badly and to an upset stomach, and between trips to the bathroom he again ventured the thought that if this is how death felt it suited him fine. After Jung departed, Freud immediately cheered up and began to muse about the mystical bent of the Swiss, also about the similarity between Adler and Jung, who were both courting popularity in America by downplaying sexuality. His newfound cheerfulness aside, however, Freud also continued his litany of psychosomatic complaints, including a claim that a migraine had once traveled down his left side only to depart through a hangnail off his little toe. Eventually the meeting broke up, and everyone boarded trains back to their home cities.

It was clear that something important had happened, but no one was quite sure what. In the weeks that followed, Freud conscientiously tried to elucidate the psychoanalytic meeting of the episode as the result of an "unruly homosexual component" in his letters to his intimates. Seif, meanwhile, conveyed to Jones his appraisal that Freud's faint reflected his "insufficiently analysed 'father complex.'" In this con-

text, Seif thought it appropriate to echo Mrs. Jung's words, "To analyze and be analyzed are far from the same." He also thought to
append the following offensive remark: "It seems that is not without
some untoward consequences that we've been saddled for two millennia with the enormous burden of the Jewish patriarchal tradition."
Seif, who otherwise thought Jung's new ideas constituted an important
advance, summarized the situation thus:

> Today one has to ask oneself: Will Freud ever rid himself of his
> conflict? Can he ever free himself of his jealousy regarding Jung at
> least to the point where he can give him his just recognition (which
> he is doing unconsciously in any case through these fainting spells).
> I think that would be the best solution.
>
> And if that is impossible then at the very least one would hope
> for some semblance of gentlemanly fair play. This is the least Jung
> deserves.

Jones elected not to tell Freud of Seif's remarks. By far the best comment belonged to Ferenczi, who declared in a letter to Freud that he
rather thought something like this might happen. Ferenczi, it will be
recalled, had been in Bremen three years before for Freud's previous
faint in Jung's presence. He knew the two men well, and if his personal
affection belonged squarely and irrevocably in Freud's corner, he un-
derestimated neither Jung's importance nor the depth of Freud's emotional involvement in the relationship.

Jung meanwhile fired off his own follow-up letter to Vienna. To
Abraham, Freud characterized Jung's letter of 26 November as "very
kind" but, at least as I read it, it was not entirely free of condescension. Jung wrote:

> I am glad we were able to meet in Munich, as this was the first
> time I have really understood you. I realized how different I am
> from you. This realization will be enough to effect a radical change
> in my whole attitude. Now you can rest assured that I shall not give
> up our personal relationship. Please forgive the mistakes which I
> will not try to excuse or extenuate. I hope the insight I have at last
> gained will guide my conduct from now on. I am most distressed
> that I did not gain this insight much earlier. It could have spared
> you so many disappointments.
>
> I have been worried about how you got back to Vienna, and
> whether the night journey may not have been too much of a strain

for you. Please let me know how you are, if only a few words on a
postcard.

Jung's display of concern was matched only by his innocence later on
in the letter: "I hope Bleuler has informed you about the articles for
the *Jahrbuch*. I myself don't know yet what will be in the January issue." The January issue would contain Maeder's "On the Function
of Dreams." Jung was pretending that he had nothing to do with it.

In fact, the situation was intolerable. "Kindly" was the last thing
Freud wanted Jung to be. Repentant, yes; kindly, no. With his faint,
Freud had surrendered whatever emotional leverage he had accrued
that very morning in Munich. And with his half-conscious remark—
"How sweet it must be to die!"—he had inadvertently provided people
like Jung and Seif with an enormous amount of ammunition. When
push came to shove, he was going to be hard pressed to account for
his utterance, even if he had gamely repeated it a second time. For he
seemed to have acted out a fantasy of being Jung's father and dying
in his son's arms.

And what of Stekel, who, had he known of the afternoon's events,
would have been fairly entitled to the last laugh? His *Zentralblatt* lasted
only two years longer, but he went on to have a splendid career as a
prolific writer on psychoanalytic topics. Here let it be said that Stekel
had a great many perceptive things to say about the human condition,
even if he sometimes wrote case material to order. It should be noted,
too, that he was a singularly unvindictive man. His autobiography,
written at the very end of his life, scarcely has a mean word to say
about anybody. At bottom, Stekel's problem was his fluency. Freudian
is a language, a language which takes symptoms and turns them into
a kind of poetry of unfulfilled wishes. But, as a language of symptoms,
Freudian is meant to be heard, not spoken; listened to, not said. Wilhelm Stekel had the uncanny knack of writing it.

"THE REST IS SILENCE"

FREUD RESPONDED to Jung's "kindly" letter on 26 November with
a less than kindly letter of his own. Having embarrassed himself thoroughly at Munich five days earlier, Freud had a lot of distance to cover
before regaining his customary composure. As usual, his prose was up
to the challenge. His letter began with faint-hearted collegiality—"for
me our relationship will always retain an echo of our past intimacy"—
before taking up the subject of his faint: "A bit of neurosis that I ought

really to look into." From there, Freud went abruptly into business matters. He hoped Jung and colleagues would be contributing to the new *Zeitschrift,* for it was up to them to keep it from starting to "look like a Viennese party organ." In particular, Jung was invited to comment on Freud's recent papers on analytic technique. Given what Freud knew about Spielrein, the invitation was rather a dare. But that was just a prelude to a far more pointed challenge:

> In the second number [of the *Zeitschrift*] Ferenczi will probably publish a study of your libido paper which, it is hoped, will do justice both to the author and to his work. I am gradually coming to terms with this paper (yours, I mean) and I now believe that in it you have brought us a great revelation, though not the one you intended. You seem to have solved the riddle of all mysticism, showing it to be based on the symbolic utilization of complexes that have outlived their function.

This, plainly, was an announcement that Jung's own psyche was still under scrutiny. Only the ground had shifted. For, in context, the complex which had outlived its function and was now being utilized symbolically was none other than the erotic one of "Siegfried." In effect, Jung was being put on notice that Freud felt free to use Spielrein's revelations as the implicit basis for a potentially devastating critique of Jung's mysticism and thus of his work generally.

Jung would have to await Ferenczi's review with a special kind of trepidation, and to read it from more than one vantage point. Three years earlier, William James had commented about psychoanalysis that its reliance on "symbolism" was methodologically "dangerous." His warning was being fulfilled in an extraordinary way: what was ostensibly pure theory was fast becoming a potential vehicle for personal insinuations. Freud evidently felt very pleased with himself at having figured out how to fashion this most unsettling challenge, for he signed his letter "Your untransformed Freud."

Jung exploded. His letter of 3 December 1912 has scrawled across the top of it: "This letter is a brazen attempt to accustom you to my new style. So look out!" Jung started out his letter by thanking Freud for his admission of a "bit" of neurosis, and then proceeded to tear into him for it:

> This "bit" should, in my opinion, be taken very seriously indeed because, as experience shows, it leads "usque ad instar voluntariae

mortis" ["To the semblance of voluntary death"—Apuleius, cited in "Transformations"]. I have suffered from this bit in my dealings with you, though you haven't seen it and didn't understand me properly when I tried to make my position clear. If these blinkers were removed you would, I am sure, see my work in a very different light.

In terms dripping with sarcasm, Jung then tossed Freud's "insight" back in his face and started in on the argument that Freud was the neurotic and that therein lay the reason why he could not appreciate Jung's work. And if Freud was going to invoke Spielrein, Jung was going to invoke what he knew about the Freud household. It took Jung only three angry paragraphs to get to the telling blow:

> Our analysis, you may remember, came to a stop with your remark that you "could not submit to analysis *without losing your* [sic] *authority.*" These words are engraved on my memory as a symbol of everything to come.

The reference, of course, was to the fateful shipboard conversation on the way back from America, when Freud refused to give his associations to a dream. Jung was announcing that he was prepared for an all-out confrontation, even if his manner of expression, appropriate to a letter, was relatively restrained.

Everything that had happened in the previous three years was now undone. The situation was worse than hopeless. They were sliding irrevocably into mutual blackmail, and if they did not find a way to stop, they could only do incalculable damage to each other—and to the common cause with which they were both still identified. As if in implicit recognition of this fact, Jung's letter went on to decry the defensive "misuse" of psychoanalysis as a means of "devaluing others and their progress by insinuations about their complexes (as though that explained anything. A wretched theory!)."

Freud's nerve did not entirely fail him, but he was quick to get out of this particular exchange. He wrote back by return post on 5 December:

> You mustn't fear that I take your "new style" amiss. I hold that in relations between analysts as in analysis itself every form of frankness is permissible. I too have been disturbed for some time by the abuse of ΨA to which you refer, that is, in polemics, especially against new ideas. I do not know if there is any way of preventing

this entirely; for the present I can only suggest a household remedy: let each of us pay more attention to his own than to his neighbor's neurosis.

The rest of the letter was taken up with business matters. There was safety in being impersonal. Only in the penultimate paragraph did Freud return to Jung's challenge:

I am sorry not to be able to discuss your remark on the neuroses of analysts at greater length, but this should not be interpreted as a dismissal. In one point, however, I venture to disagree most emphatically; you have not, as you suppose, been injured by my neurosis.

If Freud was willing to avoid personal insinuations for the time being, Jung was willing to do the same. He wrote back at once to announce his acceptance of what might be called a truce: "Since you have taken so badly to my 'new style,' I will tune my lyre a few tones lower for the present." But that said, Jung seemingly did not know what tone he should adopt next. His letter of 7 December went on to deride Adler's latest book in terms of great mockery, meant to be humorous, and to promise a review of it. Perhaps Jung longed for former days when he and Freud had joined together in deriding other men, but even today his facetiousness on the subject of Adler, whom he had noted positively at the New York Academy of Medicine and again in the German edition of his Fordham lectures, rings false.

At first glance, the letters Freud and Jung were exchanging seem to invite a military metaphor. They were testing each other's flanks, making feints, etc. And in fact the two men were negotiating with the possibility of something like war hanging over their heads. But metaphors of combat potentially distract from the essence of the confrontation. In effect, Freud and Jung were contending to see which one was the analyzer, which the one analyzed. What had once been a collaborative arrangement had collapsed into a situation in which only one of them could be the authority, only one the possessor of psychoanalytic truth. Accordingly, each man now posed a special kind of psychological threat to the other, a kind of threat that was perhaps historically unprecedented. For not only was each man claiming to know the other better than he knew himself, but by that very act he was appropriating the other's right to his own identity as a psychoanalyst. It was as though there was only one voice here, one right to speak, and the two men were struggling to see which of them possessed it. The possibility of playing for such terrible, savage stakes was implicit in how psychoanalysis had evolved—without empirical checks or methodological safeguards, the right to discern the unconscious motives of another belonged to whoever was strong enough to seize it. Yet, paradoxically, the very nature of the psychoanalytic identity they were trying to wrest from each other demanded that they not indulge their fiercer passions any further. The identity of a psychoanalyst was a corporate one. If the two men wrecked institutional psychoanalysis with their personal polemics, then neither would achieve the thing he was after.

With their latest exchange of letters, the two men had wisely called a halt to personal insinuations. But this did not mean Freud had to restrain himself on all subjects. He replied to Jung's facetious letter on 9 December by saying that a review of Adler would do some good politically as it would counteract the rumors that he, Jung, was swinging over to Adler's side. As for Jung's attempt at humor, Freud allowed simply: "I follow you with interest through all the variations of the lyre that you play with such virtuosity." Jung seemingly could not keep himself from rising to the bait and wrote back quickly to say: "Even Adler's cronies do not regard me as one of theirs." But, in making the statement, Jung accidentally capitalized the "I" of *"ihrigen,"* a slip of the pen that turned "theirs" into "yours." The slip is a common one among writers of German, it had been made several times before in their correspondence by both men, and it presented no obstacle to making out the sense of Jung's statement. But Freud couldn't resist pointing it out in his letter of 16 December:

> The habit of taking objective statements personally is not only a (regressive) human trait, but also a very specific Viennese failing. I shall be very glad if such claims are not made on you. But are you "objective" enough to consider the following slip without anger?
> "Even Adler's cronies do not regard me as one of *yours.*"

Once again, Jung exploded:

> I am objective enough to see through your little trick. You go around sniffing out all the symptomatic actions in your vicinity, thus reducing everyone to the level of sons and daughters who blushingly

admit the existence of their faults. Meanwhile you remain on top as the father, sitting pretty.

Arguably, Jung had not seen through Freud's "little trick." Freud's letter was plainly meant as a provocation. It seems never to have occurred to Jung that Freud might be circulating his letters as tangible evidence that Jung had "not outgrown his own neurosis." Gratifyingly, Jung's letter of 18 December 1912 rambled on at angry length about how this sort of behavior on Freud's part had engendered the impudence of Adler and Stekel. Freud could well have read all this with satisfaction; once more Jung was providing him with ammunition. But even more satisfying than Jung's outburst was Jung's close:

> I shall continue to stand by you publicly while maintaining my own views, but privately shall start telling you in my letters what I really think of you. I consider this procedure only decent.

That was the signal Freud had been waiting for. Jung would not go public with his personal misgivings. On 22 December, Freud drafted a letter suggesting that he, too, knew how to be discreet—"Whatever analytical remarks I have made about either [Adler and Stekel] were made to others for the most part after our relations had been broken off"—but he evidently was dissatisfied with the effort, for the letter was never sent off. To Jones, Freud volunteered that he thought the unsent letter was too mild and would only encourage Jung's outrageous behavior. The reality would seem to have been a good deal more complicated. Not only could Jung contradict Freud's claim to discretion from his own experience, but the letter also failed to send the proper signal on matters of personal disclosure. It was a delicate task, and for once Freud's prose was not equal to the occasion. Thus, while brief letters about business matters flew back and forth between Zurich and Vienna, Jung's offer to separate their private and public discussions went unanswered for ten days. Finally, Jung could stand it no longer and, under cover of sending his New Year's greetings, repeated his offer a second time:

> Don't hesitate to tell me if you want no more of my secret letters. I too can get along without them. Needless to say I have no desire to torment you. . . . If one has neurotic symptoms there will be a failure of understanding somewhere. Where, past events have al-

ready shown. So if I offer you the unvarnished truth it is meant for
your good, even though it may hurt.

   I think my honourable intentions are perfectly clear, so I need
say no more. The rest is up to you.

   By this time, however, Freud had found the right phrases. His own
letter of 3 January 1913 crossed with Jung's:

   I can answer only one point in your previous [i.e, 23 December
   1912] letter in any detail. Your allegation that I treat my followers
   like patients is demonstrably untrue. . . .

   Otherwise your letter cannot be answered. It creates a situation
   that would be difficult to deal with in a personal talk and totally
   impossible in correspondence. It is a convention among us analysts
   that none of us need feel ashamed of his own bit of neurosis. But
   one who while behaving abnormally keeps shouting that he is normal gives ground for the suspicion that he lacks insight into his
   illness. Accordingly, I propose that we abandon our personal relations entirely. I shall lose nothing by it, for my only emotional tie
   with you has long been a thin thread—the lingering effect of past
   disappointments—and you have everything to gain, in view of the
   remark you recently made in Munich, to the effect that an intimate
   relationship with a man inhibited your scientific freedom. I therefore
   say, take your full freedom and spare me your supposed "tokens of
   friendship." We are agreed that a man should subordinate his personal feelings to the general interests of his branch of endeavour.
   You will never have reason to complain of any lack of correctness
   on my part where our common undertaking and the pursuit of scientific aims are concerned; I may say, no more in the future than
   in the past. On the other hand, I am entitled to expect the same
   from you.

   Freud's letter needs to be read carefully and Jung undoubtedly
studied it hard. For his reply of 6 January, Jung finally opted for
brevity and a quotation from *Hamlet:*

   I accede to your wish that we abandon our personal relations,
   for I never thrust my friendship on anyone. You yourself are the
   best judge of what this moment means to you. "The rest is silence."

The danger had passed, but it had taken all possibility of a reconciliation with it. Except for a few unavoidable letters having to do with official business, letters which were uniformly businesslike and impersonal, the correspondence between the two men, like their friendship, was over.

The Freud-Jung correspondence has been available for nearly two decades now. Heretofore, however, the general tendency among commentators has been to focus on the stormy last two months of letters and to see therein the reasons for the end of the friendship. As though "Great is Diana of the Ephesians" had not been written a whole year earlier. In truth, the friendship between Freud and Jung had died while Spielrein was still in Vienna. What remained were the questions of how to make the rupture official and how to keep it from wrecking the International Association. The "Kreuzlingen gesture" had solved the first problem, while, as of the beginning of 1913, the second had yet to be fully addressed. But intervening between these two questions had come a third, namely what the two men knew about each other and how they would use it in their personal polemics. The question had been there all along, lying in wait, but it was not until the last two months of 1912 that it emerged from hiding. And, if we look beneath the fireworks in their correspondence during this time, beneath all the distractions about Adler and slips of the pen, we see the two men gradually working out a modus vivendi on this, the most critical question of all. The rest would be silence.

Part Five

The Aftermath

For many years now Freud has followed the same practice in his works: he pays no attention to criticisms and arguments directed at his theories, and he continues to build on the foundations which he has laid out as if they were now confirmed by scientific evidence and did not require any further discussion. The present work [*Totem and Taboo*] shows that his isolation from the scientific world is growing dramatically. The last year and a half has witnessed the abandonment of one Freudian theory after another by members of Freud's own school. It would seem obvious that major testing and revision of basic principles should be in order before another step forward is taken. And yet, just the opposite is happening. In his latest work, Freud makes his Oedipus complex theory the mainstay of his investigation without attempting in the slightest to respond to opposing arguments, let alone disprove them. He believes that his theory is logically so consistent that even the most daring hypotheses have evidential value if they merely point in the direction of the Oedipus complex

—Carl Furtmüller, 1914, review in the *Zentralblatt für Psychoanalyse and Psychotherapie*

CHAPTER 17

The History of the Psychoanalytic Movement

Scientifically I still do not understand why for you it is so important that the whole edifice should be accepted. But I remember I told you once that no matter how great your scientific accomplishments are, psychologically you impress me as an artist. From this point of view it is understandable that you do not want your art product to be destroyed. In art we have a unit which cannot be torn apart. In science you made a great discovery which has to stay. How much of what is loosely connected with it will survive is not important.

—Eugen Bleuler, letter to Sigmund Freud, 3 November 1913

W E COME NOW to the final phase of what Wittels, that early chronicler of the psychoanalytic movement, called the "unedifying struggle for supremacy." It might perhaps be more aptly termed a struggle for survival, at least as far as Jung, Freud, and Spielrein were concerned. Just as their coming together had been predicated on the dissemination of psychoanalytic theory and the gradual expansion of its institutions, their moving apart had ramifications that reached far beyond themselves. What in one context was merely a personal denouement in another created the institutional and theoretical foundations for psychoanalysis as it has come down to the present.

The next twenty months, from January 1913 to August 1914, proved to be decisive. On the personal level, the issue to be resolved during this period was how Jung and Freud—and Spielrein—would fare now that they were all irrevocably on their own. Essentially, in their different ways, each of them withdrew the love and idealization they had felt for one another—withdrew these unhappily into themselves.

It is hard to say whose was the greatest loss. Though still a relatively young man, Jung had managed to forfeit the two most important relationships of his life, relationships which had not only given him direction but which also had emotionally contained him and made him feel whole. Twelve years earlier, Jung had entered the psychiatric novitiate of the Burghölzli ostensibly because of a fascination with the mind in disorder but inwardly with the hope that he might find the key that would unlock the secrets of his own second personality. For a time, with the assistance of Freud and Spielrein, he seemed to be succeeding. Now, it fell to him to discover whether he still possessed that key, or whether, to the contrary, Freud and Spielrein had made off with it.

Freud's loss, though different, was no less great. What had begun with an excited letter to Fliess in 1904 about favorable notice of his theories in a review of another man's work in a Munich medical newsletter by a largely unknown professor of psychiatry from Zurich named Bleuler had turned into an international career far grander than anything Freud could have realistically imagined for himself. Jung had been responsible for this, responsible too for the resurgence of Freud's vitality. Now Freud was fifty-five years old and Jung was gone. Whatever the future held for Freud, it was sure to be less grand, less exciting—and less intellectually interesting—than what Jung had made possible. In the months to come, Freud would begin casting around for a substitute for the great adventure that was now over. The search would lead him to collaborate, nay conspire, with other men. For a time the excitement of that conspiracy seemed to sustain Freud—even though ultimately it depended on his feelings toward the absent Jung.

Spielrein had married in haste and soon discovered what others have discovered in similar circumstances: her former love would not die so easily, even if Jung had betrayed it and even if all reason told her it was time to move on. But her tragedy was to be compounded by events which she had inadvertently set in motion. If she was ill-fated in love, realistically she was still entitled to the career as a psychoanalyst that she imagined for herself. What she was now to discover was that psychoanalysis was becoming a house divided against itself, and that she could not pursue her chosen profession without constantly reopening the most terrible personal wounds.

The political question to be answered was obvious: Who controlled institutional psychoanalysis and what were its rules? As always this question had two dimensions: membership in formal organizations and the right to publish one's views as "discoveries" in the new science.

Jung had the presidency of the International Association at his disposal and the *Jahrbuch*. He was willing to stake the legitimacy of his rule on a policy of open inquiry and tolerance for dissent in both contexts. The reasonableness of his position notwithstanding, his credibility was undercut in some quarters by the fact that the most important dissent was now his own. Would Jung use his two positions to enforce acquiescence to his own new views? He seems never to have thought in these terms, but the suspicion that he might was roundly entertained by those who did. Freud was in command of the Vienna society, which he was continually reshaping in line with his own aims. Editorially, he had direct control only over the *Applied Psychology* monograph series, whose mythological studies had launched the project of identifying a core complex. But through his influence over the editors, he had indirect control over both *Imago*, where his work on *Totem and Taboo* was being serialized, and over the new *Zeitschrift*. Stekel had the *Zentralblatt*, which was open to Adler and his associates such as Furtmüller as well as to anyone else who cared to publish there. William Alanson White and Smith Ely Jelliffe had the new American journal, *The Psychoanalytic Review*, plus their own monograph series. (The Americans were thus players in a struggle they did not understand.)

The most important question to be answered, however, involved neither personalities nor politics, but theory and method. Here the issue to be settled was the one that Bleuler had been posing all along. Was psychoanalysis a science, in which case rival hypotheses were essential to a meaningful examination of the data? Or was it an art, in which case the original artist had the right to enforce his own views as to how his creation should best be completed?

A case could have been made that the actual practice of psychoanalysis was neither an art nor a science, but a craft. The papers Freud himself was currently publishing on technique rather suggested a craft mentality: they indicated the practical attitude which the analyst should adopt toward certain basic phenomena, like transference and dream interpretation, while they left more essential matters like hypothesis testing and issues of verification completely hanging. Moreover, in such a conception of psychoanalysis, the theoretical and practical innovations of Freud and Jung and others would still have had their place as that which distinguished the craft of psychoanalytic psychotherapy from other forms. In fact, many of the men who had aligned themselves with psychoanalysis initially thought of their affiliation this way, as something that would enhance their functioning as therapists.

They were perfectly well satisfied if Freud's concept of anal eroticism, for instance, or Jung's notion of introversion shed light on only some cases; it was not necessary that psychoanalyis be a complete, all-encompassing theory. This was Bleuler's way of conceiving psychoanalysis. He saw it as composed of numerous refinements in the conception of certain mental disorders which led to more efficacious forms of treatment. He looked forward to the day when the innovations in question would be the common property of all interested physicians.

Just this sort of compromise solution was anathema to Freud. He continued to conceive of psychoanalysis as a science in its own right, one that had its own special technical procedures capable of generating, and confirming, certain novel scientific hypotheses. Even if he had not yet made good on his promises to publish a comprehensive manual, one that would include the rules for interpretation, he seems never to have doubted that such a manual was possible. He also did not doubt that he himself was a scientist pure and simple. Nor did he question his assumption that the best way to ensure the scientific purity of psychoanalysis in the meantime was through the maintenance of a special training organization. Freud's dogged belief in the scientific status of psychoanalysis meant that for him deviant findings could be explained only by the application of a faulty technique. Just this conviction made him an artist.

Jung's attitude toward the scientific status of psychoanalysis was rapidly changing. Where Freud still clung to what were essentially nineteenth-century conceptions of the logic of scientific explanation, Jung began to interest himself in the new philosophies of science that the twentieth century was beginning to churn up, in the writings of Bergson and in the findings of the new physics, and in the relevance of hermeneutics to analytic understanding. One can only wonder what would have happened if Jung had managed to complete his forays into methodological theory while still wearing the mantle of president of the International Association. As it was, he ran out of time.

CORPSES

SPIELREIN WAS slow to realize her current predicament. During the fall of 1912, she enrolled herself in the Berlin Psychoanalytic Society, but she soon discovered that she was not really amicable with Karl Abraham, whom she knew from the Burghölzli and about whom she had undoubtedly heard much from Jung over the years. Accordingly, she continued to keep up her correspondence with Vienna, with Freud and with Rank, who was the receiving point for her submissions to the movement's journals. This meant her papers would run in organs under Freud's control. As it happened, no less than five contributions from her, most of them brief, appeared during 1913, and while none of these directly contradicted Jung to quite the degree that her paper on childhood sexual conflict inadvertently had, they decidedly did not support him, either. It is unclear how many of these papers had already been conceived by the end of 1912, when she was overtaken by illness and an operation—about both nothing further is known—and by questions. Perhaps her illness gave her time for reflection; perhaps, too, she had heard of the recent meeting at the Park Hotel in Munich. In any event, in December of 1912, she wrote to Jung asking for a clarification of the theoretical differences between him and Freud.

Jung didn't write back. For one thing he was still waiting to hear from Freud that personal attacks would cease. For another, he was beginning to become preoccupied with his own state of mind. Jung had planned to make his defense of his new views not in political caucuses nor by cultivating correspondents abroad—never his strong suit—but at the writing table. But, gradually, Jung's efforts at self-defense began to erode from within. Jung's theories represented something more than his intellectual convictions; they represented the fruit of his personal experience over the previous eight years. Both synopsis and recompense, they were now his chief means of shoring up his sense of self. So long as Jung felt confident of the choices he had made, and sure that he would yet find an audience for his new views, it all hung together reasonably well. But, for reasons he couldn't quite get ahold of, Jung was suddenly not feeling confident.

The first sign of trouble seems to have come around the time of the meeting in Munich, when Jung contemplated the fact that the prospective theory of dream interpretation would be taken up at the next congress. From Maeder, Jung knew that this topic had already been linked in Freud's mind with a suspicion that it augured a further distinction between the psychology of Jews and Christians. And as he pondered what he himself was going to say about all this—quite apart from "Siegfried," the prospective angle was integral to his own new theories—Jung seems to have realized that his own thoughts on the matter were rather too confused for a public presentation. The moment of self-recognition, if not the context, is clearly described in his memoirs:

I had explained the myths of peoples of the past; I had written a book about the hero, the myth in which man has always lived. But in what myth does man live nowadays? In the Christian myth, the answer might be. "Do *you* live in it?" I asked myself. To be honest, the answer was no. "For me, it is not what I live by." "Then do we no longer have myth?" "No, evidently we no longer have any myth." "But what then is your myth—the myth in which you do live?" At this point the dialogue with myself became uncomfortable, and I stopped thinking. I had reached a dead end.

The "dead end" was no passing moment; it was the start of a painful struggle to get ahold of himself that would occupy Jung on and off for years to come. The struggle has been poignantly, if incompletely, described in Jung's memoirs, also in the notes of his 1925 seminar portraying his own development, and in broad outline it may be familiar to many readers.

It is not too much to say that, following the final rupture with Freud, Jung very nearly went mad. Jung's own accounts make that explicitly clear. Yet Jung's accounts romanticize his struggle, making it seem almost self-willed, and in the process render it psychologically false. Madness is not something that comes of its own accord to a man of thirty-six, most especially not to a natively gifted psychologist like Jung. Even less can it be summoned up as an experiment. There were very good reasons why Jung nearly went mad. Consider just his realization that he had no myth of his own. No doubt it was an unhappy discovery for a man of Jung's temperament. And certainly, Jung is being honest when he reports that he was no Christian. But left out of his account is that Jung had in fact been tempted into experimenting with a Christianized version of psychoanalysis. Also left out of Jung's account was the fact that his mentor and his closest intimate seemed prepared to broadcast insinuations that Jung's Christianized version constituted a reaction to an affair with a Jewish girl.

While Spielrein waited for a reply to her letter, Jung began to seek internal guidance by paying more attention to his fantasies: "One fantasy kept returning: there was something dead present, but it was also still alive. For example, corpses were placed in crematory ovens, but were then discovered to be still living." Eventually these fantasies came to a head in the form of a dream. In that dream, Jung found himself amongst a row of slabs on which lay corpses, each dating from a particular century. As Jung made his way down this row, going from the nineteenth century all the way back to the twelfth, each of the corpses moved ever so slightly so as to indicate that it was still alive. Jung's conclusion was that the figures represented archaic vestiges in the unconscious, ostensibly dead but still potentially alive. In his memoirs, as in his 1925 seminar, he specifically stated that the fact that they were ostensibly dead reflected Freud's view of the matter, while to the contrary, he was now discovering that the archaic vestiges within were still alive.

In neither account did Jung mention the fact that there was another theory of the unconscious around at the time, Spielrein's, which held that archaic vestiges contained the seeds of both death and rebirth, and that both were to be understood under the sign of the sexual. The inner mental space Jung was exploring would seem to cry out for explication along Spielrein's lines: the missing ingredient, the potion that would bring the corpses truly back to life, was her company. For, according to her theory, images of death were the ego's reaction to the threat of dissolution in the sexual. Likewise, images of rebirth reflected the transforming element in sexuality, the resurrection of the individual coming with the acceptance of the collective aims of the instinct for the preservation of the species. One does not have to agree with Spielrein's thesis in all its particulars—like so much of the literature of the core complex it depends on metaphor and analogy—to know that Jung undoubtedly thought of it as he contemplated his fantasies.

And here was another hateful paradox that could not have been anticipated. Spielrein's theories, like his own and like Freud's, retained the personal stamp of their originators. Jung was not truly free to take advantage of Spielrein's perspective without feeling once more ambivalently in her thrall. Even less could he think to himself how Freud might interpret his preoccupations. Rather than constitute avenues for insight, the theories of his former intimates now constituted dangerous intrusions upon his psychic privacy.

However Jung interpreted his fantasies at the time, they were plainly odd and unhappy ones, and they did not bode well for further self-scrutiny of this kind. He decided to try another tack—travel. He made plans for yet another trip to America for March of 1913, with a stopover in Italy on the way.

WHILE JUNG wrestled with his fantasies and Spielrein waited for a reply, Freud kept busy. On 20 January, two weeks after his personal correspondence with Jung had officially ended, he wrote Spielrein to inform her of the latest:

> My personal relationship with your Germanic hero has definitely been shattered. His behavior was too bad. Since I received that first letter from you, my opinion of him has greatly altered. Scientific cooperation, however, will presumably be maintained.

Given that Spielrein still had the option of someday going into analysis with him, it was only fair for Freud to keep her abreast of his own relationship with Jung. But that was not the only thing on Freud's mind. There was also the matter of her "Destruction" paper, which had appeared side by side with Part 2 of "Transformations and Symbols" in the most recent *Jahrbuch*. *She* might be in, but her theory was out. Thus, the very same letter went on to warn her that a less-than-favorable review would appear in the new *Zeitschrift*. With surprising baldness, Freud attempted to shift the blame for it elsewhere:

> The first issue of the *Zeitschrift*, a fair proof of which lies before me already, carries a review of your last great contribution. We have taken the liberty of criticizing it freely, because the Zurich people have asked us expressly to do so. Don't be angry, and read it through with indulgence.

It would have taken more than "indulgence" for Spielrein to get through Paul Federn's review. One can scarcely imagine a more condescending or more profoundly wrongheaded reading of her work. To be sure, Spielrein's thesis was difficult on more than one level. Her paper demanded an unusually concentrated reading, and perhaps more than one, for its import to be entirely clear. Yet given that kind of reading, which she was entitled to expect from a reviewer, there could be no question of what she had accomplished. By redefining sexual desire as inherently problematic for the ego, she had indeed shed light on the prevalence of images of death, disease, and destruction in neurosis and psychosis. She had also shed light on the phenomenology of regression in schizophrenia. And her work as a whole, with its investigation into the problematics of sexual desire, had brought the problem of repression into new relief.

None of this, however, comes through in Federn's review. Instead, he caricatures her argument, making it appear as though she sought to prove that overt destructiveness was indispensable to sexuality. In effect, he construes hers as a somewhat eccentric treatise on the inevitability of sadomasochism. One can almost hear Freud's earlier comment—"She seems abnormally ambivalent"—in the background. And things only get worse when Federn tries to move into the inner workings of her theory. Among other things, he makes the point that while women may be concerned with the preservation of the species, Spielrein had failed to prove that the same thing applies to men. As if to make the contrary argument explicit, Federn goes on to argue that pleasure and fatigue are the real regulators of sexual behavior. But then in the very last sentence, he suddenly reverses himself and finds some ground for praise. The sentence reads as though it were inserted by someone else into the review: "Disregarding its objective truth, the paper seems to me, thanks to the author's sensitivity for emotional relationships, a contribution as well to the analysis of the mystical modality of thought that is so significant for humanity." Somebody in Vienna—I doubt it was Federn—had figured out how closely her monograph dovetailed with Part 2 of "Transformations and Symbols."

Having not yet seen the review, Spielrein responded to Freud's letter by sending along yet another brief article analyzing a dream of a patient she had seen while she was in Vienna. In it, Spielrein shows how the name of "Freud" together with the German word for "heathen" were used by the patient to fashion a symbolic substitute for her absent father. The analysis was convincing and it was the sort of article that was sure to please. As well, she had good news to report: Professor Friedrich Kraus of the Berlin Charité, with whom she was acquainted, was becoming interested in psychoanalysis. Freud seems to have been abashed by her indomitable eagerness. He wrote back on 9 February 1913 to thank her for her latest offering and to ask her to desist: "You have done a great deal of serious and important work and are fully entitled to take a break for a while and collect your thoughts."

BETWEEN TWO STOOLS

FREUD'S ATTITUDE toward Spielrein deserves comment. He seems never to have felt any particular personal affection toward her. Her previous intimacy with Jung seems to have constituted a liability, though paradoxically it seems also to have stirred Freud's sense of responsibility. She had thrown in her lot with him and he would honor the implied commitment, provided she was not too demanding and provided she was mature enough to see her theory discredited without protest. In fact, there was little she could do. Freud's confident disingenuousness in laying the blame for Federn's review on the "Zurich people" spoke to the heart of her predicament; she was not in close enough contact with her former mentors to know better. All she knew was that differences had arisen between Freud and Jung and that there had been a personal falling-out.

Spielrein was not the only person who was falling "between two stools," to use a favorite phrase of Freud's. Oskar Pfister seems to have been totally unsure of what to make of it all—or of what side he was on, if it came to that. James Jackson Putnam was equally at a loss. To his niece, who was in analysis with Jung, he wrote despairingly: "Why can't everyone be good?" Poul Bjerre, meanwhile, had lately had the happy thought that he might be the first to write up a history of the psychoanalytic movement. Now, he realized he would have to include a last chapter indicating that yet another split was in the making. And privately, he began to wonder if he himself might not be better off returning to the practice of hypnotism. What all these people assumed was that Jung's new ideas represented reasonable extensions of Freud's libido concept. It did not make sense to them that there should be such a sense of foreboding in the psychoanalytic air.

In Geneva, Théodore Flournoy came to his own conclusions. His own new book, *Spirits and Mediums,* had been published a year and a half earlier. In it, Flournoy had advanced a prospectus for a psychology of religious belief that would leave ultimate questions open while otherwise bringing a sturdy scientific perspective to bear. The project was dear to Flournoy, as it had been to his late friend William James, who had died of angina two years before. When Flournoy next turned his attention to current developments within psychoanalysis, made topical throughout Switzerland by the Zurich newspaper debates of the previous year, he thought to himself that his long-standing preoccupation might shed light on his new one. He got into contact with Jung, who was happy to direct him to his own new works. Flournoy now began preparing a long, thoughtful article in which he announced his agreement with the psychoanalytic vision of men like Jung and Vicar Keller as consonant with German philosophical and religious ideals while otherwise predicting that a schism between Zurich and Vienna was inevitable. What Flournoy did not say in his article, but would say in a lecture course in 1916, was that he felt that the basic split was between Jewish and Christian ideals. Despite the sincerity of his starting point, Flournoy thus made his own contribution to incivility and to the untenability of the situation.

For his part, Eugen Bleuler had come to feel that his last defense of Freudianism had been several shades too positive. Accordingly, he now presented a follow-up paper at the spring meeting of the German Psychiatrists in Breslau. Following his presentation, the luminaries of German psychiatry got up one by one to denounce the new pseudoscience. Hoche, he of the "psychic epidemic" speech two years before, rose to announce that psychoanalysis was entering its "death throes." An American assistant at Kraepelin's clinic found the denunciations long on rhetoric and short on logic and afterward said as much to Kraepelin. To this Kraepelin replied that a scientific discussion had not been in the plan. The whole point, according to the blunt-speaking North German, who had never been enamored of his Zurich colleague's plunge into "depth psychology," had been to put official psychiatry on record against Freudianism and give Bleuler a chance to backslide publicly.

In short, as word of the personal rupture between Freud and Jung began to make the rounds, the status of psychoanalysis once more became suspect. In the German preface to his Fordham lectures, Jung had specifically noted that the word "schism" was suitable only for religious movements, not scientific ones. But talk of a "schism" was in the air, and this caused friend and foe alike to have a fresh look at what psychoanalysis had become. What was falling between two stools was its scientific credibility.

"SO-CALLED FRIENDS"

FREUD SEEMS to have been well aware of how necessary it was to keep up appearances. He began churning out articles for the new *Zeitschrift,* including a paper on so-called confessional dreams, the meetings of the Vienna society proceeded apace, and his correspondences continued indefatigably. Occasionally, he would lapse into a fresh denunciation of Jung in his letters. The virulence of these private judgments of his former friend as a "brutal" man, full of "anti-Semitic condescension," diagnosable as a case of "emotional stupidity," and following Adler into outright paranoia is remarkable. Suffice it to say that on and off for the next two years Freud would be intermittently moved to fresh venom on the subject of Jung. But one garners a potentially false impression from any such catalogue of Freud's outbursts: much more often he made a point of his tolerance for open discussion, and in general his letters focused on other matters. To be through with Jung was one thing, to be preoccupied with him was another, and Freud instinctively seemed to know where the line lay between these two different postures. What was important was to keep the level of discussion at as high a level as possible, to make it seem that all differences were scientific ones and that they could be resolved in the ordinary course of further examinations of the data.

Helping Freud maintain his composure was the new secret Committee. The existence of this group—Jones, Ferenczi, Abraham, Sachs, and Rank—has been known since 1944, when Hanns Sachs first revealed it in print, but it somehow has never drawn the criticism it properly deserves. The sole purpose of this group was to guard against future deviations from Freud's views within the psychoanalytic movement. Explicitly, Freud was to tell them where to stand and they would stand there. If they found internal obstacles in the way of their mission, they were to resolve these through further self-analysis. These facts, and the fact that it operated in secrecy for over a dozen years, stamp the Committee as anything but a legitimate scientific organization. Open discussion and the honest consideration of alternative hypotheses are the hallmarks of science, not secrecy and pressure-group tactics exercised behind the scenes. The reason for this is not because scientists are exemplary citizens, open and trusting of their colleagues. The reason is that victory in a scientific dispute ultimately depends on public disclosure of findings and confirmation from other researchers. The fact that the Committee could operate in secrecy for so long—it was eventually overtaken by its own internal tensions—and that its members could believe that they were being effective in their chosen mission makes its own comment on how far psychoanalysis had moved from the normal exigencies of empirical verification.

The Committee had yet to meet in full body, but this did not keep its members from organizing through the mails. In March, while Jung was on his way to America, Abraham circulated a secret memorandum calling for the local societies in Berlin, Budapest, London, and Vienna to demand Jung's resignation in May. Understandably enough, they were counting the house to see how many votes they commanded.

There were not enough. The effort came to nothing. The historical fact should perhaps be underscored: the first time something like a straw vote was taken, the legitimacy of Jung's rule as president was endorsed by a majority of those consulted.

Also in March of 1913, Rank and Sachs finished a joint work entitled *The Significance of Psychoanalysis for the Social Sciences*. It has not heretofore been appreciated to what extent this work constitutes a point-by-point rebuttal of Jung's various theses. The tone is very dry, Jung is even cited on occasion, and the monograph easily passes itself off as an intellectual statement on the general applicability of psychoanalytic ideas to the social sciences, more or less modeled after a recent brief essay by Freud on that topic. But as one reads more closely into it, one finds revisionistic discussions of such Jungian topics as the distinction between reality and fantasy, the importance or unimportance of fantasy and imagistic thought, the motif of the hero and his companion (or twin), and, predictably, the Siegfried myth, suitably reinterpreted as a disguised Oedipal drama. There is also, for the curious, an uninspired chapter on the subject of art and poetry. Rank and Sachs continued a local tradition begun by Freud by dating their preface "Easter, 1913"—an intentionally ironic flourish for a work that went to great lengths to dismiss ethical and religious strivings as mere disguises for more fundamental wishes. The monograph was the first product of the new Committee and it defined what the tactics would be for the time being. Whatever positions Jung took would be drowned in a flood of counter-publications. America was particularly important in this strategy. Jung enjoyed a special reputation there, and with Jones's recent relocation to London, it was hard for any of the group around Freud to predict where men like Putnam, Hall, Meyer, and Hoch might stand. Accordingly, Rank's and Sachs's monograph was quickly sent off to White and Jelliffe, the editors of the newly founded *Psychoanalytic Review,* for their monograph series.

Thereafter, the various members of the Committee competed for the honor of denouncing Jung in various covert and overt ways, with Jones, Abraham, and Ferenczi, all Burghölzli-trained, taking the lead in writing hostile reviews of "Transformations and Symbols." We get only a glimpse of the bitterness of it all from the restrospectively brave sentiment expressed in Jung's memoirs:

> After the break with Freud, all my friends and acquaintances dropped away. My book was declared to be rubbish. I was a mystic,

and that settled the matter. Riklin and Maeder alone stuck by me. But I had foreseen my isolation and harbored no illusions about the reaction of my so-called friends.

For the record, the most thoughtful review was Ferenczi's. Many of Ferenczi's points followed closely the discussions in the Freud-Jung letters and it appears likely that the Hungarian was given access to the correspondence. To Ferenczi's credit; among his challenges was an empirical one: What, finally, did Jung really know of Miss Frank Miller and her actual condition? Also to Ferenczi's credit was that, quite contrary to the implication Freud had left with Jung, he did not take the opportunity to make veiled insinuations about Jung's own complexes. Jung had reason to be grateful on that score. Whether for that reason, or because the genial Hungarian was feeling rather more circumspect about the Committee's activities than he let on, Jung and Ferenczi continued to correspond privately in the years that followed.

Other works by Committee members involved covert charges of suppressed anal eroticism on Jung's part; still others were more high-minded and theoretical. Spielrein did not join in the general denunciation. On 11 April, she finally got a reply from Jung, who was back from America. From his letter one can infer first, that she had taken no glee in the hornet's nest she had helped stir up, and second, that Jung did not blame her for it:

It would have taken half a book to answer you. I was completely discouraged, since at the time everyone attacked me, and in addition in Munich I gained certainty that Freud would never understand me and would break off his personal relations with me. He wants to give me love; I want understanding. I want to be a friend on an equal footing; he wants to have me as a son. That is why he condemns everything I do, and ascribes to a complex everything I do that does not fit the framework of his doctrine. He is free to do so, but I will never accept it. During the meeting in Munich I clearly recognized that Freud is lost for me. My inner battles have so absorbed my time that I haven't written to you. It's not that I'm not open to criticism, but I know too well that the matter is too all-encompassing to go into it.

I will always remain your friend.

By this time, Jung was sufficiently composed not only to write to Spielrein, but to begin tackling his fantasies in earnest. He resolved on a method of self-therapy. On the shores of Lake Constance in Küsnacht, Jung began playing at building little stone villages, re-creating a favorite game of his boyhood. Apparently this helped for a time as Jung recovered a number of important childhood memories.

While Jung tried to hold on to his composure by playing, Freud kept busy with his correspondence. In May, he found time to address another letter to Spielrein, who now was five months pregnant and had begun to regret the deal she had made with life. Freud was consoling:

> I am sorry to hear you are consumed with longing for J., and this at a time when I am on such bad terms with him, having almost reached the conclusion that he is unworthy of all the interested concern I have bestowed on him. . . . But no doubt it is fruitless to complain about him to you. . . . I gather that you are composing your thoughts, which is bound to benefit the child. That is the right course. I hope this commitment of your libido will prove happier for you than the earlier one. . . . I imagine that you love Dr. J. so deeply still because you have not brought to light the hatred he merits.

By far the biggest event in May was the completion of the last section of *Totem and Taboo*. It contained the crux of Freud's argument, namely his contention that all religious feeling and all inherited tendencies toward the formation of conscience derived from remorse for a primordial act of parricide. Indeed, it was argued that the slain patriarch of the primal horde had been ritually eaten in a cannibalistic meal afterward and that this, too, had passed down phylogenetically, where it reappeared in disguised form in certain contemporary religious rituals. Not only did Freud's argument put the Oedipus complex on a universal footing—incredibly, he supposed that we all are descendants of that one original tribe, and thus all psychic inheritors of the same conflicted emotional constellation—but it potentially made the complex responsible for a whole gamut of religious rituals.

The methodologically dubious project of defining a "core complex" had come to an end. The outline of where he was going to finish up had long been in Freud's mind, so it is questionable how much his final formulation was affected by the mood of the moment. To Abraham, to be sure, Freud remarked in a letter of 13 May 1913 that the essay would "serve to cut us off cleanly from all Aryan religiousness." Freud's animus, however, was perhaps less important than the effect this work had on subsequent analytic theorizing. For now it was no longer a question of observing the Oedipal stage in normal development—the discovery of the "Little Hans" case—and wondering why it became psychologically important in some instances but not in others. Instead, the psychological centrality of the stage was being posited on the basis of an event in human prehistory, an imagined event at that, as though that solved either the conceptual problems of distinguishing normal from neurotic development or the methodological problems of proving that repressed Oedipal motives were indeed central to adult psychopathology.

Strictly speaking, Freud was merely multiplying hypotheses and then using that very multiplicity to seem to infer causal connections between three very different domains. The scientifically suspect endeavor of reading the psychic formations of adult nervous patients back into their childhood, and both back into ancient mythology, had been rescued only by turning the whole argument on its head and reading an imagined prehistory forward into the present. Save for Freud's justifiably great stature, and the sweet reasonableness of his prose style, the effort might have been ridiculed. Yet, this was the work that made the "Oedipus complex" central among the interpretive rubrics of psychoanalysis. Beyond trying to recover an appropriate sense of astonishment at the wholly unsatisfactory way in which this was accomplished, one also has to wonder what kind of intellectual climate allowed such a maneuver to go unquestioned.

In fact, *Totem and Taboo* was questioned—loudly—but not within the circle that mattered. By 11 June, the galleys of the *Imago* printing of the final essay were ready and Freud sent them off to each of the members of the Committee. Not surprisingly, they all liked it very much. To celebrate the occasion, they feted Freud on 30 June at a "totemic festival" at a garden restaurant outside Vienna. Years before, Freud had proposed a similar occasion to Ferenczi with the specific gloss that they might sacrifice in effigy various foes of psychoanalysis. Thus, one cannot help but suppose that as the entree was served at the totemic feast of 30 June 1913, the assembled joked about whom it stood for. This time, it was not the father who was being slain and eaten but the son. Freud distributed bound copies of his essay and urged the assembled to continue his work by contributing further to it. Loe Kann, Jones's common-law wife, who was currently in treatment with Freud, completed the occasion by presenting him with an Egyptian figurine.

These were civilized, cultivated men and their half-parody of a Last

Supper was probably less shocking in person than it might seem in the historical record. What is important to note is how rapidly the different dimensions of personal relations, politics, and theory were collapsing into one another. In the process, the crucial issues facing psychoanalysis were being disposed of in a most unsatisfactory way. Freud had become massively distrustful of Jung, and since he was no longer in contact with him, he imagined that Jung was still trying to wrest control of psychoanalysis away from him and steer it in his own directions. With that threat so vividly present in Freud's imagination, he embraced the Committee and looked forward to the distant day when he might regain direct control over all the institutions of psychoanalysis. But the members of the Committee, though capable men, had nothing more to offer Freud than their willingness to join him in his new antipathy toward Jung. None of them had made contributions like Jung's; none of them had posts like Bleuler's or Putnam's. This new inner circle was ruled by Freud's fears and by Freud's designs. Yet, *faute de mieux,* this same inner circle had become the sole meaningful sounding board for the further exposition of Freud's views. That everyone concerned easily seemed to know how to adjust to the situation is itself a comment on what institutional psychoanalysis was becoming.

PSYCHOLOGICAL TYPES

THE LAST TIME Jung and Freud were ever in the same room was the Fourth International Psychoanalytic Congress, held in Munich on 7–8 September 1913. The first such congress, it will be recalled, had been called by Jung, and bore the then outrageous name of "The Congress for Freudian Psychology." A private meeting held immediately afterward had founded the *Jahrbuch* and offended the excluded Viennese. The second such congress, with the more dignified name of "The Second Psychoanalytic Meeting in Nuremberg," had seen the beginnings of both the International Association and the Adler-Stekel *Zentralblatt.* The third such congress, the Weimar congress of September of 1911, had marked the high tide of the association. James Jackson Putnam had elicited wonderment with his keynote address on the ethical potentials of a genetic psychology, while Stekel had distinguished himself, if not the occasion, by invoking the "eagle"—in German, *Adler*— whom Freud had left behind in Vienna. As the reader may well imagine from this brief review, the fourth congress, with its slated topic of rival theories of dream interpretation, was anticipated with something less than equanimity by all concerned.

Jung continued to do almost nothing except pursuing an already painful examination of conscience and making an occasional sortie abroad. Freud, meanwhile, in collaboration with Ferenczi, who had his own correspondence going with Maeder, continued to wrestle with the "anti-Semite" issue. Freud had written Ferenczi in May that psychoanalysis should be independent of all "Aryan patronage." Then in June, after Ferenczi reported that Maeder was still writing directly about the differences in outlook between the Viennese and the Swiss, Freud gave Ferenczi the following advice:

> Certainly there are great differences between the Jewish and the Aryan spirit. We can observe that every day. Hence there would assuredly be here and there differences in outlook on life and art. But there should not be such a thing as Aryan or Jewish science. Results in science must be identical, though the presentation of them may vary.

At the beginning of August, however, Freud informed Ferenczi that he had finally examined the Fordham lectures: "I have now read the work of Jung himself and find it beyond all expectation good and harmless (innocent)!" After itemizing some criticisms, Freud closed with the admission that "On the whole I overrated the danger very much from a distance." The "danger" had indeed been overrated, but the momentum of events could not be stopped. As the congress grew nearer, Freud began to grow depressed, seriously so. Anna Freud later observed that it was the only time in her life she had ever seen him in such a state.

Spielrein, too, was depressed. Worse, she was once again ill and the complications were threatening her pregnancy. She would not be attending the congress. Freud wrote to her at the end of August:

> Let us hope that this bad period will save you an analysis. I can hardly bear to listen when you continue to enthuse about your old love and past dreams, and count on an ally in the marvelous little stranger.
>
> I am, as you know, cured of the last shred of my predilection for the Aryan cause, and would like to take it that if the child turns out to be a boy he will develop into a stalwart Zionist. . . .

We are and remain Jews. The others will only exploit us and will never understand or appreciate us.

Freud spent the final days before the Munich congress in Rome. Daily, he visited Michelangelo's statue of Moses at the church of San Pietro. He had been struck by the energy of the piece—Moses is about to hurl down the tablets containing the Ten Commandments—during his very first visit to Rome in 1901. But he had taken a wholly new liking to the statue during his last vacation there the year before, while Jung was off in America to give the Fordham lectures. Now, as Freud studied it in the summer of 1913, he considered that the figure would *not* complete its gesture, that Moses would restrain himself from smashing the new laws. It was a strange way of seeing the statue, not without its self-serving applications. Freud was furious; he imagined himself as a model of restraint.

Subsequently, for his own amusement, Freud wrote a little vignette entitled "The Moses of Michelangelo" in which he outlined his idiosyncratic view of the statue. The following year Rank talked him into publishing it anonymously in *Imago*. Appended to the piece was an editorial note unself-consciously justifying the article on the grounds that the "mode of thought" of its unidentified author was more or less identical with the "methodology of psycho-analysis." That, of course, was what was then being decided. As for Freud's daily visits to the statue in late August and early September of 1913, one may reasonably be tempted to imagine that he projected himself onto it, just as he had once projected himself onto Jung.

Freud had needed a good deal of encouragement to speak at all at the congress. For the occasion he had nothing better than a rather formulaic piece on a difficult topic, "The Disposition to Obsessional Neurosis." It was another of the sort of theoretical articles, largely devoid of illustrative case material, that were becoming, and for the next few years would principally remain, his new stock in trade. The general problem it addressed was more than a decade old and as yet unsolved—how to extend the established insights into the nature of hysteria to other neurotic syndromes. (Obsessional patients like the "Rat Man" seemed conflicted about their aggression, not their sexuality; Freud now proposed that this stemmed from a fixation to the anal stage of libidinal development.) The specific topic, moreover, had for better or worse already been swamped by the more encompassing one of how to establish psychoanalytic theory as a general psychology.

And in this larger realm Jung had already stolen a march with the Fordham lectures. Gradually, however, as the congress drew closer, Freud began to conceive of a more trenchant alternative to Jung's nascent ego psychology—a theory of narcissism. Somehow, between the daily visits to the statue of Moses and his ruminations about the piece he would write on narcissism, Freud recovered enough of his energy to sally forth to confront his former friend.

Jung prepared himself in a different way. In early August, he journeyed to London for the International Medical Congress. There he reprised the address he had given the year before at the New York Academy of Medicine. Quite interestingly, Jung now added the thought that his revised conception did *not* necessitate any change in the technique of psychoanalysis. Evidently, he was no longer pushing the idea that psychoanalysis should entail the search for spiritual potentials within the unconscious. After his return home, Jung took some friends for a four-day excursion on Lake Zurich in his sailboat. Albert Oeri, who had known Jung since boyhood, brought along a copy of Homer's *Odyssey* and read aloud as they sailed. The specific passages Oeri selected were the episode involving Circe, the enchantress, and the *Nekyia* episode, where Odysseus visits with the spirits of the dead. Between the trip abroad and the vacation at home, the outer and the inner man found their degrees of confirmation.

The Fourth International Psychoanalytic Congress was held on 7–8 September 1913, at the Hotel Bayerischer Hof in Munich. Eighty-seven persons were present, including Flournoy, who was there as Jung's guest. Rank and Maeder kicked off the first day's morning session with their respective papers on dream interpretation. Maeder would seem to have gotten rather the better of the occasion, for he took a dream from Freud's recent paper on the topic and showed how, contrary to what Freud had written, the dream did indeed manifest ethical and prospective trends. The Zurich contingent was suitably impressed. Freud later wrote that during the congress he rose to protest that all this was *not* psychoanalysis. Presumably, he did so following Maeder's talk. Maeder himself later reminisced to Henri Ellenberger that for advancing his theory in good faith he was attacked as if he had violated Holy Writ. Apparently, judging from the utter lack of positive comment about the occasion in any subsequent document, it was a most unedifying occasion. Jung chaired the meeting and he hid behind his role; he did not speak during the discussion. If the subject of racial differences came up, the fact is nowhere recorded.

In fact, the debate between Maeder and Rank represented a great lost opportunity. Here indeed were two rival hypotheses; here indeed was the chance to put each to the test and to examine their relative degrees of confirmation in actual clinical work. Nor did an examination of their respective merits require extensive investigations into far distant realms like mythology. Both the topic and the method of investigation were of the essence of psychoanalysis. Did dreams represent only attempts to discharge unfulfilled wishes? Or did they also sometimes have as their purpose attempts to anticipate and solve problems that lay in the near future? Every physician in the room potentially had ample opportunity to try out the two different modes of interpretation in his or her practice and thus to contribute the results to arriving at some tentative decision. Indeed, here was a research project very much worthy of the time and talents of the assembled. Had it been undertaken in anything like a spirit of open inquiry, moreover, it would have inevitably led to a clarification of other important issues, like when an interpretation was deemed to be confirmed and how much an investigator's own prejudices might be coercing unconscious collusion from his patients. But no such research project was proposed.

After this beginning, it was all anticlimactic. The roster of speakers for the following sessions was quite lengthy and Jung apparently had all he could do to keep the sessions moving. As he curtailed one presentation after another in order to leave time for the ensuing discussion, Viennese resentments grew. Some idea of the flavor of the occasion can be gleaned from another reminiscence of Maeder's. He bumped into Freud in one of the antechambers leading to the meeting hall and extended his hand in friendship. Freud rushed by without acknowledging Maeder's greeting and hurried out of the room. But in his haste, Freud got the pocket of his jacket hopelessly caught on the doorknob and for all his fury he couldn't get himself unstuck. Maeder had to come and get him free.

At any rate, by the beginning of the second afternoon, a plan had been hatched by Freud's contingent to protest Jung's reelection as president by handing in blank ballots. The final tally was fifty-two for reelection, twenty-two abstentions. Since Jung had been unopposed, the blank ballots would have caused a noticeable stir when they were announced. Afterward, Jung reportedly approached Jones and said, "I thought you had ethical principles," this being a favorite phrase of Jung's which he used with a deliberately comic twist in awkward situations. Here the sense was that submitting a blank ballot was a rather uncharitable thing to do. Jones's friends, however, thought the remark could be understood as "And I thought you were a Christian." That version could be given quite another twist and it later grew into a "fact," part of the official history of the occasion. For the record, Jung did not say it. Also for the record, when the matter was put to a vote, two-thirds of the membership of the International Association thought it entirely natural and fitting that Jung remain as president.

And what did Jung himself talk about on this august occasion? The title of his talk was "On the Question of Psychological Types." Jung began by comparing the dynamics of libidinal displacements in hysteria and in schizophrenia. In both there is a regression, Jung argued, but in hysteria the libido remains attached to other people via transferences, whereas in schizophrenia the libido has become so thoroughly introverted that, via the ensuing delusions, it swallows up the whole world. But after this seemingly straightforward start, Jung abruptly turned off into a protracted philosophical detour. What we have here, Jung went on to argue, is the pathological exaggeration of two fundamentally different attitudes toward the world. One is largely turned outward, the other inward. For these two different attitudes Jung now introduced the terms "extraverted" and "introverted" respectively. And, beginning with William James's distinction between the "tender-minded" and "tough-minded" dispositions in philosophy, Jung proceeded to show how the same essential polarity had turned up time and time again in a diversity of fields. Among others, he cited Schiller ("sentimental" and "naïve" poets), Nietzsche (Apollonian and Dionysian outlooks), and Otto Gross ("paranoid" versus "manic-depressive" dispositions of the "secondary cerebral processes"). It was all very interesting, but where was the man going?

Jung had saved the best for last. After completing his survey of various thinkers, he turned to his own field: "After the foregoing considerations no one will be astonished to find that in the domain of psychoanalysis we also have to reckon with the extremes of these two psychological types." And he promptly demonstrated his point all over again by using Freud and Adler as examples! Freud as the extravert naturally focused on the external world, and thus on the patient's love objects and transferences; consequently, he saw in a patient's symptoms an inability to extend his or her love. Adler as the introvert, however, naturally focused on the internal world, and thus on the patient's need to feel important and to safeguard him- or herself from attack. Consequently, he saw in symptoms various maneuvers for subtly asserting superiority. Jung's demonstration was quick and to the point. He signed off with the following simple declaration: "The difficult task of elaborating a psychology which will be equally fair to both types must be reserved for the future."

Here we have to remark on Jung's infuriating brilliance. Just when he would seem to have been down for the count, both theoretically and emotionally, he had come up with an altogether novel idea and used it to extraordinary effect. His newly coined antithesis of "introverted" and "extraverted" personality types was destined to pass into common currency. Indeed, it was one of the few insights of psychoanalysis to enjoy ready confirmation from other investigators, and even today it is spawning important new researches. Few men have ever escaped such an impossible situation more brilliantly or more creatively.

What moved Jung to come up with this brand-new theory? His own later account stresses that it was the first fruit of his private reflections upon his own fantasies and upon his differences with Freud. Quite reasonably, Jung saw himself as an introverted type and in this respect he was using Adler as his proxy. Beyond this explanation, which is more than plausible, two other considerations suggest themselves. To begin with, the new distinction allowed Jung to sidestep any question about racial differences being at the heart of the disagreements between himself and Freud. As such, it constituted a return to civility and a step back from mystification. Then, too, Jung had reason to worry about something else that might be being said behind his back. Specifically, he was liable to the charge that he had become "paranoid," with the evidence for this being that he could no longer tolerate personal intimacy with Freud. It was the old charge and the old equation, Schreber = Fliess = Adler. Jung's worry was that it was taking on a fourth term (= Jung). As far as Jung knew, this slander was already making the rounds among Freud's intimates. Arguably, then, Jung's tour de force, with its astonishing display of interpretive virtuosity, was meant to meet this charge head-on and render its absurdity all too clear.

Beyond Jung's motives, there is also the question of where he got his inspiration. The list of possible influences is long and ranges from Nietzsche and William James to Otto Gross and Adolf Meyer. Ellenberger has noted that in 1903, while Jung was enjoying a sabbatical in Paris, the great French psychologist Alfred Binet had published a work describing the "intratensive" and "extratensive" dispositions of his two young daughters. In all likelihood, Jung had cannibalized Binet's distinction in formulating his own idea of "'introversion,'" conceived of as a psychic process that might happen to anyone. But it was still a step to go from "introversion" as a process back to "introverted" as a personality type. And here let me add one more name to the list of possible influences, a surprising one at that. In a 1912 paper entitled "Types of Onset of Neurosis," Freud had attempted to integrate Jung's idea of "introversion" into a rudimentary typology describing patterns of onset for neuroses. The paper had appeared just as Jung was beginning to write up his forthcoming Fordham lectures, and as it addressed the salient issue of precipitating events in neurotic developments, Jung undoubtedly studied it closely. Quite possibly, then, the important step that Jung took at the Munich congress had occurred to him while reading Freud's paper. If so, the new theory of types might be said to be yet one more product—historically, the final one—of their collaboration.

One final comment may perhaps be in order. As brilliant as it was, Jung's innovation stopped short of truly turning psychoanalysis from the path that it was on. For he was not arguing that different types of patients might require different modes of understanding and even different types of intervention, which would have been a truly clinical approach. Instead, he was arguing that different kinds of *theorists* produce different kinds of theories. Which was a different matter. The evolution of psychoanalytic theory had been under the sway of its two giants for so long that the primacy of the theorist over the patient continued to be inadvertently maintained even as the effort was being made to understand what was going wrong.

THE DEATH OF "SIEGFRIED"

THE MUNICH congress ended in surly, sulking stalemate. There was no legitimate reason to oust Jung as president. There was no pacifying Freud. And there was no way of stopping the momentum toward schism that the failure of their collaboration had created. For her own sake, it was probably just as well that Spielrein had not been there. Her pregnancy would only have reminded the two men—with unknown consequences for herself—of how their breakup had begun, with their very different interpretations as to whether "Siegfried" was a real child or a spiritual one. Ultimately, Spielrein had been left to wrestle with this and all other issues on her own. The last months of her pregnancy had been a terrible struggle. She felt "Siegfried" was still alive in her and trying to kill the unborn baby. In psychic self-defense, she finally had a dream in which she killed off Jung. A few weeks after the congress, she gave birth. Most mercifully, her baby was both healthy and a girl. Spielrein named the girl Renate in honor of the fact that she had nearly died and thus was, as it were, "reborn." Whatever congratulatory letter Jung sent does not survive. Freud's does. It bespeaks his continuing rage at Jung:

> Well, now, my heartiest congratulations! It is far better that the child should be a "she." Now we can think again about the blond Siegfried and smash that idol before his time comes.

Jung, too, seems to have felt aftershocks from what would prove to be his last encounter with Freud on earth, an encounter to which Renate's birth provided the final punctuation. In October, while taking a train ride, Jung had a terrifying hallucination. It would seem to have depicted both his isolation and his mounting rage. He saw the whole of Europe between the North Sea and the Alps drowned by a cataclysmic flood. The Alps themselves rose higher, so that Switzerland alone was saved. The "vision," as Jung terms it in his memoirs, lasted about an hour:

> I saw the mighty yellow waves, the floating rubble of civilization, and the drowned bodies of uncounted thousands. Then the whole sea turned to blood. . . . I was perplexed and nauseated and ashamed of my weakness.

A few weeks later, the hallucination returned with the blood even more heavily emphasized. This time, Jung also heard a voice which said, "Look at it well; it is wholly real and it will be so. You cannot doubt it." Jung decided, with good reason, that he was "menaced by a psychosis."

Late in October, Jung heard from Maeder that Freud doubted his good faith in continuing as editor of the *Jahrbuch*. It is not known what Freud wrote to Maeder, nor what the context was for the charge. The most recent *Jahrbuch* issue had contained Jung's Fordham lectures, while the coming one would contain Maeder's recent address at the Munich congress. In any case, Jung could now think of no better line of self-defense than withdrawal. On 27 October, he penned an official letter to Freud announcing that he was resigning as editor. For his part, Bleuler had no stomach for continuing as director in the current climate and promptly tendered his own resignation. Freud and members of the Committee thought the resignations some kind of ploy orchestrated by Jung. Again they were imagining a wily enemy plotting to strengthen his control over the institutions of psychoanalysis. Again they were wrong. Jung was breaking into pieces. His only motive seems to have been to want to hide that fact.

After consultations with the publisher revealed nothing untoward, Freud took over as sole director, the journal was renamed the *Jahrbuch der Psychoanalyse,* and the editorship was assigned to Abraham and Hitschmann. (Like Federn, Hitschmann was endlessly loyal to Freud. Neither of them, however, knew about the Committee). But Freud was scarcely content with this, and at Ferenczi's urging he contemplated getting the societies in his control to secede from the International and form their own new body. The plan was scotched when Jones counseled that it would make no sense at all to the Americans, who would continue to affiliate themselves with the present organization.

In November, Jung's solitude became even more oppressive. It would not have been in character for Jung to seek professional help from another man. And, indeed, it was not clear that there was anybody out there who *could* help him. Accordingly, he decided to do what he had done before, give himself over to reverie:

> In order to grasp the fantasies which were stirring in me "underground," I knew I had to let myself plummet down into them, as it were. I felt not only violent resistance to this, but a distinct fear. For I was afraid of losing command of myself and becoming a prey to the fantasies—and as a psychiatrist I realized only too well what that meant. After prolonged hesitation, however, I saw that there was no other way out.

On 12 December 1913, Jung finally got up the courage to let go and give himself over to his fantasies. At once, he felt himself falling and amidst an overtaking panic he found himself living through a bizarre vision. He had landed on his feet on some soft, sticky ground; there was a dwarf with leathery, almost mummified skin guarding the entrance to an underground cave; Jung went in and found himself wading knee-deep in icy water; on a rocky promontory he found a glowing red crystal. When Jung lifted up the crystal he uncovered a hole in the rock which yielded a view into a deeper cave below. In the water of that cave, there floated the corpse of a young blond man, shot in the head. The corpse was followed by a gigantic black scarab and then a "red, newborn sun." In short order, the sun was devoured by thousands of writhing snakes. As Jung recoiled from the scene and tried to reclose the opening, first water and then blood gushed up.

One may rightly wonder what Jung might have made of his vision three years earlier, i.e., at the time he had written up his review of Morton Prince's book. For in this fantasy there were sexual symbols aplenty, that is, if one brought the same formidable style of interpretation to bear on them. But as with his dreams, one should interpret Jung's fantasies with caution. It may have equally been the case that what was fueling his desperate sense of revulsion was not his wishes and fears, whatever they were, but the very interpretive theories that he had once espoused and was still, so to speak, swimming in. In any event, as he contemplated the vision, Jung consciously tried to find a different interpretive stance. Taking his cue from the sun and the scarab (a regular feature in the sun-symbolism of Egypt), Jung attempted to interpret the dream along the lines of psychic death and rebirth. But what to make of the dead youth, an obvious embodiment of the hero-motif?

Some six days later, on 18 December, Jung had an important dream. Though the dream went far to clarify the meaning of the previous week's "vision," it was no less disturbing:

> I was with an unknown, brown-skinned man, a savage, in a lonely, rocky mountain landscape. It was before dawn; the eastern sky was already bright, and the stars fading. Then I heard Siegfried's horn sounding over the mountains and I knew that we had to kill him. We were armed with rifles and lay in wait for him on a narrow path over the rocks.
>
> Then Siegfried appeared high up on the crest of the mountain, in the first ray of the rising sun. On a chariot made of the bones of the dead he drove at furious speed down the precipitous slope. When he turned a corner, we shot at him, and he plunged down, struck dead.
>
> Filled with disgust and remorse for having destroyed something so great and beautiful, I turned to flee, impelled by the fear that the murder might be discovered. But a tremendous downfall of rain began, and I knew that it would wipe out all traces of the deed. I had escaped the danger of the discovery; life would go on, but an unbearable feeling of guilt remained.

Jung woke up. He was in his own bed in Küsnacht. In the drawer of his night table lay his service revolver, loaded and ready for use. Jung was frightened. He felt he would have to shoot himself if he did not come to terms with the dream. In his memoirs, Jung says that at this moment he realized that "Siegfried" represented his heroic ideals and his Germanic willfulness—"Where there is a will there is a way!"—both of which he now had to give up. To be sure, he mentions that when Siegfried was killed, he felt as if he himself had been shot— "a sign of my secret identity with Siegfried"—and as well that he felt "overpowering compassion" and "grief." In his memoirs, Jung interprets these feelings in terms of what ". . . a man feels when he is forced to sacrifice his ideal and his conscious attitudes." As far as this goes, Jung was telling the truth. Siegfried had indeed been the symbol for his own heroic destiny as the man who would lead psychoanalysis out of error. And Jung was in fact in the process of irrevocably giving up that identity. But, here we would be wrong not to supplement Jung's interpretation with the obvious: Jung had other reasons for wanting "Siegfried" dead, and forgotten, reasons too terrible to share even fifty years later. He had indeed escaped the "danger of discovery" and his life would in fact go on—"but an unbearable feeling of guilt remained."

In the months that followed, Jung continued to use his solitude to experiment with his fantasies and gradually disassemble the various indictments of his conscience. He found he could initiate a vision by imagining himself descending to a depth of great distance. On one occasion, he felt as if he had landed on the moon, or alternatively the "land of the dead." There, he encountered two figures, an old man who introduced himself as "Elijah" accompanied by a young blind girl who identified herself as "Salome." Jung found the pair incongruous—an elderly patriarch in the company of a young woman—but Elijah assured him that they had been together for all eternity. They had a large black snake with them which took rather a liking to Jung. Jung found he distrusted Salome, who seemed to be the seductive embodiment of evil, but he had a long conversation with Elijah, though he didn't understand what was said.

That is as far as the memoirs go. In his 1925 seminar, Jung fleshed out some of the symbols. In his slightly inaccurate retelling, Salome was the stepdaughter of King Herod who, in the pursuit of an incestuous affair with her stepfather, had gotten John the Baptist beheaded. The black snake, meanwhile, was a symbol of his own deepening introversion. To this we may add that Elijah is generally considered a precursor to the Christ. As well, certain kabbalistic traditions have it that Elijah was himself seduced by Lilith, the witch who had been Adam's first wife. In short, Jung seemed to be descending once more into something like an incestuous-religious fantasy.

Also revealed in the 1925 seminar was a second vision involving Elijah and Salome. In this one, they shrank down to a tiny size. Jung found a ancient Gnostic inscription beginning "As above, so below . . ." The same inscription, let it be noted, had turned up in Part I of "Transformations" at a point where Jung came terribly close to giving a pornographic interpretation of a Christian sermon. Salome turned to him and addressing him as "Jesus Christ," asked him to cure her blindness. Jung protested, but in short order the black snake began coiling around him, and as he struggled to extricate himself he found himself inadvertently taking the pose of the Crucifixion. Then, his face turned into the head of the lion. He realized he'd become not Jesus, but Aion, a Mithraic god of his acquaintance from the library. Salome regained her sight.

Nowhere in his later disclosures of these fantasies did Jung ever suggest that Salome and Elijah might be personifications or replacements for the two people he had recently lost. Instead, what he stressed time and again—he even coined a term, "active imagination," for it—was that by deliberately surrendering himself to his fantasies, he had managed to gain a measure of control over them. In fact, just this suggests the true value of his fantasies in helping him resolve his personal predicament. Salome and Elijah, even though they acted with a will of their own in Jung's reverie, and even if they re-created painful interactions that had previously occurred with Spielrein and Freud, lacked the capacity to do real harm. For they remained inside Jung's internal world as his "characters," so to speak, which was infinitely preferable to his being theirs.

THE END

IN MANY WAYS, Freud had sought to build his movement on the strength of Jung's endeavor to become one with himself. Both men had now turned elsewhere to accomplish their goals. For both, it was time to dissolve the partnership. On 20 April 1914, Jung took the decisive step and sent off letters to the heads of each of the local psychoanalytic societies formally announcing his resignation as president of the International Association. On the copy sent to Freud, Jung marked " +++ " at the bottom—the old symbol, used several times in their correspondence, to ward off the devil. The "unedifying struggle" was finally over.

Spielrein had helped bring the final curtain down. In April she wrote to Jung to repeat various charges that were in the air, then took his hurt and embittered reply of 15 April 1914 and forwarded it to Freud with the comment: "Everyone knows that I declare myself an adherent to the Freudian Society and J. cannot forgive me for this." By May, however, Spielrein was feeling she had been used. She wrote a letter to Freud, which does not survive, accusing him of many things. Freud wrote back on 15 May:

> Now you are going crazy yourself, and, what is more, with the same symptoms as your predecessor! One day I, all unsuspecting, received a letter from Frau Jung saying that her husband was convinced I had something against him. That was the beginning; you know the ending.
>
> And your argument that I have not yet sent you any patients? Exactly the same thing happened with Adler, who pronounced himself persecuted because I had sent him no patients. . . .
>
> What in the world could I possibly have against you after the relationship we have had up till now? Isn't it nothing more than your own bad conscience due to your failure to free yourself from your idol? Think about it again and write to me about it.

Presumably, Spielrein withdrew her charges, but no evidence survives on this point.

In June, Freud wrote her again, this time asking her if she wanted to be listed on the masthead of the new *Jahrbuch*. He went to some lengths to make it clear that he appreciated her predicament: as all the Zurich names and addresses would shortly be eliminated, should her own appear it would indicate the "clearest sort of partisanship." "And this at a time when you are still in love with Jung," Freud continued, "when you cannot be really angry with him, see in him still the hero hounded by the mob, write to me in terms of his libido theory, blame Abraham for telling the plain truth!" Freud worded it all very decently—"don't stand on ceremony"—but at bottom it was an ultimatum: was she in or was she out? Freud had his hopes: "Of course I want you to succeed in casting aside as so much trash your infantile dreams of the Germanic champion and hero, on which hinges your whole opposition to your environment and to your origins; you should not demand from this phantom the child you must once have craved from your father."

Hard words, but how did Freud know that the Zurich names would all shortly be removed? What he did not tell Spielrein was what the new *Jahrbuch* would contain. Not only had Freud completed the planned theoretical essay "On Narcissism," he had simultaneously penned a very trenchant polemic, "On the History of the Psychoanalytic Movement." The latter had been expressly designed to provoke the final resignation of the Zurichers from their membership in the association. With his fine flair for such things, Freud planned to publish both pieces in the inaugural issue of the newly reconstituted *Jahrbuch*. And did Spielrein want to be on the masthead?

Spielrein, obviously, was having a great many second thoughts about a great many things. Perhaps she was also writing Jung about her misgivings. If so, this might help explain the fact that in June, Jung's visions began turning hopeful. Lately, he had been having repeated "visions" of Europe being covered by a giant sheet of ice. Now the "vision" came to a different ending: he saw himself plucking a bunch of healing grapes from a withered tree and handing them out to a multitude.

Freud's polemic in the *Jahrbuch* had the desired effect. On 10 July, the Zurich society voted to withdraw from the International Association. "So we are rid of them at last," Freud wrote exultantly to Abraham, "the brutal holy Jung and his pious parrots." Freud and his secret Committee congratulated themselves on their tactics. The International Association was theirs. In September, at the next congress, they would begin the task of consolidating their hold over the remainder of the association. Jones, the most problematic character among them but the only Gentile, was being groomed for the presidency through an analysis with Ferenczi.

Like everyone else in Europe, they had miscalculated. There would be no congress. There would be only war, a great terrible war with machine guns which would cancel all congresses everywhere and freeze international science where it stood. Jung's dreams of carnage and devastation had been eerily prophetic, and he took heart from that, though following yet another appearance in London in August, he found himself very nearly trapped abroad. He spent more than a month riding the German rails behind the front before he made it home to Switzerland.

THE SAD SAGA of the personal disengagement of three intimates is never without its own purely human interest. But the three people in this story had done more than cast their lot together. More than anyone else, they had been responsible—Spielrein must be included in this assessment by virtue of her influence on Jung—for launching the psychoanalytic movement and for determining its essential character. As with their coming together, so with their moving apart. The manner of their disengagement was their final determining act—it gave psychoanalysis the special cast that has continued to define it down to the present. The personal denouement had determined the political one. The political outcome in turn determined the theoretical future of psychoanalyis.

It can never be said of Freud that he welcomed criticism or was open to contrary expositions, nor even that he cared much for empirical methods. All these things had their place in science, Freud knew, but first honors most often went to the visionary who had looked out ahead of the field and saw where it must go. It was a risky posture, even for so marvelously systematic a mind. There was no way of knowing ahead of time whether one's genius would generate something akin to Darwin's theory of natural selection, or something more closely resembling Charcot's theory of hysteria. In this context, it could be said of the Swiss that they had kept Freud honest, at least for a time. The practical necessity of courting them had meant paying stricter attention to the data at hand and moving ahead at a much slower, more collegial pace. The yield was not only the achievement of scientific respectability, but also confirmation of some of Freud's most important theoretical innovations, such as the presence of symbolism inside of symptoms, the silent workings of repression to evade inner conflict, and the usefulness of addressing transferences inside treatment. Even some of the failures of the period, such as Freud's inability to produce a manual of interpretation, could be said to reflect the beneficent and sobering effects of the collaboration. But now the Swiss were gone.

Henceforth psychoanalysis was whatever Freud said it was. The unfortunate but inevitable result was that psychoanalysis came to be defined neither by its methods nor by any external criteria of validation. Rather, it was and continued to be defined by membership in its exclusive guild organizations. That privilege in turn was granted only to those able to adjust themselves to the existing authority structure and to the prevailing views as to what constituted acceptable interpretation and what did not. There was no mechanism in place for orderly theory-change, no way of adjudicating disputes as to what the data of treatment might be showing. For the rest of the century, theory change in psychoanalysis was accompanied, and inevitably delayed, by the continuing threat, and many times by the actuality, of fresh heresy trials and yet more schisms.

Can one blame Jung for this? Can one say that it was his turning, for a brief historical moment, toward a Christianized version of psychoanalysis that made the adoption of authoritarian internal structures and theoretical conservatism the institutional order of the day? There is a partial truth to such a charge. But it seems most unfair to blame a man who after 1914 was no longer on the premises. In truth, the blame must be laid at the feet of both men. When they had the chance to create an open organization and to put psychoanalysis on a potentially firm scientific footing they failed. The tragedy of their collaboration was that this founding mistake could not be corrected once they could no longer talk to each other.

Three essays appeared in 1914, the last year there was any official connection between Freud and Jung. Two of the essays were by Freud, one by Otto Gross. These essays exemplify the points already made above. By way of a sad conclusion let us note how they helped to wall up the doomed collaboration in its crypt once and for all.

Both of Freud's essays ran in the inaugural issue of the reconstituted *Jahrbuch*. The first of these was "On Narcissism." In broad overview, the essay constitutes a saunter through the intricacies of psychoanalytic instinct theory. The point of the excursion, which was rather a mini-Fordham lecture, only less lucid, would seem to be to substitute narcissism, defined as libido turned back upon the self, for the older idea of ego-instincts. At another level, the essay constituted an approximate portrait of Freud's own reaction to the loss of Jung—the self-love which he had formerly invested in his Swiss friend had, he hoped, now returned to himself.

In the course of "On Narcissism," Freud disposed of a number of irritating matters in grand style. His disagreements with Adler and Jung got top billing, but there were other items perhaps worth noticing. For example, with regard to the psychoses, he continued the campaign begun in the Schreber case of resurrecting the old psychiatric term of "paraphrenia" and announcing that henceforth he would use it in preference to both Kraepelin's "dementia praecox" and Bleuler's "schizophrenia." Bleuler's term was already passing into general use as *the* term for the syndrome, as it continues to be down to this day. Evidently, Freud intended to spoil Bleuler's little triumph by requiring psychoanalysts to use *his* term. Freud kept up this campaign with regard to nomenclature for years.

Then there was Spielrein's thesis. Here more than ever Freud would seem to need her explanation of repression. For by making the ego itself a derivative of libido, he had left hanging the whole question of how conflicts with regard to sexuality might conceivably originate. The only possible solution would seem to entail the idea that the ego, however it is instinctually funded, reacts with ambivalence to its dissolution in another. But Freud did not accord Spielrein so much as a mention, even when he momentarily paused to consider the view that man's instinctive nature is divided between the instinct for self-preservation and the instinct for species-preservation. Freud gave this view, Spielrein's and Tausk's, typically elegant expression: "The individual does actually carry on a twofold existence: one to serve his own purposes and the other as a link in a chain, which he serves against his will, or at least involuntarily." In short order, however, Freud dismissed out of hand this viewpoint as a possible guide to interpretation since it was derived not from the results of psychoanalysis "but derives its principal support from biology." As though Spielrein had not defended her thesis with clinical examples.

Freud's dismissal of Spielrein's contribution may be contrasted with an article adopting an altogether different attitude toward her thesis which had lately appeared in Stekel's *Zentralblatt*. Stekel managed to keep his journal afloat up until the war, in the process publishing a number of interesting but now forgotten articles. There was, for example, an article by Putnam on his treatment philosophy, which the ethical Yankee was unwilling to withdraw after having submitted it in good faith. There was also an article by Stekel himself which claimed priority for the idea of the "prospective" function of dreams. (This, obviously, was an idea whose time had come. Adler, too, was claiming that he had introduced the idea, and Silberer was now advancing along the same lines, though he used his own term, "anagogic," instead of "prospective.") As well, in 1914, the *Zentralblatt* also carried an article, "On Destruction Symbolism," by none other than Otto Gross.

After a whirlwind career which had brought him into contact with some of the foremost political agitators in Europe, Gross had finally been arrested as an anarchist sympathizer by the Prussian police and, at the instigation of his father, forcibly interned in an asylum outside of Vienna, where Stekel was called in to analyze him. As the perceived victim of the old patriarchal order, however, Gross then became a *cause célèbre* among Europe's more radical intellectuals, rather the Patty Hearst of his day, and a movement got under way to "Free Otto Gross." Gross was moved to a more secure facility, but then a verdict was won securing his release and a happy band of radicals made the pilgrimage to Austria to present the court order in person. When they arrived, however, they found that Gross was no longer a patient. Though still interned, he had risen to the position of staff physician.

Gross's *Zentralblatt* article, "On Destruction Symbolism," is noteworthy in that it is the only paper ever written by a confessed follower of Freud's that takes up Spielrein's theory in earnest. Indeed, Gross begins by explicitly taking cognizance of her intent: she had tackled the logic of sexual repression. Unfortunately, Gross thereupon used her ideas as a pretext for developing further his own ideas about patriarchy, rape, and the violation of the natural order. In Gross, Spielrein had found an utterly useless champion.

Finally, there is Freud's other *Jahrbuch* essay to consider, "On the History of the Psycho-Analytic Movement." Compared to "On Narcissism" and other of Freud's contributions during this time, his "History" had the great virtue of a straightforward polemical style. Members of the Committee read it in galleys. In general, Freud's recounting of the vagaries of his movement demonstrated the truism that there are two sides to every story. Expectably, Freud told his side with conviction and verve. In the end he seemed to be asking nothing more than that the poor renegades who had left the true path stop calling their heresies "psychoanalysis." Along the way, he specifically decried the use of psychoanalysis itself as a weapon in polemics, though, of course, as he explained to the reader, he could not entirely keep himself from thinking about his opponents' motives. Thus, despite Abraham's explicit advice to the contrary, the exact word "persecution" was used in connection with Adler, thus making it clear to those in the know that he considered the man paranoid.

Here let us confine ourselves to some of what Freud had to say about Jung. For those readers who have found some of Jung's ramblings about symbolism and religious sublimation difficult to bear, the following blast will come as a refreshing breeze:

All the changes that Jung has proposed to make in psychoanalysis flow from his intention to eliminate what is objectionable in the family-complexes, so as not to find it again in religion and ethics. For sexual libido an abstract concept has been substituted, of which one may safely say that it remains mystifying and incomprehensible to wise men and fools alike. The Oedipus complex has a merely "symbolic" meaning: the mother in it means the unattainable, which must be renounced in the interests of civilization; the father who is killed in the Oedipus myth is the "inner" father, from whom one must set oneself free in order to become independent. . . . In this way a new religio-ethical system has been created, which, just like the Adlerian system, was bound to re-interpret, distort or jettison the factual findings of analysis. The truth is that these people have picked out a few cultural overtones from the symphony of life and have once more failed to hear the mighty and primordial melody of the instincts.

The closing metaphor would seem to invoke Wagner's operas above all, where the themes representing the characters' feelings are played by the orchestra beneath the stage while the performers are required to sing above and against them. Spielrein's "Siegfried," the reader may recall, had first come to her while she was listening to the Wagnerian theme which bears his name. Freud's was a very lovely metaphor, indeed.

This was as close as Freud would come to violating his agreement with Jung to avoid personal disclosures. In effect, he was merely reminding Jung of it. The reminders crop up elsewhere in the essay. For example, Freud quotes at length a letter from one of Jung's patients saying how demoralizing Jung's homilies had been. The patient is not Spielrein, and Freud admits that using a patient's recriminations is a questionable procedure, but then in a footnote he says, "I cannot allow that a psycho-analytic technique has any right to claim the protection of medical discretion." Then, too, there is his statement that Jung's theories are contradicted by every properly conducted psychoanalysis, "and in particular every analysis of a child." Once again, Freud avoids mentioning Spielrein's recent contribution in that area and instead mentions Jung's own published Clark lecture on the subject of his older daughter's curiosity about the birth of the family's first boy. Finally, Freud concludes by implying that all Jung's innovations constitute evasions of the reality of the patient's illness. They therefore reflect on Jung's competency as an analyst. At bottom, Freud attributes the suspect innovations either to the "physician's incapacity" to help the patient overcome the resistances "... or else to the physician's dread of the results of his own work."

This was the essay that caused Jung, and most of the rest of the Zurichers, to resign their membership in the International Association. For his part, Jung never mastered this sort of insinuating style. He did have his own views about Freud's personality, and in some ways even had gone into print with them in the abstract. The problem was that you couldn't get there from here unless you already knew what Jung did. And Jung would not be free to say what he knew for many, many years to come.

To follow Freud and Jung further in any great detail is impossible here. They remained preoccupied with each other, and embittered, but the tasks that faced them in the years ahead were entirely different. Freud had to rebuild his psychoanalytic movement and try to recoup the scientific lustre that had been largely lost during the unseemly struggle with the Swiss. Jung had to establish himself as a great psychologist in his own right, as someone who had made fundamental discoveries of his own about the inner nature of man. Both men had learned the techniques required for these different tasks during their collaboration, and both would be successful. As for Spielrein, her career needs to be outlined because it is largely unknown and because it sheds essential light on the new world she had helped bring into existence.

CHAPTER 18

In Search of a Great Destiny

I am, and most especially always was, somewhat mystical in my learnings; I violently resisted the interpretation of Siegfried as a real child, *and on the basis of my mystical tendencies* I would have simply thought that a great and heroic destiny awaited me, that I had to sacrifice myself for the creation of something great. How else could I interpret those dreams in which my father or grandfather blessed me and said, "A great destiny awaits you, my child"?

—Sabina Spielrein, letter to Carl Jung, 19 January 1918

———

O**NE WOULD LIKE** to report that Spielrein eventually found happiness in her marriage and in her children—a second daughter, Eva, was born at the end of World War I—and that she went on to have a long and distinguished career as a psychoanalyst. But, as with so many in Europe, her fate was ultimately decided by the massive upheavals by which the twentieth century gave the lie to the confident hopes of the nineteenth. Although she and all her family escaped the machine guns of the first great conflagration, something more horrible still arose in Germany and it finally caught up with her in her hometown of Rostov-on-Don in 1941. Along with the rest of the city's Jews, she and her two daughters were taken to a synagogue and shot during the Nazi occupation. Escape was no doubt impossible, but it is said that Spielrein hastened her end by accosting a Nazi officer and rebuking him in German. A long time before, she had lived in Berlin. She disbelieved that the people she had once lived among could be capable of atrocity.

By the time she was murdered, there was little left of the world she had grown up in. Her parents were already dead, their fortune lost in the Russian Revolution. (Her last known paper was dedicated to the memory of her father.) Spielrein's husband was dead, too, felled by a heart attack. For a time he had left her, but then he returned with yet another daughter by another woman. After his death, Spielrein raised the girl as her own. Spielrein's three brothers, who had taken an interest in their sister's career, with one even contributing an article to the *Zeitschrift,* found their deaths at Stalin's hands in the 1930s. In the phrase that until recently was all one could say about such things in Russia, "The threads of their lives had been cut short."

And so disappeared a world which had once sent forth an hysterical teenager who thought she was ugly and could not bear to be looked at. A world where young ladies did not perspire and in which even eating might lead to thoughts of defecation and shame. A world where the curriculum of the local Gymnasium could be altered by a rich woman so that her daughter's "purity" might not be spoiled by learning about reproduction. And yet it was also a world in which infidelity was routine and prostitution so rampant that it could be, after the tangled affairs of the Czarist state, the second-leading industry in the capital city of St. Petersburg. Likewise, it was a world where a cuckolded father could break into the all-too-pure magic circle of his wife and firstborn daughter and enjoy himself by spanking the child for his own pleasure. A world in which sexual desire permeated everywhere, but was nowhere to be named—unless it could be made artistically beautiful or philosophically wonderful.

Likewise it was a world of imagined greatness, of important destinies waiting to be fulfilled, if only one could somehow break free of the stifling comforts and cynical practicalities of the bourgeois world. Everywhere from the coffeehouses of Vienna to the officer clubs of the Kaiser's army, men imagined that they could be the next Darwin or the next Bismarck or the next Nietzsche. In having her own heroic destiny to fulfill, Spielrein was a child of her times. The only difference was that she was a woman.

THE ARTIST

A RUSSIAN NATIONAL, Spielrein relocated to neutral Switzerland shortly after World War I broke out. She stopped first in Zurich, where she made contact with Bleuler, and then with Jung and his circle. About the latter we know only that she informed Freud of the encounter. His reply of 20 April 1915 is all that survives of the incident:

> I fully agree with your treatment, but don't let's talk too much of Jung; you will always find one or more excuses for him. Your reports from Z[urich] have been supplemented recently by Dr. Pfis-

ter. . . . My impression is that those people are more stupid than we ever dared think.

From Zurich Spielrein relocated to Lausanne in French Switzerland, down the lakeshore from the city of Geneva. Her psychoanalytic publications had already begun to trail off. She contributed three articles in 1914, and one each in 1915 and 1916. The articles were brief, uninspired, and completely in line with the editorial policies of those journals. Typical was her sole contribution of 1916, "The Formation of the Oedipus Complex in Children," which was noteworthy only in her suggestion that hormonal development might play a role. There was no mention in any of her papers of "destruction," "transformation," "sacrifice," the "prophetic powers of the unconscious," or any of the other topics that had once occupied her attention.

The altogether prosaic nature of Spielrein's contributions during this period was symptomatic of a deeper malaise. Her chosen career was proving to be a dead end. Neither her heart nor her remarkable intellect was engaged. In Lausanne, she finally quit psychoanalysis altogether, going to work in a surgery clinic because she wanted to do something "useful." Her publications ceased. But the surgery clinic did not provide her with the inspiration she sought, and in a dream she saw herself as an artist. She sent the dream to Jung—his reply, if he wrote one, does not survive—but then decided on her own that she knew well what the interpretation was. She was destined to become a composer. Hastily, she composed several verses in a makeshift notation of her own and set off for the local conservatory. Somehow she found a young composer willing to take her on as a student. Some idea of the depth of her isolation can be gauged from the fact that it was literally months before she realized that she had not been to the conservatory at all, but had found her tutor in another building altogether.

Now, however, something began to stir in her. The music itself was a blessing. She would so lose herself in her lessons, her tutor too, that at the end of their sessions they had no sense of how much time had passed, and his wife had to make out the bill. Beyond consolation, the music also provided inspiration. Her new friend took some passages at random from her notebook and set them to music. Included was a line which he rendered as "I know what remorse my courage is touched by: the coward fears death and that is all he fears." Apparently the line echoed the old concerns about "consequences," "second thoughts," and fears of dying in the other. She sent the verses to Jung. He did not reply.

Next she came across a new work by Jung, "The Structure of the Unconscious," which appeared in the *Archives de Psychologie* in early 1916. In it, Jung spoke for the first time of "collective" elements in the unconscious. Jung's basic argument was that while certain material that emerged in analysis was clearly derived from the personal past, other elements reflected rather universal potentials of the human mind. Among the indications that this collective layer had been reached were feelings of both deflation and "godlikeness." Jung further argued that the application of the "nothing but" theories of Freud and Adler to the fantasies that arose from the collective layer would lead only to a life of resignation. Instead of such "semiotic" styles of interpretation, in which symbols pointed only to instincts, Jung now proposed a "hermeneutic" style, which would respect the fact that such fantasies were groping toward something yet unrealized in the person's life. Other telltale indications that one was making contact with the collective unconscious were feelings that one was either very large or small, or that one was falling, or else that one was already dead. Moreover, Jung described the state as one of "disorientation" whose resemblance to "mental derangement" was "very close." All this of course directly reflected Jung's own experiences with his fantasies during the years 1913–1914. Jung's conclusion likewise betrayed his personal hopes and fears, for he argued that during this stage of analysis, covertly his own self-analysis, "All the treasures of mythological thinking and feeling are unlocked." In any event, Spielrein found his essay entirely amicable and again wrote to him; this time for her trouble she got a collegial thank-you note on 31 May 1916.

The emotional stirrings inside Spielrein still did not stop: next she had a dream of "Siegfried." When she awoke, her first thought was, "So, he is alive after all, her Siegfried." At about the same time, Spielrein came across and read a second work by Jung, *The Psychology of the Unconscious Processes*. This monograph, an updated and much-expanded version of "New Paths in Psychology," saw Jung continuing his articulation of the idea of the collective unconscious by bringing in clinical material. First, Jung took a case of a hysterical reaction and demonstrated that it could be analyzed equally well along either Freudian or Adlerian lines. The two approaches, he suggested, were complementary, though both were restricted to the personal past. Then he went on to describe a dramatic moment from a case of his own, in which the patient confessed that she sometimes saw him as an "evil magician." Such a transference, Jung argued, could not possibly reflect her previous experience, there being no evil magicians about in the modern world. Like other such mythological projections, it betrayed, rather, the inner presence of a specific psychological structure—Jung here used the term "dominant," but in a few years' time would replace it with "archetype"—that was part of man's archaic past.

This work, too, covertly recapitulated elements taken from Jung's own secret fantasy life. Included among the "dominants" was a figure usually represented by a dream companion portrayed as a dark-skinned man of Mongoloid type. Such a figure had accompanied Jung in his 1913 dream in which he killed Siegfried. Also mentioned was Brother Medardus, the hero of E. T. A. Hoffmann's novel *The Devil's Elixirs,* which had so fascinated Jung during the scandal-plagued spring of 1909. As well, the overall thrust of Jung's argument betrayed a further debt to Hoffmann. The Freudian and Adlerian perspectives were useful for the analysis of people in the first half of life, Jung asserted, when their life-energy was still in the ascendant. But in the "afternoon of life," he argued, one had to develop a spiritual dimension and this required accessing the collective unconscious.

Between Jung's latest monograph and her own dream of "Siegfried," Spielrein had ample excuse and once more, in the early fall of 1917, she wrote to Jung. The documentary record is incomplete, but it appears that this was the occasion for his letter of 13 September 1917, which survives. Evidently, Jung wrote, he was still a figure in her unconscious; if she could decipher the "hieroglyphics" of her dream, they would serve as a link to the collective psyche and a guide to her future development. Jung added that he himself had lately lost sleep trying to grapple with these very same issues. In fact, he had.

But Spielrein did not know any of this. She was completely in the dark about Jung's personal turmoil. Even less did she know that it was in fact currently worsening. Jung had taken a double precaution: just as his ideas on the collective unconscious had stayed clear of any exegesis linking them with his previous interest in mythology, so too did his formulations about analysis avoid any personal revelations. Spielrein's only points of departure were his theoretical statements and his letter, and she found the latter somewhat mystifying as regards her own dream. She wrote back to say so—her letter does not survive—and thereby did something she dared not do: she intruded on Jung's psychic privacy. She had no clue how fragile he was, nor what a danger she represented. In his reply of 10 October 1917, Jung erupted:

Yes, my most revered, I have been blasphemed enough, mocked enough, and criticized thoroughly; therefore I will keep my runes and all my pale and thin little ideas, some of which I shared in my "Libido" work. . . . Now you may wish the sun and the eternal beauty of the mystery of the earth, you even demand it. But I do not trust your arguments, just as one does not trust Germany's pacifist ideas after it has for years prayed to the lord of wars. I do not disclose my secret to have it trampled on without any understanding. Round this garden there is now a thick, high wall, I can assure you. There is nothing behind it other than the well known old poverties and "superficial allegories" . . . You see, Freud's theory goes much deeper, even into the glands, the deepest that can be said about human psychology. Going deeper down, back into the womb, is really not possible. From there it would even be easier to explain the world. All the rest is "unscientific," symbolic lies built on repressed anal eroticism. One only has to know that everything in the end comes from the mother's womb and that it is nothing but sexuality and its unfortunate repression. All else is nothing but that. For another helpful hypothesis one can also recommend Anti-Semitism and a few other little slanders besides.

Spielrein did not answer for well over a month. Then she hit on a plan. First, she wrote to Freud, apparently to say that she was currently not doing much of anything, for his very brief reply of 18 November 1917 agrees with her: "You are right: times are hard and not favorable to scientific work." Jung had reacted to her as a member of Freud's party, which indeed she had been up to this time. Her letter to Freud thus seems to have been designed to clear her conscience on this point and to make sure that she and Jung would have their privacy, so to speak. Next, she wrote back to Jung on 27 November 1917. Adopting a dry, matter-of-fact tone, she began to outline at great length her current intellectual apprehension of his position vis-à-vis Freud and Adler, while using her little daughter as a case in point. Further, she asked Jung to return this and future letters as they would be very important for her future development. In short, she was presenting herself once more as a student.

Now they could talk. The dialogue continued intensively for at least three months, and then on and off for nearly two years afterward. Unfortunately, the documentary record, though extensive, contains numerous omissions. It is sufficient to make out the essence of the exchange, though not all of its particulars and not its ultimate resolution. On Spielrein's side, there survive eight very long letters by her, all written during a three-month period from November 1917 through

January 1918. Jung's side of the exchange is represented by ten surviving letters in all, and cover a much longer period, from November 1917 through October 1919. Sometimes, but not always, one can deduce the content of Spielrein's letters from Jung's replies.

About Spielrein's letters, it should be noted that while they are quite difficult for the modern reader, they represent an honest and intelligent effort to come to grips with the theories of Jung, Adler, and Freud. Beyond itemizing the differences, Spielrein also tried to forge a synthesis among the three, using as her point of departure the theory she had herself outlined in 1912. Moreover, whenever the task of integration seemed to get stuck, Spielrein repeatedly jumped in with practical examples so that the respective merits of the three theories could be judged on their clinical merit. In these respects, her letters are unique in the entire surviving documentary record of psychoanalysis. If anyone else made such an intensive attempt at integration during this period, their efforts have been lost. As for what they reveal of her own person, the letters show Spielrein not only to have regained her productivity, but also her intellectual incisiveness.

About Jung's letters, it should be pointed out that though he fairly quickly regained his composure, he remained prone to occasional outbursts. It should also be pointed out that he assumed that Spielrein was still seeking personal guidance from him as well as theoretical instruction. To be sure, he had some warrant for this posture, for the two did not get very far into the exchange before more intimate matters came up. The pivotal moment occurs in Spielrein's letter of 9 January 1918:

Depending on the personality of the patient and more especially that of the doctor, analysis of the "unconscious" can rob the analyzed material of its energy or "saturate it with blood." Probably the neutral attitude on the part of the doctor which Freud recommends is the best one for the average patient, for: if the doctor registers disapproval in the course of the analysis, he increases the patient's resistance and repression; if he displays too much pleasure—he encourages the patient in his self-indulgent tendencies and "saturates his desires with blood." These two extremes are especially risky in an analysis involving a doctor and a patient of different sex.

Now there is a further step, and this would be your method: Freud says one should now leave it to the patient to find a useful application for the newfound energy. You, on the other hand, feel that one should continue the analysis (analysis of the subconscious) in order to reveal to the patient his "higher goals" (vocation). This question is better resolved from experience than *a priori*. At first sight it seems to me that the Freudian method is better suited to the average patient, whereas yours applies to strong people who are capable of sublimation (here I still have in mind a doctor and a patient of different sex, because as a rule the danger of fixation is greater).

And here, finally, "Siegfried" made his appearance amidst a long discursus on whether music was indeed her vocation or whether she was deceiving herself through a faulty analysis of her dreams. The question seemed to hinge on how "Siegfried" should be interpreted:

Probably the misapprehension in regard to the Siegfried problem can be ascribed to conscious analysis, but I see it differently from the way you do: *in the beginning Siegfried was probably "real" for my subconscious,* which cleverly saw through your own subconscious attitude toward this problem. Later the difficulties of everyday life arose; you, as an adult, experienced person, could see all the ramifications. I was still much too young, and my first love and "vocation" were too sacred for me to follow your arguments and give heed to the symbols that the subconscious probably produced to warn me. I can still recall one of these warning symbols. Probably there were many of them.

So you see how I approach the problem; the subconscious can be encouraged to work through a problem in either a real or a sublimated form. Of course it can also warn one against solving the problem in a "real" form; it thereby points one toward the sublimated form. *A person's subconscious approach can, however, be completely altered by conscious processing of a problem or exposure to suggestive influences.* This is how you finally killed off the "real" Siegfried, as you explained it to me (proof that you, too, had a "real" one), i.e., sacrificed him in favor of a sublimated one. I, on the contrary, killed in my dreams the man who was supposed to become Siegfried's father, and then in reality found another man.

In an addendum written the next day, Spielrein added in italics: *"Now I would be very interested to hear what you think of my comments and how you see these matters.''* Yet another addendum indicates that she waited ten days to post the letter.

Jung drew back. "Siegfried is a symbol that ceases to be a symbol," he wrote her, "the moment it is recognized as our specific heroic attitude." If she could not get hold of this concept, he added, she would never understand his new ideas. Beyond that, he said that her music was but a "bridge" for her to make contact with her unconscious feelings.

Spielrein stayed the course. Still keeping to the format of a theoretical discussion, she replied with a number of contrary points, including the thought that perhaps music was more practical for her than psychiatry since in the latter field she always had to overcome inner resistances stemming from infancy. She used a recent dream of a cartoon to illustrate the impracticalities of her nature: ". . . in the foreground a German general, forceful, furiously determined, energetic, and behind him the Russian (Kerensky) with his army, just like Christ, full of idealism and goodness." The caption read: "Why the Russians lost." And, speaking of practicalities, would he recommend her for a psychiatric post if it came to that? Probably not, she concluded, even though he considered that she had a "heroic attitude" and even "religious feelings." Her letter ended with a sigh: "That's just the way the world is, I guess, and that is why it is so difficult to find a practical path that will lead one out of one's daydreams, other than in musical creations."

Jung thought her dream went to the heart of the matter: she lived halfway between the Russian and the German worlds, between reality and "Christification." Her mistake lay in trying to bring Siegfried into reality rather than understanding him as a bridge between the inner and outer worlds. A second letter by Jung then developed this thought unhappily further:

> Do not forget that the Jews also had prophets. You do not yet live one part of the Jewish soul because you look too much to the external. That is—regrettably—the curse of the Jew: his innermost and deepest soul he calls "infantile wish fulfillment." He murders his own prophet, murders even his Messiah.

Still Spielrein was undaunted. In her next letter, she took Jung's frightful charge, turned it on its head—the Jews had a much more profound concept of the Messiah—and forged ahead with yet more questions about theory, about her dreams, about Siegfried, and about what she should do in life. She fully accepted the prophetic function of the unconscious, she wrote, but that still left too many questions hanging:

> Does our subconscious give us any clues as to which of two noble contents we should choose, or does it say for instance, "It is your lot to create a great Aryan-Semitic hero" and then leave it to me whether I fulfill this high religious vocation by realizing this great poet, musician, and world savior in the form of a child or in the form of an artistic or a scientific work?

And just here, in the extant documents, the dialogue stops. No further letters from Spielrein to Jung survive. The next extant letter from Jung comes a full ten months later; the next after that comes more than a year later. Yet, even granted that the historical record does not permit us to eavesdrop to the extent we might like, it is sufficient to make out the essence of the conversation that went on. What had begun as a theoretical exchange was gradually turning into a subtle psychological struggle. Jung saw in Spielrein's various dreams and fantasies evidence that she was still too much in the grip of Freudianism to understand that what was stirring in her was her own inner self. He assimilated her psychic situation to his own, and encouraged her to adopt the new theories that had thus far comforted him. And to a certain extent, Spielrein understood this and was theoretically compliant. But she had other things on her mind as well. Specifically, she wanted to hear from him that long before "Siegfried" had become an emblem for her spiritual destiny, he had been a symbol of their love for each other. And she was not going to let go of the conversation until she got that satisfaction. Just this, however, threatened Jung in a way that Spielrein could not understand.

Around and around they went, kept from saying what they needed to say by, of all things, psychology.

THE BUDAPEST CONGRESS

SEVERAL HUNDRED miles to the east, Sigmund Freud was trying to get his movement back on its feet. The city of Vienna had been largely stable during the war, but the two years following the armistice brought economic ruin. Spielrein's brother Jean managed to visit Freud there in the summer of 1919. Shortly thereafter, Freud heard from Spielrein herself. She seems not to have told him of her ongoing correspondence with Jung, though she did report on happenings inside his group. With regard to Jung, she announced only that she was translating some of his works into Russian for financial reasons. In the same vein, she asked if she could continue to be enrolled as a member of the Vienna society, and keep her journal subscriptions, without paying her dues for the time being. She also announced that she would soon be sending along some new contributions. In short, Spielrein was ready to reenter the fray. Whatever else it accomplished, her dialogue with Jung had got her going again in her career. And like so many others who had been associated with psychoanalysis before the war, she was eager to pick up where she had left off.

Freud's mood during the war has been described by Jones:

> In 1917 Freud had reached the nadir of his expectations about the future of his life's work. After the defection of Alfred Adler, Wilhelm Stekel and the Swiss he felt he could almost count on the fingers of one hand the number of adherents in the whole world whom he could trust to further his work in the way he would want.

Jones does not mention where the biggest threat to Freud's vision lay. In fact, it was the same thing Jung and Spielrein were currently discussing in their letters—the prospective theory of dream interpretation. Bjerre's recently published history of psychoanalysis had described this rather as the culmination of psychoanalytic theory. Maeder's Munich presentation, which featured not only a prospective angle but also stressed an ethical dimension, was already translated into English. Jung's latest work featured a similar emphasis on spiritual development. Adler's most recent book, *The Nervous Character,* had emphasized the teleological function of neurotic symptoms in general as well as claiming priority for the prospective style of dream interpretation in particular. Stekel had independently claimed priority for the latter idea. James Jackson Putnam had recently published a major work seeking to reconcile Hegelian ethics with psychoanalytic method. G. Stanley Hall was studying Adler's writings and finding that they fit well with his own ideas about education. And Herbert Silberer had written a massive work, *Problems of Mysticism,* in which he examined an ancient alchemical tract along two separate interpretive lines, the "psychoanalytic" and the "anagogic" (Silberer's variant on the prospective style), and showed that the tract in question in fact constituted a manual for spiritual development. (Silberer's work led to an estrangement with Freud, who objected that it fell to the "psychoanalytic" method to reveal the "low" instinctual material, while the "anagogic" method uncovered the "higher" spiritual tendencies.)

What all these people basically believed was that in addition to "analysis," therapy had to be supplemented by some form of "synthesis." Freud's problem, if one can put it this way, was that once international scientific activity resumed, these thinkers would begin attending congresses and sharing their views—and Jung would presumably be there to lead them. The one advantage Freud had was the skeleton of the International Association. He stole a march on everyone by convening the Fifth International Psychoanalytic Congress in September of 1918. Held in Budapest before the Treaty of Versailles was signed, the congress was the first international scientific meeting of the postwar period. For the occasion, Freud presented "Lines of Advance in Psycho-Analytic Therapy." Calling "psycho-synthesis" an "empty phrase," Freud argued that the instinctual impulses uncovered by analysis would themselves provide all the synthetic activity needed. Freud specifically recalled his previous disagreement with the Swiss: "We refused most emphatically to turn a patient who puts himself into our hands in search of help into our private property, to decide his fate for him, to force our own ideals upon him, and with the pride of a Creator to form him in our own image and see that it is good."

For his trouble, Freud was greeted upon his return to Vienna with a new book from Pfister. What was Pfister arguing? That psychoanalysis was too one-sided in its focus on the sexual instinct. With his customary high-minded pugnaciousness, Pfister went on to demand a new method, which he proposed to call "organic," which would take into account all the instincts in psychic life. Freud fired off a letter to his clergyman friend that is celebrated for the following intemperate challenge: "Incidentally, why was it that none of all the pious ever discovered psychoanalysis? Why did it have to wait for a completely godless Jew?" Yet, if one reads the letter more clearly, one finds that in fact Freud begins to get tripped up on his own reasoning. He argues that psychoanalysis is quite right to focus on the sexual instinct because its "conservative" nature and its close connection with the "pleasure principle" make it decisive for neurosis. But this was more or less what Pfister had already argued, namely that sexuality was generally a regressive force in psychic life against which some spiritual counterweight had to be found.

The net result was that as the terrible winter of 1918–1919 began to descend on Vienna, Freud embarked on a six-month meditation upon the nature of the instincts and their relevance for treatment strategies. Along the way, he dug out of his desk drawer an old paper, "The Uncanny," that he had begun a decade earlier following Jung's second visit to Vienna. This topic was closely related to the psycho-synthesis problem, for it was precisely the intrusion of uncanny events that Jung had first used to justify his own turn toward "psycho-synthesis." Freud quickly made two discoveries of significant rhetorical import. First, as a matter of course, he reread Hoffmann's *The Devil's Elixirs* and discovered there the exact passage which had inspired Jung's dream of himself as a dead customs official. Freud published the passage in the *Zeitschrift* without comment, presumably as a signal to Jung. Second, and more important, Freud discovered that he could strip the uncanny of any spiritual implications by reinterpreting it along the lines of one of Ferenczi's ideas, namely that there was a compulsion to repeat in psychic life. (Ferenczi had advanced this idea in 1913 as part of the general campaign to discredit the Swiss. In Ferenczi's formulation, which itself was more rhetorical than substantive, the compulsion to repeat operated phylogenetically and thus generated the illusion of a progressive dimension in psychic life.) It was a tricky argument to make, since it meant reducing all uncanny phenomena to variations on *déjà vu* phenomena, but Freud soon convinced himself that it was the way to go. By the summer of 1919, he was convincing himself of something even more outrageous, namely that this compulsion to repeat constituted a basic instinctual tendency leading the individual to seek death.

"THE LOVE OF S. FOR J."

WHILE FREUD was meditating on the nature of instincts, Jung and Spielrein were continuing their long-distance discussion on "Siegfried." A brief letter from Jung of 29 November 1918 concerns a dream she had sent him; in his comment, Jung suggested that she was still too concerned with the external world. The next extant letter, dated 19 March 1919, is much graver in tone. Her dreams have taken on a "murderous" and "threatening quality," he told her, because she was still too materialistic in her attitude. She should recognize the "godlike spirit" within and not kill it with rationalizations. "I hope it is not too late," is how Jung closes.

Since no further letters from Spielrein survive, one can only surmise what she had recently communicated that might have warranted Jung's altogether graver tone. By this point Spielrein had resumed her psychoanalytic writings. In 1919 she published a review of the Russian psychoanalytic literature, and in 1920 she would publish no less than five papers. So it was not the choice of career that was at issue. However, among her 1920 papers there is one, "Little Renate's Theory of the Origin of People," that gives more than a clue. The paper, which continued in the tradition begun by Freud of documenting children's sexual researches, describes Renate's attempts to come to terms with the birth of a sister. This was the problem that was informing her letters to Jung in the spring of 1919: Spielrein was pregnant again. And once again she felt that "Siegfried" had turned into a lethal presence within who might do harm to the unborn child.

Jung's next extant letter, dated 3 April 1919, is graver still; it is also explicit. She must accept "Siegfried" as a godlike part of herself, as something which mediates between reality and the unconscious; only then would he no longer be a threat either to her or the child. Jung insisted that "Siegfried" was a representation of the "hero," at once "center point" and "saviour" and not merely a wishful fantasy. At times, Jung is quite fervent:

> Freud's opinion is a sinful rape of the holy. It spreads darkness not light . . . [o]nly out of the deepest night is new light born. Siegfried is that spark. . . . I lit in you a new light that you must safeguard for times of darkness.

Yet the letter also has a curious admission: Jung announces that he is afraid of the "frivolity" and "tyrannical self-glorification" of the female psyche. Sounding more threatened than critical, he goes on to link her "rationalistic and materialistic interpretations" to a feminine tendency to bring everything down to the realm of the "banal."

There are only two further letters of Jung's. The next, dated 1 September 1919, is brief, honest, and revealing:

> The love of S. for J. made the latter aware of something he had previously only vaguely suspected, that is, of a power in the unconscious that shapes one's destiny, a power which later led him to things of the greatest importance. The relationship had to be "subliminated" because otherwise it would have led him to delusion and madness (the concretization of the unconscious). Occasionally one must be unworthy, simply in order to be able to continue living.

One would like to know what prompted the admission. Quite possibly, it was the birth of another child to Spielrein, again a girl, again healthy. (The child grew up to be an accomplished musician.) If one reviews Jung's letters to her during the previous two years, one finds that he is repeatedly afraid of something. First, it is the Freudian school, then the German technical spirit, then materialism, then the Jewish spirit, and finally the female psyche. In each case, Jung appears to be afraid of an imagined engulfment by a point of view which, as it were, misunderstands him intimately. In each case, further, Spielrein is seen as the personification of the threat. Thus, against her own interpretations, Jung had stubbornly clung to his own view of "Siegfried." Now, however, in his letter of 1 September 1919, Jung was finally admitting that there was another side to "Siegfried" after all.

Jung's final letter, written five weeks later, is more mysterious than revealing. Apparently Spielrein had written him to ask a question about his new theory of types. That by itself suggests that they had finally resolved, as much as they ever would, who "Siegfried" was to them, and perhaps what they were to each other. In any event, Jung's letter, dated 7 October 1919, contains two diagrams schematically comparing the types of various persons; the first diagram compares himself, Bleuler, and Freud, while the second compares Goethe, Kant, Schopenhauer, and Schiller. There then follows without explanation a mysterious third diagram composed of an outer circle labeled with the symbol of masculinity and an inner circle labeled with the feminine symbol. Two x's mark the top and the bottom of the inner circle: the top x is labeled "Spielrein consc." while the bottom half of the diagram as a whole is labeled "uncs." The diagram has a vertical and a horizontal line which cross at the middle, seemingly to indicate that Jungs's theory of types is implicated here, too. Jung's only comment is that perhaps Spielrein was once more extraverted than she is now.

And that is as much as anybody knows about how the relationship between Jung and Spielrein finally ended.

SPIELREIN IN GENEVA

SPIELREIN NEXT turns up in a documentary record with her appearance on the roster of speakers at the Sixth International Psychoanalytic Congress, held at The Hague in September of 1920. It was, oddly enough, her first congress ever, and for her maiden address she lectured on "The Origin and Development of Spoken Speech." The talk was striking in its attempt to integrate Freud's notion of a primary autistic stage in infancy ruled by the pleasure principle with the findings of developmental psychology. Taking the words "mama" and "papa" as her examples, Spielrein argued that the child's first words arise out of the act of sucking and are imbued with a magical, wish-fulfilling quality. Gradually these first words become oriented to the environment, signs of a germinating hetero-eroticism. With further development, and the subconscious assimilation of the present to the past, these words give rise to the first sentences. In short, spoken speech arises in an intermediary zone between the pleasure and reality principles.

Following the congress, Spielrein relocated to Geneva, taking up residence at the Institut Rousseau, which was fast becoming the world's leading pedagogical center. In 1912, Flournoy's nephew, Edouard Claparède, had set up a pedagogical laboratory at the University of Geneva. Out of this grew the institute, which was headed jointly by Claparède and Pierre Bovet. From the first, courses in various psychotherapeutic methods, including psychoanalysis, had been part of the curriculum, not always with happy results. A lecturer on Couéism had been arrested under an old cantonal law proscribing hypnotism, while a Freudian named Schneider had alienated one and all with his unabashed proselytizing. Another Freudian, a Miss Malan, had done somewhat better, but by 1920 it was clear to men like Claparède that the sectarian zeal of the psychoanalysts was a potential threat to the spirit of open inquiry. (In Zurich, men like Binswanger and Pfister had become similarly sensitized to the threat after Committee member Hanns Sachs's unhappy stay there at the end of the war.) One consequence was that the local psychoanalytic society under Claparède's direction was kept informal. It met irregularly, it was open to all comers, and no effort was made to have it sanctioned by the International Association.

Within the society, however there was a smaller Psychoanalytic Group which met weekly and was restricted to members willing to register with the International Association. Within this group were some of the leading lights of the institute, including Bovet, currently the director; Raymond de Saussure, son of the famous linguist; Gustav Bally, a Swiss linguist; and Jean Piaget, a promising newcomer who was just beginning his pioneer researches on child development. Spielrein's stay was subsequently remembered by Bovet in somewhat ungallant terms:

But the great hopes placed in our institute were not dead. We discovered this in 1921, with the arrival in Geneva of a Russian woman, timid and tenacious, named Sabina Spielrein-Scheftel. She said she had been appointed by the International Psychoanalytic Congress in Holland to the position of assistant psychoanalyst at the J. J. Rousseau Institute. She set out to win recognition from her new province the way a bishop would take possession of his diocese. Claparède, always courteous, set up a small consulting room for her in his laboratory and Miss Spielrein began her apostolic work . . .

We were somewhat reserved in regard to this new missionary. However, we did attempt to give our students the benefits of Miss Spielrein's very real expertise by organizing some lectures for her and inviting her to the meetings of the "Psychoanalytic Group." She brought some new life to the group by having some of us analyzed regularly, following all the Freudian rules.

Miss Spielrein left the way she came. We remember her with gratitude, but her tenure here did not bring about the progress of psychoanalysis which was, it seems, expected of her in high places.

In fact, Spielrein's stay was being financed by a secret fund—there was more than one—under the control of the secret Committee. That she was temperamentally ill-suited to the job in the current political climate was not entirely her fault, but the fact is that during her stay, the smaller Psychoanalytic Group broke up. (She presented at its very last meeting: the topic was repression.) By June of 1922, she was reduced to writing to Freud asking his immediate intervention. He replied that there was little he could do:

If I did what you suggested, I should produce nothing but national-patriotic resentment against the old leader who feels entitled to play the psychoanalytic pope.

These people, it so happens, carry their political point of view over into science, and use it to conceal their total or partial ignorance. Those in Zurich are not really any different, and there is nothing we can do about it until they are joined by members who are trained in keeping with our ideas.

Yet if Spielrein's sojourn in Geneva was politically fruitless, it was intellectually productive. During the years 1921–1923, she wrote eleven psychoanalytic papers in all, including several major theoretical works.

Of these the two most important resulted from her associations respectively with the linguist Gustav Bally and with Piaget: "Time in the Unconscious Life of the Soul" and "Some Analogies Between the Thought of the Child with that of the Aphasic and with Preconscious Thought." In the former, Spielrein argued that the future tense is acquired by the child through the idea of repeated action while the past tense is acquired through analogies to spatial imagery. It was an important early contribution to the new field of psycholinguistics. In the latter paper, she analyzed a child's monologue as though it were a continuous, self-generated association experiment and then compared it with the utterances of an aphasic as he struggled to account for his performance on a simple task. Though she did not stress the point, the overall effect of the comparison was to show how both forms of thought, far from being "autistic," actually represented rudimentary attempts to come to terms with the environment.

As it happened, Spielrein's paper on children's monologues ran side by side in the *Archives de Psychologie* with an important early paper by Piaget. It is worth pausing to consider the relation between the two. Born to an eccentric, disturbed mother, Piaget came to psychology only after undergoing a profound adolescent crisis in which he struggled with fundamental philosophical questions. Recognized as a *Wunderkind* for his biological researches as a youngster, he had the good luck to study children under Binet in Paris, and then experimental psychopathology under Jung and Bleuler in Zurich. By the time Spielrein made his acquaintance, he had already hit on his revolutionary method of studying children's mistakes as a way of deducing their cognitive structures, though he was still a number of years away from the international reputation he would later command as the greatest developmental psychologist of the twentieth century.

What is not generally appreciated, however, in part due to Piaget himself, is how much his early researches grew out of a psychoanalytic perspective. In fact, Piaget initially saw himself as completing the Freudian paradigm by studying the "autistic" phase of development, when the reality principle was yet undeveloped; the notion was borrowed directly from Freud. (Spielrein's 1922 *Korrespondenzblatt* report on the situation in Geneva describes Piaget's fall lecture course in precisely these terms.) Beyond that, Piaget also derived the concept of "artificialism," one of the two distinguishing characteristics of the thought of small children, from the results of children's sexual researches as to where babies come from. The model was entirely in line with Freud's and Spielrein's views, and in his important 1926 volume of the child's conception of the world, Piaget approvingly cited her paper on little Renate's theories of birth.

But, perhaps because of his mother, Piaget had no appetite for researches into the emotions. He underwent a training analysis with Spielrein only for didactic purposes, and if one reads between the lines of his later accounts it appears that his firsthand experience of the "transference" was anything but pleasant. One anecdote, perhaps apocryphal, has it that at the moment he realized just whom he was projecting onto Spielrein's silent presence, he sat up on the couch, announced "*J'ai compris,*" and walked out of the room.

The tragedy of Spielrein's sojourn in Geneva should be underscored. If she was not the diplomat that circumstances required, she was intellectually very much the equal of the historical moment. Her papers from this period demonstrate an implicit awareness of the absolute need to square psychoanalytic theory with the new findings of developmental psychology and linguistics. They also demonstrate that she possessed the intellectual qualities needed to begin forging such a synthesis. With her departure for Russia in 1923, Western psychology lost a person it could very well have used. The important endeavor she had barely started did not resume again for decades.

It seems to have been an increasingly disappointing time for her. Thoughts of Jung crop up in her papers. A brief clinical report of 1922, "Postage Stamp Dream," is almost certainly autobiographical. A woman dreams of receiving a letter from her brother with no stamps on it; inside is a faded picture of him. The night before, the woman had reread some old letters from her former analyst, whom she regularly replaced with her brother in her dreams and with whom she had broken while still in the middle of an "intensely ambivalent transference." The dream hinges on an association from "stamps" (*Marken*) to bone marrow ("*Mark*") and to tabes, a deterioration of the bone caused by syphilis. The meaning of the dream is that the woman no longer pays attention to what the analyst, a "syphilitic Don Juan," has to say to her.

In September of 1922, Spielrein attended the Seventh International Psychoanalytic Congress in Berlin, presenting her paper on "Time in the Unconscious Life of the Soul." It was her psychoanalytic swan song and she appears to have used the occasion to present her final thoughts about Jung, and most especially about his predilection for dwelling on things past, for the following anecdote appears:

A gentleman who has decided on a definite separation from his lover, for which he suffers very much, sees this lady in a dream as an object that is overgrown with moss. This image at the same time expresses the wish that the embarrassing farewell hour might be over already, that it might become an old object overgrown with moss. This dreamer in general likes to use the past as a way of getting rid of embarrassing impressions.

By the beginning of 1923, Spielrein was ready to quit Geneva. Freud encouraged her to try Berlin, where a new clinic had been set up to offer psychoanalysis to children, but in the end she opted for Moscow, where the local psychoanalytic society was flourishing under the leadership of Mosche Wulff.

It must have been a disappointing exit. One of her brief papers of that year, "A Dream and Vision of Shooting Stars," published in the new *International Journal of Psycho-Analysis,* describes a woman who is down on her luck and who plans to move to Russia to find work. The woman is also said to be trying to resolve her feelings after an affair with a younger man. It is the first time in her life she had known passion. As she ponders her fate, she watches the raindrops beat against the window while a yellow streetlamp illuminates them from behind and she thinks to herself that they look like tiny shooting stars. She goes to bed and has a dream in which the stars in the night sky spell out a word; the word is "Love."

FROM GENEVA TO MOSCOW

PERHAPS THE MOST important thing Dr. Sabina Spielrein-Scheftel ever did was to emigrate to Moscow in the early fall of 1923. It was the time of the opening to the West, of Lenin's New Economic Policy, and of important experiments in all areas of Russian life. In this climate, psychoanalysis flourished, and talented men came from all over Russia to join the Moscow Psychoanalytic Institute. Among them were two, Alexander Luria and Lev Vygotsky, who would go on to take their place among the century's greatest psychologists. For a time, Luria served as the institute's secretary, and his periodic reports in the *International Journal of Psycho-Analysis* chronicle Spielrein's involvement in a wide variety of activities, from teaching to serving as a training analyst to working in the clinic for children.

It is astonishing in retrospect just how many people Spielrein ended up knowing firsthand. Listing the ten greatest psychologists of this century is a matter of fashion and taste but on anyone's list five names would inevitably appear and Spielrein knew them all firsthand: Freud, Jung, Piaget, Luria, and Vygotsky. But whereas with Jung and Freud, she had been their student, and with Piaget his colleague, with Vygotsky and Luria, her role was altogether different. They were the relative newcomers, she the old hand. And she had brought with her the best of Western psychology. From Zurich, she brought both the Burghölzli clinical tradition and the methods of its psychological laboratory. From Vienna, she brought orthodox Freudianism. From Geneva, the latest currents in developmental psychology. And from Jung, personally, the fruits of his ongoing self-analysis—and her trenchant criticisms. The window of time in which psychoanalysis would flourish in Russia was very short, lasting no more than three to four years, before Stalin would ban it. It was indeed fortunate that there was someone there who knew as much as Spielrein did.

Luria and Vygotsky were among the shrewd few who read the signs correctly and got out of the Moscow Institute before the Stalinist purges began in earnest. They turned to different areas, Luria to neuropsychology and Vygotsky to developmental psychology, and one would not normally connect their names with anything psychoanalytic. But Spielrein was there, they knew her, and though it soon became political and scientific suicide to admit as much, it would seem that they took advantage of what she had to offer. Here let us note only that Luria's first great work, *The Nature of Human Conflict,* involved an ingenious adaptation of—the word association experiment. And Vygotsky's seminal reflections on the development of thought in the child began with a summary rebuttal of the concept of "autistic" thought, demonstrated in detail with an examination of—a child's monologue.

It was a great destiny after all; she helped jump-start Russian psychology into the twentieth century.

THE DEATH INSTINCT

WITH SPIELREIN'S emigration back to Russia, she effectively disappeared from the annals of the psychoanalytic movement. Her papers went unread, and her memory was gradually forgotten. Eventually, she passed into almost complete obscurity and there she remained until the publication of the Freud-Jung correspondence in 1974. To be sure, her passage into undeserved oblivion was not essentially different from that of any number of Freud's early followers, both great and small.

Where she differed in her fate was that she became remembered for a single controversial contribution to psychoanalytic theory. She had, quite literally, her own footnote in the history of the psychoanalytic movement.

The footnote appeared in Freud's 1920 work, *Beyond the Pleasure Principle*. Here Freud continued his meditations on the "repetition compulsion" begun in early 1919. On the basis that inanimate life had preceded animate life—this was literally Freud's argument—he went on to argue that the compulsion to repeat ultimately constituted a tendency to return to an inorganic state. Opposed to this tendency, Freud postulated a second tendency, of which the libido was a derivative, that blindly sought to build up new structures. The interplay between the two tendencies, which are in effect transcendent biological principles, was said to determine both biological and psychological progression and regression.

About Freud's "death instinct," as it has been called, one can scarcely improve on the subsequent comment of the English psychologist William McDougall that it is "the most bizarre monster of all his gallery of monsters." The basic idea that organic processes might be balanced between two different processes, one constructive and one destructive, was a commonplace of nineteenth-century biological speculation. What Freud had done was to link the destructive tendency to a wish to die or death instinct. The later, more specific idea is generally believed to have originated with Élie Metchnikoff, the Nobel Prize-winning head of the Pasteur Institute, whose *Rhythm of Life* had appeared in 1903. Metchnikoff's agenda had been explicit. Believing that all religion represented outmoded superstition whose only real stimulus was a fear of death, Metchnikoff looked forward to a day when science would be the only faith mankind needed. But what to do about the ever-present fear of death? What Metchnikoff argued was that death was currently unpleasant and fearsome only because it came about prematurely as the result of illness and the accumulation of bodily toxins. As science advanced, he believed, and old age became less medically onerous, a natural wish to die, experienced as essentially pleasant, would become increasingly manifest at the end of a long life.

Metchnikoff goes uncited in Freud's work, but the latent polemical agenda appears to be remarkably similar. For the thrust of Freud's innovation is to create a system in which, Putnam and the Swiss notwithstanding, there is no room for any inherent instinct toward spiritual growth. True, man may appear to progress during development, but this—here Freud cites Ferenczi—was only because development must repeat the evolutionary sequence of the species, which sequence had originally been felt as frustrating and was forced upon the organism by external circumstances.

Even the title of Freud's work carries its own ironical philosophical import. For in German literary usage, the word "Beyond" (*Jenseits*) was typically used to indicate some spiritual plane above and beyond ordinary existence, sometimes even being a synonym for the "Hereafter." Thus the expectation of any reader coming naïvely to Freud's text would have been that he was going "beyond" the pleasure principle and adducing some additional principle, presumably spiritual in nature, with regard to the instincts. And this expectation would have initially been heightened when it became clear that Freud was going to talk about an urge to return to earlier states, for in German idealistic philosophy, just such an urge—to get back to the Garden before the Fall of Adam and Eve—was consistently said to drive man inexorably upward and forward—to the new Paradise of the perfected spirit. But, of course, Freud was having none of it. What was "beyond" was only what was "before," and both added up to death.

Freud never abandoned the theory. Indeed, he clung to it, even though it entailed a host of improbable assumptions and necessitated any number of unprovable assertions, all of which then needlessly complicated his next round of theory-building. (Few lay people appreciate that the familiar model of the id, the ego, and the superego, which Freud erected in the early 1920s, actually has a death instinct running around in it doing all sorts of unlikely things, such as causing regressions or untherapeutic attacks of guilt.) The reason for Freud's peculiar steadfastness is not hard to find, however. For the revised theory of the instincts inaugurated by *Beyond the Pleasure Principle* had the rhetorical advantage of allowing an altogether purified conception of the libido. In effect, Freud had taken all the problematic features of sexuality—its "conservative" nature, its tendency to become fixated, its role in fostering regression, and its romantic equation with "death"—and assigned them elsewhere. Now it could not be said against his method that it focused too exclusively on sexuality, for sexuality was no longer the problem. The real culprit in psychic life was the "death instinct," and if something went wrong with the treatment or the patient failed to improve, the "death instinct" was likely to blame.

And where does Spielrein enter into the lineaments of this improbable theory? In passing, Freud takes up the theory of masochism. Previously, he had interpreted it as sadism turned against the self, but now he reinterprets it as a primary manifestation of the death instinct. And in a footnote he announces the following:

> A considerable portion of these speculations have been anticipated by Sabina Spielrein (1912) in an interesting and instructive paper which, however, is unfortunately not entirely clear to me; she there describes the sadistic components of the sexual instinct as "destructive."

The fact that Freud cited Spielrein at all in this work, which was silently aimed at Jung and the Swiss, is of course laden with its own ironies. More pertinent still, however, is that, even granting both the context of the citation and Freud's announced perplexity about her theory, the citation is wrongfully misleading. Spielrein had not argued for anything like primary masochism. She had only been heard that way by a male Viennese audience. Even less had she in any sense "anticipated" the idea of a death instinct. What she had argued was that *sexuality* brought with it such themes as that of dying in the arms of the beloved. Which is quite a different thing.

Given the obscurity of Freud's citation, it is a little surprising that it became the basis for Spielrein's reputation ever after. But there it is: in virtually every historical work that bothers to mention Spielrein at all, she is credited, wrongly, with having anticipated Freud's theory of the death instinct. Interestingly, Spielrein is not alone in Freud's footnote. She is joined there by August Stärcke, the Dutch psychiatrist who, as it happened, had enrolled in the Vienna society the same night she did. Working independently, in 1914 he had arrived at a theory remarkably similar to hers. In his view, the "'ego instincts" were centripetal in nature—they sought to preserve and prolong life. Opposed to them were the instincts of procreation, which were centrifugal and led ultimately to renunciation and death. Accordingly, Stärcke too identified a "destructive" component in sexuality. But that was scarcely the same thing as a "death instinct," and after the appearance of *Beyond the Pleasure Principle*, Stärcke wrote to Freud specifically objecting to the citation of his work. Since there is no record of Spielrein having done the same, we will have to let Stärcke's protest stand for hers: "My objection stems from an inner observation," Stärcke wrote to Freud, " . . . loving means wanting to die." In reply to Stärcke's letter,

Freud apologized and then proposed that they break off their correspondence.

In the end, Spielrein's was a curious literary fate, to be known for a theory she did not hold. "Destruction as a Cause of Coming into Being" seeks to solve the problem of sexual repression by appealing to a portrait of sexuality as inherently ambivalent in relation to the self. There is no "death instinct" in it. Neither the term nor the idea in Freud's sense appears there.

THE ANIMA

WHILE FREUD was seeing to it that Spielrein's most important contribution would be fundamentally misunderstood by future generations, Jung was busy making her immortal—under another name. It will come as a surprise to at least some readers to learn that they are actually already surprisingly familiar with this particular Russian woman, only that they have not realized that it was her whom they knew.

In the decade following the First World War, Jung gradually formulated a new psychological system founded on the idea of "archetypes." These were said to be inherited subconscious mental structures which organized both thought and action and which might be accessed either in the later stages of treatment or else in dreams and "active imagination." Such basic structures were also said to be detectable in mythology and folklore, where their natural interplay stood revealed, and much of Jung's later work was devoted to pursuing that intriguing but methodologically dubious project. Though their number later expanded, at first there were only four basic archetypes: the "persona" (the outward personality), the "shadow" (Brother Medardus was the explicit model), the "wise old man" (a patriarchal embodiment of wisdom), and the "anima." The last-named had and continued to have a very special role to play in Jung's system, for it was the "anima" who had the power to access the images of the collective unconscious and bring them to consciousness. In essence, the "anima" was the innermost "soul" of the individual—the term was taken from Plato—and mediated between consciousness and the collective unconscious. But Jung made the further surprising claim that in men, the "anima" was always female in nature. (The corresponding male "soul" in women was termed the "animus.")

From the first, the idea of the "anima" had a romantic application, and this may in part explain its enduring popularity as a concept. The process of falling in love, according to Jung, consisted of projecting the inner anima onto a real woman, who might then become experienced as a dangerous temptress or else as an inspiratrix, as someone who could lead the man to tap the wellsprings of his creativity. For literary analogues, Jung often cited H. Rider Haggard's *She* and Pierre Benoît's *L'Atlantide,* while to his students he would explain that the anima-invested woman appears to a man as "She who must be obeyed."

The first mention of the "anima" to occur in Jung's writings came in his 1920 tome *Psychological Types* and was so cryptic that one could not have guessed the importance he already attached to the idea. As his memoirs later made clear, however, his own personal experience of the workings of this particular archetype had been the decisive event during the stormy years of his protracted "self-analysis" during World War I. And here let us be clear just how stormy this period was. By 1915, Jung's condition had so deteriorated that his wife allowed Toni Wolff openly to become his mistress and a sometime member of the household, simply because she was the only person who could calm him down. In 1916, Wolff's ministrations notwithstanding, Jung continued to be intermittently troubled by depersonalization episodes and frank hallucinations. At one point, he felt his own "soul" vanish as if it had flown away to the "land of the dead." Shortly thereafter, while his children were plagued by nightmares and the house was seemingly "haunted," he heard a chorus of spirits cry out demandingly, "We have come back from Jerusalem where we have found not what we sought." In response, Jung wrote a thoroughly grandiose, almost paranoid tract, "Seven Sermons to the Dead," that combines Gnostic terminology with the style of *Thus Spake Zarathustra* to arrive at a deliberately obscure text ringing with the plaints of self-vindication.

Jung's basic strategy for coping with himself during this time was to write down scrupulously every image and phantasy that came to him in his notebooks, sometimes with accompanying illustrations. Jung felt that it was important to try to study his own process scientifically as much as he could. It was while he was engaged in this that he first encountered the "anima" archetype:

> When I was writing down these fantasies, I once asked myself, "What am I really doing? Certainly this has nothing to do with science. But then what is it?" Whereupon a voice within me said, "It is art." I was astonished. It had never entered my head that

what I was writing had any connection with art. Then I thought,
"Perhaps my unconscious is forming a personality that is not me,
but which is insisting on coming through to expression." I knew for
a certainty that the voice had come from a woman. I recognized it
as the voice of a patient, a talented psychopath who had a strong
transference to me. She had become a living figure within my mind.

"Psychopath" here is the old term for someone with hereditary taint,
i.e., someone prone to nervous disorders. Jung's account continues:

Obviously what I was doing wasn't science. What then could it
be but art? It was as though these were the only alternatives in the
world. That is the way a woman's mind works.

I said very emphatically to this voice that my fantasies had nothing to do with art, and I felt a great inner resistance. No voice came
through, however, and I kept on writing. Then came the next assault, and again the same assertion, "That is art." This time I
caught her and said; "No, it is not art! On the contrary, it is nature," and prepared myself for an argument. When nothing of the
sort occurred, I reflected that the "woman within me" did not have
the speech centers I had. And so I suggested that she use mine. She
did so and came through with a long statement.

I was greatly intrigued by the fact that a woman should interfere
with me from within. My conclusion was that she must be the
"soul," in the primitive sense, and I began to speculate on the
reasons why the name "anima" was given to the soul. Why was it
thought of as feminine? Later I came to see that this inner feminine
figure plays a typical, or archetypal, role in the unconscious of a
man, and I called her the "anima." The corresponding figure in
the unconscious of woman I called the "animus."

At first it was the negative aspect of the anima that most impressed me. I felt a bit awed by her. It was like an invisible presence
in the room. Then a new idea came to me: in putting down all this
material for analysis I was in effect writing letters to the anima, that
is, to a part of myself with a different viewpoint from my conscious
one. I got remarks of an unusual and unexpected character. I was
like a patient in analysis with a ghost and a woman! Every evening
I wrote very conscientiously, for I thought if I did not write, there
would be no way for the anima to get at my fantasies. Also,
by writing them out I gave her no chance to twist them into
intrigues. . . .

Often as I was writing, I would have peculiar reactions that threw me off. Slowly I learned to distinguish between myself and the interruption. When something emotionally vulgar or banal came up, I would say to myself, "It is perfectly true that I have thought and felt this way at some time or other, but I don't have to think and feel that way now. I need not accept this banality of mine in perpetuity; that is an unnecessary humiliation."

Eventually Jung came to feel that the "anima" had a positive aspect and for decades to come he would turn to her whenever he felt emotionally disturbed. Typically, he would ask her to help him access his unconscious by producing an image: "As soon as the image was there, the unrest or the sense of oppression vanished. The whole energy of these emotions was transformed into interest in and curiosity about the image." But his initial experience of her was much more distrustful:

What the anima said seemed to me full of a deep cunning. If I had taken these fantasies of the unconscious as art, they would have carried no more conviction than visual perceptions, as if I were watching a movie. I would have felt no moral obligation toward them. The anima might then have easily seduced me into believing that I was a misunderstood artist, and that my so-called artistic nature gave me the right to neglect reality. If I had followed her voice, she would in all probability have said to me one day, "Do you imagine the nonsense you're engaged in is really art? Not a bit." Thus the insinuations of the anima, the mouthpiece of the unconscious, can utterly destroy a man.

Jung left very few clues as to who the "anima" might be. He states that he finally broke with the woman during the years 1918–1919 and that this helped him emerge from out of "the darkness." He also implies that he was in correspondence with the woman:

One day, for example, I received a letter from that esthetic lady in which she stubbornly maintained that the fantasies arising from my unconscious had artistic value and should be considered art. The letter got on my nerves. It was far from stupid, and therefore dangerously persuasive.

Both of these clues, that Jung was in correspondence with the woman and that he broke with her shortly after the war, point to Spielrein.

Perhaps the biggest clue, however, is the one that lies out in the open: the debate on science versus art. For it is simply not clear how or why these two different enterprises might be confused with each other. And it is even less clear what might be so disturbing about it if in fact the two were to be confused.

Just this, the identification of art with science, points decisively in Spielrein's direction. Consider that in her Transformation Journal, written in 1907, she had already discussed both science and art, explicitly equated them, and in the process described them in terms of the exact method Jung later used to defuse his anxieties:

> Every complex wants to escape the boundaries of the personality. It seeks that which resembles it, looks for its reflection, and when you hold up a mirror to it, laughter occurs even if there's nothing laughable about it for the conscious self. . . .
>
> Art is nothing but a complex which has become independent or which, "having become wild, wants to express itself to the fullest," to use your words—or "wants to be transformed," to use mine. When the artist creates, it is not at all the need to communicate to others that manifests itself. The complex simply wants to come out! . . . In science as well, the thought—or whatever it may be— that one has formulated after long torment necessarily wants to be understood by others.

But the Transformation Journal had been written in 1907 when Spielrein was still objecting to Jung's equation of the unconscious with repressed sexuality. By the time she had written her medical dissertation, Spielrein had come fully to accept his view, that the unconscious was sexual. And in her "Destruction" paper she went much further, arguing that not only was the unconscious sexual in nature, but that that very fact also made it collective in terms of its imagery. And, having gone that far, Spielrein also revamped her theory of artistic creation. Specifically, she had argued emphatically that the creative process itself was sexual, the point being that an artistic creation could be shared with the whole species. The basic process of artistic creation mirrored love-making, and indeed represented its internalized equivalent, in that there was first destruction (of the purely private perspective of the artist) and then transformation (in the form of the production of a collectively shared art product).

If Jung heard Spielrein's voice saying "It is art," then, he was simultaneously hearing the further implications of her revised theory. His ruminations were not merely the introspective adventures of an objective scientist. Whether he realized it or not, they were manifestations of the sexual instinct. In fact, the implicit accusation was graver still, and here we begin to understand what was at stake in Jung's stated determination to renounce his "banal" and "vulgar" emotions as well as his sense that the "anima" was both potentially fickle and "dangerously persuasive." For what the voice was implying was that he was once again succumbing to sexual reverie, just as he had years before, and that he was not man enough to admit it. And here, I think, it is legitimate to wonder if perhaps Jung did not deliberately misreport what the "anima" actually said. The equation in Spielrein's medical dissertation had three terms, not two, but one of them had a secret meaning known only to Spielrein and Jung. In addition to the formula "Poetry = Love," the dissertation separately specified that "Art = Poetry," this in the context of the patient's sexualized delusions. It may well be that the voice Jung heard in 1916 said: "It is not science. It is poetry."

The foregoing, I submit, forms the backdrop for understanding Jung's touching confessional letter to Spielrein of 1 September 1919, in which he admits that "the love of S. for J." showed him a truth that he had to "sublimate" lest he go mad. It may also shed light on the mysterious diagram in his final extant letter to her of 7 October 1919. Perhaps in lieu of finally confessing to her what she had become to him internally, Jung elected to act out his new method: he sent his anima an image.

In his later years, Jung spent more and more time at a private retreat on the shore in the rural town of Bollingen. There he lived simply, in a stone house he had built himself. His principal hobby during those last years was stone-carving, at which he became quite adept. Accordingly, left behind in the Bollingen retreat is a symbolic record, executed in stone, of some of Jung's preoccupations during his old age. Among these there is a stone triptych on the subject of the "anima." The initial panel shows a bear bending down, its nose nudging a ball in front of it. The inscription reads, "Russia gets the ball rolling."

It is a sad last testament to Spielrein that even in a stone monument in her honor she could not be named. Yet the bitterness was perhaps not less on the man's side. Jung's "anima," the "she who must be obeyed," finished her career as a Freudian.

Afterword

Roughly speaking we may say that the worship of Sex and Life characterized the Pagan races of Europe and Asia Minor anterior to Christianity, while the worship of Death and the Unseen has characterized Christianity. It remains for the modern nations to accept both Life and Death, both the Greek and the Hebrew elements, and all that these general terms denote, in a spirit of fullest friendliness and sanity and fearlessness.

—Edward Carpenter, *Love's Coming of Age,* 1911

ALL THIS WAS not supposed to happen in psychoanalysis, for psychoanalysis was, it was said, a science. In science neither the vision of the founder nor the counter-vision of the disciple is of any moment. This in a way is science's great consolation. What is established rests on replicatable experience, and though it may later be amended or even overthrown by yet more penetrating investigations, one does not have to worry about other issues, such as personal temperament or religious tradition, getting in the way. Indeed, this was the great hope when philosophers first began setting up laboratories of experimental psychology; perhaps finally one could put all conjectures about man's essential nature on an empirical footing. Early in their association, both Freud and Jung counted on just this protection. Psychoanalysis was a science; their differences would work themselves out as the data continued to come in. But the data came in, and things only got worse.

Transparently, the fact that Freud and Jung could ultimately arrive at two different schools of depth psychology indicates that psychoanalysis, despite its claims, was not a science. In fact, no sooner had they first institutionalized their endeavor than the two men began to realize, Freud perhaps more wittingly than Jung, that it was only by enforcing an ideological conformity upon their followers that they could create the appearance of generating homogenous results. The further history of their respective schools with the ever-present threat of new schisms—Jung's school was no more happy a place for a dissident than Freud's—only corroborates the point. Whatever it is, psychoanalysis is not a science. But if Freud and Jung were geniuses, and the beneficiaries of the best scientific educations that were available in their day, the question naturally arises as to where they went wrong.

Clearly, the data of the consulting room, from "Little Hans" 's fear of horses to Spielrein's adolescent hallucinations of a hand about to strike her, were real. And equally clearly, the two men did more than any of their contemporaries to shed light on what these and other "nervous" ailments might mean. There was no problem with the reality of the data. Then, too, the theories the two men brought to bear on that data were grounded in the best scientific wisdom of their day. A historian might point out that the phylogenetic hypothesis has no scientific standing in today's world or that Freud's dream that neurology might one day discover a specific sexual toxin in the brain, presumably of the alkaloid class, looks as if it will never be fulfilled. But that is normal in the history of science. If it was merely a question of revamping the theories of the two men in light of current scientific knowledge, there would be no problem. Indeed, it would already have happened.

The problem lay between the theory and the data; it lay in the method. Freud earnestly believed that his beloved psychoanalysis constituted a valid means of doing research on the unconscious. More, he believed that it provided the opportunity for demonstrating the worthiness of his interpretive inferences. Yet, when it came time, he found he could not even describe rules for interpretation, let alone prove their scientific sturdiness. The use of scientistic language, let it be noted, did nothing to resolve Freud's methodological problems. But Freud remained permanently uninterested in what his critics had to say on this most important point. Instead, he left behind a corpus that is almost hypnotizing in terms of its multiplications of interrelated hypotheses, dazzling in its inferential sweep. And he left the unsolved, and often unsolvable, problems of verification to the next generation of analysts, all "trained according to our ideas," as he once put it to Spielrein. The next generation would have to have had its own genius on hand if it were really to extricate Freud's legitimate clinical insights from the vast and complex web of theory with which he surrounded them. And psychoanalysis had already had two geniuses. Indeed, this is part of the tragedy of the matter; two geniuses might have been enough if one of them had not quit.

It was above all a tragedy for the field. The constriction of interpretive range, begun while Jung was still president of the International
Association, only accelerated after he left. Following the First World
War, through a combination of political shrewdness and historical accident, Freud was successful in positioning psychoanalysis at the head
of the psychotherapeutic movement, where it has since remained. But
it was decades before analysts dared to speculate about such things as
pre-Oedipal development, split object representations, the maternal
environment, separation-individuation, and the like. And only relatively recently have they been able to discuss unabashedly the significance of the "self." These are all matters which, in a sometimes terribly
muddled way, Jung had wanted to talk about a long time ago. As for
the task of verifying psychoanalytic ideas, and thereby removing them
once and for all from internecine debate, this has really only just gotten
under way recently.

Yet, we cannot end our examination of the origins of psychoanalysis without recognizing its astonishing fertility. At the very least, it
has the fruitful power that even down to the present it continues to
generate new dissensions. The secret lies not in its "method" of interpretation, and most certainly not in any of its artifacts like the use of
the couch or the rule of abstinence, but in the treatment contract.
Freud's civility is here to be praised: he hit on a form of psychical
treatment that has proved consonant with the values of the modern
world. The patient is not to be hypnotized, nor are supposedly helpful
thoughts to be put in his or her head through suggestion or persuasion.
And values are not part of the treatment, either. The therapist is a
consultant on mental matters, not a director of conscience. Psychoanalysis thus allowed a new kind of silence, a beneficent silence, into
the consulting room and thereby enabled a new kind of listening. But
in return for the freedom to be oneself, and to be oneself in any way
one likes, the patient is burdened with the obligation to be productive.
It is up to the patient to provide the material of analysis, not the
therapist. The interchange between patient and analyst, furthermore,
is conducted under the sign of a belief that whatever ails the patient
reflects his motivational history and can be cured either through a
more honest act of self-scrutiny than he or she has made heretofore or
else through abreacting the pain of his or her accumulated traumas.

The foregoing is an ideal portrait of the analytic contract, to be
sure, but insofar as it possesses any reality, two implications stand out.
The first is that there will always be patients willing to try this form of
cure. The second is that there will always be at least some analysts

who will go on to try new hypotheses when the received canon of interpretation fails to help. And so psychoanalysis survives down to the present, lagging woefully behind the science of its day, but still viable enough to attract men and women of talent and generate anew its internal controversies, and even on occasion helping people.

The real tragedy of Freud and Jung is not that they failed to create a science. It was justification enough if their ideas managed to bring some relief, and some understanding, to some people. Here let us remember that Spielrein herself was almost certainly saved by the new theories from a lifetime of invalidism or worse. The real tragedy is what they did to psychoanalysis as a clinical method. They allowed the interpretive range of psychoanalysis to become woefully constricted while simultaneously creating a political organization that ensured that this constriction would endure. The suppression of Spielrein's theory, which should invite serious consideration even in the present, was but one instance of a general pattern.

If anything emerges clearly from this study it is that psychoanalysis early ceased to be merely a clinical method—it was never a science—and became instead both a movement and a *Weltanschauung*. Freud needed Jung to get the movement going. Jung needed Freud because he wanted to live in the *Weltanschauung*, live in it and re-create it in his own image. For a time they were more than glad to accommodate each other. Ultimately, what broke them up was not their sexual secrets; these they had already fought to a draw in 1909. Nor was it the difference in their religious traditions; that, too, had been put to discussion in 1909 and seemingly resolved. Nor was it even their very real intellectual disagreements about how best to develop the canon of interpretation; these were long-standing and always secondary to the political advantages of continuing their association. What forced them apart was when these three different realms—the sexual, the religious, the theoretical—became hopelessly intertwined, and they could no longer talk about them. Not to each other and not to anyone else. It was from this more pernicious silence that psychoanalysis as we know it today, with all its contradictions, is descended.

Notes

ABBREVIATIONS

F/J Letters The Freud/Jung Letters: The Correspondence between Sigmund Freud and C. G. Jung, edited by William McGuire, translated by Ralph Mannheim and R. F. C. Hull (Princeton: Princeton University Press, 1974).

S.E. The Standard Edition of the Complete Psychological Works of Sigmund Freud, translated from the German under the general editorship of James Strachey, assisted by Alix Strachey and Alan Tyson, in collaboration with Anna Freud (London: Hogarth Press, 1953-74).

C.W. The Collected Works of C. G. Jung, edited by Sir Herbert Read, Michael Fordham, Gerhard Adler, and William McGuire, translated by R. F. C. Hull (Princeton: Princeton University Press, 1953-80).

"Transformation Journal" "Extraits inédits d'un journal: De l'Amour, de la mort et de la transformation," *Le Bloc-Notes de la Psychanalyse* 3(1983):149-70. Composed by Spielrein in 1907-1908, rediscovered and edited by Mireille Cifali, and translated by Jeanne Moll.

A Secret Symmetry Aldo Carotenuto, A Secret Symmetry: Sabina Spielrein Between Jung and Freud (New York: Pantheon, 1982; rev. ed., 1983). Revised edition contains Spielrein's diary, the Spielrein/Freud correspondence, and Spielrein's letters to Jung, plus commentary by Bruno Bettelheim and Aldo Carotenuto.

Tagebuch Aldo Carotenuto, Tagebuch einer heimlichen Symmetrie: Sabina Spielrein zwischen Jung und Freud (Freiburg im Breisgau: Kore, 1986). This, the German edition of A Secret Symmetry, contains Jung's letters to Spielrein.

Minutes Minutes of the Vienna Psychoanalytic Society, edited by Herman Nunberg and Ernst Federn, translated by M. Nunberg in collaboration with H. Collins, 4 vols. (New York: International Universities Press, 1962-75).

---

vi "I hope that Freud": William James, letter of 28 September 1909 to Théodore Flournoy, in *The Letters of William James,* ed. Henry James, 2 vols. (Boston: Atlantic Monthly Press, 1920), 2:327-28.

INTRODUCTION

4   "Sometimes a cigar is just a cigar": This remark, so well known, is probably apocryphal; it cannot be found in any primary source dealing with Freud.

"Oh, don't take that too seriously": Abram Kardiner, *My Analysis with Freud,* (New York: Norton, 1977), 75.

"I can heartily recommend the Gestapo": Ernest Jones, *The Life and Work of Sigmund Freud,* 3 vols. (New York: Basic Books, 1953–57), 3:226, gives this anecdote, but the subsequent recovery of the actual document shows no such comment by Freud. Once again, the story is probably apocryphal.

"Thank God I am not a Jungian": There are many versions of this anecdote. I first heard it from Werner Engel, but see also the interview with Wilhelm Bitter, 10 September 1970, conducted by Gene Nameche, Jung Oral History Archive, 7. Interestingly, Jung himself had forgotten that he had ever said this by the time John Billinsky interviewed him in 1957 and, according to Billinsky's unpublished notes of that interview, found the anecdote quite uproarious.

"Yes, we could—but then we would have to get up again": Robert Hobson, interview with Gene Nameche, 18 December 1969, Jung Oral History Archive, 14.

"No . . . just Jung": This anecdote I owe to Sonu Shamdasani, who further reports that it was a story Jung liked to tell about himself, especially to his British colleagues.

14   ". . . [t]he situation is not hopeless": Robert Holt, *Freud Reappraised* (New York: Guilford Press, 1989), 331.

17   "If . . . our much plagued soul": Emil Kraepelin, 1899, cited in Hannah Decker, *Freud in Germany: Revolution and Reaction in Science: 1893–1907* (New York: International Universities Press, 1977), 102.

CHAPTER I   HER FATHER'S HAND

19   "It is in the milder states of hysteria": Richard von Krafft-Ebing, 1901, cited in Jung, "On the Psychology and Pathology of So-called Occult Phenomena" (1902), *C. W.* 1:8–9.

"Puberty started when she was thirteen": See Jung, "The Freudian Theory of Hysteria" (1908), *C. W.* 4:20.

20   "her condition had got so bad": Ibid., 21.

For Aldo Carotenuto on the nature of Sabina Spielrein's disorder, see his *A Secret Symmetry*, 146–47. For Bruno Bettelheim's assessment, ibid., xvii.

"psychotic hysteria": Jung, "The Freudian Theory of Hysteria" (1908), *C.W.* 4:19.

"changed social circumstances": See Anthony Storr, "A Second Opinion," *The New York Times Book Review*, 16 May 1982, 21.

21 For a contemporaneous description of psychotic hysteria, see the epigraph to this chapter; see also the case of acute hallucinatory confusion in Freud's "The Aetiology of Hysteria" (1896), *S.E.* 3:58–60.

25 On the contemporary understanding of the role of trauma in triggering neurosis, see Albert von Schrenck-Notzing, *The Use of Hypnosis in Psychopathia Sexualis* (New York: The Institute for Research in Hypnosis Publication Society and the Julian Press, 1956), case 20, 68–72.

29 "The excess of the insistence": See Pierre Janet, *The Major Symptoms of Hysteria* (New York: Macmillan, 1924), 230–31.

30 "I have promised her": Freud cited by Albrecht Hirschmüller, document 3, in "Eine bisher unbekannte Krankengeschichte Sigmund Freuds und Joseph Breuers aus der Entstehungszeit der 'Studien über Hysterie'. " *Jahrbuch der Psychoanalyse* 10(1978):136–68.

"I am accustomed to see these hysterical manifestations": Paul DuBois, *The Psychic Treatment of Nervous Disorders* (New York: Funk & Wagnalls, 1909), 349–50.

31 "I have seen this false shame": Ibid., 355–56.

"She said that when she became bored": See A. A. Brill, *Freud's Contribution to Psychiatry* (New York: Norton, 1944), 25.

32 "They try to impress you with their grandeur or their guilt": Janet, quoted in Henri Ellenberger, *The Discovery of the Unconscious: The History and Evolution of Dynamic Psychiatry* (New York: Basic Books, 1970), 351.

33 For Krafft-Ebing on the case of a woman experiencing pleasure at the thought of blows from a hand, see his *Psychopathia Sexualis: A Medico-Forensic Study* (New York: Putnam, 1965), 179.

For childhood experiences in the life of Lou Andreas-Salomé similar to those of Spielrein, see Rudolph Binion, *Frau Lou: Nietzsche's Wayward Disciple* (Princeton: Princeton University Press, 1968), 5–7.

"Her father loved her, sexually": Franz Riklin, *Wishfulfillment and Symbolism in Fairy-Tales* (New York: Journal of Nervous and Mental Disease Publishing Co., 1915), 51, n. 3.

On the tendency toward masochism among Russian and Slavic women, see Krafft-Ebing, *Psychopathia Sexualis,* 51-52, 158, 172. See also Schrenck-Notzing, *The Use of Hypnosis in Psychopathia Sexualis,* case 7, 52.

34   For the exchange between Jung and Freud concerning Spielrein's nationality, see Freud to Jung, 30 June 1909, *F/J Letters,* 238; and Jung to Freud, 10/13 July 1909, 240.

For the patient population of the Burghölzli, see *Rechenschaftsbericht über die Zürichische Kantonale Irrenheilanstalt Burghölzli für das Jahr 1904* (Statistical report of the Burghölzli Clinic prepared for cantonal authorities) 8, 9. Information is also based on hospital records obtained for the author by Paul Schrader from Emanuel Hurwitz of Zurich, personal communication, 25 August 1984.

35   The diary appears in Carotenuto, *A Secret Symmetry,* 3-44.

For Spielrein's early childhood recollections, see her "Beiträge zur Kenntnis der kindlichen Seele," *Zentralblatt für Psychoanalyse und Psychotherapie* 3(1912):57-61.

38   For Freud's statement in Löwenfeld's book, see Jeffrey Masson, ed., *The Complete Letters of Sigmund Freud to Wilhelm Fliess: 1887-1904* (Cambridge: Harvard University Press, 1985), 343 n. 1. For the confession of Freud's former patient, ibid., 413 n. 3.

CHAPTER 2   A PSYCHIATRIC MONASTERY

39   "If I were to express briefly . . . my father's": Manfred Bleuler, "My Father's Conception of Schizophrenia," *Bulletin of the New York State Asylums* 7(1931):15.

40   On the conditions at the Burghölzli when he took over, see Auguste Forel, *Out of My Life and Work* (London: Allen & Unwin, 1937), chap. 9.

For Meyer on Forel's scientific accomplishments, see his obituary and review essays on Forel in *The Collected Papers of Adolf Meyer* (Baltimore: Johns Hopkins University Press, 1950), vol. 1.

41   On the inability of Burghölzli physicians to communicate with rural Swiss patients, see Henri Ellenberger, *The Discovery of the Unconscious: The History and Evolution of Dynamic Psychiatry* (New York: Basic Books, 1970), 286-88; and Manfred Bleuler's interview with Gene Nameche, 8 December 1969, Jung Oral History Archive, 19-20.

On Bleuler's relationship to his patients at the Rheinau asylum, ibid., 4.

43   On the Burghölzli as a teaching hospital, see Ellenberger, *The Discovery of the Unconscious,* 666-67; and Bleuler, "My Father's Conception of Schizophrenia," 1-16.

45   For Theodor Ziehen's system of psychology, see his *Introduction to Physiological Psychology* (New York: Macmillan, 1899).

46 "the sacrificed generation": Ellenberger, *The Discovery of the Unconscious,* 661.

"I always felt mistrustful": Jung, *Memories, Dreams, Reflections,* rev. ed. (New York: Pantheon, 1973), 8.

"Jesuits": Ibid., 11.

"consisted of two personalities": Ibid., 48–49.

"to the core of my being": Ibid., 48.

"I had never come across such an asocial monster": Albert Oeri, "Memories of C. G. Jung's Boyhood," *Spring* (1970):183.

"the atmosphere in the house": Jung, *Memories, Dreams, Reflections,* 18–19.

47 "The answer remained totally unclear": Ibid., 20.

On Jung building fires, ibid., 19–20.

"This possession of a secret": Ibid., 22.

"for a single moment": Ibid., 32.

On Jung's "No. 2" personality, Ibid., 32; and Ellenberger, *The Discovery of the Unconscious,* 738 n. 20.

48 On Jung's Basel Cathedral daydream and his first communion, see his *Memories, Dreams, Reflections,* 38–39, 40–43, 54–55.

"I could not plunge my dear and generous father": Ibid., 55.

On Paul Jung's loss of faith, ibid., 94.

49 On Jung's secret theological readings in his father's library, ibid., 63, 65; on reading Biedermann, 56–57; on reading Goethe, 60; on reading Krug, 61–63.

For Jung's inaugural lecture, "The Border Zone of Exact Science," see his *The Zofingia Lectures* [1896–99], *Supplement to the Collected Works* (Princeton: Princeton University Press, 1983), vol. A. chap. 1.

"The minutes read": Oeri, "Memories of C. G. Jung's Boyhood," *Spring* (1970):186–87.

50 "the Judaization of science": Jung, *The Zofingia Lectures,* 35.

"In 1875, for the first time": Ibid., 43.

On Jung's séances with his mother and cousins, see Ellenberger's "Jung's Medium," *Journal of the History of the Behavioral Sciences* 12(1976):34–42. Also see Martin Ebon, "Jung's First Medium," *Psyche* 7(1976):3–12.

50　For Jung on spiritualistic phenomena, see his "On the Psychology and Pathology of So-called Occult Phenomena" (1902), *C.W.* 1:19–43.

On Helene's hypnotic trances induced by Jung, see William McGuire, ed., *Analytical Psychology: Notes of the Seminar Given in 1925 by C. G. Jung* (Princeton: Princeton University Press, 1989), 3–4.

51　For George Hogenson on Helene's hypnotic trances, see his *Jung's Struggle with Freud* (Notre Dame, Ind.: University of Notre Dame Press, 1983), 20–22. See also William Goodheart, "C. G. Jung's First 'Patient': On the Seminal Emergence of Jung's Thought," *Journal of Analytical Psychology* 29(1984):1–34.

For Spielrein's account of Helene's trances, see her letter-drafts in *A Secret Symmetry*, 105.

53　On Jung's decision to study psychiatry, see Ellenberger, *The Discovery of the Unconscious*, 666; and Jung, *Memories, Dreams, Reflections*, 108–109.

"Owing to the peculiarity": Richard von Krafft-Ebing, *Textbook of Insanity Based on Clinical Observations for Practitioners and Students of Medicine* (Philadelphia: F. A. Davis Co., 1904), iii.

54　"in order to acquaint myself": Jung, *Memories, Dreams, Reflections*, 112.

"and gained much instruction": Ibid., 112–13.

"Speaking with her": Jung, "On the Psychology and Pathology of So-Called Occult Phenomena," *C.W.* 1:25.

For Jung on "psychopathic inferiority," ibid., 24–25, 60–65, 79–80, 87–88.

For Ellenberger on the effect of Jung's dissertation on Helene's chances of marrying, see his "Jung's Medium," *Journal of the History of the Behavioral Sciences* 12(1976):42.

55　"intensified feeling of self-importance": Krafft-Ebing, *Textbook of Insanity*, 327–28.

"We shall not be wrong": Jung, "On the Psychology and Pathology of So-called Occult Phenomena," *C.W.* 1:64.

"slave to an ideology": From Spielrein's diary, in *A Secret Symmetry*, 12.

57　"the beautiful experiments": Jung, "On Simulated Insanity" (1903), *C.W.* 1:181.

For Jung's realization that he should use the word association test in his analysis of the Ganser syndrome, ibid., 169.

58　"repressed": Jung and Franz Riklin, "The Associations of Normal Subjects" (1904), *C.W.* 2:74.

"the majority of complexes": Ibid., 82.

"had not yet outgrown": Ibid., 86.

59 For references to Freud in "The Associations of Normal Subjects," ibid., 118, 173.

"Once, while I was in my laboratory": Jung, *Memories, Dreams, Reflections,* 148.

For the belated acknowledgment of Freud's priority on the idea of repression, see Jung and Riklin, "The Associations of Normal Subjects," *C.W.* 2:191 n. 72.

60 "the strong feeling-toned complex": Riklin, "Die diagnostische Bedeutung der Assoziationen bei der Hysterie," *Psychiatrisch-neurologische Wochenschrift* 6(1904):275.

For Riklin's follow-up paper, see his "Analytische Untersuchungen der Symptome und Assoziationen eines Falles von Hysterie (Lina H.)," *Psychiatrisch-neurologische Wochenschrift* 6 (1905):449-52, 493-95, 505-11.

For an account of how Brentano's books on the mystic visions of Fräulein Emmerich attracted widespread attention, see Ellenberger, *The Discovery of the Unconscious,* 78, 159.

"staged an enormous swindle": Jung, "On Simulated Insanity," *C.W.* 1:186.

"purpose of the whole undertaking": Ibid.

"Sabina S.": Ibid., 187.

CHAPTER 3 JUNG'S TEST CASE

61 "She was, so to speak, my test case": Jung to Freud, 4 June 1909, *F/J Letters,* 228.

For Franz Riklin's analysis of "Lina H.," see his "Analytische Untersuchungen der Symptome und Assoziationen eines Falles von Hysterie (Lina H.)," *Psychiatrisch-neurologische Wochenschrift* 6(1905):449-52, 493-97, 505-11.

62 For Riklin on the role of fantasies in the etiology of Lina H.'s hysteria, ibid., 495-96.

"Freud, in his studies on hysteria": Eugen Bleuler, 1904, cited in Jeffrey Masson, ed., *The Complete Letters of Sigmund Freud to Wilhelm Fliess: 1887-1904* (Cambridge: Harvard University Press, 1985), 461 n. 3.

For Leopold Löwenfeld on Freud's failure to give a detailed discussion of psychoanalysis, see Hannah Decker, *Freud in Germany: Revolution and Reaction in Science: 1893-1907* (New York: International Universities Press, 1977), 156.

63 "There . . . some information is to be found": Freud, "Further Remarks on the Neuro-Psychoses of Defence" (1896), *S.E.* 3:162.

 "[W]e may ask that no one": Ibid., 164.

64 "If a pathological idea . . .": Freud, *The Interpretation of Dreams* (1900), *S.E.* 4:100–101.

 "The details of this technique": Freud, "Freud's Psycho-Analytic Procedure" (1904), *S.E.* 7:252.

66 "All nervous symptoms": Quoted in Eugene Taylor, "On the First Use of Psychoanalysis at the Massachusetts General Hospital: 1903–1905," *Journal of the History of Medicine and Allied Sciences* 43(1984):456.

 For Karl Abraham's account of Jung's analysis of Spielrein, see his letter to Freud, 15 January 1914, in Hilde Abraham and Ernst Freud, eds., *A Psycho-Analytic Dialogue: The Letters of Sigmund Freud and Karl Abraham: 1907–1926* (New York: Basic Books, 1965), 163.

 "The confession of her sinful thoughts": Jung, "Freud's Theory of Hysteria: A Reply to Aschaffenburg" (1906), *C.W.* 4:316.

 For Pierre Janet's rationale regarding raising the patient's energy level, see Bjorn Sjövall, *The Psychology of Tension: An Analysis of Pierre Janet's Concept of Tension Psychologique* (Stockholm: Scandanavian Universities Press, 1967), 157–58, 161–62.

67 For an account of Janet's seating arrangement with "Achilles," see Henri Ellenberger, *The Discovery of the Unconscious: The History and Evolution of Dynamic Psychiatry* (New York: Basic Books, 1970), 369–70.

68 For Spielrein's account of her ignorance of the sexual facts of life, see her "Beiträge zur Kenntnis der kindlichen Seele," *Zentralblatt für Psychoanalyse und Psychotherapie* 3(1912):57, 61.

 On the experiencing of pleasure upon giving and receiving blows to the "nates," see Albert von Schrenck-Notzing, *The Use of Hypnosis in Psychopathia Sexualis* (New York: The Institute for Research in Hypnosis Publishing Co. and the Julian Society, 1956), 291–98; and Richard von Krafft-Ebing, *Psychopathia Sexualis: A Medico-Forensic Study* (New York: Putnam, 1965), 53, 112, 117, 131, 135, 169.

69 "in my innocence": Spielrein, "Beiträge zur Kenntnis der kindlichen Seele," 66.

 "The girl was deeply rooted in him": Spielrein, letter-drafts, *A Secret Symmetry,* 105.

70 On Joseph Grasset's "polygonal" psychology, see his *Marvels Beyond Science* (New York: Rebman, 1910), iv–vi, passim; and Paul DuBois, *The Psychic Treatment of Nervous Disorders* (New York: Funk & Wagnalls, 1909), 216–18.

On Spielrein imagining a polygon, see *A Secret Symmetry,* 62–63.

"a married woman": Jung, "The Reaction-Time Ratio in the Association Experiment" (1905), *C.W.* 2:235.

On the concern with pregnancy in the analysis of "Subject No. 1," ibid., 235–46.

"He gave me some work to do": Spielrein, letter-drafts, *A Secret Symmetry,* 101–102.

71 On Jung's archaeological books, see Spielrein, "Transformation Journal," 188.

"Recently I had to treat a hysterical young lady": Jung, "On Cryptomnesia" (1905), *C.W.* 1:98.

"Anyone who has read": Ibid., 99.

On Spielrein listing her address as the Burghölzli, see Peter Swales, "What Jung *Didn't* Say," *Harvest: Journal for Jungian Studies* 38(1992):30–37.

72 "in which Dr. Jung describes me": Spielrein, *A Secret Symmetry,* 101.

73 "able so to repress": Riklin, "Cases Illustrating the Phenomena of Association in Hysteria" (1908), in Jung, ed., *Studies in Word-Association: Experiments in the Diagnosis of Psychopathological Conditions Carried Out at the Psychiatric Clinic of the University of Zurich* (London: Routledge & Kegan Paul, 1918), 322.

"Her condition was worsened": Ibid., 322–23.

74 "How else should the good man": Spielrein, letter-drafts, *A Secret Symmetry,* 101. On the significance of the letter to Freud, see Peter Swales, "What Jung *Didn't* Say," *Harvest* 38(1992):30–37.

CHAPTER 4   THE ORGANIC UNTRUTHFULNESS OF WOMAN

75 "It is thus possible for the person affected": Otto Weininger, *Sex and Character* (New York: Putnam, 1907), 266.

76 On the idea that dreams reveal wishes, prior to Freud, see Rosemarie Sand, "Pre-Freudian Discovery of Dream Meaning: The Achievements of Charcot, Janet, and Krafft-Ebing," in Toby Gelfand and John Kerr, eds., *Freud and the History of Psychoanalysis* (Hillsdale, N.J.: Analytic Press, 1992).

77 "in the Freudian world": Eugen Bleuler (1904), cited in Jeffrey Masson, ed., *The Complete Letters of Sigmund Freud to Wilhelm Fliess: 1887–1904* (Cambridge: Harvard University Press, 1985), 343 n. 1.

79 "Now I have no idea": Freud to Wilhelm Fliess, 21 September 1897, ibid., 265.

80 "before my friend": Freud, *The Interpretation of Dreams* (1900), *S.E.* 4:331.

81 On Freud and Willy Hellpach, see H. Gundlach, "Freud schreibt an Hellpach: Ein Beitrag zur Rezeptionsgeschichte der Psychoanalyse in Deutschland," *Psyche* (October 1977):909–21.

On "Human Bisexuality" and "Forgetting and Repressing," see Masson, *The Complete Letters of Sigmund Freud to Wilhelm Fliess: 1887–1904*, 448, 451; on Freud's work on the psychology of jokes, ibid., 462.

For Freud on the indispensability of the bisexual explanation of repression, ibid., 450; on its becoming a regular part of his treatments, 464, 467; on his writing it into his unpublished manuscripts, 434, 448, 450–51, 468. I am grateful to Peter Swales for bringing this aspect of Freud's theorizing to my attention.

"sexual organic foundation": Freud to Fliess, 25 January 1902, ibid., 433.

83 On Otto Weininger's theory of sexual attraction, see his *Sex and Character,* chap. 3; on repression, ibid., 265–66, 278.

84 For Weininger's ideal masculine and feminine types, ibid., 282, passim.

Peter Swales has pointed out to me that it is Freud to whom Wilhelm Stekel refers to as a "prominent neurologist" in his review of *Sex and Character,* "Otto Weininger: *Geschlecht und Charakter*" (1904), *Die Wage*, 1033.

85 "They will ask you": Freud to Fliess, 26 April 1904, in Masson, *The Complete Letters of Sigmund Freud to Wilhelm Fliess: 1887–1904*, 461.

"I am in more than one respect": Freud to Fliess, ibid., 461.

"regret": Fliess to Freud, 27 April 1904, ibid., 462.

For Fliess's accusation of Freud with regard to Weininger's theft of the bisexuality theory, see Fliess's letter of 20 July 1904, ibid., 463; for Freud's response of 23 July 1904, see 464.

86 "patented": Freud to Fliess, 27 July 1904, ibid., 466.

"the harm done to you": Freud to Fliess, ibid., 467.

"I trust you will still": Freud to Fliess, ibid., 467–68.

87 For Freud's revision of his conception of the libido, see Frank Sulloway, *Freud, Biologist of the Mind: Beyond the Psychoanalytic Legend* (New York: Basic Books, 1979), chaps. 6, 7, 8.

88 "give medical readers": Freud, "On Psychotherapy" (1905), *S.E.* 7:257.

"hint": Ibid., 266.

"re-education in overcoming": Ibid., 267.

"It seems to me": Ibid., 261.

89 "Though one may recognize": Hellpach (1906), cited in Hannah Decker, *Freud in Germany: Revolution and Reaction in Science: 1893–1907* (New York: International Universities Press, 1977), 251.

90 For Paul Möbius on hysterical attacks, see Francis Schiller, *A Möbius Strip: Fin-de-Siècle Neuropsychiatry and Paul Möbius* (Berkeley: University of California Press, 1982), 32–33.

For Otto Gross's psychology of types, see Jung, *The Psychology of Dementia Praecox* (1907), *C.W.* 3:27–28; and Martin Green, *The von Richthofen Sisters: The Triumphant and the Tragic Modes of Love* (New York: Basic Books, 1974), 32–47.

"there is very little 'nervousness' ": Paul DuBois, *The Psychic Treatment of Nervous Disorders* (New York: Funk & Wagnalls, 1909), 327.

"get your patient to confess to you": Ibid., 353.

"who seem to take a lascivious pleasure": Ibid., 329.

91 For Rank on Jews and sexuality, see Dennis Klein, *The Jewish Origins of the Psychoanalytic Movement* (New York: Praeger, 1981), 129–30.

On Freud's Jewish jokes, see John Cuddihy, *The Ordeal of Civility* (New York: Basic Books, 1974), 19–24.

On early discussions of infantile sexuality, see I. Bry and A. Rifkin, "Freud and the History of Ideas: Primary Sources, 1886–1910," in J. Masserman, ed., *Science and Psychoanalysis* (New York: Grune & Stratton, 1962), vol. 5, 6–36; Stephen Kern, "Freud and the Discovery of Child Sexuality," *History of Childhood Quarterly* 1 (1973):117–41; and Sulloway, *Freud, Biologist of the Mind,* chap. 8.

92 "the past 10 years": Freud, *Three Essays on the Theory of Sexuality* (1905), *S.E.* 7:163.

For Freud on amnesias, ibid., 174–76; on intestinal problems, 186–87; on enuresis, 191; on *globus hystericus,* 182; on examination anxiety, 203; on obsessions, 243; and on intellectual overwork, 204.

For Freud on "railway spine," ibid., 201–202.

93 "by a transference": Richard von Krafft-Ebing, *Psychopathia Sexualis: A Medico-Forensic Study* (New York: Putnam, 1965), 39.

"intervention of fancy": Ibid.

"repressed": Ibid., 123, 124–25.

"the whole thing chiefly belongs": Ibid., 137.

93   For Krafft-Ebing on infantile masturbation, ibid., 109; on erogenous zones, 49, 52–53, 131, 291; on sucking at the breast, 53; and on the role of shame, disgust, and moral education in inhibiting the libido, 35, 54, 86, 107.

94   For Jung's treatment description of his second test case, see his "Psychoanalysis and Association Experiments" (1906), *C. W.* 2:304-307.

95   "with gentle force": Ibid., 305.

"long debate on the use and purpose": Ibid., 305.

"silly": Ibid., 307.

"free associations": Ibid., 304.

"to tell me calmly": Ibid.

"The woman's complex": Jung, "The Psychopathological Significance of the Association Experiment" (1906), *C.W.* 2:422.

96   "I repeat what I have already said": Jung, "The Psychological Diagnosis of Evidence" (1905), *C.W.* 2:332–33.

97   "It is the subtlest thing": Freud to Fliess, 25 January 1901, in Masson, *The Complete Letters of Sigmund Freud to Wilhelm Fliess: 1887–1904,* 433.

For a discussion of the issues touched upon by the "Dora" case, see Stephen Kern, "Explosive Intimacy: Psychodynamics of the Victorian Family," in L. de Mause, ed., *The New Psycho-History* (New York: Psycho-History Press, 1975), 29–54.

98   "I have in this paper": Freud, *Fragment of an Analysis of a Case of Hysteria* (1905), *S.E.* 7:112.

"demands an entirely separate exposition": Ibid.

"let the patient himself": Ibid., 12.

"I came to the conclusion": Ibid., 74.

"allows us to substitute": Ibid., 97.

"I could not avoid supposing": Ibid., 57.

"a fact which I did not neglect": Ibid., 59.

"If this 'No,' ": Ibid., 58–59.

99   "spirit of contradiction": DuBois, *The Psychic Treatment of Nervous Disorders,* 355.

"You are one of those persons": Ibid.

" 'So you see that your love' ": Freud, *Fragment of an Analysis of a Case of Hysteria,* 104.

For Adolf Strümpell's concerns regarding *Studies on Hysteria*, see Decker, *Freud in Germany*, 102.

On hypnosis and erotic fixation, see Léon Chertok, "The Discovery of the Transference: Toward an Epistemological Interpretation," *International Journal of Psycho-Analysis* 49(1968):284–87; and Henri Ellenberger, *The Discovery of the Unconscious: The History and Evolution of Dynamic Psychiatry* (New York: Basic Books, 1970), 118–19, 152–55.

On the "resistance" of certain patients to hypnosis, see Auguste Forel, *Psychotherapy and Hypnotism or Suggestion* (New York: Allied Publishing Co., 1937), 100; and Albert Moll, *The Study of Hypnosis: Historical, Clinical and Experimental Research in the Techniques of Hypnotic Induction* (New York: Julian Press, 1958), 151, 166, 171.

100 On Janet and role-playing in hypnosis, see Ellenberger, *The Discovery of the Unconscious*, 367.

"The publication of the 'Dora analysis' ": Decker, *Freud in Germany*, 164.

101 For Freud on the "brutal" Fliess, see his letter to Karl Kraus, 12 January 1906, in Ernst Freud, ed., *Letters of Sigmund Freud, 1873–1939* (London: Cambridge University Press, 1975), 251.

102 "the symptoms constitute": Freud, *Fragment of an Analysis of a Case of Hysteria*, 115.

103 "Has not perhaps the gallant Viennese atmosphere": Willy Hellpach (1904), cited in Decker, *Freud in Germany*, 100.

CHAPTER 5 THE RISE OF THE ZURICH SCHOOL

105 "It is a matter of complete indifference": Eugen Bleuler (1907), cited in Hannah Decker, *Freud in Germany: Revolution and Reaction in Science: 1893–1907* (New York: International Universities Press, 1977), 171.

On the "Zurich school," see A. A. Brill, *Freud's Contribution to Psychiatry* (New York: Norton, 1944), 30, 42–43, 97–98.

106 For William Stern's criticism of Freud, see Jeffrey Masson, ed., *The Complete Letters of Sigmund Freud to Wilhelm Fliess: 1887–1904* (Cambridge: Harvard University Press, 1985), 455 n. 2; for his criticism of Jung, see Jung's "The Psychological Diagnosis of Evidence" (1905), *C.W.* 2:330.

"difficult and dangerous": Ibid., 331.

"whose life and psychological make-up": Ibid.

"a fair knowledge of certain aspects": Ibid.

"the principles of Sigmund Freud's ingenious psychoanalysis": Ibid.

106 "not an inimitable art": Ibid., 332.

"since the beginner easily loses": Jung, "Psychoanalysis and Association Experiments" (1906), *C.W.* 2:290.

"served as signposts": Ibid., 316.

"useful for facilitating": Ibid., 317.

107 "there is a particular way": Ibid., 289.

"The blood and fire dreams": Jung, "Association, Dream, and Hysterical Symptom" (1906), *C.W.* 2:384.

" 'I was outside' ": Ibid., 391.

108 "Miss L. is a patient": Ibid., 392.

"ruthlessly destroyed her illusions": Ibid., 395.

"that she is just as bad": Ibid., 406.

"Above all we see": Ibid., 400.

"The complex has an abnormal autonomy": Ibid., 406-407.

110 "The patient was unable to reveal": Ibid., 406.

111 "thinking in analogies": Jung to Freud, 6 July 1907, in *F/J Letters,* 74.

On the method of analogy in linguistic disciplines, see Steinthal, in I. Goldhizer, *Mythology Among the Hebrews and Its Historical Development* (New York: Cooper Square Publishers, 1967), 365-446.

112 "I saw horses being hoisted": Jung, *The Psychology of Dementia Praecox* (1907), *C.W.* 3:57-58.

113 For Jung's interpretation of his horse dream, ibid., 58-62; specifically regarding the prospect of too many children, 61-62.

For Jung's letters to Freud regarding his horse dream, see his letters of 26 December 1906 and 8 January 1907 in *F/J Letters,* 14-15, 20.

"merely a convenient screen": Jung to Freud, ibid., 20.

"A certain young lady": Jung, *The Psychology of Dementia Praecox,* 46.

114 "Many thanks for sending me": Freud to Jung, 11 April 1906, *F/J Letters,* 3.

115 "an exactly similar method": Freud, "Psycho-Analysis and the Establishment of the Facts in Legal Proceedings" (1906), *S.E.* 9:107.

"I can assure you": Jung, *The Psychology of Dementia Praecox,* 3-4.

117 For Gustav Aschaffenburg's criticisms of Freud, see Decker, *Freud in Germany,* 103, 137-38, 165-67; and Henri Ellenberger, *The Discovery of the Uncon-*

scious: The History and Evolution of Dynamic Psychiatry (New York: Basic Books, 1970), 793–94.

"moderate and cautious criticism": Jung, "Freud's Theory of Hysteria: A Reply to Aschaffenburg" (1906), *C.W.* 4:3.

"somewhat one-sided": Ibid., 4.

"An indefinitely large": Ibid.

118 "Recently I conducted a lively correspondence": Jung to Freud, 5 October 1906, *F/J Letters*, 4–5.

119 "Your letter gave me great pleasure": Freud to Jung, 7 October 1906, ibid., 5.

"I venture to hope": Ibid.

"two warring worlds": Ibid., 6.

"he shows no understanding": Ibid.

"My 'transference' ": Ibid.

"one feels alarmed": Jung to Freud, 23 October 1906, ibid., 7.

"At the risk of boring you": Jung to Freud, 26 October 1906, ibid.

121 "indescribable relief": Jung, *Memories, Dreams, Reflections,* rev. ed. (New York: Pantheon, 1973), 40.

"You certainly did not show": Freud to Jung, 27 October 1906, *F/J Letters*, 8.

122 "I am glad to hear": Ibid., 8–9.

123 "Transference provides the impulse": Freud to Jung, 6 December 1906, ibid., 12–13.

124 For Ludwig Binswanger's account of Jung's associations, see William McGuire, "Jung's Complex Reactions (1907): Word Association Experiments Performed by Binswanger," *Spring* (1984):1–34. See also Ludwig Binswanger, "On the Psychogalvanic Phenomenon in Association Experiments," in C. G. Jung, ed., *Studies in Word Association* (London: Routledge & Kegan Paul, 1918), 457–468, 512–513.

For Sabina Spielrein's reaction to the "ruefulness-faithfulness" complex, also to the reactions, "child-have, cap-put on," see *A Secret Symmetry,* 102; see also McGuire, "Jung's Complex Reactions," 2–4.

126 For Spielrein's associations, see Binswanger, "On the Psychogalvanic Phenomenon in Association Experiments," 514.

"two strong complexes": Ibid.

126   ". . . he is contemplating": Ibid., 468.

127   "lacks any understanding of sexual matters": Freud, in *Minutes* 1:33.

"The sexual component of psychic life": Freud, ibid., 99.

On the consensus that neuroses were more prevalent among Jews, ibid., 94.

128   "Our cures are cures of love": Freud, ibid., 101.

For Freud's criticism of Jung's theory of a dementia praecox toxin, ibid., 101.

"painting, music or psychology": Alfred Adler, ibid., 96.

"vague and incomprehensible": Max Eitingon, Ibid., 96.

CHAPTER 6   JUNG AND FREUD

129   ". . . modern European society": Iwan Bloch, *The Sexual Life of Our Times in Its Relations to Modern Civilization* (1906; London: Rebman, 1910), 276.

For Otto Weininger on "emancipated women," see his *Sex and Character* (New York: Putnam, 1907), 64-75.

130   "a simple evolutionary necessity": Bloch, *The Sexual Life of Our Times*, 278.

"It would be an interesting task": Ibid.

On Auguste Forel's visit to Vienna during his student years, see his *Out of My Life and Work* (London: Allen & Unwin, 1937), 81.

For Bloch on Viennese married life, see his *The Sexual Life of Our Times*, 221-31.

For Hanns Sachs on Freud's ideas and the double consciousness of Viennese life, see his *Freud, Master and Friend* (Cambridge: Harvard University Press, 1944), chap. 2.

131   "the first man of real importance": Jung, *Memories, Dreams, Reflections,* rev. ed. (New York: Pantheon, 1973), 149.

". . . Jung gave me a lively account": Ernest Jones, *The Life and Work of Sigmund Freud,* 3 vols. (New York: Basic Books, 1955), 2:32.

For Freud on Jung's grasp of the neuroses, see Vincent Brome, *Ernest Jones: Freud's Alter Ego* (New York: Norton, 1983), 93.

"in my experience": Jung, *Memories, Dreams, Reflections,* 149.

132   "dethrone him and take his place": Ludwig Binswanger, *Sigmund Freud: Reminiscences of a Friendship* (New York: Grune & Stratton, 1957), 2.

"The easy-going, friendly atmosphere": Ibid., 2–3.

For Adler's presentation, see *Minutes* 1:138–40.

"3 may perhaps stand": Freud, ibid., 142.

"Professor Freud points out": Ibid., 145.

133 For Max Graf on Jung and Binswanger's visit, see his "Reminiscences of Professor Sigmund Freud," *The Psychoanalytic Quarterly* 11(1942):472.

For Jung on Freud being "handsome," see Richard Evans, interview with Gene Nameche, 25 November 1971, Jung Oral History Archive, 18.

"degenerate and Bohemian crowd": Jung, cited in Ernest Jones, *Free Associations: Memoirs of a Psychoanalyst* (New York: Basic Books, 1959), 167.

134 "the drive to explore other possibilities": Spielrein, diary, in *A Secret Symmetry*, 30.

For Jones on the Jewishness of Freud's Viennese group, see his *Free Associations*, 167.

"sulky and pathetically eager for recognition": Ibid., 169.

"morose, pathetic figure": Ibid.

"dry, witty, and somewhat cynical": Ibid.

"The egregious Stekel": Ibid.

For Jones's lengthy treatment of Wilhelm Stekel, ibid., 219–21.

"The reader may perhaps gather": Ibid., 169–70.

"took me aside afterward": Binswanger, *Sigmund Freud*, 4.

"keen": Ibid.

136 "In 1907 I arrived": Jung to John Billinsky, quoted by Billinsky, unpublished notes of 1957 interview provided to the author by John Billinsky, Jr.

"When, a few days later": Jung to Billinsky, quoted in Billinsky, "Jung and Freud," *Andover Newton Quarterly* 10(1969):42.

137 For Freud's upbraiding his patient Eva Rosenfeld for dismissing the story too easily, see Paul Roazen, *Freud and His Followers* (New York: Knopf, 1975), 62.

"For children, Freud went with Martha": Oskar Rie's comment to Pauline Fliess, as reported by Peter Swales, personal communication, 15 September 1989.

On Jung's testimony, see Henry Murray, interview with Nameche, 11 November 1968, Jung Oral History Archive, 59; Hugo Charteris's statement occurs in passing in Vincent Brome, *Jung: Man and Myth* (New York: Atheneum, 1978), 264; and John Phillips related his account in a personal interview with the author, 27 September 1984.

137 "Jung had hardly known him": Carl Meier, interview with Nameche, 11 September 1970, Jung Oral History Archive, 59.

138 For Swales on Freud and Minna Bernays, see his "Freud, Minna Bernays and the Imitation of Christ" (presentation at the New School for Social Research, New York, 20 May 1982); "Freud, Minna Bernays and the Conquest of Rome," *New American Review* 1(1982):1–23; and "Freud, Martha Bernays, and the Language of Flowers: Masturbation, Cocaine, and the Inflation of Fantasy" (1983, privately published).

139 "free of cost," see *On Dreams* (1901), *S.E.* 5:638–57.

"absent for purposes of cure": Swales, "Freud, Minna Bernays and the Conquest of Rome," 10.

"serious mischief in important directions": Freud, *On Dreams*, 671; and Swales, "Freud, Minna Bernays and the Conquest of Rome," 10.

For a demonstration of the autobiographical nature of Freud's "Aliquis" episode, ibid., 3–8.

140 "Later generations who try to find out": Rosemary Dinnage, "Declarations of Dependence," *Times Literary Supplement,* 10 December 1982:1351.

On Jung's "compulsive infatuation," see his letter to Freud, 4 June 1909, *F/J Letters,* 229.

141 "The Jews, who have preserved their race": Auguste Forel, *The Sexual Question: A Scientific, Psychological, Hygienic and Sociological Study* (New York: Physicians & Surgeons Book Co., 1905), 189.

142 "It is the courage of making a clean breast": Schopenhauer to Goethe, cited in Sandor Ferenczi, "A Little Chanticleer," *First Contributions to Psycho-Analysis* (1912; New York: Bruner/Mazel, 1980), 254.

"Oedipus, his father's murderer": Nietzsche, *The Birth of Tragedy and The Genealogy of Morals* (1872; New York: Anchor Books, 1956), 61.

"psychoanalytic frankness": See Freud's letter to Jung, 7 April 1907, *F/J Letters,* 28.

"You will doubtless have drawn": Ibid., 25.

143 "I am choosing different paper": Ibid., 27.

"Many thanks for your long": Ibid., 30.

144 "You see, my view of our relationship": Ibid., 32–33.

"Your *Gradiva* is magnificent": Ibid., 49.

146 "One question which you leave open": Ibid., 49.

"a statement such as yours": Freud to Jung, 26 May 1908, ibid., 52.

"You are right": Freud to Jung, ibid., 52.

147 For Jung's anecdotes, see Freud, *The Psychopathology of Everyday Life* (1901; material added in 1907 rev. ed.), *S.E.* 6:18, 25, 215.

"First they write": Freud to Jung, 26 May 1907, *F/J Letters*, 54–55.

148 "In my entourage": Jung to Freud, 30 May 1907, ibid., 55–56.

"The remark in your last letter": Jung to Freud, 4 June 1907, ibid., 56.

"I'd like to make an amusing picture-book": Ibid., 57.

"A picture-book such as the one": Freud to Jung, 6 June 1907, ibid., 59.

149 "It is amusing to see": Jung to Freud, 12 June 1907, ibid., 63.

"a very bad *blague*": Jung to Freud, 28 June 1907, ibid., 67.

150 "I am going to write": Emma Jung, cited in Jung's letter to Freud, 6 July 1907, ibid., 72.

"Vienna complex might have to share": Freud to Jung, 1 July 1907, ibid., 68.

"Now for a bit of historical mysticism": Jung to Freud, 6 July 1907, ibid., 73.

"what a frightful tussle": Ibid.

"An hysterical patient": Ibid., 72–73.

151 "You will then see": Ibid., 74.

"I am writing to you": Freud to Jung, 10 July 1907, ibid., 74.

152 "Don't despair": Freud to Jung, 18 August 1907, ibid., 77.

". . . I have unpleasant presentiments": Jung to Freud, 19 August 1907, ibid., 78.

"surface psychology": See Freud to Jung, 27 August 1907, ibid., 80.

"Whether you have been": Freud to Jung, 2 September 1907, ibid., 82.

153 "bad joke": Pierre Janet, see Jung, "New Paths in Psychology" (1912), *C.W.* 7:248.

For Jung's follow-up reports to Freud on the Amsterdam congress, see his letters of 4 September 1907 and 11 September 1907, *F/J Letters*, 83–84, 84–85.

153 "it still needs a bit of polishing": Jung to Freud, 30 November 1907, ibid., 102

"an indefinitely large number": Jung, "The Freudian Theory of Hysteria" (1908), *C.W.* 4:23. See also Jung, "Freud's Theory of Hysteria: A Reply to Aschaffenburg" (1906), *C.W.* 4:4.

"The public can forgive Freud": Jung, "The Freudian Theory of Hysteria," 23.

"When real sexual demands": Ibid., 22.

155 For Freud's letter to Karl Abraham of 5 July 1907 regarding the seduction theory, see Hilde Abraham and Ernst Freud, eds., *A Psycho-Analytic Dialogue: The Letters of Sigmund Freud and Karl Abraham: 1907–1926* (New York: Basic Books, 1965), 1–4.

"I intend to leave Zurich": Abraham to Freud, 7 October 1907, ibid., 8–9.

"I quickly suppressed the first impulse": Freud to Abraham, 8 October 1907, ibid., 9.

156 On Abraham's "resistances," see E. Glover, ibid., xiv.

For Abraham's reaction to Freud's praise, see H. Abraham, "Karl Abraham: An Unfinished Biography," *International Review of Psycho-Analysis* 1(1974):35.

For an example of the "Jewish" dimension in the Freud/Abraham correspondence, see Freud's letter of 3 May 1908 and Abraham's reply of 11 May 1908, in Abraham and Freud, *A Psycho-Analytic Dialogue*, 33–36.

CHAPTER 7 THE SCIENCE OF FAIRY TALES

158 "In Psychiatry": Franz Riklin, *Wishfulfillment and Symbolism in Fairy-Tales* (1908; New York: Journal of Nervous and Mental Disease Publishing Co., 1915), 1.

"the human psyche": Ibid., 3

For Riklin on sexual symbols being clear to "the initiated," ibid., 29, 31.

159 "Abasia dream motive": Ibid., 56.

"Anxiety? Bad conscience": Ibid., 67.

"Symbol for the hymen": Ibid., 53.

161 "It was Wagner": Spielrein, letter-drafts, in *A Secret Symmetry*, 107.

162 "Thus Siegfried came into being": Ibid., 108.

163 "sacrifice": Spielrein, diary, ibid., 21–25.

For a discussion of the effects of puberty on hysterical women, see Charles Mercier, *Sanity and Insanity* (New York: Scribners, 1889), 220–22, 240–42.

"When I confessed this complex": Spielrein, letter-drafts, *A Secret Symmetry*, 108.

164 On Spielrein's "prophetic" dreams concerning Jung's desire for a son, see her diary, ibid., 30; and her letter to Jung, 6/16 January 1918, 77.

On Spielrein and Jung's diary, see her letter-drafts, ibid., 105.

"I was able to read": Spielrein, letter-drafts, ibid., 109.

165 "Without your instruction": Spielrein, letter to Jung, 19 January 1918, ibid., 79–80.

For Spielrein's description of the symbols for "Siegfried," such as a "book" or as an "Aryan-Semitic minstrel," ibid., 86–87. For Jung's comment "in her dreams she is merged with me," see *F/J Letters*, 72.

166 For Spielrein's folio from the Claparède cache, see "Extraits inédits d'un journal: De l'Amour, de la mort et de la transformation," J. Moll, trans., *Le Bloc-Notes de la Psychanalyse* 3(1983):149–70. Folio is hereafter abbreviated as "Transformation Journal."

"That he could say such a thing": Spielrein, letter-drafts, *A Secret Symmetry*, 96.

For a discussion of when the three parts of Spielrein's folio were written, see Moll, translator's note, "Transformation Journal," 147–48.

167 "the instinct for species preservation": Ibid., 161.

For Spielrein on the unintended attraction between doctor and patient, ibid., 158.

For Spielrein on sexuality being "demonic" and "destructive," ibid., 154; on sexuality at individual differentiation, 156; on sexuality and "sacrifice," 156; on part of the sexual instinct being repressed, 156.

"to express themselves": Ibid., 153.

"this state is worse than death": Ibid., 160.

"I have to take an extreme position": Ibid., 165.

168 "Understand me well": Ibid., 165–66.

169 "a long cherished": Jung to Freud, 11 September 1907, *F/J Letters*, 86.

"uninhibited abreaction": Jung to Freud, 25 September 1907, ibid., 90.

"Dr. Gross tells me": Ibid.

170 For Jung's report on the meetings of the "Freudian Society of Physicians," see his letter to Freud of 25 September 1907, ibid., 89.

"priceless doggerel": Jung to Freud, 10 October 1907, ibid., 101.

"If only his respectable colleagues": Ernest Jones, *Free Associations: Memoirs of a Psychoanalyst* (New York: Basic Books, 1959), 164.

"I would like to ask": Jung to Freud, 10 October 1907, *F/J Letters*, 93.

"For a long time": Spielrein, letter-drafts, *A Secret Symmetry*, 100.

171 "Actually—and I confess": Jung to Freud, 28 October 1907, *F/J Letters*, 95.

"downright disgusting": Ibid.

"all the agonies": Jung to Freud, 2 November 1907, ibid., 95.

"your +++ dangerousness": Ibid., 96.

"Here too your discoveries": Ibid.

172 "In the hospital": A. A. Brill, *Lectures on Psychoanalytic Psychiatry* (New York: Knopf, 1946), 27.

"enthusiasm and brilliance": Ibid., 26.

"Jung was at that time": Ibid.

173 "My old religiosity": Jung to Freud, 8 November 1907, *F/J Letters*, 97.

"What you say of your inner developments": Freud to Jung, 15 November 1907, ibid., 98.

"Congress of Freudian followers": Jung to Freud, 30 November 1907, ibid., 101.

"magnificent plans": Freud to Jung, 21 December 1907, ibid., 104.

"I have a sin to confess": Jung to Freud, 25 January 1908, ibid., 115.

"a complex connected with my family": Jung to Freud, 15 February 1908, ibid., 117.

174 "At last I come to science": Freud to Jung, 17 February 1908, ibid., 120–21.

On Wilhelm Fliess's fear that Freud wanted to kill him, see Swales, "Freud, Fliess, and Fratricide: The Role of Fliess in Freud's Conception of Paranoia," in Lawrence Spurling, ed., 4 vols. *Sigmund Freud: Critical Assessments* (London: Routledge, 1989). Here and elsewhere in the text, I am grateful to Peter Swales for sharing his extensive researches into Fliess's life.

175 "I thank you with all my heart": Jung to Freud, 20 February 1908, *F/J Letters*, 122.

176 "Jung and Jünger": Jung to Freud, undated postcard, ibid., 125.

"You really are the only one": Freud to Jung, 25 February 1908, ibid., 126.

"Of course the devil": Jung to Freud, 11 March 1908, ibid., 134.

"Your last letter upset me": Jung to Freud, 18 April 1908, ibid., 138.

177 "Don't act on the first impulse": Spielrein, "Transformation Journal," 166.

178 "Before you could converse": Ibid., 167.

"I don't feel very much at ease": Ibid., 168.

179 ". . . *We either decide*": Ibid., 169–70.

For Spielrein and her exams, see her letter-drafts, *A Secret Symmetry*, 109–11.

181 On Abraham's complaints about the Swiss, see Ernest Jones, *The Life and Work of Sigmund Freud*, 3 vols. (New York: Basic Books, 1955), 2:46, 138.

"Do you think Jung can escape": Abraham to Jones, quoted in Vincent Brome, *Ernest Jones: Freud's Alter Ego* (New York: Norton, 1983), 55.

182 "fits a case of hysteria": Abraham to Freud, 4 April 1908, Hilde Abraham and Ernst Freud, eds., *A Psycho-Analytic Dialogue: The Letters of Sigmund Freud and Karl Abraham: 1907–1926* (New York: Basic Books, 1965), 32.

On Jung and the Viennese at Salzburg, see Jones, *The Life and Work of Sigmund Freud*, vol. 2, 44.

"Transformations in the (conception and)": Freud to Jung, 5 March 1908, *F/J Letters*, 132.

For Freud's comments on technique, see *Minutes* 1:180, 250, 335–36.

183 "Associations as well as free thoughts": Freud, ibid., 250.

185 "splitting of the personality": Freud, "Notes Upon a Case of Obsessional Neurosis" (1909), *S.E.* 11:177.

"repressed complexes": Ibid., 181.

"diversion of . . . attention": Ibid., 223.

"complex sensitiveness": Ibid., 210.

"symbolism": Ibid., 217.

"perfect analogy": Ibid., 220.

"It was almost as though Fate": Ibid., 216.

186 "the nearest approach": Jones, *Free Associations*, 172–73.

186   For an account of the influence of Otto Gross's theories, see Martin Green, *The Von Richthofen Sisters: The Triumphant and the Tragic Modes of Love* (New York: Basic Books, 1974), 32–45.

187   "We are doctors": Ibid., 45.

188   "like nodding automata": Jung to Jones, quoted in Jones, *Free Associations*, 174.

"I have let everything drop": Jung to Freud, 25 May 1908, *F/J Letters*, 153.

"Still, I have never had": Freud to Jung, 29 May 1908, ibid., 155.

"He is addicted": Freud to Jung, 30 June 1908, ibid., 162.

189   "One thing and another": Freud to Jung, 13 August 1908, ibid., 169.

"an analysis carried out conjointly": Jung, "The Significance of the Father in the Destiny of the Individual" (1909), *C. W.* 4:304.

"A man disillusioned in love": Ibid., 303.

190   "The infantile attitude": Ibid., 320.

"the history of the fantasy systems": Ibid., 320.

For Jung on the alternating cycle between periods of the father and of the prophets and reformers, ibid., 320–21.

"Like everything that has fallen": Ibid., 321.

191   For Jung's complaint to Freud of his lack of an intellectual companion, see his letter of 9 September 1908, *F/J Letters*, 171.

"I told him how my exams": Spielrein, letter-drafts, *A Secret Symmetry*, 107.

CHAPTER 8   SEXUAL AND PSYCHOLOGICAL RESEARCHES

193   "Thus at that time I learned": Josef Breuer, quoted in Paul Cranefeld, "Josef Breuer's Evaluation of His Contribution to Psycho-Analysis" (1958), *The International Journal of Psycho-Analysis* 39(1958):319.

194   "shock the bourgeoisie": Ibid., 320.

"I confess that the plunging": Ibid.

195   "you have revenged yourself": Freud to Jung, 22 January 1909, *F/J Letters*, 201.

196   For Aldo Carotenuto's description of Jung's letters to Spielrein, see his *A Secret Symmetry*, xlvi.

"you have vigorously taken my unconscious": Jung to Spielrein, 20 June 1908, in Carotenuto, *Tagebuch einer heimlichen Symmetrie: Sabina Spielrein zwischen*

Jung und Freud (Freiburg im Breisgau: Kore, 1986), 189. Hereafter abbreviated as *Tagebuch*.

"find a clear way out": Ibid.

197 "strong spirit": Ibid.

"You cannot imagine": Jung to Spielrein, 30 June 1908, *A Secret Symmetry*, 167.

"many disappointments": Jung to Spielrein, 4 July 1908, *Tagebuch*, 190.

"calmer and freer": Ibid.

"shifting volcanically from grey to gold": Jung to Spielrein, 12 August 1908, ibid., 192.

"beam of light": Ibid., 191.

"the devil had gotten": Ibid.

"generous spirit": Ibid.

198 "I notice how much": Jung to Spielrein, 12 August 1908, Ibid., 167–68.

For Jung's letter to Spielrein, 2 September 1908, ibid., 194.

"because of the": Jung to Spielrein, 28 September 1908, ibid., 195.

199 "Why, of course": Freud to Jung, 30 June 1908, *F/J Letters*, 161.

"to demolish the resentment": Freud to Jung, 13 August 1908, ibid., 167.

"a few personal concessions": Ibid.

"My selfish purpose": Ibid., 168.

200 "Prof. Bleuler has nothing": Jung to Freud, 28 August 1908, ibid., 169–70.

"I am looking forward": Ibid., 171.

"insofar as his unapproachability": Freud to Abraham, 11 October 1908, in Hilde Abraham and Ernst Freud, eds., *A Psycho-Analytic Dialogue: The Letters of Sigmund Freud and Karl Abraham: 1907–1926* (New York: Basic Books, 1965), 54.

201 For Freud on language fragmentation, see his letter to Jung, 15 October 1908, *F/J Letters*, 172–73.

"in analysis we guide": Jung's remark, as remembered by Freud in his letter of 15 October 1908, ibid., 173.

Regarding the discussion of Jung's "star complex," see Freud's letter to Jung, 29 November 1908, ibid., 183.

"has done me so much good": Jung to Freud, 24 October 1908, ibid., 173.

201 "Freud seems to be an idea": Abraham to Freud, 31 July 1908, in Abraham and Freud, *A Psycho-Analytic Dialogue,* 44.

"been reverting to his": Abraham to Freud, 16 July 1908, ibid., 44.

"Moreover, he can hardly back out": Freud to Abraham, 23 July 1907, ibid., 47.

"I am glad to say": Freud to Abraham, 29 September 1908, ibid., 51–52.

202 "high regard": Ibid., 52.

For Auguste Forel's reservations regarding Freudian analysis, see John Kerr, "*The Devil's Elixirs,* Jung's 'Theology,' and the Dissolution of Freud's 'Poisoning Complex,' " *The Psychoanalytic Review* 75(1988):9–10.

"Forel's attacks": Freud to Jung, 8 November 1908, *F/J Letters,* 175.

203 "I stood in lonely opposition": Abraham to Freud, 10 November 1909, in Abraham and Freud, *A Psycho-Analytic Dialogue,* 56.

"I hear from Abraham": Freud to Jung, 12 November 1908, *F/J Letters,* 178.

For Henri Ellenberger on Abraham's presentation to the Berlin Association of Psychiatrists and Nerve-Specialists, see his *The Discovery of the Unconscious: The History and Evolution of Dynamic Psychiatry* (New York: Basic Books, 1970), 799–800.

"every last hillbilly": Jung to Freud, 27 November 1908, *F/J Letters,* 180.

"the only thing he understood": Ibid.

204 "*Magna est vis veritatis*": Jung to Freud, 11 November 1908, ibid., 176.

"the star": Freud to Jung, remembering an earlier conversation, 29 November 1908, ibid., 183.

"You can imagine our joy": Jung to Freud, 3 December 1908, ibid., 184.

"I must say": Freud to Jung, 11 December 1908, ibid., 186.

"My father begot me": Ibid., 186 n. 2.

205 For Jung's letter to Spielrein, 4 December 1908, see *Tagebuch,* 195–96.

For Jung's childhood incident, ibid., 196.

"I am looking for a person": Jung to Spielrein, 4 December 1908, *A Secret Symmetry,* 168–69.

"Therefore when one": Jung to Spielrein, 4 December 1908, *Tagebuch,* 196.

206 "birth of Jung's *Jahrbuch*": Freud to Jung, 17 December 1908, *F/J Letters,* 188.

"if I am Moses": Freud to Jung, 17 January 1909, ibid., 196-97.

"I moved from being her doctor": Jung to Frau Spielrein, cited in Spielrein, letter-drafts, *A Secret Symmetry*, 94.

"the prosaic solution": Ibid.

207   "I have always told": Ibid., 95.

208   "he gave me a long sermon": Spielrein, letter-drafts, ibid., 96.

"can only do great harm": Freud to Jung, 30 June 1908, *F/J Letters*, 162.

"Both with students": Jung to Jones, 25 February 1909, quoted in Ernest Jones, *The Life and Work of Sigmund Freud*, 3 vols. (New York: Basic Books, 1955), 2:139.

"The last and worst straw": Jung to Freud, 7 March 1909, *F/J Letters*, 207.

209   "the buffetings fate has given me": Ibid., 208.

"to recuperating from all my batterings": Ibid., 209.

"To be slandered and scorched": Freud to Jung, 9 March 1909, ibid., 210.

210   "traumatic hyperaesthesia": Ibid., 209.

"Oddly enough": Jung to Freud, 19 January 1909, ibid., 197.

"And another thing": Freud to Jung, 9 March 1909, ibid., 210-11.

"I must answer you at once": Jung to Freud, 11 March 1909, ibid., 211-12.

211   "whole tangle of neurotic problems": Jung to Freud, 11 March 1909, *F/J Letters*, 212.

"Lately I visited Häberlin": Jung to Freud, 21 March 1909, ibid., 214.

212   "It interested me to hear": Jung, *Memories, Dreams, Reflections,* rev. ed. (New York: Pantheon, 1973), 155-56.

213   For Jung's "great dream" as it was reported to the 1925 seminar, see William McGuire, ed., *Analytical Psychology: Notes of the Seminar Given in 1925* by C. G. Jung, (Princeton: Princeton University Press, 1989), 38-39.

For Jung's account of the "great dream" in his memoirs, see his *Memories, Dreams, Reflections,* 163-65.

214   On Jung and *The Devil's Elixirs*, see Kerr, *"The Devil's Elixirs,* Jung's 'Theology,' and the Dissolution of Freud's 'Poisoning Complex,' " *The Psychoanalytic Review* 75(1988):1-34.

"the miserable activity": E. T. A. Hoffmann, *The Devil's Elixirs* (1816; London: John Calder, 1963), 321.

214   "This may well explain": Ibid., 210.

"spookery": Jung to Freud, 2/12 April 1909, *F/J Letters*, 216.

"I had the feeling": Ibid., 217.

215   "It is strange": Freud to Jung, 16 April 1909, ibid., 218.

". . . I confront the despiritualized": Ibid., 218-19.

216   "the specifically Jewish nature": Ibid., 220.

"I have not gone over": Jung to Freud, 12 May 1909, ibid., 220.

217   "Dear Professor Freud": Spielrein to Freud, letter-drafts, *A Secret Symmetry*, 91.

218   "Weird!": Freud to Jung, 3 June 1909, *F/J Letters*, 226.

"At the moment": Jung to Freud, 4 June 1909, ibid., 228-29.

219   "come very close to it": Freud to Jung, 7 June 1909, ibid., 230.

"I believe that only": Ibid., 231.

". . . it is too stupid": Jung to Freud, 12 June 1909, Ibid., 232.

"Fräulein Spielrein has admitted": Freud to Jung, 18 June 1909, ibid., 234-35.

220   "the old legal dictum": Freud to Spielrein, 8 June 1909, *A Secret Symmetry*, 114.

"From the enclosures": Ibid., 114.

"whenever you like": Freud to Jung, 18 June 1909, *F/J Letters*, 235.

221   "He loves him": Spielrein, letter-drafts, *A Secret Symmetry*, 93.

"a piece of knavery": Jung to Freud, 21 June 1909, *F/J Letters*, 236.

"[S]he has freed herself": Ibid.

"perfect honesty": Ibid.

"the fact that I was wrong": Freud to Spielrein, 24 June 1909, *A Secret Symmetry*, 115.

222   "Amazingly awkward": Freud to Jung, 30 June 1909, *F/J Letters*, 238.

223   "To suffer this disdain": Spielrein, letter-drafts, *A Secret Symmetry*, 93.

"Four and a half years ago": Ibid.

224   "I begged him": Ibid., 96-97.

"Later generations": Rosemary Dinnage, "Declarations of Dependence," *Times Literary Supplement*, 10 December 1982, 1351.

"For 'poetry' we must surmise": *A Secret Symmetry*, 219 n. 20.

225 For appearances of the word "poetry" in Spielrein's dissertation, see her "Über den psychologischen Inhalt eines Falles von Schizophrenie (Dementia Praecox)," *Jahrbuch für psychoanalytische und psychopatholgische Forschungen* 3(1911):332–34, 364, 368, 377, *passim*.

"Poetry = Love": Ibid., 364 n. 1.

For Richard von Krafft-Ebing's use of the word "poetry," see his *Psychopathia Sexualis: A Medico-Forensic Study* (New York: Putnam, 1965), 23, 28, 31, 32; on the "poetry" of the symbolic act of subjection, ibid., 178.

"still always a fairy poetess": Franz Riklin, *Wishfulfillment and Symbolism in Fairy-Tales* (1908; New York: Journal of Nervous and Mental Disease Publishing Co., 1915), 3.

"poet": Jung, "Psychoanalysis and Association Experiments" (1906), *C.W.* 2:289.

226 For Forel on sexual influences over poetry, see his *The Sexual Question: A Scientific, Psychological, Hygienic and Sociological Study* (New York: Physicians and Surgeons Publishing Co., 1905), chap. 18.

"the poetry of love": Ibid., 498.

"the poetry of amorous intoxication": Ibid., 290.

"we could sit in speechless ecstasy": Spielrein, letter-drafts, *A Secret Symmetry*, 96.

For Spielrein's confession that she identified Jung with her father and brother, ibid., 105. For Jung's identifying her with his mother, ibid.

For the substitution of Spielrein's brother for Jung in her dreams, see her diary, ibid., 40.

For Spielrein's "Siegfried" fantasies, ibid., 30, 34–35.

229 "At the time Dr. Jung": Spielrein to Freud, letter-drafts, ibid., 106.

"Honegger has fathomed": Freud to Oskar Pfister, 12 July 1909, Ernst Freud and H. Meng, eds., *Psycho-Analysis and Faith: The Letters of Sigmund Freud and Oskar Pfister* (New York: Basic Books, 1963), 26.

For François Roustang on Honegger's analysis of Freud, see his *Dire Mastery: Discipleship from Freud to Lacan* (Baltimore: Johns Hopkins University Press, 1976), 87–88.

230 "I am celibate": Jung, "The Analysis of Dreams" (1909), *C.W.* 4:32.

230 For examples of the usage of "Pope," see Freud's letters of 21 April 1907 and 1 July 1907, *F/J Letters*, 42, 69.

"the surprising gift": Freud to Jung, 19 July 1909, ibid., 242.

On Jung trying to introduce Spielrein into his household, see Spielrein's diary, *A Secret Symmetry*, 12.

231 ". . . it's so nice when someone": Spielrein, ibid., 4.

"Mother says it is impossible": Ibid., 6.

233 "Finally, to judge": James Jackson Putnam (1906), "Recent Experiences in the Study and Treatment of Hysteria at Massachusetts General Hospital," in Ernest Jones, ed., *Addresses on Psychoanalysis* (London: International Psycho-Analytic Press, 1921), 40.

CHAPTER 9 AMERICA AND THE CORE COMPLEX

235 "Our own soul": G. Stanley Hall, *Adolescence: Its Psychology, and Its Relations to Physiology, Anthropology, Sociology, Sex, Crime, Religion and Education*, 2 vols. (New York: Appleton, 1904), 2:64–65.

"American colitis": Ernest Jones, *The Life and Work of Sigmund Freud*, 3 vols. (New York: Basic Books, 1955), 2:90.

For Jung's view of Freud's "neurosis," see his interview with John Billinsky, infra. this book, page 267 (original interview notes, 1957, supplied by John Billinsky, Jr.).

237 "maternal nurturance": J. Lears, *No Place of Grace: Antimodernism and the Transformation of American Culture* (New York: Pantheon, 1981), 250.

"sad new light": Hall, *Adolescence*, 121.

238 "one must combine": Edward Thorndike, cited in Frank Sulloway, *Freud, Biologist of the Mind: Beyond the Psychoanalytic Legend* (New York: Basic Books, 1979), 458.

"chock full of errors": Thorndike, cited in Peter Gay, *Freud: A Life for Our Time* (New York: Norton, 1988), 207.

241 "We owe to our European guests": Adolf Meyer, *Collected Papers of Adolf Meyer*, 2 vols. (Baltimore: Johns Hopkins University Press, 1950), 1:454–55.

243 "the fruit of an unprejudiced examination": Freud, "Five Lectures on Psycho-Analysis" (1910), *S.E.* 11:20.

"sublimation": Ibid., 52–54.

"You will find it worthwhile": Jones, *Life and Work* 2:58.

244 "visibly moved": Ibid., 57.

"This is the first": Ibid.

"Freud is in seventh heaven": Jung, letter to Emma Jung, 14 September 1909, cited in *Memories, Dreams, and Reflections*, rev. ed. (New York: Pantheon, 1973), 368.

"Kill his father": Freud, in Jones, *Life and Work* 2:58.

"The future of psychology": James, quoted in Jones, ibid., 59.

245   "I hope that Freud": James to Théodore Flournoy, 28 September 1909, in Henry James, ed., *The Letters of William James*, 2 vols. (Boston: Atlantic Monthly Press, 1920), 2:327-28.

"It is true that Freud": Albert Moll, *The Sexual Life of the Child* (New York: Macmillan, 1912), 190-91.

246   "I have started work": Freud to Jung, 8 November 1908, *F/J Letters*, 175.

For Freud's mention that the "General Exposition" would have a section on transference, see his letter to Jung, 30 December 1908, ibid., 193.

"I am having trouble finishing [it]": Freud to Jung, 25 January 1909, ibid. 202.

247   For Freud's "complex" additions to the 1907 revised edition of *The Psychopathology of Everyday Life*, see *S.E.* 6:23-25, 40.

For Freud's mention of his "money" complex, see his letter to Jung, 2 December 1909, *F/J Letters*, 270.

248   "The entire theory": Freud, in *Minutes* 2:323.

250   For Peter Rudnytsky on the importance of Sophocles' *Oedipus Rex* in German literature and philosophy during the latter half of the nineteenth century, see his *Freud and Oedipus* (New York: Columbia University Press, 1987), chaps. 4-8.

"(Oedipus Saga!)": Franz Riklin, *Wishfulfillment and Symbolism in Fairy-Tales* (1908; New York: Journal of Nervous and Mental Disease Publishing Co., 1915), 65.

"a typical personification": Sandor Ferenczi, "The Analytic Interpretation and Treatment of Psychosexual Impotence" (1908), in Ernest Jones, ed. and trans., *First Contributions to Psycho-Analysis* (New York: Bruner/Mazel, 1980), 26.

"one thing and another": Freud to Jung, 13 August 1908, *F/J Letters*, 169.

251   "These myths are a combination": Freud, *Minutes* 2:72.

252   "Shortly after": Auguste Forel, *Out of My Life and Work* (London: Allen & Unwin, 1937), 29-30.

252   "the inferences and constructions": Freud, "On the Sexual Theories of Children" (1908), *S.E.* 9:209.

"I can only give an assurance": Ibid.

253   "from the time of this first deception": Ibid., 213–14.

255   "Does the Professor talk to God": cited in Freud, "Analysis of a Phobia in a Five-Year-Old Boy" (1909), *S.E.* 10:42–44.

"I am so obsessed": Freud to Jung, 11 December 1909, *F/J Letters,* 186.

"little Oedipus": Freud, "Analysis of a Phobia in a Five-Year-Old Boy," 97, 111.

256   "He [the father] not only prevented": Ibid., 134.

"I am therefore tempted": Ibid., 147.

"Now I hope": Freud to Jung, 4 October 1909, *F/J Letters,* 250.

"pleasant and affectionate": Freud to Jung, 4 October 1909, ibid., 249.

257   "beastly non-paying patient": Wilhelm Stekel, quoted in letter of Freud to Jung, 17 October 1909, ibid., 255.

"my many, absolutely necessary": Freud to Jung, 4 October 1909, ibid., 248.

"The nuclear complex": Freud, "Notes upon a Case of Obsessional Neurosis" (1909), *S.E.* 10:208 n.

"The feelings which are aroused": Freud, "Five Lectures on Psycho-Analysis" (1910), *S.E.* 11:47–48.

258   "In general": Freud, *Minutes* 2:286.

For Freud's advice to Ludwig Binswanger on the core complex, see Binswanger, *Sigmund Freud: Reminiscences of a Friendship* (New York: Grune & Stratton, 1957), 11–19.

"A little less loneliness": Freud to Jung, 11 November 1909, *F/J Letters,* 260.

"I hope you will soon come": Ibid.

For Freud on "Oedipus," see his letters to Jung of 11 November and 21 November 1909, ibid., 260, 266.

For Freud directing Jung to the 1908 paper on children's sexual researches, see his letters of 17 October, 21 November, and 21 December 1909, ibid., 255, 266, 276.

259   "general method": Freud to Jung, 2 February 1910, ibid., 291.

"faulty interpretive technique": Freud to Jung, 13 January 1910, ibid., 287.

260 "The transition to mythology": Jung to Freud, 17 June 1910, ibid., 329.

CHAPTER 10   THE HOUSE WITH TWO SKULLS

263 "Time here is so frightfully": Jung, letter to Emma Jung, 31 August 1909, in Aniela Jaffé, *C. G. Jung: Word and Image* (Princeton: Princeton University Press, 1979), 47.

"spoke most intelligently": Jung, quoted in Barbara Hannah, *Jung: His Life and Work* (New York: Putnam, 1976), 98.

264 "Here we meet with an important new feature": Jung, "Psychic Conflicts in a Child" (1910), *C.W.* 17:129.

"When life comes up against an obstacle": Ibid., 129 n. 4.

265 "the poetry of fairytale": Ibid., 141.

". . . I had the impression": Jung, *Memories, Dreams, Reflections,* rev. ed. (New York: Pantheon, 1973), 161.

266 "Certain questions had been": Ibid.

"Freud had a dream": Ibid., 158.

267 "mostly concerned with cares": Jung, quoted in Jones, *The Life and Work of Sigmund Freud,* 3 vols. (New York: Basic Books, 1955), 2:55.

"On the trip": Jung interview with John Billinsky, 10 May 1957. Original notes supplied by John Billinsky, Jr.

268 ". . . would have dismissed it": Jung, "Symbols and the Interpretation of Dreams" (1961; 1975), *C.W.* 18:452.

"My wife and my sister-in-law": Jung, *Memories, Dreams, Reflections,* 159.

"I was quite aware": Ibid., 160.

"On the journey back": Jung to Freud, 1 October 1909, *F/J Letters,* 247.

"The analysis on the way home": Jung to Freud, 14 October 1909, ibid., 250.

"I am feeling in top form": Jung to Freud, 1 October 1909, ibid, 247.

269 "Monakow & Co. lay on the floor": Jung to Freud, 22 November 1909, ibid., 268.

"Your (that is, our) cause": Ibid.

270 "Archaeology or rather mythology": Jung to Freud, 14 October 1909, ibid., 251-52.

"Rich lodes open up": Jung to Freud, 8 November 1909, ibid., 258.

270 "For me there is no longer": Jung to Freud, 15 November 1909, ibid., 263.

"Only the great": Jung to Freud, 30 November 1909, ibid., 269.

"elemental": Ibid.

"I often wish I had": Ibid., 270.

"I feel more and more": Ibid., 269.

271 "a prolonged face-to-face": Freud to Jung, 19 December 1909, ibid., 277.

"I am turning over and over": Jung to Freud, 25 December 1909, ibid., 279.

"mythologically typical": Jung to Freud, 30 January 1910, ibid., 289.

"The supporting material": Ibid.

"During the time I didn't write": Ibid.

272 "the Walpurgis nights": Jung to Freud, 20 February 1910, ibid., 296.

"the overflowing delights": Jung to Freud, 6 April 1910, ibid., 305.

"At present I am pursuing": Jung to Freud, 17 April 1910, ibid., 308.

"I explained there": Jung to Freud, 2 March 1910, ibid., 298–99.

For Miss Miller's paper, see appendix: "Some Instances of Subconscious Creative Imagination" in the revised verion of Jung's text *Symbols of Transformation* (1952), *C.W.* 5:447–62.

273 "I read like mad": Jung, *Memories, Dreams, Reflections*, 162–63.

275 "aroused great applause": Jung to Freud, 24 May 1910, *F/J Letters*, 319.

276 For John Forrester on Freud's objection to Jung's two ways of thinking between the symbolic and the verbal, see his *Language and the Origins of Psychoanalysis* (New York: Columbia University Press, 1980), 101. See also Freud to Jung, undated comments, *F/J Letters*, 333.

". . . don't accuse me of plagiarism": Freud to Jung, 19 June 1910, ibid., 332.

"I conceived and wrote it": Ibid.

"like a blocked bowel movement": Freud to Jung, 10 August 1910, ibid., 343.

277 "This would be more apt": Freud to Jung, undated comments, ibid., 333.

"Basically, a part of the castration complex": Ibid., 334.

"Hence the comforting": Jung to Freud, 26 June 1910, ibid., 336.

"The Christian identifies": Ibid., 336–37.

"a good letter": Freud to Jung, 5 July 1910, ibid., 338.

"ample proof": Ibid.

CHAPTER II   THE INTERNATIONAL
PSYCHOANALYTIC ASSOCIATION

280   "Our psychology is a science": Jung, "Marginal Notes on Wittels, *The Sexual Need*" (1910), *C. W.* 18:927.

For Ernest Jones's claim of having been included in a discussion of forming an official organization, see his *Free Associations: Memoirs of a Psychoanalyst* (New York: Basic Books, 1959), 214.

281   "be devoted to other tasks": Freud to Jung, 2 January 1910, *F/J Letters*, 282.

For Jung's efforts to get Freud to lecture on case material, see his letter to Freud, 10 January 1910, ibid., 285.

"organization and propaganda": Freud to Jung, 2 February 1910, ibid., 292.

"How could you have been so mistaken": Jung to Freud, 2 March 1910, ibid., 298.

For Freud's anger at Ludwig Binswanger, see his letter to Jung, 12 December 1909, ibid., 273.

For Jung on printing Eugen Bleuler's discussion of psychoanalysis in the *Jahrbuch*, see his letter to Freud, 8 November 1909, ibid., 257.

282   "so dull and colourless": Freud to Jung, 13 February 1910, ibid., 296.

"absolutely frivolous and faulty": Freud to Jung, 2 February 1910, ibid., 91.

"Sadger's writing is unsufferable": Ibid.

"the only one who can be accepted": Ibid.

"I suggest that you and I": Freud to Jung, 11 November 1909, ibid., 259.

"external matters": See appendix 3: "Statutes of the International Psychoanalytic Association," ibid., 569.

284   "bad joke": Jung to Freud, 23 October 1910, ibid., 361.

285   "I still have not got over": Freud to Oskar Pfister, 17 March 1910, in Ernst

Freud and H. Meng, eds., *Psycho-Analysis and Faith: The Letters of Sigmund Freud and Oskar Pfister* (New York: Basic Books, 1963), 35.

285 "Anyone who fails to produce results": Freud, "The Future Prospects of Psycho-Analytic Therapy" (1910), *S. E.* 11:145.

"I should therefore": Ibid., 151.

286 For the attribution of Sandor Ferenczi's dictatorial streak, see Jones, *The Life and Work of Sigmund Freud,* 3 vols. (New York: Basic Books, 1955), 2:69.

"heralded by the appearance of Jung": Ferenczi "On the Organization of the Psycho-Analytic Movement" (1910), in M. Balint, ed., *Final Contributions to the Problems and Methods of Psycho-Analysis* (New York: Bruner/Mazel, 1980), 300.

"guerrilla warfare": Ibid., 301.

"It would be a family": Ibid., 304–305.

287 "It can readily be imagined": Fritz Wittels, *Sigmund Freud: His Personality, His Teaching, and His School* (London: Allen & Unwin, 1924), 139–40.

288 "the outcome of my statesmanship": Freud to Jung, 12 April 1910, *F/J Letters,* 306.

289 "Today we must play highschool fraternity": Freud, quoted in Hanns Sachs, *Freud, Master and Friend* (Cambridge: Harvard University Press, 1944), 62.

"energetically protested against belonging": Jung to Freud, 6 August 1910, *F/J Letters,* 341.

On Muthmann's "courage," see Freud's letter to Jung, 14 June 1907, ibid., 64.

290 "empire": Binswanger, *Sigmund Freud: Reminiscences of a Friendship* (New York: Grune & Stratton, 1957), 32.

"It seems to give people": Jung to Freud, 6 August 1910, *F/J Letters,* 341.

"[O]ne didn't want to sit down": Bleuler to Jung, quoted in Jung's letter to Freud, 30 April 1910, ibid., 313.

291 "the inevitable collapse": Willy Hellpach, quoted by William McGuire, ibid., 367 n. 7.

"the transmission of specific representations": Hoche, quoted in Henri Ellenberger, *The Discovery of the Unconscious: The History of Dynamic Psychiatry* (New York: Basic Books, 1970), 806.

292 "I object that a man": Oskar Vogt, ibid.

"Maybe I am to blame": Freud to Jung, 10 August 1910, *F/J Letters,* 343.

"I heartily agree": Jung to Freud, 10 August 1910, ibid., 345.

"Moreover ΨA is too great a truth": Jung to Freud, 11 August 1910, ibid., 346.

293   "Yesterday I got an epistle": Freud to Ferenczi, 14 August 1910, cited in Jones *Life and Work* 2:140.

"he [Freud] regarded the coming together": Alphonse Maeder, interview with Gene Nameche, 28 January 1970, Jung Oral History Archive, 16.

"The three travellers": Wittels, *Sigmund Freud*, 137–38.

294   "I send you kind regards": Freud to Jung, 24 September 1910, *F/J Letters*, 355.

"Despair gave me courage": Spielrein, diary, *A Secret Symmetry*, 8.

CHAPTER 12   THE SPIRITUAL TREND IN PSYCHOANALYSIS

296   "Finally, I want to emphasize": Spielrein, "Über den psychologischen Inhalt eines Falles von Schizophrenie (Dementia Praecox)," *Jahrbuch für psychoanalytische und psychopatholgische Forschungen* 3(1912):400.

For Spielrein on her patient's "Catholicizing" complex, ibid., 332–34.

"mythological experiments": Ibid., 336–37.

297   "Sistine experiments": Ibid., 334–36, 338.

"flogged though Basel": Ibid., 332, 339–40.

"Dr. J.'s father": Ibid., 376.

"Dr. J. who has prostituted me": Ibid., 375; see also 387, 393.

298   "In general, the schizophrenic likes": Ibid., 398–99.

299   "had thrown him into raptures": Spielrein, diary, *A Secret Symmetry*, 14.

"he is miffed": Ibid.

"I explained to him": Ibid., 14–15.

"Between the two ladies": Jung to Freud, 8 September 1910, *F/J Letters*, 352.

"bent my umbrella": Spielrein, diary, *A Secret Symmetry*, 15.

"that my mother's umbrella": Ibid., 16.

300   "He laughed at my accident": Ibid.

"We discussed so many interesting issues": Ibid.

300 "Yes, my dear, good friend": Ibid., 18.

301 "We were supposed to sit down": Ibid., 20.

302 "a good letter": Freud to Jung, 5 July 1910, *F/J Letters,* 338.

303 "I think my conjecture": Jung to Freud, 29 September 1910, ibid., 355-56.

304 "Rome in particular": Jung to Freud, 11 August 1910, ibid., 346.

"In the dream": Jung, *Memories, Dreams, Reflections,* rev. ed. (New York: Pantheon, 1973), 307.

305 For Jung on his Arona dream, ibid., 292-93, 301, 302.

306 "spiritual forefather": Ibid., 307.

"Since term time is starting": Jung to Freud, 20 October 1910, *F/J Letters,* 359.

307 "The earlier lecture": Jung to Freud, 13 December 1910, ibid., 378.

"I lectured at the ΨA Society": Jung to Freud, 23 December 1910, ibid., 383.

"Should I tell everything in order": Spielrein, diary, *A Secret Symmetry,* 21.

308 "Many stories were told": Ibid.

"The Christian in it": Ibid., 30.

309 ". . . I intend to cling": Ibid.

". . . can lead to parapsychological phenomena": Jung, *Memories, Dreams, Reflections,* 137.

"I never try to convert": Ibid., 138-40.

312 "The two of us love each other": Spielrein, diary, *A Secret Symmetry,* 33.

"Since yesterday": Ibid.

313 "Adieu, my little son": Ibid., 34.

"My friend said in parting": Ibid., 37.

"He is gone": Ibid., 38.

314 "I remain defiant": Ibid., 39.

"could hear": Ibid., 39.

"Either the gods are too weary": Ibid., 40.

315 "If I want to remain true to myself": Bleuler to Freud, 13 October 1910, in

Franz Alexander and Selesnick, "Freud-Bleuler Correspondence," *Archives of General Psychiatry* 12(1965):3.

". . . it is amazing how he works": Freud to Jung, 19 December 1910, *F/J Letters*, 381.

316 "conformance to certain *technical rules*": Freud, "On 'Wild' Psycho-Analysis" (1910), *S.E.* 11:222.

"yet be learnt from books": ibid., 226.

"Neither I myself nor my friends": Ibid.

"After his Defense of my ΨA": Freud to Ludwig Binswanger, 1 January 1911, cited in Binswanger, *Sigmund Freud: Reminiscences of a Friendship* (New York: Grune & Stratton, 1957), 28.

". . . he is only a poor devil": Freud to Sandor Ferenczi, 29 December 1910, cited in Ernest Jones, *The Life and Work of Sigmund Freud*, 3 vols. (New York: Basic Books, 1955), 2:140.

"discover and maintain the correct attitude": Freud to Binswanger, 1 January 1911, cited in Binswanger, *Reminiscences of a Friendship*, 28.

317 "the same paranoia": Freud to Jung, 3 December 1910, *F/J Letters*, 376.

"I can still recall vividly": Jung, *Memories, Dreams, Reflections*, 150.

318 "After a few stammering attempts": Ibid.

"Don't be dismayed": Freud to Jung, 22 December 1910, *F/J Letters*, 387.

"strange headaches . . . lapses of memory": Freud to Jung, 17 February 1911, ibid., 393.

"I still owe you a mountain": Jung to Freud, 18 January 1910, ibid., 386.

"the refreshing hours in Munich": Freud to Jung, 22 January 1911, ibid., 386–87.

"He was magnificent": Freud to Ferenczi, 29 December 1910, cited in Jones, *Life and Work* 2:140.

CHAPTER 13   THE DYING AND RESURGENT GOD

319 "This immortal saying": Spielrein, letter-drafts, *A Secret Symmetry*, 107–108.

321 "the indissoluble connection": Freud to Oskar Pfister, 12 March 1909, in Ernst Freud and H. Meng, eds., *Psycho-Analysis and Faith: The Letters of Sigmund Freud and Oskar Pfister* (New York: Basic Books, 1963), 20.

323 "In the Nibelungen myth": Spielrein, "Die Destruktion als Ursache des

Werdens," *Jarhbuch für Psychoanalytische und Psychopathologische Forschungen* 4(1912):494.

323 "Wagner's heroes have in common": Ibid., 496.

324 "Receive now the product": Spielrein to Jung, undated cover letter, *A Secret Symmetry*, 48.

325 "I am surprised by the abundance": Jung to Spielrein, 8 August 1911, *Tagebuch,* 199-200.

326 "Anyone who can read": Jung, "Transformations and Symbols of the Libido," part 1 (1911), in Beatrice Hinkle, trans., *Psychology of the Unconscious: A Study of the Transformations and Symbolisms of the Libido: Contribution to the History of the Evolution of Thought* (New York: Moffat, Yard & Co., 1916), 3.

For Jung's citation of Jakob Burckhardt's maxim, ibid., 40-41 n. 42.

For Jung on Faust, ibid., 68-69, 88-92.

"prospective potency of subliminal combinations": Ibid., 64.

327 "This time I shall hardly be spared": Ibid., 493 n. 17.

"The passionate longing": Ibid., 116-17.

328 "The prophetic visions": Ibid., 126.

329 "In effect it simply uses": Peter Homans, *Jung in Context: Modernity and the Making of a Psychology* (Chicago: University of Chicago Press, 1979), 65-66.

"I have never felt happy": *Symbols of Transformation* (1952 revision of "Transformations and Symbols"), *C.W.* 5:xxiii.

330 "Something should come of it": Jung to Freud, 28 February 1911, *F/J Letters,* 397.

". . . a parallel investigation": Jung to Freud, 19 March 1911, Ibid., 407.

"Please don't worry": Jung to Freud, 8 May 1911, ibid., 421.

332 "How extraordinary": Jung, cited in Barbara Hannah, *Jung: His Life and Work: A Biographical Memoir* (New York: Putnam, 1976), 99.

"He was haunted by bad dreams": Ibid., 110.

"She took over my fantasy": Jung, cited in William McGuire, ed., *Analytical Psychology: Notes of the Seminar Given in 1925* (Princeton: Princeton University Press, 1989), 27.

333 "It is a well-recognized fact": Jung, "Transformations and Symbols of the Libido," 392.

334 "Brünnhilde's sin": Ibid., 395.

"We can now answer": Ibid., 428.

335 "flabbergasted": Jung to Freud, 8 March 1911, *F/J Letters,* 401.

"The Freudian adepts": Wilhelm Stekel, quoted in Fritz Wittels, *Sigmund Freud: His Personality, His Teaching, and His School* (London: Allen & Unwin, 1924), 150–51.

"There was an atmosphere of the foundation of a religion": Max Graf, "Reminiscences of Professor Sigmund Freud," *The Psychoanalytic Quarterly* 11(1942):471.

"as head of a church": Ibid., 473.

"When the empire I have founded": Freud to Ludwig Binswanger, 23 March 1911, cited in Binswanger, *Sigmund Freud: Reminiscences of a Friendship* (New York: Grune & Stratton, 1957), 56.

336 "A man who had once nursed his father": Freud, "Formulations on the Two Principles of Mental Functioning" (1911), *S.E.* 12:225–26.

337 "In these few remarks": Ibid., 226.

"I have taken your": Jung to Freud, 19 March 1911, *F/J Letters,* 408.

338 For Henri Ellenberger on the lack of a thorough dream analysis emphasizing the sexual element in the original *Interpretation of Dreams,* see his *The Discovery of the Unconscious: The History and Evolution of Dynamic Psychiatry* (New York: Basic Books, 1970), 451.

"I simply cannot expose": Freud to Jung, 17 February 1911, *F/J Letters,* 395.

339 "I am trying to be popular": Jung to Freud, 8 May 1911, ibid., 421.

"As the latest researches": Jung, "New Paths in Psychology" (1912), *C.W.* 7:264.

340 "Everything I am doing": Jung to Freud, 12 June 1911, *F/J Letters,* 426.

"I gather that you have": Freud to Jung, 15 June 1911, ibid., 429.

"by no means everything": Jung, "New Paths in Psychology," 264.

"the mystery of self-sacrifice": Ibid., 265.

341 "an arrogant ass": Freud to Jung, 1/3 March 1911, *F/J Letters,* 399.

342 "A few rather useless members": Freud to Jung, 15 June 1911, ibid., 428.

343 "Since my mental powers revived": Freud to Jung, ibid., 438.

344 "unleash your associations": Jung to Freud, 29 August 1911, ibid., 439.

344 "your embargo on discussion": Ibid.

"Sister Moltzer, Dr. Hinkle-Eastwick": Jung to Freud, 29 August 1911, ibid., 440.

345 "We Viennese have nothing": Freud to Jung, 1 September 1911, ibid., 442.

"So you too are aware": Ibid., 441.

"There were of course seminars": Ernest Jones, *The Life and Work of Sigmund Freud,* 3 vols. (New York: Basic Books, 1955), 2:101.

346 "It's a healthy coarseness": Freud, cited in Jones, ibid., 86.

"They have learned to tolerate": Ibid., 85.

347 "All criticisms coming from without": Poul Bjerre, *The History and Practice of Psychanalysis* (Boston: Richard Badger, 1916), 321.

CHAPTER 14 ON TRANSFORMATION

349 "I allow myself to write": Jung to Spielrein, 21–22 September 1911, *Tagebuch,* 202.

"Freud will certainly accept you": Ibid., 202.

354 "The feud broke up": Mrs. Hanns Sachs, cited in Paul Roazen, *Freud and His Followers* (New York: Knopf, 1971), 186.

355 ". . . and Sabina Spielrein": Freud to Jung, 12 October 1911, *F/J Letters,* 447.

"She said I didn't look malicious": Ibid.

"which unfortunately will soon become": Freud to Jung, 13 October 1911, ibid., 449.

"It's a pity": Ibid.

"the so-called 'early memories of childhood' ": Jung to Freud, 17 October 1911, ibid., 450.

On Emma Jung's letter to Sandor Ferenczi regarding Jung's problem with Freud's authority, see L. Donn, *Jung and Freud: Years of Friendship, Years of Loss* (New York: Scribners, 1988), 137.

356 On Freud's reply to Ferenczi regarding Emma Jung's concerns, ibid., 138.

"You see how petty": Freud to Jung, 20 October 1911, *F/J Letters,* 451.

"My Dear, Under the circumstances": Jung to Spielrein, circa mid-October 1911, *Tagebuch,* 202.

357 "A few words in haste": Jung to Freud, 30 October 1911, *F/J Letters,* 452.

"Dear Professor Freud, I don't really know": Emma Jung to Freud, 30 October 1911, ibid., 452-53.

358 "My psychology of religion": Freud to Jung, 2 November 1911, ibid., 453.

"Your nice kind letter": Emma Jung to Freud, 6 November 1911, ibid., 456.

359 "Dr. Spielrein prefaces her comments": *Minutes* 3:302-303. Incidentally, both here and in reporting Freud's comments (next note), Rank misidentifies Groos as "Gross."

360 "The interpretation of children's play": Freud, ibid., 306-307.

For Freud's remarks on Spielrein's point about the unconscious not knowing time, ibid., 308.

361 "I pray you to send": Jung to Spielrein, 13 November 1911, *Tagebuch*, 203.

"At the last meeting": Freud to Jung, 12 November 1911, *F/J Letters*, 458.

"The reading for my psychology of religion": Ibid., 459.

362 "You were really annoyed": Emma Jung to Freud, 14 November 1911, ibid., 462-63.

363 "death instinct": *Minutes* 1:175-77.

"Spielrein has dealt with": *Minutes* 3:316-17.

364 "You are a dangerous rival": Jung to Freud, 14 November 1911, *F/J Letters*, 460.

"But papers like Spielrein's": Ibid., 461.

"In my second part": Ibid.

"Strictly business": Freud to Jung, 16 November 1911, ibid., 464.

"Spielrein's paper certainly belongs": Ibid.

365 "I am writing in my own style": Jung to Spielrein, 24 November 1911, *Tagebuch*, 204.

"Out of such an attitude": Ibid.

"Heartfelt thanks for your letter": Emma Jung to Freud, 24 November 1911, *F/J Letters*, 467.

366 "ΨA is beginning to shape destinies": Freud to Jung, 20 October 1911, ibid., 451.

367 "This 'who is not for us is against us' ": Eugen Bleuler to Freud, 11 March 1911, cited in Franz Alexander and Sheldon Selesnick, "Freud-Bleuler Correspondence," *Archives of General Psychiatry*, 12(1965):5.

367 "I venture to hope": Bleuler to Freud, 30 November 1911, cited in *F/J Letters,* 469.

368 "Taking as her point of departure": *Minutes* 3:329–31. Incidentally, the minutes use the alternative spelling "Mechnikov."

369 "biological straightjacket": Jung to Freud, 29 November 1910, *F/J Letters,* 374.

370 "that resistance to sexuality": Viktor Tausk, in *Minutes* 3:332.

     "this presentation as an attempt": Josef Friedjung, ibid., 333.

     "Dr. (Mrs.) Stegmann remarks": Ibid., 333–34.

     "According to him": Stegmann, ibid., 334.

371 "The presentation itself": Freud, ibid., 335.

     "The material has been transmitted": Ibid.

     For Freud on the Book of Genesis, see his letter to Jung, 17 December 1911, *F/J Letters,* 473.

     "The question of whether": Freud, in *Minutes* 3:334.

     "Spielrein, in her concluding words": Ibid., 335.

372 "I very much hope": Jung to Freud, 24/27 November 1911, *F/J Letters,* 465.

373 For Henri Ellenberger on the resentment within the German-speaking medical community against the spread of psychoanalytic ideas to a larger, nonmedical community, see his *The Discovery of the Unconscious: The History and Evolution of Dynamic Psychiatry* (New York: Basic Books: 1970), 805.

374 "Here nothing much has happened": Freud to Jung, 30 November 1911, *F/J Letters,* 468–69.

375 "I read between the lines": Ibid.

     For Freud's "offer," ibid., 459.

     "I should be very much interested": Freud to Jung, 30 November 1911, ibid., 469.

     For Jung's references to Freud's theory of libido, see Jung, "The Freudian Theory of Hysteria" (1908), *C.W.* 4:18, 19 n. 7.

     "preservation of the species": Ibid., 19 n. 7.

     "This letter must yield": Freud to Jung, 30 November 1911, *F/J Letters,* 470.

376 "You will see from the letterhead": Jung to Freud, 11 December 1911, ibid.

     "I'll gladly take Spielrein's new paper": Ibid., 470–71.

"My Dear, Do not get too depressed": Jung to Spielrein, 11 December 1911, *Tagebuch,* 205.

377   "Freud has spoken very positively": Ibid.

"Prof. Freud in his letter spoke very flatteringly": Ibid., 206.

"Prof. Freud, of whom I have become very fond": Spielrein, diary entry for 7 January 1912, *A Secret Symmetry,* 41.

378   On the fact that paying patients were in very short supply, see *F/J Letters,* 450, 473.

"[O]nce I brought Freud": Spielrein to Jung, 15 December 1917, *A Secret Symmetry,* 60.

"Once, when for purely scientific reasons": Spielrein to Jung, 6/16 January 1918, ibid., 71.

"when I was not even that close": Ibid.

380   "I am very much impressed": Freud to Jung, 17 December 1911, *F/J Letters,* 472.

"You have asked for an example": Ibid., 473.

381   For Jung on the problems of variants and distortions, see his letters to Freud of 8 November 1909, Ibid., 258; 15 November 1909, 263–64; 30 November 1909, 269; and 10 January 1910, 285.

382   "for the exploration of whose ruins": Freud, "Great is Diana of the Ephesians" (1912), *S.E.* 12:342.

"Paul was too strict a Jew": Ibid., 343–44.

"Why did Freud publish": Ellenberger, *The Discovery of the Unconscious,* 816.

384   "There one hears just the argument": Freud to Ferenczi, 24 April 1910, cited in Ernest Jones, *The Life and Work of Sigmund Freud,* 3 vols. (New York: Basic Books, 1955), 2:116.

"Our Aryan comrades": Freud to Abraham, letter of 26 December 1908, in Hilde Abraham and Ernst Freud, eds. *A Psycho-Analytic Dialogue: The Letters of Sigmund Freud and Karl Abraham, 1907–1926* (New York: Basic Books, 1965), 64.

386   "Your little piece from Rascher's *Jahrbuch*": Freud to Jung, 31 December 1911, *F/J Letters,* 475.

"of a specifically Swiss character": Jung to Freud, 10 January 1912, ibid., 481.

CHAPTER 15　THE DEATH OF A FRIENDSHIP

388　"The whole idea": Eugen Bleuler, *Dementia Praecox, or the Group of Schizophrenias* (1911; New York: International Universities Press, 1950), 1–2.

"Perhaps you need to justify": Freud to Ludwig Binswanger, 23 November 1911, cited in Binswanger, *Sigmund Freud: Reminiscences of a Friendship* (New York: Grune & Stratton, 1957), 37.

389　"In his last letter of that year": Ibid., 38.

For Henri Ellenberger on the absence of Freud's name from the list of contributors to the *Breuer-Stiftung,* see his *The Discovery of the Unconscious: The History and Evolution of Dynamic Psychiatry* (New York: Basic Books, 1970), 809.

390　"sentimental donkey": Freud to Sandor Ferenczi, 23 January 1912, cited in Phyllis Grosskurth, *The Secret Ring: Freud's Inner Circle and the Politics of Psychoanalysis* (New York: Addison-Wesley, 1991), 43.

"Do *I* always have to be right": Freud to Ferenczi, 2 February 1912, ibid., 44.

391　"Of course she is right": Freud to Jung, 17 December 1911, *F/J Letters,* 473–74.

"Frau C. has told me": Freud to Jung, 31 December 1911, ibid., 475–76.

"The problem with you younger men": Ibid., 476.

"What you write about the Frau C. incident": Freud to Jung, 10 January 1911, ibid., 479.

"I have been racking my brains": Ibid.

392　"*For me* the cardinal rule": Jung to Freud, 9 January 1911, Ibid., 479.

For Ellenberger on the controversy regarding psychoanalysis in the *Neue Zürcher Zeitung,* see his *Discovery of the Unconscious,* 810–14.

"I must definitely declare": Auguste Forel, ibid., 814.

For an account of Adolf Keller's defense of the Zurich brand of psychoanalysis, see Mireille Cifali, "Le fameux couteau de Lichtenberg," *Le Bloc-Notes de la Psychanalyse* 4(1984):177.

393　"blackmail": Jung to Freud, 23 January 1912, *F/J Letters,* 482.

"I am not giving out": Ibid., 483.

"I have no desire to intrude": Freud to Jung, 24 January 1912, ibid., 483.

"grisly fights with the hydra": Jung to Freud, circa 15 February 1912, ibid., 483–84.

394 "a woman in love identifies": Spielrein, in *Minutes* 4:25.

"Now I want to be happy": Spielrein, *A Secret Symmetry*, 41.

395 "I hereby confirm the receipt": Jung to Spielrein, cited in diary, ibid., 42.

"Today there was another unpleasantness": Ibid.

"Further analysis superfluous": Ibid., 43.

396 "I was very glad to receive": Freud to Jung, 18 February 1912, *F/J Letters*, 484.

"I have edited Bjerre's piece": Ibid., 484–85.

"It seems to me": Ibid., 485.

397 On Spielrein's name being struck from the book version of *Totem and Taboo*, see McGuire, ibid., 485 n. 3.

"I think I am not wrong": Jung to Freud, 25 February 1912, ibid., 487–88.

"What you say about my resentment": Freud to Jung, 29 February 1912, ibid., 488.

398 "Your letter has made me pensive": Jung to Freud, 3 March 1912, ibid., 490.

"I have not kept up": Ibid., 491.

"Why so 'pensive' ": Freud to Jung, 5 March 1912, ibid., 492–93.

399 "imitating Adler": Jung to Freud, 10 March 1912, ibid., 493.

"I have finished my work": Ibid., 494.

"I'm afraid I shall have to trim": Jung to Freud, 10 March 1912, *F/J Letters*, 494.

"I knew in advance": Jung, *Memories, Dreams, and Reflections*, rev. ed. (New York: Pantheon, 1973), 167.

400 "phantastic self-oblivion": Jung, "Transformations and Symbols of the Libido," part 2 (1912), in Beatrice Hinkle, trans., *Psychology of the Unconscious: A Study of the Tranformations and Symbolisms of the Libido: Contribution to the History of the Evolution of Thought* (New York: Moffat, Yard & Co., 1916), 432.

"individual erotic conflict": Ibid., 433.

"It is not to be forgotten": Ibid.

400 "Marvel not that I said": Ibid., 252.

"... I take it to be a wise counsel": Ibid., 453-55.

401 "The comparison of the Mithraic": Ibid., 478.

402 "will for life and [the will] for death": Ibid., 464. See also 480.

403 "incredible parallels": Jung to Spielrein, 18 March 1912, *Tagebuch*, 206.

"One wants not only the ascent": Ibid., 207.

"When I said that there were": Jung to Spielrein, 25 March 1912, ibid., 208.

"swallowed": Ibid.

"not for the public": Ibid.

"Represent me to Freud": Ibid.

"As for Speilrein's paper": Freud to Jung, 21 March 1912, *F/J Letters*, 494.

"My paper on Taboo": Ibid., 495.

404 "The problem of why the individual": Spielrein, *Minutes* 4:84-85.

405 "Dr. Spielrein was right in stating": Freud, ibid., 86.

406 "Phobia or Jungianism?": Wilhelm Stekel to Spielrein, unpublished letter provided by Paul Schrader courtesy of Aldo Carotenuto.

For Spielrein on Paul Scheftel, see her diary, *A Secret Symmetry*, 45-46. I am also grateful to V. Zelensky of Moscow and A. Etkind of St. Petersburg for sharing information with me about Spielrein's marriage.

"I was working on Spielrein's paper": Jung to Freud, 1 April 1912, *F/J Letters*, 498.

"Her tomb seemed to me": Jung, *Memories, Dreams, Reflections*, 286.

407 "Spielrein, to whom I was glad": Freud to Jung, 21 April 1912, *F/J Letters*, 499.

"what I had interpreted as flagging interest": Ibid.

408 "Although no longer as satisfied": Binswanger, *Reminiscences of a Friendship*, 40.

"The tremendous role of the mother": Jung to Freud, 27 April 1912, *F/J Letters*, 502.

"It will surely come as no surprise": Freud to Jung, 14 May 1912, ibid., 504.

409 "about that which is close": Freud to Binswanger, 16 May 1912, *Reminiscences of a Friendship*, 41.

"Just as *cum grano salis*": Jung to Freud, 17 May 1912, *F/J Letters*, 506.

"In the libido question": Freud to Jung, 23 May 1912, ibid., 507.

410 "disastrous similarity to a theorem": Ibid.

"In light of your hints": Ibid.

"But I repeat": Ibid., 508.

"I shall be closer to you": Ibid.

411 "On the question of incest": Jung to Freud, 8 June 1912, ibid., 509.

"pleased if you yourself": Freud to Jung, 13 June 1912, ibid., 510.

"Your remark pains me": Ibid., 511.

"When I saw that it would be possible": Ibid., 510.

"About the libido question": Ibid.

"I, too, was very gratified": Freud to Spielrein, 14 June 1912, *A Secret Symmetry*, 116.

412 "have to amend my praises of Jung": Ibid.

"I look forward as October approaches": Ibid.

413 "It is a pity": Freud to Oskar Pfister, 4 July 1912, in Ernst Freud and H. Meng, eds., *Psycho-Analysis and Faith: The Letters of Sigmund Freud and Oskar Pfister* (New York: Basic Books, 1963), 56–57.

"Until now I didn't know": Jung to Freud, 18 July 1912, *F/J Letters*, 511.

"but be construed into a formal disavowal": Freud to Ernest Jones, 23 July 1912, cited in Gay, *Freud: A Life for Our Time*, 230.

"They separate like oil and water": Freud to Ferenczi, 29 July 1912, cited in ibid., 231.

"Jews and anti-Semites": Freud to Otto Rank, 15 July 1912, cited in Gay, *A Life for Our Time*, 231.

414 "So you are a married woman now": Freud to Spielrein, letter dated only "August 1912," *A Secret Symmetry*, 117.

415 "I have answered Maeder's letter": Freud to Ferenczi, 20 October 1912, cited in Ernest Jones, *The Life and Work of Sigmund Freud*, 3 vols. (New York: Basic Books, 1955), 2:455.

"You, sir, are an anti-Semite": Freud to Alphonse Maeder, date uncertain, see Maeder, interview with Gene Nameche, 28 January 1970, Jung Oral History Archive, 20.

CHAPTER 16   THE REST IS SILENCE

416   "I know that your ideal": Freud to James Jackson Putnam, 20 August 1912, in Nathan G. Hale, ed., *James Jackson Putnam and Psychoanalysis: Letters between Putnam and Sigmund Freud, Ernest Jones, William James, Sandor Ferenczi, and Morton Prince, 1877–1917* (Cambridge: Harvard University Press, 1971), 146.

"tear each other to pieces": Freud to Alphonse Maeder, date unknown, referred to in Maeder to Freud, 24 October 1912, published by Mireille Cifali in *Le Bloc-Notes de la Psychanalyse* 9(1989):221.

418   "neurosis": A. A. Brill volunteered this to Ernest Jones, who shared it with Freud in his letter of 20 November 1912, cited in Andrew Paskauskas, *Ernest Jones: A Critical Study of His Scientific Development (1896–1913)*, doctoral diss. (University of Toronto, 1987), 331.

419   "I am unable to vindicate": Jung, New York Academy of Medicine address, 8 October 1912, 5. From unpublished typescript of Jung's address, original in the Jung Archives, Library of Congress. I am grateful to Sonu Shamdasani for sharing this. Compare with Jung, "Psychoanalysis" [retitled "General Aspects of Psychoanalysis"] (1913), *C.W.* 4:229–42.

"What Dr. Jung said, in effect": Putnam to Jones, 24 October 1912, in Hale, *James Jackson Putnam and Psychoanalysis: Letters*, 276–77.

420   "Elektra complex": Jung, "The Theory of Psychoanalysis" (1913), *C.W.* 4:154.

"genetic conception": Ibid., 122.

"presexual stage": Ibid., 117.

421   "sacrifice": Ibid., 151.

"castration complex": Ibid.

422   "Such schisms can only exist": Ibid., 86.

"I found that my version": Jung to Freud, 11 November 1912, *F/J Letters*, 515–16.

423   "I greet you on your return": Freud to Jung, 14 November 1912, ibid., 517.

"your harping on the 'Kreuzlingen gesture' ": Ibid.

424   "unable to prevent them": Ibid., 519.

424   "I am convinced that ΨA": Meader to Freud, 24 October 1912, in *Les Bloc-Notes de la Psychanalyse* 9(1989):223.

"Most of the analysts": Ibid.

425   For Hanns Sachs's announcement that Wilhelm Stekel had been removed as editor of the *Zentralblatt,* see *Minutes* 4:103.

426   "secret contract": see Freud's letter to Jung, 27 January 1913, *F/J Letters,* 541.

"treachery": Ibid.

"You will learn sooner or later": Stekel to Jones, 12 October 1912, cited in Paskauskas, *Ernest Jones: A Critical Study,* 337.

427   "A gentleman should not": Freud, quoted in Jones, *The Life and Work of Sigmund Freud,* 3 vols. (New York: Basic Books, 1955), 2:145.

429   "The story may be crude": Jung, quoted by Leonhard Seif to Jones, unpublished letter, 26 December 1912. I am grateful to Andrew Paskauskas for sharing this letter with me; the original is in the Ernest Jones Archive, London.

"I picked him up": Jung, *Memories, Dreams, Reflections,* rev. ed. (New York: Panetheon, 1973), 157.

"How sweet it must be": Freud, quoted by Jones, *The Life and Work of Sigmund Freud,* 1:317.

"unruly homosexual component": Ibid.

"insufficiently analysed 'father complex' ": Seif to Jones, unpublished letter, 26 December 1912.

430   "To analyze and be analyzed": undated comment by Emma Jung, ibid.

"Today one has to ask oneself": Ibid.

"very kind": Freud to Karl Abraham, 3 December 1912, in Hilde Abraham and Ernst Freud, eds., *A Psycho-Analytic Dialogue: The Letters of Sigmund Freud and Karl Abraham: 1907–1926* (New York: Basic Books, 1965), 128.

"I am glad we were able": Jung to Freud, 26 November 1912, *F/J Letters,* 522.

431   "I hope Bleuler has informed you": Ibid., 523.

"for me our relationship": Freud to Jung, 29 November 1912, ibid., 523.

"A bit of neurosis": Ibid., 524.

432   "look like a Viennese party organ": Ibid.

432   "In the second number": Ibid.

      "Your untransformed Freud": Ibid., 525.

      "This letter is a brazen attempt": Jung to Freud, 3 December 1912, ibid., 525.

      "This 'bit' should": Ibid.

433   "Our analysis, you may remember": Ibid., 526.

      "devaluing others and their progress": Ibid.

      "You mustn't fear that I take": Freud to Jung, 5 December 1912, ibid., 529.

434   "I am sorry not to be able": Ibid., 530.

      "Since you have taken so badly": Jung to Freud, 7 December 1912, ibid., 530.

435   "I follow you with interest": Freud to Jung, 9 December 1912, ibid., 533.

      "Even Adler's cronies": Jung to Freud, undated letter written between 11 and 14 December 1912, ibid., 533.

      "The habit of taking objective statements": Freud to Jung, 16 December 1912, ibid., 534.

      "I am objective enough to see": Jung to Freud, 18 December 1912, ibid., 535.

436   "I shall continue to stand": Ibid.

      "Whatever analytical remarks": Freud, letter-draft, ibid., 537.

      "Don't hesitate to tell me": Jung to Freud, 3 January 1913, ibid., 539–40.

437   "I can answer only one point": Freud to Jung, 3 January 1913, ibid., 539.

      "I accede to your wish": Jung to Freud, 6 January 1912, ibid., 540.

439   "For many years now Freud": Carl Furtmüller (1914), cited in N. Kiell, *Freud Without Hindsight: Reviews of His Work* (Madison: International Universities Press, 1988), 393.

CHAPTER 17   THE HISTORY OF THE
PSYCHOANALYTIC MOVEMENT

441   "Scientifically I still do not understand": Eugen Bleuler to Freud, 3 November 1911, cited in Alexander and Sheldon Selesnick, "Freud-Bleuler Correspondence," *Archives of General Psychiatry* 12(1965):6.

446 "I had explained the myths": Jung, *Memories, Dreams, Reflections,* rev. ed. (New York: Pantheon, 1973), 171.

"One fantasy kept returning": Ibid., 172.

448 "My personal relationship": Freud to Spielrein, 20 January 1913, *A Secret Symmetry,* 118.

"The first issue of the *Zeitschrift*": Ibid.

449 "Disregarding its objective truth": Paul Federn, "Sabina Spielrein: Die Destruktion als Ursache des Werdens," *Internationale Zeitschrift für ärztliche Psychoanalyse* 1(1913):93.

"You have done a great deal": Freud to Spielrein, 9 February 1913, Freud/ Spielrein letters, in *A Secret Symmetry,* 119.

450 "Why can't everyone be good": James Jackson Putnam to Fanny Bowditch, unpublished letter, Fanny Bowditch Katz Archive, Countway Library, Harvard Medical School.

Théodore Flournoy's book was retitled in English as *Spiritism and Psychology,* ed. and trans. H. Carrington (New York: Harper & Brothers, 1912).

452 Peter Gay has chronicled Freud's various denunciations of Jung in his *Freud: A Life for Our Time* (New York: Norton, 1988), 240–42.

453 "After the break with Freud": Jung, *Memories, Dreams, Reflections* 167–68.

454 For the fact that Sandor Ferenczi continued to correspond with Jung, I am grateful to Martin Stanton.

"It would have taken half a book": Jung to Spielrein, 11 April 1913, *Tagebuch,* 209. See also *A Secret Symmetry,* 184.

455 "I am sorry to hear you are consumed": Freud to Spielrein, 8 May 1913, *A Secret Symmetry,* 119–20.

"serve to cut us off": Freud to Karl Abraham, 13 May 1913, in Hilde Abraham and Ernst Freud, eds., *A Psycho-Analytic Dialogue: The Letters of Sigmund Freud and Karl Abraham: 1907–1926* (New York: Basic Books, 1965), 139.

458 "Aryan patronage": Freud to Ferenczi, 4 May 1913, cited in Gay, *A Life for Our Time,* 239.

"Certainly there are great differences": Freud to Ferenczi, 8 June 1913, cited in Ernest Jones, *The Life and Work of Sigmund Freud,* 3 vols. (New York: Basic Books, 1955), 2:149.

"On the whole I overrated": Freud to Ferenczi, 5 August 1913, cited in

Andrew Paskauskas, "Freud's Break with Jung: The Crucial Role of Ernest Jones," *Free Associations* 11(1988):12.

458 "Let us hope that this bad period": Freud to Spielrein, 28 August 1913, *A Secret Symmetry*, 120–21.

459 "methodology of psycho-analysis": Editorial comment, appended to Freud, "The Moses of Michelangelo" (1914), *S. E.* 13:211.

460 For Freud's account of the Fourth Psychoanalytic Congress and Alphonse Maeder's talk, see his "On the History of the Psychoanalytic Movement" (1914), *S.E.* 14:60.

For Maeder's recollection of the reception given his talk, see Henri Ellenberger, *The Discovery of the Unconscious: The History and Evolution of Dynamic Psychiatry* (New York: Basic Books, 1970), 815.

461 For Maeder's recollection of Freud's snubbing him at the congress, see Maeder, interview with Gene Nameche, 28 January 1970, 29.

"I thought you had ethical principles": Jung, cited by Jones, *Free Associations: Memoirs of a Psychoanalyst* (New York: Basic Books, 1959), 224.

462 On the Christian twist of Jung's remark, see Jones, *The Life and Work of Sigmund Freud* 2: 102–103.

"After the foregoing considerations": Jung, "On the Question of Psychological Types" (1913) [retitled: "A Contribution to the Study of Psychological Types"], *C. W.* 6:508.

463 "The difficult task of elaborating": Ibid., 509.

465 "Well, now, my heartiest congratulations": Freud to Spielrein, 29 September 1913, *A Secret Symmetry*, 121.

"I saw the mighty yellow waves": Jung, *Memories, Dreams, Reflections*, 175.

"Look at it well": Ibid.

"menaced by a psychosis": Ibid., 176.

466 "In order to grasp the fantasies": Ibid., 178.

467 "I was with an unknown, brown-skinned man": Ibid., 180.

468 "Where there is a will": Ibid.

"a sign of my secret identity": Ibid.

". . . a man feels when he is forced": Ibid.

"land of the dead": Ibid., 181.

470 "Everyone knows that I declare myself": Spielrein to Freud, undated ad-

dendum to a letter from Jung to Spielrein, 15 April 1914, *A Secret Symmetry*, 112.

"Now you are going crazy yourself": Freud to Spielrein, 15 May 1914, ibid., 122.

"when you cannot be really angry": Freud to Spielrein, 12 June 1914, ibid., 122.

"Of course I want you to succeed": Ibid.

471 "So we are rid of them": Freud to Abraham, 12 July 1914, cited in Gay, *Freud: A Life for Our Time*, 241.

474 "The individual does actually carry on": Freud, "On Narcissism: An Introduction" (1914), *S.E.* 14:78.

"but derives its principal support": Ibid., 79.

475 "persecution": Freud, "On the History of the Psycho-Analytic Movement" (1914), *S.E.* 14:50.

"All the changes that Jung": Ibid., 62.

476 "I cannot allow": Ibid., 64 n. 2.

"and in particular": Ibid., 65.

477 ". . . or else to the physician's dread": Ibid., 66.

CHAPTER 18 IN SEARCH OF A GREAT DESTINY

478 "I am, and most especially always was": Spielrein to Jung, 19 January 1918, Spielrein/Jung Letters, *A Secret Symmetry*, 79–80.

479 "I fully agree with your treatment": Freud to Spielrein, 20 April 1915, ibid., 123.

480 "useful": Spielrein to Jung, ca. 27 January 1918, ibid., 87.

"I know what remorse my courage": recalled in Spielrein letter to Jung, circa 27 January 1918, ibid., 88.

481 "godlikeness": Jung, "The Structure of the Unconscious" (1916), *C. W.* 7:280.

"nothing but": Ibid., 283.

For "semiotic" versus "hermeneutic," ibid., 291–93.

"very close": Ibid., 283.

"All the treasures of mythological feeling": Ibid., 282.

481   "So, he is alive after all": recalled in Spielrein to Jung, 28 January 1918, *A Secret Symmetry*, 88.

482   "dominant": Jung, *The Psychology of the Unconscious Processes* (1917), C.W. 7:65–66.

"afternoon of life": Ibid., 74.

"hieroglyphics": Jung to Spielrein, 13 September 1917, *Tagebuch*, 212.

"Yes, my most revered": Jung to Spielrein, 10 October 1917, ibid., 214.

483   "You are right": Freud to Spielrein, 18 November 1917, *A Secret Symmetry*, 124.

484   "Depending on the personality": Spielrein to Jung, 9 January 1918, *A Secret Symmetry*, 70–71.

485   "Probably the misapprehension": Ibid., 77–78.

"Now I would be very interested": Ibid., 78.

486   "Siegfried is a symbol": Jung to Spielrein, cited in Spielrein's letter to Jung, 19 January 1918, ibid., 78.

". . . in the foreground a German general": Spielrein to Jung, 19 January 1918, ibid., 81.

"That's just the way the world is": Ibid., 82.

"Christification": Jung to Spielrein, 21 January 1918, *Tagebuch*, 218.

"Do not forget that the Jews": Jung to Spielrein, circa 25 January 1918, ibid., 219–20.

487   "Does our subconscious give us any clues": Spielrein to Jung, 28 January 1918, *A Secret Symmetry*, 88.

488   "In 1917 Freud had reached": Ernest Jones, *The Life and Work of Sigmund Freud*, 3 vols. (New York: Basic Books, 1957), 3:7.

489   "empty phrase": Freud, "Lines of Advance in Psycho-Analytic Therapy" (1919), *S.E.* 17: 161.

"We refused most emphatically": Ibid., 164.

"Incidentally, why was it": Freud to Oskar Pfister, 9 October 1918, in Ernst Freud and H. Meng, eds., *Psycho-Analysis and Faith: The Letters of Sigmund Freud and Oskar Pfister* (New York: Basic Books, 1963), 63.

490   "murderous" and "threatening": Jung to Spielrein, 19 March 1919, *Tagebuch*, 221.

"godlike spirit": Ibid.

491 "center point" and "saviour": 3 April 1919, ibid., 222.

"Freud's opinion is a sinful rape": Ibid.

"The love of S. for J.": Jung to Spielrein, 1 September 1919, *A Secret Symmetry*, 190.

492 "Spielrein consc.": Jung to Spielrein, 7 October 1919, *Tagebuch*, 225. Compare with diagrams in William McGuire, ed., *Analytical Psychology: Notes of the Seminar Given in 1925* (Princeton: Princeton University Press, 1989), 108–10.

494 "But the great hopes": Pierre Bovet, *Vingt Ans de Vie de l'Institute Rousseau* (Genève: Université du Genève, 1932), 101.

"If I did what you suggested": Freud to Spielrein, 12 June 1922, *A Secret Symmetry*, 126.

496 "intensely ambivalent transference": Spielrein, "Briefmarkentraum," *Internationale Zeitschrift für ärztliche Psychoanalyse* 8(1922):244.

"syphilitic Don Juan": Ibid.

497 "A gentleman who has decided on a definite separation from his lover": Spielrein, "Die Zeit im unterschwelligan Seelenleben," *Imago* 9(1923):303.

"Love": Spielrein, *"Rêve et vision des étoiles filantes,"* *International Journal of Psycho-Analysis* 4(1923):132.

499 "the most bizarre monster of all": William McDougall, cited in Frank Sulloway, *Freud, Biologist of the Mind: Beyond the Psychoanalytic Legend* (New York: Basic Books, 1979), 345.

501 "A considerable portion of these speculations": Freud (1920), *Beyond the Pleasure Principle*, S.E. 18:55 n. 1.

"loving means wanting to die": August Stärcke, cited in Spanjaard, "August Stärcke," in Franz Alexander, Samuel Eisenstein, and Martin Grotjahn, eds., *Psychoanalytic Pioneers* (New York: Basic Books, 1966), 330.

503 "We have come back from Jerusalem": Jung, *Memories, Dreams, Reflections*, rev. ed. (New York: Pantheon, 1973), 190–91.

"When I was writing down these fantasies": Ibid., 185.

504 "Obviously what I was doing": Ibid., 185–87.

505 "As soon as the image": Ibid., 187.

"What the anima said seemed to me full of a deep cunning": Ibid., 187.

"the darkness": Ibid., 195.

"One day, for example": Ibid.

506 "Every complex wants to escape": Spielrein, "Transformation Journal," 153.

507 "Art = Poetry": Spielrein, "Über den psychologischen Inhalt eines Falles von Schizophrenie (Dementia Praecox)," *Jahrbuch für psychoanalytische und psychopathologische Forschungen* 3(1912):333.

AFTERWORD

508 "Roughly speaking we may say": Edward Carpenter, *Love's Coming of Age* (New York: Boni & Liveright, 1911), 163.

Bibliographical Essay

This book has undergone multiple revisions designed to sharpen the narrative and to clarify its import for the general reader. A specialist will immediately grasp that embedded in the narrative are numerous topics that would profit from more extensive and detailed discussions. Among those topics are the evolution of the core complex, the significance of Adler, the psychoanalytic interpretations of autism and paranoia, the relation of drive theory to affects, introversion, and ambivalence, the prospective style of interpretation, theories of the death instinct—and still others.

The bibliography that follows is designed to serve two masters: to orient the general reader to what is an overwhelming literature and to point out to the specialist certain sources of interest that are sometimes overlooked. This book relies principally on published primary sources. Crucial is Aldo Carotenuto's *A Secret Symmetry: Sabina Spielrein Between Freud and Jung* (New York: Pantheon, 1982; rev. ed., 1983), which contains the extant portions of Spielrein's diary during the years 1909–12 as well as her letters to both Freud and Jung. Jung's letters to Spielrein are not yet available in English and can be found only in the German edition of Carotenuto's book, *Tagebuch einer heimlichen Symmetrie: Sabina Spielrein zwischen Jung und Freud* (Frieburg im Breisgau: Kore, 1986). Spielrein's "Transformation Journal," composed by her during 1907–1908, was rediscovered by Mireille Cifali and published in a French translation by Jeanne Moll as "Extraits inédits d'un journal: De l'Amour, de la mort et de la transformation," *Le Bloc-Notes de la Psychanalyse* 3 (1983): 149–70. Spielrein's participation in the Vienna Psychoanalytic Society during 1911–12 is charted in volume 3 (1975) of the *Minutes of the Vienna Psychoanalytic Society,* ed. Herman Nunberg and Ernst Federn, trans. M. Nunberg with H. Collins (New York: International Universities Press, 1962–75). No less important, obviously, are *The Freud/Jung Letters: The Correspondence Between Sigmund Freud and C. G. Jung* (Princeton: Princeton University Press, 1974). Translated by Ralph Manheim and R. F. C. Hull, the letters have been exquisitely edited and annotated by William McGuire.

The following sources have been utilized with regard to other correspondences: Jeffrey Masson, ed., *The Complete Letters of Sigmund Freud to Wilhelm Fliess, 1887–1904* (Cambridge: Harvard University Press, 1985); Hilde Abraham and Ernst Freud, eds., *A Psycho-Analytic Dialogue: The Letters of Sigmund Freud and Karl Abraham: 1907–1926* (New York: Basic Books, 1965); Ludwig Binswanger, *Sigmund*

Freud: Reminiscences of a Friendship (New York: Grune & Stratton, 1957), which contains excerpts from correspondence plus personal reminiscences; Franz Alexander and Sheldon Selesnick, "Freud-Bleuler Correspondence," *Archives of General Psychiatry* 12(1965):1–9, which contains excerpts from letters plus commentary; Ernst Freud and H. Meng, eds., *Psychoanalysis and Faith: The Letters of Sigmund Freud and Oskar Pfister* (New York: Basic Books, 1963); Nathan G. Hale, ed., *James Jackson Putnam and Psychoanalysis: Letters Between Putnam and Sigmund Freud, Ernest Jones, William James, Sandor Ferenczi, and Morton Prince, 1877–1917* (Cambridge: Harvard University Press, 1975); Ernst Freud, ed., *Letters of Sigmund Freud, 1873–1939* (London: Cambridge University Press, 1975); Gerhard Adler, ed., with Aniela Jaffé, *C. G. Jung Letters,* 2 vols. (Princeton: Princeton University Press, 1973–75); John Burnham, *Jelliffe: American Psychoanalyst and Physician & His Correspondence with Sigmund Freud and C. G. Jung,* ed. William McGuire (Chicago: University of Chicago Press, 1983).

The Freud-Ferenczi correspondence is not yet published, but I am indebted to the coeditor, Ernst Falzeder, for answering my queries about it on several points. Selections and excerpts from this correspondence have already appeared in: Ernest Jones, *The Life and Work of Sigmund Freud,* 3 vols. (New York: Basic Books, 1953–57); Peter Gay, *Freud: A Life for Our Time* (New York: Norton, 1989); Ilse Grubrich-Simitis, "Six Letters of Sigmund Freud and Sandor Ferenczi on the Interrelationship of Psychoanalytic Theory and Technique," *International Review of Psycho-Analysis* 13(1986): 259–77; Sandor Ferenczi, "Ten Letters to Freud," *International Journal of Psycho-Analysis* 40(1959): 243–50; and Phyllis Grosskurth, *The Secret Ring: Freud's Inner Circle and the Politics of Psychoanalysis* (New York: Addison-Wesley, 1991). The Freud-Jones correspondence is also not yet published; here I am grateful to Andrew Paskauskas for answering my queries. Selections and excerpts from the correspondence have already appeared in: Jones, *Life and Work* (ibid.); Gay, *Freud* (ibid.); Andrew Paskauskas, "Freud's Break with Jung: The Crucial Role of Ernest Jones," *Free Associations* 11(1988):7–34; and Paskauskas, "Ernest Jones: A Critical Study of His Scientific Development (1896–1913)" (Ph.D. diss., University of Toronto, 1985).

The published works of both Freud and Jung have received loving care from those charged with the English editions. *The Standard Edition of the Complete Psychological Works of Sigmund Freud* (London: Hogarth Press, 1953–74) was published under the general editorship of James Strachey, who doubled as chief translator, with Alix Strachey and Alan Tyson in collaboration with Anna Freud. *The Collected Works of C. G. Jung* (Princeton: Princeton University Press, 1953–80) was edited by Sir Herbert Read, Michael Fordham, Gerhard Adler, and William McGuire, with R. F. C. Hull as translator. Jung's "Transformations and Symbols of the Libido," 1911–12, originally appeared in English as *Psychology of the Unconscious,* trans. Beatrice Hinkle (New York: Moffat, Yard & Co., 1916), and has recently been reissued under the same title, William McGuire, ed., (Princeton: Princeton University Press, 1991).

Spielrein's published works are not yet available in English; I have relied on translations prepared by Ursula Ofman and Peter Gachot. A listing of Spielrein's papers can be found in Carotenuto's *A Secret Symmetry,* 238–39 (ibid.). Specifically cited in this work are: "Über den psychologischen Inhalt eines Falles von Schizophrenie (Dementia Praecox)," *Jahrbuch für psychoanalytische und psychopathologische Forschungen* 3(1911): 329–400; "Die Destruktion als Ursache des Werdens," *Jahrbuch für psychoanalytische und psychopathologische Forschungen* 4(1912):465–503; "Beiträge zur Kenntnis der kindlichen Seele," *Zentralblatt für Psychoanalyse und Psychotherapie* 3(1912):57–72; "Traum vom *Vater Freudenreich*," *Internationale Zeitschrift für ärztliche Psychoanalyse* 1(1913):484–86; "Das unbewusste Träumen in Kuprins *Zweikampf*" (actually a communication from her brother Jean), *Imago* 2(1913):524–25; "Die Äusserungen des Oedipuskomplexes im Kindersalter," *Internationale Zeitschrift für ärztliche Psychoanalyse* 4(1916):44–48; "Zur Frage der Entstehung und Entwicklung der Lautsprache," *Internationale Zeitschrift für ärztliche Psychoanalyse* 6(1920):401; "Renatchens Menschenentstehungstheorie," *Internationale Zeitschrift für ärztliche Psychoanalyse* 6(1920):155–57; "Briefmarkentraum," *Internationale Zeitschrift für ärztliche Psychoanalyse* 8(1922):342–43; "Die Entstehung der kindlichen Worte Papa und Mama," *Imago* 8(1922):345–67; "Schweize," *Internationale Zeitschrift für ärztliche Psychoanalyse* 8(1922):234–35; "Rêve et vision des étoiles filantes," *International Journal of Psycho-Analysis* 4(1923):129–32; "Quelques analogies entre la pensée de l'enfant, celle de l'aphasique et la pensée subconsciente," *Archives de psychologie* 18(1923):306–22; "Die Zeit im unterschwelligen Seelenleben," *Imago* 9(1923):300–17. Not included in Carotenuto's list is the very revealing paper "Qui est l'auteur du crime?," discovered by Mireille Cifali and republished in *Le Bloc-Notes de la Psychanalyse* 2(1982):141–46. Many, but not all, of Spielrein's papers were abstracted in English in the early issues of *Psychoanalytic Review*. Abstracts can be found in the following volumes: 1:470; 5:434; 6:106; 7:95–100; 12:353–55; 14:338–39; 16:444; 20:233–34; 25:547–48.

The authority on Spielrein's later career in Geneva is Mireille Cifali. See her essay "Une femme dans la psychanalyse, Sabina Spielrein: Un autre portrait," *Le Bloc-Notes de la Psychanalyse* 8(1988):253–66. Also worth consulting are Fernando Vidal, "Piaget et la Psychanalyse: Premières rencontres," *Le Bloc-Notes de la Psychanalyse* 6(1986):171–89; and Pierre Bovet, *Vingt ans de vie de L'institut Rousseau* (Genève: Université du Genève, 1932). With regard to her later career, indications of her activities can be derived from reports in the *International Journal of Psycho-Analysis* 1:359–60; 3:280, 513–20; 4:241, 524; 5:123, 261–66; 6:258–61; 7:151. I am grateful to A. Etkind, Valerie Zelensky, and Magnus Ljunggrien for sharing information with me concerning Spielrein's activities in Russia. For general background, see also: Martin Miller, "Freudian Theory Under Bolshevik Rule: The Theoretical Controversy During the 1920's," *Slavic Review* 44(1985):625–46; and Hans Lobner and Vladimir Levitin, "A Short History of Freudism: Notes on the History of Psychoanalysis in the U.S.S.R.," *Sigmund Freud House Bulletin* 2(1978):5–30.

The secondary literature on Freud and Jung is vast and not untainted by polemics. Several works are fundamental to this study and therefore are singled out here. Indispensable for basic historical information are Ernest Jones, *The Life and Work of Sigmund Freud*, 3 vols. (New York: Basic Books, 1953–57), and Henri Ellenberger's massive gift to future generations of scholars, *The Discovery of the Unconscious: The History and Evolution of Dynamic Psychiatry* (New York: Basic Books,

1970). Hannah Decker's *Freud in Germany: Revolution and Reaction to Science: 1893–1907* (New York: International Universities Press, 1977) is invaluable. Also important is Paul Roazen's *Freud and His Followers* (New York: Knopf, 1975). Following in Decker's footsteps is Norman Kiell, whose *Freud Without Hindsight: Reviews of His Work, 1893–1939* (Madison: International Universities Press, 1988), contains much useful material. Central to the conceptual origins of this study was Peter Homans, *Jung in Context: Modernity and the Making of a Psychology* (Chicago: University of Chicago Press, 1979). With regard to the interpretive stance taken toward the scientific status of psychoanalysis, I have taken my cue from three authors: Robert Holt, whose articles have recently been collected in an important volume, *Freud Reappraised* (New York: Guilford Press, 1989); Frank Sulloway, whose *Freud, Biologist of the Mind: Beyond the Psychoanalytic Legend* (New York: Basic Books, 1979) has lately been complemented by the author's equally trenchant assessment of the relation between Freud's failure to publish a manual of technique and the inner organization of his group, "Reassessing Freud's Case Histories: The Social Construction of Psychoanalysis," in Toby Gelfand and John Kerr, eds., *Freud and the History of Psychoanalysis* (Hillsdale, N.J.: Analytic Press, 1992); and Adolf Grünbaum, whose *The Foundations of Psychoanalysis: A Philosophical Critique* (Berkeley: University of California Press, 1984) has come to define contemporary debate over the evidentiary status of Freud's claims.

Peter Swales, a friend as well as a colleague, deserves separate mention. Swales's papers include: "Freud, Johann Weier, and the Status of Seduction" (privately published, 1982), condensed as "A Fascination with Witches; The Role of the Witch in the Conception of Fantasy," *The Sciences* 22(1982)21–25; "Freud, Cocaine, and Sexual Chemistry: The Role of Cocaine in Freud's Conception of the Libido" (privately published, 1983); "Freud, Minna Bernays and the Conquest of Rome: New Light on the Origins of Psychoanalysis," *New American Review* 1(1982):1–23; "Freud, Fliess, and Fratricide: The Role of Fliess in Freud's Conception of Paranoia" (privately published, 1982); "Freud, Minna Bernays and the Imitation of Christ," presentation at the New School for Social Research, New York, 20 May 1982; "Freud, Martha Bernays, and the Language of Flowers: Masturbation, Cocaine, and the Inflation of Fantasy" (privately published, 1983); "Freud, Krafft-Ebing, and the Witches: The Role of Krafft-Ebing in Freud's Flight into Fantasy" (privately published, 1983); "Freud, Professor Diogenes Teufelsdröckh, and the Garden of Eden: Primal Innocence, Carnal Knowledge and Original Sin," presentation before the History of Psychiatry section, New York/Cornell Medical Center, 7 January 1988; "Fliess, Freud, and the Skull on the Lido," presentation at the Third Hannah Conference in the History of Medicine, Trinity College, Toronto, 15 October 1991; "Freud, His Teacher, and the Birth of Psychoanalysis" (1986, vol. 1:3–82) and "Freud, Katharina, and the First 'Wild Analysis'" (1988, vol. 3:81–164), both in Paul Stepansky's series *Freud: Appraisals and Reappraisals* (Hillsdale, N.J.: Analytic Press); "Freud, His Origins, and Family History; The Freuds, the Nathansohns, and the Bernays," presentation at the Center for Israel and Jewish Studies, Columbia University, New York, 26 January 1987; "Freud and the Unconscionable: The Obstruction of Freud Studies, 1946–2113," presentation before the National Psychological Association for the

Advancement of Psychoanalysis, New York, 25 January 1992; "What Jung *Didn't Say*," *Harvest: Journal for Jungian Studies* 38(1992):30–37. Of the privately published papers, those on cocaine, Weier, Krafft-Ebing, and Fliess and fratricide are all available in Laurence Spurling, ed., *Sigmund Freud: Critical Assessments*, vol. 1 (London: Routledge, 1989). In addition, Swales made available to me a draft of his manuscript for his forthcoming study, *Wilhelm Fliess: Freud's Other* (New York: Farrar, Straus & Giroux).

Also deserving separate mention is Sonu Shamdasani, whose work is only now beginning to come into print. His signal essay, "A Woman Called Frank," *Spring* (1990):26–56, was indispensable in bringing into new relief the nature of Jung's clinical prediction in "Transformations and Symbols." See also his "Two Unknown Early Cases of Jung," *Harvest: Journal for Jungian Studies* 38(1992):38–43. Beyond that, Shamdasani has generously shared with me much basic archival information as well as his preparations for his important forthcoming intellectual biography of Jung.

The two most essential biographical sources concerning Jung are his memoirs, written with the help of Aniela Jaffé, *Memories, Dreams, Reflections* (1962, with final, rev. ed. in 1973, New York: Pantheon), and the notes of his 1925 seminar, taken by Cary de Angulo and reviewed by Jung himself, which have long been available as a typescript in the Kristine Mann Library of the C. G. Jung Institute of New York and which have recently been published as *Analytical Psychology: Notes of the Seminar Given in 1925 by C. G. Jung*, William McGuire, ed. (Princeton: Princeton University Press, 1989). No comparable texts of public self-revelation exist for any other psychoanalytic figure, Freud included. For a brief but illuminating commentary, see D. W. Winnicott's review of the memoirs, *International Journal of Psycho-Analysis* 45(1964):450–55.

A single biography of Jung comparable to Jones's work on Freud does not yet exist. The most important basic reference works include: "Carl Gustav Jung and Analytic Psychology," which constitutes chapter 9 (657–748) of Ellenberger's *Discovery of the Unconscious* (ibid.), and which Jung reviewed in manuscript; Barbara Hannah, *Jung: His Life and Work, A Biographical Memoir* (New York: Putnam, 1976); Anthony Storr, *C. G. Jung* (New York: Viking, 1973); E. A. Bennett, *C. G. Jung* (New York: Dutton, 1962); Vincent Brome, *Jung: Man and Myth* (New York: Atheneum, 1978); Laurens van der Post, *Jung and the Story of Our Time* (New York: Random House, 1975); and Paul Stern, *C. G. Jung–The Haunted Prophet* (New York: Braziller, 1976). Hannah, Bennett, and van der Post had the advantage of being close associates of Jung's. Brome's is a workmanlike study by a professional biographer while Storr's brief overview of the man and his work brings a psychiatrically informed perspective to bear. Stern's book, which appears to rely on an unnamed informant, is at once the most vivid and devastating of all accounts. Two other works which contain a great deal of useful information, some of it nowhere else available, are *C. G. Jung: Word and Image*, edited by Aniela Jaffé (Princeton: Princeton University Press, 1979), and *C. G. Jung Speaking: Interviews and Encounters*, edited by William McGuire and R. F. C. Hull (Princeton: Princeton University Press, 1977). The Jung Oral History Archive contains almost two hundred interviews with persons who knew Jung personally. The interviews were conducted by Gene Nameche under the auspices of the Frances Wickes Foundation. The collection of typescripts, only some of which are restricted, is housed at the Rare Books Department, Countway Library, Harvard Medical School. Linda Donn has made good use of some of the interviews in her sympathetic account, *Freud and Jung: Years of Friendship, Years of Loss* (New York: Scribners, 1988). Otherwise the material has not yet made its way into the mainstream of Jung scholarship. The following interviews are particularly important: Henry Murray (4 November 1968); C. A. Meier (11 September 1970); Ruth Bailey (17 February 1969); Robert Hobson (18 December 1969); Wolfgang Binswanger (13 September 1970); Herman Müller (4 May 1970); Jolande Jacobi (13 December 1969; 26 January 1970); Alphonse Maeder (11 January 1970), Michael Fordham (12 February 1969), Richard Evans (25 November 1971), and James Hillman (1 January 1970).

Works on the Freud-Jung relationship that reward scrutiny include: George Hogenson, *Jung's Struggle with Freud* (Notre Dame, Ind.: University of Notre Dame Press, 1983); Robert Steele, *Freud and Jung: Conflicts of Interpretation* (with consulting editor Susan Swinney; London: Routledge & Kegan Paul, 1982); Duane Schultz, *Intimate Friends, Dangerous Rivals: The Turbulent Relationship Between Freud and Jung* (Los Angeles: Tarcher, 1990). Schultz joins Donn in providing a narrative overview of the relationship, while Hogenson and Steele are more interested in disentangling the theoretical struggle. More partisan in nature are Liliane Frey-Rohm, *From Freud to Jung: A Comparative Study of the Psychology of the Unconscious* (New York: Putnam, 1974), and Edward Glover, *Freud or Jung?* (London: Allen & Unwin, 1950), written from a Jungian and a Freudian perspective respectively. Nandor Fodor's *Freud, Jung, and Occultism* (New York: New York University Press, 1971) is still worth consulting, though as with Glover and Frey-Rohm, his study came out before the publication of the correspondence. Two excellent and provocative articles directly concern the correspondence: Paul Stepansky, "The Empiricist as Rebel: Jung, Freud and the Burden of Discipleship," *Journal of the History of the Behavioral Sciences* 12(1976):216–39; Patrick Mahony, "The Budding International Association of Psychoanalysis and Its Discontents," *Psychoanalysis and Contemporary Thought* 2(1977):551–90. Four more works in particular attempt to capture the psychological flavor of the relationship: Mikkel Borch-Jacobsen, *The Freudian Subject* (Stanford: Stanford University Press, 1988); François Roustang, *Dire Mastery: Discipleship from Freud to Lacan* (Baltimore: Johns Hopkins University Press, 1976); Peter Homans, "Narcissism in the Jung-Freud Confrontations," *American Imago* 38(1974):81–95; and John Gedo, "Magna Est Vis Veritas Tuae et Praevalebit," *The Annual of Psychoanalysis*, vol. 7 (New York: International Universities Press, 1979).

The standard reference works with regard to Freud are: Jones, *Life and Work* (ibid.); "Sigmund Freud and Psychoanalysis," a book-length study which comprises chapter 7 (418–570) of Ellenberger's *Discovery of the Unconscious* (ibid.); Ronald Clark, *Freud: The Man and the Cause* (New York: Random House, 1980); and Max Schur, *Freud: Living and Dying* (New York: Basic Books, 1972), an important and eye-opening work when it appeared. For an appraisal of Clark's work, see Robert Holt's review, *Review of Psychoanalytic Books* 1(1982):3–13. In some ways, the more interesting works on Freud are not the recent ones, which have to contend with a confusing, and now overwhelming, secondary literature, but the works written in the pre-Jones era. The most important and most readable of these works is also the earliest: Fritz Wittels, *Sigmund Freud: His Personality, His Teaching, and His School* (London: Allen & Unwin, 1924). Wittels's companion volume, *Freud and His Time* (New York: Liveright, 1931), also rewards careful scrutiny. (I do not take seriously Wittels's retraction of the first work, "Revision of a Biography," *The Psychoanalytic Review* 20(1933):361–74, which was apparently extracted from him when he moved to New York from Europe.) Helen Walker Puner's biography, *Freud: His Life and His Mind* (New York: Howell, Soskin, 1947) is provocative and was once important enough, as Gay points out, for Jones to debate in his biography. Hanns Sachs, *Freud, Master and Friend* (Cambridge: Harvard University Press, 1944), presents Freud as only a disciple can see him. Theodore Reik's *From Thirty Years with Freud* (New York: International Universities Press, 1940) is an interesting hodgepodge of anecdotes and theorems which renders well the psychoanalytic vision on the eve of the Second World War. Erich Fromm's *Sigmund Freud's Mission: An Analysis of His Personality and Influence* (New York: Grove, 1963) trenchantly captures several important dimensions in Freud's personality. Fromm's de-idealized view is all the more interesting in that his principal informant was Sachs. Less colorful than the foregoing but quite remarkable are Siegfried Bernfeld's path-breaking papers: "Freud's Earliest Theories and the School of Helmholtz," *The Psychoanalytic Quarterly* 13(1944):341–62; "Freud's Scientific Beginnings," *American Imago* 6(1949):163–96; "Sigmund Freud, M.D., 1882–1885," *The International Journal of Psycho-Analysis* 32(1951):204–17; "Freud's Studies on Cocaine, 1884–1887," *Journal of the American Psychoanalytic Association* 1(1953):581–613; and, with Suzanne Cassirer Bernfeld, "Freud's First Year in Practice, 1886–1887," *Bulletin of the Menninger Clinic* 16(1952):37–49.

For general background on the phenomenology and scientific understanding of nervous disorders as they were understood at the time, one can do no better than consult the texts of the period, most especially those of Pierre Janet and Paul Dubois. Dubois's *The Psychic Treatment of Nervous Disorders,* originally published in 1904 as *Les Psychonévroses et Leur Traitement Morale,* English translation by Smith Ely Jelliffe (New York: Funk & Wagnalls, 1909), is evenly divided between scientific history and the treatment (via "persuasion") of focal complaints. Janet's major descriptive texts are *L'Automatisme Psychologique, Essaie de Psychologie Expérimentale sur les Formes Inférieurs de l'Activité Humaine* (Paris: Alcan, 1889) and *The Major Symptoms of Hysteria,* 2nd ed. (New York: Macmillan, 1924). See also Théodule Ribot, *The Diseases of Personality,* 1891 (Chicago: Open Court Publishing Co., 4th rev. ed., 1910). Also to be consulted are Janet's autobiographical statement in Carl Murchison, ed., *History of Psychology in Autobiography,* vol. 1 (123–33) (Worcester: Clark University Press, 1923), as well as "Pierre Janet and Psychological Analysis," which forms chapter 6 (341–417) in Ellenberger's *Discovery of the Unconscious.* For Joseph Grasset and his "polygonal" psychology, see his *The Semi-Insane and the Semi-Responsible,* trans. S. Ely Jelliffe (New York: Funk & Wagnalls, 1912), and his *Marvels Beyond Science,* 1902, trans. R. Tubeuf (New York and London: Rebman, 1910). For the debate on hypnotism, similarly, one should consult

Hippolyte Bernheim, *Suggestive Therapeutics: A Treatise on the Nature and Uses of Hypnotism,* trans. Christian Herter from the second French revised edition (New York: Putnam, 1889), and *New Studies in Hypnotism,* trans. Richard Sandor from the 1891 French edition (New York: International Universities Press, 1980). Some further information on hypnotic practice is contained in passing in Poul Bjerre's *The History and Practice of Psychanalysis* (Boston: Richard Badger, 1916). Richard von Krafft-Ebing's two great texts and the companion study by his disciple Albert von Schrenck-Notzing are equally important. See Krafft-Ebing, *Textbook of Insanity Based on Clinical Observations for Practitioners and Students of Medicine,* trans. C. Chadock from the 1901 German ed. (Philadelphia: F. A. Davis Co., 1904) and *Psychopathia Sexualis: A Medico-Forensic Study,* trans. H. Wedeck from the 1902 German edition (New York: G. P. Putnam's Sons, 1965), and Schrenck-Notzing, *The Use of Hypnosis in Psychopathia Sexualis,* trans. C. Chaddock from the 1889 German ed. (New York: Institute for Research in Hypnosis Publication Society and the Julian Press, 1956).

On hysteria in particular see Ilse Veith's historical study, *Hysteria: The History of a Disease* (Chicago: University of Chicago Press, 1965). A rewarding survey of the landscape of nervousness is George Drinka's *The Birth of Neurosis: Myth, Malady, and the Victorians* (New York: Simon & Schuster, 1984). More scholarly is Malcolm Macmillan's "Delboeuf and Janet as Influences in Freud's Treatment of Emmy von N.," *Journal of the History of the Behavioral Sciences* 15(1979):299–309; see, too, chapter 2, "Charcot, Hypnosis, and Determinism," in Macmillan's trenchant *Freud Evaluated: The Closing Arc* (Amsterdam: North Holland, 1990). Worth consulting for general background are: Jeffrey Boss, "The Seventeenth-Century Transformation of the Hysteric Affection, and Sydenham's Baconian Medicine," *Psychological Medicine* 1(1979):221–34, which charts the gradual reconception of the role of the womb in hysteria; Nathan Kravis, "James Braid's Psychophysiology: A Turning Point in the History of Dynamic Psychiatry," *American Journal of Psychiatry* 145(1988):1191–1206; Toby Gelfand, "Réflexions sur Charcot et la famille névropathique," *Histoire des Sciences Medicales* 21(1987):245–50; Mark Micale, "Charcot and the Idea of Hysteria in the Male: Gender, Mental Science, and Medical Diagnosis in Late-Nineteenth-Century France," *Medical History* 34(1990):363–441.

The literature on turn-of-the-century theories of nervous ailments and hereditary degeneration makes more sense if one recognizes how recently the modern clinical approach to disease evolved and how relatively badly psychiatry and neurology lagged behind in their conceptualizations. Here basic, indispensable sources include: Erwin Ackerknecht, *A Short History of Medicine* (New York: Ronald Press, 1955); Erwin Ackerknecht, *A Short History of Psychiatry* (London: Hafner, 1959); Michel Foucault, *The Birth of the Clinic* (New York: Vintage, 1975); Fielding Garrison, *Contributions to the History of Medicine* (New York: Hafner, 1966). Also worth consulting is Franz Alexander and Sheldon Selesnick, *The History of Psychiatry* (New York: Harper & Row, 1966). For more background, see: L. S. Jacyna, "Principles of General Physiology: The Comparative Dimension to British Neuroscience in the 1830's and 1840's," *Studies in the History of Biology,* 7(1983):47–92), and Charles Mercier's thoughtful and essentially modern *Sanity and Insanity*

(New York: Scribners, 1889) in Havelock Ellis's *Contemporary Science* series. For Ellis himself, incidentally, the key source remains Phyllis Grosskurth's *Havelock Ellis: A Biography* (New York: Knopf, 1980). For the relation of hereditary degeneration to racism, see above all George Mosse's two works, *The Crisis of German Ideology* (New York: Grosset & Dunlap, 1964) and *Toward the Final Solution: A History of European Racism* (Madison: University of Wisconsin Press, 1985), and Sander Gilman's richly rewarding *Difference and Pathology: Stereotypes of Sexuality, Race, and Madness* (Ithaca: Cornell University Press, 1983). Also important is Leon Poliakov, *The Aryan Myth: A History of Racist and Nationalist Ideas in Europe* (New York: Basic Books, 1974).

On Spielrein's diagnosis, see especially Anthony Storr, "A Second Opinion," *The New York Times Book Review*, 16 May 1982, 1–2, 21. On "lovesickness" and Avicenna, I am indebted to Fady Hajal's presentation on "Lovesickness, a Major Health Hazard for Medieval Middle Eastern Youth," 19 June 1987, History of Psychiatry Section, New York Hospital/Cornell Medical Center. On Robert Carter, see Alison Kane and Eric Carlson, "A Different Drummer: Robert B. Carter and Nineteenth-Century Hysteria," *Bulletin of the New York Academy of Sciences* 58(1982):510–34. Concerning the importance of the Gymnasium degree, see Frau C. A. Meier, interview with Gene Nameche, 19–23 March 1970, Jung Oral History Archive, 44. On the general literary conception of Russians and "the Russian soul," see Robert Williams, "The Russian Soul: A Study in European Thought and Non-European Nationalism," *Journal of the History of Ideas* 31(1970):573–88. On the history of attitudes toward masturbation, see Robert MacDonald, "The Frightful Consequences of Onanism: Notes on the History of a Delusion," *Journal of the History of Ideas* 28(1967)423–31. Rosemary Dinnage's review of Carotenuto's book is illuminating: "Declarations of Dependence," *London Times Literary Supplement*, 10 December 1982: 1351.

On the distinctiveness of the Swiss psychiatric tradition, see Oskar Diethelm's "Switzerland" (chapter 9:238–55), in *World History of Psychiatry*, edited by John G. Howells (New York: Bruner/Mazel, 1975); the same volume also contains essays on "Germany and Austria" (chapter 10:256–90) by Esther Fischer-Homberger, and "Union of Soviet Socialist Republics" (chapter 12:308–33) by Joseph Wortis and A. G. Galach'yan. Also important are Henri Ellenberger's two essays "The Scope of Swiss Psychology" in Henry David and Helmut von Braken, eds., *Perspectives in Personality Theory* (New York: Basic Books, 1961) and "Carl Gustav Jung: His Historical Setting," in Hertha Riese, ed., *Historical Explorations in Medicine and Psychiatry* (New York: Springer, 1978). The former essay on Swiss psychology is reprinted as chapter 6 in Mark Micale, ed., *Beyond the Discovery of the Unconscious: Selected Essays on the History of Psychiatry by Henri Ellenberger* (Princeton: Princeton University Press, forthcoming).

For Auguste Forel the most accessible source is Ellenberger, *Discovery of the Unconscious* (ibid.). But Adolf Meyer's essays in the *Collected Papers of Adolf Meyer*, vol. 1, ed. E. Winters (Baltimore: Johns Hopkins University Press, 1950), are equally informative. Forel's own autobiography is *Out of My Life and Work*, trans. B. Miall (London: Allen & Unwin, 1950). Forel's text *Psychotherapy and Suggestion or Hypnosis* (1889; New York: Allied Publishing Co., 1937) compares favorably with Albert Moll's *The Study of Hypnosis: Historical, Clinical and Experimental Research in the Techniques of Hypnotic Induction* (1889; New York: Julian Press, 1958). Forel's *Hygiene of Nerves and Mind in Health and Disease,* trans. H. A. Aikens (New York: Putnam, 1907), was intended to be an introductory text on the new conception of the nervous system. More important still is Forel's *The Sexual Question: A Scientific, Psychological, Hygienic and Sociological Study* (1904; New York: Physicians & Surgeons Book Co., 1905), which should be read in conjunction with Albert Moll's *The Sexual Life of the Child* (1907; New York: Macmillan, 1912).

The Bleulers, father and son, have a record of continuous service to successive generations in their community that is unmatched in the history of psychiatry. See: Manfred Bleuler: "Eugen Bleuler's Conception of Schizophrenia—An Historical Sketch," *Bulletin of the Isaac Ray Medical Library* 1(1953):47–60; "My Father's Conception of Schizophrenia," *Bulletin of the New York State Asylums* 7(1931):1–16; "Eugen Bleuler," *Archives of Neurology and Psychiatry* 26(1934):610–28; and his interview with Gene Nameche, 8 December 1969, Jung Oral History Archive. Eugen Bleuler's two great texts, *Dementia Praecox, or the Group of Schizophrenias* (1911; New York: International Universities Press, 1950) and *Textbook of Psychiatry* (1916; New York: Arno Press, 1976), contain clinical observations that still command interest; they also, of course, establish for the historian Bleuler's mature attitudes toward the theories of his three great colleagues and collaborators, Kraepelin, Jung, and Freud. Also worth consulting is Manfred Bleuler's important clinical work, *The Schizophrenic Disorders: Long-Term Patient and Family Studies,* trans. Siegfried Clemens (New Haven: Yale University Press, 1978), with its multiple discussions of Jung's and Eugen Bleuler's mutual influence. With regard to ambivalence, in English one should consult: "Bleuler versus Jung on Negativism," an abstract in *The Psycho-Analytic Review* 7(1920):106–108; Eugen Bleuler, *The Theory of Schizophrenic Negativism,* trans. W. A. White (New York: Nervous and Mental Disease Publishing Co., 1912), and the abstract by M. Karpas in *The Psychoanalytic Review* 2(1915):466–68. Bleuler's "Defense and Critical Remarks of Freud's Psychoanalysis" is available in English only as an abstract in *The Psycho-Analytic Review* 5(1918):238–42.

Readers interested in the historical development of the dementia praecox diagnosis can do no better than to consult Jacques Quen's introductory essay in vol. 1 (vii–xxxii) of Emil Kraepelin's *Psychiatry: Textbook for Students and Physicians,* based on the sixth German edition (1899; Canton, Mass.: Science History Publications, 1990). Kraepelin's other great work, *Lectures on Clinical Psychiatry,* trans. Thomas Johnstone (New York: William Wood, 1912), has attracted the wrath of antipsychiatry commentators, though it remains a model of clinical-phenomenological description. Kraepelin's own *Memoirs* (New York and Berlin: Springer-Verlag, 1987) are of keen interest to the historian of psychiatry.

For Jung's early development, both personally and theoretically, there are a number of especially rewarding articles. Quite disarming are Albert Oeri's reminiscences, "Memories of C. G. Jung's Boyhood," *Spring* (1970): 182–89, reprinted in McGuire and Hull, eds., *C. G. Jung Speaking* (ibid.), 3–10. Much worth reading are: Martin Ebon, "Jung's First Medium," *Psyche* 7(1970):3–15; James Hillman, "Some Early Background to Jung's Ideas: Notes on *C. G. Jung's Me-*

dium by Stephanie Zumstein-Preiswerk,'' *Spring* (1976):123–36; William B. Good-heart, "C. G. Jung's First 'Patient': On the Seminal Emergence of Jung's Thought," *Journal of Analytical Psychology* 29(1984):1–34; Aniela Jaffé, "Details about C. G. Jung's Family," *Spring* (1984): 35–43; Phillip Wolf-Windegg, "C. G. Jung—Bachofen, Burckhardt, and Basel," *Spring* (1976): 137–47; Adolf Portmann, "Jung's Biology Professor: Some Reflections," *Spring* (1976):148–54; J. Marvin Spiegelman, "Psychology and the Occult," *Spring* (1976):104–22. Aubrey Lewis' essay, "Jung's Early Work," *Journal of Analytical Psychology* 2(1957):119–36, is a model of scholarship that combines historical information with critical review.

Very much worth consulting are the contributions of Jung's collaborators on the word association experiment. These can be found in English only in the original compendium, *Studies in Word Association: Experiments in the Diagnosis of Psychopathological Conditions Carried Out at the Psychiatric Clinic of the University of Zurich Under the Direction of C. G. Jung*, trans. M. D. Eder (London: Routledge & Kegan Paul, 1918). See therein: Eugen Bleuler, "Upon the Significance of Association Experiments," chapter 1 (1–7), and "Consciousness and Association," chapter 6 (266–96); Franz Riklin, "Cases Illustrating the Phenomenon of Association in Hysteria," chapter 8 (322–52); Emma Fürst, "Statistical Investigations in Word Association and in Familial Agreement," chapter 11 (407–45); Ludwig Binswanger, "On the Psychogalvanic Phenomenon in Association Experiments," first published in 1907, chapter 12 (446–530). Only in German can one find Riklin's important "Analytische Untersuchungen der Symptome und Assoziationen eines Falles von Hysterie (Lina H.)," *Psychiatrisch-neurologische Wochenschrift* 6(1904–1905):449–52, 493–95, 505–11. With regard to Binswanger's paper see also McGuire, "Jung's Complex Reactions (1907): Word Association Experiments Performed by Binswanger," *Spring* (1984):1–34. Herbert Lehman has implicated Spielrein in Jung's early contact with Freud in interesting, informed ways in his "Jung Contra Freud/Nietzsche Contra Wagner," *International Review of Psycho-Analysis*, 13(1986):201–209. For the Burghölzli milieu during the period, A. A. Brill's two volumes are extremely valuable: *Lectures on Psychoanalytic Psychiatry* (New York: Knopf, 1946) and *Freud's Contribution to Psychiatry* (New York: Norton, 1944). The statistical report for the year 1904 prepared for the cantonal authorities, *Rechenschaftsbericht über die Zürichische Kantonale Irrenheilanstalt Burghölzli für das Jahr 1904,* is available from the University of Zurich. Bleuler's *Affectivity, Suggestibility, and Paranoia,* originally 1906, trans. C. Ricksher (Utica: New York State Hospitals Press, 1912) is a model example of the Zurich School's theoretical program.

On the scientific study of occultism in the last decades of the nineteenth century, one can consult Jung's own detailed review in his 1902 dissertation, *On the Psychology and Pathology of So-called Occult Phenomena,* in vol. 1 of the *Collected Works* (ibid.). Interestingly, like Janet, Jung was himself an excellent historian, at least early in his career. See also Jung's *The Zofingia Lectures,* W. McGuire, ed. and J. van Heurck, trans. which is now available as *Supplementary Volume A* (1983) to the Collected Works (op. cit.). Théodore Flournoy's masterpiece, *From India to Planet Mars,* trans. D. B. Vermilye (New Hyde Park, N.Y.: University Books, 1963), is credulous at times, but fascinating; Flournoy has some of the good-natured and writerly qualities of his close friend William James. Flournoy's paper

"L'Automatisme teleologique anti-Suicide," originally published in 1908 in the *Archive de Psychologie*, has been printed as "Anti-suicidal Hallucinations" in H. Carrington, ed. and trans., *Spiritism and Psychology* (New York: Harper & Brothers, 1912). That Freud was well aware of Flournoy's ongoing relation to Jung is attested to by Mireille Cifali's insightful article: "Le fameux couteau de Lichtenberg," *Le Bloc-Notes de la Psychanalyse* 4(1984):171–88, and by Theodore Reik's chapter, "An Unknown Lecture of Freud's" (63–93), in Reik's *From Thirty Years with Freud* (ibid.).

Edwin Boring's *A History of Experimental Psychology* (New York: Appleton-Crofts, 1950) is the standard work in the field, a lucid account which Boring modestly brings to a close just when he would have had to discuss his own contributions. Also relevant are Théodule Ribot's *German Psychology of To-Day: The Empirical School*, trans. from the second French edition by James Mark Baldwin (New York: Scribners, 1899), and Theodore Ziehen's *Introduction to Physiological Psychology*, trans. C. Van Liew and O. Beyer (New York: Macmillan, 1899). Ziehen's autobiographical statement, which features a description of the "transposition" concept, appears in vol. 1 (122–33) of Carl Murchison's *A History of Psychology in Autobiography* (ibid.); also to be found there is Edouard Claparède's self-effacing account of his own contribution (63–97). See also Raymond Fancher, *Pioneers of Psychology* (New York: Norton, 1990).

On Janet's therapies, which Jung was familiar with, see, first of all, Janet's *Psychological Healing: A Historical and Clinical Study*, 1925 (Salem, N.H.: Arno Press, 1976) and *Principles of Psychotherapy*, trans. H. M. and E. R. Guthrie (New York: Macmillan, 1924). The latter work is especially relevant as it is based on Janet's 1904 Lowell Lectures in Boston and thus is roughly contemporaneous with Jung's treatment of Spielrein. Unfortunately for the historian, however, new material was clearly added prior to the 1920 French edition upon which this translation is based. Bjorn Sjövall's hard-to-find *The Psychology of Tension: An Analysis of Pierre Janet's Concept of Tension Psychologique*, trans. A. Dixon (Stockholm: Scandinavian University Books, 1967), is excellent.

Instructive for the comparison case it provides is Eugene Taylor's "On the First Use of 'Psychoanalysis' at the Massachusetts General Hospital, 1903–1905," *Journal of the History of Medicine and Allied Sciences*, 43(1984):447–71. The reader interested in understanding the American dimensions of Jung's context should consult the following papers by Taylor: "James Jackson Putnam's Fateful Meeting with Freud: The 1909 Clark University Conference," *Voices* 21(1985):78–89; "Jung and His Intellectual Context: The Swedenborgian Connection," *Studia Swedenborgiana* 7(1991):47–69; "C. G. Jung and the Boston Psychopathologists, 1902–1912," *Voices* 21(1985):131–44; "William James and C. G. Jung," *Spring* (1980): 157–69; "The American Society for Psychical Research, 1884–1889," in D. Radin and N. Weiniger, eds., *Annual Review in Parapsychology* (Secaucus, N.J.: Secaucus Press, 1986); "Psychotherapy, Harvard, and the American Society for Psychical Research, 1884–1889," in *Proceedings of the 28th Annual Convention of the Parapsychological Association* (Medford, Mass.: Tufts University Press, 1985); "William James on Consciousness and Freud's Reply," address before the American Psychological Association, Washington, D.C., 16 August 1992. Putnam's original paper,

"Recent Experiences in the Study and Treatment of Hysteria at the Massachusetts General Hospital, with Remarks on Freud's Method of Treatment by 'Psycho-Analysis,'" *Journal of Abnormal Psychology* 1(1906):26–41, should be read in conjunction with his later ones, collected posthumously by Ernest Jones as *Addresses on Psychoanalysis* (New York: International Psycho-Analytic Press, 1921). Putnam deserves to be rediscovered by a scholar equipped to extract his clinical views from his Hegelianism. Boris Sidis's *Philistine and Genius* (New York: Moffat, Yard & Co., 1911) can be taken as representative of a typical, non-Freudian, American psychological work during this period. On Beard and neurasthenia, see Malcolm Macmillan's "Beard's Concept of Neurasthenia and Freud's Concept of the Actual Neuroses," *Journal of the History of the Behavioral Sciences* 12(1976):376–90. G. Stanley Hall's *Adolescence: Its Psychology and Its Relations to Physiology, Anthropology, Sociology, Sex, Crime, Religion and Education*, 2 vols. (New York: D. Appleton, 1904), has to be read to be believed. For Hall's context, see J. J. Lears, *No Place of Grace: Antimodernism and the Transformation of American Culture* (New York: Pantheon, 1981). For a parallel work by one of Hall's students, see A. F Chamberlain, *The Child: A Study in the Evolution of Man* (London: Walter Scott, 1906). For Freud's reception in America, before, during and after the Clark congress, two works are indispensable: Nathan G. Hale's *Freud and the Americans: The Beginnings of Psychoanalysis in the United States* (New York: Oxford University Press, 1971) and John Burnham's *Psychoanalysis in American Medicine, 1894–1918: Medicine, Science, and Culture* (New York: International Universities Press, 1976). Eugene Taylor's forthcoming study, *The Development of Scientific Psychotherapy in America* (New York: Addison-Wesley) will join Hale's and Burnham's accounts as definitive when it appears. See also Taylor's reconstruction of William James's 1896 Lowell Lectures, *William James on Exceptional Mental States* (Amherst: University of Massachusetts Press, 1984), and *The Letters of William James*, ed. Henry James (Boston: Atlantic Monthly Press, 1920).

The recent controversy over the "seduction" theory was inspired in no small part by Jeffrey Masson's *Assault on Truth: Freud's Suppression of the Seduction Theory* (New York: Farrar, Straus and Giroux, 1984), a book that is seriously flawed but was nonetheless useful in getting the topic of childhood sexual abuse back on the psychoanalytic agenda. For a clear-headed critique, see Arnold Davidson's review in *London Review of Books*, 19 July 1984:9–11. The authority on Freud's original "seduction" theory, its genesis and its ultimate fate, is surely Anthony Stadlen of London. I am grateful to Stadlen for sharing with me his as-yet-unpublished researches on both the seduction theory and the "Aliquis" episode.

The literature on Freud's milieu is quite overwhelming; the following is but a sample. The interested reader should consult Carl Schorske's elegant *Fin-de-Siècle Vienna: Politics and Culture* (New York: Vintage, 1981), which never grows out of date. Hannah Decker's study *Freud, Dora, and Vienna 1900* (New York: Free Press, 1991) provides a multifaceted look at the world of Freud and the Bauers. William McGrath's *Freud's Discovery of Psychoanalysis: The Politics of Hysteria* (Ithaca: Cornell University Press 1986) is a treasure-trove of unanticipated finds all intelligently contextualized. McGrath has also recently contributed an important statement of the impact of Austrian politics on Freud's theorizing, "Freud and the Force of History," in Toby Gelfand and John Kerr, eds., *Freud and the History of Psychoanalysis* (Hillsdale: Analytic Press, 1992). Frederick Morton's labor of love, *A Nervous Splendor: Vienna 1888-1889* (London: Weidenfeld & Nicholson, 1979), is so entertaining with its abundance of colorful detail that one readily forgives the author his thumbnail sketch of Freud as an obsessed young physician furiously pacing the Ringstrasse oblivious to his surroundings. Far more daunting is Erna Lesky's *The Vienna Medical School of the 19th Century*, trans. L. Williams and I. S. Levij (Baltimore: Johns Hopkins University Press, 1976), a work of enduring greatness by a preeminent historian of medicine. Francis Schiller's *A Möbius Strip: Fin-de-Siècle Neuropyschiatry and Paul Möbius* (Berkeley: University of California Press, 1982) is short, clear, and delightful. Dennis Klein's *The Jewish Origins of the Psychoanalytic Movement* (New York: Praeger, 1981) remains a very important study, as does Marianne Krüll's *Freud and His Father* (New York: Norton, 1986). See also Hugo Knoepfmacher, "Freud and the B'nai B'rith," *Journal of the American Psychoanalytic Association* 27(1979):447-59. John Cuddihy's *The Ordeal of Civility* (New York: Basic Books, 1974) is provocative. So, too, in a different way is David Bakan's *Sigmund Freud and the Jewish Mystical Tradition* (Princeton: Van Nostrand, 1958). Paul Vitz's *Sigmund Freud's Christian Unconscious* (New York: Guilford Press, 1988) contains much interesting material. See also Yosef Yerushalmi's important new work, *Freud's Moses: Judaism Terminable and Interminable* (New Haven: Yale University Press, 1991), a work by a distinguished scholar. Independently covering much of the same ground as Yerushalmi is Emanuel Rice's parallel book *Freud and Moses: The Long Journey Home* (Albany: State University of New York Press, 1991). Peter Gay's *A Godless Jew: Freud, Atheism, and the Makings of Psychoanalysis* (New Haven: Yale University Press, 1987) offers yet another perspective. A very important background study is John Efron's remarkable "Defining the Jewish Race: The Self-Perceptions and Response of Jewish Scientists to Scientific Racism in Europe, 1882-1933 (Ph.D. dissertation, Columbia University, 1991; Baltimore: Johns Hopkins University Press, forthcoming).

On Freud's person, a useful source is Hendrik Ruitenbeek's collection, *Freud as We Knew Him* (Detroit: Wayne State University Press, 1973). Two articles that often get overlooked are Franz Alexander's "Recollections of Berggasse 19," *Psychoanalytic Quarterly* 9(1940):197-206, and Bruno Goetz, "That's All I Have to Say About Freud," *International Review of Psycho-Analysis* 3(1975):139-43. See also Abram Kardiner, *My Analysis with Freud* (New York: Norton, 1977), and H. Gundlach, "Freud schreibt an Hellpach: Ein Beitrag zur Rezeptionsgeschichte der Psychoanalyse in Deutschland," *Psyche* (October 1977): 909-21. On Freud as a writer, a topic which resurfaces with each new generation of commentators, three works usefully define the current parameters of discussion: Robert Holt, "Freud's Cognitive Style," which is combined with "On Reading Freud" in *Freud Reappraised* (ibid.); Patrick Mahony, *Freud as a Writer* (New York: International Universities Press, 1982); François Roustang, *Psychoanalysis Never Lets Go* (Baltimore: John Hopkins University Press, 1982).

Informed discussions of Freud's early theorizing abound; the reader inclined to go into this area must gear up for a full campaign. The Freud-Fliess letters are indispensable, but also worth consulting are two standard works, Walter

Stewart, *Psychoanalysis: The First Ten Years, 1888-1898* (London: Allen & Unwin, 1969), and Kenneth Levin, *Freud's Early Psychology of the Neuroses: A Historical Perspective* (Pittsburgh: University of Pittsburgh Press, 1979). On the importance of Freud's neurological training, see Peter Amacher, *Freud's Neurological Education and Its Influence on Psychoanalytic Theory* (New York: International Universities Press, 1962), and Paul Cranefeld, "Freud and the 'School of Helmholtz,'" *Gesnerus* 23(1966):35-39. Larry Stewart's conjectures in "Freud Before Oedipus: Race and Heredity in the Origins of Psychoanalysis," *Journal of the History of Biology* 9(1966):215-28, should be read in connection with Toby Gelfand's essays, "Mon Cher Docteur Freud: Charcot's Unpublished Correspondence to Freud, 1888-1893," *Bulletin of the History of Medicine* 62(1988):563-88; and "Sigmund-sur-Seine: Fathers and Brothers in Charcot's Paris," in Toby Gelfand and John Kerr, eds., *Freud and the History of Psychoanalysis* (ibid.). On the opposite side of the aisle are those who emphasize Freud's allegiance to romantic biological concepts, such as Madeleine and Henri Vermorel, "Was Freud a Romantic?" *International Review of Psycho-Analysis* 13(1986):15-37, and those for whom cultural influences are more important, such as Ernst Ticho, "The Influence of the German-Language Culture on Freud's Thought," *International Journal of Psycho-Analysis* 67(1986):227-36, and Didier Anzieu, "The Place of Germanic Lanuage and Culture in Freud's Discovery of Psychoanalysis Between 1895 and 1900," *International Journal of Psycho-Analysis* 67(1986):219-26. A valuable volume that tries to synthesize these varying approaches is John Gedo and George Pollack, eds., *Freud: The Fusion of Science and Humanism* (New York: International Universities Press, 1975).

The reader interested in Freud's clinical concepts might best begin with part 1 of Macmillan's *Freud Evaluated*, Swales's papers, and Ola Andersson's *Studies in the Prehistory of Psychoanalysis* (Stockholm: Norstedts, 1962). Very much worth consulting are three excellent contributions by Rosemarie Sand: "Early Nineteenth Century Anticipation of Freudian Theory," *International Review of Psycho-Analysis* 15(1988):465-79; "Confirmation in the Dora Case," *International Review of Psycho-Analysis* 10(1983):333-57; and "Pre-Freudian Discovery of Dream Meaning: The Achievements of Charcot, Janet, and Krafft-Ebing," in Gelfand and Kerr, eds., *Freud and the History of Psychoanalysis* (ibid.). The last paper provides a taste of Sand's important forthcoming book on nineteenth-century theories of the dream. See also: Léon Chertok, "On the Discovery of the Cathartic Method," *International Journal of Psycho-Analysis* 42(1961):284-87, and "The Discovery of the Transference: Toward an Epistemological Interpretation," *International Journal of Psycho-Analysis* 49(1968):560-76; Suzanne Reichard, "A Re-Examination of 'Studies in Hysteria,'" *Psychoanalytic Quarterly* 25(1956):155-77; Lindsay Hurst, "Freud and the Great Neurosis: Discussion Paper," *Journal of the Royal Society of Medicine* 76(1983):57-61; Charles Goshen, "The Original Case Material of Psychoanalysis," *American Journal of Psychiatry* 108(1952):829-34. An excellent paper too often overlooked is Abram de Swaan, "On the Sociogenesis of the Psychoanalytic Setting," in P. Gleichman, J. Goudsblom, and H. Korte, eds., *Human Figurations: Essays for Norbert Elias* (Amsterdam: Amsterdams Sociologisch Tijdschrift, 1977). One should also see I. Bry and A. Rifkin, "Freud and the History of Ideas: Primary Sources," in J. Masserman, ed., *Science and Psychoanalysis* (New

York: Grune & Stratton, 1962), vol. 5. Excellent are Stephen Kern's two papers, "Explosive Intimacy: Psychodynamics of the Victorian Family," in L. de Mause, ed., *The New Psycho-History* (New York: Psychohistory Press, 1975), and "Freud and the Discovery of Child Sexuality," *History of Childhood Quarterly* 1(1973):117–41. Very much worth consulting is Mark Kanzer and Jules Glenn, eds., *Freud and His Patients* (New York: International Universities Press, 1983). On the subject of "the Rat Man," see Patrick Mahony's important study, *Freud and the Rat Man* (New Haven: Yale University Press, 1986). Mahony's companion study, *Cries of the Wolf Man* (New York: International Universities Press, 1984), should be read in conjunction with Karin Obholzer's *The Wolf-Man Sixty Years Later* (London: Routledge & Kegan Paul, 1982). On Schreber, one should consult his original text, *Memoirs of My Nervous Illness,* ed. and trans. by Ida Macalpine and Richard Hunter (Cambridge: Harvard University Press, 1988). The basic secondary texts are: William Niederland, *The Schreber Case: Psychoanalytic Profile of a Paranoid Personality* (New York: Quadrangle, 1974; reprinted, Hillsdale: Analytic Press, 1988); Morton Schatzman, *Soul Murder: Persecution in the Family* (Middlesex: Penguin Books, 1976); Han Israëls, *Schreber: Father and Son* (privately published by author, 1981; reprinted, Madison: International Universities Press, 1989); and Zvi Lothane, *In Defense of Schreber: Soul Murder and Psychiatry* (Hillsdale: Analytic Press, 1992). Beyond its historical sweep, Lothane's text usefully surveys the vast secondary literature on Schreber.

Weininger scholarship has become an industry but the reader is encouraged to plunge into the work itself: Otto Weininger, *Sex and Character,* originally 1903 (New York: Putnam 1907). On the more general question of biological theories of femininity, see Susan Mondal, "Science Corrupted: Victorian Biologists Consider 'The Woman Question,' " *Journal of the History of Biology* 11(1978):1–55. With regard to the putative relation between femininity and Judaism, see Sander Gilman's provocative and insightful essay "The Struggle of Psychiatry with Psychoanalysis: Who Won?" in F. Meltzer, ed:, *The Trials of Psychoanalysis* (Chicago: University of Chicago Press, 1988). The same volume contains Arnold Davidson's extraordinary paper "How to Do the History of Psychoanalysis: A Reading of Freud's *Three Essays on the Theory of Sexuality.*" Three works not easily classified but very much worth consulting in understanding the general culture and its attitudes toward sexuality are Edward Carpenter, *Love's Coming of Age* (1905; New York: Boni & Liveright, 1911), Thomas Szasz, *Karl Kraus and the Soul-Doctors* (London: Routledge & Kegan Paul, 1977), and Iwan Bloch, *The Sexual Life of Our Times in Its Relations to Modern Civilization,* trans. M. Eden Paul (1906; London: Rebman, 1910).

On the subject of Freud's collaborators, Roazen's *Freud and His Followers* (ibid.) is the place to begin. Albrecht Hirschmüller's scholarly *The Life and Work of Josef Breuer: Physiology and Psychoanalysis* (New York: New York University Press, 1989) is the definitive work on Breuer and "Anna O." See also Hirschmüller's "Eine bisher unbekannte Krankengeschichte Sigmund Freuds und Josef Breuers aus der Entstehungszeit der 'Studien über Hysterie'." *Jahrbuch der Psychoanalyse* 10(1978):136–68, and Paul Cranefeld, "Josef Breuer's Evaluation of His Contribution to Psycho-Analysis," *International Journal of Psycho-Analysis* 39(1958):317–22.

On Rank's early career, the basic sources are the relevant passages in Klein, *The Jewish Origins of Psychoanalysis* (ibid.), in Jessie Taft, *Otto Rank: A Biographical Study* (New York: Julian Press, 1958), and in Esther Menaker, *Otto Rank: A Rediscovered Legacy* (New York: Columbia University Press, 1982). Peter Rudnytsky, a literary scholar with a broad background in psychoanalytic history, has joined Menaker, a prominent analyst, in trying to revive Rank's contributions with his thoughtful study *The Psychoanalytic Vocation: Rank, Winnicott, and the Legacy of Freud* (New Haven: Yale University Press, 1991). Ferenczi is next on the list to be rediscovered: see Lewis Aron and Adrienne Harris, eds., *The Theoretical and Clinical Contributions of Sandor Ferenczi* (Hillsdale: Analytic Press, forthcoming), especially the historical contributions therein by Judith Meszaros, André Haynal, Axel Hoffer, Arnold Rachman, and Christopher Fortune. See also Martin Stanton, *Sandor Ferenczi: Reconsidering Active Intervention* (New York: Aronson, 1991). Ferenczi's papers have been reprinted in a three-volume set: *First, Further,* and *Final Contributions to Psycho-Analysis* (New York: Bruner/Mazel, 1980). For Ernest Jones, in addition to Paskauskas's contributions, see Jones's own *Free Associations: Memoirs of a Psychoanalyst* (New York: Basic Books, 1959) and Vincent Brome, *Ernest Jones: Freud's Alter Ego* (New York: Norton, 1983). Hilde Abraham's tribute to her father, "Karl Abraham: An Unfinished Biography," *International Review of Psycho-Analysis* 1(1974):12–72, contains much of relevance concerning the Burghölzli milieu and Abraham's relation to it as well as his relation to Freud. For more on Abraham, see: Ernest Jones's "Introductory Memoir" (9–41) in Jones, ed., *Selected Papers of Karl Abraham* (London: Hogarth Press, 1927); E. Glover, introduction, in Hilde Abraham, ed., *Clinical Papers and Essays on Psychoanalysis* (New York: Basic Books, 1955); and Vincent Brome, *Freud and His Early Circle* (New York: Morrow, 1969). Stekel's memoirs reward scrutiny: *The Autobiography of a Psychoanalyst,* E. Gutheil, ed. (New York: Liveright, 1950). Stekel's magnum opus is *The Language of Dreams,* partially reprinted in English as *Sex and Dreams: The Language of Dreams,* trans. J. van Teslar (Boston: Richard Badger, 1911). Stekel's review of Weininger appeared in 1904 in *Die Wage* (1033). On Adler, Phyllis Bottome's outspoken defense, *Alfred Adler: Apostle of Freedom* (London: Faber & Faber, 1939) attempts to deal with the "biology" charge among other things, and should be read in conjunction with Chapter 8, "Alfred Adler and Individual Psychology" (571–656), in Ellenberger's *Discovery of the Unconscious.* Paul Stepansky's *In Freud's Shadow: Adler in Context* (Hillsdale, N.J.: Analytic Press, 1983) is the definitive examination of Adler's rise and fall within Freud's circle. Also worth consulting is Leo Lobl, "Otto Rank and Alfred Adler," *Journal of the Otto Rank Association* 9(1974):49–64. Two readily available collections of Adler's early and late writings respectively are those edited by Heinz and Rowena Ansbacher, *The Individual Psychology of Alfred Adler* (New York: Harper Torchbooks, 1964), and *Superiority and Social Interest* (New York: Norton Paperbacks, 1979). On Otto Gross, the authority is Emanuel Hurwitz of Zurich; in English, his researches have been summarized by Kurt Eisler in his *Viktor Tausk's Suicide* (New York: International Universities Press, 1983). Another very good source is Martin Green, *The Von Richthofen Sisters: The Triumphant and the Tragic Modes of Love* (New York: Basic Books, 1974). For Gross's political connections, see Arthur Mitzman, "Anarchism, Expressionism, and Psychoanalysis,"

New German Critique 10(1977):77–104. On Freud's shifting relationships with his followers one might also consult Richard Evans, *Conversations with Carl Jung and Reactions from Ernest Jones* (Princeton: Van Nostrand, 1964). Phyllis Grosskurth in her *The Secret Ring: Freud's Inner Circle and the Politics of Psycho-Analysis* (ibid.) has charted the formation and further adventures of the Committee. Three works which provide interesting overviews of the development of the psychoanalytic movement are: Marthe Robert, *Sigmund Freud's Life and Achievement* (New York: Harcourt, Brace & World, 1966); Edith Kurzweil, *The Freudians: A Comparative Perspective* (New Haven: Yale University Press, 1989); and the important biographical compendium edited by Franz Alexander, Samuel Eisenstein, and Martin Grotjahn, *Psychoanalytic Pioneers* (New York: Basic Books, 1966). On the composition of the Vienna Psychoanalytic Society, three articles worth consulting are: Max Graf, "Reminiscences of Professor Sigmund Freud," *The Psychoanalytic Quarterly* 11(1942):465–76; Edward Shorter, "The Two Medical Worlds of Sigmund Freud," in Gelfand and Kerr, eds., *Freud and the History of Psychoanalysis* (ibid.); and Harald Leopold-Löwenthal, "The Minutes of the Vienna Psycho-Analytic Society," *Sigmund Freud House Bulletin* 4(1980):23–41. Another interesting source is *The Freud Journal of Lou Andreas-Salomé,* trans. Stanley Leavy (New York: Basic Books, 1964). Rudolph Binion's magnificent biography, *Frau Lou: Nietzsche's Wayward Disciple* (Princeton: Princeton University Press, 1968), comes as close to a psychobiography as any work possibly can. Russell Jacoby's *The Repression of Psychoanalysis: Otto Fenichel and the Political Freudians* (New York: Basic Books, 1983) contains, among other things, useful information about contemporary literary and student movements. Niles Holt similarly provides insight into the inspiration for the Haeckel Bunds in "Ernst Haeckel's Monistic Religion," *Journal of the History of Ideas* 32(1971):265–305.

On Toni Wolff's early association with Jung, see her sister's interview with Gene Nameche (Frau Susanne Trüb, 21 September 1970) at the Jung Oral History Archive. For Trigant Burrow's association with Jung, see chapter 3, "The Year with Jung," in *A Search for Man's Sanity: The Selected Letters of Trigant Burrow with Biographical Notes,* ed. Sir Herbert Read (New York: Oxford University Press, 1958). Honegger's death has been sensitively studied by Hans Walser, "An Early Psychoanalytic Tragedy: J. J. Honegger and the Beginnings of Training Analysis," *Spring* (1974): 243–55.

John Billinsky's article "Jung and Freud" appeared in 1969 in the *Andover Newton Quarterly* 10:3–34. I am grateful to John Billinsky, Jr., who after a long search discovered his father's original manuscript, apparently composed in Zurich in 1957. Confirming testimony is to be found in Gene Nameche's interviews with Henry Murray (4 November 1968) and Carl Meier (11 September 1970) at the Jung Oral History Archive. Peter Gay, both in the bibliographic essay in his *Freud: A Life for Our Time* (ibid.) and in his article "Sigmund and Minna? The Biographer as Voyeur," *The New York Times Book Review* (29 January 1989):1, 43–45, has taken a dismissive stance toward the possibility of an affair. To be noted is that a large portion of the correspondence between Freud and Minna Bernays, that is, after the letter of 27 April 1893 up to the letter of 25 July 1910, is still restricted at the Sigmund Freud archives at the Library of Congress. Discussion of this issue will remain more a matter of opinion than of reasoned argument until Anthony Stadlen publishes his detailed and illuminating analysis of the text of the "Aliquis" episode as it relates to Freud's own biography.

On a different topic, Nora Crow Jaffé has questioned Freud's reading of *Gradiva*, arguing that Jensen means for the illusion itself to be seen as healing: see "A Second Opinion on Delusions and Dreams: A Reading of Freud's Interpretation of Jensen," in Anne Hudson Jones, ed., *Images of Healers* (Albany: State University of New York Press, 1983). The three founding works for applied psychoanalysis in relation to myths and folktales are: Franz Riklin, *Wishfulfillment and Symbolism in Fairy-Tales*, 1908, ed. and trans. S. Jelliffe and W. A. White (New York: Journal of Nervous and Mental Disease Publishing Co., 1915); Karl Abraham, *Dreams and Myth*, 1909, retitled *Dreams and Myths: A Study in Race Psychology*, ed. and trans. S. Jelliffe and W. A. White (New York: Journal of Nervous and Mental Disease Publishing Co., 1913); Otto Rank, *The Myth of the Birth of the Hero*, 1909, in P. Freund, ed., The *Myth of the Birth of the Hero and Other Writings* (New York: Vintage Books, 1969). Oskar Pfister's study of Count Zinzendorf, *Die Frömmigkeit des Grafen Ludwig von Zinzendorf: Ein Psychoanalytischer Beitrag zur Kenntnis der religiösen Sublimierungsprozesse und zur Erklärung des Pietismus*, exists only in the original German edition as volume 9 in Freud's series *Schriften zur angewandten Seelenkunde* (Leipzig & Wien: Franz Deuticke, 1910). The book informs much of Jung's criticism of Christianity in "Transformations and Symbols." Rank's compendium, *The Incest-Motif in Literature and Legend*, has now happily appeared in English translation with an introduction by Peter Rudnytsky (Baltimore: Johns Hopkins University Press, 1992). Freud's dependence on Frazer is clear enough in the pages of *Totem and Taboo*, but the modern reader supposes that Freud has gone well beyond Frazer when actually many of the psychological interpretations are to be found in the anthropologist's text. The only cure is to consult the original: James Frazer, *The Golden Bough* (London: Macmillan, 1922). Freud's reliance on phylogenetic rationales did not stop with *Totem and Taboo;* see Ilse Grubrich-Simitis, *Sigmund Freud: A Phylogenetic Fantasy* (Cambridge: Harvard University Press, (1987), and Barry Silverstein's two papers, "Oedipal Politics and Scientific Creativity: Freud's 1915 Phylogenetic Fantasy," *Psychoanalytic Review* 76(1989):403–24, and "Now Comes a Sad Story: Freud's Lost Metapsychological Papers," in Paul Stepansky, ed., *Freud: Appraisals and Reappraisals* (Hillsdale, N.J.: Analytic Press, 1988), vol. 1. For an informed treatment of more basic issues, see Edmund Wallace, *Freud and Anthropology: A History and Reappraisal* (New York: International Universities Press, 1983). Among Jung's many sources, two important ones are available in English: Franz Cumont, *The Mysteries of Mithra*, trans. from the second French edition by T. J. McCormack (Chicago: Open Court Publishing Co., 1910), and Leo Frobenius, *The Childhood of Man: A Popular Account of the Lives, Customs, and Thoughts of the Primitive Races*, trans. A. H. Keane (London: Seeley & Co., 1908). Frank Miller's essay, "Some Instances of Subconscious Creative Imagination," can be found as an appendix (447–62) to Jung's 1952 *Symbols of Transformation*, vol. 5 of the *Collected Works* (ibid). Steinthal's analysis of the Prometheus legend has been reprised in I. Goldhizer, *Mythology Among the Hebrews and its Historical Development* (1877; New York: Cooper Square Publishers, 1967). Extremely useful for background information are L. Sahakian, *History and Systems of Social Psychology*, 2d ed. (New York: Hemisphere Publishing Co., 1982), which links Stenthal, Lazarus, and Wundt to Herbart, and Kurt Danziger's important essay, "Origins and Basic Principles of Wundt's *Völkerpsychologie*," *British Journal of Social Psychology* 22(1983):301–13, which serves as a needed corrective to the only English version of Wundt's folk psychology, *Elements of Folk Psychology* (London: Allen & Unwin, 1912). With regard to the idea of the "core complex," William McGuire deserves credit for having identified it as the exact phrase being used in his editorial notes to *The Freud/Jung Letters* (ibid.). The single author who has most assiduously pursued the ramifications of the core complex idea is John Forrester. I have relied upon his *Language and the Origins of Psychoanalysis* (New York: Columbia University Press, 1980) in my treatment of the topic. Martin Bergmann's *The Anatomy of Loving: The Story of Man's Quest to Know What Love Is* (New York: New York University Press, 1987) contains, among other insights, an interesting analysis of Freud's "A Special Type of Choice of Object Made by Men." For a more detailed account of E. T. A. Hoffmann's *The Devil's Elixirs* and Jung's dream of the knight and the customs official, see my own "*The Devil's Elixirs*, Jung's "Theology," and the Dissolution of Freud's "Poisoning Complex," *The Psychoanalytic Review* 75(1988):1–34. Both Dmitri Merejkowski's *The Romance of Leonardo da Vinci*, trans. G. Guerney (Garden City, N.Y.: Garden City Publishing Co., 1928), and Hoffmann's *The Devil's Elixirs*, trans. R. Taylor (London: John Calder, 1963), are available in English. Two works worth consulting on the collateral influence of Greek thought during the period are E. M. Butler, *The Tyranny of Greece over Germany* (Cambridge: Cambridge University Press, 1935), and William Heinrich Roscher, *Ephialtes: A Pathological Mythological Treatise on the Nightmare of Classical Antiquity*, trans. A. V. O'Brien (1900; New York: Spring Publications, 1972).

Spielrein's ideas on destruction, sacrifice, and transformation show an obvious debt to Nietzsche, who was equally an important source for Jung, but they were also informed by contemporary developments in her home country. See: Friedrich Nietzsche, *The Birth of Tragedy and The Geneaology of Morals* (New York: Anchor Books, 1956); "The Russian Student Movement: The Heroic Will to Martyrdom," chapter 4 of Lewis Feuer's *The Conflict of Generations: The Character and Significance of Student Movements* (New York: Basic Books, 1969); James Rice, "Russian Stereotypes in the Freud-Jung Correspondence," *Slavic Review* 41(1983):19–34. Parallel ideas on destruction and transformation can also be found in Eduard von Hartmann's three-volume compendium, *Philosophy of the Unconscious: Speculative Results According to the Induction Method of the Physical Sciences*, trans. William Copeland (London: Kegan Paul, Trench, Trubner & Co., 1893). For background on the "death instinct," see Élie Metchnikoff, *The Nature of Man*, trans. P. C. Mitchell (New York: Putnam, 1908), and my own "Beyond the Pleasure Principle and Back Again: Freud, Jung, and Sabina Spielrein," in Paul Stepanksy, ed., *Freud: Appraisals and Reappraisals*, vol. 3 (ibid.)

On the question of dream function and the prospective style of interpretation generally, see Alphonse Maeder's three contributions: "Zur Traumfunktion," *Jahrbuch für psychoanalytische und psychopathologische Forschungen* 4(1912): 692–707; "Zur

Frage der Traumfunktion teleologik," *Jahrburch für psychoanalytische und psychopathologische Forschungen* 5(1913):453–54: and *On the Function of Dreams*, 1913, ed. and trans. S. Jelliffe and W. A. White (New York: Journal of Nervous and Mental Disease Publishing Co., 1915). See also: Herbert Silberer, *Problems of Mysticism and Its Symbolism* (New York: Moffat, Yard & Co., 1917) and Wilhelm Stekel, "Religious Symbolism in Dreams," in *The Interpretation of Dreams*, trans. E. Paul and C. Paul (New York: Liveright, 1947). Maeder's letter to Freud of October 1912 has been published by Mireille Cifali in *Le Bloc-Notes de la Psychanalyse* 9(1989):219–26. Seif's letter to Jones of December 1912, which praises Jung's symbolic extension of the libido concept, has not been published; I am grateful to Andrew Paskauskas for sharing its contents with me. Oskar Pfister's challenge to Freud on interpretive method can be found in his *Psycho-Analysis in the Service of Education: Being an Introduction to Psycho-Analysis*, trans. B. Low and H. Geschwind (1917; London: Henry Kimpton, 1922).

On Jung's dream of killing Siegfried, see Michael Vannoy Adams, "My Siegfried Problem—And Ours: Jungians, Freudians, Anti-Semitism and the Psychology of Knowledge," in Aryeh Maidenbaum and Stephen Martin's *Lingering Shadows: Jungians, Freudians, and Anti-Semitism* (Boston: Shambhala, 1991). The same volume contains valuable information about Jung's later anti-Semitism from a diversity of viewpoints. See especially Jay Sherry's "The Case of Jung's Alleged Anti-Semitism," 117–32.

The publications of Committee members during this period deserve a separate study. Ernest Jones's "The God Complex," in *Essays in Applied Psycho-Analysis*, vol. 2 (244–65), retitled *Psycho-Myth, Psycho-History* (New York: Stonehill, 1974), was expressly meant as a portrait of Jung—and of Jones himself. Rank's important work *The Double: A Psychoanalytic Study*, ed. and trans. Harry Tucker (1913; Chapel Hill: University of North Carolina Press, 1971), betrays an implicit inclination to eclipse many of Jung's formulations. Rank's and Sachs's *The Significance of Psychoanalysis for the Mental Sciences*, trans. Charles Payne (1913; New York: Journal of Nervous and Mental Disease Publishing Co., 1916) is far more blatant, though it has to be read carefully. Even non-Committee members jumped in. In addition to his review "Sabina Spielrein: Die Destruktion als Ursache des Werden," *Internationale Zeitschrift für ärztliche Psychoanalyse* 1(1913):92–93, Paul Federn also weighed in with "Some General Remarks on the Principles of Pain-Pleasure and of Reality," *Psychoanalytic Review* 2(1914):1–11. Ferenczi's review of "Transformations," which ran in the *Internationale Zeitschrift für ärztliche Psychoanalyse* 1(1913):132–48, has not been published in English. Abraham combined both the Fordham lectures and "Transformations" in his review, which appears in English translation in his *Clinical Papers and Essays on Psychoanalysis* (New York: Basic Books, 1955). For Otto Gross's review of Spielrein, see "Über Destruktionssymbolik," *Zentralblatt für Psychoanalyse und Psychotherapie* 4(1914): 525–34.

The reader interested in brief overviews of the contemporary state of Freud scholarship might consult Paul Stepansky, "Series Introduction" (xi–xix), and John Gedo, "On the Origins of the Theban Plague: Assessment of Freud's Character" (241–59), both in vol. 1 of Stepansy, ed., *Freud: Appraisals and Reappraisals* (ibid.), as well as my own "History and the Clinician," in Gelfand and Kerr, eds., *Freud and the History of Psychoanalysis* (ibid.). For a comprehensive understanding of basic source material, the best course might be to follow Ellenberger through his notes to *The Discovery of the Unconscious* (ibid.). Similarly with regard to German medical opinion, Hannah Decker's bibliography in *Freud in Germany: Revolution and Reaction in Science: 1893–1907* (ibid.) is definitive. With regard to secondary scholarship, four excellent bibliographies may usefully be consulted. Mark Micale has compiled a thoughtful, annotated bibliography, comprising both European and American sources and following the outline of Ellenberger's general historiographic program, in *Beyond the Discovery of the Unconscious: Selected Essays on the History of Psychiatry by Henri Ellenberger* (ibid.). (Micale's introduction to this volume, "Henri F. Ellenberger and the Origins of European Psychiatric Historiography," is itself an important essay.) The bibliography in Frank Sulloway's *Freud, Biologist of the Mind: Beyond the Psychoanalytic Legend* (ibid.) constitutes a valuable combination of primary reference material and secondary discussions thereof, including some material gleaned from the professional psychoanalytic literature. Yet more exhaustive with regard to the psychoanalytic literature is the bibliography contained in Malcolm Macmillan's *Freud Evaluated: The Closing Arc* (ibid.). One more excellent listing of both primary and secondary works is the bibliographical essay in Peter Gay's *Freud: A Life for Our Time* (ibid.).

Index